BUSINESS STATISTICS

BUSINESS STATISTICS

An Introductory Course

KEN BLACK
University of Houston—Clear Lake

WEST PUBLISHING COMPANY

St. Paul   New York   Los Angeles   San Francisco

Text design: Sylvia Dovner/Technical Texts
Copy editing: Jerrold Moore
Artwork: DBA Design & Illustration
Composition: Graphic World, Inc.
Cover illustration and design: Stacey Lewis
Indexing: Schroeder Editorial

Library of Congress Cataloging-in-Publication Data

Black, Ken.
   Business statistics : an introductory course / Ken Black.
    p. cm.
   Includes bibliographical references and index.
   ISBN 0-314-92219-9
   1. Commercial statistics.   I. Title.
HF1017.B57   1992
519.5′02465—dc20   91-26873
                         ∞   CIP

Photo Credits: *Page 1,* Michael Beasley/Tony Stone Worldwide; *page 17,* Tim Brown/ Tony Stone Worldwide; *page 45,* Peter Poulides/Tony Stone Worldwide; *page 99,* © 1991, Chris Gilbert, San Francisco; *page 159,* © 1991, Chris Gilbert, San Francisco; *page 207,* © 1991, Martin Rogers/FPG International, Corp.; *page 251,* Frost Publishing; *page 319,* © The Stock Market/Tim Young, 1991; *page 365,* © The Stock Market/Brownie Harris, 1991; *page 421,* © The Stock Market/Ted Horowitz, 1991; *page 495,* © The Stock Market/Thaine Manske, 1991; *page 573,* Courtesy of Dow Chemical, USA.

To my girls, Carolyn, Caycee, and Wendi

Contents

Preface

The main objective of this textbook is to help every business student to become statistically literate. That is, this text is intended to help every student appreciate the potential applications of statistics, to understand and use the vocabulary and symbology of statistics, and to learn when and where to apply statistical techniques appropriately. To accomplish these objectives, the text has been organized and developed around real-life business examples, business settings, and business applications.

The text is written for a one-semester statistics course, with the idea that this semester may be the only exposure some students will ever have to the field of statistics. Therefore, some topics that are rarely covered in the first semester have been deleted. The focus here is on thoroughly presenting those topics that are crucial for all business students to explore. The material has been written with the assumption that the student has mastered algebra but not calculus.

This textbook is the culmination of many years of observation and experimentation in the teaching of business statistics. My intent is to transfer many of the techniques and ideas that have been successful in the classroom to the textbook. It is my belief that a good text complements the instructor as part of a two-pronged effort to communicate knowledge and information. Thus I have written this text with the notion that it will serve to reexplain and reinforce topics presented in the classroom. I also hope that it will kindle an interest in statistics and research through the use of business vignettes, historical notes, and problems containing up-to-date, real-life data. The text is replete with demonstration problems and examples to help the students visualize and conceptualize the topics and ideas.

Coverage

This text contains twelve chapters, which the instructor should be able to complete in one semester. The intent of Chapter 1 is to convince the student of the importance and widespread use of statistics in the contemporary business world. Included are specific examples of data analysis in several areas of business. Chapter 1 introduces the paradigm of inferential statistics, which is extremely important in this course and which is referred to several other times in the text. In addition, Chapter 1 discusses levels of data and the importance of understanding the type of data before determining a method of analysis.

Chapter 2 is a collection of data summary and graphic depiction techniques. Its premise is that virtually every professional in the business world eventually is asked to present data orally or in writing so as to capture and communicate the essence of the information effectively, accurately, and succinctly.

Chapter 3 presents techniques that can be used to describe data statistically. The topics in Chapter 3 are standard descriptive statistical tools, such as mean, median, mode, range, variance, and standard deviation.

The main topic of Chapter 4 is probability, which undergirds the concept of inferential statistics. Because of the variety of types and combinations of probability problems, they are often the most difficult for students to solve in statistics. My objective in this chapter is to present techniques for solving probability problems so that the student has a core of mechanisms for approaching these problems. The chapter discusses varied probability methods, such as sample space, classical formulas, matrix approach, and tree diagrams. A special section in Chapter 4 deals with multiple trials. The formal treatment of this topic is unique in its inclusion to this text. This topic serves as an intuitive bridge to Chapter 5.

Chapters 5 and 6 include the standard topics of discrete and continuous distributions. Chapter 7 is an expanded version of sampling. I believe that students too often are asked to compute statistical solutions without regard to where the data came from and how the data were gathered. This chapter covers the major ways of gathering data through sampling. It discusses the sampling distribution of several statistics, including the four statistics presented later as large sample statistics, to prepare students for what follows in later chapters. Chapter 7 also includes some of the more pertinent aspects of quality control. Quality control and total quality management are important concepts in business and will continue to be throughout the 1990s. In addition to exposing students to quality control, the construction of control charts logically follows the discussion of sampling distributions presented early in the chapter.

Chapters 8, 9, and 10 are organized so that students can understand more effectively the topics of confidence interval estimation and hypothesis testing. Because I believe that attempting to learn these topics simultaneously is confusing, I dedicated Chapter 8 to confidence interval estimation and Chapter 9 to hypothesis testing, using, in each, large sample statistical tests. I reserved small sample analysis for Chapter 10. Hypothesis testing and confidence interval estimation for small sample statistics are presented together in Chapter 10. By the time the student has reached Chapter 10, hypothesis testing and confidence interval estimation have been introduced thoroughly enough to justify the inclusion of both topics in the chapter on small sampling statistics.

Chapter 11 presents regression and correlation techniques. Because I assume that much of the student's use of regression analysis will be primarily on a computer, the chapter emphasizes understanding regression concepts and being able to locate key regression items in a computer printout.

Chapter 12 presents several important nonparametric statistical techniques. I placed particular emphasis on chi-square methodology.

Chapter Organization

Each chapter begins with vignette. This brief business scenario sets the stage for the work undertaken in the chapter. The vignette should help the student understand the type of issues explored in the chapter. Most sections in each chapter contain demonstration problems. These demonstration problems are located after topics are explained in a section. They are formal presentations of how examples from that section should be worded, analyzed, and solved. Practice problems are provided after virtually every section in the text. With problems after each section, the student does not have to wait until the end of the chapter to practice skills learned in a section. Additional problems are given for practice at the end of each chapter. Most chapters contain between 50 and 100 practice problems. Many of the problems in the text use data from current surveys and research projects. My intent is to expose students to current data from the field of business as they work the problems. In addition, most chapters contain a historical note, which helps generate interest and an appreciation for the origin of statistical thought. Each chapter ends with a chapter summary, a list of key words, and a section on using the computer to solve problems presented in that chapter.

Appendices

There are five appendices in the text. Appendix A contains the statistical tables. Table A.1 is a table of random numbers. The digits in this table are random in all directions. This table is particularly useful as a resource for researchers who are undertaking random sampling or the instructor can use the table to demonstrate random sampling in a statistics course. A.2 is tables of binomial probability distributions. The tables contain exact probabilities for X values. Each table of binomial distribution probabilities has nine P values. Tables are given for n values from 1 to 20 and for 25. Table A.3 contains Poisson probabilities. Probabilities are listed for lambda values from 0 to 10. This table contains exact probabilities. Table A.4 is a table of e^{-x} values. This table is provided because these values are not accessible on all calculators, and they can be used to compute Poisson probabilities of exponential distribution probabilities.

Table A.5 is the standard normal distribution table. It contains probabilities for Z values up through 3.50 and for some selected Z values to 5.00. The table is also included inside the back cover for students' and instructors' convenience since the table is so frequently used. Table A.6 gives critical values of t. This table contains probability values for five values of alpha and 33 different degrees of freedom. This table is also used quite frequently in the course and is included inside the back cover for the user's convenience. Table A.7 contains two F distribution tables, one for alpha of .05 and one for alpha of .01. Table A.8 is a table of values of chi-square for selected probabilities. For each degree of freedom, nine values of chi-square are given. Table A.9 is a table of factors for control charts. This table contains the A and d values that are used to construct quality control charts.

Appendix B contains two databases with actual measurements from the business world. Database 1 contains personal income data, bank deposit data, FSLIC data, and data about business failures for the 50 states. Database 2 contains production data for over 135 manufacturing industries on six variables. These databases can be used in the instructional process in a number of ways. Instructors can assign portions of the databases to be analyzed by techniques presented in the text. Sampling techniques can be applied to the data to demonstrate the methodology of random sampling. The databases can be loaded into computers and analyzed by computer packages. A copy of the databases is available to each instructor in disk form. Access to these databases affords students an additional opportunity to see real data and get hands-on experience in managing the data.

Appendix C contains additional explanation on summation notation. Summations are introduced in Chapter 3. However, it is not appropriate to include a detailed explanation in the main text on summations. Included in Appendix C, are several of the laws of summations and some examples of how summations are determined.

Appendix D is a supplementary *t* test formula, which can be used in situations where the *t* test for independent samples is appropriate but the assumption of equal variances in the populations cannot be met. Appendix E contains the answers for most of the odd-numbered problems. In cases where the problem answer is not numerical, the answer is not given. However, the *Student's Solution Manual and Study Guide* contains the work for all odd-numbered problems including those which have graphical and non-numerical solutions.

The appendices are followed by a glossary of terms and an index.

Using the Computer

Many business statistics instructors utilize at least one statistical software package as part of the course. These instructors often find that they must either provide supplementary computer materials or require their students to purchase extra materials, including extra texts. Recognizing this, I created a section entitled Using the Computer for most chapters. These end-of-chapter sections were prepared carefully so that extra computer materials are not needed. These sections explain the use of the statistical software package, Minitab. Minitab is a user-friendly package that was created as a pedagogical tool. My intent in including Using the Computer sections in the text is to provide all the material necessary for the student to utilize Minitab successfully to analyze data with many of the techniques in the text. In these sections line-by-line commands are explained. Demonstration problems from the chapters are worked, showing the exact Minitab commands required. The output is given for the computerized demonstration problems. The main task for the instructor will be to log students into the local system and show them how to access Minitab or to allow students the opportunity to purchase a PC version of Minitab. One of my goals is to encourage more statistics instructors to use the computer packages in class by making the Minitab commands readily available and familiar to both instructors and students.

Supplements

To supplement this text, an instructor's manual, a student's solutions manual and study guide, transparency masters, and a test bank are available. The instructor's manual contains chapter objectives, chapter teaching strategies, chapter outlines, key words, and worked-out solutions to all problems in the text. The student's solutions manual and

Preface

study guide contains the worked-out solutions to all odd-numbered problems in the text, chapter objectives, chapter outlines, key words, and study questions on key words and concepts. The test bank contains more than 50 test questions for each chapter, along with an answer key. It is available on Westest, a microcomputer version, on request. The test bank will include questions about key terms, key ideas, main concepts, when to use what type of analysis, problem solving, analyzing output, making a decision from the analysis, reading tables, and mathematical calculation.

Recognizing the importance of visualizing important statistical concepts, West Publishing Company is pleased to offer a selection of video segments to supplement business statistics courses. *Against All Odds: Inside Statistics* is a visual introduction to statistics produced by the Annenberg CPB Collection. Qualified adopters of the text may select—free of charge—from the twenty-six segments for in-class use. For more information, please contact your West representative.

Acknowledgments.   Many people assisted me in this project. I would like to commend particularly the people at West Educational Publishing for the professional manner in which they have assisted me in this project. A special plaudit goes to my editor, Rick Leyh, for his encouragement, enthusiasm, and guidance in this project. I would like to also thank Jessica Evans, developmental editor, for her continued support and assistance. In addition, I want to credit Tom Hilt, production editor, for his suggestions and capable direction in bringing the manuscript to production.

I want to thank my colleagues at the University of Houston—Clear Lake for their interest, encouragement, and support in bringing this text to completion. I am thankful for my wife, Carolyn, whose professional opinion I value and who carried an extra parenting burden while I wrestled with this manuscript. Thanks to my daughters, Caycee and Wendi, for being patient with their dad while he was spending time with the text rather than with them.

I am grateful to the Literary Executor of the late Sir Ronald A. Fisher, F.R.S., to Dr. Frank Yates, F.R.S., and to the Longman Group Ltd, London for permission to reprint work from their book *Statistical Tables for Biological, Agricultural, and Medical Research* (6th Edition 1974) for Table A.8 in this text.

In addition, I want to acknowledge the outstanding work done by my reviewers. I know that their reviews were done with diligence and a high standard of excellence. I want them to know that their comments and suggestions were taken seriously and given the highest consideration in manuscript revisions. I believe that these reviewers helped to make the text significantly better. These reviewers are

Steven Bajgier, Drexel University;
Mohammad S. Bajwa, Northampton Community College;
Robert Barringer, Southern Illinois University, Edwardsville;
Dale M. Bryson, Umpqua Community College;
Walter Johnson, Southwest Texas State University;
Robert Lacher, South Dakota State University;
Daniel McGee, University of Arizona at Tucson;

John Meisel, Southern Illinois University, Edwardsville;
Carolyn Monroe, Baylor University;
Ron Morgan, West Chester University;
James Pool, University of Northern Colorado;
Russ Robins, Tulane University;
Don Satterfield, Memphis State University;
Sam Seaman, Baylor University;
Vivek Shah, Southwest Texas State University;
Don Shriner, Frostburg State College;
Justin Stolen, University of Nebraska at Omaha;
Scott Urquhart, New Mexico State University;
Peter Westfall, Texas Tech University.

BUSINESS STATISTICS

INTRODUCTION TO STATISTICS

CHAPTER LEARNING OBJECTIVES

The primary objective of Chapter 1 is to introduce you to the world of statistics, enabling you to

1. Be aware of a wide range of applications of statistics in business.
2. Define statistics.
3. Differentiate between descriptive and inferential statistics.
4. Classify numbers by level of data and understand why doing so is important.

JACOBSON, DICKERSON, AND JIMENEZ: A DATA DILEMMA

Edward Jacobson is president of a telemarketing company in New York. He wants to create a new division in the company and increase overall market share by adding a new product. Jacobson knows that start-up for this project will require a substantial investment in time and capital.

Across the country on the West Coast, Jennifer Dickerson, an expert in economic modeling, has been given the task of developing a model that can be used to forecast the cost of aerospace projects. She believes that in order to accomplish this task she will need to gather data from previously completed aerospace projects. She also believes that data from related industries outside the aerospace arena might be useful to her in developing the model.

Meanwhile, Marco Jimenez, who is a human resources manager with a large manufacturing firm in the South, is struggling to utilize effectively a large database of employee information that has been gathered and stored over time. He has available to him statistics about employee age, years of experience, absenteeism, family responsibilities, job preference, managerial experience, and other characteristics.

Managerial Questions

- Will the payoff justify the investment for Jacobson's company? What is the potential market for the telemarketing company's new product? How can Jacobson effectively gather useful market information to help him in his decision making?
- What type of data should Dickerson gather to proceed with her project? How should it be gathered? What level of data can be used in Dickerson's project? What statistical techniques are appropriate and useful in the development of her cost model?
- How can Jimenez make sense out of the data available to him? How can the employee information data be analyzed and presented in a manner which is most helpful to the firm?

Welcome to the world of statistics! Almost daily, the importance of statistics for business and other aspects of society increases. Advances in information processing and storage technology make statistics readily available for consumers, researchers, and decision makers. The computer affords data users easy access to analytic tools that make widespread application of statistics feasible. As more and more people are exposed to the study of statistics, greater awareness of their potential leads to ever widening use of statistics. Virtually all fields of endeavor use statistics, including science, education, business, technology, psychology, and sociology.

STATISTICS IN BUSINESS 1.1

This text focuses on the applications of statistics in business. Statistics are widely used in business; virtually all business disciplines apply statistical techniques in some decision-making situations. Such use is made possible, in part, by the requirement that most business majors in the United States take a statistics course as part of their curriculum. In addition, easy access to computing facilities and statistical software enables decision makers to utilize statistical analysis fully. Availability of tools and a receptive audience generate a steadily increasing use of statistics in business.

Examples of Statistics in Business

Accounting. Statistics are widely applied in accounting. One example is their use in a recent survey by the Federal Reserve bank system (the Fed) to determine the extent to which banks are using off-balance-sheet activities. The international banking industry uses off-balance-sheet activities to increase earnings and diversify operations. Some estimates indicate that the top twenty-five banks have committed as much as $1.5 trillion in the United States to off-balance-sheet activities. From the statistics generated by this survey, the Fed determined that Citibank holds the largest market share of off-balance-sheet international banking activity with almost 17% of the total.

Finance. Statistics are used in the financial world in many different ways, including projecting economic trends. Data provided by the U.S. Labor Department contain several leading indicators of the country's economy. These indicators are calculated from a variety of statistical data. One of the more widely used financial statistics is the Consumer Price Index (CPI), which business analysts often cite as an indicator of inflation in the economy.

Management. Management uses statistics as a decision-making aid in such diverse areas as human resource allocation, organizational behavior, and labor relations, among others. Statistics generated for an employment survey conducted by the National Federation of Independent Business indicated sharp cuts in hiring in the fourth quarter of 1989. Eight industries experienced cutbacks of 10% or more. The construction industry suffered the greatest cutbacks: a 30% slash in jobs. The other seven industries experiencing cutbacks included manufacturing, agriculture, wholesale, services, retailing, finance, and professional.

Management Information Systems. A 1989 statistical survey taken by Data Quest, Inc., in the management information systems area, revealed that manufacturers shipped a total of 192,000 computer workstations in 1988. During that same year, they shipped 9,960,000 personal computers. The firm used statistical techniques to predict that the ratio of workstations to personal computers will increase over time.

Marketing.   Market analysts use statistics to measure consumer attitudes, market share, and advertising potential. They often use statistical analysis to help determine consumer motivation. For example, trade show sales managers wanted to know what motivates people to attend trade shows. The Trade Show Bureau conducted a statistical survey that asked respondents to rank the factors in their decision to attend trade shows. A five-point scale was used to measure these factors, with a 1 indicating that the factor was of little importance and a 5 meaning that the factor was of great importance. The bureau contacted people in seven industries, including health care, manufacturing, communication, transportation, computers, food and beverage, and banking/finance/insurance. Some of the factors measured included general curiosity, speakers, history of attendance, new products, and meeting other professionals. Results varied by industry.

1.2   WHAT IS STATISTICS?

statistics

The word statistics has many different meanings in our culture. *Webster's Third New International Dictionary* gives a comprehensive definition of **statistics** as *"a science dealing with the collection, analysis, interpretation, and presentation of numerical data."* Viewed from this perspective, statistics includes all the topics presented in this text. Statistics also is a branch of mathematics, and most of the science of statistics is based on mathematical thought and derivation. Many academic areas, including business, offer statistics courses within their own disciplines. However, statistics has become a course of study in its own right.

People often use the word statistics to refer to a group of data. They may say, for example, that they gathered statistics from their business operation. What they are referring to are measured facts and figures. The media and others also use the word *statistic* to refer to a death. Becoming a statistic in this sense of the word obviously is undesirable.

The expression statistics is used in at least two other important ways. First, statistics is a descriptive measure computed from a sample and is used to make determinations about a population. This usage is discussed later. Second, statistics refers to the distribution being used in the analysis of data. For example, a researcher using the t distribution to analyze data might refer to use of the t statistic in analyzing the data.

The following are some of the common uses of the word *statistics.*

1. Science of gathering, analyzing, interpreting, and presenting data
2. Branch of mathematics
3. Course of study
4. Facts and figures
5. A death
6. Measurement taken on a sample
7. Type of distribution being used to analyze data

DESCRIPTIVE VERSUS INFERENTIAL STATISTICS | **1.3**

The study of statistics can be organized in a variety of ways. One of the main ways is to subdivide statistics into two branches: descriptive statistics and inferential statistics. In order to understand the difference between descriptive and inferential statistics, definitions of population and sample are helpful. *Webster's Third New International Dictionary* defines **population** as *"a collection of persons, objects, or items of interest."* The population can be a widely defined category, such as "all automobiles," or it can be narrowly defined, such as "all Ford Mustang cars produced from 1970 to 1974." A population can be a group of people, such as "Hispanic registered voters in New York," or it can be a set of objects, such as "all light bulbs produced on April 19, 1990 by the Lumino Company at the Cleveland plant." The researcher defines the population to be whatever he or she is studying. When a researcher *gathers data from the whole population for a given measurement of interest*, it is called a **census.** Most people are familiar with the U.S. Census. It is an attempt made every ten years to measure all persons living in this country. If a researcher is interested in ascertaining the Scholastic Aptitude Test (SAT) scores for all students at the University of Kansas, one way to do so is to conduct a census of all students currently enrolled at that university.

    A **sample** is *a portion of the whole* and, if properly taken, is representative of the whole. For various reasons (explained in Chapter 7), a researcher sometimes prefers to work with a sample of the population instead of dealing with the entire population. For example, in conducting quality control experiments to determine the average life of light bulbs, a light bulb manufacturer might randomly sample only seventy-five light bulbs during a production run. Because of time and money limitations, a human resources manager might take a random sample of forty employees instead of using a census to measure company morale.

    If a researcher is *using data gathered on a group to describe or reach conclusions about that same group only*, the statistics are called **descriptive statistics.** For example, if a teacher produces statistics to summarize a class's examination effort and uses those statistics to reach conclusions about that class only, the statistics are descriptive. The teacher can use these statistics to discuss class average, talk about the range of class scores, or present any other data measurements for the class based on the test.

    Most athletic statistics, such as batting average, rebounds, and first downs, are descriptive statistics, because they are used to describe an individual or team effort. Many of the statistical data generated by businesses are descriptive in nature. They might include number of employees on vacation during June, average salary at the Denver office, corporate sales for 1990, average managerial satisfaction score on a companywide census of employee attitudes, and average return on investment for the Lofton Company for the years 1980 through 1989.

    Inferential statistics and descriptive statistics are utilized differently. If a researcher *gathers data from a sample and uses the statistics generated to reach*

population

census

sample

descriptive statistics

inferential statistics
conclusions about the population from which the sample was taken, the statistics are **inferential statistics.** The data gathered are being used to *infer* something about a larger group. Inferential statistics are sometimes referred to as inductive statistics. The use and importance of inferential statistics are ever growing.

One application of inferential statistics is in pharmaceutical research. An important new drug being tested in cancer research is interferon. It is very expensive to produce, and therefore tests must be limited to small samples of patients. Utilizing inferential statistics, researchers can design experiments with small randomly selected samples of cancer patients and attempt to reach conclusions and make inferences about the population of cancer victims.

Market researchers use inferential statistics to study the impact of advertising on various market segments. Suppose that a soft drink company creates an advertisement depicting teenagers playing in the ocean surf drinking a cola product, and market researchers want to measure the impact of the new advertisement on various age groups. The researcher could randomly sample people from the population, stratify the population into age categories ranging from young to old, and use inferential statistics to determine the effectiveness of the advertisement for the various age groups in the population. The advantage of using inferential statistics is that they allow the researcher to study effectively a wide range of phenomena without having to conduct a census. Most of the topics discussed in this text deal with inferential statistics.

parameter

statistic

A *descriptive measure of the population* is called a **parameter.** Parameters are usually denoted by Greek letters. Examples of parameters are population mean (μ), population variance (σ^2), and population standard deviation (σ). A *descriptive measure of a sample* is called a **statistic.** Statistics are usually denoted by Roman letters. Examples of statistics are sample mean $(\overline{X})$, sample variance (S^2), and sample standard deviation *(S).*

Differentiation between the terms parameter and statistic is important only in the use of inferential statistics. A statistician often wants to estimate the value of a parameter or conduct tests about the value of a parameter. However, the calculation of parameters is usually either impossible or infeasible because of the amount of time and money required to take a census. In such cases, the statistician can take a random sample of the population, calculate a statistic on the sample, and infer by estimation the value of the parameter. The basis for inferential statistics, then, is the ability to make decisions about parameters without having to complete a census of the population.

For example, a manufacturer in the washing machine business might need to determine the average number of loads that a new machine can wash before it has to be repaired. The parameter is the population mean or average number of washes per machine before repair. A company statistician takes a sample of machines, computes and averages the number of washes before repair for each machine, and estimates the population value or parameter by using the statistic, which in this case is the sample average. Figure 1.1 demonstrates this process.

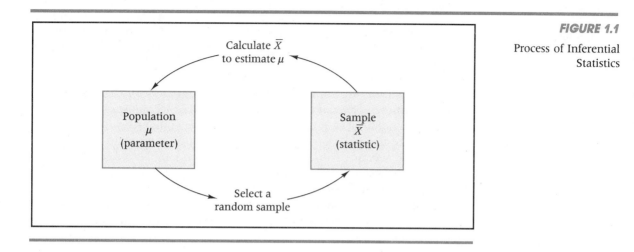

FIGURE 1.1

Process of Inferential
Statistics

Inferences about parameters are made under uncertainty. Unless parameters are computed directly from the population, the statistician never knows
with certainty whether the estimates or inferences made from samples are true
or not. In an effort to help estimate the error of confidence in the result of the
process, statisticians use probability statements. Therefore part of this text is
devoted to probability (Chapter 4).

**Demonstration
Problem 1.1**

Company relocation is usually an extremely important decision. Many
factors have to be considered, including proximity to suppliers, proximity to markets, availability of skilled workers, nearness to transportation facilities, community and state business environments, livability
of community (schools, shopping, housing, etc.) and others. Certainly
one important factor in relocation can be the cost of leasing office
space.

Information-gathering firms can conduct studies to estimate the
cost of office space in various locations. For example, Reis Reports,
Inc., a real estate research group, produced a study in which it estimated
the average asking price for renting office space in major U.S. cities.
This study showed that the average asking price in Atlanta for renting
business real estate is $18.04 per square foot. In New York City, it is
$36.22 and in Los Angeles, it is $25.00. How can a research organization use statistics to generate these decision-making data?

Solution:

The researcher should identify the metropolitan areas under consideration and then randomly select some office buildings from each area. Carefully prepared telephone interviews or written questionnaires should be utilized, asking respondents to report the rental price per square foot for office space in their buildings. Figures for the random sample of each city can then be averaged, and other statistics, such as range, standard deviation, and median, can be computed.

The researcher then uses inferential statistics to estimate citywide price. The averages computed from the random samples are compared by city to determine whether a difference in rental prices exists between two or more cities. An estimate is produced for the average office rental price for metropolitan areas of the United States. Decision makers can then use the sample data and population estimates as input in making relocation decisions.

1.4   LEVELS OF DATA MEASUREMENT

Millions of numerical data are gathered in businesses every day, representing myriad items. For example, numbers represent dollar costs of items produced, geographical locations of retail outlets, weights of shipments, and rankings of subordinates at yearly reviews. All such data should not be analyzed the same way statistically because the entities represented by the numbers are different. For this reason, the statistician needs to know the *level of data measurement* represented by the numbers being analyzed.

The disparate use of numbers can be illustrated by the numbers 40 and 80, which could represent the weights of two objects being shipped, the ratings received on a consumer test by two different products, or the football jersey numbers of a fullback and a wide receiver. Although 80 pounds is twice as much as 40 pounds, the wide receiver is probably not twice as big as the fullback! Averaging the two weights seems reasonable but averaging the football jersey numbers makes no sense. The appropriateness of the data analysis depends on the level of measurement of the data gathered. The phenomenon represented by the numbers determines the level of data measurement. Four common levels of data measurement are as follows:

1. nominal
2. ordinal
3. interval
4. ratio

Nominal Level

The lowest level of data measurement is **nominal level data.** Numbers representing nominal data (the word *level* often is omitted) can be used only to classify or categorize. Jersey numbers used to identify athletes are an example of nominal data. The numbers are used only to differentiate players or positions and not to make a value statement about them. Many demographic questions in surveys result in data that are nominal because the questions are used for classification only. An example of such a question is:

nominal level data

> Which of the following employment classifications best describes your area of work?
>
> A. Educator
> B. Construction worker
> C. Manufacturing worker
> D. Lawyer
> E. Doctor
> F. Other

Suppose that, for computing purposes, an educator is assigned a 1, a construction worker is assigned a 2, a manufacturing worker is assigned a 3, and so on. These numbers should be used only to classify respondents. The number 1 does not denote the top classification. It is used only to differentiate an educator (1) from a lawyer (4).

Some other types of measurement questions that often are nominal in measurement are gender, religion, ethnicity, geographic location, and place of birth. Social security numbers, telephone numbers, employee ID numbers, and ZIP code numbers are further examples of nominal data. Statistical techniques that are appropriate for analyzing nominal data are limited. However, some of the more widely used statistics, such as the chi-square statistic, can be applied to nominal data, often producing useful information.

Ordinal Level

Ordinal level data measurement is a level higher than that for nominal level data. In addition to the capabilities of nominal data, ordinal data can be used to rank or order objects. For example, using ordinal data, a supervisor can evaluate three employees by ranking their productivity with the numbers 1 through 3. The supervisor could identify one employee as the most productive, one as the least productive, and one as middling by using ordinal data. However, the supervisor could not use ordinal data to establish that the intervals between the employees ranked 1 and 2 and between the employees ranked 2 and 3 are equal. That is, she could not say that the differences in the amount

ordinal level data

of productivity between workers ranked 1, 2, and 3 are the same. With ordinal data, the distances or spacing represented by consecutive numbers are not necessarily equal.

Another example of ordinal measurement is the order of finish of runners in a race. Suppose that, in a 100 meter dash, the finish places are 1, 2, 3, 4, 5, and 6. Obviously, the runner finishing first won the gold medal and was the fastest. The runner finishing second was next fastest and so on. The finishes are shown graphically in Figure 1.2. There is no reason to believe that each pair of runners finished the same distance apart. Indeed, the first and second place finishers might have had a photo finish while the third place finisher trailed by 5 meters. The finish place numbers (1, 2, 3, 4, 5, and 6) are ordinal.

Some questionnaire Likert-type scales are considered by many researchers to be ordinal in level. The following is an example of one such type scale:

This class is ___ ___ ___ ___ ___
              awful   bad   okay   good   outstanding
                1   2   3   4   5

When this survey question is coded for the computer, only the numbers 1 through 5 will remain, not the adjectives. Virtually everyone would agree that a 5 is higher than a 4 on this scale and that ranking responses is possible. However, most respondents would not consider the differences between awful, bad, okay, good, and outstanding to be equal. Certain statistical techniques are specifically suited to ordinal data.

Interval Level

interval level data   **Interval level data** are next to the highest level of data. Interval measurements have the properties of ordinal data measurements, but, in addition, the distances between consecutive numbers are equal. That is, interval data have *equal intervals*. An example of interval measurement is Fahrenheit temperature.

FIGURE 1.2

An Example of Ordinal
Measurement

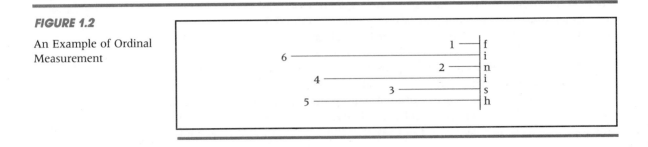

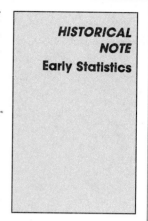

When was the study of statistics first developed? Much of the science of statistics is based on probability, which arose from rudimentary beginnings thousands of years ago. Although the person who invented the first random event is unknown, game playing was highly developed in Egypt by 3500 B.C. Some believe that gaming, usually involving some type of wager, was introduced by Ptolemy in Greece in 300 B.C. In the Roman Empire, gaming was common recreation everywhere until eventually laws were passed forbidding it. The evolution of the die took place over thousands of years. The earliest dice unearthed were made of well-fired buff pottery that likely existed as early as 3000 B.C. Thus the claim that statistics, in one form or another, has been around for more than 5000 years might well be valid.

David, F. N., *Games, Gods and Gambling* (New York: Hafner, 1962).

**HISTORICAL NOTE
Early Statistics**

With Fahrenheit temperature numbers, the temperatures can be ranked, and the amounts of heat between consecutive readings, such as 20°, 21°, and 22°, are the same.

Ratio Level

Ratio level data represent the highest level of measurement. Ratio data have the same properties as interval data, except that ratio data have an *absolute zero* as the lowest value. The implication of absolute zero is that there are no negative values in ratio measures. This definition allows the statistician to create *ratios* with the data. The difference between interval and ratio data is slight (interval data can contain negatives). Some authors combine the two levels into one level: an interval/ratio level.

ratio level data

Examples of ratio data are height, weight, time, volume, Kelvin temperature, and many others. With ratio data, a researcher can state that 180 pounds of weight is twice as much as 90 pounds or, in other words, make a ratio of 180:90. Many of the data gathered by machines in industry are ratio data.

Another example of ratio data is the time required for runners to complete a 100 meter dash. Zero is an absolute, because a runner cannot complete the race in negative time. Equal intervals exist between consecutive times in the race (10 seconds, 11 seconds, 12 seconds). In addition, if a runner completes the race in 10 seconds and a second runner completes it in 20 seconds, the first runner is said to be twice as fast as the second runner. Time is ratio level data in most cases, except in situations such as a NASA launch countdown that involves negative time (time minus 10 and counting—in which case, time is interval level data).

Comparison of the Four Levels of Data

metric data

nonmetric data

The highest levels of data—interval and ratio—are called **metric data** because they are *quantitative* in nature. Nominal and ordinal data are **nonmetric data** and are sometimes referred to as *qualitative* data. Interval and ratio data are usually gathered by precise instruments that often are used in production and engineering processes or in national standardized testing. Nominal and ordinal measurements are derived from imprecise measurements, such as demographic questions or the categorization of people or objects.

Figure 1.3 shows the relationships of the usage potential among the four levels of data measurement. The concentric squares denote that each higher level of data can be analyzed by any of the techniques used on lower levels of data. That is, ratio data can be analyzed by any statistical technique applicable to the other three levels of data.

Nominal data are the most limited data in terms of the types of statistical analysis that can be used with them. Ordinal data allow the researcher to perform any analysis that can be done with nominal data and some additional analyses. With ratio data, a statistician can make ratio comparisons and appropriately do any analysis that can be performed on nominal, ordinal, or interval data. Some statistical techniques require ratio data and cannot be used to analyze other levels of data.

Statistical techniques can be categorized according to different systems. One breakdown of statistics is into two subcategories: parametric statistics and nonparametric statistics. **Parametric statistics** require that data be interval or ratio. If the data are nominal or ordinal, **nonparametric statistics** must

parametric statistics

nonparametric statistics

FIGURE 1.3

Usage Potential of Various Levels of Data

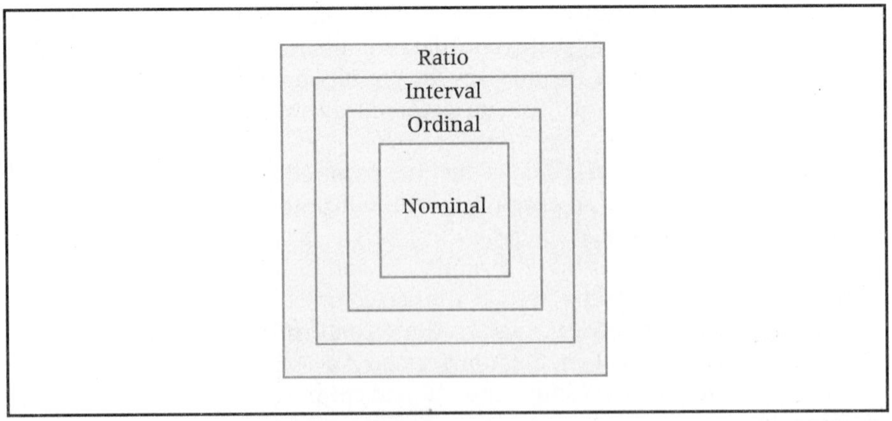

be used. Nonparametric statistics can also be used to analyze interval or ratio data. This text focuses largely on parametric statistics, with the exception of Chapter 12, which contains nonparametric techniques. Thus much of the material in this text requires that data be interval or ratio level data.

CHAPTER SUMMARY

Understanding what statistics are may be difficult sometimes, because the word has so many different connotations. Among the more common uses of the word statistics are (1) the science of gathering, analyzing, interpreting, and presenting data; (2) a branch of mathematics; (3) a course of study; (4) facts and figures; (5) a death; (6) sample measurement; and (7) type of distribution being used. Statistics are broadly used in business, including the disciplines of accounting, decision sciences, economics, finance, management, management information systems, marketing, production, and others.

The study of statistics can be subdivided into two main areas: descriptive statistics and inferential statistics. Descriptive statistics result from gathering data from a body, group, or population and reaching conclusions only about that group. Inferential statistics are generated from the process of gathering sample data from a group, body, or population and reaching conclusions about the larger group from which the sample was drawn.

The type of statistical analysis that is appropriate depends on the level of data measurement, of which there are four: (1) nominal, (2) ordinal, (3) interval, and (4) ratio. Nominal is the lowest level of data, representing classification only of data such as geographic location, gender, or social security number. The next level is ordinal data, which can be used to rank measurements, but the intervals between consecutive numbers do not necessarily represent equal distances. Interval is the next to highest level of data measurement, in which the distances represented by consecutive numbers are equal. The highest level of data measurement is ratio, which contains all the qualities of interval data, except that ratio data also contain an absolute zero. The lowest value of ratio data is zero; that is, ratio data have no negative values. Interval and ratio data sometimes are called metric, or quantitative, data. Nominal and ordinal data sometimes are referred to as nonmetric, or qualitative, data.

The two major types of inferential statistics are (1) parametric statistics and (2) nonparametric statistics. Use of parametric statistics requires interval or ratio data and certain assumptions about the distribution of the data. The techniques presented in this text are largely parametric. If data are only nominal or ordinal in level, nonparametric statistics must be used.

Key Words

Statistics	Nominal level data
Population	Ordinal level data
Census	Interval level data
Sample	Ratio level data
Descriptive statistics	Metric data
Inferential statistics	Nonmetric data
Parameter	Parametric statistics
Statistic	Nonparametric statistics

USING THE COMPUTER

Advent of the modern computer opened many new opportunities for statistical analysis. The computer allows for storage, retrieval, and transference of large data sets. Furthermore, computer software has been developed to analyze data by means of sophisticated statistical techniques. Some widely used statistical techniques, such as multiple regression, are so tedious and cumbersome to compute manually that they were of little practical use to researchers before development and utilization of computers.

Many statistical software packages are now available. Three particular statistical packages that are widely used by business statisticians are Minitab, SAS, and SPSS. These packages have been utilized for more than a decade. Many computer spreadsheet software packages also have the capability of analyzing data statistically. Among the more widely used spreadsheet packages is Lotus 1-2-3.

In this text, the focus is on Minitab, because it is particularly useful as a teaching tool; it was specifically written to enable students to learn how to analyze statistical data by computer. As applicable, the Minitab commands pertinent to the analysis presented in a chapter are explained. Exposure to Minitab should foster your appreciation and understanding of the capabilities of statistical software packages.

SUPPLEMENTARY PROBLEMS

1.1 Give a specific example of data that might be gathered from each of the following business disciplines: accounting, human resources, organizational behavior, sales, consumer behavior, physical distribution, finance, and information systems.

1.2 State examples of data that can be gathered for decision-making purposes from each of the following industries: manufacturing, insurance, travel, retailing, communications, computing, mining, agriculture, banking, and aerospace.

1.3 Give an example of *descriptive* statistics in the recorded music industry. Give an example of how *inferential* statistics could be used in the recorded music industry. Compare the two examples. What makes them different?

1.4 Suppose that you are an operations manager for a plant that manufactures batteries. Give an example of how you could use *descriptive* statistics to make better managerial decisions. Give an example of how you could use *inferential* statistics to make better managerial decisions.

1.5 Classify each of the following as nominal, ordinal, interval, or ratio level data:

    a. The time required to produce each tire on an assembly line
    b. The number of quarts of milk that a family drinks in a month
    c. The age of each of your employees
    d. The ranking of four machines in your plant after they have been designated as excellent, best, satisfactory, and worst
    e. The telephone area code of clients in the United States
    f. The dollar sales at the local pizza house each month
    g. The sizes of men's shoes
    h. The volume of fill in soft drink bottles in ounces
    i. The ranking of a company in the *Fortune 500*
    j. The number of tickets sold at a movie theater on any given night
    k. The employee's ID number
    l. The identification number on a questionnaire
    m. The size of a company as measured by the number of employees

1.6 The Rathburn manufacturing company makes electric wiring, which it sells to contractors in the construction industry. Approximately 900 electric contractors purchase wire from Rathburn annually. Rathburn's director of marketing wants to determine electric contractors satisfaction with Rathburn's wire. He developed a satisfaction scale that yields a satisfaction score of between 10 and 50 for participant responses. A random sample of 35 of the 900 contractors is asked to complete the satisfaction survey. The satisfaction scores for the 35 participants are averaged to produce a mean satisfaction score.

    a. What is the population for this study?
    b. What is the sample for this study?
    c. What is the statistic for this study?
    d. What is the parameter for this study?

CHARTS AND GRAPHS

2

CHAPTER LEARNING OBJECTIVES

The overall objective of Chapter 2 is for you to master several techniques for summarizing and depicting data, enabling you to

1. Recognize the difference between grouped and ungrouped data.
2. Construct a frequency distribution.
3. Construct a histogram, a frequency polygon, an ogive, a pie chart, and a stem and leaf plot.

JASON JACKSON'S PRESENTATION FOR REGIONAL MANAGEMENT

Jason Jackson is assistant district manager for the Atwater Company in a district that spans Colorado and Wyoming. In his district are seventeen Atwater retail outlets of varying sizes. Jackson's boss has asked him to prepare an annual district sales report and to present it at the annual regional management meeting in Phoenix. Jackson knows that this is a great opportunity for him to display his skills as an organizer and presenter. He also knows that he will be alloted only a few minutes to make his presentation. The computer information system contains weekly sales figures for all seventeen district stores. Jackson realizes that, with these figures alone, he has 884 pieces of data (17 stores, each of which has 52 weeks of sales figures). Jackson wants to make a strong impression on regional management so that he will be considered seriously as district management material.

Managerial Questions

- How can Jackson reduce and synthesize the 884 pieces of data into meaningful summaries without losing the essence of the information?
- Is graphic display the most effective means of communicating the information represented by these data?
- What other measurements of these district stores contain information that would be useful to regional management?

N umbers are everywhere! The massive amounts of data being produced is a phenomenon of the computer and new communication tools. The need to manage data has spawned entirely new disciplines. In the field of statistics,

frequency distribution

one mechanism for reducing and summarizing data is the **frequency distribution.** Presentation of statistical data using graphic depictions can often communicate information in a manner that is effective, efficient, and meaningful to the receiver.

ungrouped data

Raw data sometimes are referred to as **ungrouped data.** Ungrouped data is information that has not been summarized in any way. Most data used by researchers are ungrouped. Table 2.1 contains the ages of fifty managers of child care centers in five U.S. cities. The data are ungrouped. *Data that have*

grouped data

been organized into a frequency distribution are called **grouped data.** Table 2.2 presents the frequency distribution for the data from Table 2.1 as an example of grouped data. The distinction between ungrouped and grouped data is important, because the calculation of statistics for the two types of data is different. The focus of this chapter is on organizing ungrouped data into grouped data and displaying them graphically.

(+50)

Raw Data

42	26	32	34	57
30	58	37	50	30
53	40	30	47	49
50	40	32	31	40
52	28	23	35	25
30	36	32	26	50
55	30	58	64	52
49	33	43	46	32
61	31	30	40	60
74	37	29	43	54

TABLE 2.1

Ages of a Sample of Managers from Urban Child Care Centers in the United States

Class Interval	Frequency
20–under 30	6
30–under 40	18
40–under 50	11
50–under 60	11
60–under 70	3
70–under 80	1

TABLE 2.2

Frequency Distribution of Child Care Managers' Ages

FREQUENCY DISTRIBUTIONS | 2.1

Frequency distributions are relatively easy to construct. Although there are some guidelines for their construction, the final shape and design of a distribution varies from researcher to researcher, even when the original raw data are identical. In a sense, frequency distributions are constructed according to individual taste.

When constructing a frequency distribution, the researcher should first determine the range of the raw data. The **range** often is defined as *the difference between the largest and smallest numbers*. The range for the data in Table 2.1 is 51 (74 − 23).

range

The second step in constructing a frequency distribution is to determine how many classes it will have. One rule of thumb is that the number of classes selected be between 5 and 15. If the frequency distribution has too few classes, the data may be too general to be useful. Too many classes may result in a frequency distribution that does not aggregate the data enough to be helpful. The final number of classes is arbitrary; the researcher determines it by examining the range and deciding on a number of classes that will span the range adequately and also will be meaningful to the user. The data in Table 2.1 were grouped into six classes for Table 2.2.

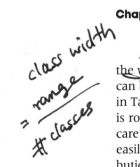

$$\text{class width} = \frac{\text{range}}{\text{\# classes}}$$

After determining the number of classes, the researcher must determine the width of the class interval. An approximation of the size of the class width can be calculated by dividing the range by the number of classes. For the data in Table 2.1, this approximation would be 51/6 or 8.5. Normally, the number is rounded up to the next whole number, which in this case is 9. In the child care manager example, ten-year intervals are used, because most people can easily recognize and understand ten-year age intervals. The frequency distribution must start at a value equal to or lower than the lowest number of the ungrouped data and end at a value equal to or higher than the highest number. The youngest age is 23 and the oldest is 74, so the researcher starts the frequency distribution at 20 and ends it at 80. Table 2.2 contains the completed frequency distribution for the data in Table 2.1. Class endpoints are selected so that no value of the data can fall into more than one class. The class interval expression, (–under), in the distribution of Table 2.2 avoids such a problem.

Class Midpoint

class midpoint

The *midpoint of each class interval* is called the **class midpoint.** It is the value halfway across the class interval and can be calculated as the average of the two class endpoints. For example, in the distribution in Table 2.2, the midpoint of the class interval (30−under 40) is 35, or (30 + 40)/2. A second way to obtain the class midpoint is to calculate one-half the distance across the class interval (half the class width) and add it to the class beginning point, as for the child care managers' distribution:

Class beginning point = 30;

Class width = 10;

Class midpoint = $30 + \frac{1}{2}(10) = 35$.

The class midpoint is important, because it becomes the representative value for each class in most group statistics calculations. The third column in Table 2.3 contains the class midpoints for all classes of the data from Table 2.2.

TABLE 2.3	Class Interval	Frequency	Midpoint	Relative Frequency	Cumulative Frequency
Class Midpoints, Relative Frequencies, and Cumulative Frequencies for Child Care Data	20−under 30	6	25	.12	6
	30−under 40	18	35	.36	6+18> 24
	40−under 50	11	45	.22	35
	50−under 60	11	55	.22	46
	60−under 70	3	65	.06	49
	70−under 80	1	75	.02	50
	Totals	50		1.00	

Relative Frequency

Relative frequency is *the proportion of the total frequencies which fall in any*
given class interval. Relative frequency is the individual class frequency divided
by the total frequency. For example, from Table 2.3, the relative frequency for
the class interval (40–under 50) is 11/50, or .22. Consideration of the relative
frequency is preparatory to the study of probability in Chapter 4. Indeed, if
values were randomly selected from the data presented in Table 2.1, the probability of drawing a number that is "40 and under 50" would be .22, the
relative frequency for that class interval. Column 4 of Table 2.3 displays the
relative frequencies for the frequency distribution of Table 2.2.

Cumulative Frequency

The **cumulative frequency** is a *running total* of frequencies through the
classes. The cumulative frequency for each class interval is the frequency for
that class interval added to the preceding cumulative total. In Table 2.3 the
cumulative frequency for the first class is the same as the class frequency: 6.
The cumulative frequency for the second class interval is the frequency of that
interval (18) plus the frequency of the first interval (6), which yields a new
cumulative frequency of 24. This process continues through the last interval,
at which point the cumulative total equals the sum of the frequencies (50).
The concept of cumulative frequency is used in many areas, including sales
cumulated over a fiscal year, sports scores during a contest (cumulated points),
years of service, points earned in a course, and costs of doing business over a
period of time. Table 2.3 displays cumulative frequencies for the data from
Table 2.2.

> **Demonstration
> Problem 2.1**

The following data give the average weekly mortgage interest rates for
a 60-week period:

10.29	10.03	10.14	9.77	9.35
9.69	10.02	10.40	10.16	9.96
9.98	10.56	9.75	9.87	10.11
10.39	10.28	9.97	9.90	9.57
10.11	9.95	10.23	10.31	10.00
10.30	10.17	9.96	9.78	10.30
10.16	9.78	9.79	10.07	10.03
9.87	9.80	10.10	10.13	9.95
10.08	10.24	10.34	10.47	10.31
9.96	9.70	9.57	9.88	9.84
10.02	10.40	10.12	10.16	10.16
9.99	9.94	10.29	10.05	9.84

$(12 \times 6) = 7^2$

$$\begin{array}{r} 10.56 \\ 9.35 \\ \hline 1.23 \end{array}$$

Construct a frequency distribution for these data. Calculate and display the class midpoints, relative frequencies, and cumulative frequencies for this frequency distribution.

Solution:

How many classes should this frequency distribution contain? The range of the data is 1.21 (10.56 − 9.35). If 13 classes are used, each class width is approximately:

$$\text{Class width} = \frac{\text{Range}}{\text{Number of classes}} = \frac{1.21}{13} = 0.093.$$

If a class width of 0.1 is used, a frequency distribution can be constructed with endpoints that are more uniform looking and allow presentation of the information in categories more familiar to mortgage interest rate users.

The first class endpoint must fall on or before 9.35 in order to include the smallest value; the last endpoint must fall on or after 10.56 in order to include the largest value. In this case the frequency distribution begins at 9.30 and ends at 10.60. The resulting frequency distribution, class midpoints, relative frequencies, and cumulative frequencies are as follows:

Class Interval	Frequency	Class Midpoint	Relative Frequency	Cumulative Frequency
9.30–under 9.40	1	9.35	.0167	1
9.40–under 9.50	0	9.45	.0000	1
9.50–under 9.60	2	9.55	.0333	3
9.60–under 9.70	1	9.65	.0167	4
9.70–under 9.80	6	9.75	.1000	10
9.80–under 9.90	6	9.85	.1000	16
9.90–under 10.00	10	9.95	.1667	26
10.00–under 10.10	8	10.05	.1333	34
10.10–under 10.20	11	10.15	.1833	45
10.20–under 10.30	5	10.25	.0833	50
10.30–under 10.40	6	10.35	.1000	56
10.40–under 10.50	3	10.45	.0500	59
10.50–under 10.60	1	10.55	.0167	60
Totals	60		1.0000	

The frequencies and relative frequencies of these data reveal the mortgage interest rate classes that are likely to occur during this period. Most of the mortgage interest rates (52 of the 60) fall in the classes starting with (9.70–under 9.80) and going through (10.30–under 10.40). The most frequently occurring rates, 11, fall in the (10.10–under 10.20) class.

2.1 The following data represent the afternoon high temperatures for fifty construction days during a year in St. Louis:

42	70	64	47	66
55	85	10	24	45
16	40	81	15	35
38	79	35	36	23
31	38	52	16	81
69	73	38	48	25
31	62	47	63	84
17	40	36	44	17
64	75	53	31	60
12	61	43	30	33

a. Construct a frequency distribution for the data using five class intervals.

b. Construct a frequency distribution for the data using ten class intervals.

c. Examine the results of (a) and (b) and comment on the usefulness of the frequency distribution in terms of temperature summarization capability.

2.2 A packaging process is supposed to fill small boxes of raisins with approximately fifty raisins so that each box will weigh the same. Suppose that 100 boxes of raisins are randomly sampled, and the raisins are counted. The following data are the result of this study:

57	51	53	52	50	60	51	51	52	52
44	53	45	57	39	53	58	47	51	48
49	49	44	54	46	52	55	54	47	53
49	52	49	54	57	52	52	53	49	47
51	48	55	53	55	47	53	43	48	46
54	46	51	48	53	56	48	47	49	57
55	53	50	47	57	49	43	58	52	44
46	59	57	47	61	60	49	53	41	48
59	53	45	45	56	40	46	49	50	57
47	52	48	50	45	56	47	47	48	46

Construct a frequency distribution for these data. What does the frequency distribution reveal about the box fills?

2.3 The owner of a fast food restaurant ascertains the ages of a sample of her customers. From these data, she constructs the frequency distribution shown. For each class interval of the frequency distribution, determine the class midpoint, the relative frequency, and the cumulative frequency.

Class Interval	Frequency
0– 5	6
5–10	8
10–15	17
15–20	23
20–25	18
25–30	10
30–35	4

What does the relative frequency tell the fast food restaurant owner about customer ages?

2.4 The semiprofessional bowling league in a city held a tournament, and from the scores, the league's president constructed the frequency distribution shown. For each class of the frequency distribution, determine the class midpoint, the relative frequency, and the cumulative frequency.

Class Interval	Frequency
140–165	93
165–190	107
190–215	46
215–240	55
240–265	80
265–290	16

2.5 List three specific uses of cumulative frequencies in business.

2.2   GRAPHIC DEPICTION OF DATA

Today, decision makers are being blitzed by data. Hence the medium of information communication can be essential. One of the most widely used mediums of transferring information is graphic depiction. Converting data to graphics can be creative and artful. Often the most difficult and crucial step in this process is reducing important and sometimes expensive data to a graphic picture in a manner that is both clear and concise and yet consistent with the message of the original data. Five types of graphic depictions are presented: (1) histogram, (2) frequency polygon, (3) ogive, (4) pie chart, and (5) stem and leaf plot.

Histograms

A **histogram** is a type of vertical bar chart. Construction involves labeling the X axis (abscissa) with the class endpoints and the Y axis (ordinate) with the frequencies; drawing a horizontal line segment from class endpoint to class endpoint at each frequency value; and connecting each line segment vertically from the frequency value to the X axis, forming a series of rectangles. Figure 2.1 contains a histogram of the frequency distribution in Table 2.2.

A histogram is a useful tool for differentiating the frequencies of class intervals. A quick glance at a histogram reveals which class intervals produce the highest frequency totals. Figure 2.1 clearly shows that the class interval (30−under 40) yields by far the highest frequency count (18). Recall that these data points represent ages of the managers of child care centers; thus more managers were in the (30−under 40) age class than any other class. Note also that the (40−under 50) class and the (50−under 60) class contain the same number of frequencies. Examination of the histogram reveals where large increases or decreases occur between classes, such as from the (20−under 30)

histogram

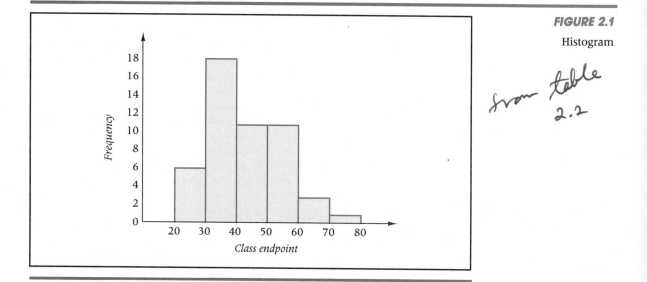

FIGURE 2.1

Histogram

from table 2.2

class to (30—under 40) class, an increase of 12, or from the (50—under 60) class to the (60—under 70) class, a decrease of 8.

Sometimes, creating graphs with identical scales on both axes is desirable. However, because the range of meaningful numbers for the two variables being graphed often differ considerably, the resulting graph contains X and Y axes with different scales. Note that the scales of the axes used to construct the histogram in Figure 2.1 are different. The user of the graph should have a clear understanding of the scales used for the axes. Otherwise, a graph's creator can "lie with statistics" by stretching or compressing a graph to make a point. For example, if the histogram presented in Figure 2.1 is compressed so that the Y axis has the same scale as the X axis, the resulting histogram—Figure 2.2— shows little difference in the frequencies of ages for the various class intervals and conveys a picture much different from that of Figure 2.1.

Frequency Polygons

frequency polygon   Construction of a **frequency polygon** begins—as with a histogram—with the scaling of class endpoints along the X axis and the frequency values along the Y axis. A dot is graphed for the frequency value at the midpoint of each class interval (class midpoint), and connecting these midpoint dots completes the graph. Figure 2.3 contains a frequency polygon of the distribution in Table 2.2. The information gleaned from frequency polygons and histograms is about the same.

If no other frequency values lie outside the range of the class intervals being graphed in the frequency polygon, a zero frequency can be graphed at the class midpoint of the class before the lowest class interval (10—under 20) and the class after the highest class interval (80—under 90). Connecting the endpoints of the frequency polygon to these two zero frequencies closes off the frequency polygon (the line segments from frequencies 6 to 0 and 1 to 0 in Figure 2.3). Many researchers prefer to close off the frequency polygon. In

---

FIGURE 2.2

Histogram with Equal
Scales on the Axes

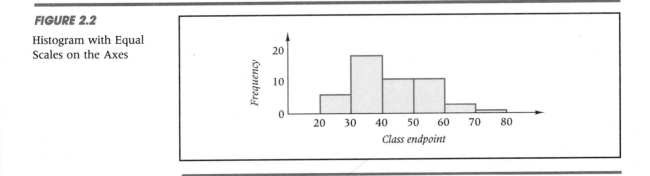

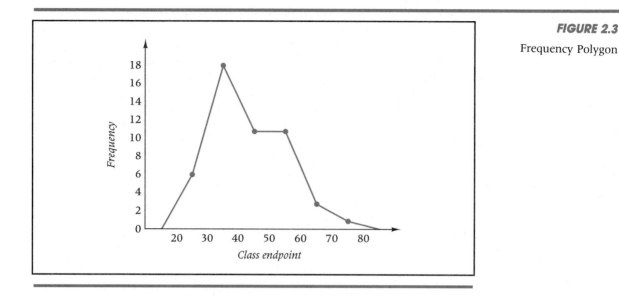

FIGURE 2.3

Frequency Polygon

a manner similar to the histogram, changing the axes scales can compress or stretch a frequency polygon, affecting the user's impression of what the graph represents.

Ogives

An **ogive** (o-jive) is a *cumulative or decumulative frequency polygon*. Again, construction begins with the labeling of the X axis with the class endpoints and the Y axis with the frequencies. However, the use of cumulative frequency values requires that the scale along the Y axis be great enough to include the frequency total. Ogive construction begins with the plotting of a dot of zero frequency at the beginning of the first class and proceeds by marking a dot at the *end* of each class interval for the cumulative value. Connecting the dots then completes the ogive. Figure 2.4 depicts an ogive for the data in Table 2.2.

Ogives are most useful when the decision maker wants to see *running totals*. For example, if a comptroller is interested in controlling costs, an ogive could depict cumulative costs over a fiscal year.

ogive

Pie Charts

A **pie chart** is *a circular depiction of data where the area of the whole pie represents 100% of the data being studied and slices represent a percentage breakdown of the sublevels*. Pie charts clearly show the relative magnitudes of parts to a whole.

pie chart

They are especially useful in displaying items such as budget categories and time and resource allocations.

Construction begins by determining the proportion of each subunit to the whole. Table 2.4 contains a breakdown of a hypothetical college student's time schedule for a typical weekday. Note conversion of the raw hours to proportions (relative frequencies). Because there are 360 degrees in a circle, each proportion is multiplied by 360 to obtain the correct number of degrees to represent each item. For example, the student sleeps 8 hours per day, which is 8/24 or 0.333 of the total day. Multiplying this value by 360 degrees results in 120 degrees.

FIGURE 2.4

Ogive

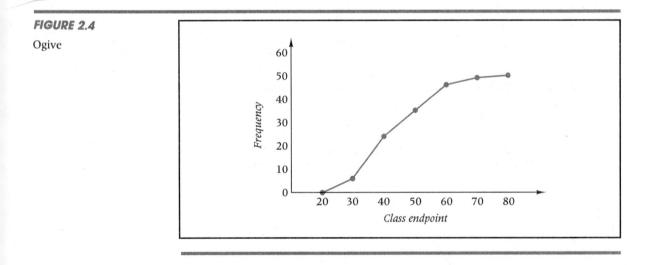

TABLE 2.4

Daily Schedule for a
College Student

Item	Hours	Proportion	Degrees
Class	3.6	.150	54
Eat	3.0	.125	45
Lab	0.4	.017	6
Library	1.0	.042	15
Relax	4.0	.167	60
Sleep	8.0	.333	120
Study	3.0	.125	45
Travel	1.0	.042	15
Totals	24.0	1.000	360

FIGURE 2.5

Pie Chart of Student's Time

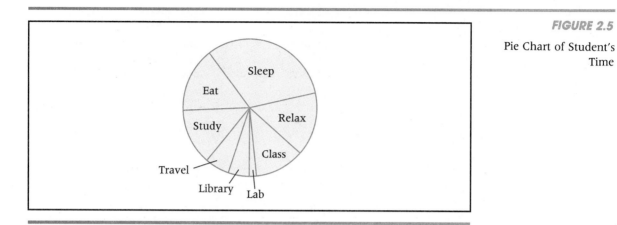

FIGURE 2.5

Pie Chart of Student's Time

Thus sleep is represented by 120 degrees, or 1/3, of the pie. The pie chart is then completed by using a compass to lay out the slices. The pie chart in Figure 2.5 represents the data in Table 2.4.

Demonstration Problem 2.2

In 1990, a survey by Drake Beam Morin, Inc., of its middle-aged clients who had been laid off, revealed that the new jobs obtained for clients aged 50 and over included positions in the following areas:

General management	28%
Corporate staff	4%
Finance/accounting	10%
Marketing/sales	18%
Science/engineering/information systems	12%
All other	28%

Construct a pie chart to depict these figures.

Solution:

Convert each percentage to degrees by converting the percentages to proportions and multiplying the proportions by 360°:

General management	$360°(0.28) = 100.8°$
Corporate staff	$360°(0.04) = 14.4°$
Finance/accounting	$360°(0.10) = 36.0°$
Marketing/sales	$360°(0.18) = 64.8°$
Science/engineering/information systems	$360°(0.12) = 43.2°$
All other	$360°(0.28) = 100.8°$

Construct the pie chart:

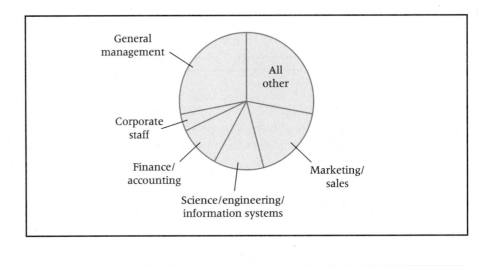

Stem and Leaf Plots

stem and leaf plot Another way to organize raw data into groups is by a **stem and leaf plot.** This technique is simple and provides a unique view of the data. A stem and leaf plot is constructed by dividing the digits for each number of the data into two groups, a stem and a leaf. The stem consists of the higher valued digits and the leaf contains the lower values. If a set of data has only two digits, the stem is the value on the left and the leaf is the value on the right. For example, if 34 is one of the numbers, the stem is 3 and the leaf is 4. For numbers with more than two digits, division of stem and leaf is a matter of researcher preference.

Table 2.5 contains scores from an examination given to a group of thirty-five job trainees over plant safety policy and rules. A stem and leaf plot of these data is displayed in Table 2.6. One advantage of such a distribution is that the instructor can readily see whether the scores are in the upper or lower end of

86	77	91	60	55	**TABLE 2.5**
76	92	47	88	67	Safety Examination
23	59	72	75	83	Scores for Plant Trainees
77	68	82	97	89	
81	75	74	39	67	
79	83	70	78	91	
68	49	56	94	81	

Stem	*Leaf*		**TABLE 2.6**
2	3		Stem and Leaf Plot for
3	9		Plant Safety Examination
4	7 9		Data
5	5 6 9		
6	0 7 7 8 8		
7	0 2 4 5 5 6 7 7 8 9	(×10)	
8	1 1 2 3 3 6 8 9		
9	1 1 2 4 7		

each bracket and also determine the spread of the scores. A second advantage of stem and leaf plots is that the values of the original raw data are retained (unlike most frequency distributions and graphic depictions, which use the class midpoint to represent the values in a class).

Demonstration Problem 2.3

The following data represent the costs of a sample of 30 parcel postage mailings by a company:

$3.67	$10.94	$3.20	$8.64	$2.84
1.83	7.80	5.42	1.97	2.09
3.34	4.95	5.11	3.32	2.78
3.64	3.45	4.65	7.20	3.53
9.15	5.47	3.89	3.55	4.10
2.75	1.93	3.21	4.84	4.15

Using dollars as a stem and cents as a leaf, construct a stem and leaf plot of the data.

Solution:

Stem	Leaf
1	83, 93, 97
2	09, 75, 78, 84
3	20, 21, 32, 34, 45, 53, 55, 64, 67, 89
4	10, 15, 65, 84, 95
5	11, 42, 47
6	
7	20, 80
8	64
9	15
10	94

**PROBLEMS
Section 2.2**

2.6 Construct a histogram and a frequency polygon for the following data:

Class Interval	Frequency
30–32	5
32–34	7
34–36	15
36–38	21
38–40	34
40–42	24
42–44	17
44–46	8

2.7 Construct a histogram and a frequency polygon for the following data:

Class Interval	Frequency
10–20	9
20–30	7
30–40	10
40–50	6
50–60	13
60–70	18
70–80	15

2.8 Construct an ogive for the following data:

Class Interval	Frequency
3– 6	2
6– 9	5
9–12	10
12–15	11
15–18	17
18–21	5

2.9 According to *Fortune* magazine, Japan is the world's fastest-growing major market for imported cars. The increased status of imported cars along with the strong buying power of the yen have contributed to this demand. The following numbers of foreign cars were imported and registered in Japan in 1989:

Company	Number of Cars Sold in Japan in 1989
Volkswagen-Audi	48,980
BMW	33,076
Mercedes-Benz	31,511
Rover	10,655
Citroen-Peugeot	8,494
General Motors	7,231
Volvo	7,122
Ford Motor	5,967
Others	22,943

Construct a pie chart showing the percentage each company has of the Japanese imported car market.

2.10 The following is a list of the top ten record labels for chart share of Billboard's weekly top pop album list between January 7 and December 23, 1989:

Record Company	Number of Albums
Columbia	51
Atlantic	38
Geffen	24
MCA	34
Elektra	23
Warner Brothers	36
Epic	32
Capitol	33
Mercury	28
Arista	24

Use the number of albums appearing on the charts and construct a pie chart for these record companies.

2.11 Construct a stem and leaf chart using two digits for the stem:

212	239	240	218	222	249	265
224	257	271	266	234	239	219
255	260	243	261	249	230	
246	263	235	229	218	238	
254	249	250	263	229	221	
253	227	270	257	261	238	
240	239	273	220	226	239	
258	259	230	262	255	226	

2.12 The following data represent the number of passengers per flight in a sample of 50 flights from Wichita, Kansas, to Kansas City, Missouri:

23	65	44	37	23	45	70
46	17	29	52	38	47	19
66	25	48	80	52	49	
67	20	29	59	50	19	
13	47	69	51	17	32	
58	28	34	33	57	64	
19	16	35	48	41	27	
17	38	60	46	77	61	

Construct a stem and leaf plot for these data. What does the stem and leaf plot tell you about the number of passengers per flight?

CHAPTER SUMMARY

There are two types of data: grouped and ungrouped. Most statistical analysis is performed on ungrouped, or raw, data. Grouped data are data that have been organized into a frequency distribution. Differentiating between grouped and ungrouped data is important, because statistical operations on the two types are computed differently.

Constructing a frequency distribution involves several steps. The first step is to determine the range of the data, which is the difference between the largest value and the smallest value. Next, the number of classes is determined, which is an arbitrary choice of the researcher. However, too few classes overaggregate the data into meaningless categories; too many classes do not summarize the data enough to be useful. The third step in constructing the frequency distribution is determining the width of the class interval. Dividing the range of values by the number of classes yields the approximate width of the class interval.

The class midpoint is the midpoint of a class interval. It is the average of the class midpoints and it represents the halfway point of the class interval. Relative frequency is a value computed by dividing an individual frequency by the sum of the frequencies. Relative frequency represents the proportion of total values that fall in a given class interval, and it is analagous to the probability of randomly drawing a value from a given class interval out of all values. The cumulative frequency is a running total frequency tally that starts with the first frequency value and adds each ensuing frequency to the total.

The types of graphic depictions presented in this chapter were histograms, frequency polygons, ogives, pie charts, and stem and leaf plots. A histogram is a vertical bar chart in which a line segment connects class endpoints at the value of the frequency. Two vertical lines connect this line segment down to the X axis, forming rectangles. A frequency polygon is constructed by graphing a dot at the midpoint of each class interval for the value of each frequency and then connecting the dots. Ogives are cumulative or decumulative frequency polygons. Points on an ogive are graphed at the class endpoints. The ogive graph starts at the beginning of the first class interval with a value of zero and continues through the values of the cumulative frequencies to the class endpoints.

A pie chart is a circular depiction of data. The amount of each category is represented as a slice of the pie proportionate to the total. The slices are determined by multiplying the proportion of each category by 360° to compute the number of degrees of the circle allotted to each category. Stem and leaf plots are another way to organize data. The numbers are divided into two parts: a stem and a leaf. The stems are the leftmost digits of the numbers and the leaves are the rightmost digits. The researcher determines how to divide the digits into stems and leaves. The stems are individually listed, with all leaf values corresponding to each stem displayed beside that stem.

Key Words

Frequency distribution	Cumulative frequency
Ungrouped data	Histogram
Grouped data	Frequency polygon
Range	Ogive
Class midpoint	Pie chart
Relative frequency	Stem and leaf plot

USING THE COMPUTER

Beginning with Chapter 2, you can use the computer to perform at least some of the statistical operations discussed in many of the chapters. Where applicable, chapters contain a section explaining how to use Minitab to work problems in that chapter. In Chapter 2, you can use Minitab to construct histograms and to make stem and leaf plots. The process begins by calling up Minitab or loading Minitab into your computer. When Minitab is on-line, you will get a Minitab prompt (MTB >) after which you can type the desired command.

Histograms

Minitab can produce a histogram from raw data. First, load the raw data into Minitab. You can do so with either a SET command or a READ command.* The READ command is more useful when loading multiple columns of data when the column sizes are equal. The SET command allows you to load only one column at a time but is preferred for single column entry or when the column sizes are unequal. To load data using the SET command, type SET after the MTB prompt followed by the column location where the data are to

*Minitab commands can be in either uppercase or lowercase form. In this text uppercase letters are used for Minitab commands.

be stored for further use. For example, if the data are to be stored in column 1, the command is

    MTB > SET C1

    After you enter this command, the prompt will change to **DATA**. **DATA** is the prompt that is specifically used with the **SET** and **READ** commands. Enter values following the **DATA** prompt and separate them by spaces, commas, or slashes. When you strike the return button, you will continue to get **DATA** prompts until you enter **END** after a **DATA** prompt. When you have typed "end" after a **DATA** prompt, you will again get a Minitab prompt. An example of using the **SET** command is:

    MTB > SET C1
    DATA > 12 31 44 68 96
    DATA > 23 49 54
    DATA > END
    MTB >

From these commands, the data 12, 31, 44, 68, 96, 23, 49, and 54 will be stored in column 1.

    To construct a histogram, use the Minitab command **HISTOGRAM**, followed by the column in which the data are stored. For example:

    MTB > HISTOGRAM C1

Using this command, Minitab will determine the class interval width, determine a starting point, and compute a histogram. Minitab often provides subcommands for a given command. Subcommands can be used with the **HISTO-GRAM** command to specify the width of class intervals and a starting point for the histogram if you so desire.

    To get a subcommand prompt, **SUBC**, you need to end the Minitab command with a semicolon. You end each subcommand with either a semicolon or a period. If you end a subcommand with a semicolon, the subcommand prompts will continue. If you end a subcommand with a period, the next command will be a Minitab command prompt, **MTB**. **HISTOGRAM** has two subcommands: **INCREMENT** and **START**. The **INCREMENT** subcommand allows you to preset the class interval width. The **START** command allows you to determine the value of the first class midpoint. For example, if you want to construct a histogram from the data in column 1 with a class width of 5 and a starting midpoint of 20, the commands are

    MTB > HISTOGRAM C1;
    SUBC > INCREMENT 5;
    SUBC > START 20.
    MTB >

Note that, in order to get the SUBC prompt, the HISTOGRAM command ends with a semicolon. The semicolon at the end of the INCREMENT command allows for another SUBC prompt. The period after the START command causes Minitab to return to the MTB prompts. This pattern holds for all Minitab subcommands.

The Minitab HISTOGRAM command generates output automatically on the screen, including the size of the database being used and a rather crude histogram constructed with small asterisks in the form of a horizontal bar graph. The count (frequency) values for each class are given along with the midpoint values (class midpoint). Following are the statements and the output for Minitab histogram analysis of the data in Table 2.1:

Commands

```
MTB  > SET C1
DATA > 42  26  32  34  57  30  58  37  50  30
DATA > 53  40  30  47  49  50  40  32  31  40
DATA > 52  28  23  35  25  30  36  32  26  50
DATA > 55  30  58  64  52  49  33  43  46  32
DATA > 61  31  30  40  60  74  37  29  43  54
DATA > end
MTB  > HISTOGRAM C1;
MTB  > INCREMENT 10;
MTB  > START 10.
```

Output

```
Histogram of C1   N = 50

Midpoint Count
       15.0      7*******
       25.0      6******
       35.0      5*****
       45.0      8********
       55.0     10**********
       65.0      3***
       75.0      3***
       85.0      5*****
       95.0      3***
```

Stem and Leaf Plots

Minitab can also produce stem and leaf plots. You begin the process by loading the data, using either the SET or READ command. The SET command is preferred in constructing stem and leaf plots, because these plots are usually constructed for a single set of data. After you load the data, you can construct the stem and leaf plot by using the Minitab command, STEM AND LEAF. Actually, Minitab needs only the first four letters of a command, so it makes no difference whether you use STEM or STEM AND LEAF. The STEM AND

LEAF portion of the command is followed by the column location of the data. For example,

MTB > STEM AND LEAF C1

The following Minitab commands and output are required to produce a stem and leaf plot for the data in Table 2.5:

Commands

MTB > SET C1
DATA > 86 77 91 60 55 76 92 47 88 67 23 59 72 75 83
DATA > 77 68 82 97 89 81 75 74 39 67
DATA > 79 83 70 78 91 68 49 56 94 81
DATA > END
MTB > STEM AND LEAF C1

Output

Stem and leaf of C1   N = 35
Leaf Unit = 1.0

```
   1    2  3
   2    3  9
   4    4  79
   7    5  569
  12    6  07788
 (10)   7  0245567789
  13    8  11233689
   5    9  11247
```

The first column of the stem and leaf output contains the running sum totals of frequencies from the top of the distribution down to the middle and from the bottom of the distribution up to the middle. The value in the parentheses is the frequency total for the row containing the median (10). The second column of the output contains the stem values. The numbers to the right of the stems are the leaf values. The leaf unit tells where the decimal place goes. The 1.0 leaf unit denotes that the leaf values are in the 1's place for this problem.

SUPPLEMENTARY PROBLEMS

2.13 The Olson Company manufactures a metal ring for industrial engines that usually weighs about 50 oz. A random sample of fifty of these metal rings produced the following weights (in ounces):

51	46	41	47	62
53	55	52	52	39
56	41	69	53	44
50	44	53	46	55
44	52	57	36	43
47	56	51	58	52
53	50	54	51	43
53	57	63	38	42
42	44	42	49	57
57	46	47	50	49

Construct a frequency distribution for these data using eight classes.

2.14 A northwestern distribution company surveyed fifty-three of its mid-level managers. The survey obtained the ages of these managers, which later were organized into the frequency distribution shown. Determine the class midpoint, relative frequency, and cumulative frequency for these data.

Class Interval	Frequency
20–25	8
25–30	6
30–35	5
35–40	12
40–45	15
45–50	7

2.15 The following data are shaped roughly like a normal distribution (discussed in Chapter 6):

61.4	26.4	30.4	63.9	67.9
81.6	73.4	65.1	71.6	57.3
71.1	48.9	54.8	32.5	55.1
56.8	52.9	55.6	76.4	19.9
77.4	32.1	32.7	52.7	35.3
27.3	37.4	47.5	46.8	19.1
47.9	54.6	53.3	58.6	87.8
74.1	60.2	60.5	61.7	48.2
60.1	60.5	38.1	46.8	27.3
58.1	54.9	40.1	32.5	39.1

Construct a frequency distribution starting with 10 as the lowest class beginning point and use a class width of 10. Construct a histogram and a frequency polygon for this frequency distribution and observe the shape of a normal distribution. Based on your results from these graphs, what does a normal distribution look like?

2.16 Use the data from Problem 2.14.

a. Construct a histogram and a frequency polygon.

b. Construct an ogive.

2.17 In a medium-sized southern city, there are 86 houses for sale, each having about 2,000 square feet of floor space. The asking prices vary. The frequency distribution shown contains the price categories for the 86 houses. Construct a histogram, a frequency polygon, and an ogive from these data.

Asking Price	Frequency
$ 50,000–under $ 60,000	21
60,000–under 70,000	27
70,000–under 80,000	18
80,000–under 90,000	11
90,000–under 100,000	6
100,000–under 110,000	3

2.18 Good, relatively inexpensive prenatal care often can prevent a lifetime of expense owing to complications resulting from low baby birth weights. A survey of a random sample of fifty-seven new mothers asked them to estimate how much they spent on prenatal care. The researcher tallied the results and presented them in the frequency distribution shown. Use these data to construct a histogram, a frequency polygon, and an ogive.

Amount Spent on Prenatal Care	Frequency of New Mothers
$ 0–$100	3
100– 200	6
200– 300	12
300– 400	19
400– 500	11
500– 600	6

2.19 A consumer group surveyed food prices at eighty-seven stores on the East Coast. Among the food prices being measured was that of sugar. Based on the data collected, the group constructed the frequency distri-

bution of the prices of five pounds of Domino's sugar in the stores surveyed. Compute a histogram, a frequency polygon, and an ogive for the
following data:

Price	Frequency
$1.75–under $1.90	9
1.90–under 2.05	14
2.05–under 2.20	17
2.20–under 2.35	16
2.35–under 2.50	18
2.50–under 2.65	8
2.65–under 2.80	5

2.20 The Quaker Oats Company is a relatively diverse company. The following
tabulation shows several of the businesses the Quaker Oats Company
owns and their sales figures for 1989:

Business	1989 Sales (millions)
International	$1,249.5
Fisher-Price Toys	844.8
Grocery specialties (Gatorade, Van Camp's)	739.0
Pet foods	608.4
Ready-to-eat cereals	443.5
Food service	414.7
Hot cereals	377.1
Others (including Aunt Jemima products, Celeste Pizza, etc.)	1,047.2

Construct a pie chart displaying the percentage that each of these businesses is of the whole.

2.21 Some forecasters believe that the 1990s will be a decade of environmental
concerns. The following list shows the number of oil spills by the largest
U.S. oil companies between 1984 and 1988. (Note that these data reflect
the fact that oil companies do not all transport the same amounts of oil
over the same number of miles.) Construct a pie chart to display the
following numbers:

Company	Number of Spills
Chevron	1,221
Amoco	314
Texaco	500
Exxon	611
Shell	567
Mobil	421
Arco	24
Tenneco	145

2.22 According to the *Oil and Gas Journal,* at the end of 1990 the oil reserves for the Arabian Gulf region were as follows:

Country	Billions of Barrels
Saudi Arabia	257.5
Iraq	100.0
Kuwait	94.5
Iran	92.9
Abu Dhabi	92.2
Others	23.7

Construct a pie chart to depict the portion of the total Arabian Gulf region oil reserves in each of these countries.

2.23 BAA PLC., owner and operator of Heathrow Airport, released the following figures on the origin of travelers passing through Heathrow for the year ending March 31, 1990:

Origin	Percentage
Europe	51.2
Britain	17.9
Other international	15.5
North America	15.4

Construct a pie chart to represent these percentages.

2.24 A research organization selected 50 U.S. towns with 1990 populations of between 4,000 and 6,000 as a sample to represent small towns for survey purposes. The populations of these towns are as follows:

4,420	5,221	4,299	5,831	5,750
5,049	5,556	4,361	5,737	4,654
4,653	5,338	4,512	4,388	5,923
4,730	4,963	5,090	4,822	4,304
4,758	5,366	5,431	5,291	5,254
4,866	5,858	4,346	4,734	5,919
4,216	4,328	4,459	5,832	5,873
5,257	5,048	4,232	4,878	5,166
5,366	4,212	5,669	4,224	4,440
4,299	5,263	4,339	4,834	5,478

Construct a stem and leaf plot for the data, letting each leaf contain two digits.

2.25 Listed here are thirty different weekly Dow Jones Industrial stock averages:

2,656	2,301	2,975	3,002	2,468
2,742	2,830	2,405	2,677	2,990
2,200	2,764	2,337	2,961	3,010
2,976	2,375	2,602	2,670	2,922
2,344	2,760	2,555	2,524	2,814
2,996	2,437	2,268	2,448	2,460

Construct a stem and leaf plot for these thirty values. Let the stem contain two digits.

2.26 The U.S. Department of Transportation keeps track of the percentage of flights arriving within 15 minutes of their scheduled arrivals. The following data are for 1990:

Airline	On-time Percentage	Airline	On-time Percentage
Pan Am	83.8	Alaska	79.7
America West	83.8	American	79.0
Northwest	82.1	United	77.4
Eastern	81.2	TWA	77.1
USAir	80.8	Delta	77.1
Southwest	80.8	Continental	76.9

Use this information to construct a stem and leaf plot. Let the leaf be the tenths of a percent.

DESCRIPTIVE STATISTICS

3

CHAPTER LEARNING OBJECTIVES

The focus of Chapter 3 is on the use of statistical techniques to describe data. Its intent is to enable you to

1. Distinguish between central tendency and variability.
2. Understand conceptually the meaning of mean, median, mode, and range.
3. Compute a mean, a median, a mode, a range, a variance, a standard deviation, a mean absolute deviation, and a coefficient of variation.
4. Differentiate between sample and population variance and standard deviation.
5. Understand the meaning of standard deviation as it is applied using the empirical rule and Chebyshev's theorem.

LISA MYERS: A DATA DILEMMA

The Britavia Corporation faces a financial "belt tightening." The company officers are taking a close look at all areas of expenditures, including managerial travel expenses. In an effort to get a handle on them, a vice president asked that Lisa Myers, a mid-level manager, be put on a special short-term project to compile a report on 1990 company management's travel expenses. She has been asked to focus her report on per diem expenses.

Myers discovered that the accounting office has figures in the computer for multiple day travel to various cities in the United States. In examining some of the data, she observed that travel to certain cities in the northeast exceeds $200 per day, whereas travel to certain southern cities is closer to $100 per day. A wealth of information is available to her. One of her tasks is to take the unorganized and unsummarized data and begin to make sense of it.

Managerial Questions

- Which data descriptors should Myers prefer? Which would be more meaningful to her audience?
- How can she take a set of numbers on a variable such as cost per meal and summarize the set using a single data descriptor?
- If some of the data are already in frequency distribution form, how can she compute statistics that will further describe the data?

Chapter 2 described graphic techniques for organizing and presenting data. However, to be able to develop *numerical* values that can describe a data set also is important. This chapter presents statistical descriptive measures that can be used to analyze data numerically in several different ways, including measures of central tendency and measures of variability. The computation of measures of central tendency and variability is different for ungrouped data and grouped data. Hence grouped data and ungrouped data are treated separately.

3.1 MEASURES OF CENTRAL TENDENCY FOR UNGROUPED DATA

measures of central tendency

One type of measure that can be used to describe a set of data is the measure of central tendency. **Measures of central tendency** yield information about *the center or the middle of a group of numbers.* Suppose, for example, that a market researcher is interested in targeting the ages of purchasers of compact discs.

28	23	27	30	24
35	29	21	25	18
21	31	19	22	44
17	24	29	42	31
24	41	34	24	27
32	28	25	25	35
25	17	24	29	22

TABLE 3.1

Ages of Purchasers of
Compact Discs

She conducts a survey of thirty-five compact-disc buyers and records buyers' ages (Table 3.1). For these data, measures of central tendency can yield the average age of these purchasers, the age of the middle purchaser, or the most frequent age. A measure of central tendency yields information about where the center of the group tends to fall. Measures of central tendency do not focus on the outer parts of the data set or the span of the data set. The measures of central tendency presented here for ungrouped data are the mode, the median, and the mean.

Mode

The **mode** is *the most frequently occurring value* in a set of data. For the data in Table 3.1, the mode is 24 years, because there are more twenty-four-year-olds (5) than any other age. Organizing the data into an *ordered array*—an ordering of the numbers in magnitude from smallest to largest—helps to locate the mode. The following is an ordered array of the values in Table 3.1:

mode

```
17  17  18  19  21  21  22  22  23  24  24  24
24  24  25  25  25  25  27  27  28  28  29  29
29  30  31  31  32  34  35  35  41  42  44
```

Another mechanism that can be helpful in the selection of the mode is a stem and leaf plot. Utilizing the process presented in Chapter 2 yields the stem and leaf plot for the data in Table 3.1 shown in Table 3.2. The most frequently occurring leaf under any stem is the leaf of 4 associated with the stem of 2, so the mode is 24.

Stem	Leaf
1	7, 7, 8, 9
2	1, 1, 2, 2, 3, 4, 4, 4, 4, 4, 5, 5, 5, 5, 7, 7, 8, 8, 9, 9, 9
3	0, 1, 1, 2, 4, 5, 5
4	1, 2, 4

TABLE 3.2

Stem and Leaf Plot for
Ages of Compact-Disc
Purchasers

If there is a tie for the most frequently occurring value, there are two modes. In that case the data are said to be *bimodal*. If a set of data is not exactly bimodal but contains two values that are more dominant than others, some researchers take the liberty of referring to the data set as bimodal even though there is not an exact tie for the mode. Data sets with more than two modes are referred to as *multimodal*.

In the world of business, the concept of mode is often used in determining sizes. For example, shoe manufacturers might produce less expensive shoes in three widths only: small, medium, and large. Each width size represents a modal width of feet. By reducing the number of sizes to a few modal sizes, companies can reduce total product costs by limiting machine setup costs. Similarly the garment industry produces shirts, dresses, suits, and many other clothing products in modal sizes. For example, all size M shirts in a given lot are produced in the same size. This size is some modal size for medium-sized men.

Median

median

The **median** is *the middle value in an ordered array of numbers*. If there is an odd number of terms in the array, the median is the middle number. If there is an even number of terms, the median is the average of the two middle numbers. The following steps are used to determine the median:

- *Step 1.* Arrange the observations in an ordered data array.
- *Step 2.* If there is an odd number of terms, find the middle term of the ordered array. It is the median.
- *Step 3.* If there is an even number of terms, find the average of the middle two terms. This average is the median.

Suppose that a statistician wants to determine the median for the following numbers:

15   11   14   3   21   17   22   16   19   16   5   7   19   8   9   20   4

He arranges the numbers in an ordered array:

3   4   5   7   8   9   11   14   15   16   16   17   19   19   20   21   22

There are seventeen terms (an odd number of terms), so the median is the middle number, or 15.

If the number 22 is eliminated from the list, there are only sixteen terms:

3   4   5   7   8   9   11   14   15   16   16   17   19   19   20   21

Now there is an even number of terms, and the statistician determines the median by averaging the two middle values, 14 and 15. The resulting median value is 14.5.

Another way to locate the median is by finding the $(n + 1)/2$ term in an ordered array. For example, if a data set contains 77 terms, the median is the 39th term. That is,

$$\frac{n + 1}{2} = \frac{77 + 1}{2} = \frac{78}{2} = 39\text{th term.}$$

This formula is helpful when a large number of terms must be manipulated or when a computer program is being written to compute the median.

The median is unaffected by the magnitude of extreme values. This characteristic is an advantage, because large and small values do not inordinately influence the median. For this reason, the median is often the best measure of central tendency to use in the analysis of variables such as house costs, income, and age. For example, suppose that a real estate broker wants to determine the median selling price of ten houses listed at the following prices:

$67,000	$105,000	$ 148,000
91,000	116,000	167,000
95,000	122,000	189,000
		5,250,000

With ten terms, the median is the average of the two middle terms, $116,000 and $122,000, or $119,000. This price is a reasonable representation of the prices of the ten houses. Note that the house priced at $5,250,000 did not enter into the analysis other than to count as one of the ten houses. If the price of the tenth house were $200,000, the results would be the same. However, if all the house prices were averaged, the resulting average price of the original ten houses would be $635,000, or more expensive than nine of the ten.

A disadvantage of the median is that all the information from the numbers is not used. That is, information about the specific asking price of the most expensive house does not really enter into the computation of the median.

Mean

The **arithmetic mean** is synonymous with the *average* and is computed by *summing all numbers and dividing by the number of numbers.* Because the arithmetic mean is so widely used, most statisticians refer to the arithmetic mean simply as the *mean*.

arithmetic mean

The population mean is represented by the Greek letter mu (μ). The sample mean is represented by $\overline{X}$. The formulas for computing the population mean and the sample mean are given in the boxes that follow.

Population Mean	$$\mu = \frac{\Sigma X}{N} = \frac{X_1 + X_2 + X_3 + \cdots + X_N}{N}.$$

Sample Mean	$$\overline{X} = \frac{\Sigma X}{n} = \frac{X_1 + X_2 + X_3 + \cdots + X_n}{n}.$$

The capital Greek letter sigma (Σ) is commonly used in mathematics to represent a summation of all the numbers in a grouping.* Also, N is the number of terms in the population, and n is the number of terms in the sample. The algorithm for computing a mean is to sum all the numbers in the population or sample and divide by the number of terms.

A more formal definition of the mean is

$$\mu = \frac{\sum_{i=1}^{N} X_i}{N}.$$

However, for the purposes of this text,

$$\Sigma X \quad \text{denotes} \quad \sum_{i=1}^{N} X_i.$$

Suppose that five chiropractors practice in a certain town. Last Tuesday they saw 24, 13, 19, 26, and 11 patients, respectively. The *population* mean number of patients seen on Tuesday by a chiropractor in this town was 18.6 patients. The computations are

$$
\begin{array}{r}
24 \\
13 \\
19 \\
26 \\
\underline{11} \\
\Sigma X = 93
\end{array}
$$

and

$$\mu = \frac{\Sigma X}{N} = \frac{93}{5} = 18.6.$$

*The mathematics of summations is not discussed here. A more detailed explanation is given in Appendix C.

To compute the arithmetic mean of the *sample* of numbers,

$$57 \quad 86 \quad 42 \quad 38 \quad 90 \quad 66,$$

sum the numbers:

$$
\begin{array}{r}
57 \\
86 \\
42 \\
38 \\
90 \\
\underline{66} \\
\Sigma X = 379.
\end{array}
$$

Then calculate the *sample* mean:

$$\overline{X} = \frac{\Sigma X}{n}$$

$$= \frac{379}{6} = 63.167.$$

**Demonstration
Problem 3.1**

Compute the mean value of age for the sample of thirty-five purchasers of compact discs listed in Table 3.1.

Solution:

For these data,

$$\Sigma X = 952 \qquad \text{and} \qquad n = 35.$$

Then

$$\overline{X} = \frac{952}{35} = 27.2 \text{ years old.}$$

For the group of compact-disc purchasers, the average age is 27.2 years.

The mean is affected by each and every value, which is an advantage. The mean uses all the data and each data item influences the mean. It is also a disadvantage, because extremely large or small values can cause the mean to be pulled toward the extreme value; in that case, the mean becomes less representative of the middle values. Recall the preceding discussion of the ten house prices. If the mean is computed on the ten houses, the mean price is larger than the price of nine of the houses, because the $5,250,000 house is included in the calculation. The total price of the ten houses is $6,350,000, and the mean price is

$$\overline{X} = \frac{\Sigma X}{n}$$
$$= \frac{\$6,350,000}{10} = \$635,000.$$

The mean is the most commonly used measure of central tendency because it utilizes each data item in its computation, it is a familiar measure, and it possesses mathematical properties that make it attractive to use in inferential statistics analysis.

Demonstration Problem 3.2

Lisa Myers of the Britavia Corporation gathered a sample of per diem expenses (in dollars) from managerial records:

150	165
110	180
180	200
215	125
150	150
160	190

Compute the mode, median, and mean for these data.

Solution:

- *Mode:* The most frequently occurring value is 150 which is the mode. The modal per diem expense is $150.00.
- *Median:* Arrange the data in an ordered array:

    110   125   150   150   150   160
    165   180   180   190   200   215

    The number of terms is 12. The median is located at the $(12 + 1)/2 = 6.5$th term. The median is the average of

160 and 165, or 162.5. The median per diem expense
is $162.50.

• *Mean:* The sample mean is

$$\overline{X} = \frac{\Sigma X}{n}$$

$$= \frac{1{,}975}{12} = 164.6.$$

The mean per diem expense is $164.60.

3.1 Determine the mode for the following numbers:

2 4 8 4 6 2 7 8 4 3 8 9 4 3 5

3.2 Determine the median for the numbers in Problem 3.1.

3.3 Determine the median for the following numbers:

213 345 609 073 167 243 444 524 199 682

3.4 Compute the mean for the following numbers:

17.3 44.5 31.6 40.0 52.8 38.8 30.1 78.5

3.5 Compute the mean for the following numbers:

7 −2 5 9 0 −3 −6 −7 −4 −5 2 −8

3.6 Assume that the following data represent the number of glasses of water
consumed per week by a sample of athletes:

41	57	32	38	22
23	30	25	40	25
33	29	25	23	24
50	28	31	24	47
38	22	23	27	25

Calculate the mode, median, and mean for the data. Compare the three
answers. Which of the three is most useful in describing the data? Why?

3.7 The following tabulation shows the top eight amusement/theme parks ranked by *Amusement Business* magazine according to their 1989 attendance:

Rank	Park	Attendance
1	Walt Disney World (Fla.)	30,000,000
2	Disneyland (Calif.)	14,400,000
3	Universal Studios (Calif.)	5,100,000
4	Knott's Berry Farm	5,000,000
5	Sea World of Florida	4,000,000
6	Sea World of California	3,800,000
7	Busch Gardens the Dark Continent (Fla.)	3,500,000
8	Kings Island (Ohio)	3,200,000

Compute a mean and a median attendance. Of the two statistics, which is more meaningful in this situation? How can the arithmetic mean and the median each be used in different but meaningful ways with these data?

3.8 The reported average median income for baby boomers for the years 1983–1985 was $22,333. What do you think an average median income is? Why is it advantageous to use a median to compute income?

3.9 According to the U.S. Army Corps of Engineers, the top ten U.S. ports, ranked by total tonnage in 1987 (in 100,000 tons) were as follows:

New Orleans, La.	167.9
New York, N.Y.	154.5
Houston, Tx.	112.5
Valdez Harbor, Alas.	106.9
Baton Rouge, La.	73.4
Corpus Christi, Tx.	53.5
Long Beach, Calif.	45.9
Tampa Harbor, Fla.	44.3
Los Angeles, Calif.	40.5
Norfolk Harbor, Va.	40.0

What is the mean tonnage figure for these U.S. ports? What is the median? How do the mean and the median compare?

3.10 According to *Fortune* magazine, the top fifteen U.S. industrial exporters had the following export sales in 1988:

Company	($ millions)
General Motors	9,392
Ford	8,822
Boeing	7,849
General Electric	5,744
IBM	4,951
Chrysler	4,344
E.I. duPont de Nemours	4,196
McDonnell Douglas	3,471
Caterpillar	2,930
United Technologies	2,848
Eastman Kodak	2,301
Digital Equipment	2,083
Hewlett-Packard	2,064
Unisys	2,013
Philip Morris	1,863

What is the average 1988 dollar export sales for these companies? What is the median export dollar sales for 1988 for these companies? How do the mean and median differ? Why?

COMPUTING THE MEAN FOR GROUPED DATA · **3.2**

Grouped data do not provide information about individual values. Hence the mean for grouped data must be calculated by a different method than that used for ungrouped or raw data. The mean for grouped data is computed by *summing the products of the class midpoint and the class frequency for each class and dividing that sum by the total number of frequencies.*

$$\mu_{grouped} = \frac{\Sigma fM}{\Sigma f} = \frac{f_1 M_1 + f_2 M_2 + f_3 M_3 + \cdots + f_N M_N}{f_1 + f_2 + f_3 + \cdots + f_N}.$$

Mean for Grouped Data

Examination of a frequency distribution reveals that the actual values of the original raw data used to construct the distribution are unavailable from the grouped data. Therefore, computing a mean for grouped data requires use of the class midpoint to represent each value in a class interval.

Table 3.3 contains a frequency distribution of ages from a sample of radio station KWOW listeners. What is the mean age of a KWOW listener based on these data?

TABLE 3.3

Frequency Distribution
of Radio Station KWOW
Listener Ages Taken
from a Sample of 122

Age	Frequency (f)
10–15	6
15–20	22
20–25	35
25–30	29
30–35	16
35–40	8
40–45	4
45–50	2
	$\Sigma f = 122$

The first step in the process is to determine the class midpoints of the frequency distribution and multiply each midpoint by its associated frequency. Table 3.4 contains the class midpoints and the products of each midpoint and its associated frequency (columns 3 and 4). Multiplying a class midpoint (M) by its class frequency (f) weights each class midpoint by the number of values in that class (fM). The reason for weighting each class is to avoid representing each class as the same if there are, say, six frequencies in one class but thirty-five frequencies in another class. Next, the fM terms are summed, and the total fM is divided by the total number of frequencies. The result is the grouped data mean, which for these data, is 25.66.

The grouped mean is only an approximation, because it is based on the assumption that the mean of the values in a class interval equals the class midpoint. There is no guarantee that the values in a class interval will be distributed in such a way that the average value is the class midpoint. In some cases, the values in a class interval may actually fall at one end of the interval; in those cases, the grouped mean contains considerable error.

TABLE 3.4

Computation of Group
Arithmetic Mean for
Data in Table 3.3

Age	Frequency (f)	Midpoint (M)	fM
10–15	6	12.5	75.0
15–20	22	17.5	385.0
20–25	35	22.5	787.5
25–30	29	27.5	797.5
30–35	16	32.5	520.0
35–40	8	37.5	300.0
40–45	4	42.5	170.0
45–50	2	47.5	95.0
	$\Sigma f = 122$		$\Sigma fM = 3,130.0$

$$\mu_{grouped} = \frac{\Sigma fM}{\Sigma f} = \frac{3,130}{122} = 25.66.$$

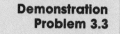

The frequency distribution of per farm crop income in 1988 shown for
49 states (excluding California) is based on data from the Economic
Research Service of the U.S. Department of Agriculture. Compute a
group mean for the following data:

Income ($ thousands)	f
0–under 500	18
500–under 1,000	13
1,000–under 1,500	5
1,500–under 2,000	8
2,000–under 2,500	1
2,500–under 3,000	1
3,000–under 3,500	0
3,500–under 4,000	2
4,000–under 4,500	1

Solution:

Determine the class midpoints and compute $\mu_{grouped} = \Sigma fM / \Sigma f$ as follows:

Income ($ thousands)	f	M	fM
0–under 500	18	250	4,500
500–under 1,000	13	750	9,750
1,000–under 1,500	5	1,250	6,250
1,500–under 2,000	8	1,750	14,000
2,000–under 2,500	1	2,250	2,250
2,500–under 3,000	1	2,750	2,750
3,000–under 3,500	0	3,250	0
3,500–under 4,000	2	3,750	7,500
4,000–under 4,500	1	4,250	4,250
	$\Sigma f = 49$		$\Sigma fM = 51,250$

$\Sigma f = 49$ states (California excluded)

$$= \frac{\Sigma fM}{\Sigma f} = \frac{51,250}{49} = 1045.9 \text{ (thousands)} = 1,045,900.$$

The average per farm crop income for 49 of the states is $1,045,900.

3.11 Compute the mean for the following data:

Class	f
0– 2	39
2– 4	27
4– 6	16
6– 8	15
8–10	10
10–12	8
12–14	6

3.12 Compute the mean for the following data:

Class	f
1.2–1.6	220
1.6–2.0	150
2.0–2.4	90
2.4–2.8	110
2.8–3.2	280

3.13 The following data represent the number of appointments made per fifteen minute interval by telephone solicitation for a lawn care company:

Number of Appointments	Frequency of Occurrence
0–1	31
1–2	57
2–3	26
3–4	14
4–5	6
5–6	3

Compute the mean number of appointments per interval.

3.14 In order to determine the average number of photo sittings per day for studios in the United States a marketing firm conducted a survey of studios. The following tabulation shows the resulting distribution of sittings. Compute the mean number of sittings per day.

Number of Sittings	Frequency of Occurrence
12–17	48
17–22	57
22–27	60
27–32	55

3.15 The frequency distribution shown contains information about the number of farms per state for the fifty states, based on information from the U.S. Department of Agriculture. Determine the average number of farms per state from these data. The mean computed from the original ungrouped data was 43,464.4. How does your answer for these grouped data compare? Why might they differ?

Number of Farms per State	f
0–under 20,000	16
20,000–under 40,000	11
40,000–under 60,000	9
60,000–under 80,000	4
80,000–under 100,000	7
100,000–under 120,000	2
120,000–under 140,000	0
140,000–under 160,000	0
160,000–under 180,000	0
180,000–under 200,000	1

MEASURES OF VARIABILITY FOR UNGROUPED DATA | 3.3

Measures of central tendency yield information about the center or central portion of a data set. However, researchers use another group of analytic tools to describe a set of data. These tools are **measures of variability,** which *describe the spread or the dispersion of a set of data.* Using measures of variability in conjunction with measures of central tendency makes possible locating the center of the data *and* determining how far the data spread from the center.

measures of variability

For example, a company has twenty-five sales people in the field, and the median annual sales figure for these people is $1,200,000. Are the sales people being successful as a *group* or not? The median provides information about the sales of the person in the middle, but what about the other sales people? Are all of them selling $1,200,000 annually, or do the sales figures vary widely, with one person selling $5,000,000 annually and another selling only $150,000 annually? Measures of variability provide the additional information necessary to answer that question.

As another example, suppose that a student is taking an accounting class and the instructor has just graded the midterm examination. The instructor reports that the class average score on the test was 74.6%. What does this score mean to the student? Should she be satisfied with this information? Virtually everyone in the class might have scored about 75%, in which case almost the entire class has earned a C on the test. Or the scores could have ranged from zero to 100%! The measure of central tendency does not yield sufficient information to describe the data set. What is needed is the second dimension of measurement, a measure of variability or dispersion of the data. Figure 3.1 shows three distributions in which the mean of each distribution is the same but the dispersions vary. Observation of these distributions shows that a measure of dispersion is necessary to complement the mean value in describing the data. Methods of computing measures of variability differ for ungrouped data and grouped data. This section focuses on four measures of variability for ungrouped data: range, mean absolute deviation, variance, and standard deviation.

Range

The **range** is *the difference between the largest value of a data set and the smallest value.* Although it is usually a single numeric value, some researchers define the range as *the ordered pair of smallest and largest numbers (smallest, largest).* It is a crude measure of variability, describing the distance to the outer bounds of the data set. It reflects those extreme values, because it is constructed from them. An advantage of the range is its ease of computation. One important

FIGURE 3.1

Three Distributions with the Same Mean but Different Dispersions

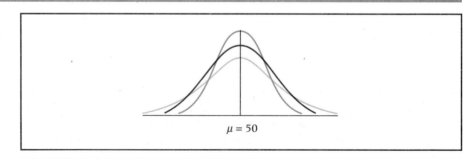

$\mu = 50$

City	1989	TABLE 3.5
San Antonio	$14.50	Average Cost of Office Rental Space per Square Foot
Houston	15.00	
Fort Worth	16.50	
Philadelphia	25.25	
San Francisco	27.00	
Washington, D.C.	28.00	
Chicago	33.72	
New York (midtown)	42.52	

use of the range is in quality assurance, where the range is used to construct control charts.

The data in Table 3.5 represent the 1989 average cost of office rental space in dollars per square foot for eight U.S. cities. What is the range of the rental costs for these cities? The highest cost is $42.52 per square foot in New York, and the lowest cost is $14.50 per square foot in San Antonio. Thus the range for these data is $42.52 − $14.50 = $28.02.

Demonstration Problem 3.4

Determine the range of ages for the 35 purchasers of compact discs listed in Table 3.1.

Solution:

The youngest purchaser is a 17-year-old, and the oldest is a 44-year-old. The range for this data set is 27 years.

$$\text{Range} = 44 - 17 = 27 \quad \text{or} \quad (17, 44).$$

Mean Absolute Deviation, Variance, and Standard Deviation

Three other measures of variability are the mean absolute deviation, the variance, and the standard deviation. These three measures can be obtained through a similar process and are therefore presented together. The variance and standard deviation are widely used in statistics. Although the standard deviation has some stand-alone potential, the importance of variance and standard deviation lies mainly in their role as tools used in conjunction with other statistical devices.

Suppose that a small company has started a production line to build guitars. During the first five weeks of production, the output is 5, 9, 16, 17, and 18 guitars, respectively. Which descriptive statistics could the owner use to measure the early progress of production? In an attempt to summarize these figures, he could compute an arithmetic mean:

$$\underline{X} \quad guitars$$

X
5
9
16
17
18

$$\Sigma X = 65 \qquad \mu = \frac{\Sigma X}{N} = \frac{65}{5} = 13.$$

**deviations from the
mean**

How much variability exists in these five weeks of data? One way for the owner to begin to look at the spread of the data is to subtract the mean from each data value. *Subtracting the mean from each value of data yields the* **deviations from the mean** $(X - \mu)$. Table 3.6 shows these deviations for the guitar company production in the third column. Note that some deviations from the mean are positive and some are negative. Figure 3.2 shows that geometrically the negative deviations represent values that fall below (to the left of) the mean and positive deviations represent values that lie above (to the right of) the mean.

An examination of deviations from the mean can reveal information about the variability of data. However, the deviations mostly are used as a tool to compute other measures of variability. Note that in both column 3 of Table 3.6 and Figure 3.2 these deviations total zero. This phenomenon applies to all cases: For a given set of data, *the sum of all deviations from the arithmetic mean is always zero*, or

$$\Sigma(X - \mu) = 0.$$

This property requires consideration of alternative ways to obtain measures of variability.

TABLE 3.6

Deviations from the
Mean for Guitar
Production

Number (X)	Mean (μ)	Deviations from the Mean (X − μ)
5	$\mu = \dfrac{65}{5} = 13$	−8
9		−4
16		+3
17		+4
18		+5
$\Sigma X = 65$		$\Sigma(X - \mu) =$ 0

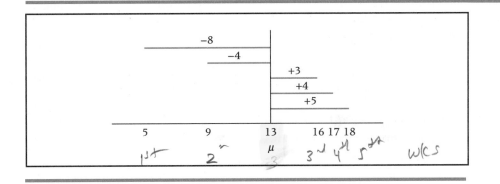

FIGURE 3.2

Geometric Distances
from the Mean (from
Table 3.6)

One obvious way to force the sum of deviations to have a nonzero total
is to take the absolute value of each deviation around the mean. Utilizing the
absolute value of the deviations about the mean makes solving for the mean
absolute deviation possible.

Mean Absolute Deviation. The **mean absolute deviation** (M.A.D.) is *the*   **mean absolute
average of the absolute values of the deviations from the mean.*   deviation**

$$\text{M.A.D.} = \frac{\Sigma|X - \mu|}{N}.$$

**Mean Absolute
Deviation**

Using the data from Table 3.6, the guitar company owner can compute a
mean absolute deviation by taking the absolute values of the deviations and
averaging them, as shown in Table 3.7. The mean absolute deviation for the
guitar production data is 4.8. The average deviation is 4.8 guitars per week.
Because it is computed using absolute values, the mean absolute deviation
loses much of its potential usefulness in statistics and is not as widely used as

X	μ	$X - \mu$	$|X - \mu|$	**TABLE 3.7**
5	$\frac{65}{5} = 13$	-8	$+8$	M.A.D. for Guitar Production Data
9		-4	$+4$	
16		$+3$	$+3$	
17		$+4$	$+4$	
18		$+5$	$+5$	
$\Sigma X = 65$		$\Sigma(X - \mu) = 0$	$\Sigma|X - \mu| = 24$	

$$\text{M.A.D.} = \frac{\Sigma|X - \mu|}{N} = \frac{24}{5} = 4.8.$$

other measures of dispersion. However, those in the field of forecasting occasionally use the mean absolute deviation as a measure of error.

Variance.   Because absolute values are not conducive to easy manipulation, mathematicians developed an alternative mechanism for overcoming the zero-sum property of deviations from the mean. This approach utilizes the square of the deviations from the mean. The result is the variance, an important measure of variability.

variance   The **variance** is the *average of the squared deviations from the arithmetic mean.* The population variance is denoted by σ^2.

**Population
Variance**

$$\sigma^2 = \frac{\Sigma(X - \mu)^2}{N}.$$

Table 3.8 shows the original production numbers for the guitar company, the deviations from the mean, and the squared deviations from the mean.

The sum of the squared deviations—called the *sum of squares of X* and sometimes abbreviated as SS_X—is used throughout statistics. For the guitar production company, this value is 130. Dividing it by the number of data values (5 weeks) yields the variance for guitar production:

$$\sigma^2 = \frac{130}{5} = 26.0 \text{ guitars}^2.$$

Standard Deviation.   The standard deviation is a popular measure of variability. In a one-semester statistics course, the standard deviation is the most

---

TABLE 3.8		X	$X - \mu$	$(X - \mu)^2$
Computing a Variance from the Guitar Production Data		5	-8	64
		9	-4	16
		16	$+3$	9
		17	$+4$	16
		18	$+5$	25
		$\Sigma X = 65$ $\Sigma(X - \mu) = 0$		$\Sigma(X - \mu)^2 = 130$

$$= (8)^2 + (4)^2 + (3)^2 + (4)^2 + (5)^2$$
$$= 130$$

$$SS_x = (X - \mu)^2 = 130.$$

$$\text{Variance} = \sigma^2 = \frac{SS_x}{N} = \frac{\Sigma(X - \mu)^2}{N} = \frac{130}{5} = 26.0.$$

$$\text{Standard deviation} = \sigma = \sqrt{\frac{\Sigma(X - \mu)^2}{N}} = \sqrt{\frac{130}{5}} = 5.1.$$

widely used measure of variability. It is used both as a separate entity and as a part of other analyses, such as computing confidence intervals and in hypothesis testing (see Chapters 8, 9, and 10).

The **standard deviation** is *the square root of the variance.* The population standard deviation is denoted by σ.

standard deviation

$$\sigma = \sqrt{\frac{\Sigma(X - \mu)^2}{N}}.$$

Population Standard Deviation

Like the variance, the standard deviation utilizes the sum of the squared deviations about the mean (SS_x). It is computed by averaging these square deviations (SS_x/N) and taking the square root of that average. The process of computing a standard deviation always involves computing a variance. One feature of the standard deviation distinguishes it from a variance: The standard deviation is expressed in the same units as the raw data, whereas the variance is expressed in those units squared. Table 3.8 shows the standard deviation for the guitar production company: $\sqrt{26}$, or 5.1.

What does a standard deviation of 5.1 mean? The meaning of standard deviation is more readily understood from its use, which is explored in a later section. Although the standard deviation and the variance are closely related and can be computed from each other, differentiating between them is important, because both are widely used in statistics.

Population Versus Sample Variance and Standard Deviation

The sample variance is denoted by S^2 and the sample standard deviation by S. Computation of the sample variance and standard deviation differ slightly from computation of the population variance and standard deviation. The main use for sample variances and standard deviations is as estimators of population variances and standard deviations. Using $n - 1$ in the denominator of a sample variance or standard deviation, rather than n, results in a better estimate of the population values.

$$S^2 = \frac{\Sigma(X - \bar{X})^2}{n - 1}.$$

Sample Variance

$$S = \sqrt{S^2}.$$

Sample Standard Deviation

	I.Q. Scores (X)	Squared Deviations $(X - \overline{X})^2$
TABLE 3.9	106	138.06
Sample Variance and	109	76.56
Sample Deviation for	114	14.06
I.Q. Scores	116	3.06
	121	10.56
	122	18.06
	125	52.56
	129	126.56
	$\Sigma X = 942$	$SS_x = \Sigma(X - \overline{X})^2 = 439.48$

$$\overline{X} = 117.75.$$

$$S^2 = \frac{\Sigma(X - \overline{X})^2}{n - 1} = \frac{439.48}{7} = 62.78.$$

$$S = \sqrt{S^2} = \sqrt{62.78} = 7.92.$$

A college's records reveal the I.Q. scores shown in Table 3.9 for a sample of eight students. The mean I.Q. score for this sample of eight college students is 117.75. The sample variance is 62.78, and the sample standard deviation is 7.92.

Computational Formulas for Variance and Standard Deviation

An alternative method of computing variance and standard deviation, sometimes referred to as the computational method or shortcut method, is available. Algebraically,

$$\Sigma(X - \mu)^2 = \Sigma X^2 - \frac{(\Sigma X)^2}{N},$$

and

$$\Sigma(X - \overline{X})^2 = \Sigma X^2 - \frac{(\Sigma X^2)}{n}.$$

Computational Formula for Population Variance and Standard Deviation

$$\sigma^2 = \frac{\Sigma X^2 - \dfrac{(\Sigma X)^2}{N}}{N};$$

$$\sigma = \sqrt{\sigma^2}.$$

Substituting these equivalent expressions into the original formulas for variance and standard deviation yields the following computational formulas.

$$S^2 = \frac{\Sigma X^2 - \frac{(\Sigma X)^2}{n}}{n-1};$$

$$S = \sqrt{S^2}.$$

Computational Formula for Sample Variance and Standard Deviation

These computational formulas utilize the sum of the X values and the sum of the X^2 values instead of the difference between the mean and each value and computed deviations. In the precalculator/computer era, this method usually was faster and easier than using the original formulas. Computer programmers prefer to use the computational method to calculate variance or standard deviation, because it requires less computer time.

Using the computational method, the guitar company owner can compute a population variance and standard deviation for the production data, as shown in Table 3.10. (Compare these results with those in Table 3.8.)

X	X^2
5	25
9	81
16	256
17	289
18	324
$\Sigma X = 65$	$\Sigma X^2 = 975$

$$\sigma^2 = \frac{975 - \frac{(65)^2}{5}}{5} = \frac{975 - 845}{5} = \frac{130}{5} = 26.$$

$$\sigma = \sqrt{26} = 5.1.$$

TABLE 3.10

Computational Formula Calculations of Variance and Standard Deviation for Guitar Production Data

Demonstration Problem 3.5

The effectiveness of district attorneys can be measured by several variables, including the number of convictions per month, the number of cases handled per month, and the total number of years of conviction per month. A researcher uses a sample of five district attorneys in a city. She determines that the total number of years of conviction that each attorney won against defendants during the past month is that shown in column 1 in the following tabulations.

Solution:

The researcher computes the mean absolute deviation, the variance, and the standard deviation for these data in the following manner.

X	$\|X - \bar{X}\|$	$(X - \bar{X})^2$
55	41	1,681
100	4	16
125	29	841
140	44	1,936
60	36	1,296
$\Sigma X = 480$	$\Sigma\|X - \bar{X}\| = 154$	$SS_x = 5,770$

$$\bar{X} = \frac{\Sigma X}{n} = \frac{480}{5} = 96.$$

$$\text{M.A.D.} = \frac{154}{5} = 30.8.$$

$$S^2 = \frac{5,770}{4} = 1,442.5 \quad \text{and} \quad S = \sqrt{S^2} = 37.98.$$

She then uses computational formulas to solve for S^2 and S and compares the results.

X	X^2
55	3,025
100	10,000
125	15,625
140	19,600
60	3,600
$\Sigma X = 480$	$\Sigma X^2 = 51,850$

$$S^2 = \frac{51,850 - \frac{(480)^2}{5}}{4} = \frac{51,850 - 46,080}{4} = \frac{5,770}{4} = 1,442.5$$

$$S = \sqrt{1,442.5} = 37.98.$$

The results are the same: The sample standard deviation obtained by both methods is 37.98, or 38, years.

Meaning of Standard Deviation

What is a standard deviation? What does it do, and what does it mean? There is no precise way of defining a standard deviation other than reciting the formula used to compute it. However, insight into the concept of standard deviation can be gleaned by viewing the manner in which it is applied. Two ways of applying the standard deviation are the empirical rule and Chebyshev's theorem.

Empirical Rule The **empirical rule** is a guideline that states the approximate percentage of values that fall within a given number of standard deviations of the mean of a set of data if the data are normally distributed. The empirical rule is used only for three numbers of standard deviations: 1σ, 2σ, and 3σ. More detailed analysis of other numbers of σ values is presented in Chapter 6. Also discussed in further detail in Chapter 6, the normal distribution is a unimodal, symmetrical distribution that is bell (or mound) shaped. The requirement that the data be normally distributed contains some tolerance, and the empirical rule generally applies so long as the data are approximately mound shaped.

empirical rule

Distance from the Mean	Percentage of Values Falling Within Distance
$\mu \pm 1\sigma$	68
$\mu \pm 2\sigma$	95
$\mu \pm 3\sigma$	99.7

Empirical Rule*

*Based on the assumption that the data are approximately normally distributed.

If a set of data is normally distributed, or bell shaped, approximately 68% of the data values fall within one standard deviation of the mean, 95% within two standard deviations, and almost 100% within three standard deviations. I.Q. test scores tend to be normally distributed. If an I.Q. test has a mean of 100 and a standard deviation of 15, then 68% of the I.Q. scores fall between scores of 85 and 115 (100 ± 15, one standard deviation), as shown in Figure 3.3(a); 95% of the I.Q. scores fall between 70 and 130 [$100 \pm 2(15)$, two standard deviations], as shown in Figure 3.3(b); and 99.7% fall between 55 and 145 [$100 \pm 3(15)$, three standard deviations].

Note that, if 95% of the scores fall within two standard deviations of the mean, approximately 5% fall outside this range. The normal distribution is symmetrical, so the 5% can be split, with 2.5% of the values falling outside

$\mu = 100$
$\sigma = 15$

$\mu \pm \sigma \quad 100 \pm 15$
$\qquad\qquad 85 < x < 115$

FIGURE 3.3

Empirical Rule for One
and Two Standard De-
viations of I.Q. Scores

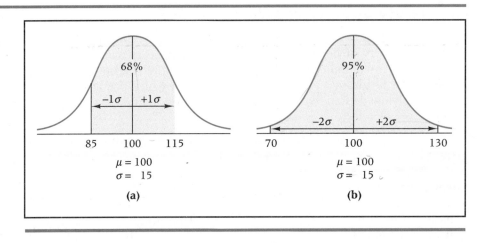

(a)   (b)

$Z = \dfrac{X - \mu}{\sigma}$

$\dfrac{115 - 100}{15}$

$= \dfrac{15}{15} = 1$

the $\mu \pm 2\sigma$ range in each tail of the distribution. Some school districts use an I.Q. score of 70 as a cutoff for special education, with students scoring below 70 on the I.Q. test qualifying for special education. As 2.5% of the I.Q. scores fall below 70, these districts, in effect, are offering special education opportunities to the students whose I.Q. scores fall in the lowest 2.5%.

Because many phenomena are distributed approximately in a bell shape, including most human characteristics such as height and weight, the empirical rule applies in many situations and is widely used. In the area of quality control, many American companies have been using $\mu \pm 2\sigma$ or $\mu \pm 3\sigma$ as cutoff points for accepting produced items or batches. These firms, in a sense, are using the empirical rule to establish critical values. Manufactured items having characteristics (dimensions, weight, finish, and the like) outside this range ($\mu \pm 2\sigma$ or $\mu \pm 3\sigma$) are considered unacceptable.

**Demonstration
Problem 3.6**

According to the Energy Information Administration, the average fuel rate of automobiles in the United States was 19.2 miles per gallon for 1988. Suppose that the standard deviation of fuel rate was 6.3 miles per gallon. If the distribution of fuel rate is bell shaped, between what fuel rate limits would (a) 68%, (b) 95%, and (c) 99.7% of the cars fall?

Solution:

According to the empirical rule, 68% of the values of a normal distribution fall within $\mu \pm 1\sigma$.

a. For $\mu = 19.2$ and $\sigma = 6.3$, 68% of the values should fall within $19.2 \pm 1(6.3) = 19.2 \pm 6.3 = 12.9$ miles per gallon to 25.5 miles per gallon.

$+\ 31.8$
-6.6

b. 95% of the values should fall within $\mu \pm 2\sigma$, or $19.2 \pm 2(6.3) = 19.2 \pm 12.6 = 6.6$ miles per gallon to 31.8 miles per gallon;

c. 99.7% of the values should fall within $\mu \pm 3\sigma$, or $19.2 \pm 3(6.3) = 19.2 \pm 18.9 = 0.3$ mile per gallon to 38.1 miles per gallon.

Chebyshev's Theorem. Chebyshev's theorem applies to all distributions regardless of their shape. Because it must apply to all distributions, the theorem is more conservative than the empirical rule. **Chebyshev's theorem** states that, within k standard deviations of the mean, at least $1 - 1/k^2$ proportion of the values occur.

Chebyshev's theorem

Chebyshev's Theorem

Number of Standard Deviations (k)	Distance from the Mean $(\mu \pm k\sigma)$	Minimum Proportion of Values Falling Within Distance $(1 - 1/k^2)$
$k = 2$	$\mu \pm 2\sigma$	$1 - 1/2^2 = 0.75$
$k = 3$	$\mu \pm 3\sigma$	$1 - 1/3^2 = 0.89$
$k = 4$	$\mu \pm 4\sigma$	$1 - 1/4^2 = 0.94$

Assumption: $k > 1$.

Chebyshev's theorem says that at least 75% of all values fall within $\pm 2\sigma$ of the mean regardless of the shape of a distribution. In contrast, the empirical rule states that, if the data are normally distributed, 95% of all values fall within $\mu \pm 2\sigma$. According to Chebyshev's theorem, the percentage of values falling within three standard deviations of the mean is at least 89%, compared to 99.7% for the empirical rule. Since a formula is used to compute proportions with Chebyshev's theorem, any value of k greater than 1 $(k > 1)$ can be used. For example, if $k = 2.5$, at least 0.84 of all values fall within $\mu \pm 2.5\sigma$. If $k = 2.5$, $1 - 1/k^2 = 1 - 1/2.5^2 = 0.84$.

**Demonstration
Problem 3.7**

Suppose that the average fuel rate for automobiles in the United States is 19.2 miles per gallon, with a standard deviation of 6.3 miles per gallon. Suppose further that the distribution of fuel rates is unknown. Within what fuel rate limits would at least 85% of the values be expected to fall?

Solution:

Because the distribution of fuel rates is unknown, use of the empirical rule is *not* appropriate; Chebyshev's theorem must be applied. It states that at least $1 - 1/k^2$ proportion of the values fall within $\mu \pm k\sigma$. Since 85% of the values fall within this range, let

$$1 - \frac{1}{k^2} = 0.85.$$

Solving for k yields

$$0.15 = \frac{1}{k^2}$$
$$k^2 = 6.667$$
$$k = 2.58.$$

Chebyshev's theorem says that at least 0.85 of the values fall within 2.58σ of the mean. For $\mu = 19.2$ and $\sigma = 6.3$, at least 0.85 of all values lie within $19.2 \pm 2.58(6.3) = 19.2 \pm 16.25$, or from 2.95 miles per gallon to 35.45 miles per gallon.

Z Scores

Z score

A **Z score** represents *the number of standard deviations a value (X) is above or below the mean.* Using Z scores allows translation of a value's raw distance from the mean into units of standard deviations.

Z Scores

$$Z = \frac{X - \mu}{\sigma}.$$

If a Z score is negative, the raw value *(X)* is below the mean. If the Z score is positive, the raw value *(X)* is above the mean.

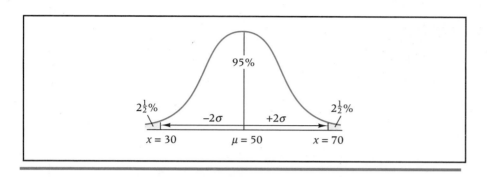

For example, for a data set that is normally distributed with a mean of 50 and a standard deviation of 10, a statistician wants to determine the Z score for a value of 70. This value ($X = 70$) is 20 units above the mean, so the Z value is

$$Z = \frac{70 - 50}{10} = \frac{+20}{10} = +2.00.$$

This Z score signifies that the raw score of 70 is two standard deviations above the mean. How is this Z score interpreted? The empirical rule states that 95% of all values fall within two standard deviations of the mean if the data are approximately normally distributed. Figure 3.4 shows that, because the value of 70 lies two standard deviations above the mean, 95% of the values fall between 70 and the value ($X = 30$) that is two standard deviations below the mean. As 5% of the values fall outside the range of two standard deviations from the mean and the normal distribution is symmetrical, 2½% (½ of the 5%) fall below the value of 30. Thus 97½% of the values fall below the value of 70. The topic of Z scores is discussed more extensively in Chapter 6.

**Demonstration
Problem 3.8**

Values that come from distributions with different means and standard deviations can be compared by means of Z scores. The average age of a worker at the Anaheim plant is 32.3 years, with a standard deviation of 8.7 years. The Fresno plant has older workers, and the average age at that plant is 34.6 years, with a standard deviation of 7.9 years. Is a 45-year-old worker at the Anaheim plant or a 46-year-old worker at the Fresno plant older in comparison to the other workers at their respective plants?

Solution:

Determine the Z score for the worker at each plant. The worker with the largest positive Z score is the one who is older relative to people at his plant.

Plant A	Plant B
$\mu_A = 32.3$	$\mu_B = 34.6$
$\sigma_A = 8.7$	$\sigma_B = 7.9$
$X_A = 45$	$X_B = 46$

$$Z_A = \frac{45 - 32.3}{8.7} = 1.46 \quad \text{and} \quad Z_B = \frac{46 - 34.6}{7.9} = 1.44.$$

The Z score of 1.44 for the worker at the Fresno plant is smaller than the Z score of 1.46 for the worker at the Anaheim plant. That is, the age of the worker at the Fresno plant is slightly nearer to the mean age of the workers at that plant than the age of the worker from the Anaheim plant is to the mean age of workers at that plant. Even though the worker at the Fresno plant is older (46) than the worker at the Anaheim plant (45), the worker at the Fresno plant is closer in age to the mean of his group than is the worker at the Anaheim plant, because the Fresno plant worker's Z score is smaller.

Coefficient of Variation

coefficient of variation

The **coefficient of variation** is *the ratio of the standard deviation to the mean expressed in percentage* and is denoted C.V.

Coefficient of Variation

$$\text{C.V.} = \frac{\sigma}{\mu}(100).$$

The coefficient of variation essentially is a relative comparison of a standard deviation to its mean. The coefficient of variation can be useful in comparing standard deviations that have been computed from different means.

Demonstration Problem 3.9

A professor teaches two sections of statistics. She gives each section a different examination covering the same material. The mean raw score on the examination for section 1 is 29.0, with a standard deviation of 4.6. The mean raw score for section 2 is 84.0, with a standard deviation of 10.0. Which section has the greatest dispersion of scores?

Solution:

Section 1	Section 2
$\mu_1 = 29$	$\mu_2 = 84$
$\sigma_1 = 4.6$	$\sigma_2 = 10$

Direct comparison of the standard deviations of 4.6 and 10.0 indicates that section 2 has the greater dispersion ($\sigma_2 = 10.0$). However, computing the coefficients of variation and comparing them reveal quite different results:

$$C.V._1 = \frac{4.6}{29}(100) = 15.86 \quad \text{and} \quad C.V._2 = \frac{10}{84}(100) = 11.90.$$

Thus the professor finds that the section 2 examination results have a smaller dispersion relative to its mean than do the section 1 examination results, based on the size of the coefficients of variation.

The choice of whether to use coefficient of variation or raw standard deviations to compare multiple standard deviations is a matter of preference. The coefficient of variation also provides an optional method of interpreting the value of a standard deviation.

**PROBLEMS
Section 3.3**

3.16 A data set contains seven values:

$$6 \quad 2 \quad 4 \quad 9 \quad 1 \quad 3 \quad 5$$

a. Find the range.
b. Find the mean absolute deviation.
c. Find the population variance.
d. Find the population standard deviation.

3.17 A data set contains eight values:

$$4 \quad -3 \quad 0 \quad -5 \quad 2 \quad 9 \quad -4 \quad 5$$

    a. Find the range.

    b. Find the mean absolute deviation.

    c. Find the sample variance.

    d. Find the sample standard deviation.

3.18 A data set contains six values:

$$12 \quad 23 \quad 19 \quad 26 \quad 24 \quad 23$$

    a. Find the population standard deviation using the formula containing the mean (the original formula).

    b. Find the population standard deviation using the computational formula.

    c. Compare the results. Which formula was faster to use? Which formula do you prefer? Why do you think the computational formula is sometimes referred to as the "shortcut" formula?

3.19 Use your calculator to find the sample variance and sample standard deviation for the following data:

57	88	68	43	93	44	18	39	40	59
63	51	37	77	83	46	59	37	15	73
66	60	38	52	28	23	19	90	58	35
34	52	60	57	29	82	14	38	27	24
92	37	38	17	67	71	25	39	84	70

3.20 Use your calculator to find the population variance and population standard deviation for the following data:

123	090	546	378	259	639	533	309
392	280	179	601	446	277	983	349
572	953	749	075	127	198	520	668
303	468	531	646	079	035	178	478

3.21 The savings rate for baby boomers in 1989 was 5.3%. Wanting to measure the savings rates for baby boomers today, a researcher takes a random sample of twelve baby boomers and records the following savings rates.

4.8%	3.6%	6.7%	5.4%
1.3%	5.1%	4.8%	8.3%
6.0%	3.9%	7.1%	2.2%

   a. Determine the mean absolute deviation.

   b. Determine the variance.

   c. Determine the standard deviation.

3.22 A distribution of numbers is approximately bell shaped. If the mean of the numbers is 125 and the standard deviation is 12, between what two numbers would approximately 68% of the values fall? Between what two numbers would 95% of the values fall? Between what two values would 99.7% of the values fall?

3.23 A distribution of numbers is not normally distributed. If the mean of the numbers is 38 and the standard deviation is 6, what proportion of values would fall between 26 and 50? What proportion of values would fall between 14 and 62? Between what two values would 89% of the values fall?

3.24 According to Chebyshev's theorem, how many standard deviations from the mean would include at least 80% of the values?

3.25 Environmentalists are concerned about emissions of sulfur dioxide into the air. The average number of days per year in which sulfur dioxide levels exceed 150 micrograms per cubic meter in Milan, Italy is 29. The number of days per year in which emission limits are exceeded is normally distributed with a standard deviation of 4.0 days. What percentage of the years would average between 21 and 37 days of excess emissions of sulfur dioxide? What percentage of the years would exceed 37 days? What percentage of the years would exceed 41 days? In what percentage of the years would there be fewer than 25 days with excess sulfur dioxide emissions?

3.26 Use the data in Problem 3.16 and determine the Z score for each value. Use the *population* standard deviation.

3.27 According to the National Center for Education Statistics, the average number of pupils per teacher in U.S. public schools is 17.6. Assume that the number of pupils per teacher is normally distributed, with a standard deviation of 2.9. Find the Z scores for the following classroom sizes:

   19 students   22 students   15 students   10 students

   What do these Z scores tell you about each classroom?

3.28 What is the relationship between a Z score of 2.00 and the empirical rule? A Z score of 1.00? A Z score of -1.00?

3.29 The average daily high temperature for January in Mobile, Alabama, is 61 degrees. The average daily high temperature for January in New York City is 37 degrees. The standard deviation for January highs in Mobile is 12 degrees, and for New York City it is 9 degrees. Use the coefficient of variation to determine which city has a higher relative variability of daily high temperatures in January.

<table>
<tr><td>3.4</td><td>MEASURES OF VARIABILITY FOR GROUPED DATA</td></tr>
</table>

Two measures of variability for grouped data are presented here: the variance and the standard deviation. Again, the standard deviation is the square root of the variance. Both measures have original and computational formulas. In this text, only the computational versions are used to compute variance and standard deviation for grouped data.

Formulas for Population Variance and Standard Deviation of Grouped Data	Original Formula	Computational Version
	$\sigma^2 = \dfrac{\Sigma f(M - \mu)^2}{N}$ $\sigma = \sqrt{\sigma^2}$	$\sigma^2 = \dfrac{\Sigma fM^2 - \dfrac{(\Sigma fM)^2}{N}}{N}$

Formulas for Sample Variance and Standard Deviation for Grouped Data	Original Formula	Computational Version
	$S^2 = \dfrac{\Sigma f(M - \bar{X})^2}{n - 1}$ $S = \sqrt{S^2}$	$S^2 = \dfrac{\Sigma fM^2 - \dfrac{(\Sigma fM)^2}{n}}{n - 1}$

Demonstration Problem 3.10

Solve for the population variance and standard deviation for the data from Table 3.3:

Age	f	Age	f
10–15	6	30–35	16
15–20	22	35–40	8
20–25	35	40–45	4
25–30	29	45–50	2

8 class

Solution:

The class midpoint represents all values in a class interval. The computational formula utilizes the products fM and fM^2. To compute fM^2, first square M and then multiply the result by f. Multiplying the fM column by the M column gives the same result.

$$\Sigma x^2 - (\Sigma x)^2$$

Age	f	M	fM	fM^2
10–15	6	12.5	75.0	937.50
15–20	22	17.5	385.0	6,737.50
20–25	35	22.5	787.5	17,718.75
25–30	29	27.5	797.5	21,931.25
30–35	16	32.5	520.0	16,900.00
35–40	8	37.5	300.0	11,250.00
40–45	4	42.5	170.0	7,225.00
45–50	2	47.5	95.0	4,512.50
	$\Sigma f = 122$		$\Sigma fM = 3{,}130.0$	$\Sigma fM^2 = 87{,}212.50$

$$\sigma^2 = \frac{\Sigma fM^2 - \dfrac{(\Sigma fM)^2}{N}}{N} = \frac{87{,}212.5 - \dfrac{(3{,}130)^2}{122}}{122} = \frac{6{,}910.04}{122} = 56.64.$$

$$\sigma = \sqrt{56.64} = 7.53.$$

As with the mean for grouped data, the variance and standard deviations may be only approximate. The reason is that the actual values in any class interval do not necessarily average to the class midpoint that represents them.

**PROBLEMS
Section 3.4**

3.30 Find the population variance and standard deviation for the following data:

Class	f	Class	f
20–30	7	50–60	13
30–40	11	60–70	6
40–50	18	70–80	4

3.31 Find the sample variance and standard deviation for the following data:

Class	f
5– 9	20
9–13	18
13–17	8
17–21	6
21–25	2

3.32 From a random sample of voters in Nashville, Tennessee, voters are classified by age group, as shown by the following data. What are the mean and standard deviation of this sample?

Age Group	Frequency
18–under 24	17
24–under 30	22
30–under 36	26
36–under 42	35
42–under 48	33
48–under 54	30
54–under 60	32
60–under 66	21
66–under 72	15

3.33 The Air Transport Association of America publishes figures on the busiest airports in the United States. The following frequency distribution has been constructed from these figures for the year 1988:

Number of Passengers Arriving and Departing (millions)	Number of Airports
10–under 20	7
20–under 30	6
30–under 40	3
40–under 50	3
50–under 60	1

Use these data to compute a population mean and standard deviation for the total number of passengers arriving at and departing from these twenty airports.

SKEWNESS **3.5**

A normal distribution is perfectly symmetrical because when it is divided vertically in the middle, the right half of the distribution is identical to the left half. Figure 3.5 shows a symmetric distribution.

Skewness is *the lack of symmetry of a distribution of values.* The distribution in Figure 3.5 has no skewness because it is symmetric. Figure 3.6 shows a distribution that is skewed left, or negatively skewed, and Figure 3.7 shows a distribution that is skewed right, or positively skewed.

skewness

FIGURE 3.5

Normal Distribution

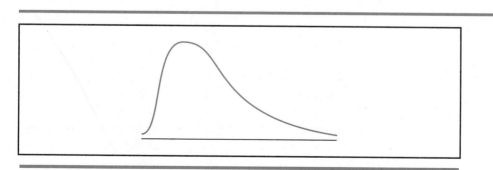

FIGURE 3.6

Distribution Skewed Left, or Negatively Skewed

FIGURE 3.7

Distribution Skewed Right, or Positively Skewed

FIGURE 3.8

Relationship of Mean,
Median, and Mode

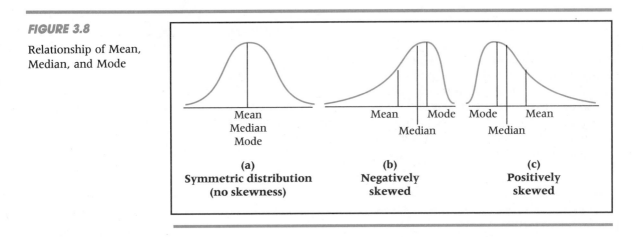

The skewed portion is the long, thin part of the curve. Many researchers use *skewed distribution* to mean that the data are sparse at one end of the distribution and piled up at the other end. Instructors sometimes refer to a grade distribution as *skewed,* meaning that few students scored at one end of the grading scale, and many students scored at the other end.

Skewness and the Relationship of the Mean, Median, and Mode

The concept of skewness helps in understanding the relationship of the mean, median, and mode. In a unimodal distribution (distribution with a single peak or mode) that is skewed, the mode is the apex (high point) of the curve, and the median is the middle value. The mean tends to be located toward the tail of the distribution, because the mean is affected by all values, including the extreme ones. Because a bell-shaped or normal distribution has no skewness, the mean, median, and mode all fall at the center of the distribution. Figure 3.8 displays the relationship of the mean, median, and mode for different types of skewness.

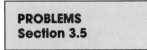

**PROBLEMS
Section 3.5**

3.34   A restaurant manager analyzes customer bills for one day and determines that the mean bill per customer is $27.85, the median bill is $25.61, and the modal bill is $23.10. Discuss the skewness of this distribution of bills. What decision-making information does this analysis give the restaurant manager?

The oldest measure of descriptive statistics is probably the arithmetic mean. Pythagoras knew about the arithmetic mean in the sixth century, B.C. Several of the more popular descriptive statistical measures were in use long before they were given a name. Sir Francis Galton gave the median its name in 1883, even though it had been in use for a long time before his work. Karl Pearson designated the value with the most frequencies as the mode in 1894.

Carl Gauss (1777–1855), recognized as one of the most brilliant mathematicians of all time, worked on the development of several measures of variability. One of his students, J. F. Enke, formally recorded a formula for standard deviation in 1832. Enke learned or modified the formula from Gauss. Sir Ronald A. Fisher gave birth to the term variance in 1891. Pearson coined the term standard deviation in 1894.

Source: Adapted from Dudycha, Arthur L., and Linda W. Dudycha, "Behavioral Statistics: An Historical Perspective," in *Statistical Issues: A Reader for the Behavioral Sciences,* edited by Roger Kirk (Monterey, Calif.: Brooks/Cole, 1972).

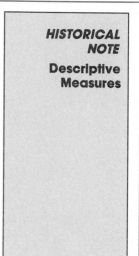

HISTORICAL NOTE
Descriptive Measures

3.35 A local hotel offers ballroom dancing on Friday nights. A researcher observes the customers and estimates their ages. Discuss the skewness of the distribution of ages, if the mean age is 51, the median age is 54, and the modal age is 59.

3.36 On a certain day the average closing price of a group of stocks on the New York Stock Exchange is $35.00 (to the nearest dollar). If the median value is $33.00 and the mode is $21.00, is the distribution of these stock prices skewed? If so, how?

CHAPTER SUMMARY

Statistical descriptive measures include measures of central tendency and measures of variability. Measures of central tendency and measures of variability are computed differently for ungrouped and grouped data. Measures of central tendency are useful in describing data, because these measures communicate the size or location of the center of the data. The most common measures of central tendency are the three m's: mode, median, and mean.

The mode is the most frequently occurring value in a set of data. If two values tie for the mode, the data are bimodal. Data sets can be multimodal. Among other things, the mode is used in business for determining sizes.

The median is the middle term in an ordered array of numbers, if there is an odd number of terms. If there is an even number of terms, the median is the average of the two middle terms in an ordered array. The formula $(n + 1)/2$ specifies the location of the median. A median is unaffected by the magnitude of extreme values. This characteristic makes the median a most useful and appropriate measure of central tendency when reporting such things as income, age, and price of houses.

The arithmetic mean is widely used and is usually what researchers are referring to when they use the word *mean*. The arithmetic mean is the *average*. The population mean and the sample mean are computed in the same way but are denoted by different symbols. The arithmetic mean is affected by *every* value and can be inordinately influenced by extreme values.

Only one measure of central tendency was presented for grouped data: the mean. The grouped data mean is only approximate, because the computation of the mean involves the assumption that the class midpoint represents all the data in a class.

Measures of variability are statistical tools used in combination with measures of central tendency to describe data. Measures of variability provide a description of data that measures of central tendency cannot do: information about the spread of the data values. These measures include the range, mean absolute deviation, variance, standard deviation, and coefficient of variation for ungrouped data. The variance and standard deviation for grouped data also were included in the chapter.

One of the most elementary measures of variability is the range. It is the difference between the largest and smallest values. Although the range is easy to compute, it has limited usefulness.

The mean absolute deviation (M.A.D.) is the average deviation from the mean. It is computed by averaging the absolute values of the deviations from the mean. The mean absolute deviation provides the magnitude of the average deviation but without specifying its direction. The mean absolute deviation has limited usage in statistics, but interest is growing in the use of M.A.D. in the field of forecasting.

Variance is widely used as a tool in statistics but is little used as a stand-alone measure of variability. The variance is the average of the squared deviations about the mean.

The square root of the variance is the standard deviation. It also is a widely used tool in statistics. It is used more often than the variance as a stand-alone measure. The standard deviation is best understood by examining its applications in determining where data fall with regard to the mean. The empirical rule and Chebyshev's theorem are statements relating the number of data values to various numbers of standard deviations from the mean.

The empirical rule reveals the percentage of values that fall within one, two, or three standard deviations of the mean for a set of data. The empirical rule applies only if the data are in a bell-shaped distribution. According to the empirical rule, approximately 68% of all values of a normal distribution fall within plus or minus one standard deviation of the mean. Ninety-five percent of all values fall within two standard deviations either side of the mean, and virtually all values fall within three standard deviations of the mean.

Chebyshev's theorem also delineates the proportion of values that fall within a given number of standard deviations from the mean. However, it applies to any distribution. According to Chebyshev's theorem, at least $1 - 1/k^2$ values fall within k standard deviations of the mean. Chebyshev's theorem says that at least 75% of all values fall within two standard deviations of the mean, and at least 89% fall within three standard deviations of the mean. The Z score represents the number of standard deviations a value is from the mean.

The coefficient of variation is a ratio of a standard deviation to its mean, given as a percentage. It is especially useful in comparing standard deviations or variances that have come from data with different means.

Two measures of variability for grouped data are the variance and standard deviation. These two measures often are only approximate for grouped data, because they are based on the assumption that the class midpoint represents the average of all values in a class interval.

Skewness is the lack of symmetry in a unimodal distribution. If a distribution is skewed, it is stretched in one direction or the other. The skewed part of a graph is its long, thin portion.

Key Words

Measures of central tendency	Variance
Mode	Standard deviation
Median	Empirical rule
Arithmetic mean	Chebyshev's theorem
Measures of variability	Z score
Range	Coefficient of variation
Deviations from the mean	Skewness
Mean absolute deviation	

USING THE COMPUTER

You can use Minitab to compute several of the statistics discussed in Chapter 3, including the mean, the median, the range, and the standard deviation. Other statistics that cannot be computed directly by Minitab can be computed by manipulating various operations within Minitab. Several Minitab commands can assist you in performing these calculations: **MEAN, MEDIAN, DESCRIBE, RANK, SORT, RANGE, STANDARD DEVIATION**, and **LET**.

Mean

You can compute an arithmetic mean (average) in Minitab by using the command, **MEAN**. A Minitab prompt precedes this Minitab command, which is followed by the column location(s) of the data. The general form of the command is

MTB > MEAN Cn

When using any of these Minitab commands, you must first enter the data into a column or columns. You can use either the **SET** command or the **READ** command to meet this requirement. The **SET** command is preferred for single data sets. After the **MEAN** command is performed, the output is printed automatically (although if you want to see the original data, you must perform a print command on the column where the data are stored, MTB > PRINT C1). If the data from Table 3.1 are entered into column 1 and analyzed using the **MEAN** command, the command statements and output are

Commands

```
MTB  > SET C1
DATA > 28   23   27   30   24   35   29   21   25   18   21   31   19
DATA > 22   44   17   24   29   42   31   24   41   34   24   27   32
DATA > 28   25   25   35   25   17   24   29   22
DATA > end
MTB  > MEAN C1
```

Output

```
MEAN = 27.200
```

Median

You can compute a median for a data set by utilizing the same process you used to compute a mean, with the exception that the Minitab command is

MTB > MEDIAN Cn

The output is the median value, and it is printed automatically. To compute a median for the data in Table 3.1, the commands and output are

Commands

```
MTB  > SET C1
DATA > 28   23   27   30   24   35   29   21   25   18   21   31   19
DATA > 22   44   17   24   29   42   31   24   41   34   24   27   32
DATA > 28   25   25   35   25   17   24   29   22
DATA > End
MTB  > MEDIAN C1
```

Output

```
MEDIAN = 25
```

Describe

The **DESCRIBE** command computes several descriptive statistics at one time, including the mean, median, minimum value, maximum value, and standard deviation. You use the same method to implement this command that you used to compute a mean, except that the Minitab command is

MTB > DESCRIBE Cn

The output is printed automatically. If the data from Table 3.1 are entered into column 2, the command statements and output for using **DESCRIBE** are

Commands

```
MTB  > SET C2
DATA > 28   23   27   30   24   35   29   21   25   18   21   31   19
DATA > 22   44   17   24   29   42   31   24   41   34   24   27   32
DATA > 28   25   25   35   25   17   24   29   22
DATA > End
MTB  > DESCRIBE C2
```

Output

	N	MEAN	MEDIAN	TRMEAN	STDEV	SEMEAN
C1	35	27.20	25.00	26.84	6.66	1.13
	MIN	MAX	Q1	Q3		
C1	17.00	44.00	23.00	31.00		

Rank

The Minitab **RANK** command takes the data stored in one column, ranks the values from 1 to n, and stores the ranks in another column. The rank of 1 is given to the smallest number and n is the rank of the largest number. In the case of ties, the command averages the ranks for those values and assigns that average rank to all the tied values. The output consists of the ranks for the values in the order that the original values are stored in Minitab. The output is *not* printed automatically on the screen. Because the output is stored in a column, you must use the **PRINT** command to produce output on the screen.

You use the **RANK** command with a Minitab prompt (**MTB >**). It is followed by the column in which the data are stored and the column in which the ranks are to be stored. A space separates each column location. For example, if the data set is stored in column 1 and the ranks are to be stored in column 2, the command is

MTB > RANK C1 C2

Suppose that the data from Table 3.1 are set into column 1 and Minitab is used to rank these data. The commands to do so and the output from the results are

Commands

```
MTB  > SET C1
DATA > 28   23   27   30   24   35   29   21   25   18   21   31   19
DATA > 22   44   17   24   29   42   31   24   41   34   24   27   32
DATA > 28   25   25   35   25   17   24   29   22
DATA > End
MTB  > RANK C1 C2
MTB  > PRINT C2
```

Output

```
C2
    21.5    9.0   19.5   26.0   12.0   31.5   24.0
     5.5   15.5    3.0    5.5   27.5    4.0    7.5
    35.0    1.5   12.0   24.0   34.0   27.5   12.0
    33.0   30.0   12.0   19.5   29.0   21.5   16.5
    16.5   31.5   16.5    1.5   12.0   24.0    7.5
```

Sort

Minitab has a command that can sort a set of data values in order from smallest to largest: SORT. It allows you to take data that have been entered and stored in any order and make an ordered array from them. Like the RANK command, the SORT command requires the column location of the data that are being analyzed and a column into which the sorted data are stored. The output from SORT is not printed out automatically. To show the output on the screen or on hardcopy, you must perform a PRINT command on the column in which the output is stored.

The SORT command follows a Minitab (MTB) prompt. It requires two column locations following the word SORT. The first column is the location of the data set to be sorted. The second column is where the output is to be stored. If the data set is located in column 1 and the output is to be stored in column 2, the command to do a sort routine is

```
MTB > SORT C1 C2
```

Suppose that the data from Table 3.1 are set into Minitab in column 1. If a SORT is to be performed on these data, the results are to be stored in column 2, and the output is to be printed, the commands and output are

Commands

```
MTB  > SET C1
DATA > 28   23   27   30   24   35   29   21   25   18   21   31   19
DATA > 22   44   17   24   29   42   31   24   41   34   24   27   32
DATA > 28   25   25   35   25   17   24   29   22
DATA > End
```

MTB > SORT C1 C2
MTB > PRINT C2

Output

C2
```
    17  17  18  19  21  21  22  22  23  24  24  24  24
    24  25  25  25  25  27  27  28  28  29  29  29  30
    31  31  32  34  35  35  41  42  44
```

Range

Minitab can directly compute and yield a range value for a set of data in the same manner that it computes the mean and median. After loading the data into a column location, use the Minitab command, **RANGE**, to compute the range. This command requires the column location of the stored data:

MTB > RANGE Cn

Minitab automatically prints the range on the screen. If the data from Table 3.1 are loaded into column 1, the commands and resulting output from computing a range are

Commands

```
MTB  > SET C1
DATA > 28  23  27  30  24  35  29  21  25  18  21  31  19
DATA > 22  44  17  24  29  42  31  24  41  34  24  27  32
DATA > 28  25  25  35  25  17  24  29  22
DATA > End
MTB  > RANGE C1
```

Output

RANGE = 27.000

Standard Deviation

You can compute a standard deviation in Minitab by using the **STANDARD DEVIATION** command followed by the location of the data. As with the range, you must first **SET** or **READ** the data into a column(s). The entire command **STANDARD DEVIATION** can be used, but *Minitab always requires only the first four letters of a command,* so you can reduce the command to **STAN**. The command is

MTB > STANDARD DEVIATION Cn

or

MTB > STAN Cn

The output for this command consists solely of the value of the standard deviation. It is printed automatically on the screen. To compute a standard deviation from the data in Table 3.6, use the following commands. Assume that the data have been set into column 2.

Commands

```
MTB  > SET C2
DATA > 5 9 16 17 18
DATA > end
MTB  > STANDARD DEVIATION C2
```

Output

```
ST.DEV. = 5.7009
```

Store a Constant or Integer Value

You can store any value as a constant by using a LET command and a K_n location. For example, to store the number 12 in location K_1, use

```
MTB > LET K1 = 12
```

Variance

Minitab has no variance command. You compute a variance by manipulating other Minitab commands. The easiest way to do so is to implement a standard deviation command and then square the value, which you can do by using a LET command. First, use the STANDARD DEVIATION command to compute the standard deviation:

```
(STAN Cn)
```

Next, square the value of the standard deviation. Use of the expression **2 to square a value is almost universal in computing practice:

```
(STAN(Cn))**2
```

Then store that value as an integer in a constant location, K_n:

```
LET Kₙ = (STAN(Cn))**2
```

You actually accomplish these three steps simultaneously with one command (the last command). The LET command allows you to *let* a constant location contain the result of an operation on a column or other constants. The result is stored in the constant location and not automatically printed on the screen. To obtain the results, you must follow the LET command with a PRINT command. To compute a variance for the data from Table 3.6, the command statements and the output are

Commands

```
MTB  > SET C2
DATA > 5 9 16 17 18
DATA > end
MTB  > LET K3 = (STAN(C2))**2
MTB  > PRINT K3
```

Output

```
K3   32.500
```

<hr>

SUPPLEMENTARY PROBLEMS

3.37 The 1990 U.S. Census asked every household to report information on each person living there. Suppose that a sample of 30 households is selected and the number of persons living in each is as follows:

2	3	1	2	6	4	2	1	5	3	2	3	1	2	2
1	3	1	2	2	4	2	1	2	8	3	2	1	1	3

Compute the arithmetic mean, mode, and median for these figures.

3.38 According to Alexander and Associates, the all-time top video rentals as of June 1990 were the following:

Movie	Rentals (millions)
Top Gun	105.5
Crocodile Dundee	66.2
Dirty Dancing	62.6
Three Men and a Baby	52.8
Platoon	50.2
The Color Purple	49.5
Robocop	47.8
Die Hard	47.8
Fatal Attraction	45.7
Lethal Weapon	45.7

If you were asked to summarize these data, using a measure of central tendency, would you use the mean, median, or mode? Compute each and comment on the outcome.

3.39 The 1990 U.S. Census also asked for each person's age. Suppose that a sample of 40 households is taken from the census data and the age of the first person recorded on the census form is given as follows:

42	29	31	38	55	27	28	33	49	70
25	21	38	47	63	22	38	52	50	41
19	22	29	81	52	26	35	38	29	31
48	26	33	42	58	40	32	24	34	25

Compute the variance and standard deviation for this sample.

3.40 According to the National Association of Realtors, the top states for resale of existing single-family houses, condominiums, and co-ops in 1989 were: California, Florida, Illinois, Michigan, New York, Ohio, Pennsylvania, and Texas. The data shown are the number of units resold for each of these states. Compute an arithmetic mean and a sample standard deviation for these data. Note that the numbers are quite large. You might try recoding the data to reduce the values of the numbers to make the data more manageable. One simple way of recoding these numbers is to move the decimal point three places to the left (e.g., 197,000 becomes 197). If you recode the data this way, the resulting mean and standard deviations will be correct for the recoded data. To convert the answers back so that they are correct for the original data, move the decimal point back to the right three places in the answers (e.g., 243 becomes 243,000).

State	Home Sales
California	516,000
Florida	184,000
Illinois	197,000
Michigan	171,000
New York	199,000
Ohio	214,000
Pennsylvania	239,000
Texas	243,000

3.41 Listed are the top ten rated shows of all time for the Public Broadcasting Service. Determine the average audience share (in percent), the population variance, and the population standard deviation for the following ten shows:

Title	Audience (percent)
"National Geographic 'The Sharks'"	17.4
"National Geographic 'The Grizzlies'"	17.0
"National Geographic 'Land of the Tiger'"	16.5
"National Geographic 'Incredible Machine'"	16.0
"Great Moments with National Geographic"	15.7
"Best of Wild America: The Babies"	14.7
"The Music Man"	14.7
"Live from the Grand Ole Opry"	14.6
"Live from the Grand Ole Opry"	14.2
"National Geographic 'Lions of . . . African Night'"	13.8

3.42 A movement is under way in the United States to lessen airport noise. In an attempt to cut noise, airlines are switching to quieter planes, known as Stage 3 aircraft. The following tabulation shows twelve major U.S. airlines and the number of Stage 3 aircraft they operate, as reported by Avmark, Inc.:

Airline	Number of Stage 3 Aircraft
American	333
America West	44
Continental	155
Delta	183
Eastern	54
Midway	9
Northwest	111
Pan American	66
Southwest	48
TWA	96
United	215
US Air	175

a. Find the arithmetic mean and median of these data.

b. Determine the population variance and population standard deviation for these data.

3.43 Each major league baseball stadium has its own unique dimensions. In some stadiums the distance to the fence is shorter than in others. The following data are the distances from home plate to the fence in center field for each of the National League stadiums as listed in the *Sports Encyclopedia of Baseball:*

City	Stadium	Center Field Distance (feet)
Atlanta	Atlanta–Fulton County	402
Chicago	Wrigley	400
Cincinnati	Riverfront	404
Houston	Astrodome	400
Los Angeles	Dodger	395
Montreal	Olympic	404
New York	Shea	410
Philadelphia	Veterans	408
Pittsburgh	Three Rivers	400
St. Louis	Busch	414
San Diego	Jack Murphy	405
San Francisco	Candlestick	400

a. Compute an arithmetic mean for these distances.

b. Determine the median of these distances.

c. What is the mean absolute deviation of these distances?

d. Compute the population variance and standard deviation for these figures.

e. What is the Z score of the center field distance at Wrigley Field in Chicago?

3.44 National Park Service records contain the following 1989 summer sulfate concentration levels for nine national parks:

Park	Sulfate Level
Grand Canyon	1.4
Shenandoah	11.1
Acadia	4.9
Yellowstone	0.9
Yosemite	1.7
Mesa Verde	1.4
Crater Lake	0.8
Great Smoky Mountains	10.4
Mount Rainier	2.8

The health standard for the United States for sulfate concentrations is 0.2. Treat the data as population data.

a. Compute the mean.

b. Compute the median.

c. Compute the variance.

d. Compute the standard deviation.

e. Using the answers for (a) and (d), determine the Z scores for Grand Canyon Park and the Shenandoah Park.

3.45 The Lundberg Survey measures the average retail prices for a gallon of gasoline in several key U.S. cities. The data gathered on March 22, 1991 for regular unleaded gasoline is as follows:

City	Price
Atlanta	$0.94
Los Angeles	0.94
Dallas	0.98
Miami	1.03
San Francisco	1.05
Philadelphia	1.08
Las Vegas	1.12
Long Island, N.Y.	1.15
Boston	1.15
Chicago	1.19

a. Compute the mean.

b. Compute the median.

c. Compute the mode.

d. Compute the variance.

e. Compute the standard deviation.

f. What is the Z score for Atlanta? What does this Z score indicate about the price of regular unleaded gasoline in Atlanta?

3.46 Company reports in 1990 listed the following numbers of McDonald's restaurants in seven foreign countries:

Country	Number of Restaurants
Japan	653
Canada	568
West Germany	295
Britain	289
Australia	225
France	84
Netherlands	49

Compute the population mean and standard deviation for these data. Use the computational formula to determine the standard deviation. Determine the Z scores for Japan, Britain, and the Netherlands. If you did not have access to the raw data, what would these Z scores tell you about the number of McDonald's restaurants in these three countries compared to the others? Why?

3.47 According to the National Association of Realtors, in the Spring of 1989 the highest median house prices in the United States were in San Francisco, where the median price was $266,000. A sample of twelve homes in San Francisco produced these prices:

$201,900	$261,000	$239,000
297,000	303,000	259,000
255,000	335,000	275,000
179,000	279,000	250,000

Determine the mean, median, range, and standard deviation of these data.

3.48 The cellular phone market has grown phenomenally during the past few years. According to the Cellular Telecommunications Industry Association, the top eleven markets for cellular phones in 1989 were (alphabetically): Boston, Chicago, Dallas, Detroit, Houston, Los Angeles, New York, Philadelphia, San Francisco, St. Louis, and Washington, D.C. The average number of subscribers in 1989 for the top ten companies was 277,500, with a standard deviation of 99,268.

a. If the distribution of the number of subscribers per company is known to be bell shaped, between what two numbers of subscribers would 95% of the companies fall? 68% of the companies?

b. If the shape of the distribution of subscribers is unknown, approximately what proportion of the companies would fall between 78,964 subscribers and 476,036 subscribers?

c. The largest cellular phone company in the United States in 1989 was BellSouth, with 419,000 subscribers. What is the Z score for the number of BellSouth's subscribers? The eighth largest cellular phone company in 1989 was Bell Atlantic with 189,000. What is the Z score for Bell Atlantic's number of subscribers?

3.49 The radio music listener market is diverse. Listener formats might include adult contemporary, album rock, top 40, oldies, soul, country and western, classical, and jazz. In targeting audiences, market researchers need to be concerned about the ages of the listeners attracted to particular formats. In 1990, the trend was toward more "oldies" format stations. A market researcher surveyed a sample of 170 listeners of oldies stations and obtained the following age distribution:

Age	Frequency
15–20	5
20–25	12
25–30	19
30–35	29
35–40	44
40–45	37
45–50	18
50–55	6

a. What is the mean age of an oldies format listener?

b. What are the variance and standard deviation of the age of oldies format listeners?

3.50 A research agency administers a demographic survey to ninety telemarketing companies to determine the size of their operations. When asked to report "How many employees now work in your telemarketing operation?" their responses varied from 1 to 100. The agency's analyst organizes the figures into a frequency distribution:

Number of Employees Working in Telemarketing	Number of Companies
0– 20	32
20– 40	16
40– 60	13
60– 80	10
80–100	19

a. Compute the arithmetic mean for this distribution.

b. Compute the standard deviation for these data.

3.51 An accounting professor taught three sections of principles of accounting. She gave a midterm examination in each of the three sections. The mean scores for the three sections were 29, 41, and 37, respectively. The standard deviations for the three sections were 8.2, 8.7, and 11.0, respectively.

a. Which section had the highest coefficient of variation?

b. Which section had the lowest coefficient of variation?

c. What do the coefficients of variation tell us about the sections?

3.52 Eight of the top sprinters for midwestern universities ran in the conference finals of the 100 meter dash. Their average time in the race was 10.39 seconds, with a standard deviation of .11. Meanwhile, in the intramural meet at one of the universities, the eight finalists in the 100 meter dash averaged a time of 11.75 seconds, with a standard deviation of .63. Compute the coefficients of variation for each of the two races and compare the results.

3.53 Financial analysts like to use the standard deviation as a measure of risk for a stock. The greater the deviation in a stock price over a period of time, the more risky it is to invest in the stock. However, the average prices of some stocks are considerably higher than the average price of others, allowing for the potential of a greater standard deviation of price. For example, a standard deviation of $5.00 on a $10.00 stock is considerably different from a $5.00 standard deviation is on a $40.00 stock. In this situation, a coefficient of variation might provide insight into risk. Suppose that stock X costs an average of $32.00 per share and has varied with a standard deviation of $3.45 for the past 60 days. Suppose that stock Y costs an average of $84.00 per share and has had a standard deviation of $5.40 for the past 60 days. Use the coefficient of variation to determine the coefficient of variability for each stock.

3.54 During the 1990s, businesses are expected to show a lot of interest in Central and Eastern European countries. As new markets begin to open up, American business people need to gain a better understanding of the market potential there. The following are the per capita income figures for eight of these European countries published by the *World Almanac* prior to German reunification:

Country	Per Capita Income
Albania	$ 900
Bulgaria	2,806
Czechoslovakia	8,300
East Germany	10,000
Hungary	4,180
Poland	2,000
Romania	2,020
Yugoslavia	3,109

Compute the mean and standard deviation for Albania, Bulgaria, Czechoslovakia, and East Germany. Compute the mean and standard deviation for Hungary, Poland, Romania, and Yugoslavia. Use a coefficient of variation to compare the two standard deviations.

3.55 A U.S. Census Bureau report showed that the median income for men aged 25 or older with four or more years of college was $35,700. Suppose that the mean income for this group is $41,600 and the mode is $33,000. Is the distribution of incomes for this group skewed? If so, how and why? Which of these measures of central tendency would you use to describe these data? Why?

PROBABILITY

4

CHAPTER LEARNING OBJECTIVES

The main objective of Chapter 4 is to help you understand the basic principles of probability, specifically enabling you to

1. Comprehend the different ways of assigning probability.
2. Utilize the four main types of probability.
3. Select the appropriate law of probability to use in solving problems.
4. Solve problems using the laws of probability.

**KIM NGUYEN
DETERMINES
PROBABILITIES FOR
FIRE EXTINGUISHING
SYSTEMS**

The Federal Corporation is taking an inventory of the fire extinguisher sprinkler system in its Atlanta high-rise building. Concerned about the reliability and readiness of the building's sprinkler system, the operations manager assigned Kim Nguyen to analyze the situation. She contacted the sprinkler system's manufacturers and interviewed other people knowledgeable about the system. They told her about redundant devices on the sprinklers that reduce the probability of sprinkler failure. However, Nguyen is concerned about the independence of sprinklers. If one fails, will that cause others to fail? She also wonders about the other fire prevention and fire fighting systems in the building that complement the sprinkler system. She can gather information regarding these systems and the likelihood that they will work if a fire breaks out. She recognizes, however, that the company will never know for certain whether the systems work until there is a fire. Kim Nguyen's final report to the company will contain many uncertainties and probabilities.

**Managerial
Questions**

- What is the probability of fire in the building?
- What is the probability of a sprinkler working if there is a fire?
- What is the probability of all sprinkler activation devices failing for a specific sprinkler?
- What is the probability of at least one fire prevention system working?

In business, most decision making involves uncertainty. For example, an operations manager does not know definitely whether a valve in the plant is going to malfunction or continue to function—and, if so, for how long. Should it be replaced? What is the chance that the valve will malfunction within the next week? In the banking industry, what are the new vice president's prospects for successfully turning a department around? The answers to these questions are uncertain.

In the case of the high-rise building that Kim Nguyen is studying, what are the chances that a fire extinguishing system will work when needed if redundancies are built in? Business people must deal with these and thousands of similar questions daily. Since most such questions do not have definite answers, the decision making is based on uncertainty. In many of these situations, a probability can be assigned to the likelihood of an outcome. This chapter is about learning how to determine or assign probabilities.

INTRODUCTION TO PROBABILITY | 4.1

Chapter 1 discussed the difference between descriptive and inferential statistics. Much statistical analysis is inferential, and probability is the basis for inferential statistics. Recall that inferential statistics involves taking a sample from a population, computing a statistic on the sample, and inferring from the statistic the value of the corresponding parameter of the population. The reason for doing so is that the value of the parameter is unknown. Because it is unknown, the analyst conducts the inferential process under uncertainty. However, based on rules and laws, the analyst can assign a probability of obtaining the results. Figure 4.1 depicts this process.

Suppose that a quality control inspector selects a random sample of forty light bulbs from a population of brand X bulbs and computes the average number of hours of lumination for the sample bulbs. By using techniques discussed later in this text, the specialist estimates the average number of lumination hours for the *population* of brand X light bulbs from this *sample* information. Because the light bulbs being analyzed are only a sample of the population, the average number of lumination hours for the forty bulbs may or may not accurately estimate the average for all bulbs in the population. The results are uncertain. Based on the laws presented in this chapter, the inspector can assign a value of probability to this estimate.

METHODS OF ASSIGNING PROBABILITIES | 4.2

The three general methods of assigning probabilities are (1) classical probability, (2) relative frequency of occurrence, and (3) subjective probability.

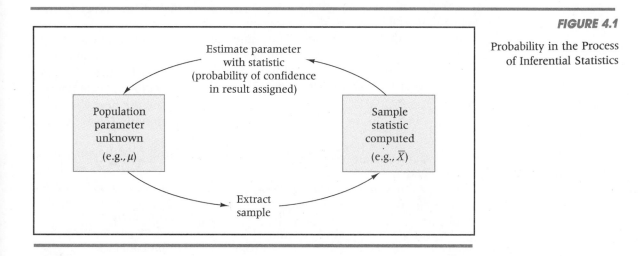

FIGURE 4.1

Probability in the Process
of Inferential Statistics

Estimate parameter
with statistic
(probability of confidence
in result assigned)

Population
parameter
unknown

(e.g., μ)

Sample
statistic
computed

(e.g., $\bar{X}$)

Extract
sample

Classical Method of Assigning Probabilities

classical probability
experiment
event

The classical method of assigning probabilities is based on the assumption that each outcome is equally likely to occur. **Classical probability** utilizes rules and laws. It involves an **experiment,** which is *a process that produces outcomes,* and an **event,** which is *an outcome of an experiment.*

Classical Method of Assigning Probabilities

$$P(E) = \frac{n_e}{N},$$

where: N = total possible number of outcomes of an experiment

n_e = the number of outcomes in which the event occurs out of N outcomes

---

a priori

In a coin tossing experiment, the classical method determines the probability of getting a head on one toss of the coin. There are two possible outcomes—heads and tails—but only one of those possible outcomes is the desired event (head). Hence the probability of getting a head is 1/2. Similarly, the probability of obtaining an even number from a throw of a die is 3/6. The outcome from the roll of a die can be determined by the classical method **a priori,** meaning before or prior to the experiment. Of six possible outcomes from the die (1, 2, 3, 4, 5, 6), three are even numbers (2, 4, 6). From the classical method, also, the probability a priori of drawing an ace on one draw from a standard deck of cards is 4/52, because, of the 52 cards in a standard deck of cards, 4 are aces.

As n_e can never be greater than N (no more than N outcomes in the population could possibly possess attribute e), the highest value of any probability is 1. If the probability of an outcome occurring is 1, the event is certain to occur. The smallest possible probability is 0. If none of the outcomes of the N possibilities possesses the desired characteristic, e, the probability is $0/N = 0$, and the event is certain not to occur. The range of possibilities for probabilities is

$$0 \leq P(E) \leq 1.$$

Thus probabilities are nonnegative proper fractions or nonnegative decimal values less than or equal to 1.

Probability values may be converted to percentages by multiplying by 100. Meteorologists often report weather probabilities in percentage form. For example, when they forecast a 60% chance of rain for tomorrow, they are saying that the probability of rain tomorrow is .60.

Relative Frequency of Occurrence

The **relative frequency of occurrence** method of assigning probabilities is based on cumulated historical data. With this method, the probability of an event occurring is equal to the number of times the event has occurred in the past divided by the total number of opportunities for the event to have occurred:

$$\begin{array}{c}\text{Probability by}\\ \text{relative frequency}\\ \text{of occurrence}\end{array} = \frac{\begin{array}{c}\text{number of}\\ \text{times an event occurred}\end{array}}{\begin{array}{c}\text{total number of opportunities}\\ \text{for the event to occur}\end{array}}.$$

Relative frequency of occurrence is not based on rules or laws but on what has occurred in the past. For example, a company wants to determine the probability that its inspectors are going to reject the next batch of raw materials from a supplier. Data gathered from company record books show that the supplier had sent the company ninety batches in the past, and inspectors had rejected 10 of them. By the method of relative frequency of occurrence, the probability of the inspectors rejecting the next batch is 10/90 or .11. If the next batch is rejected, the relative frequency of occurrence probability for the subsequent shipment would change to $11/91 = .12$.

A baseball player's batting average can be viewed as a relative frequency of occurrence probability. If a player has batted 310 times this season and has 85 hits, his batting average is $85/310 = .274$, and the probability of his getting a hit the next time up is .274. After he bats the next time, the relative frequency of occurrence probability will change unless he walks or sacrifices (walks and sacrifices do not count as official times at bat).

Weather probabilities also can be viewed as relative frequency of occurrence probabilities. Forecasters could take the predicted conditions for today, look in the meteorological records, and find days with similar conditions. Suppose that, of the last seventy days with conditions like those forecast for today, it rained on twelve days. The probability of having rain today based on those historical days is $12/70 = .17$.

Most people agree that the probability of tossing a fair coin and getting heads is 1/2. Although usually determined by probability laws, this probability also can be determined by using relative frequency of occurrence. A coin could be tossed 500 times and the number of heads determined. The number of heads tossed divided by 500 is the relative frequency of occurrence probability.

Subjective Probability

The subjective method of assigning probability is based on the feelings or insights of the person determining the probability. **Subjective probability** comes from the person's intuition or reasoning. Although not a scientific approach to probability, the subjective method often is based on the accumulation of knowledge, understanding, and experience stored and processed in the human mind. At times it is merely a guess. At other times, subjective probability can potentially yield accurate probabilities. Suppose that a director of transportation for an oil company is asked the probability of getting a shipment of oil out of Saudi Arabia to the United States within three weeks. If he has scheduled many such shipments, has a knowledge of Saudi politics, and has an awareness of current climatological and economic conditions, he may be able to give an accurate probability that the shipment can be made on time.

Subjective probability can be a potentially useful way of tapping a person's experience, knowledge, and insight and using them to forecast the occurrence of some event. An experienced airline mechanic can usually assign a meaningful probability that a particular plane will experience a certain type of mechanical difficulty. Physicians sometimes assign subjective probabilities to the length of life expectancy for people having cancer.

Subjective probabilities can be used as a mechanism to utilize the background of experienced workers and managers in decision making. Weather forecasting is a version of subjective probability when the forecast is based on an *educated guess*. Subjective probabilities can provide useful information in making decisions but should be backed with as many facts as possible.

4.3   STRUCTURE OF PROBABILITY

In the study of probability, developing a language of terms and symbols is helpful. The structure of probability provides a common framework within which the topics of probability can be explored.

Experiment

Most people think of an experiment as a scientific experiment, such as those conducted in laboratories, rather than as a process that produces outcomes. Some types of experiments explore ways to improve health. Other types of experiments involve mental capabilities. Aerospace companies experiment with new types of aircraft. In probability, an experiment takes the form of an activity, such as tossing a coin, selecting a part from an assembly line, or drawing a card. In statistics experiments can vary from studying the impact of colors on consumers to studying the effects of the consumer price index on the stock market.

Event

Because an event is an outcome of an experiment, if the experiment is to toss two coins, an event could be to get two tails. In an experiment to roll a die, one event could be to roll an even number, and another event could be to roll a number greater than 2. If the experiment is to sample five bottles coming off a production line, an event could be to get one defective and four good bottles. Events are denoted by uppercase letters; italic capital letters (e.g., A and E_1, E_2, . . .) represent the general or abstract case, and roman capital letters (e.g., H and T for heads and tails) denote specific things and people.

Elementary Events

Events that cannot be decomposed or broken down into other events are called **elementary events.** Elementary events are denoted by lowercase letters (e.g., e_1, e_2, e_3, . . .). Suppose that the experiment is to roll a die. The elementary events for this experiment are to roll a 1 or roll a 2 or roll a 3, and so on. Rolling an even number is an event, but it is not an elementary event, because the even number can be broken down further into events 2, 4, and 6. In the experiment of rolling a die, there are six elementary events {1, 2, 3, 4, 5, 6}.

Rolling a pair of dice results in thirty-six possible elementary events (outcomes). For each of the six elementary events possible on the roll of one die, there are six possible elementary events on the roll of the second die as depicted in Figure 4.2. Table 4.1 contains a list of these thirty-six outcomes.

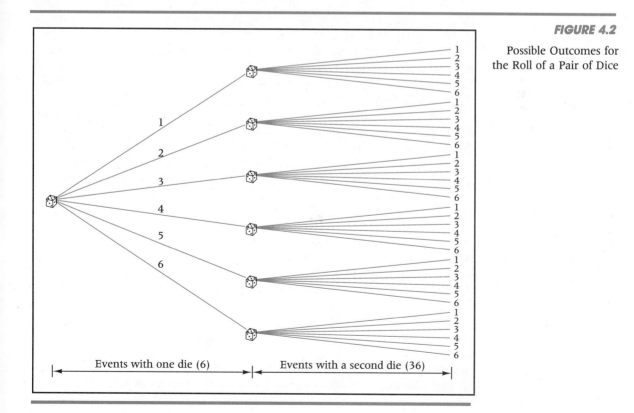

FIGURE 4.2

Possible Outcomes for the Roll of a Pair of Dice

Events with one die (6)   Events with a second die (36)

TABLE 4.1	(1,1)	(2,1)	(3,1)	(4,1)	(5,1)	(6,1)
All Possible Elementary	(1,2)	(2,2)	(3,2)	(4,2)	(5,2)	(6,2)
Events in the Roll of a	(1,3)	(2,3)	(3,3)	(4,3)	(5,3)	(6,3)
Pair of Dice	(1,4)	(2,4)	(3,4)	(4,4)	(5,4)	(6,4)
	(1,5)	(2,5)	(3,5)	(4,5)	(5,5)	(6,5)
	(1,6)	(2,6)	(3,6)	(4,6)	(5,6)	(6,6)

In the experiment of rolling a pair of dice, other events could include outcomes such as two even numbers, a sum of 10, a sum greater than 5, and others. However, none of these events is an elementary event, because each can be broken down into several of the elementary events displayed in Table 4.1.

Sample Space

sample space

A **sample space** is *a complete roster or listing of all elementary events for an experiment.* Table 4.1 is the sample space for the roll of a pair of dice. The sample space for the roll of a single die is {1, 2, 3, 4, 5, 6}. The sample space for the experiment of tossing a coin is {H, T}. If two coins are tossed, the sample space is {H_1H_2, H_1T_2, T_1H_2, and T_1T_2}.

Sample space can aid in finding probabilities. For an equal likelihood of outcomes, the probability of tossing two coins and getting *both* heads is ¼. The sample space for this experiment contains four elementary events, and one of them is H_1H_2. The probability of tossing two coins and getting *one* head is ²⁄₄, which can be obtained by examining the sample space. There are two elementary events in which there is one head (H_1T_2 and T_1H_2) out of four total elementary events. However, using the sample space to determine probabilities is unwieldy and cumbersome when the sample space is large. Hence statisticians usually use other, more effective methods of determining probability.

Unions and Intersections

set notation
union

The **set notation** for unions and intersections is used as a symbolic tool in this chapter. The **union** of X, Y is denoted X ∪ Y. An element qualifies for the union of X, Y if it is in either X or Y or in both X and Y. The union expression X∪Y can be translated to X or Y. For example, if

$$X = \{1, 4, 7, 9\} \quad \text{and} \quad Y = \{2, 3, 4, 5, 6\},$$

$$X∪Y = \{1, 2, 3, 4, 5, 6, 7, 9\}.$$

Note that all the values of X and all the values of Y qualify for the union. In Venn diagrams, the shaded regions denote the union, as in Figure 4.3.

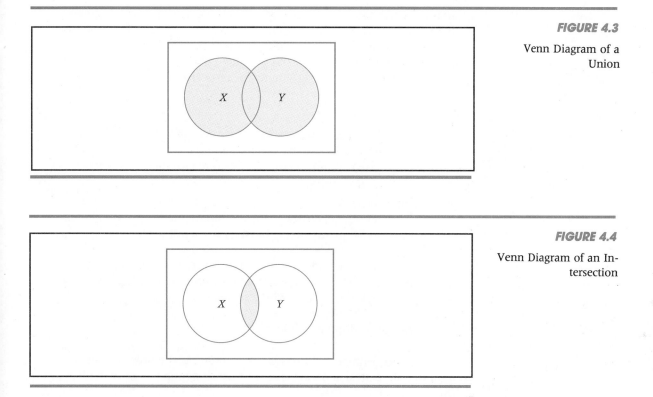

FIGURE 4.3

Venn Diagram of a
Union

FIGURE 4.4

Venn Diagram of an In-
tersection

An **intersection** is denoted $X \cap Y$. To qualify for intersection, an element must be in *both X and Y*. The intersection contains the elements common to both sets. Thus the intersection symbol, $\cap$, is often read as *and*. The intersection of *X, Y* is referred to as *X and Y*. For example, if

Intersection

$$X = \{1, 4, 7, 9\} \quad \text{and} \quad Y = \{2, 3, 4, 5, 6\},$$

$$X \cap Y = \{4\}.$$

Note that only the value of 4 is common to both sets *X* and *Y*. The intersection is more exclusive and thus, is smaller than the union. That is, elements must be characteristic of both *X* and *Y* to qualify. In Venn diagrams, the shaded area denotes the intersection, as in Figure 4.4.

**Demonstration
Problem 4.1**

A town of 25,000 people has two home improvement-type stores. The line of goods carried in each store is similar but not the same. Store 1 on the west side of town stocks lumber, plumbing supplies, building tools, roofing materials, sheetrock, concrete blocks, nails, and screws. Store 2 on the east side of town stocks garden tools, plants, trees, lumber, building tools, and lawn equipment. Determine the union and intersection for the items stocked by these two stores. What might the union or intersection of these items mean to the customer?

Solution:

Store 1.   {lumber, plumbing supplies, building tools, roofing materials, sheetrock, concrete blocks, nails, screws}

Store 2.   {garden tools, plants, trees, lumber, building tools, lawn equipment}

Union.   {lumber, plumbing supplies, building tools, roofing materials, sheetrock, concrete blocks, nails, screws, garden tools, plants, trees, lawn equipment}

To the consumer, the union represents the total possible types of home improvement supplies available for purchase in this city. It is a roster of available items somewhere in the city.

Intersection.   {lumber, building tools}

To the consumer, the intersection represents the only items common to both stores, allowing comparative shopping for those items in this city.

Mutually Exclusive Events

mutually exclusive events

Two or more events are **mutually exclusive events** if *the occurrence of one event precludes the occurrence of the other events.* This characteristic means that mutually exclusive events cannot occur simultaneously and therefore can have no intersection.

In the toss of a single coin, the events of heads and tails are mutually exclusive. The person tossing the coin gets either a head or a tail but never both. On a toss of a pair of dice, the event (6,6) *boxcars* is mutually exclusive with the event (1,1) *snake eyes.* Getting both boxcars and snake eyes on the same roll of the dice is impossible. In a sample of manufactured products, the product either is or is not defective; the outcome cannot be both on one draw. The event of selecting a defective part is mutually exclusive with the event of selecting a nondefective part.

In baseball, the event of the Chicago Cubs winning the National League East title is mutually exclusive of the event of the New York Mets winning the

National League East title. One of these teams can win the division but not both. In case of a tie, the league has a playoff to ensure mutual exclusivity. The event of the Chicago Cubs winning the National League East title is *not* mutually exclusive with the event of the Chicago White Sox winning the American League West title. Because they are in different divisions (and leagues), both may win, both may lose, or one may win and one may lose. The probability of two mutually exclusive events occurring at the same time is zero. In terms of set notation, if events X and Y are mutually exclusive,

$$P(X \cap Y) = 0,$$

or the probability of X intersecting Y is zero.

Independent Events

Two or more events are **independent events** if *the occurrence or nonoccurrence of one of the events does not affect the occurrence or nonoccurrence of the others.* Certain experiments, such as rolling dice, yield independent events; each die is independent of the other. Whether a 6 is rolled on the first die has no influence on whether a 6 is rolled on the second die. Coin tosses always are independent of each other. The event of getting a head on the first toss of a coin is independent of getting a head on the second toss.

Independent events

The impact of independent events on probability is that, if two events are independent, the probability of attaining the second event is the same regardless of the outcome of the first event. The probability of tossing a head is always $\frac{1}{2}$, regardless of what was tossed previously. Thus, if someone tosses a coin six times and gets six heads, the probability of tossing a head on the seventh time is still $\frac{1}{2}$, because coin tosses are independent.

Many experiments using random selection can produce either independent or nonindependent events. In these experiments, the outcomes are independent if sampling is done *with replacement*. That is, after each item is selected and the outcome is determined, the item is restored to the population, and the population is shuffled. This way, each draw becomes independent of the previous draw. Suppose that an inspector is randomly selecting bolts from a bin that contains 5% defects. If the inspector samples a defective bolt and returns it to the bin, on the second draw there are still 5% defects in the bin regardless of the fact that the first outcome was a defect. If the inspector does *not* replace the first draw, the second draw is not independent of the first; in this case, fewer than 5% defects remain in the population. Thus the probability of the second outcome is dependent on the first outcome. In terms of symbolic notation, if X and Y are *independent*:

$$P(X|Y) = P(X) \quad \text{and} \quad P(Y|X) = P(Y),$$

where $P(X|Y)$ denotes the probability of X occurring given that Y has occurred, and $P(Y|X)$ denotes the probability of Y occurring given that X has occurred.

Collectively Exhaustive Events

**collectively
exhaustive events**

A list of **collectively exhaustive events** contains *all possible elementary events for an experiment.* Thus all sample spaces are collectively exhaustive lists. The list of possible outcomes for the tossing of a pair of dice contained in Table 4.1 is a collectively exhaustive list. The sample space for an experiment can be described as a list of events that are mutually exclusive and collectively exhaustive. Sample space events do not overlap or intersect, and the list is complete.

Complementary Events

complement

The **complement** of event A is denoted $\overline{A}$. All the elementary events of an experiment not in A comprise its complement. For example, if in rolling one die, event A is getting an even number, the complement of A is getting an odd number. If event A is getting a 5 on the roll of a die, the complement of A is getting a 1, 2, 3, 4, or 6. The complement of event A contains whatever portion of the sample space that event A does not contain, as the Venn diagram in Figure 4.5 shows.

Using the complement of an event can be helpful sometimes in solving for probabilities because of the rule:

$$P(\overline{A}) = 1 - P(A).$$

Suppose that a pair of coins is tossed. If A is the event of getting two heads and the probability of getting A is $\frac{1}{4}$, the complement of A is not getting two heads and the probability of the complement of A is $1 - \frac{1}{4} = \frac{3}{4}$. The sample space for this experiment validates this probability:

$$\{H_1H_2,\ H_1T_2,\ T_1H_2,\ T_1T_2\}.$$

FIGURE 4.5

The Complement of
Event A

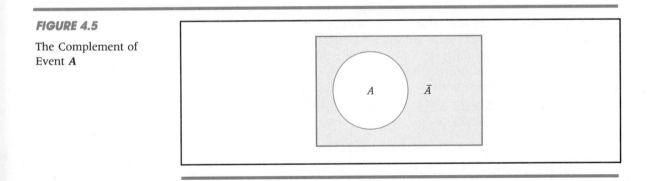

Event A is the outcome, H_1H_2. The complement of A is all the rest of the outcomes: H_1T_2, T_1H_2, T_1T_2. The use of the law of the probability of complements at times can be helpful in solving tedious probability problems. Solving for the probability of $\overline{A}$ rather than solving for the probability of A may be simpler on occasion.

**PROBLEMS
Section 4.3**

4.1 For the experiment of tossing three different coins at the same time, what is the sample space? Based on the sample space, what is the probability of tossing one head in this experiment?

4.2 Kelli and Craig have just gotten married. They plan to have two children. Suppose that having a boy and having a girl are equally likely and that each baby's gender is independent of the other's. What is the sample space of possible outcomes for Kelli and Craig's potential family? From this sample space, determine the probability that they will have one boy and one girl but not necessarily in that order.

4.3 For the experiment of rolling three dice simultaneously, how many elementary events are in the sample space? Name two events that are mutually exclusive in this experiment. How does independence of events enter into this experiment?

4.4 A bin contains six parts. Two of the parts are defective and four are acceptable. If three of the six parts are selected from the bin, what is the sample space? For this sample space, what is the probability that one of the three sampled parts is defective?

4.5 Given $X = \{1, 3, 5, 7, 8, 9\}$, $Y = \{2, 4, 7, 9\}$, and $Z = \{1, 2, 3, 4, 7\}$, solve the following:

   a. $X \cup Z = \underline{\hphantom{xx}}$ **b.** $X \cap Y = \underline{\hphantom{xx}}$

   c. $X \cap Z = \underline{\hphantom{xx}}$ **d.** $X \cup Y \cup Z = \underline{\hphantom{xx}}$

   e. $X \cap Y \cap Z = \underline{\hphantom{xx}}$ **f.** $(X \cup Y) \cap Z = \underline{\hphantom{xx}}$

   g. $(Y \cap Z) \cup (X \cap Y) = \underline{\hphantom{xx}}$

4.6 What is independent about the experiment of tossing two coins? What events could be mutually exclusive in this experiment?

4.7 Name two events in your everyday life that are independent. Name two events in your everyday life that are mutually exclusive.

4.8 If an experiment is to toss a coin three times in a row, what is the complement of getting three tails?

4.9 If a population consists of the positive even numbers through 30 and if $A = \{2, 6, 12, 24\}$, what is $\overline{A}$?

FOUR TYPES OF PROBABILITY

marginal probability

Four particular types of probability are presented in this chapter. The first type is **marginal probability.** Marginal probability is denoted $P(E)$, where E is some event. A marginal probability is usually computed by dividing some subtotal by the whole. An example of marginal probability is the probability that a person owns a Ford car. This probability is computed by dividing the number of Ford owners by the total number of car owners. The probability of a person wearing glasses is also a marginal probability. This probability is computed by dividing the number of people wearing glasses by the total number of people.

union probability

A second type of probability is the union of two events. **Union probability** is denoted $P(E_1 \cup E_2)$, where E_1 and E_2 are two events. $P(E_1 \cup E_2)$ is the probability that E_1 will occur or that E_2 will occur or that both E_1 and E_2 will occur. An example of union probability is the probability that a person owns a Ford or a Chevrolet. To qualify for the union, the person only has to possess at least one of these cars. Another example is the probability of a person wearing glasses or having red hair. All people wearing glasses are included in the union along with all redheads and all redheaded people who wear glasses.

joint probability

A third type of probability is the intersection of two events or **joint probability.** The joint probability of events E_1 and E_2 occurring is denoted $P(E_1 \cap E_2)$. Sometimes $P(E_1 \cap E_2)$ is read as the probability of E_1 *and* E_2. To qualify for the intersection, both events *must* occur. An example of joint probability is the probability of a person owning both a Ford and a Chevrolet. Owning one type of car is not sufficient. A second example of joint probability is the probability that a person is a redhead and wears glasses.

conditional probability

The fourth type is **conditional probability.** Conditional probability is denoted $P(E_1 | E_2)$. This expression is read: *the probability that E_1 will occur given that E_2 is known to have occurred.* Conditional probabilities involve knowledge of some prior information. The information that is known or given is to the right of the vertical line in the probability statement. An example of conditional probability is the probability that a person owns a Chevrolet given that she owns a Ford. This conditional probability is only a measure of the proportion of Ford owners who have a Chevrolet—not the proportion of total car owners who own a Chevrolet. Conditional probabilities are computed by determining the number of items that possess an outcome out of some subtotal of the population. In the car owner example, the possibilities are reduced to Ford owners, and then the number Chevrolet owners out of those Ford owners is determined. Of the four probability types, only conditional probability does not have the population total as its denominator. Conditional probabilities use a population subtotal in the denominator. Figure 4.6 summarizes the four types of probability.

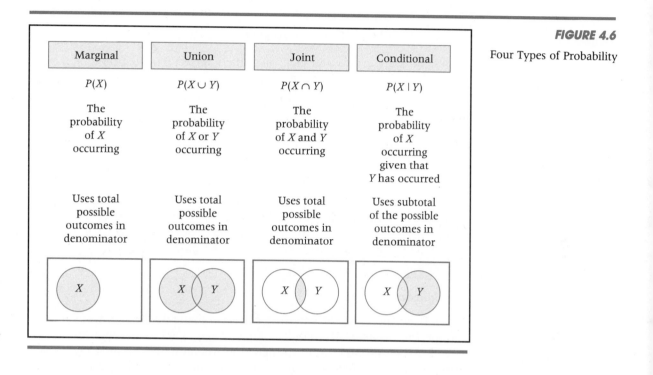

FIGURE 4.6

Four Types of Probability

Marginal	Union	Joint	Conditional
$P(X)$	$P(X \cup Y)$	$P(X \cap Y)$	$P(X \mid Y)$
The probability of X occurring	The probability of X or Y occurring	The probability of X and Y occurring	The probability of X occurring given that Y has occurred
Uses total possible outcomes in denominator	Uses total possible outcomes in denominator	Uses total possible outcomes in denominator	Uses subtotal of the possible outcomes in denominator

ADDITION LAW   **4.5**

Several tools are available for use in solving probability problems. These techniques include the laws of probability, tree diagrams, probability matrices, sample space, and insight. Because of the individuality and variety of probability problems, some techniques apply more readily in certain situations than in others. There is no best method for solving all probability problems. In some instances, the probability matrix lays out a problem in a readily solvable manner. In other cases, setting up the probability matrix is more difficult than solving the problem in another way. The probability laws almost always can be used to solve probability problems. However, for some problems the solution can be determined without formally applying the laws.

One of the tools already presented is sample space; others include the laws of probability. Four general laws of probability are presented in this chapter: the addition law, the multiplication law, the conditional law, and Bayes's rule. The addition law and the multiplication law each have a general law and a special law. The general law of addition is used to find the probability of the union of two events, $P(X \cup Y)$.

General Law of Addition	$P(X \cup Y) = P(X) + P(Y) - P(X \cap Y),$ where X, Y are events and $(X \cap Y)$ is the intersection of X and Y.

The expression $P(X \cup Y)$ denotes the probability of X occurring or Y occurring or both X and Y occurring.

**Demonstration
Problem 4.2**

n = 100
Hispanic — 23
— 35
women

The Omega Corporation has an opening for a pipefitter. One hundred people applied for the position, of which twenty-three are Hispanic and thirty-five are women. If the selection is random, what is the probability that the person selected for the position is Hispanic or a woman?

Solution:

Let H be the event of choosing a Hispanic and W be the event of choosing a woman. The problem is to find $P(H \cup W)$. Of the applicants, 23 are Hispanic and 35 are women. The answer to the question might seem to be 23 + 35 = 58 Hispanic or women applicants out of the 100. However, there might be some Hispanic applicants who are women and who have been counted on both lists. Suppose that 9 Hispanic applicants actually are women. The correct solution for the problem is

$$P(H \cup W) = P(H) + P(W) - P(H \cap W) = \frac{23}{100} + \frac{35}{100} - \frac{9}{100}$$

$$= \frac{49}{100} = .49.$$

In terms of a Venn diagram, the solution is as follows:

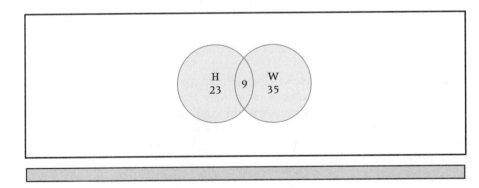

Note that the addition law subtracts the intersection from the probability. It is not a matter of getting rid of the intersection. It *is* the need not to count the intersection twice.

A probability matrix can be formed for the pipefitter applicant example. Probability matrices can sometimes be economical ways to solve probability problems (in this text, only two-dimensional matrices will be used). The pipefitter applicant problem has two variables: Hispanic and woman. Each variable can be placed along a dimension. A contingency table of raw values for the pipefitter problem is shown in Table 4.2.

The probability matrix is determined by taking the contingency table of raw values and dividing all numbers by the total (100), as shown in Table 4.3. Table 4.4 shows that the probability of the union of Hispanic and woman is the sum of the Hispanic row (yes) and the woman column (yes), minus the

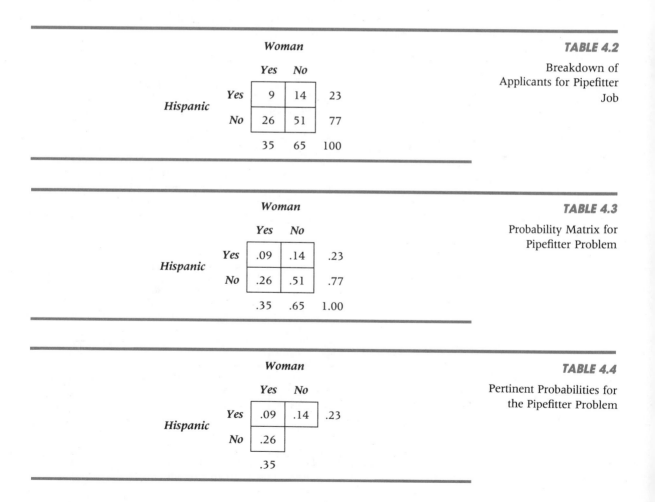

TABLE 4.2

Breakdown of Applicants for Pipefitter Job

		Woman		
		Yes	No	
Hispanic	Yes	9	14	23
	No	26	51	77
		35	65	100

TABLE 4.3

Probability Matrix for Pipefitter Problem

		Woman		
		Yes	No	
Hispanic	Yes	.09	.14	.23
	No	.26	.51	.77
		.35	.65	1.00

TABLE 4.4

Pertinent Probabilities for the Pipefitter Problem

		Woman		
		Yes	No	
Hispanic	Yes	.09	.14	.23
	No	.26		
		.35		

intersection of the two (yes, yes), or in set notation,

$$P(H \cup W) = .35 + .23 - .09 = .49.$$

In probability matrices, the subtotals in the *margins* are the marginal probabilities. The $P(H)$ in the margin is .23. The $P(W)$ in the margin is .35. Solving for probabilities of unions requires adding the two marginal probabilities and subtracting the intersection probability, which is located in a *cell* of the probability matrix.

Demonstration Problem 4.3

The following tables contain the raw values and corresponding probability matrix for the results of a national survey of 200 executives. They were asked to identify the geographic locale of their company and their company's industry type.

Raw Values

		Geographic Location				
		Northeast D	Southeast E	Midwest F	West G	
	Finance A	24	10	8	14	56
Industry Type	Manufacturing B	30	6	22	12	70
	Communications C	28	18	12	16	74
		82	34	42	42	200

Probability Matrix

		Geographic Location				
		Northeast D	Southeast E	Midwest F	West G	
	Finance A	.12	.05	.04	.07	.28
Industry Type	Manufacturing B	.15	.03	.11	.06	.35
	Communications C	.14	.09	.06	.08	.37
		.41	.17	.21	.21	1.00

(a) If a respondent is randomly selected from these data, what is the probability that this executive is from the Midwest? (b) What is the probability that a respondent is from the communications industry (C) or from the Northeast (D)? (c) What is the probability that a respondent is from the Southeast (E) or from the finance industry (A)?

Solution:

a. $P(\text{Midwest}) = P(F) = .21$.

b. $P(C \cup D) = P(C) + P(D) - P(C \cap D) = .37 + .41 - .14 = .64$.

c. $P(E \cup A) = P(E) + P(A) - P(E \cap A) = .17 + .28 - .05 = .40$.

> **Demonstration
> Problem 4.4**

A standard deck of cards contains 52 playing cards of four suits (hearts, diamonds, spades, clubs). Each suit has 13 cards (ace, king, queen, jack, 10, 9, 8, 7, 6, 5, 4, 3, 2). There are 26 red cards (hearts and diamonds) and 26 black cards (spades and clubs). If a card is drawn from a well-shuffled standard deck of playing cards, what is the probability of drawing a heart or a queen? That is,

$$P(\heartsuit \cup Q) = ?$$

Red Cards		Black Cards	
Hearts	*Diamonds*	*Spades*	*Clubs*
Ace	Ace	Ace	Ace
King	King	King	King
Queen	Queen	Queen	Queen
Jack	Jack	Jack	Jack
10	10	10	10
9	9	9	9
8	8	8	8
7	7	7	7
6	6	6	6
5	5	5	5
4	4	4	4
3	3	3	3
2	2	2	2

Solution:

$$P(\heartsuit \cup Q) = P(\heartsuit) + P(Q) - P(\heartsuit \cap Q).$$

There are thirteen hearts, so $P(\heartsuit) = 13/52$. There are four queens, so $P(Q) = 4/52$. However, the queen of hearts ($\heartsuit \cap Q$) is on both lists and must be subtracted out:

$$P(\heartsuit \cup Q) = \frac{13}{52} + \frac{4}{52} - \frac{1}{52} = \frac{16}{52} = \frac{4}{13}.$$

Special Rule of Addition

If two events are mutually exclusive, the probability of the union of the two events is the probability of the first event plus the probability of the second event. Because mutually exclusive events do not intersect, nothing has to be subtracted out.

Special Law of Addition	If X, Y are mutually exclusive, $$P(X \cup Y) = P(X) + P(Y).$$

The special law of addition is a special case of the general law of addition. In a sense, the general law fits all cases. However, when the events are mutually exclusive, a zero is inserted into the general law formula for the intersection, resulting in the special law formula.

Demonstration Problem 4.5

If the probability of the Los Angeles Dodgers winning the National League West title is .12 and the probability of the San Diego Padres winning the National League West title is .18, what is the probability of the Dodgers or the Padres winning the National League West title?

Solution:

Both the Dodgers and the Padres are in the same division. Because of the playoff format, no two teams in the same division can be champions of that division. Thus the two events of the Dodgers winning the title and the Padres winning the title are mutually exclusive. The answer to the question is

$$P(\text{Dodgers} \cup \text{Padres}) = P(\text{Dodgers}) + P(\text{Padres}) = .12 + .18 = .30.$$

What is the probability of drawing a king or an ace on one draw from a well-shuffled standard deck of playing cards?

Solution:

$$P(K \cup A) = P(K) + P(A).$$

There are no kings that are also aces, so the two events are mutually exclusive. There are 4 kings and 4 aces in a 52-card deck of standard playing cards. The solution is

$$\frac{4}{52} + \frac{4}{52} = \frac{8}{52}.$$

Use the data from the tables in Demonstration Problem 4.3. What is the probability that a randomly selected respondent is from the Southeast or the West? That is,

$$P(E \cup G) = ?$$

Solution:

As geographic location is mutually exclusive (the work location is either in the Southeast or in the West but not in both),

$$P(E \cup G) = P(E) + P(G) = .17 + .21 = .38.$$

4.10 Given $P(A) = .10$, $P(B) = .12$, $P(C) = .21$, $P(A \cap C) = .05$, and $P(B \cap C) = .03$, solve the following:
   a. $P(A \cup C) = $ __   **b.** $P(B \cup C) = $ __
   c. If A and B are mutually exclusive, $P(A \cup B) = $ __

4.11 Use the values in the table to solve the equations given.

	D	E	F
A	5	8	12
B	10	6	4
C	8	2	5

a. $P(A \cup D) =$ __
b. $P(E \cup B) =$ __
c. $P(D \cup E) =$ __
d. $P(A \cup B \cup C) =$ __
e. $P(B \cup E \cup F) =$ __

4.12 Use the values in the table to solve the equations given.

	E	F
A	.10	.03
B	.04	.12
C	.27	.06
D	.31	.07

a. $P(A \cup F) =$ __
b. $P(E \cup B) =$ __
c. $P(B \cup C) =$ __
d. $P(B \cup C \cup D) =$ __
e. $P(E \cup F) =$ __

4.13 Suppose that 47% of all Americans have flown in an airplane at least once and that 28% of all Americans have ridden on a train at least once. What is the probability that a randomly selected American has either ridden a train or flown in an airplane? Can this problem be solved? Under what conditions can it be solved? If the problem cannot be solved, what information is needed to make it solvable?

4.14 According to the New York Stock Exchange, 76% of all shareholders have some college education, which holds for American shareholders. Suppose that 37% of all adult Americans have some college education and that 22% of all adult Americans are shareholders. For a randomly selected adult American:

a. What is the probability that the person did not own shares of stock?

b. What is the probability that the person owns shares of stock or had some college education?

c. What is the probability that the person has neither some college education nor owns shares of stock?

d. What is the probability that the person does not own shares of stock or has no college education?

4.15 According to the U.S. Bureau of Labor Statistics, in 1990, 75% of the women aged 25–49 participated in the labor force. At the same time the figure for men was 90%. Suppose that 78% of the women and 74% of the men in this age group are married. Suppose also that 61% of all women aged 25–49 are married and are participating in the labor force. Suppose further that 65% of all men aged 25–49 are married and are participating in the labor force.

a. What is the probability that a randomly selected woman aged 25–49 is married or is participating in the labor force?

b. What is the probability that a randomly selected woman aged 25–49 is married or is participating in the labor force but not both?

c. What is the probability that a randomly selected man aged 25–49 is married or is participating in the labor force?

d. What is the probability that a randomly selected man aged 25–49 is neither married nor participating in the labor force?

e. What is the probability that a randomly selected man aged 25–49 is both married *and* participating in the labor force?

4.16 A 1990 survey of 55,000 sales professionals conducted by Dartnell Corporate/Personnel Corporation of America found that 15% of all sales professionals have home fax machines and 35% use car phones. Suppose that 6% of all sales professionals both have home fax machines and use car phones.

a. What is the probability that a randomly selected sales professional has a home fax machine?

b. What is the probability that a randomly selected sales professional has a home fax machine or uses a car phone?

c. What is the probability that a randomly selected sales professional neither has a home fax machine nor uses a car phone?

d. Suppose that no sales professional has both a home fax machine *and* uses a car phone. What is the probability that a randomly selected sales professional has a home fax machine or uses a car phone?

4.17 A survey conducted by the Northwestern University Lindquist–Endicott Report asked 320 companies about the procedures they use in hiring. Only 54% of the responding companies review the applicant's college transcript as part of the hiring process, and only 44% consider faculty references. Assume that these percentages are true for the population of companies in the United States and that 35% of all companies use both the applicant's college transcript and faculty references.

a. What is the probability that a randomly selected company uses faculty references as part of the hiring process?

b. What is the probability that a randomly selected company uses both faculty references and college transcript as part of the hiring process?

c. What is the probability that a randomly selected company uses either faculty references or college transcript as part of the hiring process?

d. What is the probability that a randomly selected company uses either faculty references or college transcript but not both as part of the hiring process?

e. What is the probability that a randomly selected company uses neither faculty references nor the college transcript as part of the hiring process?

| 4.6 | MULTIPLICATIVE LAW |

The probability of the intersection of two events $(X \cap Y)$ is called the joint probability. The general law of multiplication is used to find the probability of the intersection of two events or the joint probability.

General Law of Multiplication

$$P(X \cap Y) = P(X) \cdot P(Y|X) = P(Y) \cdot P(X|Y).$$

The occurrence of $X \cap Y$ means that both X and Y must happen. The general law of multiplication gives the probability that both event X and event Y will occur at the same time.

Demonstration Problem 4.8

A company has 140 employees, of which 30 are supervisors. Eighty of the employees are married, and 20% of the married employees are supervisors. If a company employee is randomly selected, what is the probability that the employee is married *and* is a supervisor?

Solution:

Let M denote married and S denote supervisor.

$$P(M \cap S) = ?$$

First, calculate the marginal probabilities:

$$P(M) = \frac{80}{140}$$
$$= .5714.$$

Then, 20% of the married employees are supervisors, which is the conditional probability: $P(S|M) = .20$. Finally, applying the general law of multiplication gives

$$P(M \cap S) = P(M) \cdot P(S|M)$$
$$= (.5714)(.20) = .1143.$$

Thus 11.43% of the 140 employees are married and are supervisors.

The intersection probability can be found in the cell of a probability matrix. A probability matrix is constructed of two types of probabilities: *joint* (intersection) probabilities in the cells and *marginal* probabilities in the margins. If a probability matrix can be constructed for a joint probability problem, the answer for the joint probability question can be obtained in a cell. Sometimes, however, constructing the probability matrix is more difficult than solving the problem directly.

Demonstration Problem 4.9

From the data obtained from the interviews of 200 executives previously used, find (a) $P(B \cap E)$, (b) $P(G \cap A)$, and (c) $P(B \cap C)$.

Raw Values

Geographic Location

			Northeast D	Southeast E	Midwest F	West G	
	Finance	A	24	10	8	14	56
Industry Type	Manufacturing	B	30	6	22	12	70
	Communications	C	28	18	12	16	74
			82	34	42	42	200

Probability Matrix

Geographic Location

			Northeast D	Southeast E	Midwest F	West G	
	Finance	A	.12	.05	.04	.07	.28
Industry Type	Manufacturing	B	.15	.03	.11	.06	.35
	Communications	C	.14	.09	.06	.08	.37
			.41	.17	.21	.21	1.00

Solution:

a. From the cell of the probability matrix, $P(B \cap E) = 6/200 = .03$.
Solve by the formula $P(B \cap E) = P(B) \cdot P(E|B)$:

$$P(B) = \frac{70}{200} = .35.$$

The probability of E occurring given that B has occurred, $P(E|B)$, can be determined from the probability matrix. How many B's are there? The probability matrix shows .35 of B. As B is given, $P(E|B) = E/.35$. What are the E's in the B row? .03. Thus $P(E|B) = .03/.35$. Therefore

$$P(B \cap E) = P(B) \cdot P(E|B) = (.35)\left(\frac{.03}{.35}\right) = .03.$$

Although the formula works, the probability matrix makes finding the joint probability in the cell of the matrix faster than using the formula.

An alternative is to use $P(B \cap E) = P(E) \cdot P(B|E)$, but $P(E) = .17$. Then $P(B|E)$ means the probability of B if E is given. There are .17 E's in the probability matrix and .03 B's in these E's. Thus

$$P(B|E) = \frac{.03}{.17}, \text{ and } P(B \cap E) = P(E) \cdot P(B|E) = (.17)\left(\frac{.03}{.17}\right) = .03.$$

b. To obtain $P(G \cap A)$, find the intersecting cell of G and A in the probability matrix, .07, or use the formula:

$$P(G \cap A) = P(G) \cdot P(A|G) = (.21)\left(\frac{.07}{.21}\right) = .07,$$

or

$$P(G \cap A) = P(A) \cdot P(G|A) = (.28)\left(\frac{.07}{.28}\right) = .07.$$

c. The probability $P(B \cap C)$ means that one respondent would have to work both in the manufacturing industry *and* the communications industry. The survey used to gather data from the 200 executives, however, requested that each respondent specify only one industry type for his or her company. Thus B and C are mutually exclusive. None of the respondents is in both manufacturing *and* communications. Hence

$$P(B \cap C) = .0.$$

Demonstration Problem 4.10

If one card is drawn at random from a standard deck of 52 playing cards what is the probability that the card is a 9 *and* a club?

$$P(9 \cap \clubsuit) = ?$$

Solution:

Only one card is both a 9 and a club: the 9 of clubs. Fifty-two cards are available to draw from, so

$$P(9 \cap \clubsuit) = \frac{1}{52}.$$

Use of the formula gives $P(9 \cap \clubsuit) = P(9) \cdot P(\clubsuit|9)$. $P(9) = 4/52$, because there are four 9's in a deck of 52 cards. Then, $P(\clubsuit|9) = 1/4$, because there are four 9's (that there is a 9 is given) and of the four 9's, one is a club. Thus

$$P(9 \cap \clubsuit) = P(9) \cdot P(\clubsuit|9) = \frac{4}{52} \cdot \frac{1}{4} = \frac{1}{52}.$$

Use of the other version of the formula yields $P(9 \cap \clubsuit) = P(\clubsuit) \cdot P(9|\clubsuit)$. Here, $P(\clubsuit) = 13/52$, because there are 13 clubs in a deck of 52 cards. Then, $P(9|\clubsuit) = 1/13$, because of 13 clubs only one of them is a 9. Thus

$$P(9 \cap \clubsuit) = P(\clubsuit) \cdot P(9|\clubsuit) = \frac{13}{52} \cdot \frac{1}{13} = \frac{1}{52}.$$

Special Law of Multiplication

If events X and Y are independent, a special law of multiplication can be used to find the intersection of X and Y.

If X, Y are independent,

$$P(X \cap Y) = P(X) \cdot P(Y).$$

Special Law of Multiplication

Coin tosses and dice throws are experiments that naturally produce independent events. Other experiments produce independent events if the experiments are conducted *with replacement*.

Demonstration Problem 4.11

If two coins are tossed, what is the probability of getting a head on the first coin and a head on the second coin?

$$P(H_1 \cap H_2) = ?$$

Solution:

The two coins are independent, so

$$P(H_1 \cap H_2) = P(H_1) \cdot P(H_2) = \frac{1}{2} \cdot \frac{1}{2} = \frac{1}{4}.$$

**Demonstration
Problem 4.12**

A manufacturing firm produces pads of bound paper. Three percent of all paper pads produced are improperly bound. An inspector randomly samples two pads of paper, one at a time. Because a large number of pads are being produced during the inspection, the sampling being done, in essence, is *with* replacement. What is the probability that the two pads selected are both improperly bound?

Solution:

Let I denote improperly bound. The problem is to determine

$$P(I_1 \cap I_2) = ?$$

The probability of I = .03, or 3% are improperly bound. As the sampling is done *with* replacement, the two events are independent. Thus

$$P(I_1 \cap I_2) = P(I_1) \cdot P(I_2) = (.03)(.03) = .0009.$$

**Demonstration
Problem 4.13**

What is the probability of throwing a pair of dice and rolling two 6's (boxcars)? That is,

$$P(6_1 \cap 6_2) = ?$$

Solution:

Because the dice are independent,

$$P(6_1 \cap 6_2) = P(6_1) \cdot P(6_2) = \frac{1}{6} \cdot \frac{1}{6} = \frac{1}{36}.$$

Suppose that two cards are drawn, one at a time, *with replacement*, from a standard deck of playing cards. What is the probability of drawing a queen first and a 5 second? That is,

$$P(Q_1 \cap 5_2) = ?$$

Solution:

The cards are being drawn with replacement, so the events (the two draws of cards) are independent. Therefore

$$P(Q_1 \cap 5_2) = P(Q_1) \cdot P(5_2) = \frac{4}{52} \cdot \frac{4}{52} = \frac{16}{2704}.$$

Most probability matrices contain variables that are not independent. If a probability matrix contains independent events, the special law of multiplication can be applied. If not, the special law cannot be used. In Section 4.7 we explore a technique for determining whether events are independent. Table 4.5 contains data from independent events.

	D	E	
A	8	12	20
B	20	30	50
C	6	9	15
	34	51	85

TABLE 4.5

Contingency Table of Data from Independent Events

Use the data from Table 4.5 and the special law of multiplication to find $P(B \cap D)$.

Solution:

$$P(B \cap D) = P(B) \cdot P(D) = \frac{50}{85} \cdot \frac{34}{85} = .2353.$$

This approach works *only* for contingency tables and probability matrices in which the variable along one side of the matrix is *independent* of the variable along the other side of the matrix. Note that the answer obtained by using the formula is the same as the answer obtained by using the cell information from Table 4.5:

$$P(B \cap D) = \frac{20}{85} = .2353.$$

**PROBLEMS
Section 4.6**

4.18 **a.** A batch of fifty parts contains six defects. If two parts are randomly drawn, one at a time without replacement, what is the probability that both parts are defective? $\frac{6}{50} \times \frac{5}{50} = \frac{36}{250} .0149$

b. If this experiment is repeated, but *with* replacement, what is the probability that both parts are defective?

4.19 A child is playing with a pair of dice, one of which is green and the other white. If he rolls this pair of dice, what is the probability of his rolling a 5 on the green die and a 4 on the white die? What is the probability of his rolling a 3 on one die and a 1 on the other?

4.20 Three coins are tossed. What is the probability of getting heads on the first, heads on the second, and tails on the third?

4.21 A student shuffles a standard deck of playing cards and draws three cards, one at a time, without replacement. What is the probability that she will draw three aces in a row? What is the probability that she will draw a jack first, a queen second, and a king third? With replacement, does the probability of drawing three consecutive aces go up or down?

4.22 Use the values in the table to solve the equations given.

	C	D	E	F
A	5	11	16	8
B	2	3	5	7

a. $P(A \cap E) = $ __
b. $P(D \cap B) = $ __
c. $P(D \cap E) = $ __
d. $P(A \cap B) = $ __

4.23 Use the values in the table to solve the equations given.

	D	E	F
A	.12	.13	.08
B	.18	.09	.04
C	.06	.24	.06

a. $P(E \cap B) = $ __
b. $P(C \cap F) = $ __
c. $P(E \cap D) = $ __

4.24 According to the nonprofit group, Zero Population Growth, 78% of the U.S. population now lives in urban areas. Suppose that this figure holds for both adults and children. Scientists at Princeton University and the University of Wisconsin report that about 15% of all U.S. adults care for ill relatives. Suppose that 11% of adults living in urban areas care for ill relatives.

    a. Use the general law of multiplication to determine the probability of randomly selecting an adult from the U.S. population who lives in an urban area *and* is caring for an ill relative.

    b. Construct a probability matrix and show where the answer to this problem lies in the matrix.

4.25 Cans now account for 48% of all U.S. soft-drink containers. Suppose that 94% of all cans used as U.S. soft-drink containers are made of aluminum. If a U.S. soft-drink container is blindly selected:

    a. What is the probability that the container is not a can?

    b. What is the probability that the container is not aluminum (assume that only cans can be aluminum)?

    c. What is the probability that the container is an aluminum can?

    d. What is the probability that the container is a can and is not aluminum?

    e. What is the probability that the container is aluminum or not a can? (Assume again that only cans can be aluminum)

4.26 A recent study by Becker Associates, a San Diego travel consultant, found that 30% of the traveling public said that their flight selections are influenced by perceptions of airline safety. Thirty-nine percent want to know the age of the aircraft, and 22% think that the crew's flight experience should be available to the public. Suppose that 87% of the traveling public who say that their flight selections are influenced by perceptions of airline safety want to know the age of the aircraft, and 63% of the traveling public who say that their flight selections are influenced by perceptions of airline safety want to know the crew's flight experience record.

    a. What is the probability of randomly selecting a member of the traveling public and finding out that he or she says that flight selection is influenced by perceptions of airline safety *and* wants to know the crew's flight experience record?

    b. What is the probability of randomly selecting a member of the traveling public and finding out that he or she says that flight selection is influenced by perceptions of airline safety *and* does *not* want to know the age of the aircraft?

    c. A researcher randomly selects two members of the traveling public, one at a time. What is the probability that both want to know the age of the aircraft?

4.7 | LAW OF CONDITIONAL PROBABILITY

Conditional probabilities are based on knowledge of one of the variables. If X, Y are two events, the conditional probability of X occurring given that Y is known or has occurred is expressed as $P(X|Y)$.

Law of Conditional Probability

$$P(X|Y) = \frac{P(X \cap Y)}{P(Y)} = \frac{P(Y|X) \cdot P(X)}{P(Y)}.$$

The conditional probability of $(X|Y)$ is *not* the probability that X will occur. It *is* the probability that X will occur given Y. For example, suppose that an applicant's name has been randomly selected from the Omega Corporation pool of 100 pipefitter applicants. The name of the person is unknown, but the applicant is known to be a woman. Given that the applicant is a woman, what is the probability that she is Hispanic? This is the conditional probability, $P(H|W)$. The knowledge that the applicant is a woman now limits the pool list to the women applicants. Of the 35 women, how many are Hispanic? Nine of the 35 women are Hispanic. Thus the conditional probability, $P(H|W)$, is $9/35$. Note that the denominator of the answer is not the population total, 100, but a subtotal of the population, 35. The conditional probability is the only one of the four types of probability mentioned in Section 4.4 in which the denominator of the probability is not the population total but a subtotal.

The Omega Corporation problem also can be solved by formula. The data for the pipefitter job applicants are shown in Table 4.6.

$$P(H|W) = \frac{P(H \cap W)}{P(W)} = \frac{\dfrac{9}{100}}{\dfrac{35}{100}} = \frac{9}{35}.$$

TABLE 4.6

Raw Data Matrix for Pipefitter Problem

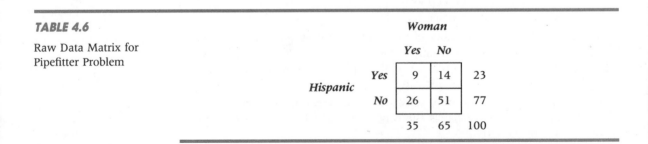

		Woman		
		Yes	No	
Hispanic	Yes	9	14	23
	No	26	51	77
		35	65	100

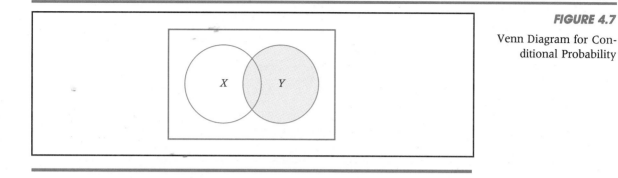

FIGURE 4.7

Venn Diagram for Conditional Probability

The second version of the conditional law formula is

$$P(X|Y) = \frac{P(Y|X) \cdot P(X)}{P(Y)}.$$

This version is more complex than the first version, $[P(X \cap Y)]/[P(Y)]$. However, sometimes the second version must be used because of the information given in the problem—for example, when solving for $P(X|Y)$ but $P(Y|X)$ is given. The second version of the formula is obtained from the first version by substituting the formula for $P(X \cap Y) = P(Y|X) \cdot P(X)$ into the first version. Using the second version of the formula to solve the Omega Corporation problem yields

$$P(H|W) = \frac{P(W|H) \cdot P(H)}{P(W)} = \frac{\left(\frac{9}{23}\right)\left(\frac{23}{100}\right)}{\frac{35}{100}} = \frac{\frac{9}{100}}{\frac{35}{100}} = \frac{9}{35}.$$

The Venn diagram in Figure 4.7 shows a conditional probability, $P(X|Y)$. As the diagram shows, because Y is given, the only concern is measuring the amount of X contained in Y.

Table 4.7 contains the probability matrix for the Omega Corporation problem. These values are not conditional probabilities. The cell values are joint probabilities; and the values in the margins are marginal probabilities. To obtain a conditional probability in a probability matrix requires manipulating the values in the tables. For example, to solve for $P(H|W)$, the total probability of being a woman (the given part) is located first. In the matrix in Table 4.8, that value is the column 1 marginal total, .35. The focus here is on column 1 in the matrix, because the applicant is known to be a woman, and thus all other columns are irrelevant.

TABLE 4.7

Probability Matrix for
the Omega Corporation
Pipefitter Problem

		Woman		
		Yes	*No*	
Hispanic	*Yes*	.09	.14	.23
	No	.26	.51	.77
		.35	.65	1.00

TABLE 4.8

Portion of Omega
Corporation Pipefitter
Applicants Who Are
Women

		Woman	
		Yes	*No*
Hispanic	*Yes*	.09	—
	No	.26	—
		.35	

In this column, how many are Hispanic? The answer is .09. So the probability of getting a Hispanic given that the applicant is a woman is .09 out of .35. This result is consistent with that from the formula, which yields

$$P(\text{H}|\text{W}) = \frac{P(\text{H} \cap \text{W})}{P(\text{W})} = \frac{.09}{.35} = \frac{9}{35}.$$

**Demonstration
Problem 4.16**

Again, use the data from the executive interviews to find $P(\text{B}|\text{F})$, $P(\text{G}|\text{C})$, and $P(\text{D}|\text{F})$.

Raw Values

			Geographic Location				
			Northeast D	*Southeast* E	*Midwest* F	*West* G	
	Finance	A	24	10	8	14	56
Industry Type	*Manufacturing*	B	30	6	22	12	70
	Communications	C	28	18	12	16	74
			82	34	42	42	200

Probability Matrix

Geographic Location

		Northeast D	Southeast E	Midwest F	West G	
Finance	A	.12	.05	.04	.07	.28
Manufacturing	B	.15	.03	.11	.06	.35
Communications	C	.14	.09	.06	.08	.37
		.41	.17	.21	.21	1.00

Industry Type labels the rows Finance/Manufacturing/Communications.

Solution:

$$P(B|F) = \frac{P(B \cap F)}{P(F)} = \frac{.11}{.21} = .524.$$

Determining conditional probabilities from a probability matrix by using the formula is a relatively painless process. In this case, the joint probability, $P(B \cap F)$, appears in a cell of the matrix (.11); the marginal probability, $P(F)$, appears in a margin (.21). Bringing these two probabilities together by formula produces the answer, $.11/.21 = .524$. This answer means that 52.4% of the F values (the Midwest executives) are B (in manufacturing).

Solution:

$$P(G|C) = \frac{P(G \cap C)}{P(C)} = \frac{.08}{.37} = .216.$$

This result means that 21.6% of the responding communications industry executives (C) were from the West (G).

Solution:

$$P(D|F) = \frac{P(D \cap F)}{P(F)} = \frac{.00}{.21} = .00.$$

Because D and F are mutually exclusive, $P(D \cap F)$ is zero and so is $P(D|F)$. The rationale behind $P(D|F) = .00$ is that, if F is given (the respondent is known to be located in the Midwest), he or she could not be located in D (the Northeast).

Demonstration Problem 4.17

If a single card is randomly drawn from a standard deck of playing cards,

$$P(J \mid \Diamond) = ?$$

Solution:

$$P(J \mid \Diamond)$$

The card has been drawn, and it is a diamond. What is the probability that the card is a jack given that it is a diamond?

$$P(J \mid \Diamond) = \frac{P(J \cap \Diamond)}{P(\Diamond)}.$$

There are thirteen diamonds. Thus $P(\Diamond) = 13/52$, and

$$P(J \mid \Diamond) = \frac{P(J \cap \Diamond)}{\dfrac{13}{52}}.$$

But $(J \cap \Diamond)$ is the jack of diamonds, and there is only one, so

$$P(J \cap \Diamond) = \frac{1}{52}.$$

Using these values gives

$$P(J \mid \Diamond) = \frac{\dfrac{1}{52}}{\dfrac{13}{52}} = \frac{1}{13}.$$

Demonstration Problem 4.18

Suppose that two cards are drawn, one at a time without replacement, from a standard deck of playing cards.

$$P(J_2 \mid A_1) = ?$$
$$P(\Diamond_2 \mid \Diamond_1) = ?$$

Solution:

The expression $P(J_2 \mid A_1)$ is the probability of the second card being a jack if the first card drawn was an ace. If the first card drawn was an ace and was not replaced, only 51 cards are left, including the 4 Jacks. Thus

$$P(J_2|A_1) = \frac{4}{51}.$$

Solution:

$P(\diamondsuit_2|\diamondsuit_1)$. What is the probability of drawing a diamond on the second draw if the first card drawn was a diamond. After the first draw, only 51 cards are left, and only 12 diamonds are left. Thus

$$P(\diamondsuit_2|\diamondsuit_1) = \frac{12}{51}.$$

Independent Events

If X and Y are independent events,

$$P(X|Y) = P(X), \quad \text{and} \quad P(Y|X) = P(Y).$$

It does not matter that X or Y is given in either case, because X and Y are independent. In these cases, the conditional probability is solved as a marginal probability.

Sometimes, testing a contingency table of raw data is important in order to determine whether events are independent. If *any* combination of two events from the different sides of the matrix fail the test, $P(X|Y) = P(X)$, the matrix does *not* contain independent events.

Demonstration Problem 4.19

Test the matrix for the 200 executive responses to determine whether industry type is independent of geographic location.

Raw Values

			Northeast D	Southeast E	Midwest F	West G	
	Finance	A	24	10	8	14	56
Industry Type	Manufacturing	B	30	6	22	12	70
	Communications	C	28	18	12	16	74
			82	34	42	42	200

Geographic Location

Probability Matrix

Geographic Location

		Northeast D	Southeast E	Midwest F	West G	
Finance	A	.12	.05	.04	.07	.28
Manufacturing	B	.15	.03	.11	.06	.35
Communications	C	.14	.09	.06	.08	.37
		.41	.17	.21	.21	1.00

Industry Type (row label at left)

Solution:

Select one industry and one geographic location (say, A—Finance and G—West). Does $P(A|G) = P(A)$?

$$P(A|G) = \frac{14}{42}, \quad \text{and} \quad P(A) = \frac{56}{200}.$$

Does $14/42 = 56/200$? No: .33 ≠ .28. Industry and geographic location are not independent, because there is at least one exception to the test.

Demonstration Problem 4.20

Determine whether Table 4.5 contains independent events.

	D	E	
A	8	12	20
B	20	30	50
C	6	9	15
	34	51	85

Solution:

Check the first cell in the matrix to find whether $P(A|D) = P(A)$.

$$P(A|D) = \frac{8}{34} = .2353;$$

$$P(A) = \frac{20}{85} = .2353.$$

The checking process must continue until all the events are determined to be independent. In this matrix, all the possibilities check out.

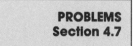

4.27 Use the values in the table to solve the equations given.

	E	F	G
A	15	12	8
B	11	17	19
C	21	32	27
D	18	13	12

a. $P(G|A) = $ ___
b. $P(B|F) = $ ___
c. $P(C|E) = $ ___
d. $P(E|G) = $ ___

4.28 Use the values in the table to solve the equations given.

	C	D
A	.36	.44
B	.11	.09

a. $P(C|A) = $ ___
b. $P(B|D) = $ ___
c. $P(A|B) = $ ___

4.29 A player has just drawn a queen from a standard deck of playing cards. What is the probability that she will now draw a second queen if she does not replace the first card? What is the probability that she will draw a second queen if she *does* replace the first card and reshuffles the deck.

4.30 If a Monopoly player rolls a pair of dice, what is the probability of rolling a 5 on one die if the other die yields a 3?

4.31 A lake contains 1,000 fish, of which 300 are undersize. Suppose that a fisherman is equally likely to catch any of the 1,000 fish. If he has just caught an undersized fish and decides to keep it, what is the probability that the next fish caught will be undersize? What is the probability that the fisherman's first catch would be an undersized fish *and* that his second catch also would be an undersized fish if he did not throw the first fish back.

4.32 The results of a survey asking, "Do you have a calculator and/or a computer in your home?" are as follows:

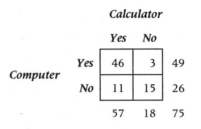

Calculator

		Yes	No	
	Yes	46	3	49
Computer	No	11	15	26
		57	18	75

Is the variable *calculator* independent of the variable *computer?* Why or why not?

4.33 In 1988, of the approximately 13,500 banks in the United States, 200 failed. Suppose that 20% of all the banks were classified as large banks, 35% were classified as medium-sized banks, and 45% were considered small banks. Suppose also that 125 of the bank failures were small banks. A bank is randomly selected from the 1988 U.S. roster.

a. What is the probability that the bank failed?

b. If the bank failed, what is the probability that it is a small bank?

c. If the bank is either medium-sized or large, what is the probability that the bank did not fail?

4.34 According to a *Reader's Digest* survey conducted by Gallup International, only 30% of the Swiss live in houses, compared to 55% of Europeans in general. Some 15.1% of the Swiss live in houses that have three or more bedrooms, whereas some 27% of the Europeans in general live in houses that have three or more bedrooms.

a. If a Swiss is randomly selected, what is the probability that he or she does not live in a house?

b. If a Swiss is randomly selected, what is the probability that he or she lives in a house with three or more bedrooms if the sampler knows that he or she lives in a house?

c. If a European is randomly selected, what is the probability that he or she lives in a house with less than three bedrooms if the sampler knows that he or she lives in a house?

4.35 People in relatively new countries move around more than people in older, more settled countries, and young people tend to move more than older people. New Zealanders seem to move the most: 19% of New Zealanders move annually. The United States follows New Zealand with an 18% mobility rate. People in their twenties are more likely to move than any other group. Suppose that 14% of all Americans are in their twenties and that 16% of all New Zealanders are in their twenties. Suppose further that 3% of all Americans are in their twenties and have moved during the last year and that 5% of all New Zealanders are in their twenties and have moved during the last year.

   a. What is the probability that a randomly selected American has moved during the last year if he is in his twenties?

   b. What is the probability that a randomly selected American is in her twenties if she did not move last year?

   c. What is the probability that a randomly selected New Zealander is in his twenties if he moved last year?

REVISION OF PROBABILITIES: BAYES' RULE   *4.8*

An extension to the conditional law of probabilities is Bayes' rule, which was developed by and named for Thomas Bayes (1702–1761). **Bayes' rule** is a formula that extends the use of the law of conditional probabilities to allow revision of original probabilities with new information.

Bayes' rule

$$P(X_i|Y) = \frac{P(Y|X_i) \cdot P(X_i)}{P(Y|X_1) \cdot P(X_1) + P(Y|X_2) \cdot P(X_2) + \cdots + P(Y|X_n) \cdot P(X_n)}.$$

General Bayes' Rule

$$P(X_i|Y) = \frac{P(Y|X_i) \cdot P(X_i)}{P(Y|X_1) \cdot P(X_1) + P(Y|X_2) \cdot P(X_2)}.$$

Bayes' Rule for Two Events

    A particular type of printer ribbon is produced only by two companies: Alamo Ribbon Company and South Jersey Products. Suppose that Alamo produces 65% of the ribbons and that South Jersey produces 35%. Eight percent of the ribbons produced by Alamo are defective and 12% of the South Jersey ribbons are defective. A customer purchases a new ribbon. What is the probability that Alamo produced the ribbon? What is the probability that South Jersey produced the ribbon? The ribbon is tested, and it is defective. Now what is the probability that Alamo produced the ribbon? That South Jersey produced the ribbon?

    The probability was .65 that the ribbon came from Alamo and .35 that it came from South Jersey. These are called *prior* probabilities, because they are based on the original information.

    The new information that the ribbon is defective changes the probabilities, because one company produces a higher percentage of defective ribbons than the other company does. How can this information be utilized to update or revise the original probabilities? Bayes' Rule allows such updating. One way to lay out a revision of probabilities problem is to use a table. Table 4.9 shows the analysis for the ribbon problem.

The process begins with the prior probabilities: .65 Alamo and .35 South Jersey. Because the product is found to be defective, the conditional probabilities, $P(\text{defective}|\text{Alamo})$ and $P(\text{defective}|\text{South Jersey})$ should be used. Eight percent of Alamo's ribbons are defective: $P(\text{defective}|\text{Alamo}) = .08$. Twelve percent of South Jersey's ribbons are defective: $P(\text{defective}|\text{South Jersey}) = .12$. Eight percent of Alamo's 65% of the ribbons are defective: $(.08)(.65) = .052$, or 5.2% of the total. This figure appears in column 4 of Table 4.9; it is the joint probability of getting a ribbon that was made by Alamo *and* is defective. Because the purchased ribbon is defective, these are the only Alamo ribbons of interest. Twelve percent of South Jersey's 35% of the ribbons are defective. Multiplying these two percentages yields the joint probability of getting a South Jersey ribbon that is defective. This answer also appears in column 4 of Table 4.9: $(.12)(.35) = .042$. That is, 4.2% of all ribbons are made at South Jersey *and* are defective. These are the only South Jersey ribbons of interest because the ribbon purchased is defective.

Column 4 is totaled to get .094 or 9.4% of all ribbons are defective (Alamo *and* defective = .052 + South Jersey *and* defective = .042). The other 90.6% of the ribbons, which are acceptable, are not of interest because the ribbon purchased is defective. To compute column 5, the posterior or revised probabilities, involves dividing each value in column 4 by the total of column 4. That is, for the Alamo company, .052 of the total ribbons are Alamo *and* defective out of the total of .094 that are defective. Dividing .052 by .094 yields .553 as a revised probability that the ribbon was made by Alamo. This probability is lower than the prior or original probability of .65, because fewer of Alamo's ribbons (as a percentage) are defective than those produced by South Jersey. The defective ribbon is now less likely to have come from Alamo than before the knowledge of the defective ribbon. South Jersey's probability is revised by dividing the .042 joint probability of the ribbon being made by South Jersey *and* defective by the total probability of the ribbon being defective (.094).

	Event	*Prior Probability* $P(E_i)$	*Conditional Probability* $P(d\|E_i)$	*Joint Probability* $P(E_i \cap d)$	*Posterior or Revised Probability*
TABLE 4.9 Bayesian Table for Revision of Ribbon Problem Probabilities	Alamo	.65	.08	.052	$\dfrac{.052}{.094} = .553$
	South Jersey	.35	.12	.042	$\dfrac{.042}{.094} = .447$
				$P(\text{defective}) = .094$	

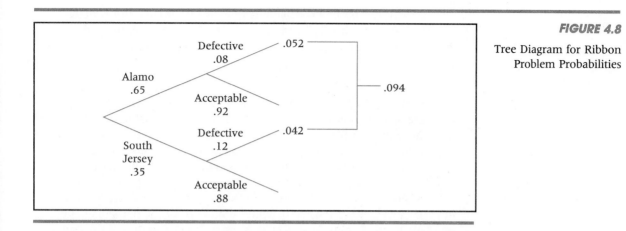

FIGURE 4.8

Tree Diagram for Ribbon
Problem Probabilities

The result is .042/.094 = .447. The probability that the defective ribbon is from South Jersey has increased, because a higher percentage of South Jersey ribbons are defective.

Tree diagrams are another common way to solve Bayes' rule problems. Figure 4.8 shows the solution for the ribbon problem. Note that the tree diagram contains all possibilities, including both defective and acceptable ribbons. When new information is given, only the pertinent branches are selected and used. The joint probability values at the end of the appropriate branches are used to revise and compute the posterior possibilities. The total number of defective ribbons = .052 + .042 = .094.

Revised probabilities: Alamo $= \dfrac{.052}{.094} = .553$

$$\text{South Jersey} = \dfrac{.042}{.094} = .447.$$

**Demonstration
Problem 4.21**

Machines A, B, and C all produce the same two parts, X and Y. Of all the parts produced, machine A produces 60%, machine B produces 30%, and machine C produces 10%.

40% of the parts made by machine A are part X.

50% of the parts made by machine B are part X.

70% of the parts made by machine C are part X.

A part produced by this company is randomly sampled and is determined to be an X part. With the knowledge that it is an X part, revise the probabilities that the part came from machine A, B, or C.

Solution:

The prior probability of the part coming from machine A is .60, because machine A produces 60% of all parts. The prior probability that the part came from B is .30 and that it came from C is .10. These prior probabilities are more pertinent if nothing is known about the part. However, the part is known to be an X part. The conditional probabilities show that different machines produce different proportions of X parts. For example, .40 of the parts made by machine A are X parts, but .50 of the parts made by machine B and .70 of the parts made by machine C are X parts. It makes sense that the probability of the part coming from machine C would increase and that the probability that the part was made on machine A would decrease because the part is an X part.

The following table shows how the prior probabilities, conditional probabilities, joint probabilities, and marginal probability, $P(X)$, can be used to revise the prior probabilities to obtain posterior probabilities.

Event	Prior $P(E_i)$	Conditional $P(X|E_i)$	Joint $P(X \cap E_i)$	Posterior
A	.60	.40	$(.60)(.40) = .24$	$\dfrac{.24}{.46} = .52$
B	.30	.50	.15	$\dfrac{.15}{.46} = .33$
C	.10	.70	.07	$\dfrac{.07}{.46} = .15$
			$P(X) = .46$	

After the probabilities have been revised it is apparent that the probability of the part being made at machine A has decreased and that the probabilities that the part was made at machines B and C have increased. A tree diagram presents another view of this problem.

Revised probabilities: Machine A $\dfrac{.24}{.46} = .52.$

Machine B $\dfrac{.15}{.46} = .33.$

Machine C $\dfrac{.07}{.46} = .15.$

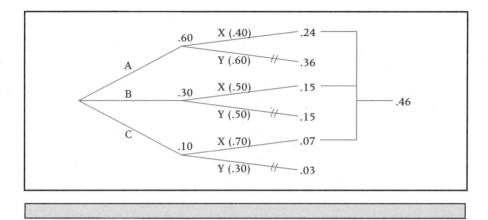

4.36 In a manufacturing plant, machine A produces 10% of a certain product, machine B produces 40% of this product, and machine C produces 50% of this product. Five percent of the products produced by machine A are defective, 12% of machine B products are defective, and 8% of machine C products are defective. The company inspector has just sampled a product from this plant and has found it to be defective. Based on this new information, revise the probabilities that the product was produced by machine A, machine B, or machine C.

4.37 Alex, Alicia, and Juan fill orders in a fast food restaurant. Alex fills incorrectly 20% of the orders he takes. Alicia fills incorrectly 12% of the orders she takes. Juan fills incorrectly 5% of the orders he takes. Alex fills 30% of all orders, Alicia fills 45% of all orders, and Juan fills 25% of all orders. An order has just been filled.

a. What is the probability that Alicia filled the order?

b. If the order was filled by Juan, what is the probability that it was filled correctly?

c. Who filled the order is unknown, but the order was filled incorrectly. What are the revised probabilities that Alex, Alicia, or Juan filled the order?

d. Who filled the order is unknown, but the order was filled correctly. What are the revised probabilities that Alex, Alicia, or Juan filled the order?

4.38 In a small town, two lawn companies fertilize lawns during the summer. Tri-State lawn service has 72% of the market. Thirty percent of the lawns fertilized by Tri-State could be rated as very healthy one month after service. Greenchem has the other 28% of the market. Twenty percent of the lawns fertilized by Greenchem could be rated as very healthy after one month of service. A lawn that has been treated with fertilizer by one of these companies within the last month is randomly selected. If the lawn is rated as very healthy, what are the revised probabilities that Tri-State or Greenchem treated the lawn?

4.39 A major league baseball team has four starting pitchers: Gomez, Jackson, Smith and Alvarez. Each pitcher starts every fourth game. The team wins 60% of all games that Gomez starts, 45% of the games that Jackson starts, 35% of the games that Smith starts, and 40% of the games that Alvarez starts. An avid fan has just returned from a three-week vacation in the wilderness and finds out that the team played yesterday.

a. What is the probability that Gomez started the game?

b. What is the probability that Jackson started the game?

c. If the team won yesterday, revise the probability of each pitcher starting the game.

4.9   USING THE MULTIPLICATIVE LAW WITH MULTIPLE TRIALS

The multiplicative law of probability is used to solve for joint probabilities or intersections. Whenever two or more trials involving joint probabilities are being analyzed, the process often becomes complicated by multiple sequences of occurrence. If a particular order of occurrence is *specified*, multiple sequence is not a problem, because the outcome can occur in only one way. For example, suppose that 11% of all television viewers watch NBC's nightly news. The probability of interviewing three television viewers at random and finding that the first one watches NBC's nightly news, the second one does not watch NBC's nightly news, and the third one watches NBC's nightly news is

$$P(NBC_1 \cap \text{not } NBC_2 \cap NBC_3).$$

However, *not* specifying a particular sequence complicates the problem. For example, suppose that three viewers are randomly selected. What is the probability that two of the viewers watch NBC's nightly news? The procedure is more complicated because which two of the three viewers who watch NBC's nightly news were not specified. In fact, the sequence can occur in three different ways:

Sequence 1	(NBC_1)	(NBC_2)	$(\text{not } NBC_3)$
Sequence 2	(NBC_1)	$(\text{not } NBC_2)$	(NBC_3)
Sequence 3	$(\text{not } NBC_1)$	(NBC_2)	(NBC_3)

Unless a particular order of occurrence is specified, the procedure that uses the multiplicative law to solve for probabilities when there is more than one trial must provide for order of occurrence. There are two categories of these problems: (1) problems with replacement and (2) problems without replacement.

Problems with Replacement

In probability problems when the events are independent the probability of a particular outcome does not depend on the outcome of the other events. The special law of multiplication is used to determine the specific probability, and then that probability is weighted by the number of ways the outcomes can occur.

For example, an experiment is conducted in which three coins are tossed. What is the probability of tossing three coins and getting one head? This outcome could occur by getting heads on the first coin, tails on the second coin, and tails on the third coin. This joint probability is

$$P(H_1 \cap T_2 \cap T_3) \quad \text{or} \quad P(H_1) \cdot P(T_2) \cdot P(T_3) = \left(\frac{1}{2}\right)\left(\frac{1}{2}\right)\left(\frac{1}{2}\right) = \frac{1}{8}.$$

However, ⅛ is only the probability of getting a head on the first coin, a tail on the second coin, and a tail on the third coin. The coin tosser could have gotten the head on the second coin $(T_1 \cap H_2 \cap T_3)$ or on the third coin $(T_1 \cap T_2 \cap H_3)$. The probability of each of these events occurring is ⅛. Thus there are three ways to get one head in a toss of three coins. For each sequence, the probability is ⅛. The total probability of getting one head in three coin tosses is 3(⅛) = ⅜. Each possibility and its associated probability have been enumerated:

$$P(H_1 \cap T_2 \cap T_3) = \frac{1}{2} \cdot \frac{1}{2} \cdot \frac{1}{2} = \frac{1}{8};$$

$$P(T_1 \cap H_2 \cap T_3) = \frac{1}{2} \cdot \frac{1}{2} \cdot \frac{1}{2} = \frac{1}{8};$$

$$P(T_1 \cap T_2 \cap H_3) = \frac{1}{2} \cdot \frac{1}{2} \cdot \frac{1}{2} = \frac{1}{8}.$$

The three ⅛ values have summed, because one head can be obtained the first way *or* the second way *or* the third way. In reality, because there are multiple ways of getting the desired outcome, the addition law and the special multiplication law are being used. The addition law is for the multiple sequences, and the special law of multiplication is used to determine the probability of a particular sequence occurring.

Instead of enumerating each possible way to get one head in three coin tosses, **combinations** can be used to determine how many ways the outcome can happen. The combination of n things taken r at a time is expressed as $_nC_r$.

combinations

$$_nC_r = \frac{n!}{r!(n-r)!},$$

Combination Formula

where: $0 \leq r \leq n$.

For the three coin toss problem, $_3C_1 = (3!)/(1!2!) = 3$ indicates without listing all the possibilities that the desired outcome could have occurred in three different ways (sequences). If three coins are being tossed and the outcome is to get *two* heads, the combination of three things taken two at a time, $_3C_2 = 3$, yields the number of ways (sequences) in which that can occur.

**Demonstration
Problem 4.22**

Suppose that 3% of all VCRs made by a particular company in 1991 are defective. If five of these VCRs are randomly selected from across the country and tested, what is the probability that two of them are defective? Assume that each VCR is made independently of the others.

Solution:

Let D be a defective VCR and G be a good VCR. One way to get two defectives would be

$$D_1 \cap D_2 \cap G_3 \cap G_4 \cap G_5.$$

Because the VCRs are made independently, the probability of getting the first two defective and the last three good is

$$(.03)\,(.03)\,(.97)\,(.97)\,(.97) = .00082,$$

which is *not* the answer to the problem. It *is* the probability of getting two defects in *that* order or sequence. Regardless of the order in which two defects and three good VCRs occur, two (.03) probabilities and three (.97) probabilities will be multiplied. The question becomes: How many different ways can two defects be obtained from a total of five VCRs? There are ten ways to get two defects:

D_1	D_2	G_3	G_4	G_5	
D_1	G_2	D_3	G_4	G_5	
D_1	G_2	G_3	D_4	G_5	
D_1	G_2	G_3	G_4	D_5	
G_1	D_2	D_3	G_4	G_5	
G_1	D_2^r	G_3	D_4	G_5	10 ways
G_1	D_2	G_3	G_4	D_5	
G_1	G_2	D_3	D_4	G_5	
G_1	G_2	D_3	G_4	D_5	
G_1	G_2	G_3	D_4	D_5	

Using combinations to enumerate all possibilities yields

$$_5C_2 = \frac{5!}{2!3!} = 10 \text{ ways.}$$

Multiplying the ten ways by the probability of getting one of these ways gives (10) (.00082) = .0082, which is the answer for drawing five VCRs and getting two defectives (in any order).

Problems Without Replacement

When events are not independent, the general multiplicative law is used to determine joint probabilities. If the number of trials is greater than one, sequence must be taken into consideration in the determination of the probability.

For example, an experimenter is going to draw three cards without replacement from a standard deck of playing cards. What is the probability that one card will be a king? There are three ways to get one king in a draw of three cards:

$$K_1 \cap N_2 \cap N_3$$
$$N_1 \cap K_2 \cap N_3$$
$$N_1 \cap N_2 \cap K_3$$

where K is a king and N is not a king.

In the first sequence, the probability of drawing these three cards in that order is

$$\frac{4}{52} \cdot \frac{48}{51} \cdot \frac{47}{50} = .06805.$$

Note the impact that each card has on the next card's probability, because the cards are being drawn without replacement. The second and third sequences of drawing one king in three cards produce the following probabilities, respectively:

$$\frac{48}{52} \cdot \frac{4}{51} \cdot \frac{47}{50} = .06805, \quad \text{and} \quad \frac{48}{52} \cdot \frac{47}{51} \cdot \frac{4}{50} = .06805.$$

In each of these three sequences the order is different and the cards are being selected without replacement, so the individual probabilities are different. However, the final outcome of each sequence shows that the probability for each sequence of three cards is the same. In such problems—while producing different individual fractional probabilities—each sequence will produce the same overall probability, because ultimately each sequence contains the same values in the numerator and the same values in the denominator. Thus computing the probability of only one of the sequences and weighing the answer by the number of ways the sequences can occur is necessary. In this problem, each sequence yields .06805 as a probability. Because there are three ways of getting one king in a draw of three cards, the total probability of getting one king is $3(.06805) = .20415$.

Fifty identical TV sets are stored in a warehouse. Five of the TV sets are defective, but the five defective sets are unlabeled. If the stock clerk randomly selects four TV sets from the stock without replacement, what is the probability that two of the sets selected are defective?

Solution:

Enumerated are the possible ways that four sets can be drawn with two defective sets. Let D denote a defective set and G denote a good set.

$$D_1 \cap D_2 \cap G_3 \cap G_4$$
$$D_1 \cap G_2 \cap D_3 \cap G_4$$
$$D_1 \cap G_2 \cap G_3 \cap D_4$$
$$G_1 \cap D_2 \cap D_3 \cap G_4$$
$$G_1 \cap D_2 \cap G_3 \cap D_4$$
$$G_1 \cap G_2 \cap D_3 \cap D_4$$

$$P(D_1 \cap D_2 \cap G_3 \cap G_4) = \frac{5}{50} \cdot \frac{4}{49} \cdot \frac{45}{48} \cdot \frac{44}{47} = .007165.$$

Solving for any of the other five sequences yields the same answer. Weighting the first sequence probability (.007165) by the six sequences yields the final answer:

$$(.007165)(6) = .04299.$$

Combinations could have been used to enumerate the possibilities: $_4C_2 = 6$.

Chapter 5 contains more formalized procedures for working the problems in Section 4.9.

4.40 If you roll a die six times in a row, what is the probability that you will get four 3's? What is the probability that you will get one or more 3's?

4.41 According to the U.S. Bureau of Labor Statistics, union membership in the United States represents approximately 17% of the total labor force. If five people are randomly selected from the U.S. labor force, what is the probability that two of the five are members of a union?

4.42 A poker player has just been dealt a five-card hand from a standard deck of cards. What is the probability that she has been dealt three aces?

4.43 The college bookstore has thirty copies of a statistics computer package for sale. The manager suspects that six of them are defective. If so and if a student purchases four of these packages:

a. What is the probability that one of the packages is defective?

b. What is the probability that two or more of the packages are defective?

4.44 At the DuPont Company, a recent survey revealed that 55% of the company's male employees favor flexible work options. A personnel analyst randomly selects eight male employees for interviews. None is interviewed more than once.

a. What is the probability that five of the eight favor flexible work options?

b. What is the probability that none of the eight favors flexible work options?

c. What is the probability that six or more favor flexible work options?

4.45 In forty-four states, bar associations offer counseling and hot lines to lawyers struggling to overcome depression, alcoholism, or drug abuse. A study in Washington state revealed that 18% of the lawyers in that state have an alcohol problem. If seven lawyers in Washington state are randomly selected, assuming that no lawyer can be selected twice:

a. What is the probability of selecting seven lawyers with alcohol problems?

b. What is the probability of selecting no lawyers with alcohol problems?

c. What is the probability of selecting two lawyers with alcohol problems? and

d. What is the probability of selecting fewer than two lawyers with alcohol problems?

e. How many lawyers with alcohol problems would you expect to get in a random sample of seven lawyers if the statewide percentage holds?

4.46 According to Cargo Facts, 10% of all overnight shipments in Europe are handled by Federal Express. A random sample of eleven cargo items is selected one at a time *with replacement* from across Europe.

a. What is the probability that four of the items were shipped by Federal Express?

b. What is the probability that more than two items were shipped by Federal Express?

c. How many items of the eleven could be expected to have been shipped by Federal Express?

CHAPTER SUMMARY

The study of probability addresses ways of assigning probabilities, types of probabilities, and laws of probabilities. Probabilities undergird the notion of inferential statistics. Using sample data to estimate and test hypotheses about population parameters is done with uncertainty. If samples are taken at random, probabilities can be assigned to outcomes of the inferential process.

Three ways of assigning probabilities are: (1) classical method; (2) relative frequency of occurrence; and (3) subjective probabilities. The classical method can assign probabilities a priori, or before the experiment takes place. It relies on the laws and rules of probability. The relative frequency of occurrence method assigns probabilities based on historical data or empirically derived data. Subjective probabilities are based on the feelings, knowledge, and experience of the person determining the probability.

Certain special types of events effect amendments to some of the laws of probability: mutually exclusive events and independent events. Mutually exclusive events are events that cannot occur at the same time, so the probability of their intersection is zero. In determining the union of two mutually exclusive events, the addition law is amended by the deletion of the intersection. Independent events are events in which the occurrence of one event has no impact or influence on the occurrence of the other. Certain experiments, such as those involving coins or dice, naturally produce independent events. Other experiments produce independent events when the experiment is conducted *with* replacement. If events are independent, the joint probability is computed by multiplying the individual probabilities, which is a special case of the law of multiplication.

Four types of probability are marginal probability, joint probability, conditional probability, and union probability. The general law of addition is used to compute the probability of a union. The general law of multiplication is used to compute joint probabilities. The conditional law is used to compute conditional probabilities.

Bayes' rule is a method that can be used to revise probabilities when new information becomes available; it is a variation of the conditional law. Bayes' rule takes prior probabilities of events occurring and adjusts or revises those probabilities based on information about what subsequently occurs.

When the multiplicative law is used with multiple trials, the process of determining the total probability answer for a problem gets more complicated, because the number of sequences of occurrence become part of the problem. However, the probability of one sequence can be computed, and the total probability of the problem can be determined by weighting the probability of the one sequence by the number of sequences. The number of sequences can be determined by using combinations.

Key Words

Classical probability

Experiment

Event

A priori

Relative frequency of occurrence

Subjective probability

Elementary events

Sample space

Set notation

Union

Intersection

Mutually exclusive events

Independent events

Collectively exhaustive events

Complement of an event

Marginal probability

Union probability

Joint probability

Conditional probability

Bayes' rule

Combinations

SUPPLEMENTARY PROBLEMS

4.47 Use the values in the table to solve the equations given.

Variable 1

		D	E
	A	10	20
Variable 2	B	15	5
	C	30	15

a. $P(E) =$ ___

b. $P(B \cup D) =$ ___

c. $P(A \cap E) =$ ___

d. $P(B|E) =$ ___

e. $P(A \cup B) =$ ___

f. $P(B \cap C) =$ ___

g. $P(D|C) =$ ___

h. $P(A|B) =$ ___

i. Are variables 1 and 2 independent? Why?

4.48 Use the values in the table to solve the equations given.

	D	E	F	G	
A	3	9	7	12	3١
B	8	4	6	4	22 ٫28
C	10	5	3	7	25
	2١	١8	١6	2³	7·8

a. $P(F \cap A) =$ ___

b. $P(A|B) =$ ___

c. $P(B) =$ ___

d. $P(E \cap F) =$ ___

e. $P(D|B) =$ ___

f. $P(B|D) =$ ___

g. $P(E \cup F \cup G) =$ ___

h. $P(D \cup C) =$ ___

i. $P(F) =$ ___

4.49 The following table presents income and age characteristics of some stock shareholders in the United States in 1985, as published in the *World Almanac:*

		Income				
		<15K	*15–25K*	*25–50K*	*>50K*	
	<21	1,446	655	140	19	2,260
	21–34	226	5,295	3,733	1,839	11,093
Age (years)	*35–44*	207	1,550	5,711	3,514	10,982
	45–54	1,026	1,975	2,370	2,528	7,899
	≥55	740	3,702	5,922	4,442	14,806
		3,645	13,177	17,876	12,342	47,040

   a. Create a probability matrix.

   b. What is the probability that a randomly selected stock owner is 21–34 years old?

   c. What is the probability that a randomly selected stock owner is <21 years old and has an income of 15–25K?

   d. What is the probability that a randomly selected stock owner is <21 years old or has an income of 25–50K?

   e. What is the probability that a randomly selected stock owner has an income >50K if he or she is known to be 35–44 years old?

   f. What is the probability of randomly selecting a person who is 35–44 years old and who is 45–54 years old. Are the age categories mutually exclusive or independent?

   g. Are the age and income categories independent? Use the formulas to show why or why not.

4.50 Two elevators are located side by side in a three-story building. A person goes into the building and pushes the button to call an elevator. Each elevator is independent and is equally likely to be on a given floor.

   a. What is the probability that both elevators will already be on the first floor?

   b. What is the probability that at least one elevator will be on the first floor?

   c. What is the probability that neither elevator will be on the first floor?

   d. If one elevator is on the first floor, what is the probability that the other elevator also is on the first floor?

4.51 The following table contains a breakdown on the age and gender of U.S. physicians in 1988, as reported by the American Medical Association:

U.S. Physicians in 1988

		Age (years)					
		<35	*35–44*	*45–54*	*55–64*	*>65*	
Gender	*Man*	.18	.25	.17	.13	.12	.85
	Woman	.07	.05	.02	.01	.00	.15
		.25	.30	.19	.14	.12	1.00

a. What is the probability that one randomly selected physician is 35–44 years old?

b. What is the probability that one randomly selected physician is both a woman and 45–54 years old?

c. What is the probability that one randomly selected physician is a man or is 35–44 years old?

d. What is the probability that one randomly selected physician is less than 35 years old or 55–64 years old?

e. What is the probability that one randomly selected physician is a woman if she is 45–54 years old?

4.52 Suppose that three dice are rolled. What is the probability that the sum of the three dice will equal 10?

4.53 In a standard deck of playing cards, what is the probability of drawing four cards in a row without replacement and getting in this order an ace, a king, a queen, and a jack? What is the probability if the experiment is done with replacement? Which has a higher probability?

4.54 In an effort to save letter carriers time and energy, many newer mailboxes serve several households at once. One such mailbox in a residential area contains sixteen boxes. One of the sixteen boxes is for outgoing mail. The rest of the boxes are used by residents for mail delivery. In addition to the sixteen boxes, the end of the mailbox has two large compartments for packages, which can be opened only if the resident is given a key in his or her own box. Suppose that the letter carrier never uses both large compartments for one resident. That is, on any one day that the compartments are used, two different residents are given keys. What is the probability a resident will get one of these keys today (have packages in one of the large compartments) if both large compartments have packages in them? Assume that any one of the residents is equally likely to get a key.

4.55 A recent survey commissioned by *The World Almanac* and Maturity News Service reported that 51% of the respondents did not believe that the

Social Security system will be secure in 20 years. Of the respondents who were under age 45, 67% believed that the system will not be secure in 20 years. Of the respondents who were age 45 or older, 70% believed the system will be secure in 20 years. Of the people surveyed, 57% were under age 45. One respondent is randomly selected.

a. What is the probability that the person is older than age 45?

b. What is the probability that the person is younger than age 45 and believes that the Social Security system will be secure in 20 years?

c. If the person selected believes that the Social Security system will be secure in 20 years, what is the probability that the person is more than 45 years old?

d. What is the probability that the person is younger than age 45 or believes that the Social Security system will not be secure in 20 years?

4.56 Foreign investment in U.S. industries has been increasing. Direct investment of foreign companies in U.S. companies rose from $90 billion in 1980 to $304 billion in 1988, according to the U.S. Commerce Department. In 1986, 33% of all U.S. chemical manufacturing business was foreign owned, as was 21% of primary metals, 12% of printing and publishing, and 10% of food manufacturing. Suppose that 14% of all U.S. manufacturing is food, 4% is primary metals, 5% is printing and publishing, and 10% is chemical. A U.S. manufacturing firm is randomly selected from one of these industries.

a. What is the probability that the company is a chemical firm or a food manufacturing firm?

b. What is the probability that the company is a printing and publishing company and is foreign owned?

c. What is the probability that the company is foreign owned?

d. What is the probability that the company is a primary metals firm or is foreign owned?

e. If the company is not foreign owned, what is that probability that it is a chemical company?

4.57 In a certain city, 30% of the families have a Mastercard, 20% have an American Express card, and 25% have a Visa card. Eight percent of the families have both a Mastercard and an American Express card. Twelve percent have both a Visa card and a Mastercard. Six percent have both an American Express card and a Visa card.

a. What is the probability of selecting a family that has either a Visa card or an American Express card?

b. If a family has a Mastercard, what is the probability that it also has a Visa card?

c. If a family has a Visa card, what is the probability that it also has a Mastercard.

d. Is possession of a Visa card independent of possession of a Mastercard? Why?

e. Is possession of an American Express card mutually exclusive of possession of a Visa card?

4.58 A survey conducted for Lifetime's daily half-hour series, "The Great American TV Poll" asked Americans what they consider to be the most important thing in their lives. Twenty-nine percent said "good health," 21% responded "a happy marriage," and 40% replied "faith in God." Because they were asked which of these things is *the most* important thing, a respondent could not select more than one answer.

a. What is the probability that a person replied "a happy marriage" or "faith in God"?

b. What is the probability that a person replied "a happy marriage" or "faith in God" or "good health"?

c. What is the probability that a person replied "faith in God" and "good health"?

d. What is the probability that a person replied neither "faith in God" nor "good health" nor "a happy marriage"?

4.59 A telephone survey conducted by the Maritz Marketing Research company found that 43% of Americans expect to save more money next year than they saved last year. Forty-five percent of those surveyed plan to reduce debt next year. Of those who expect to save more money next year, 81% also plan to reduce debt next year. An American is randomly selected.

a. What is the probability that this person expects to save more money next year and plans to reduce debt next year?

b What is the probability that this person expects to save more money next year or plans to reduce debt next year?

c. What is the probability that this person neither expects to save more money next year nor plans to reduce debt next year?

d. What is the probability that this person expects to save more money next year and does not plan to reduce debt next year?

4.60 According to U.S. Bureau of the Census surveys, the Asian populations of Vermont and Virginia doubled during the 1980s. Asians currently account for 2.6% of Virginia's population. Some 75% of the Asians living in Virginia live in urban areas. Some 48% of the non-Asians living in Virginia live in urban areas.

a. What is the probability of randomly selecting a person from Virginia who is Asian and lives in an urban area?

b. What is the probability of randomly selecting a person from Virginia who is non-Asian and lives in a nonurban area?

c. A person from Virginia is randomly selected. If that person is from an urban area, revise the probabilities that the person is Asian and that the person is non-Asian.

4.61 According to the Public Voice for Food and Health Policy, approximately 27% of all soup products in 1990 did not carry nutritional labeling. Approximately 83% of breakfast meats did not carry nutritional labeling, and about 59% of hot dog products did not have nutritional labeling. Assume that if these three goups of foods were combined, 60% would be soup products, 35% would be breakfast meats, and 5% would be hot dogs. A researcher is blindly given a food product from these three groups and told that the product *does* have nutritional labeling. Revise the probabilities that the product is a soup product, a breakfast meat, and a hot dog product.

4.62 According to the Nielsen ratings for February 1989, approximately 27% of all U.S. households watch the "Cosby Show." Based on this figure, what is the probability of randomly selecting *four* U.S. households and

  a. getting two households that watched Cosby?

  b. getting two or more households that watched Cosby?

  c. getting one household that watched Cosby?

  d. finding out that none of the households watched Cosby?

4.63 According to Nielsen Media Research, 63% of all U.S. households have two or more television sets. Three American households are randomly selected.

  a. What is the probability that all three households have two or more television sets?

  b. What is the probability that one household has two or more television sets?

  c. What is the probability that two or more households have two or more television sets?

4.64 The U.S. Bureau of the Census reports that approximately 11% of the population of Little Rock, Arkansas, is more than 65 years old. A researcher randomly selects six people from the population of Little Rock.

  a. What is the probability that none of the six is more than 65 years old?

  b. What is the probability that all six are more than 65 years old?

  c. What is the probability that two are more than 65 years old?

  d. What is the probability that three or more are more than 65 years old?

4.65 The chance of spotting an American-made car in Bangkok is estimated to be 1 in 250. A researcher sat at a busy location in Bangkok and randomly selected every 100th car that passed by until she had selected 10 cars. What is the probability that, of the 10 cars,

    a. one is American made?

    b. none is American made?

    c. more than two are American made?

4.66 A survey by Leo J. Shapiro & Associates, Inc., during and after the Persian Gulf War showed that at the peak of the war 82% of all consumers were less willing to travel by air. After the war, this figure dropped to 65%.

    a. If three consumers were randomly selected after the war, what is the probability that all three were less willing to travel by air?

    b. At the height of the war, what would the probability have been of randomly selecting five people and all five were less willing to travel by air?

DISCRETE DISTRIBUTIONS

5

CHAPTER LEARNING OBJECTIVES

The overall learning objective of Chapter 5 is to help you understand a category of distributions that produces only discrete outcomes, thereby enabling you to:

1. Distinguish between discrete random variables and continuous random variables.
2. Identify the type of statistical experiments that can be described by the binomial distribution, and know how to work such problems.
3. Decide when to use the Poisson distribution in analyzing statistical experiments, and know how to work such problems.
4. Decide when binomial distribution problems can be approximated by the Poisson distribution, and know how to work such problems.
5. Decide when to use the hypergeometric distribution, and know how to work such problems.

CLINT McCARTY DECIDES TO ADVERTISE

Clint McCarty owns a sporting goods store in a suburb of Boston. He is interested in increasing customer traffic into his store, hoping for a surge in sales. From time to time in the past he has taken informal counts of customer arrivals at his store during one-minute intervals. The store seems to average about 1.4 customers per minute during the early evening hours.

McCarty decides to spend a portion of the store's revenues on advertising and chooses television as the medium. He is also interested in gaining some local visibility by appearing in the ads himself. He tapes several advertisements and selects one to appear several times on a late night wrestling program. The next day during the early evening business hours, Clint counts the number of store arrivals during a one-minute interval. Three people enter into the store.

Managerial Questions

- What is the probability that three people would arrive at the store during a one-minute interval by chance, if the average arrival rate is only 1.4 customers per minute?
- Does the sudden slight increase in arrivals for a one-minute interval indicate a change in the arrival rate of customers?
- Did the advertising affect the number of arrivals?
- Do the numbers of people arriving at the store vary according to different times of the day?

S tatistical experiments produce outcomes. Some experiments generate a small number of possible outcomes, such as the experiment of tossing a single coin once. In the single coin toss experiment, there are only two possible outcomes: heads or tails. However, other types of experiments produce a large number of possible outcomes. One such experiment involves tossing five coins, which results in thirty-two possible outcomes:

$H_1 H_2 H_3 H_4 H_5$	$H_1 T_2 H_3 H_4 T_5$	$H_1 H_2 T_3 T_4 T_5$	$T_1 T_2 H_3 T_4 H_5$
$H_1 H_2 H_3 H_4 T_5$	$T_1 H_2 H_3 H_4 T_5$	$H_1 T_2 H_3 T_4 T_5$	$T_1 T_2 T_3 H_4 H_5$
$H_1 H_2 H_3 T_4 H_5$	$H_1 H_2 T_3 T_4 H_5$	$T_1 H_2 H_3 T_4 T_5$	$H_1 T_2 T_3 T_4 T_5$
$H_1 H_2 T_3 H_4 H_5$	$H_1 T_2 H_3 T_4 H_5$	$H_1 T_2 T_3 H_4 T_5$	$T_1 H_2 T_3 T_4 T_5$
$H_1 T_2 H_3 H_4 H_5$	$T_1 H_2 H_3 T_4 H_5$	$T_1 H_2 T_3 H_4 T_5$	$T_1 T_2 H_3 T_4 T_5$
$T_1 H_2 H_3 H_4 H_5$	$H_1 T_2 T_3 H_4 H_5$	$T_1 T_2 H_3 H_4 T_5$	$T_1 T_2 T_3 H_4 T_5$
$H_1 H_2 H_3 T_4 T_5$	$T_1 H_2 T_3 H_4 H_5$	$H_1 T_2 T_3 T_4 H_5$	$T_1 T_2 T_3 T_4 H_5$
$H_1 H_2 T_3 H_4 T_5$	$T_1 T_2 H_3 H_4 H_5$	$T_1 H_2 T_3 T_4 H_5$	$T_1 T_2 T_3 T_4 T_5$

DISCRETE VERSUS CONTINUOUS DISTRIBUTIONS | *5.1*

Both of the coin toss experiments produce distributions that have discrete outcomes. In an experiment of chance, outcomes occur randomly. For example, rolling a pair of dice is a chance experiment: Any one of thirty-six possibilities can occur at random. A **random variable** is *a variable which contains the outcomes of a chance experiment.*

random variable

For example, suppose that an experiment is to measure the arrivals of automobiles at a turnpike toll booth during a thirty-second period. The possible outcomes are: 0 cars, 1 car, 2 cars, . . . , *n* cars. These numbers (0, 1, 2, . . . , *n*) are the values of a random variable. Suppose that another experiment is to measure the time between the completion of two tasks in a production line. The values will vary from 0 seconds to *n* seconds. These time measurements are the values of another random variable. There are two categories of random variables: (1) discrete random variables and (2) continuous random variables.

Discrete random variables *take on values only at certain points over a given interval.* Thus there are gaps or voids in them along an interval. In statistics, discrete random variables produce values that are nonnegative whole numbers. For example, if six people are randomly selected from a population and how many of the six are left-handed is to be determined, the random variable produced is discrete. The only possible numbers of left-handed people in the sample of six are 0, 1, 2, 3, 4, 5, and 6. There cannot be 2.75 left-handed people in a group of six people. Obtaining non-whole-number values is impossible. Other examples of experiments that yield discrete random variables include the following.

discrete random variables

1. Tossing ten coins and determining how many of the coins are tails
2. Randomly selecting twenty-five people who consume soft drinks and determining how many prefer *diet* soft drinks
3. Determining the number of defects in a batch of fifty items
4. Sampling 100 registered voters and determining how many voted for President Bush
5. Counting the number of people who arrive at a store during a five-minute period

Continuous random variables *take on values at every point over a given interval.* Thus continuous random variables have no gaps or unassumed values. For example, if a person is to run a 1500-meter race, any possible value could occur beyond the world record. A person could run it in 4 minutes, 37.9456 seconds or 6 minutes, 11.9471 seconds. A noninclusive list of measures for which continuous random variables might be generated is time, height, weight, and volume. Other examples of experiments that yield continuous random variables include the following.

continuous random variables

1. Sampling the volume of liquid nitrogen in a storage tank
2. Measuring the time between customer arrivals at a retail outlet
3. Determining the money earned by a company each month over period of many months
4. Measuring the lengths of newly designed automobiles
5. Measuring the weight of grain in a grain elevator at different points of time

Once continuous data are measured and recorded, they become discrete data, because the data are rounded off to a discrete number. Thus in actual practice, virtually all business data are discrete. However, for practical reasons, data analysis is facilitated greatly by using continuous distributions on data that were continuous originally.

discrete distributions
continuous distributions

The outcomes for random variables and their associated probabilities can be organized into distributions. The two types of distributions are **discrete distributions,** constructed from discrete random variables, and **continuous distributions,** based on continuous random variables. Discrete distributions include the binomial distribution, Poisson distribution, and hypergeometric distribution. Continuous distributions include the normal distribution, uniform distribution, exponential distribution, t distribution, Chi-square distribution, and F distribution. Chapter 5 covers discrete distributions, and Chapter 6 addresses continuous distributions.

5.2   BINOMIAL DISTRIBUTION

binomial distribution

Perhaps the most widely known of all discrete distributions is the **binomial distribution.** The binomial distribution has been used for hundreds of years. Several assumptions underlie the use of the binomial distribution:

- The experiment involves n identical trials.
- Each trial has only two possible outcomes.
- Each trial is independent of the previous trials.
- The term p is the probability of getting a success on any one trial; the term $q = (1 - p)$ is the probability of getting a failure on any one trial.
- The terms p and q remain constant throughout the experiment.

As the word *bi*nomial indicates, any single trial of a binomial experiment contains only two possible outcomes. These two outcomes are labeled *success* or *failure.* Usually the outcome of interest to the researcher is labeled a success. For example, if a quality control analyst is looking for defective products, she would consider finding a defective product a success even though the company would not consider a defective product a success. If researchers are studying left-handedness, the outcome of getting a left-handed person in a trial of an experiment is a success. The other possible outcome of a trial in a binomial experiment is called a failure. The word failure is only used in opposition to success. In the preceding experiments, a failure could be to get an acceptable part (as opposed to a defective part) or to get a right-handed person (as opposed to a left-handed person). In a binomial distribution experiment there are only two possible, mutually exclusive outcomes to any one trial (heads/tails, right handed/left handed, defective/good, male/female, etc.).

The binomial distribution is a discrete distribution. In n trials, only X successes are possible, where X is a whole number between zero and n. For example, if five parts are randomly selected from a batch of parts, only 0, 1, 2, 3, 4, or 5 defects are possible in that sample. In a sample of five parts, getting 2.356 defects is not possible.

In a binomial experiment, the trials must be independent. This constraint means that either the experiment is by nature one that produces independent trials (such as tossing coins or rolling dice), or it means that the experiment is conducted with replacement. The effect of the independent trial requirement is that p, the probability of getting a success on one trial, remains constant from trial to trial. For example, suppose that 5% of all parts in a bin are defective. The probability of drawing a defective part on the first draw is $p = .05$. If the first part drawn is not replaced, the second draw is not independent of the first, and the p value will change for the next draw. The binomial distribution does not allow for p to change from trial to trial within an experiment. If a coin is tossed all day long, the probability of obtaining a head on the next toss is still .50, because coin tosses are always independent of each other. In other experiments, as in drawing parts from the bin, the parts must be replaced in order to maintain a constant value of p. However, if the population is large compared to the sample size, the effect of sampling without replacement is minimal, and the independence assumption essentially is met. That is, p remains relatively constant.

Generally, if the sample size, n, is less than 5% of the population, the independence assumption is not of great concern. Therefore the acceptable sample size for using the binomial distribution with samples taken *without* replacement is

$$n < 5\% \; N$$

where: $n =$ sample size
$N =$ population size

For example, suppose that 10% of the population of the world is left-handed and that a sample of twenty people is randomly selected from the world's population. If the first person selected is left-handed—and the sampling is conducted without replacement—the value of $p = .10$ is virtually unaffected, because the population of the world is so large. In addition, with many experiments, the population is continually being replenished, even as the sampling is being done. This condition often is the case with quality control sampling of products from large production runs. Other examples of binomial distribution problems include the following.

1. Suppose that 40% of all teenagers in Denver go skiing once a year. If twenty Denver teenagers are randomly sampled, what is the probability ten of them will have gone snow skiing during the past year?
2. Suppose that a machine producing computer chips has a 6% defective rate. If a company purchases thirty of these chips, what is the probability that none is defective?
3. Suppose that there is a runoff for the Democratic nomination for governor in the state of Georgia. The polls show that candidate A has 57% of the vote. If a random sample of fifteen voters is taken, what is the probability that fewer than seven of these voters support candidate A?
4. Suppose that brand X car battery has a 35% market share. If seventy cars are selected at random, what is the probability that at least thirty cars have a brand X battery?

Solving a Binomial Problem

Some energy companies have issued debit cards with which consumers can purchase gasoline. The clerk in the station where the gasoline is purchased enters the debit card information into a computer system through which the customer's bank account is debited for the price of the purchase. In essence, the customer is paying cash for the gas, so there is usually a cash discount for using a debit card. Suppose that, for a particular brand, an estimated 4% of all customers purchasing gasoline use a debit card. If five customers are randomly selected, what is the probability that one of these customers uses a debit card?

Solving this problem first requires taking one possible sequence of customers. Suppose that the first customer used the debit card, and the next four customers did not. Letting D stand for debit and N represent not debit, the sequence is

$$D_1 \quad N_2 \quad N_3 \quad N_4 \quad N_5$$

The probability of getting this sequence of customers is calculated by using the special rule of multiplication for independent events. All five of these events must happen to achieve this sequence, and each event is independent of the others. If 4% of all customers purchasing gasoline use a debit card, the probability of one person using a debit card is .04, which is the value of p. Ninety-six percent of the customers do not use debit cards. Thus the probability of getting a non-debit-card user, q, in any one trial is $1 - .04 = .96$. The probability of obtaining the sequence of five customers with the first being a debit card user is

$$P(D_1 \cap N_2 \cap N_3 \cap N_4 \cap N_5) = (.04)(.96)(.96)(.96)(.96) = .03397.$$

Obviously in a sample of five gasoline customers the debit card user could be the second customer or the third customer, etc. All the possible sequences of getting one debit card user out of five customers are

D_1	N_2	N_3	N_4	N_5
N_1	D_2	N_3	N_4	N_5
N_1	N_2	D_3	N_4	N_5
N_1	N_2	N_3	D_4	N_5
N_1	N_2	N_3	N_4	D_5

The probability of each of these sequences occurring is

$$(.04)(.96)(.96)(.96)(.96) = .03397$$
$$(.96)(.04)(.96)(.96)(.96) = .03397$$
$$(.96)(.96)(.04)(.96)(.96) = .03397$$
$$(.96)(.96)(.96)(.04)(.96) = .03397$$
$$(.96)(.96)(.96)(.96)(.04) = .03397$$

Note that in each case the probability is the same. Each of the five sequences contains the product of .04 and four .96's. The commutative property of multiplication allows for the reordering of the five individual probabilities in any one sequence. The probabilities in each of the five sequences may be reordered and summarized as $(.04)^1(.96)^4$. Each sequence contains the same five probabilities, so there is no point in recomputing the probability of each sequence. What *is* important is to determine how many different ways the sequences can be formed and multiply that figure by the probability of one sequence occurring. For the five sequences of this problem, the total probability of getting one debit card user in a sample of five customers is

$$5(.04)^1(.96)^4 = .16985.$$

An easier way to determine the number of sequences than by listing all possibilities is to use *combinations* to calculate them. Five customers are being sampled, so $n = 5$, and the problem is to get one debit card user, $X = 1$. Hence $_nC_X$ will yield the number of possible ways to get X successes in n trials. For this problem, $_5C_1$, tells the number of sequences of possibilities:

$$_5C_1 = \frac{5!}{1!(5-1)!} = 5.$$

Putting the combination with the probability of each sequence yields

$$_5C_1(.04)^1(.96)^4 = .16985.$$

Now suppose that 70% of all Americans believe that cleaning up the environment is an important issue. What is the probability of randomly sampling four Americans and having two of them say that they believe that cleaning up the environment is an important issue? Let E represent the success of getting a person who believes that cleaning up the environment is an important issue. For this example, $p = .70$. Let N represent the failure of not getting a person who believes that cleaning up is an important issue (N denotes not important). The probability of getting one of these persons is $q = .30$.

The various sequences of getting two E's in a sample of four are:

$$
\begin{array}{cccc}
E_1 & E_2 & N_3 & N_4 \\
E_1 & N_2 & E_3 & N_4 \\
E_1 & N_2 & N_3 & E_4 \\
N_1 & E_2 & E_3 & N_4 \\
N_1 & E_2 & N_3 & E_4 \\
N_1 & N_2 & E_3 & E_4
\end{array}
$$

Two successes in a sample of four can be obtained six ways. Using combinations, the number of sequences is

$$_4C_2 = 6 \text{ ways.}$$

The probability of selecting any individual sequence is

$$(.70)^2(.30)^2 = .0441.$$

Thus the overall probability of getting two people who believe that cleaning up the environment is important out of four randomly selected people, when 70% of Americans believe that cleaning up the environment is important, is

$$_4C_2(.70)^2(.30)^2 = .2646.$$

Generalizing from these two examples yields the binomial formula, which can be used to solve binomial problems.

Binomial Formula

$$_nC_X \cdot p^X \cdot q^{n-X} = \frac{n!}{X!(n-X)!} \; p^X \cdot q^{n-X},$$

where: n = the number of trials (or the number being sampled)

X = the number of successes desired

p = the probability of getting a success in one trial

$q = 1 - p$ = the probability of getting a failure in one trial

The binomial formula summarizes the steps presented so far to solve binomial problems. The formula allows the solution of these problems quickly and efficiently.

A researcher wants to test the claim that 10% of all people are left-handed by randomly selecting forty students at a university. What is the probability of getting six left-handed students among the forty?

Solution:

The value of $p = .10$ (left-handed), the value of $q = 1 - p = .90$ (right-handed), $n = 40$, and $X = 6$. The binomial formula yields the final answer:

$$_{40}C_6(.10)^6(.90)^{34} = .1068.$$

If 10% of the population is left-handed, about 10.68% of the time the researcher would get six who are left-handed in a sample of forty people.

Suppose these results actually occurred. What would they tell the researcher? With a probability of .1068, the odds are against getting this number of left-handed people by chance. How many left-handed people would the researcher have expected to find in forty people? If 10% of the population is left-handed, the researcher would have expected to find about four who were left-handed in forty people (10% of 40). Is the proportion of left-handed students at a university higher than the proportion in the general population? The sample results might cause the researcher to investigate this idea further.

According to the U.S. Bureau of the Census, approximately 6% of all workers in Jackson, Mississippi, are unemployed. In conducting a random telephone survey in Jackson, what is the probability of getting two or fewer unemployed workers in a sample of 20?

Solution:

This problem must be worked as the union of three problems: (1) zero unemployed, $X = 0$; (2) one unemployed, $X = 1$; and (3) two unemployed, $X = 2$. In each problem, $p = .06$, $q = .94$, and $n = 20$. The binomial formula gives

$$
\begin{array}{ccc}
X = 0 & X = 1 & X = 2 \\
{}_{20}C_0(.06)^0(.94)^{20} + & {}_{20}C_1(.06)^1(.94)^{19} + & {}_{20}C_2(.06)^2(.94)^{18} = \\
.2901 \quad + & .3703 \quad + & .2246 \quad = .8850.
\end{array}
$$

If 6% of the workers in Jackson, Mississippi, are unemployed, the telephone surveyor would get zero, one, or two unemployed workers 88.5% of the time in a random sample of twenty workers. The requirement of getting two or fewer is satisfied by getting zero, one, or two unemployed workers. Thus this problem is the union of three probabilities. Whenever the binomial formula is used to solve for cumulative success (not an exact number), the probability of each X value must be solved and the probabilities summed. If an actual survey produced such a result, it would serve to validate the census figures.

Using the Binomial Table

Anyone who works enough binomial problems will begin to recognize that the probability of getting $X = 5$ successes from a sample size of $n = 30$ when $p = .10$ is the same no matter whether the five successes are left-handed people, defective parts, brand X purchasers, or any other variable. Sampling thirty people or thirty parts does not matter in terms of the final probabilities. Whether 10% of the population is left-handed or 10% of the parts produced are defective makes no difference in the final probabilities. The essence of the problem is the same: $n = 30$, $X = 5$, and $p = .10$. Recognizing this fact, mathematicians constructed a set of binomial tables containing presolved probabilities.

Two parameters, n and p, describe or characterize a binomial distribution. Binomial distributions actually are a family of distributions. Every different value of n and/or every different value of p gives a different binomial distribution, and tables are available for various combinations of n and p values. Because of space limitations, the binomial tables presented in this text are limited. Table A.2 in Appendix A contains binomial tables. Each table is headed by a value of n. Nine values of p are presented in each table of size n. In the column below each value of p is the binomial distribution for that value of n and p. Table 5.1 contains a segment of Table A.2: the binomial probabilities for $n = 20$.

n = 20

TABLE 5.1

Probability

Excerpt from Table A.2,
Appendix A

X	.1	.2	.3	.4	.5	.6	.7	.8	.9
0	.122	.012	.001	.000	.000	.000	.000	.000	.000
1	.270	.058	.007	.000	.000	.000	.000	.000	.000
2	.285	.137	.028	.003	.000	.000	.000	.000	.000
3	.190	.205	.072	.012	.001	.000	.000	.000	.000
4	.090	.218	.130	.035	.005	.000	.000	.000	.000
5	.032	.175	.179	.075	.015	.001	.000	.000	.000
6	.009	.109	.192	.124	.037	.005	.000	.000	.000
7	.002	.055	.164	.166	.074	.015	.001	.000	.000
8	.000	.022	.114	.180	.120	.035	.004	.000	.000
9	.000	.007	.065	.160	.160	.071	.012	.000	.000
10	.000	.002	.031	.117	.176	.117	.031	.002	.000
11	.000	.000	.012	.071	.160	.160	.065	.007	.000
12	.000	.000	.004	.035	.120	.180	.114	.022	.000
13	.000	.000	.001	.015	.074	.166	.164	.055	.002
14	.000	.000	.000	.005	.037	.124	.192	.109	.009
15	.000	.000	.000	.001	.015	.075	.179	.175	.032
16	.000	.000	.000	.000	.005	.035	.130	.218	.090
17	.000	.000	.000	.000	.001	.012	.072	.205	.190
18	.000	.000	.000	.000	.000	.003	.028	.137	.285
19	.000	.000	.000	.000	.000	.000	.007	.058	.270
20	.000	.000	.000	.000	.000	.000	.001	.012	.122

**Demonstration
Problem 5.3**

Solve the binomial probability for $n = 20$, $p = .40$, and $X = 10$ by using Table A.2, Appendix A.

Solution:

To use Table A.2, first locate the value of n. As $n = 20$ for this problem, the portion of the binomial tables containing values for $n = 20$ presented in Table 5.1 can be used. After locating the value of n, search horizontally across the top of the table for the appropriate value of p. In this problem, $p = .40$. The column under .40 contains the probabilities for the binomial distribution of $n = 20$ and $p = .40$. To get the probability of $X = 10$, find the value of X in the leftmost column and locate the probability in the table at the intersection of $p = .40$ and $X = .10$. The answer is .117. Working this problem by the binomial formula yields the same results:

$$_{20}C_{10}(.40)^{10}\ (.60)^{10} = .1171.$$

Demonstration Problem 5.4

Suppose that 70% of all cola drinkers select nondiet colas. If twenty cola drinkers are randomly selected, what is the probability that more than fifteen of them will be nondiet cola drinkers?

Solution:

For this problem, $n = 20$, $p = .70$, and $X > 15$. Because $n = 20$, that portion of the binomial tables presented in Table 5.1 can be used to work this problem. Search along the row of p values for .70. The problem is to locate the probability of getting $X > 15$, so getting the final answer involves summing the probabilities for $X = 16$, 17, 18, 19, and 20. These values appear in the X column at the intersection of each X value and $p = .70$.

X value	Probability
16	.130
17	.072
18	.028
19	.007
20	.001
$X > 15$	.238

If 70% of all cola drinkers drink nondiet colas and twenty cola drinkers are selected, the probability is .238 that more than fifteen of the cola drinkers selected drink nondiet cola.

Mean and Standard Deviation of a Binomial Distribution

A binomial distribution has an expected value or long-run average, which is denoted by μ. The value of μ is determined by $n \cdot p$. For example, if $n = 10$ and $p = .4$, then $\mu = n \cdot p = (10)(.4) = 4$. The long-run average or expected value means that, if n items are sampled over and over for a long time and if p is the probability of getting a success on one trial, the average number of successes per sample is expected to be $n \cdot p$. If 40% of all graduate business students at a large university are women and if random samples of ten graduate business students are selected many times, the expectation is that, on average, four of the ten students would be women.

$$\mu = n \cdot p;$$
$$\sigma = \sqrt{n \cdot p \cdot q}.$$

Mean and Standard Deviation of a Binomial Distribution

Examining the mean of a binomial distribution gives an intuitive feeling about the likelihood of a given outcome. For example, suppose that researchers generally agree that 10% of all people are left-handed. However, suppose that a researcher believes, as some have theorized, that this figure is higher for children who are born to women over the age of 35. In an attempt to gather evidence, she randomly selects 100 children who were born to women over the age of 35 and 20 turn out to be left-handed. Is it likely that she would have gotten 20 left-handed people in a sample of 100? How many would she have expected to get in a sample of 100? The mean or expected value for $n = 100$ and $p = .10$ is $(100)(.10) = 10$ left-handed people. Did the 20 left-handed children in a sample of 100 happen by chance or is she drawing from a different population than the general population that produces 10% left-handed people? She can investigate this outcome further by examining the binomial probabilities for this problem. However, the mean of the distribution gives her an expected value from which to work.

The standard deviation of a binomial distribution is denoted σ and is equal to $\sqrt{n \cdot p \cdot q}$. For this example, $\sigma = \sqrt{100(.10)(.90)} = 3$. If the binomial distribution, $n = 100$ and $p = .10$, were bell shaped, the empirical rule would say that $\mu \pm 3\sigma$ or $10 \pm 3(3)$ contains 99.7% of the values. That is, 99.7% of the time when 100 people are sampled, between 1 and 19 would be left-handed. The figure of 20 left-handed children obtained from the sample of 100 children of mothers over 35 years of age falls outside the range of $\mu \pm 3\sigma$. That indicates that the population from which the sample was drawn may be different than the population from which the 10% left-handed p value was calculated.

Chapter 6 shows that some binomial distributions are bell-shaped and can be approximated by using the normal curve. The mean and standard deviation of a binomial distribution are the tools used to convert these binomial problems to normal curve problems.

Graphing Binomial Distributions

The graph of a binomial distribution can be constructed by using all the possible X values of a distribution and their associated probabilities. The X values are usually graphed along the X axis, and the probabilities are graphed along the Y axis. Table 5.2 shows the X values and their probabilities for a binomial distribution of $n = 5$ and $p = .40$. Figure 5.1 presents the graph of this binomial distribution.

The graph of the binomial distribution of $n = 5$ and $p = .4$ in Figure 5.1 shows that the most likely occurrence in this distribution is $X = 2$. This outcome makes sense, because the mean of this distribution, $\mu = n \cdot p = 5(.4) = 2.0$, is the expected value.

In any binomial distribution the largest X value that can occur is n and the smallest value is zero. Thus the graph of any binomial distribution is constrained by 0 and n. If the p value of the distribution is not .50, this constraint will result in the graph "piling up" at one end and being skewed at the other end.

Examine the probabilities and the resulting graph for the binomial distribution of $n = 8$ and $p = .20$ presented in Table 5.3 and Figure 5.2, respectively.

TABLE 5.2

Binomial Distribution for $n = 5$ and $p = .40$

X value	Probability
0	.078
1	.259
2	.346
3	.230
4	.077
5	.010

FIGURE 5.1

Graph of the Binomial Distribution with $n = 5$ and $p = .40$

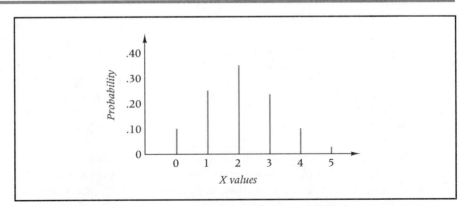

X value	Probabilities
0	.168
1	.336
2	.294
3	.147
4	.046
5	.009
6	.001
7	.000
8	.000

TABLE 5.3

Binomial Distribution for
$n = 8$ and $p = .20$

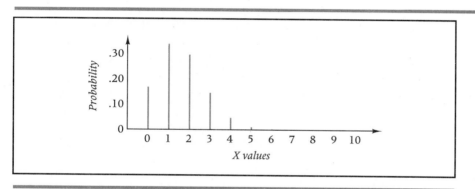

FIGURE 5.2

Graph of the Binomial
Distribution with $n = 8$
and $p = .20$

The expected value for this distribution is 1.6. What are the most probable X values? Is this distribution skewed? Figure 5.2 reveals that the most probable X values (1 and 2) occur near the mean. Because the p value is nearer 0 than n (8), the graph "piles up" near 0 and is skewed toward 8.

**Demonstration
Problem 5.5**

A manufacturing company produces 10,000 plastic mugs per week. This company supplies mugs to another company, which packages the mugs as part of picnic sets. The second company randomly samples ten mugs sent from the supplier. If two or less of the sampled mugs are defective, the second company accepts the lot. What is the probability that the lot will be accepted if the mug manufacturing company actually is producing mugs that are 10% defective? 20% defective? 30% defective? 40% defective?

Solution:

In this series of binomial problems, $n = 10$, $X \leq 2$, and p varies from .10 to .40. From Table A.2—and cumulating the values—the probability of $X \leq 2$ for each p value and the expected value is as follows:

p	Lot Accepted $P(X \leq 2)$	Expected Number of Defects (μ)
.10	.930	1.0
.20	.677	2.0
.30	.382	3.0
.40	.167	4.0

These values indicate that if the manufacturing company is producing 10% defectives, there is a relatively high possibility (.930) that the lot will be accepted by chance. For higher values of p, the probability of lot acceptance by chance decreases.

**PROBLEMS
Section 5.2**

5.1 Solve the following problems using the binomial formula.
   a. If $n = 4$ and $p = .10$, $P(X = 3) =$
   b. If $n = 7$ and $p = .80$, $P(X = 4) =$
   c. If $n = 10$ and $p = .60$, $P(X \geq 7) =$
   d. If $n = 12$ and $p = .45$, $P(5 \leq X \leq 7) =$

5.2 Solve the following problems using the binomial tables (Table A.2).
   a. If $n = 20$ and $p = .50$, $P(X = 12) =$
   b. If $n = 20$ and $p = .30$, $P(X > 8) =$
   c. If $n = 20$ and $p = .70$, $P(X < 12) =$
   d. If $n = 20$ and $p = .90$, $P(X \leq 16) =$
   e. If $n = 15$ and $p = .40$, $P(4 \leq X \leq 9) =$
   f. If $n = 10$ and $p = .60$, $P(X \geq 7) =$

5.3 Solve for the mean and standard deviation of the following binomial distributions.
   a. $n = 20$ and $p = .70$
   b. $n = 70$ and $p = .35$
   c. $n = 100$ and $p = .50$

5.4 Use the probability tables in Table A.2 and sketch the graph of each of the following binomial distributions. Note on the graph where the mean of the distribution falls.

    a. $n = 6$ and $p = .70$

    b. $n = 20$ and $p = .50$

    c. $n = 8$ and $p = .80$

5.5 According to some merchandising sources, 11% of all U.S. camcorder units shipped for sale are VHS-C format. A researcher randomly samples twenty individual camcorder units across the United States.

    a. What is the probability that none of the sampled camcorder units is VHS-C format?

    b. What is the probability that four are of the VHS-C format?

    c. What is the probability that fifteen or more are of the VHS-C format? (Compute the answer to four decimal places only.)

    d. How many VHS-C format units would the researcher expect to get in a sample of twenty?

5.6 Raising money for charitable causes is a competitive activity. However, in America certain causes receive much more support than others. For example, almost 53% of all American households contribute to some religion. Twenty-four percent of the households give to some health cause. Education receives charitable contributions from 15% of all American households. Suppose that a professional fund raiser conducts a nationwide telephone survey of twelve American households.

    a. What is the probability that ten of these households made charitable contributions to religion?

    b. What is the probability that ten of these households contributed to some health cause?

    c. What is the probability that two or fewer households made charitable contributions to education?

    d. Based on the findings in (a), (b), and (c), what would the telephone surveyor conclude about the stated percentages?

5.7 In 1988, George Bush campaigned on a no-new-taxes platform. However, in 1990, President Bush acknowledged that tax increases were needed to reduce the budget deficit. A poll of U.S. voters showed that 70% favored increasing the tax rate on corporations, and 20% opposed increasing the income tax rate for upper-income individuals. Suppose that you wondered whether people in your city felt the same as other American voters and that you took a random survey of twenty-five voters in your city.

    a. What would the probability be of getting fifteen or more voters in the sample who favor increasing the tax rate on corporations?

    b. What is the probability of getting more than twenty who favor increasing the tax rate on corporations?

    c. What is the probability of getting fifteen or fewer who do *not* favor increasing the tax rate on corporations?

5.8 Referring to Problem 5.7, what is the probability of randomly sampling ten people and getting fewer than three who oppose increasing the income tax rate for upper-income individuals? What is the probability of getting eight or more people who oppose increasing the income tax rate for upper-income individuals?

5.9 What are the values of n and p in Problem 5.8? Graph this binomial distribution. Could you have ascertained the answers in Problem 5.8 intuitively from the graph?

5.10 The Home Improvement Research Institute conducted a survey of 6,000 homeowners who completed do-it-yourself projects during the past year. Among other things, the survey found that 25% of the respondents had completed some type of interior painting job in the past year. Suppose that eight homeowners who had completed a do-it-yourself project in the past year were randomly contacted.

    a. What is the expected number of those who have completed some type of interior painting job during the past year?

    b. Compute the binomial probabilities for each possibility and graph the results (compute only to four decimal places).

    c. Suppose that six of the eight respondents said that they had completed some type of interior painting job during the past year. What might the institute's researchers conclude about the 25% proportion determined in the survey of 6,000?

5.11 According to the American Hospital Association, in the late 1980s, approximately 55% of all U.S. hospitals contained 100 or more beds. A researcher draws a sample of fifteen hospitals by randomly selecting names from a directory of U.S. hospitals.

    a. What is the probability of selecting ten or more hospitals that have 100 or more beds?

    b. What is the probability of selecting less than five hospitals that have 100 or more beds?

    c. What is the probability of selecting from six to ten hospitals, inclusive, that have 100 or more beds?

    d. What are the mean and standard deviation for this problem?

    e. Use the empirical rule from Chapter 3 to determine within what values of x approximately 95% of the values would fall.

5.12 In 1987, nearly 11% of the population of the United States underwent inpatient surgery according to the National Center for Health Statistics. This type of surgery is done in nonfederal, short-stay hospitals and excludes infants. Suppose that you observe in your community an apparently higher proportion of inpatient surgery than the U.S. figure indicates. To test this idea, you randomly interview twenty-five people in your community; four reply that they have had inpatient surgery. Use the 11% figure and a sample size of twenty-five to determine the probability of getting four or more people who have had inpatient surgery during the past year.

POISSON DISTRIBUTION | **5.3**

The Poisson distribution is another discrete distribution. It is named after Simeon-Denis Poisson (1781–1840), a French mathematician, who published its essentials in a paper in 1837. The Poisson distribution and the binomial distribution have some similarities, but they also have several differences. The binomial distribution describes a distribution of two possible outcomes designated as successes and failures from a given number of trials. The **Poisson distribution** *focuses only on the number of discrete occurrences over some interval or continuum.* A Poisson experiment does not have a given number of trials *(n),* as a binomial experiment does. For example, whereas a binomial experiment might be used to determine how many American-made cars there are in a random sample of twenty cars, a Poisson experiment might focus on the number of cars randomly arriving at an automobile repair facility during a ten-minute interval.

Poisson distribution

The Poisson distribution describes the occurrence of *rare events.* In fact, the Poisson formula has been referred to as the *law of improbable events.* For example, serious accidents at a chemical plant are rare, and the number per month might be described by the Poisson distribution. The Poisson distribution often is used to describe the number of random arrivals per some *time* interval. If the number of arrivals per interval is too frequent, the time interval can be reduced enough so that a rare number of occurrences is expected. Another example of a Poisson distribution is the number of random customer arrivals per five-minute interval at a small boutique on weekday mornings.

The Poisson distribution also has an application in the field of management science. The models utilized in queuing theory (theory of waiting lines) usually are based on the assumption that the Poisson distribution is the proper distribution to describe random arrival rates over a period of time.

The Poisson distribution has the following characteristics.

- It is a discrete distribution.
- It describes rare events.
- Each occurrence is independent of the other occurrences.
- It describes discrete occurrences over a continuum or interval.
- The occurrences in each interval can vary from zero to infinity.
- The expected number of occurrences must hold constant throughout the experiment.

Examples of Poisson-type situations include the following.

1. Number of AIDS cases per 10,000 people
2. Number of hazardous waste sites per county in the United States
3. Number of major oil spills in the New England region per month
4. Number of arrivals at a turnpike toll booth per minute between 3 A.M. and 4 A.M. in January on the Kansas Turnpike
5. Number of times a one-year-old personal computer printer breaks down per quarter (three months)
6. Number of sewing flaws per pair of jeans during production
7. Number of times a meteor strikes a populated area of the world per year
8. Number of times a tire blows on a commercial airplane per week
9. Number of paint spots per new automobile
10. Number of flaws per bolt of cloth

Each of these examples deals with a rare occurrence of events for some interval. Note that, although time is a more common interval for the Poisson distribution, intervals can vary from a county in the United States to a pair of jeans. Some of the intervals in these examples might have zero occurrences. Moreover, the average occurrence per interval for many of these examples is probably in the single digits (1–9).

lambda   If a Poisson distributed phenomenon is studied over a long period of time, a long-run average can be determined. This average is denoted **lambda** (λ). Each Poisson problem contains a lambda value from which the probabilities of particular occurrences are determined. Although n and p are required to describe a binomial distribution, a Poisson distribution can be described by λ alone. The Poisson formula is used to compute the probability of occurrences over an interval for a given lambda value.

Poisson Formula

$$P(X) = \frac{\lambda^X e^{-\lambda}}{X!},$$

where: $X = 0, 1, 2, 3, \ldots$
λ = long-run average
$e = 2.718282$

Here, X is the number of occurrences per interval for which the probability is being computed, λ is the long-run average, and $e = 2.718282$ is the base of natural logarithms.

A word of caution about using the Poisson distribution to study various phenomena is necessary. The λ value must hold constant throughout a Poisson experiment. The researcher must be careful not to apply a given lambda to intervals for which lambda changes. For example, the average number of customers arriving at a Sears' store during a one-minute interval will vary from hour to hour, day to day, and month to month. Different times of the day or week might produce different lambdas. The number of flaws per pair of jeans might vary from Monday to Friday. The researcher should be very specific in describing the interval for which lambda is being used.

Working Poisson Problems by Formula

Suppose that bank customers arrive randomly on weekday afternoons at an average of 3.2 customers every four minutes. What is the probability of five customers arriving in a four-minute interval on a weekday afternoon? The lambda for this problem is 3.2 customers per four minutes. The value of X is five customers per four minutes. The probability of five customers randomly arriving during a four-minute interval when the long-run average has been 3.2 customers per four-minute interval is

$$\frac{(3.2^5)(e^{-3.2})}{5!} = \frac{(335.54)(.0408)}{120} = .1141.$$

Bank customers arrive randomly on weekday afternoons at an average of 3.2 customers every four minutes. What is the probability of having more than seven customers in a four-minute interval on a weekday afternoon?

Solution:

$$\lambda = 3.2 \text{ customers/4 minutes;}$$
$$X > 7 \text{ customers/4 minutes.}$$

In theory, the solution requires obtaining the values of $X = 8, 9, 10, 11, 12, 13, 14, \ldots, \infty$. In actuality, each X value is determined until the values are so far away from $\lambda = 3.2$ that the probabilities approach zero. The exact probabilities are then summed to find $X > 7$:

$$P(X = 8 | \lambda = 3.2) = \frac{(3.2^8)(e^{-3.2})}{8!} = .0111;$$

$$P(X = 9 | \lambda = 3.2) = \frac{(3.2^9)(e^{-3.2})}{9!} = .0040;$$

$$P(X = 10 | \lambda = 3.2) = \frac{(3.2^{10})(e^{-3.2})}{10!} = .0013;$$

$$P(X = 11 | \lambda = 3.2) = \frac{(3.2^{11})(e^{-3.2})}{11!} = .0004;$$

$$P(X = 12|\lambda = 3.2) = \frac{(3.2^{12})(e^{-3.2})}{12!} = .0001;$$

$$P(X = 13|\lambda = 3.2) = \frac{(3.2^{13})(e^{-3.2})}{13!} = \underline{.0000};$$

$$P(X > 7) = P(X \geq 8) \qquad\qquad\quad = .0169.$$

If the bank has been averaging 3.2 customers every 4 minutes on weekday afternoons, it is unlikely that more than 7 people would randomly arrive in any one 4-minute period. This answer indicates that more than 7 people would randomly arrive in a 4-minute period only 1.69% of the time. Bank officers could use these results to help them make staffing decisions.

Demonstration Problem 5.7

A bank has been averaging a random arrival rate of 3.2 customers every four minutes. What is the probability of getting 10 customers during an eight-minute interval?

Solution:

$$\lambda = 3.2 \text{ customers}/4 \text{ minutes};$$
$$X = 10 \text{ customers}/8 \text{ minutes}.$$

This example is different from the first two Poisson examples in that the intervals for lambda and the sample are different. The intervals must be the same in order to use λ and X together in the probability formula. There is a right way and a wrong way to approach this dilemma. The right way is to adjust the interval for lambda so that it and X have the same interval. The interval for X is eight minutes, so lambda should be adjusted to an eight-minute interval. Logically, if the bank averages 3.2 customers every four minutes, it should average twice as many, or 6.4 customers, every eight minutes. If X were for a two-minute interval, the value of lambda could have been halved from 3.2 to 1.6 customers per two-minute interval. The wrong way is to equalize the intervals by changing the X value. *Never adjust or change X* in a problem. Always adjust the lambda value. After lambda has been adjusted for an eight-minute interval, the solution is

$$\lambda = 6.4 \text{ customers}/8 \text{ minutes};$$
$$X = 10 \text{ customers}/8 \text{ minutes};$$
$$\frac{(6.4)^{10}e^{-6.4}}{10!} = .0528.$$

Using the Poisson Tables

Every value of lambda determines a different Poisson distribution. Regardless of the nature of the interval associated with a lambda, the Poisson distribution for a particular lambda is the same. Table A.3, Appendix A, contains the Poisson distributions for selected values of lambda. Probabilities are displayed in the table for each X value associated with a given lambda if the probability has a nonzero value to four decimal places. Table 5.4 is a portion of Table A.3 that contains the probabilities of $X \le 9$ if lambda is 1.6.

X	*Probability*	TABLE 5.4
		Poisson Table for
0	.2019	$\lambda = 1.6$
1	.3230	
2	.2584	
3	.1378	
4	.0551	
5	.0176	
6	.0047	
7	.0011	
8	.0002	
9	.0000	

Demonstration Problem 5.8

If a real estate office sells 1.6 houses on an average weekday and sales of houses on weekdays are Poisson distributed, what is the probability of selling four houses in one day? What is the probability of selling no houses in one day? What is the probability of selling more than five houses in a day? What is the probability of selling ten or more houses in a day? What is the probability of selling four houses in two days?

Solution:

$$\lambda = 1.6/\text{day};$$
$$P(X = 4 | \lambda = 1.6) = ?$$

Table 5.4 contains the probabilities for $\lambda = 1.6$. The left column contains the X values. The line $X = 4$ yields the probability .0551. If a real estate firm has been averaging 1.6 houses sold per day, only on 5.51% of the days would it sell four houses and still maintain the lambda value. Line 1 shows the probability of selling no houses in a day (.2019). That is, on 20.19% of the days, the firm would sell no houses if sales are Poisson distributed with $\lambda = 1.6$ houses per day. More than five houses is the same as $X > 5$. Table 5.4 is *not* cumulative. To determine $P(X > 5)$, find the probabilities of $X = 6$, $X = 7$, $X = 8$, $X = 9, \ldots, X = \infty$. However, at $X = 9$, the probability to four decimal places is zero, and Table 5.4 stops when an X value zeros out at four decimal places. The answer for $X > 5$ is

X	Probability
6	.0047
7	.0011
8	.0002
9	.0000
	$X > 5 = .0060$

What is the probability of selling ten or more houses in one day? As the table zeros out at $X = 9$, the probability of $X \geq 10$ is essentially .0000. What is the probability of selling four houses in two days? In this case, the interval has been changed from one day to two days. Lambda is for one day, so an adjustment must be made: A lambda of 1.6 for one day converts to a lambda of 3.2 for two days. Table 5.4 no longer applies, so Table A.3 must be used to solve this problem. The answer is found by looking up $\lambda = 3.2$ and $X = 4$ in Table A.3: the probability is .1781.

Mean and Standard Deviation of a Poisson Distribution

The mean or expected value of a Poisson distribution is λ. It is the long-run average of occurrences for an interval if many random samples are taken. Lambda usually is not a whole number, so most of the time actually observing lambda occurrences in an interval is impossible.

For example, suppose that $\lambda = 6.5$/interval for some Poisson distributed phenomenon. The resulting number of X occurrences for twenty different random samples from a Poisson distribution with $\lambda = 6.5$ might be

6 9 7 4 8 7 6 6 10 6 5 5 8 4 5 8 5 4 9 10

Computing the mean number of occurrences from this group of twenty intervals gives 6.6. In theory, for infinite sampling, the long-run average is 6.5. Note from the samples that, when λ is 6.5, several 5's and 6's occur. Rarely would sample occurrences of 1, 2, 3, 11, 12, 13, . . . , occur when $\lambda = 6.5$. Understanding the mean of a Poisson distribution gives a feel for the actual occurrences that are likely to happen.

The variance of a Poisson distribution also is λ. The standard deviation is $\sqrt{\lambda}$. Combining the standard deviation with Chebyshev's theorem indicates the spread or dispersion of a Poisson distribution. For example, if $\lambda = 6.5$, the variance also is 6.5, and the standard deviation is $\sqrt{6.5} = 2.55$. Chebyshev's theorem states that at least $1 - 1/k^2$ values fall within k standard deviations of the mean. The interval $\mu \pm 2\sigma$ contains at least $1 - (1/2)^2 = 0.75$ of the values. For $\mu = \lambda = 6.5$ and $\sigma = 2.55$, 75% of the values should fall within the $6.5 \pm 2(2.55) = 6.5 \pm 5.1$ range. That is, the range from 1.4 to 11.6 should include at least 75% of all the values. An examination of the twenty values randomly generated for a Poisson distribution with $\lambda = 6.5$ shows that, actually, 100% of the values fall within this range.

Graphing Poisson Distributions

The values in Table A.3, Appendix A, can be used to graph a Poisson distribution. The X values are graphed along the X axis and the probabilities along the Y axis. Figure 5.3 depicts the graph for the distribution of values for $\lambda = 1.6$.

The graph reveals a Poisson distribution skewed to the right. With a mean of 1.6 and a possible range of X from zero to infinity, the values obviously will "pile up" at 0 and 1. Consider, however, the graph of the Poisson distribution for $\lambda = 6.5$ shown in Figure 5.4. Note that with $\lambda = 6.5$, the probabilities are greatest for the values of 5, 6, 7, and 8. The graph has very little skewness, because the probability of occurrence of values near zero is small, as are the probabilities of large values of X.

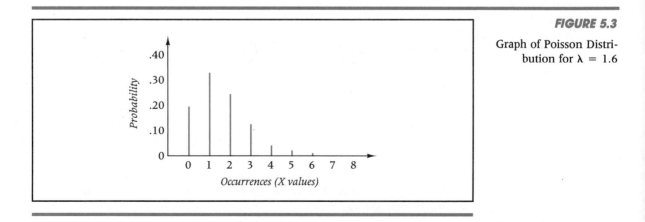

FIGURE 5.3

Graph of Poisson Distribution for $\lambda = 1.6$

FIGURE 5.4

Graph of Poisson Distri-
bution for $\lambda = 6.5$

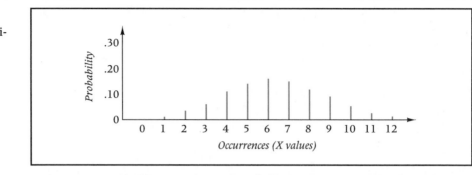

Approximating Binomial Problems by the Poisson Distribution

Certain types of binomial distribution problems can be approximated by using
the Poisson distribution. Binomial problems with large sample sizes and small
p values, which then generate rare events, are potential candidates for use of
the Poisson distribution. As a rule of thumb, if $n > 20$ and $n \cdot p \leq 7$, the
approximation is close enough to use the Poisson distribution for binomial
problems.

If these conditions are met and the binomial problem is a candidate for
this process, the procedure begins with computation of the mean of the binomial distribution, $\mu = n \cdot p$. Because μ is the expected value of the binomial,
it translates to the expected value, λ, of the Poisson distribution. Using μ as
the λ value and using the X value of the binomial problem allows approximation of the probability from a Poisson table or by the Poisson formula.

Demonstration Problem 5.9

Work the following binomial distribution problem by using the Poisson
distribution: $n = 50$ and $p = .03$. What is the probability that $X = 4$?
That is, $P(X = 4 | n = 50$ and $p = .03) = ?$

Solution:

$$\lambda = \mu = n \cdot p = (50)(.03) = 1.5.$$

As $n > 20$ and $n \cdot p \leq 7$, this problem is a candidate for the Poisson
approximation. For $X = 4$, Table A.3 yields a probability of .0471 for
the Poisson approximation. For comparison, working the problem by
the binomial formula yields

$$_{50}C_4\ (.03)^4(.97)^{46} = .0459.$$

The Poisson approximation is .0012 different from the result obtained by using the binomial formula to work the problem.

Large values of n and small values of p usually are not included in binomial distribution tables. Using the Poisson distribution as an approximation can be very helpful in these situations. As n gets large ($n \geq 70$), most calculators cannot compute the factorials needed to use the binomial formula, making use of the formula difficult for large n values and making the Poisson approximation more attractive.

> **Demonstration Problem 5.10**

Suppose that the probability of a bank making a mistake processing a deposit is .0003. If 10,000 deposits (n) are audited, what is the probability that more than six mistakes were made in processing deposits?

Solution:

$$\lambda = \mu = n \cdot p = (10,000)(.0003) = 3.0.$$

Because $n > 20$ and $n \cdot p \leq 7$, the Poisson approximation is close enough to analyze $X > 6$. Table A.3 yields the following probabilities.

$\lambda = 3.0$	
X	**Probability**
7	.0216
8	.0081
9	.0027
10	.0008
11	.0002
12	.0001
	$X > 6 = .0335$

To work this problem by using the binomial formula requires starting with $X = 7$:

$$_{10,000}C_7(.0003)^7(.9997)^{9993}.$$

This process would continue for X values of 8, 9, 10, 11, ..., until the probabilities approach zero. Obviously, this process is impractical, making the Poisson approximation an attractive alternative.

**PROBLEMS
Section 5.3**

5.13 Solve the following problems by using the Poisson formula.
  a. $P(X = 5 | \lambda = 2.3) =$
  b. $P(X = 2 | \lambda = 3.9) =$
  c. $P(X \le 3 | \lambda = 4.1) =$
  d. $P(X = 0 | \lambda = 2.7) =$
  e. $P(X = 1 | \lambda = 5.4) =$
  f. $P(4 < X < 8 | \lambda = 4.4) =$

5.14 Solve the following problems by using the Poisson tables in Appendix A.
  a. $P(X = 6 | \lambda = 3.8) =$
  b. $P(X > 7 | \lambda = 2.9) =$
  c. $P(3 \le X \le 9 | \lambda = 4.2) =$
  d. $P(X = 0 | \lambda = 1.9) =$
  e. $P(X \le 6 | \lambda = 2.9) =$
  f. $P(5 < X \le 8 | \lambda = 5.7) =$

5.15 Sketch the graphs of the following Poisson distributions. Compute the mean and standard deviation for each distribution. Locate the mean on the graph. Note how the probabilities are graphed around the mean.
  a. $\lambda = 6.3$
  b. $\lambda = 1.3$
  c. $\lambda = 8.9$
  d. $\lambda = 0.6$

5.16 On Monday mornings, the First National Bank only has one teller window open for deposits and withdrawals. Experience has shown that the average number of arriving customers in a four-minute interval on Monday mornings is 2.8, and each teller can serve more than that number efficiently. These random arrivals at this bank on Monday mornings are Poisson distributed.
  a. What is the probability that on a Monday morning six customers will arrive in a four-minute interval?
  b. What is the probability that no one will arrive at the bank for deposit or withdrawal during a four-minute interval?

c. Suppose that the teller can serve no more than four customers in any four-minute interval at this window on a Monday morning. What is the probability that, during any given four-minute interval, the teller will be unable to meet the demand? What is the probability that the teller *will* be able to meet the demand? When demand cannot be met during any given interval, a new window is opened. What percentage of the time will a second window have to be opened?

d. What is the probability that three people will arrive during a two-minute period at the bank on Monday mornings to make a deposit or a withdrawal? What is the probability that five or more customers will arrive during an eight-minute period?

5.17 No-hit games are relatively rare events in major league baseball. A database for no-hit games can be established by using the number of no-hit games per season over a long period of time. The following list shows the number of no-hit games pitched in the major leagues each year for the twenty years from 1957 through 1976. Assume that no-hit games are Poisson distributed. Compute λ from the data and answer the questions using this computed λ. Assume that no-hit games are random occurrences and are equally as likely to occur in one year as the next.

Year	Number of No-Hit Games Pitched
1957	1
1958	2
1959	3
1960	3
1961	1
1962	5
1963	3
1964	3
1965	4
1966	1
1967	4
1968	5
1969	6
1970	4
1971	3
1972	3
1973	5
1974	3
1975	2
1976	3

a. Based on these data and the Poisson distribution, what is the probability of having a season with no no-hit games?

b. What is the probability of having ten no-hit games occur in three seasons?

5.18 According to the United Nations Environment Program and World Health Organization, in Bombay, India, air pollution standards for particulate matter are exceeded an average of 5.6 days in every three-week period. Assume that the distribution of number of days exceeding the standards per three-week period is Poisson distributed.

a. What is the probability that the standard is not exceeded on any day during a three-week period?

b. What is the probability that the standard is exceeded six days of a three-week period?

c. What is the probability that the standard is exceeded fifteen or more days during a three-week period? If this outcome actually occurred, what do you conclude?

5.19 The average number of annual trips per family to amusement parks in the United States is Poisson distributed, with a mean of 0.6 trip per year. What is the probability of randomly selecting an American family and finding that:

a. The family did not make a trip to an amusement park last year?

b. The family took one trip to an amusement park last year?

c. The family took two or more trips to amusement parks last year?

d. The family took three or fewer trips to amusement parks over a three-year period?

e. The family took exactly 4 trips to amusement parks during a six-year period?

5.20 Ship collisions in the Houston Ship Channel are rare. Suppose that the number of collisions are Poisson distributed, with a mean of 1.2 collisions every four months.

a. What is the probability of having no collisions occur over a four-month period?

b. What is the probability of having two collisions in a two-month period?

c. What is the probability of having one or less collisions in a six-month period? If this outcome occurs, what do you conclude about ship channel conditions during this period? What do you conclude about ship channel safety awareness during this period? What do you conclude about weather conditions during this period? What do you conclude about lambda?

5.21 A pen company averages 1.2 defective pens per carton produced (200 pens). The number of defects per carton are Poisson distributed.

a. What is the probability of selecting a carton and finding no defective pens?

b. What is the probability of finding eight or more defective pens in a carton?

c. Suppose that a purchaser of these pens will quit buying from the company if a carton contains more than three defectives. What is the probability that a carton contains more than three defective pens?

5.22 A medical researcher estimates that .00004 of the population has a rare blood disorder. If the researcher randomly selects 100,000 people from the population, what is the probability that 7 or more people will have the rare blood disorder? What is the probability that more than 10 people will have the rare blood disorder? Suppose that the researcher gets more than ten people who have the rare blood disorder in the sample of 100,000 but that the sample was taken from a particular geographic region. What might the researcher conclude from the results?

5.23 Based on historical studies, every time a major league batter goes to the plate to bat the probability that he will hit a triple is approximately .009. From a random sample of 300 at bats from baseball history books, what is the probability of finding six or more triples? Assume that every time at bat is independent of all other times at bat.

5.24 According to the Nielsen ratings in 1989, 4.5% of all households watched the "Today Show" on morning television. In an effort to validate this figure for the local television station, a market analyst randomly selects and contacts eighty households on a given day.

a. What is the probability that more than six households watched the "Today Show" that day?

b. What is the probability that none of the households watched the "Today Show" that day?

c. If the Nielsen ratings are correct, how many households would the analyst expect to have watched the "Today Show" on that day?

HYPERGEOMETRIC DISTRIBUTION **5.4**

hypergeometric distribution

Another discrete statistical distribution is the hypergeometric distribution. Statisticians often use the **hypergeometric distribution** to complement the types of analyses that can be made by using the binomial distribution. Recall that the binomial distribution applies, in theory, only to those experiments in which the trials are done with replacement (independent events). The hypergeometric distribution applies only to experiments in which the trials are done without replacement.

The hypergeometric distribution, like the binomial distribution, consists of two possible outcomes: success and failure. However, the user must know the size of the population and the proportion of successes and failures in the population in order to apply the hypergeometric distribution. That is, because the hypergeometric distribution is utilized when sampling is done without replacement, information about population makeup must be known in order to redetermine the probability of a success in each successive trial as the probability changes. The hypergeometric distribution has the following characteristics.

- It is a discrete distribution.
- Each outcome consists of either a success or a failure.
- Sampling is done *without* replacement.
- The population, N, is finite and known.
- The number of successes in the population, X, is known.

Hypergeometric Formula	$$p = \frac{{}_xC_x \cdot {}_{N-x}C_{n-x}}{{}_NC_n},$$ where: N = size of the population
	     n = sample size
	     X = number of successes in the population
	     x = number of successes in the sample; sampling is done *without* replacement

   A hypergeometric distribution is characterized or described by three parameters: N, X, and n. Because of the multitude of possible combinations of these three parameters, creating tables for the hypergeometric distribution is practically impossible. Thus the researcher who selects the hypergeometric distribution for analyzing data must use the hypergeometric formula to calculate each probability. Because this task can be tedious and time-consuming, most researchers use the hypergeometric distribution as a fall-back position when working binomial problems without replacement. Even though the binomial distribution theoretically applies only when sampling is done *with* replacement and p stays constant, recall that, if the population is large enough compared to the sample size, the impact of sampling *without* replacement on p is minimal. Thus the binomial distribution can be used in some situations when sampling is done *without* replacement. Because of the tables available, using the binomial distribution instead of the hypergeometric distribution whenever possible is preferable. As a rule of thumb, if the sample size is less than 5% of the population, use of the binomial distribution rather than the hypergeometric distribution is acceptable when sampling is done *without* replacement. The hypergeometric distribution yields the exact probability, and the binomial distribution yields a good approximation of the probability in these situations. In summary, the hypergeometric distribution should be used instead of the binomial distribution when

1. sampling is being done *without* replacement *and*
2. $n \geq 5\%$ N.

Demonstration Problem 5.11

Twenty-four people, of which eight are women, have applied for a job. If five of the applicants are randomly sampled, what is the probability that three of those sampled are women?

Solution:

This problem contains a small, finite population of twenty-four, or $N = 24$. A sample of five applicants is taken, or $n = 5$. The sampling is being done *without* replacement, because the five applicants selected for the sample are five different people. The sample size is 21% of the population, with is $\geq 5\%$ of the population ($n/N = 5/24 = .21$). The hypergeometric distribution is the appropriate distribution to use. The population breakdown is $X = 8$ women (successes) and $N - X = 24 - 8 = 16$ men. The probability of getting $x = 3$ women in the sample of $n = 5$ is

$$\frac{{}_8C_3 \cdot {}_{16}C_2}{{}_{24}C_5} = \frac{(56)(120)}{42,504} = .1581.$$

Conceptually, the combination in the denominator of the hypergeometric formula yields all the possible ways of getting n samples from a population, N, including the ones with the desired outcome. In Demonstration Problem 5.11, there are 42,504 ways of selecting five people from twenty-four people. The numerator of the hypergeometric formula computes all the possible ways of getting x successes from the X successes available and $n - x$ failures from the $N - X$ available failures in the population. There are 56 ways of getting 3 women from a pool of 8 and there are 120 ways of getting 2 men from a pool of 16. The combinations of each are multiplied in the numerator, because the joint probability of getting x successes *and* $n - x$ failures is being computed.

Demonstration Problem 5.12

Suppose that there are eighteen major computer companies in the United States and that twelve are located in California's Silicon Valley. If three computer companies are randomly selected from the entire list, what is the probability that one or more of the selected companies are located in the Silicon Valley?

Solution:

$$N = 18, \quad n = 3, \quad X = 12, \quad \text{and} \quad x \geq 1.$$

This is actually three problems in one: $x = 1$, $x = 2$, and $x = 3$. Sampling is being done without replacement, and the sample size is 16.6% of the population. Hence this problem is a candidate for the hypergeometric distribution. The solution is

$$\begin{array}{ccc} x = 1 & x = 2 & x = 3 \\ \dfrac{_{12}C_1 \cdot {}_6C_2}{_{18}C_3} + & \dfrac{_{12}C_2 \cdot {}_6C_1}{_{18}C_3} + & \dfrac{_{12}C_3 \cdot {}_6C_0}{_{18}C_3} = \\ .2206 \ + & .4853 \ + & .2696 \ = .9755. \end{array}$$

An alternative solution method using the law of complements would be 1 minus the probability that none of the companies is located in Silicon Valley, or

$$1 - P(x = 0 | N = 18, n = 3, X = 12).$$

Thus

$$1 - \frac{_{12}C_0 \, {}_6C_3}{_{18}C_3} = 1 - .0245 = .9755.$$

PROBLEMS Section 5.4

5.25 Compute the following probabilities by using the hypergeometric formula.

a. The probability of $x = 3$ if $N = 11$, $X = 8$, and $n = 4$

b. The probability of $x < 2$ if $N = 15$, $X = 5$, and $n = 6$

c. The probability of $x = 0$ if $N = 9$, $X = 2$, and $n = 3$

d. The probability of $x > 4$ if $N = 20$, $X = 5$, and $n = 7$

5.26 Listed are the thirteen largest two-year colleges in the United States. According to Peterson's Guides, each of these colleges has an enrollment of more than 25,000 students. Six different two-year colleges are randomly selected for representation on a national committee of educators to discuss the issues of two-year colleges. What is the probability that two of the six are California colleges?

Two-Year Colleges	Enrollment
Community College of the Air Force (Alabama)	389,000
Miami–Dade Community College (Florida)	46,035
Portland Community College (Oregon)	34,400
Northern Virginia Community College (Virginia)	33,466
Houston Community College (Texas)	30,236
Oakland Community College (Michigan)	27,827
San Diego Mesa College (California)	27,000
Pima Community College (Arizona)	26,810
El Camino College (California)	26,784
Long Beach City College (California)	26,044
City College of San Francisco (California)	25,900
Tarrant County Junior College (Texas)	25,857
De Anza College (California)	25,546

5.27 Use the list of two-year colleges in Problem 5.26 to answer the following questions.

a. If four of the colleges are randomly selected, what is the probability that at least two of them have enrollments of more than 28,000 students?

b. If three of the colleges are randomly selected, what is the probability that all three have enrollments of less than 27,000 students?

c. If five of the colleges are randomly selected, what is the probability that San Diego Mesa College is one of the colleges selected?

5.28 W. Edward Deming in his red bead experiment has a box of 4,000 beads, of which 800 are red and 3,200 are white.* Suppose that a researcher were to conduct a modified version of the red bead experiment. In her experiment, she has a bag of 20 beads, of which four are red and 16 are white. This experiment requires a participant to reach into the bag and randomly select 5 beads without replacement.

*Walton, Mary, "Deming's Parable of the Red Beads," *Across the Board* (February 1987):43–48.

James Bernoulli was born in Basel, Switzerland, on Christmas Day in 1654. He was the first of nine distinguished mathematicians with the Bernoulli name. His parents wanted him to become a minister of the Reformed Church, and they encouraged him to study theology. Bernoulli is believed to have become interested in mathematics after he studied some of Euclid's writings. He later became interested in astronomy.

By the time he was twenty-two, Bernoulli had become a scholar and a teacher. For the next five years, he traveled while studying and tutoring. He returned to Basel at the age of twenty-seven and started corresponding with Leibnitz. Bernoulli was one of the first to learn and apply what was then the new differential calculus. He applied calculus to the laws of probability and contributed significantly to the field of statistics from this work. In 1687, he was appointed chair of mathematics of the University of Basel. His teaching was renowned, and students came from all over Europe to study under him.

He wrote his most famous work, *Ars Conjectandi*, during the latter part of his life, but it was not published until after his death in 1705. The fourth part of *Ars Conjectandi* contains Bernoulli's *golden theorem*, which since has become known as Bernoulli's theorem. Bernoulli advanced many other statistical ideas, including the binomial theorem. As a result, binomial trials often are referred to as Bernoulli trials.

Source: Adapted from David, F. N. *Games, Gods, and Gambling* (New York: Hafner, 1962), and Dudycha, Arthur L., and Linda W. Dudycha, "Behavioral Statistics: An Historical Perspective," in *Statistical Issues: A Reader for the Behavioral Sciences*, edited by Roger Kirk (Monterey, Calif.: Brooks/Cole, 1972).

a. What is the probability that the participant will select four white beads?

b. What is the probability that the participant will select four red beads?

c. What is the probability that the participant will get all red beads?

5.29 According to the U.S. Environmental Protection Agency, the top nine cars in fuel economy are the Honda Civic CRX, Honda Civic CRX HF, Geo Metro XFI, Volkswagen Jetta, Chevrolet Corsica, Volkswagen Passat, Honda Civic Wagon, Plymouth Colt Wagon, and Volvo 740 Wagon. Four cars are randomly selected from this list. What is the probability of getting:

a. Two Hondas?

b. At least two Hondas?

c. Zero Hondas?

5.30 A company produces and ships sixteen personal computers knowing that four of them have defective wiring. The company that has purchased the computers is going to thoroughly test three of the computers. The purchasing company can detect the defective wiring when it is there. What is the probability that the purchasing company will find:

a. No defective computers?

b. Three defective computers?

c. Two or more defective computers?

d. One or less defective computer?

5.31 A western city has eighteen police officers who are eligible for promotion. Eleven of the eighteen are Hispanic. Suppose that only five of the police officers are chosen for promotion and that one is Hispanic. If the officers chosen for promotion had been selected by chance alone, what is the probability that one or less of the five promoted officers is Hispanic? What might this result indicate?

CHAPTER SUMMARY

Probability experiments produce random outcomes. A variable that contains the outcomes of a random experiment is called a random variable. Random variables that take on values only at certain points are called discrete random variables. Random variables that take on values at all points over a given interval are called continuous random variables. Discrete distributions are constructed from discrete random variables. Continuous distributions are constructed from continuous random variables. Three discrete distributions are the binomial distribution, Poisson distribution, and hypergeometric distribution.

The binomial distribution fits experiments when only two mutually exclusive outcomes are possible. Each trial in a binomial experiment must be independent of the other trials, and the probability of getting a desired outcome on any one trial is p. The binomial distribution can be used to analyze discrete studies involving such things as heads/tails, defective/good, and male/female. The binomial formula is used to determine the probability of obtaining X outcomes in n trials. Binomial distribution problems can be solved more rapidly with the use of binomial tables than by formula. A binomial table can be constructed for every different pair of n and p values. Table A.2 of Appendix A contains binomial tables for selected values of n and p. The mean or long-run average of a binomial distribution is $\mu = n \cdot p$. The standard deviation of a binomial distribution is $\sqrt{n \cdot p \cdot q}$.

The Poisson distribution usually is used to analyze phenomena that produce rare occurrences. The only information required to generate a Poisson distribution is the long-run average, which is denoted by lambda (λ). The Poisson distribution deals with occurrences over some interval. The assumptions are that each occurrence is independent of the other occurrences and that the value of lambda remains constant throughout the experiment. Some examples of Poisson type experiments are number of flaws per page of paper, number of crashes per 1,000 commercial airline flights, and number of calls per minute to a switchboard. Poisson probabilities can be determined by either the Poisson formula or the Poisson tables in Table A.3 of Appendix A. Lambda is both the mean and the variance of a Poisson distribution. The Poisson distribution can be used to approximate binomial distribution problems when n is large ($n > 20$), p is small, and $n \cdot p \leq 7$.

The hypergeometric distribution is a discrete distribution. It usually is used when the population is small and finite and sampling is done without replacement. Because using the hypergeometric distribution is a tedious process, using the binomial distribution whenever possible usually is more advantageous. Although an assumption underlying the binomial distribution is that the sampling is done with replacement, if the sample size is less than 5% of the population, the approximation is close enough to justify the use of the binomial distribution and to avoid using the hypergeometric distribution.

Key Words

Random variable	Binomial distribution
Discrete random variables	Poisson distribution
Continuous random variables	Lambda
Discrete distributions	Hypergeometric distribution
Continuous distributions	

USING THE COMPUTER

You can manipulate Minitab to produce several of the statistics in Chapter 5. Moreover, you can use Minitab to solve directly two main types of problems: the binomial distribution and the Poisson distribution. Essentially what Minitab can do in these two areas is to produce a table of values for any binomial or Poisson distribution. The main command that you use to accomplish this result is the probability density function, or PDF, command. It produces probabilities for various distributions, depending on the given parameters. For example, to produce a binomial distribution, you need to know the values of n and p. To produce a Poisson distribution, you need to know the value of lambda. The general form of the PDF command is

```
MTB > PDF;
SUBC > (type of distribution) (parameters of that distribution).
```

The PDF command uses a subcommand to delineate the type of distribution requested and the parameters of that distribution. Subcommands can be used when the subcommand prompt is given (SUBC >). To access the subcommand prompts, end the Minitab command with a semicolon (;). The next prompt will be a subcommand prompt (SUBC >), and you will be able to execute the appropriate subcommands. You will continue to get subcommand prompts until a subcommand prompt is terminated by a period (.), in which case the prompt returns to a Minitab command prompt (MTB >).

Using PDF to Generate Binomial Distribution Values

To generate binomial distribution values with Minitab, use the Minitab command: MTB > PDF;. The semicolon at the end of the command will generate a subcommand prompt. The subcommand used to generate binomial distributions is BINOMIAL n p. Insert the values of n and p after the BINOMIAL subcommand with a space, comma, or slash between them. The value of p must have the decimal point. The general form of the commands in Minitab to produce a binomial distribution are

MTB > PDF;
SUBC > BINOMIAL n p.

One of the examples in Chapter 5 uses a binomial distribution with $n = 20$ and $p = .06$. The Minitab commands used to produce this distribution are

MTB > PDF;
SUBC > BINOMIAL 20 .06.

The resulting output is

```
BINOMIAL WITH N = 20   P = 0.060000
      K              P(X = K)
      0                0.2901
      1                0.3703
      2                0.2246
      3                0.0860
      4                0.0233
      5                0.0048
      6                0.0008
      7                0.0001
      8                0.0000
```

Note that the Minitab output stops when the probability zeros out at four decimal places.

Using Minitab to Produce Poisson Distribution Values

In a manner similar to that used with the binomial distribution, you can use Minitab to generate values for the Poisson distribution. The general forms of the commands are

```
MTB > PDF;
SUBC > POISSON λ.
```

Note that the subcommand, POISSON, requires only one parameter following it: the value of lambda. One of the examples in Chapter 5 utilized a Poisson distribution with a lambda value of 1.6. The Minitab commands needed to generate the values of this distribution are

```
MTB > PDF;
SUBC > POISSON 1.6.
```

The resulting output for this Poisson distribution is

```
POISSON WITH MEAN =   1.600
     K              P(X = K)
     0               0.2019
     1               0.3230
     2               0.2584
     3               0.1378
     4               0.0551
     5               0.0176
     6               0.0047
     7               0.0011
     8               0.0002
     9               0.0000
```

SUPPLEMENTARY PROBLEMS

5.32 Solve for the probabilities of the following binomial distribution problems using the binomial formula.
   a. If $n = 11$ and $p = .23$, what is the probability that $X = 4$?
   b. If $n = 6$ and $p = .50$, what is the probability that $X \geq 1$?
   c. If $n = 9$ and $p = .85$, what is the probability that $X > 7$?
   d. If $n = 14$ and $p = .70$, what is the probability that $X \leq 3$?

5.33 Use Table A.2, Appendix A, to solve for the probabilities of the following binomial distribution problems.

a. $P(X = 14 | n = 20 \text{ and } p = .60) =$

b. $P(X < 5 | n = 10 \text{ and } p = .30) =$

c. $P(X \geq 12 | n = 15 \text{ and } p = .60) =$

d. $P(X > 20 | n = 25 \text{ and } p = .40) =$

5.34 Use the Poisson formula to solve for the probabilities of the following Poisson distribution problems.

a. If $\lambda = 1.25$, what is the probability that $X = 4$?

b. If $\lambda = 6.37$, what is the probability that $X \leq 1$?

c. If $\lambda = 2.4$, what is the probability that $X > 5$?

5.35 Use Table A.3, Appendix A, to solve the following Poisson distribution problems.

a. $P(X = 3 | \lambda = 1.8) =$

b. $P(X < 5 | \lambda = 3.3) =$

c. $P(X \geq 3 | \lambda = 2.1) =$

d. $P(2 < X \leq 5 | \lambda = 4.2) =$

5.36 Solve the following problems by using the hypergeometric formula.

a. If $N = 6$, $n = 4$, and $X = 5$, what is the probability that $x = 3$?

b. If $N = 10$, $n = 3$, and $X = 5$, what is the probability that $x \leq 1$?

c. If $N = 13$, $n = 5$, and $X = 3$, what is the probability that $x \geq 2$?

5.37 A beautician has been in business for one year. Sixty percent of her customers are walk-in business. If she randomly samples eight of the people from last week's list of customers, what is the probability that three or less were walk-ins? If this outcome actually occurred, what are some of the explanations for it?

5.38 According to the American Medical Association, as of January 1, 1988, slightly more than 26% of all U.S. physicians under the age of 35 are women. Your company has just hired eight physicians under the age of 35 and none is a woman. If a group of women physicians under the age of 35 want to sue your company for discriminatory hiring practices, would they have a strong case based on these numbers? Use the binomial distribution to determine the probability of the company's hiring result occurring randomly and comment on the potential justification for a lawsuit.

5.39 In a nationwide federal survey of 24,600 eighth graders in 1,000 public and private schools, only about one-half (50%) of the students indicated that their parents had *any* contact with the schools. You believe that your city is different from the national norm, so you randomly sample 25 eighth graders from schools in your city. What is the probability that at least 13 of them would reply that their parents had some contact with the schools last year? Suppose that your survey resulted in 20 saying that their parents had some involvement with the schools last year. What is the probability that you would get 20 or more such parents by chance if the national figures also were true for your city? What is the expected number of parents who had contact with the schools in a sample of 25?

5.40 The National Center for Health Statistics reports that 25% of all Americans between the ages of 65 and 74 have a chronic heart condition. Suppose that you live in a state where the environment is conducive to good health and low stress and that you believe that the conditions in your state promote healthy hearts. To investigate this theory, you conduct a random telephone survey of twenty 65- to 74-year-olds in your state.

   a. Based on the figure from the National Center for Health Statistics, what is the expected number of 65- to 74-year-olds in your survey who have a chronic heart condition?

   b. Suppose that only one person in your survey has a chronic heart condition. What is the probability of getting one or fewer people with chronic heart conditions in a sample of twenty if 25% of the population in this age bracket has this health problem? What do you conclude about your state from the sample data?

5.41 Analysts estimate that AT&T has a 70% share of the U.S. long distance market. If twenty long distance calls are randomly sampled from around the United States, what is the expected number of AT&T calls? What are the mean and standard deviations of the binomial distribution for this sample? Graph the binomial distribution of this sample. Are only ten of the calls likely to be on AT&T's network? Calculate the probability.

5.42 One of viewers' favorite commercials of 1990 was the Eveready battery commercial featuring the obnoxious pink bunny. Unfortunately for Eveready, 40% of the people who named the commercial as the most outstanding ad were sure that it was a Duracell ad. This result is not unusual. According to the *Wall Street Journal,* when number two brands challenge the number one brand by mocking them in ads, consumers often remember the name of the number one brand rather than the number two brand. Suppose that the 40% figure is true for all people who view the ad. If twelve people are randomly selected who have viewed the ad, what is the probability that none says that the commercial is an ad for Duracell? What is the probability that eight or more of the twelve would say that it is a Duracell ad?

5.43 According to the U.S. Bureau of the Census, about 20% of Idaho residents live in metropolitan areas. This percentage is the lowest of all fifty states. A catalog sales company in Georgia has just purchased a list of Idaho consumers. Its market analyst randomly selects twenty-five people from this list.

   a. What is the probability that eight of these people live in metropolitan areas?

   b. What is the probability that the analyst would get more than ten people in this sample who live in metropolitan areas?

c. Suppose that the analyst got more than ten people who live in metropolitan areas from the group of twenty-five. What might he conclude about the company's list of Idaho consumers? What might he conclude about the census figure?

5.44 A survey conducted for the Northwestern National Life Insurance Company early in 1991 revealed that 70% of American workers say that job stress caused frequent health problems. One in three said that they expected to burn out in the job in the near future. Thirty-four percent said that they thought seriously about quitting their job last year because of workplace stress. Fifty-three percent said that they were required to work more than forty hours a week very often or somewhat often.

   a. Suppose that a random sample of ten American workers is selected. What is the probability that more than seven of them say that job stress caused frequent health problems? What is the expected number of workers who say that job stress caused frequent health problems?

   b. Suppose that a random sample of fifteen American workers is selected. What is the expected number of these sampled workers who say that they will burn out in the near future? What is the probability that ten or more say that they will burn out in the near future? What is the probability that none of the fifteen say that they will burn out in the near future?

   c. Suppose that a sample of seven workers is randomly selected. What is the probability that all seven say they are asked very often or somewhat often to work more than forty hours a week? If this outcome actually happened, what do you conclude?

5.45 In previous semesters, during the last hour and a half of a three-hour final test in statistics, examinations were turned in according to a Poisson distribution, with an average of 1.8 tests per five-minute interval.

   a. What is the probability that four tests will be turned in during a five-minute interval?

   b. What is the probability that nine or more tests will be turned in during a fifteen-minute interval?

   c. What is the probability that no one will turn in an examination during a ten-minute interval? During a five-minute interval?

   d. What is the expected number of examinations to be turned in during a five-minute interval? Sketch the graph of this distribution and note the expected number. What is the value with the highest probability of occurrence during a five-minute interval?

5.46 A service station has a pump that distributes diesel fuel to automobiles. The station owner estimates that only about 3.2 cars use the diesel pump every two hours. Assume that the arrivals of diesel pump users are Poisson distributed.

a. What is the probability that three cars will arrive to use the diesel pump during a one-hour period?

b. Suppose that the owner needs to shut down the diesel pump for half an hour to make repairs. However, the owner hates to lose any business. What is the probability that no cars will arrive to use the diesel pump during a half-hour period?

c. Suppose that five cars arrive during a one-hour period to use the diesel pump. What is the probability of five or more cars arriving during a one-hour period to use the diesel pump? If this outcome actually occurs, what might you conclude?

5.47 One of the earliest applications of the Poisson distribution was in analyzing incoming calls to a telephone switchboard. Analysts generally believe that random phone calls are Poisson distributed. Suppose that phone calls to a switchboard arrive at an average rate of 2.4 calls per minute.

a. If an operator wants to take a one-minute break, what is the probability that there will be no calls during a one-minute interval?

b. If an operator can handle at most five calls per minute, what is the probability that the operator will be unable to handle the calls in any one-minute period?

c. What is the probability that three calls will arrive in a two-minute interval?

d. What is the probability that one or less calls will arrive in a fifteen-second interval?

5.48 Suppose that, for every family vacation trip by car of more than 2,000 miles, an average of .60 flat tires occurs. Suppose also that the distribution of the number of flat tires per trip of more than 2,000 miles is Poisson. What is the probability that a family will take a trip of more than 2,000 miles and have no flat tires? What is the probability that the family will have three or more flat tires on such a trip? Suppose that trips are independent and that the value of lambda holds for all trips of more than 2,000 miles. If a family takes two trips of more than 2,000 miles during a summer, what is the probability that the family will experience no flat tires on either trip?

5.49 Suppose that, for every lot of 100 computer chips a company produces, an average of 1.4 are defective. Another company buys many lots of these chips at a time from which one lot is randomly selected and tested for defects. If the tested lot contains more than 3 defects, the buyer will reject all the lots sent in that batch. What is the probability that the buyer will accept the lots? Assume that the defects per lot are Poisson distributed.

5.50 A binomial distribution problem has $n = 1,000$ and $p = .005$. Use the Poisson distribution to approximate the probability that $x < 4$.

5.51 Suppose that the probability of finding a four-leaf clover among clovers is .0002. If a naturalist randomly examined 10,000 clovers, what is the probability that she would find no four-leaf clovers? What is the probability that she would find three or more four-leaf clovers?

5.52 Only 3% of all American households have only a black-and-white television. A television marketing analyst randomly selects 160 American households.

   a. How many households would she expect to have only a black-and-white television?

   b. What is the probability that ten or more households have only a black-and-white television?

   c. What is the probability that between two and eight households (inclusive) have only a black-and-white television set?

5.53 The following table lists the twenty-six largest U.S. universities according to enrollment figures from the *World Almanac*:

University	Enrollment
Ohio State University—Columbus	53,669
University of Texas at Austin	50,107
Arizona State University	43,426
Michigan State University	42,695
University of Wisconsin—Madison	40,949
Texas A & M University—College Station	39,163
University of Minnesota	38,172
Pennsylvania State—University Park	37,269
University of Maryland—College Park	36,681
University of Illinois—Champaign	36,036
San Diego State University	35,821
University of California at Los Angeles	35,730
University of Michigan	35,220
California State University, Long Beach	35,363
Purdue University—West Lafayette	34,969
University of Arizona	34,725
University of Florida	34,021
Indiana University—Bloomington	33,776
University of Washington	33,460
Northeastern University	32,389
New York University	31,690
University of California at Berkeley	31,612
California State University, Northridge	31,531
Wayne State University	30,751
University of Houston	30,372
University of South Florida	30,003

a. If five different universities are randomly selected from the list, what is the probability that three of them have enrollments of 40,000 or more?

b. If eight different universities are randomly selected from the list, what is the probability that two or fewer are universities in Arizona or California?

c. Suppose that universities are being randomly selected from this list *with* replacement. If five universities are sampled, what is the probability that the sample will contain two universities in Texas?

5.54 According to a 1988 survey commissioned by Cushman and Wakefield, a real estate firm, the sixteen favorite business locations in the United States are as follows:

1. Atlanta, Georgia
2. San Diego, California
3. Boston, Massachusetts
4. Chicago, Illinois
5. Dallas/Fort Worth, Texas
6. Los Angeles, California
7. Washington, D.C.
8. Phoenix, Arizona
9. Columbus, Ohio
10. Minneapolis/St. Paul, Minnesota
11. Norfolk, Virginia
12. Seattle, Washington
13. Sacramento, California
14. New York, New York
15. Tampa, Florida
16. San Francisco, California

Suppose that a company's president decides to use this master list to determine the site location for a new office headquarters. She plans to reduce the list by randomly sampling six cities. What is the probability that the sample will contain one Arizona city? What is the probability that the sample will contain two or more cities that begin with the letter *S*? Suppose that the president defines a city as eastern if it is in Georgia, Massachusetts, Virginia, New York, or Florida, or is the District of Columbia. What is the probability that the sample of six cities will contain at least one eastern city?

5.55 In one midwestern city, the government has fourteen repossessed houses, which are evaluated to be worth about the same. Ten of the houses are located on the north side of town and the rest on the west side. A local contractor has submitted a bid in which he offered to purchase four of the houses. Which houses the contractor will get is subject to a random draw.

a. What is the probability that all four houses selected for the contractor will be located on the north side of town?

b. What is the probability that all four houses selected for the contractor will be located on the west side of town?

c. What is the probability that half of the houses selected for the contractor will be on the west side and half on the north side of town?

5.56 According to the *World Almanac,* twenty-four people work in the Office of the Vice President of the United States. Suppose that six of these people live in Washington, D.C., and the rest live in Virginia. If eight of the twenty-four people are randomly selected, what is the probability that exactly half of the eight live in Washington, D.C.? What is the probability that all of the eight live in Virginia?

5.57 The audiovisual department of a university has thirteen VCRs in its inventory. Because of state contracts, the audiovisual department stocks only two brands. Six of the thirteen VCRs stocked are Toshiba brand, and the others are Zenith brand. A conference is being conducted at the university, and five VCRs will be needed. The five VCRs are randomly selected.

a. What is the probability that all five are Zenith VCRs?

b. What is the probability that all five are Toshiba VCRs?

c. What is the probability that exactly three are Toshiba VCRs?

6

CONTINUOUS DISTRIBUTIONS

CHAPTER LEARNING OBJECTIVES

The primary learning objective of Chapter 6 is to help you understand continuous distributions, thereby enabling you to

1. Appreciate the importance of the normal distribution.
2. Recognize normal distribution problems, and know how to solve such problems.
3. Decide when to use the normal distribution to approximate binomial distribution problems, and know how to work such problems.
4. Decide when to use the exponential distribution to solve problems in business, and know how to work such problems.

THE BATTERY EXPIRATION PROBLEM

The Northwest Battery Company produces a broad line of batteries. The company has developed a new type of AA battery, which it believes has a significantly longer shelf life than others. The manufacturing division is concerned with the expiration date to be printed on the side of the battery. The company wants an expiration date by which no more than 10% of the batteries will lose full power.

Shannon Russell has been given the task of overseeing the research to determine appropriate expiration times. Russell believes that battery shelf life is normally distributed:

Managerial Questions

- Do all batteries have the exact same shelf life?
- What is the average shelf life of an AA battery? How can that value be determined?
- What is the minimal shelf life during which only 10% of the batteries fail to operate?

Whereas Chapter 5 focused on the characteristics and applications of discrete distributions, Chapter 6 concentrates on information about continuous distributions. The many continuous distributions in statistics include the normal distribution, exponential distribution, uniform distribution, t distribution, chi-square distribution, and F distribution. This chapter presents the normal distribution and one other continuous distribution: the exponential distribution.

6.1   NORMAL DISTRIBUTION

normal distribution

Probably the most widely known and used of all distributions is the **normal distribution.** It fits many human characteristics, such as height, weight, length, speed, IQ, scholastic achievement, years of life expectancy, among others. Like their human counterparts, living things in nature, such as trees, animals, insects, and others, possess many characteristics that are normally distributed. Most items produced or filled by machines are normally distributed. Chapter 7 addresses the fact that, when large enough sample sizes are taken, many statistics are normally distributed regardless of the shape of the underlying distribution. Because of its many applications, the normal distribution is an extremely important distribution. Figure 6.1 shows the graphic representation of the normal distribution: the normal curve.

FIGURE 6.1

The Normal Curve

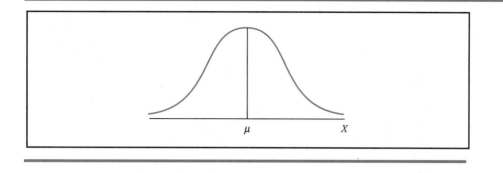

History of the Normal Distribution

Discovery of the normal curve of errors is generally credited to Karl Gauss (1777–1855), mathematician and astronomer, who recognized that the errors of repeated measurement of objects are often normally distributed.[1] Thus the normal distribution is sometimes referred to as the Gaussian distribution or the normal curve of error. A modern day analogy of Gauss's work might be the distribution of measurements of machine produced parts, which often yield a normal curve of error around a mean specification.

To a lesser extent, some credit has been given to Pierre-Simon de Laplace (1749–1827) for discovering the normal distribution. However, many now believe that Abraham de Moivre (1667–1754), a French mathematician, first understood the normal distribution. De Moivre determined that the binomial distribution approached the normal distribution as a limit. De Moivre worked with remarkable accuracy: His published table values for the normal curve are only a few ten-thousandths off the values of presently published tables.[2] The following are the characteristics of the normal distribution.

- It is a continuous distribution.
- It is a symmetrical distribution.
- It is asymptotic to the axis.
- It is unimodal.
- It is a family of curves.
- Area under the curve sums to 1.

The normal distribution is symmetrical. Each half of the distribution is a mirror image of the other half. Many normal distribution tables contain prob-

[1] Ingram, John A., and Joseph G. Monks, *Statistics for Business and Economics* (San Diego: Harcourt Brace Jovanovich, Publishers, 1989).

[2] Kirk, Roger E., *Statistical Issues: A Reader for the Behavioral Sciences* (Monterey, Calif.: Brooks/Cole Publishing Co., 1972).

ability values for only one side of the distribution, because probability values for the other side of the distribution are identical owing to symmetry.

In theory, the normal distribution is asymptotic to the axis. Thus the distribution goes forever in each direction. The reality is that most applications of the normal curve are experiments that have finite limits of potential outcomes. For example, even though SAT scores are analyzed by the normal distribution, the range of SAT scores is only from 200 to 800.

The normal curve sometimes is referred to as the bell-shaped curve. It is unimodal in that values *mound up* in only one portion of the graph—the center of the curve. The normal distribution actually is a family of curves. Every unique value of the mean and every unique value of the standard deviation has a different normal curve. In addition, the total area under any normal distribution sums to 1. The area under the curve yields the probabilities, so the total of all probabilities for a normal distribution is 1. Because the distribution is symmetric, the area of the distribution on each side of the mean is 0.5.

Probability Density Function of the Normal Distribution

The normal distribution is described or characterized by two parameters: μ and σ. The values of μ and σ produce a normal distribution. The mathematical function of the normal distribution is

$$f(X) = \frac{1}{\sigma\sqrt{2\pi}}e^{-(1/2)[(X-\mu)/\sigma]^2},$$

where: μ = mean of X
σ = standard deviation of X
σ^2 = variance of X
π = 3.14159 . . .
e = 2.71828 . . .

Because the formula is so complex, using it to determine areas under the curve is difficult. Virtually all researchers use table values to analyze normal distribution problems rather than this formula.

Standardized Normal Distribution

Every unique pair of μ and σ values has a different normal distribution. Figure 6.2 shows the graphs of normal distributions for three pairs of parameters:

1. μ = 50 and σ = 5
2. μ = 80 and σ = 5
3. μ = 50 and σ = 10

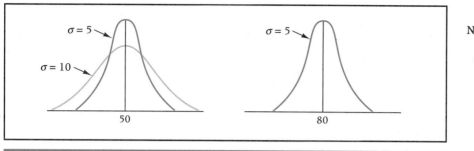

FIGURE 6.2

Normal Curves for Three
Different Combinations
of Means and Standard
Deviations

Note that every change in a parameter (μ or σ) determines a different normal distribution. This characteristic of the normal curve (a *family* of curves) could make analysis by the normal distribution tedious, because volumes of normal curve tables—one for each different combination of μ and σ—would be required. Fortunately, a mechanism was developed by which all normal distributions can be converted into a single distribution: the Z distribution. This process yields the **standardized normal distribution** (or curve). The conversion formula for any X value of a given normal distribution is

standardized normal distribution

$$Z = \frac{X - \mu}{\sigma}.$$

Z Formula

A **Z score** is the number of standard deviations that a value, X, is away from the mean. If the value of X is less than the mean, the Z score is negative; if the value of X is more than the mean, the Z score is positive. This formula allows conversion of the distance of any X value from its mean into standard deviation units. A standard Z table can be used to find probabilities for any normal curve problem that has been converted to Z scores. The **Z distribution** is a normal distribution with a mean of 0 and a standard deviation of 1. That is, any value of X at the mean of a normal curve is 0 standard deviations from the mean. Also, about 68% of the Z scores fall within a range of ± 1, because 1 is the value of the standard deviation of the Z distribution.

Z score

Z distribution

The Z distribution probability values are given in Table A.5. Because it is so frequently used, the Z distribution is also printed inside the back cover of this text. For discussion purposes, a copy of Z distribution values is presented in Table 6.1.

TABLE 6.1

Z Distribution

Second Decimal Place in Z

Z	0.00	0.01	0.02	0.03	0.04	0.05	0.06	0.07	0.08	0.09
0.0	.0000	.0040	.0080	.0120	.0160	.0199	.0239	.0279	.0319	.0359
0.1	.0398	.0438	.0478	.0517	.0557	.0596	.0636	.0675	.0714	.0753
0.2	.0793	.0832	.0871	.0910	.0948	.0987	.1026	.1064	.1103	.1141
0.3	.1179	.1217	.1255	.1293	.1331	.1368	.1406	.1443	.1480	.1517
0.4	.1554	.1591	.1628	.1664	.1700	.1736	.1772	.1808	.1844	.1879
0.5	.1915	.1950	.1985	.2019	.2054	.2088	.2123	.2157	.2190	.2224
0.6	.2257	.2291	.2324	.2357	.2389	.2422	.2454	.2486	.2517	.2549
0.7	.2580	.2611	.2642	.2673	.2704	.2734	.2764	.2794	.2823	.2852
0.8	.2881	.2910	.2939	.2967	.2995	.3023	.3051	.3078	.3106	.3133
0.9	.3159	.3186	.3212	.3238	.3264	.3289	.3315	.3340	.3365	.3389
1.0	.3413	.3438	.3461	.3485	.3508	.3531	.3554	.3577	.3599	.3621
1.1	.3643	.3665	.3686	.3708	.3729	.3749	.3770	.3790	.3810	.3830
1.2	.3849	.3869	.3888	.3907	.3925	.3944	.3962	.3980	.3997	.4015
1.3	.4032	.4049	.4066	.4082	.4099	.4115	.4131	.4147	.4162	.4177
1.4	.4192	.4207	.4222	.4236	.4251	.4265	.4279	.4292	.4306	.4319
1.5	.4332	.4345	.4357	.4370	.4382	.4394	.4406	.4418	.4429	.4441
1.6	.4452	.4463	.4474	.4484	.4495	.4505	.4515	.4525	.4535	.4545
1.7	.4554	.4564	.4573	.4582	.4591	.4599	.4608	.4616	.4625	.4633
1.8	.4641	.4649	.4656	.4664	.4671	.4678	.4686	.4693	.4699	.4706
1.9	.4713	.4719	.4726	.4732	.4738	.4744	.4750	.4756	.4761	.4767
2.0	.4772	.4778	.4783	.4788	.4793	.4798	.4803	.4808	.4812	.4817
2.1	.4821	.4826	.4830	.4834	.4838	.4842	.4846	.4850	.4854	.4857
2.2	.4861	.4864	.4868	.4871	.4875	.4878	.4881	.4884	.4887	.4890
2.3	.4893	.4896	.4898	.4901	.4904	.4906	.4909	.4911	.4913	.4916
2.4	.4918	.4920	.4922	.4925	.4927	.4929	.4931	.4932	.4934	.4936
2.5	.4938	.4940	.4941	.4943	.4945	.4946	.4948	.4949	.4951	.4952
2.6	.4953	.4955	.4956	.4957	.4959	.4960	.4961	.4962	.4963	.4964
2.7	.4965	.4966	.4967	.4968	.4969	.4970	.4971	.4972	.4973	.4974
2.8	.4974	.4975	.4976	.4977	.4977	.4978	.4979	.4979	.4980	.4981
2.9	.4981	.4982	.4982	.4983	.4984	.4984	.4985	.4985	.4986	.4986
3.0	.4987	.4987	.4987	.4988	.4988	.4989	.4989	.4989	.4990	.4990
3.1	.4990	.4991	.4991	.4991	.4992	.4992	.4992	.4992	.4993	.4993
3.2	.4993	.4993	.4994	.4994	.4994	.4994	.4994	.4995	.4995	.4995
3.3	.4995	.4995	.4995	.4996	.4996	.4996	.4996	.4996	.4996	.4997
3.4	.4997	.4997	.4997	.4997	.4997	.4997	.4997	.4997	.4997	.4998
3.5	.4998									
4.0	.49997									
4.5	.499997									
5.0	.4999997									

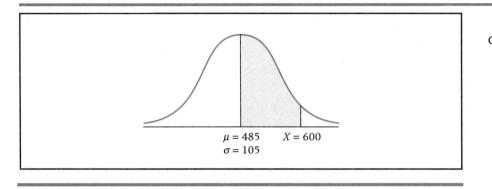

FIGURE 6.3

Graphical Depiction of
the Area Between a
Score of 600 and a
Mean on a GMAT

Working Normal Curve Problems

The mean and standard deviation of a normal distribution and the Z formula
and table allow a researcher to determine the probabilities for intervals of any
particular values of a normal curve. Let's examine some possible probability
values of Graduate Management Aptitude Test (GMAT) scores.* The GMAT is
widely used by graduate schools of business in the United States as an entrance
requirement. In one particular year, the mean score for the GMAT was 485,
with a standard deviation of 105. For these parameters—and assuming that
GMAT scores are normally distributed—what is the probability that a randomly
selected score from this administration of the GMAT falls between 600 and the
mean? That is,

$$P(485 \leq X \leq 600 | \mu = 485 \text{ and } \sigma = 105) = ?$$

Figure 6.3 shows a graphic representation of this problem.

The Z formula yields the number of standard deviations that the X value,
600, is away from the mean:

$$Z = \frac{X - \mu}{\sigma} = \frac{600 - 485}{105} = \frac{115}{105} = 1.10.$$

The Z value of 1.10 reveals that the GMAT score of 600 is 1.1 standard deviations more than the mean. The Z distribution values in Table 6.1 give the
probability. The whole number and tenths place portion of the Z score appear
in the first column of Table 6.1 (the 1.1 portion of this Z score). Across the
top of the table are the values of the hundredths place portion of the Z score.
For this Z score, the hundredths place value is 0, so the first column contains
the answer. The probability value in Table 6.1 for $Z = 1.10$ is .3643. The shaded
portion of the curve at the top of the table indicates that the probability value

The Official Guide for GMAT Review (Princeton, N.J.: Educational Testing Service, 1988).

FIGURE 6.4

Graphical Solutions to
GMAT Problem

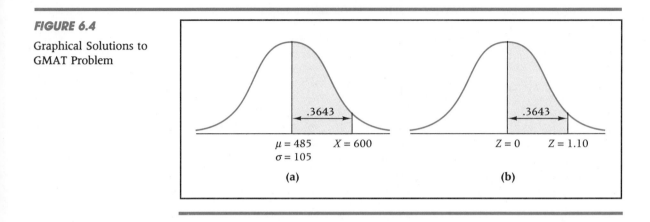

given *always* is the probability or area between an X value and the mean. In this particular example, that is the desired area. Thus the answer is that .3643 of the scores on the GMAT fall between a score of 600 and the mean of 485. Figure 6.4(a) depicts graphically the solution in terms of X values. Figure 6.4(b) shows the solution in terms of Z values.

**Demonstration
Problem 6.1**

What is the probability of obtaining a score greater than 700 on a GMAT test that has a mean of 485 and a standard deviation of 105? Assume that GMAT scores are normally distributed.

$$P(X > 700 | \mu = 485 \text{ and } \sigma = 105) = ?$$

Solution:

Examine the following diagram.

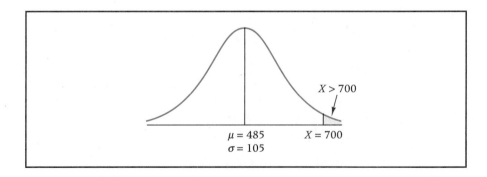

This problem calls for determining the area of the upper tail of the distribution. The Z score for this problem is

$$Z = \frac{X - \mu}{\sigma} = \frac{700 - 485}{105} = \frac{215}{105} = 2.05.$$

Table 6.1 gives a probability of .4798 for this Z score. However, the table gives the area between an X value and the mean, which in this case is .4798. This value is the probability of randomly drawing a GMAT with a score between the mean and 700. Finding the probability of getting a score greater than 700, which is the tail of the distribution, requires subtracting the probability value of .4798 from .5000, because each half of the distribution contains .5000 of the area. The result is .0202. Note that an attempt to determine the area of $X \geq 700$ instead of $X > 700$ would have made no difference, because, in continuous distributions, the area under an exact number such as $X = 700$ is zero. A line segment has no width and hence no area.

$$\begin{array}{l} .5000 \text{ (probability of } X \text{ greater than the mean)} \\ \underline{-.4798} \text{ (probability of } X \text{ between 700 and the mean)} \\ .0202 \text{ (probability of } X \text{ greater than 700)} \end{array}$$

The solution is depicted graphically in (a) for X values and in (b) for Z values.

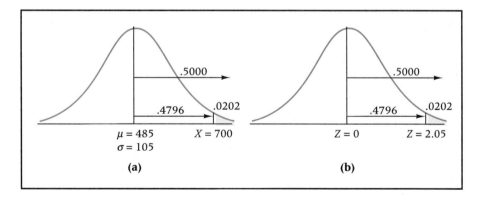

For the same GMAT examination, what is the probability of randomly drawing a score that is 550 or less?

$$P(X \leq 550 | \mu = 485 \text{ and } \sigma = 105) = ?$$

Solution:

A sketch of this problem is shown. Determine the area under the curve for all values of less than or equal to 550.

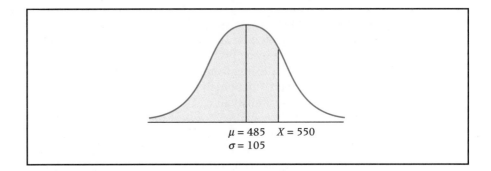

$$\mu = 485 \quad X = 550$$
$$\sigma = 105$$

The Z formula yields the area between 550 and the mean:

$$Z = \frac{X - \mu}{\sigma} = \frac{550 - 485}{105} = \frac{65}{105} = 0.62.$$

The area under the curve for $Z = 0.62$ is .2324, which is the probability of getting a score between 550 and the mean. However, obtaining the probability for all values less than or equal to 550 also requires including the values less than the mean. Because one-half or .5000 of the values are less than the mean, the probability of $X \leq 550$ is

.5000 (probability of values less than the mean)
+.2324 (probability of values between 550 and the mean)
.7324 (probability of values $\leq$ 550)

This solution is depicted graphically in (a) for X values and in (b) for Z values.

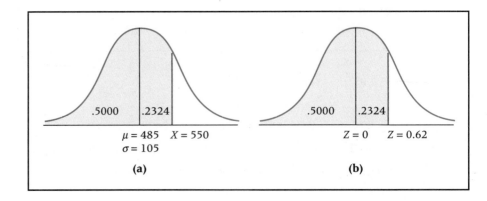

.5000   .2324   .5000   .2324

$\mu = 485 \quad X = 550$ $Z = 0 \quad\quad Z = 0.62$
$\sigma = 105$

(a)   (b)

What is the probability of getting a score of less than 400 on the same GMAT test?

$$P(X < 400 | \mu = 485 \text{ and } \sigma = 105) = ?$$

Solution:

The sketch reveals that the problem is to determine the area of the lower tail of the distribution.

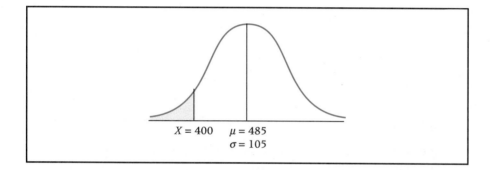

$$X = 400 \qquad \mu = 485$$
$$\sigma = 105$$

The Z score for this problem is

$$Z = \frac{X - \mu}{\sigma} = \frac{400 - 485}{105} = \frac{-85}{105} = -0.81.$$

Note that this Z value is negative and that none of the Z values in Table 6.1 is negative. However, because the normal distribution is symmetric, probabilities for X values on the left, or negative, side of the distribution are the same as the values on the right, or positive, side of the distribution. The negative sign in the Z value merely indicates that the area is on the left side of the distribution. Table 6.1 yields a probability of .2910 for a Z value of 0.81. The problem is to find the area in the lower tail of the distribution, so the probability, .2910, must be subtracted from .5000 to obtain the answer.

     .5000 (probability of a value less than the mean)
   $-$.2910 (probability of a value between 400 and the mean)
     .2090 (probability of a value less than 400)

Graphically, the solution is shown in (a) for X values and in (b) for Z values.

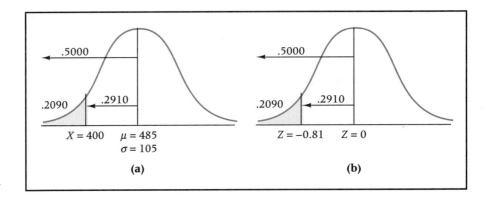

(a)   (b)

Demonstration Problem 6.4

What is the probability of randomly obtaining a score between 300 and 600 on the same GMAT exam?

$$P(300 < X < 600 | \mu = 485 \text{ and } \sigma = 105) = ?$$

Solution:

The sketch depicts the problem graphically: Determine the area between $X = 300$ and $X = 600$, which spans the mean value. As areas in the Z distribution are given in relation to the mean, this problem must be worked as two separate problems and the results combined.

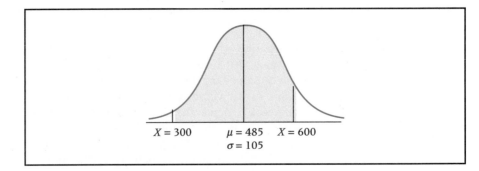

A Z score is determined for each X value:

$$Z = \frac{X - \mu}{\sigma} = \frac{600 - 485}{105} = \frac{115}{105} = 1.10,$$

and

$$Z = \frac{X - \mu}{\sigma} = \frac{300 - 485}{105} = \frac{-185}{105} = -1.76.$$

The probability for $Z = 1.10$ is .3643; the probability for $Z = -1.76$ is .4608. The solution of $P(300 < X < 600)$ is obtained by summing the probabilities:

.3643 (probability of a value between the mean and 600)
+.4608 (probability of a value between the mean and 300)
.8251 (probability of a value between 300 and 600)

Graphically, the solution is shown in (a) for X values and in (b) for Z values.

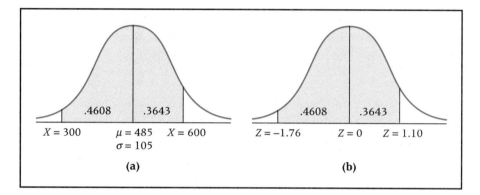

**Demonstration
Problem 6.5**

What is the probability of getting a score between 350 and 450 on the same GMAT exam?

$$P(350 < X < 450 | \mu = 485 \text{ and } \sigma = 105) = ?$$

Solution:

The sketch reveals that the solution to the problem involves determining the area of the shaded slice in the lower half of the curve.

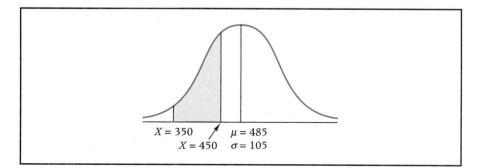

In this problem, the two X values fall on the same side of the mean. The areas or probabilities of each X value must be determined and the final probability found by determining the difference between the two areas.

$$Z = \frac{X - \mu}{\sigma} = \frac{350 - 485}{105} = \frac{-135}{105} = -1.29,$$

and

$$Z = \frac{X - \mu}{\sigma} = \frac{450 - 485}{105} = \frac{-35}{105} = -0.33.$$

The probability associated with $Z = -1.29$ is .4015.
The probability associated with $Z = -0.33$ is .1293.

Subtracting gives

    .4015 (probability of a value between 350 and the mean)
  $-$.1293 (probability of a value between 450 and the mean)
    .2722 (probability of a value between 350 and 450)

Graphically, the solution is shown in (a) for X values and in (b) for Z values.

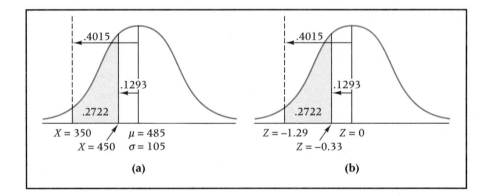

	(a)		(b)

Demonstration
Problem 6.6

According to the National Park Service, the 1989 summer average concentration of sulfates as measured in micrograms per cubic meter for the Shenandoah National Park was 11.1. Suppose that the standard deviation of sulfate concentration for that summer was 3.25. What is the probability that the level of sulfates for a randomly selected day during that summer was between 12 and 15?

$$P(12 \le X \le 15 \mid \mu = 11.1 \text{ and } \sigma = 3.25) = ?$$

Solution:

The diagram shows the mean and standard deviation of the curve, along with the shaded area for which the probability is to be determined.

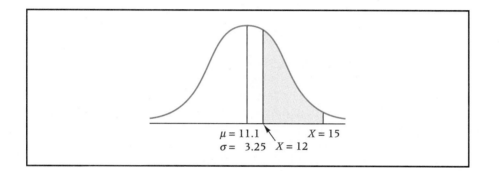

This problem involves two X values and thus requires two different Z scores. The probabilities of these Z scores are then used to solve for the final probability.

$$Z = \frac{X - \mu}{\sigma} = \frac{15 - 11.1}{3.25} = \frac{3.9}{3.25} = 1.20,$$

and

$$Z = \frac{X - \mu}{\sigma} = \frac{12 - 11.1}{3.25} = \frac{0.9}{3.25} = 0.28.$$

Area between $X = 15$ and the mean:	.3849
Area between $X = 12$ and the mean:	$-.1103$
Area between $X = 12$ and $X = 15$:	.2746

The answer is .2746, or 27.46% of all days during the summer of 1989 had sulfate levels between 12 and 15 in the Shenandoah National Park. Graphically, the solution is depicted in (a) for X values and in (b) for Z values.

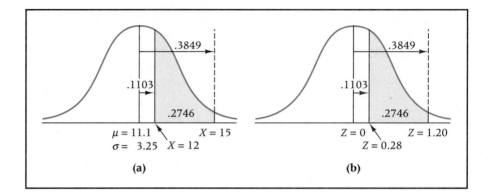

(a)   (b)

**Demonstration
Problem 6.7**

The differences between the rise and fall of ocean tides along the U.S.
coasts vary considerably. The tides on the upper coast of Maine produce
some of the greatest differences between high and low tides in the
country. Suppose that the differences between high and low tides for
a given location on the coast are normally distributed. If 86.65% of
the differences in high and low tides in Eastport, Maine, are less than
21.52 ft and if the standard deviation of these differences is 2.9 ft, what
is the average difference in high and low tides in Eastport, Maine?

Solution:

In this problem, the standard deviation and an X value are given; the
object is to determine the value of the mean. Examination of the Z-
score formula reveals four variables: X, μ, σ, and Z. In this problem,
only two of the four variables are given. Because solving one equation
with two unknowns is impossible, one of the other unknowns must
be determined. The value of Z can be determined from the normal
distribution table (Table 6.1).

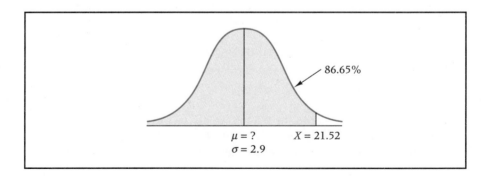

As 86.65% of the values are less than $X = 21.52$, 36.65% of the tidal differences lie between 21.52 ft and the mean. The other 50% of the differences lies in the lower half of the distribution. Converting the percentage to a proportion yields .3665 of the values between the X value and the mean. What Z value is associated with this area? This area, or probability, of .3665 in Table 6.1 is associated with the Z value of 1.11. This Z value is positive, because it is in the upper half of the distribution. Using the Z value of 1.11, the X value of 21.52, and the σ value of 2.9 allows solving for the mean algebraically:

$$Z = \frac{X - \mu}{\sigma},$$

$$1.11 = \frac{21.52 - \mu}{2.9},$$

and

$$\mu = 21.52 - (2.9)(1.11) = 18.3.$$

The mean tidal difference in Eastport, Maine, is 18.3 ft.

Demonstration Problem 6.8

The U.S. Environmental Protection Agency publishes figures on solid waste generation in the United States. In 1986, the average amount of waste generated per person per day was 3.58 lb. Suppose that the daily amount of waste generated per person is normally distributed, with a standard deviation of 1.04 lb. Of the daily amounts of waste generated per person, 67.72% would be greater than what amount?

Solution:

The mean and standard deviation are given, but X and Z are unknown. The problem is to solve for an X value that has .6772 of the X values greater than that value.

If .6772 of the values are greater than X, then .1772 lie between X and the mean (.6772 − .5000). Table 6.1 shows that the probability of .1772 is associated with a Z value of 0.46. As X is less than the mean, the Z value actually is −0.46. Whenever an X value is less than the mean, its associated Z value is negative and should be reported that way.

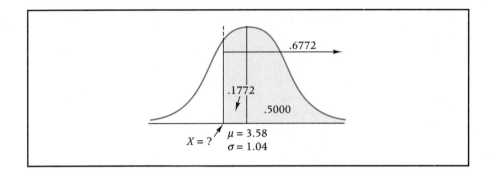

Solving the Z equation yields

$$Z = \frac{X - \mu}{\sigma},$$

$$-0.46 = \frac{X - 3.58}{1.04},$$

and

$$X = 3.58 + (-0.46)(1.04) = 3.10.$$

Thus 67.72% of the daily average amounts of solid waste per person weighs more than 3.10 lb.

PROBLEMS
Section 6.1

6.1 Find the table values for the following Z scores.
   a. $Z = 2.34$
   b. $Z = 1.64$
   c. $Z = 0.81$
   d. $Z = -2.93$
   e. $Z = -0.42$

6.2 Determine the probability or area for the portions of the normal distribution described.
   a. $Z \geq 1.96$
   b. $Z < 0.73$
   c. $1.46 < Z \leq 2.84$
   d. $-2.67 \leq Z \leq 1.08$
   e. $-2.05 < Z \leq -0.87$

6.3 Find the Z scores for the following normal distribution problems.

    a. $\mu = 100, \sigma = 9, X = 115$

    b. $\mu = 34, \sigma = 2.16, X = 35$

    c. $\mu = 259, \sigma = 30.6, X = 251$

    d. $\mu = 157, \sigma = 3.45, X = 145$

6.4 Determine the probabilities for the following normal distribution problems.

    a. $\mu = 604, \sigma = 56.8, X \leq 635$

    b. $\mu = 48, \sigma = 12, X < 20$

    c. $\mu = 111, \sigma = 33.8, 100 \leq X < 150$

    d. $\mu = 264, \sigma = 10.9, 250 < X < 255$

    e. $\mu = 37, \sigma = 4.35, X > 35$

    f. $\mu = 156, \sigma = 11.4, X \geq 170$

6.5 Suppose that you are working with a data set that is normally distributed, with a mean of 200 and a standard deviation of 47. Determine the value of X from the following information.

    a. 60% of the values are greater than X.

    b. X is less than 17% of the values.

    c. 22% of the values are less than X.

    d. X is greater than 55% of the values.

6.6 Work the following problems, assuming that the data are normally distributed.

    a. The standard deviation of the distribution is 12.56, and 71.97% of the values are greater than 56. What is the value of μ?

    b. The mean of the distribution is 352, and only 13.35% of the values are less than 300. What is the value of σ?

6.7 The U.S. Environmental Protection Agency reports the average annual fuel costs for various makes of cars. For the 1990 Oldsmobile Custom Cruiser the average is $788. Suppose that annual fuel costs for any make of automobile are normally distributed and that the standard deviation of annual fuel costs for the 1990 Oldsmobile Custom Cruiser is $113. A 1990 Oldsmobile Custom Cruiser is randomly selected from those that were sold.

    a. What is the probability that the annual fuel cost is greater than $700?

    b. What is the probability that the annual fuel cost is less than $500?

    c. What is the probability that the annual fuel cost is between $800 and $1,000?

6.8 Suppose that the standard deviation for Problem 6.7 is unknown. If 72.4% of all 1990 Oldsmobile Custom Cruisers had an annual fuel cost greater than $650, what would be the value of the standard deviation?

6.9 Suppose the average annual fuel cost for Problem 6.7 is unknown. Using the standard deviation of Problem 6.7, what is the value of the mean annual fuel cost for the Oldsmobile Custom Cruiser if 31% of the annual fuel costs are less than $700?

6.10 According to Ronald T. Reuther, the average life of a cow is 15 years with a maximum longevity of 30 years. Suppose that the average life spans of cows are normally distributed, with a standard deviation of 4.87 years.

   a. What is the probability that a cow will live to be more than 25 years old?

   b. What is the probability that a cow will live to be between 10 and 20 years old?

   c. What is the probability that a cow will live to be no more than 5 years old?

   d. What is the probability that a cow will live to be between 17 and 19 years old?

6.11 Data accumulated by the National Climatic Data Center shows that the average wind speed in miles per hour for St. Louis, Missouri, is 9.7 mph. Suppose that wind speed measurements are normally distributed for a given geographical location. If 22.45% of the time the wind speed measurements are more than 11.6 mph, what is the variance of wind speed in St. Louis?

6.12 According to the Internal Revenue Service, 1990 income tax returns averaged $911 in refunds for taxpayers. One explanation of this figure is that taxpayers would rather have the government keep back too much money during the year than to owe it money at the end of the year. Suppose that the average amount of tax at the end of a year is a refund of $911, with a standard deviation of $525. Assume that amounts owed or due on tax returns are normally distributed.

   a. What proportion of tax returns show a refund of greater than $1,500?

   b. What proportion of the tax returns show that the taxpayer owes money to the government?

   c. What proportion of the tax returns show a refund of between $100 and $500?

6.13 Suppose that hourly prime interest rates for 1991 are normally distributed with a mean of 10.1% and a standard deviation of 0.4%.

   a. What proportion of the hours registered a prime interest rate of more than 9.5%?

   b. What proportion of the hours registered a prime interest rate of between 10% and 11%?

   c. What proportion of the hours registered a prime interest rate of less than 9%?

   d. What proportion of the hours registered a prime interest rate of between 9.5% and 10.5%?

6.14 Toolworkers are subject to work-related injuries. One disorder, caused by strains to the hands and wrists, is called carpel tunnel syndrome. This disorder strikes as many as 23,000 workers per year. The U.S. Labor Department estimates that the average cost of this disorder to employers and insurers is approximately $30,000 per injured worker. Suppose that these costs are normally distributed, with a standard deviation of $9,000.

a. What proportion of the costs fall between $15,000 and $45,000?

b. What proportion of the costs are greater than $50,000?

c. What proportion of the costs fall between $5,000 and $20,000?

d. Suppose that the standard deviation was unknown but that 90.82% of the costs were more than $7,000. What would be the value of the standard deviation?

e. Suppose that the mean value was unknown but that the standard deviation was still $9,000. How much would the average cost be if 79.95% of the costs were less than $33,000?

USING THE NORMAL CURVE TO WORK BINOMIAL DISTRIBUTION PROBLEMS | **6.2**

For certain types of binomial distribution problems, the normal distribution can be used to approximate the probabilities. As sample sizes get large, binomial distributions approach the normal distribution in shape regardless of the value of p. This phenomenon occurs faster (for smaller values of n) when p is near .50. Figures 6.5–6.7 show three binomial distributions. Note that in Figure 6.5 even though the sample size, n, is only 10, the binomial graph bears a strong resemblance to a normal curve.

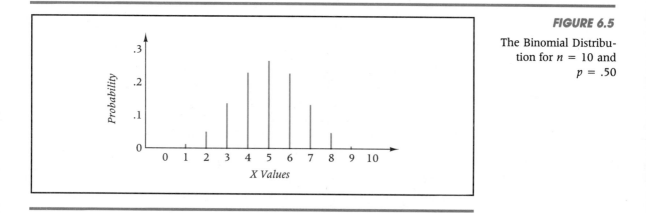

FIGURE 6.5

The Binomial Distribution for $n = 10$ and $p = .50$

FIGURE 6.6

The Binomial Distribution for $n = 10$ and $p = .20$

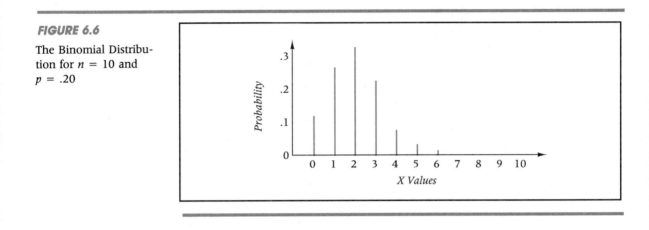

FIGURE 6.7

The Binomial Distribution for $n = 100$ and $p = .20$

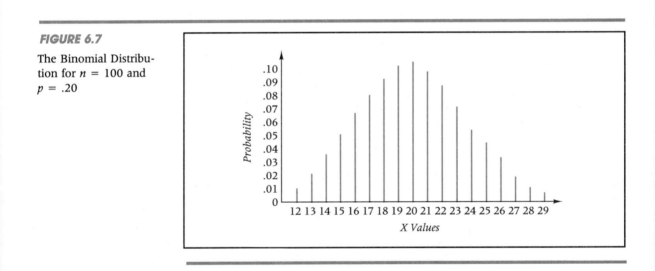

The graph in Figure 6.6 ($n = 10$ and $p = .20$) is skewed to the right because of the low p value and the small sample size. For this distribution, the expected value is only 2 and the probabilities pile up at $X = 0$ and 1. However, when n gets large enough, as in the binomial distribution ($n = 100$ and $p = .20$) presented in Figure 6.7, the graph becomes relatively symmetrical around the mean ($\mu = n \cdot p = 20$), because there are enough possible outcome values to the left of $X = 20$ to allow the curve to fall back to the X axis.

For large n values, the binomial distribution is cumbersome to analyze without a computer. Table A.2 only goes to $n = 25$. Because of the size of the factorials involved, using calculators to work binomial problems when n is large is difficult or impossible. Fortunately, the normal distribution is a good approximation for binomial distribution problems for large values of n.

To work a binomial problem by the normal curve requires a translation process. The first part of this process is to convert the two parameters of a binomial distribution, n and p, to the two parameters of the normal distribution, μ and σ. This conversion utilizes formulas from Chapter 5:

$$\mu = n \cdot p \quad \text{and} \quad \sigma = \sqrt{n \cdot p \cdot q}.$$

Conversion of a Binomial Problem to the Normal Curve

After completion of this conversion, a test must be made to determine whether the normal distribution is a good enough approximation of the binomial distribution:

Does the interval $\mu \pm 3\sigma$ lie between 0 and n?

Recall that the empirical rule states that approximately 99.7%, or almost all, of the values of a normal curve lie within three standard deviations of the mean. For a normal curve approximation of a binomial distribution problem to be acceptable, all possible X values should fall between 0 and n, which are the lower and upper limits, respectively, of a binomial distribution. If $\mu \pm 3\sigma$ does not lie between 0 and n, do *not* use the normal distribution to work a binomial problem, because the approximation is not good enough. Upon demonstration that the normal curve is a good approximation for a binomial problem, the procedure continues.

The process can be illustrated in the solution of the binomial distribution problem:

$$P(X \geq 25 | n = 60 \text{ and } p = .30) = ?$$

Note that this binomial problem contains a relatively large sample size and that none of the binomial tables in Appendix A.2 can be used to solve the problem. This problem is a good candidate for use of the normal distribution.

Translating from a binomial problem to a normal curve problem gives

$$\mu = n \cdot p = (60)(.30) = 18 \quad \text{and} \quad \sigma = \sqrt{n \cdot p \cdot q} = 3.55.$$

The binomial problem becomes a normal curve problem:

$$P(X \geq 25 | \mu = 18 \text{ and } \sigma = 3.55) = ?$$

Next, the test is made to determine whether the normal curve sufficiently fits this binomial distribution to justify the use of the normal curve:

$$\mu \pm 3\sigma = 18 \pm 3(3.55) = 18 \pm 10.65;$$
$$7.35 \le \mu \pm 3\sigma \le 28.65.$$

This interval lies between 0 and 60, so the approximation is sufficient to allow use of the normal curve. Figure 6.8 depicts the apparent graph of the normal curve version of this problem.

Correcting for Continuity

correction for continuity

The translation of a discrete distribution to a continuous distribution is not completely straightforward. A correction of $+.50$ or $-.50$ or $\pm.50$, depending on the problem, is required. This correction ensures that most of the binomial problem's information is correctly transferred to the normal curve analysis. This correction is called the **correction for continuity**, which is made during conversion of a discrete distribution into a continuous distribution.

Figure 6.9 shows a portion of the graph of the binominal distribution, $n = 60$ and $p = .30$. Note that with a binomial distribution, all the probabilities are concentrated on the whole numbers. Thus the answers for $X \ge 25$ are found by summing the probabilities for $X = 25, 26, 27, \ldots, 60$. There are *no* values between 24 and 25, 25 and 26, ..., 59 and 60. Yet, the normal distribution is continuous, and values exist all along the X axis. A correction must be made for this discrepancy in order for the approximation to be as accurate as possible.

As an analogy, visualize the process of melting iron rods in a furnace. The iron rods are like the probability values on each whole number of a binomial distribution. Note that the binomial graph in Figure 6.9 looks like a series of iron rods in a line. When the rods are placed in a furnace, they melt down and spread out. Each rod melts and moves to fill the area between it and the adjacent rods. The result is a continuous sheet of solid iron (continuous iron) that looks like the normal curve. The melting of the rods is analogous to spreading the binomial distribution to approximate the normal distribution.

FIGURE 6.8

Graph of Apparent Solution of Binomial Problem Worked by the Normal Curve

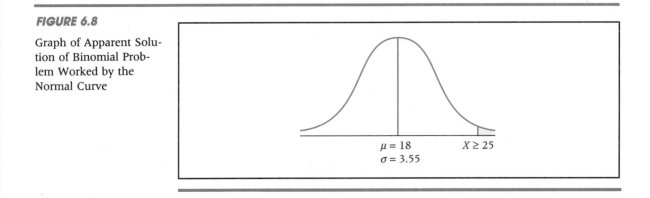

$\mu = 18$ $X \ge 25$
$\sigma = 3.55$

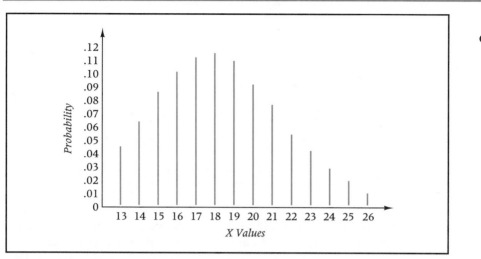

FIGURE 6.9

Graph of the Binomial Problem: $n = 60$ and $p = .30$

How far does each rod spread toward the others? A good estimate is that each rod goes about half way toward the adjacent rods. In other words, a rod that was concentrated at $X = 25$ spreads to cover the area from 24.5 to 25.5; $X = 26$ becomes continuous from 25.5 to 26.5; and so on. For the problem $P(X \geq 25 \mid n = 60$ and $p = .30)$, conversion to a continuous normal curve problem yields $P(X \geq 24.5 \mid \mu = 18$ and $\sigma = 3.55)$. The correction for continuity was $-.50$, because the problem called for the inclusion of the value of 25 along with all greater values; the binomial value of $X = 25$ translates to the normal curve value of from 24.5 to 25.5. Had the binomial problem been to analyze $P(X > 25)$, the correction would have been $+.50$, resulting in a normal curve problem of $P(X \geq 25.5)$. This latter case would begin at more than 25, because the value of 25 would not be included.

The decision to correct for continuity depends on the equality sign and the direction of the desired outcomes of the binomial distribution. Table 6.2 contains a list of some rules of thumb that can help in the application of the correction for continuity.

Values Being Determined	Correction
$X >$	$+.50$
$X \geq$	$-.50$
$X <$	$-.50$
$X \leq$	$+.50$
$\leq X \leq$	$-.50$ and $+.50$
$< X <$	$+.50$ and $-.50$

TABLE 6.2

Some Rules of Thumb for the Correction for Continuity

FIGURE 6.10

Graph of the Solution to
the Binomial Problem
Worked by the Normal
Curve

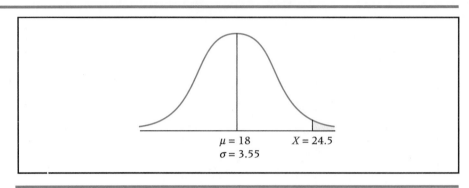

$\mu = 18$ $X = 24.5$

$\sigma = 3.55$

For the binomial problem, $P(X \geq 25 \mid n = 60$ and $p = .30)$, the normal curve becomes $P(X \geq 24.5 \mid \mu = 18$ and $\sigma = 3.55)$, as shown in Figure 6.10, and

$$Z = \frac{X - \mu}{\sigma} = \frac{24.5 - 18}{3.55} = 1.83.$$

The probability (Table 6.1) of this Z value is .4664. The answer to this problem lies in the tail of the distribution, so the final answer is

$$
\begin{array}{r}
.5000 \\
- .4664 \\
\hline
.0336
\end{array}
$$

Had this problem been worked using the binomial formula, the solution would have been as shown in Table 6.3. The difference between the normal distribution approximation and the actual binomial values is only 0.0025 (.0361 − .0336).

TABLE 6.3

Probability Values for
the Binomial Problem of
$n = 60$, $p = .30$, and
$X \geq 25$

X Value	Probability
25	0.0167
26	0.0096
27	0.0052
28	0.0026
29	0.0012
30	0.0005
31	0.0002
32	0.0001
33	0.0000
$X \geq 25$	0.0361

Work the following binomial distribution problem by using the normal distribution.

$$P(X = 12 | n = 25 \text{ and } p = .40) = ?$$

Solution:

Find μ and σ.

$$\mu = n \cdot p = (25)(.40) = 10.0;$$
$$\sigma = \sqrt{n \cdot p \cdot q} = \sqrt{(25)(.40)(.60)} = 2.45.$$
$$\text{Test: } \mu \pm 3\sigma = 10.0 \pm 3(2.45) = 2.65 \text{ to } 17.35.$$

This range falls between 0 and 25, so the approximation is close enough. Correct for continuity next. Because the problem is to determine the probability of X being exactly 12, the correction entails both $+.50$ and $-.50$. That is, a binomial probability at $X = 12$ translates to a continuous normal curve area that lies between 11.5 and 12.5. Graphing the problem gives:

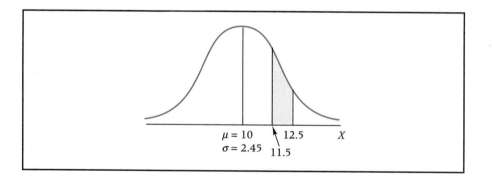

$$Z = \frac{X - \mu}{\sigma} = \frac{12.5 - 10}{2.45} = 1.02,$$

and

$$Z = \frac{X - \mu}{\sigma} = \frac{11.5 - 10}{2.45} = 0.61.$$

$Z = 1.02$ produces a probability of .3461.
$Z = 0.61$ produces a probability of .2291.

The difference in areas yields the answer:

$$.3461 - .2291 = .1170.$$

Had the problem been worked using the binomial tables, the resulting answer would have been .114. The difference between the normal curve approximation and the value obtained using binomial tables is only .003.

**Demonstration
Problem 6.10**

Solve the following binomial distribution problem by using the normal distribution.

$$P(X < 27 | n = 100 \text{ and } p = .37) = ?$$

Solution:

Neither the sample size nor the p value is contained in Table A.2; thus working this problem using binomial distribution techniques is impractical. It is a good candidate for the normal curve. Calculating μ and σ yields

$$\mu = n \cdot p = (100)(.37) = 37.0;$$
$$\sigma = \sqrt{n \cdot p \cdot q} = \sqrt{(100)(.37)(.63)} = 4.83.$$

Testing to determine the closeness of the approximation gives

$$\mu \pm 3\sigma = 37 \pm 3(4.83) = 37 \pm 14.49.$$

The range 22.51 to 51.49 lies between 0 and 100. This problem satisfies the conditions of the test. Next, correct for continuity: $X < 27$ as a binomial problem translates to $X \leq 26.5$ as a normal distribution problem. The graph of the problem is as follows:

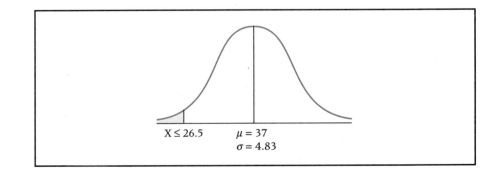

$X \leq 26.5$ $\mu = 37$
$\sigma = 4.83$

Solving for the answer yields

$$Z = \frac{X - \mu}{\sigma} = \frac{26.5 - 37}{4.83} = -2.17.$$

Table 6.1 shows a probability of .4850. Solving for the tail of the distribution gives

$$.5000 - .4850 = .0150,$$

which is the answer. Had this problem been solved by the binomial formula, the probabilities would have been:

X value	Probability
26	.0059
25	.0035
24	.0019
23	.0010
22	.0005
21	.0002
20	.0001
X < 27	.0131

The answer obtained by using the normal curve approximation (.0150) compares favorably to this exact binomial answer. The difference is only .0019.

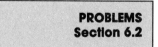

**PROBLEMS
Section 6.2**

6.15 Convert the following binomial distribution problems to normal distribution problems. Use the correction for continuity.
 a. $P(X \le 16 | n = 30 \text{ and } p = .70)$
 b. $P(10 < X \le 20) | n = 25 \text{ and } p = .50)$
 c. $P(X = 22 | n = 40 \text{ and } p = .60)$
 d. $P(X > 14 | n = 16 \text{ and } p = .45)$

6.16 Use the test $\mu \pm 3\sigma$ to determine whether the following binomial distributions can be approximated by using the normal distribution.
 a. $n = 8 \text{ and } p = .50$
 b. $n = 18 \text{ and } p = .80$

    c. $n = 12$ and $p = .30$

    d. $n = 30$ and $p = .75$

    e. $n = 14$ and $p = .50$

6.17 Where appropriate, work the following binomial distribution problems by using the normal curve. Also, use Table A.2 to find the answers using the binomial distribution and compare the answers obtained by the two methods.

    a. $P(X = 8 | n = 25$ and $p = .40) =$

    b. $P(X \geq 13 | n = 20$ and $p = .60) =$

    c. $P(X = 7 | n = 15$ and $p = .50) =$

    d. $P(X < 3 | n = 10$ and $p = .70) =$

6.18 According to a survey reported by Wertheim Schroeder & Company, "Huggies" diapers produced by Kimberly-Clark Corporation had 32.5% of the disposable diaper market in 1989. If forty-five families were randomly selected and interviewed in 1989, what is the probability that eighteen or more families used Huggies?

6.19 In the survey presented in Problem 6.18, "Pampers" diapers held 25.5% of the market. If seventy families were randomly selected, what is the probability that less than fifteen families used Pampers?

6.20 According to a recent survey by the U.S. Bureau of Labor Statistics, 87% of all the part-time college students enrolled in the fall of 1989 also worked. If this figure still holds and if 120 part-time college students are randomly selected, what is the probability that less than 100 also work?

6.21 Mexican food is becoming a mainstream American food group. A recent survey of homemakers revealed that 41% buy fixings for Mexican food in food stores. If this is true and thirty-five homemakers are randomly sampled, what is the probability that fewer than five homemakers buy fixings for Mexican food in food stores?

6.22 According to Dataquest, Inc., Cray controlled 36.7% of the worldwide market share in supercomputers in 1990. Researchers obtained a master list of all supercomputers in the world and randomly selected fifty of these supercomputers.

    a. What is the probability that less that fifteen are Cray computers?

    b. What is the probability that between fifteen and twenty-five (inclusive) are Cray computers?

    c. What is the probability that more than twenty-five are Cray computers?

6.23 In a travel study, Leo J. Shapiro and Associates, Inc., reported that on February 10, 1991, during the Persian Gulf war, 29% of Americans said that the Gulf crisis would affect their vacation plans.

    a. At the end of the war if the figure was still 29%, in a random sample of 150 travelers, what is the probability that 20 or less responded *yes* that the Gulf crisis would affect their vacation plans?

b. However, a study at the end of the war indicated that only 7% of the travelers felt at that time that the Gulf crisis would affect their vacation plans. What is the probability that a random sample of 150 travelers would result in 20 or less travelers saying *yes* the Gulf crisis would affect their vacation plans?

EXPONENTIAL DISTRIBUTION | *6.3*

Another continuous distribution is the exponential distribution. It is closely related to the Poisson distribution. Whereas the Poisson distribution is discrete and describes random occurrences over some interval, the **exponential distribution** is continuous and describes the times between random occurrences. The following are the characteristics of the exponential distribution.

exponential distribution

- It is a continuous distribution.
- It is a family of distributions.
- It is skewed to the right.
- The X values vary from 0 to ∞.
- Its apex is always at $X = 0$.
- The curve steadily decreases as X gets larger.

The exponential probability distribution is determined by

$$f(X) = \lambda e^{-\lambda X},$$

where: $X \geq 0$

$\lambda > 0$

An exponential distribution can be characterized by the one parameter, λ. Each unique value of λ determines a different exponential distribution. Thus there is actually a family of exponential distributions. Figure 6.11 shows graphs of exponential distributions for four values of λ. The points on the graph are determined by using λ and various values of X in the probability density formula. The mean of an exponential distribution is $\mu = 1/\lambda$, and the standard deviation of an exponential distribution is $\sigma = 1/\lambda$.

Probabilities of the Exponential Distribution

Probabilities are computed for the exponential distribution by determining the amount of area under the curve between two points. Applying calculus to the exponential probability formula produces a formula that can be used to calculate the probabilities of an exponential distribution.

FIGURE 6.11

Graphs of Some Expo-
nential Distributions

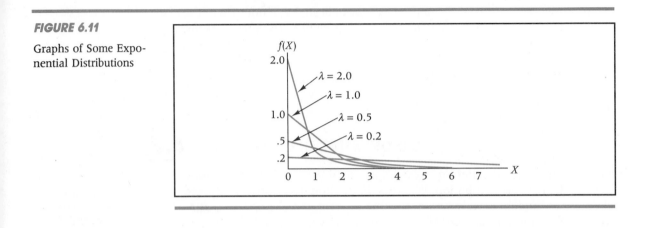

**Probabilities of
the Right Tail of
the Exponential
Distribution**

$$P(X \geq X_0) = e^{-\lambda X_0},$$

where: $X_0 \geq 0.$

To use this formula requires finding values of e^{-X}. These values can be computed
on most calculators or obtained from Table A.4, which contains the values of
e^{-X} for selected values of X.

For example, arrivals at a bank are Poisson distributed with a λ of 1.2
customers every minute. What is the average time between arrivals and what
is the probability that at least 2 minutes will elapse between one arrival and
the next arrival?

Interarrival times of random arrivals are exponentially distributed. The
mean of this exponential distribution is $\mu = 1/\lambda = 1/1.2 = 0.833$ min (50
sec). On average, .833 min, or 50 sec, will elapse between arrivals at the bank.
The probability of an interval of 2 min or more between arrivals can be calculated by

$$P(X \geq 2 | \lambda = 1.2) = e^{-1.2(2)} = .0907.$$

About 9.07% of the time when the rate of random arrivals is 1.2/min will 2
min or more elapse between arrivals, as shown in Figure 6.12.

This problem underscores the potential of using the exponential distribution in conjunction with the Poisson distribution to solve problems. In operations research and management science, these two distributions are used
together to solve queuing problems (theory of lines). The Poisson distribution
is used to analyze the arrivals to the queue, and the exponential distribution
is used to analyze interarrival time.

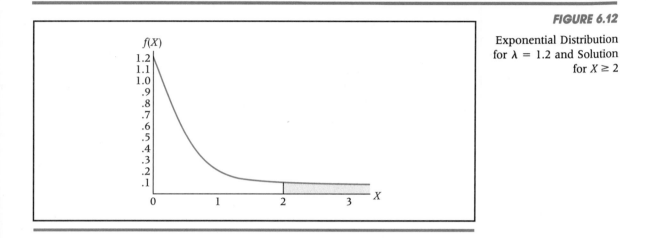

FIGURE 6.12

Exponential Distribution
for $\lambda = 1.2$ and Solution
for $X \geq 2$

**Demonstration
Problem 6.11**

A company that manufactures washing machines makes them to last an average of six years before they have a major breakdown. The manufacturer offers a free warranty against major breakdowns. However, the company only wants to guarantee the machine against major breakdowns for no more than 20% of the machines. For how many years should the warranty be promised?

Solution:

The exponential distribution is used to analyze the times between major breakdowns. The mean time is six years, so $\mu = 6$ for this exponential distribution. Lambda then is

$$\lambda = \frac{1}{\mu} = \frac{1}{6} = 0.167/\text{yr}.$$

The problem is to find a number of years, X_0, so that no more than 20% of the machines have a major breakdown before that time. Thus X_0 in the exponential probability formula represents the time after which 80% or more of the machines may be expected to break down. That is,

$$P(X \geq X_0) = e^{-\lambda X_0} = e^{-(0.167)X_0} \geq .80.$$

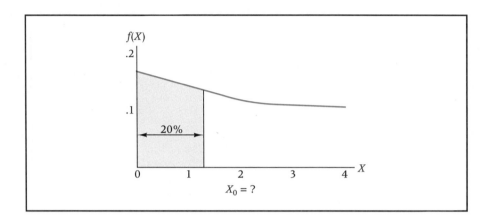

The table shows several values of X_0 and their associated probabilities. Thus if a one-year warranty is given with the product, 84.62% of the breakdowns will occur after that time, and less than 20% of the machines will have major breakdowns before the warranty has expired.

X_0	$P(X \geq X_0)$	$P(X < X_0) = 1 - P(X \geq X_0)$	
1	.8462	.1538	(less than 20%)
2	.7161	.2839	
3	.6059	.3941	
4	.5127	.4873	

**PROBLEMS
Section 6.3**

6.24 Use the probability density formula to sketch the graphs of the following exponential distributions.

  a. $\lambda = 0.1$

  b. $\lambda = 0.3$

  c. $\lambda = 0.8$

  d. $\lambda = 3.0$

6.25 Determine the mean and standard deviation of the following exponential distributions.

  a. $\lambda = 3.25$

  b. $\lambda = 0.7$

    c. $\lambda = 1.1$

    d. $\lambda = 6.0$

6.26 Determine the following exponential probabilities.

    a. $P(X \geq 5 | \lambda = 1.35) =$

    b. $P(X < 3 | \lambda = 0.68) =$

    c. $P(X > 4 | \lambda = 1.7) =$

    d. $P(X < 6 | \lambda = 0.80) =$

6.27 In Mrs. Centrito's class at the Jackson Elementary School in Oceanside, Oregon, 0.3 children get sick in class during any particular week. Assume that the occurrences of children getting sick in class are Poisson distributed.

    a. What is the probability that the interval between occurrences will be a week or less?

    b. What is the probability that more than a month (four weeks) will elapse between class illnesses?

    c. What is the probability that thirty-six weeks (an entire school year) can go by between class illnesses?

6.28 The average length of time between arrivals at a turnpike toll booth is 23 sec. Assume that the time between arrivals at the toll booth is exponentially distributed.

    a. What is the probability that a minute or more will elapse between arrivals?

    b. If a car has just passed through the toll booth, what is the probability that no car will show up for at least five more minutes?

6.29 The Foundation Corporation specializes in constructing the concrete foundations for new houses in the South. The company knows that, because of soil types, moisture conditions, variable construction, and other factors, eventually most foundations will need major repair. Based on its records, the company's president believes that a new house foundation on average will not need major repair for 20 years. If she wants to guarantee the company's work against major repair but only wants to have to honor no more than 10% of its jobs, for how many years should the company guarantee its work?

6.30 During the dry month of August, one U.S. city has measurable rain on average only two days per month. If the arrival of rainy days is Poisson distributed in this city during the month of August, what is the average number of days that will pass between measurable rain? What is the standard deviation? What is the probability during this month that no more than two days will elapse between rainy days?

6.31 During the summer at a small private airport in western Nebraska, the unscheduled arrival of airplanes is Poisson distributed with an average arrival rate of 1.12 planes/hr.

HISTORICAL NOTE

Abraham de Moivre

Abraham de Moivre was born at Vitry in Champagne, France, on May 26, 1667. His father was a surgeon. At the age of eleven, de Moivre went to college and studied the humanities. Later, studying under Ozanam, a famous mathematician, in Paris, de Moivre became interested in mathematics.

After the Edict of Nantes, de Moivre was imprisoned at the age of eighteen in Priory of St. Martin. Set free at the age of twenty-one, he left France, never returned, and never published in French. He went to England with nothing but his knowledge of mathematics and became a visiting tutor of noblemen's children. The famous astronomer Edmund Halley befriended him and helped introduce de Moivre to the Royal Society. In 1697, he was elected as a Fellow of the Royal Society and became a friend of Sir Isaac Newton. Many people now credit Abraham de Moivre with discovering the normal curve.

Source: Adapted from Dudycha, Arthur L., and Linda W. Dudycha, "Behavioral Statistics: An Historical Perspective," in *Statistical Issues: A Reader for the Behavioral Sciences*, edited by Roger Kirk (Monterey, Calif.: Brooks/Cole, 1972), and David, F. N., *Games, Gods, and Gambling* (New York: Hofner, 1962).

a. What is the average interarrival time between planes?

b. What is the probability that at least two hours will elapse between plane arrivals?

c. What is the probability of two planes arriving less than ten minutes apart?

6.32 A busy city restaurant has determined that between 6:30 P.M. and 9:00 P.M. on Friday nights, the arrivals of customers are Poisson distributed, with an average arrival rate of 2.44/min.

a. What is the probability that at least ten minutes would elapse between arrivals?

b. What is the probability that at least five minutes would elapse between arrivals?

c. What is the probability that at least one minute would elapse between arrivals?

d. What is the expected amount of time between arrivals?

CHAPTER SUMMARY

The most widely used of all distributions probably is the normal distribution. Many phenomena are normally distributed, including most machine produced parts; many measurements of the biological and natural environment; and many human characteristics such as height, weight, IQ, and achievement test scores. The normal curve is continuous, symmetrical, unimodal, and asymptotic to the axis; actually, it is a family of curves.

The parameters necessary to describe a normal distribution are the mean and the standard deviation. In order to analyze data by the normal curve, they must be standardized by using the mean and the standard deviation to compute Z scores. A Z score is the distance that a value is from the mean in units of standard deviations. Using the Z score of a value, the probability of that value occurring by chance from a given normal distribution can be determined by using a table of Z scores and their associated probabilities.

The normal distribution can be used to work certain types of binomial distribution problems. Doing so requires converting the n and p values of the binomial distribution to μ and σ of the normal distribution. When worked by using the normal distribution, the binomial distribution solution is only an approximation. If the values of $\mu \pm 3\sigma$ lie within a range from 0 to n, the approximation is reasonably accurate. Adjusting for the fact that a discrete distribution problem is being worked by a continuous distribution requires a correction for continuity. The correction for continuity involves adding and/or subtracting 0.50 to the X value being analyzed. This correction usually improves the normal curve approximation.

Another continuous distribution is the exponential distribution. It complements the discrete Poisson distribution. The exponential distribution is used to compute the probabilities of times between random occurrences. The exponential distribution is a family of distributions described by one parameter, λ. The distribution is skewed to the right and always has its highest value at $X = 0$.

Key Words

Normal distribution	Z distribution
Standardized normal distribution	Correction for continuity
Z score	Exponential distribution

USING THE COMPUTER

You can analyze two types of problems in Chapter 6 with Minitab: normal distribution problems and exponential distribution problems. You can utilize Minitab to analyze normal curve problems directly. However, you must manipulate Minitab commands in order to analyze exponential distribution problems.

Analyzing Normal Curve Problems with Minitab

Using the CDF command, you can determine normal curve probabilities with Minitab. The abbreviation CDF stands for *cumulative probabilities for distribution functions*. The CDF command requires the value of X for which the probability is being determined and a subcommand. The form of the CDF command is **MTB > CDF X;**. The CDF command ends with a semicolon, which signals Minitab to produce a subcommand prompt. The subcommand for a normal distribution is the word **NORMAL**, followed by the value of the mean and the standard deviation and a period, which signals Minitab to go back to Minitab command prompts. For example, one of the Chapter 6 demonstration problems is to determine the probability of getting a GMAT score greater than 700 when the mean GMAT score is 485 and the standard deviation is 105. The commands necessary to analyze this problem are:

```
MTB > CDF 700;
SUBC > NORMAL 485 105.
```

The output is:

```
700.0000   0.9797
```

The probability is 0.9797. However, Minitab produces cumulative probabilities from the left end of the normal distribution. This answer, 0.9797, is the probability that $X \leq 700$. Because the problem asks for the probability that $X > 700$, you must subtract: $1 - .9797 = .0203$. You may need to manipulate the Minitab probability output to obtain the desired probability, because the CDF output *always* yields the probability of a value being $\leq X$.

Solving for Exponential Distribution Probability Values

Minitab does not directly compute probability values for the exponential distribution. However, using a few of Minitab's capabilities, you can manipulate Minitab commands to produce exponential probabilities. Suppose that the object is to determine the interarrival time probabilities when the arrivals are Poisson distributed with a λ of 1.2/min. First, select the interarrival times of interest: $X = 1$ min, 2 min, 3 min, 4 min, 5 min, 6 min, and 7 min. **READ** or **SET** these X values into a column.

```
MTB > SET C1
DATA > 1, 2, 3, 4, 5, 6, 7
DATA > END
```

The probability formula of the exponential distribution requires $e^{-\lambda x}$. Use another Minitab command, **LET**, to multiply each X value by $-\lambda$ and take the exponential power of that answer. You can accomplish these two steps with one **LET** command by using parentheses and special symbols. To multiply the X value by $-\lambda$, use a * symbol, the Minitab symbol for multiplication. Use $-\lambda$*C1 to multiply each value in column 1 by $-\lambda$. Specifically, for $\lambda = 1.2$: -1.2*C1. You raise the exponent base e to the power of X by using the Minitab command, **EXPO**, followed by a parenthesis with the desired power. For this problem, **EXPO(-1.2*C1)** yields the exponential probabilities for the desired X values in column 1. Because the answers must be placed temporarily in a location, the **LET** command requires the column number of the location where the answers are to be stored. For this problem, the command that computes exponential probabilities is:

MTB > LET C2 = EXPO(-1.2*C1)

If the contents of column 2 are printed out, the results are:

C2
  0.30119 0.09072 0.02732 0.00823 0.00248 0.00075
  0.00022

In general, to compute probabilities for the exponential distribution, enter the desired values of X into a column, multiply the column by $-\lambda$, and raise the results to the exponential power.

SUPPLEMENTARY PROBLEMS

6.33 Assume a normal distribution and find the following probabilities.
    a. $P(X < 21 | \mu = 25$ and $\sigma = 4)$
    b. $P(X \geq 77 | \mu = 50$ and $\sigma = 9)$
    c. $P(X > 47 | \mu = 50$ and $\sigma = 6)$
    d. $P(13 < X < 29 | \mu = 23$ and $\sigma = 4)$
    e. $P(X \geq 105 | \mu = 90$ and $\sigma = 2.86)$

6.34 Work the following binomial distribution problems by using the normal distribution. Check your answers by using Table A.2 to solve for the probabilities.
    a. $P(X = 12 | n = 25$ and $p = .60)$
    b. $P(X > 5 | n = 15$ and $p = .50)$
    c. $P(X \leq 3 | n = 10$ and $p = .50)$
    d. $P(X \geq 8 | n = 15$ and $p = .40)$

6.35 Find the probabilities for the following exponential distribution problems.
    a. $P(X \geq 3 | \lambda = 1.3)$
    b. $P(X < 2 | \lambda = 2.0)$
    c. $P(1 \leq X \leq 3 | \lambda = 1.65)$
    d. $P(X > 2 | \lambda = 0.405)$

6.36 *The Sports Encyclopedia: Baseball* presents a historical record of players who have had more than 3,000 at bats in the major leagues. It shows that the mean lifetime batting average for these players was .26125. The standard deviation of these batting averages was .020133. If a player is randomly selected from the list of hitters, what is the probability that he had a career batting average higher than .300? What is the probability that his average was lower than .300? What is the probability that his average was lower than .250? What is the probability that his average was lower than .200? What is the probability that his average was between .280 and .290? Assume that these batting averages are normally distributed for the population.

6.37 In another study of major league baseball players from the same sources, the ERAs (earned run averages, or number of earned runs given up by a pitcher per nine innings) were computed for pitchers who had pitched more than 1,000 innings. The researchers found that the average ERA for a major league pitcher with more than 1,000 innings was 3.482. If 93.19% of all pitchers with more than 1,000 innings had an ERA higher than 2.50, what is the standard deviation of ERAs for major league pitchers who have pitched more than 1,000 innings?

6.38 According to the U.S. Bureau of Labor Statistics, the average unemployment rate over many years for the United States by quarters was 6.73% with a variance of 0.4624. Assuming that these unemployment rates are normally distributed, what is the probability of randomly selecting a quarter that has an unemployment rate lower than 6.25? What is the probability of selecting a quarter with an unemployment rate higher than 7? What is the probability of randomly selecting a quarter having a rate between 6.5 and 6.6?

6.39 The Federal Deposit Insurance Corporation conducted a study of U.S. bank failures between 1985 and 1988. It revealed that the average number of bank failures was 161 per year, with a standard deviation of 32.63. Suppose that the number of bank failures in the United States per year was normally distributed with the above mean and standard deviation. If a year is randomly selected, how many bank failures would have to occur for only 20% of the other years to have fewer bank failures?

6.40 According to the U.S. Department of Agriculture, Alabama egg farmers produce millions of eggs every year. Suppose that egg production per year in Alabama is normally distributed, with a standard deviation of 83 million eggs. If during only 3% of the years Alabama egg farmers produce more than 2,900 million eggs, what is the mean egg production by Alabama farmers?

6.41 The National Climate Data Center reports that the average annual snowfall at Boston, Massachusetts, is 42 in. Suppose that average annual snowfall figures for a given location are normally distributed. What is the variance of annual snowfall for Boston if 60% of the years have an annual snowfall of between 33 in. and 51 in?

6.42 According to the Audit Bureau of Circulations, the average daily circulation of the *Wall Street Journal* based on 1988–1989 figures is 1,931,410. The standard deviation is 50,940. Assume that the paper's daily circulation is normally distributed. What percentage of days would it surpass a circulation of 2,000,000? Suppose that the paper cannot support the fixed expenses of a full-production setup if the circulation drops below 1,800,000. If the probability of this event occurring is low, the production manager might try to keep the full crew in place and not disrupt operations. How often will this event happen, based on the historical information?

6.43 According to the National Center for Education Studies, the annual tuition and fees at four-year universities averaged $1,750 in 1988. Suppose that the figures for tuition and fees at four-year universities are normally distributed, with a standard deviation of $475. The average annual tuition and fees at two-year colleges was $650 in 1988. Suppose that the figures for tuition and fees at two-year colleges also are normally distributed, with a standard deviation of $215. Based on these two distributions and probabilities, is there much chance that a two-year college would have higher annual tuition and fees than any of the four-year universities?

6.44 Some U.S. colleges and universities require that entering students take the ACT (American College Testing) examination. In 1988, the mean score for the ACT was 18.8 for the composite test. If 14% of the composite scores were higher than 26, what was the standard deviation for the 1988 ACT examination?

6.45 Suppose that the average speeds of passenger trains traveling from Newark, New Jersey, to Philadelphia, Pennsylvania, are normally distributed, with a mean average speed of 88 mph and a standard deviation of 6.4 mph.
   a. What is the probability that a train will average less than 70 mph?
   b. What is the probability that a train will average more than 80 mph?
   c. What is the probability that the train will average between 90 and 100 mph?

6.46 U.S. Bureau of Labor Statistics data show that the average production worker put in 40.9 hours of work per week in 1989. Suppose that the number of hours worked by a production worker are normally distributed, with a mean of 40.9 hours and variance of 27.6 hours.

    a. What is the probability that a randomly selected worker worked 45 or more hours last week?

    b. What is the probability that a randomly selected worker worked between 35 and 45 hours last week?

    c. The mean number of hours worked by production workers in 1992 is unknown. If the standard deviation of hours worked is 6.92 hours and if 23% of the workers worked less than 34 hours, what is the mean number of hours worked?

6.47 Average precipitation for Duluth, Minnesota, during the summer months is 4.03 in. per month. Suppose that the amount of rainfall per month in the summer for Duluth is normally distributed, with a standard deviation of 1.3 in.

    a. What is the probability of getting more than 6 in. of rainfall in a summer month?

    b. What is the probability of getting between 3 and 4 in. of rainfall in a summer month?

    c. What is the probability of having less than 1 in. of rainfall in a summer month?

    d. Suppose that the standard deviation of rainfall is unknown. If during 85% of the summer months the rainfall is more than 2.7 in., what is the standard deviation of rainfall? Assume that the mean rainfall for summer months is still 4.03 in.

6.48 A 1989 U.S. Bureau of Labor Statistics survey showed that one in five people 16 years old or older volunteers some of his or her time. If this figure holds for the entire population and if a random sample of 150 people age 16 years old or older is taken, what is the probability that more than 50 of those sampled do volunteer work?

6.49 Domestic brands of clothing dominate the Japanese market. In 1989, domestic brands accounted for 62.9% of the Japanese market. During the same year, U.S. brands accounted for only 7.5% of the Japanese market, showing considerable potential for market share growth. Suppose that market share could be measured by asking each Japanese buyer which country's brand of clothing they prefer. If the market share percentages cited hold true, what is the probability of randomly selecting 200 Japanese buyers and having more than 100 of them say that they do not prefer to buy Japanese clothing?

6.50 Based on the information in Problem 6.49, what is the probability of randomly sampling 300 Japanese buyers and finding that between 20 and 30 (inclusive) prefer to buy U.S. clothing?

6.51 The U.S. Equal Employment Opportunity Commission reported that, in 1988, 2% of all management jobs of companies with more than 100 employees were held by black women. If that proportion still holds and a random sample of 500 managers from companies with more than 100 employees is taken, what is the probability that there would be no black women managers? What is the expected number of black women managers in a sample of 500?

6.52 In an effort to be more responsive to employee needs, companies have begun developing optional types of flexible scheduling to employees. According to a survey of companies, 17% of all companies offer *job sharing* as an option to employees. If a researcher called fifty randomly selected companies from across the country in an effort to validate this finding, how many companies would she expect to offer job sharing? What is the probability that more than ten of the companies offer job sharing?

6.53 In an effort to determine if parental-leave laws had increased administrative costs to companies, the Families and Work Institute conducted a survey. It reported that in Rhode Island 56% of the companies had experienced no increase in administrative costs as a result of these laws. The figure for Oregon was 66%. If a random sample of seventy-five companies is taken in each of the two states, what is the expected number of companies that would have increased administrative costs? What is the probability that in Rhode Island forty-two or more companies would report that they experienced no increase in administrative costs because of these laws?

6.54 Incoming phone calls generally are thought to be Poisson distributed. If an operator averages 2.2 phone calls every 30 sec, what is the expected (average) amount of time between calls? What is the probability that a minute or more would elapse between incoming calls? Two minutes?

6.55 Suppose that interarrival times at a hospital emergency room during a weekday are exponentially distributed, with an average interarrival time of nine minutes. If the arrivals are Poisson distributed, what would the average number of arrivals per hour be? What is the probability that it will be less than five minutes between any two arrivals?

6.56 Supermarkets usually get very busy at about 5 P.M. on weekdays as many workers stop by on the way home to shop. Suppose that at that time arrivals at a supermarket's express checkout station are Poisson distributed with an average of 0.8 person/min. If the clerk has just checked out the last person in line, what is the probability that at least 1 min will elapse before the next customer arrives? Suppose that the clerk needs to go to the manager's office to ask a quick question and that 2.5 min are needed to do so. What is the probability that the clerk will get back before the next customer arrives?

6.57 Suppose that, between midnight and 3 A.M., meteor arrivals in the summer sky are Poisson distributed with an average arrival of 1 meteor every 20 min. What is the probability that at least 1 hr will elapse between meteor arrivals? What is the probability that a meteor will arrive between 10 and 30 min? What is the probability that less than 5 min will elapse between meteor arrivals?

6.58 Coastal residents along the Gulf of Mexico from Texas to Florida worry about the threat of hurricanes during the season from June through October. Residents get especially nervous when hurricanes enter the Gulf of Mexico. Suppose that the arrival of hurricanes during this season is Poisson distributed, with an average of three hurricanes entering the Gulf of Mexico during the five-month season. If a hurricane has just entered the Gulf of Mexico, what is the probability that it will be at least one month until the next hurricane enters the Gulf? What is the probability that another hurricane will enter the Gulf of Mexico in two weeks or less? What is the average amount of time between hurricanes entering the Gulf of Mexico?

6.59 A convention holds its registration on Wednesday morning from 9:00 A.M. until 12:00 noon. Past history has shown that registrants arrive following a Poisson distribution at an average rate of 1.8 every 15 sec. Fortunately, several service facilities are available to register convention members.

a. What is the average number of seconds between arrivals to the registration area for this conference based on past results?

b. What is the probability that it would be 25 sec or more between registration arrivals?

c. What is the probability that less than 5 sec will elapse between arrivals?

d. Suppose that the registration computers went down for a 1-min period. Would this condition pose a problem? What is the probability that at least 1 min will elapse between arrivals?

7

SAMPLING, SAMPLING DISTRIBUTIONS, AND QUALITY CONTROL

CHAPTER LEARNING OBJECTIVES

The three main learning objectives for Chapter 7 are to give you (a) an appreciation for the proper application of sampling techniques, (b) an understanding of the sampling distributions of several statistics, and (c) the ability to apply several quality control techniques—thereby enabling you to

1. Distinguish between random and nonrandom sampling.
2. Decide when to use various sampling techniques.
3. Use the sampling distributions of $\overline{X}$, $\hat{p}$, $\overline{X}_1 - \overline{X}_2$, and $\hat{p}_1 - \hat{p}_2$ to analyze data.
4. Use quality control terminology, and construct control charts.

**HEALTHCARE
AMERICA MARKETS
A NEW BLOOD
PRESSURE PRODUCT**

**HEALTHCARE
AMERICA MARKETS
A NEW BLOOD
PRESSURE PRODUCT**

The Healthcare America Corporation has developed a new product to measure blood pressure and is in the process of developing a market strategy for the product. Luisa Carmillo, Vice President of Marketing, is consulting with her team of market managers in an attempt to determine how large the market is for the new product and where the target market exists. Carmillo and her team believe that physicians might be the prime target for this new product. However, she is uncertain about geographic and specialty differences in the potential target audience. A well-prepared market strategy could spell the difference between success and failure for this new product. Carmillo and her team might be able to gather market data through the use of sampling.

**Managerial
Questions**

- What is the target market for this product and how large is it?
- What competing products are already in existence?
- What demographic variables influence buyers?
- What distribution network would be most effective?
- Is it feasible to conduct a census of potential consumers or should a sample be taken?
- What sampling techniques would yield adequate information for this study at a reasonable price?
- What are some possible frames for this study?
- What measurements can be taken in order to determine the answers to the marketing questions?

This chapter explores the process of sampling, the sampling distributions of some statistics, and the use of sampling in quality control. How are the data used in statistical analysis obtained? Why do researchers often take a sample rather than conduct a census? What are the differences between random and nonrandom sampling? Chapter 7 addresses these questions and others about sampling. Included in this chapter is a discussion of particular sampling techniques.

It has been determined that statistics such as the sample mean have particular distributions when a large number of certain types of samples are taken. Knowledge of these distributions is important in the study of statistics and the distributions are basic to much of the statistical analysis that is done. Chapter 7 contains a presentation of some of these distributions. In addition, this chapter provides a discussion of several of the key topics in quality control. Statistical quality control is based on sampling, and the discussion of quality control methods such as quality control charts is related directly to the topics on sampling.

SAMPLING | **7.1**

Sampling is widely used in business as a means of gathering useful information about a population. Data are gathered from samples and conclusions are drawn about the population as a part of the inferential statistics process. In the Healthcare America example, area samples of physicians could be taken from a few states, such as California, Florida, and Michigan. Product purchase responses along with customer demographics could be recorded for physicians in the sample. From these responses the marketing team could develop a *customer profile* of physicians that describes the attributes of purchasers and nonpurchasers. Sales representatives could then use the sample information to determine which types of physicians to concentrate their sales activity on. Often, the sample provides a reasonable means for gathering useful decision-making information that might be otherwise unattainable and unaffordable.

Reasons for Sampling

There are several good reasons for taking a sample instead of conducting a census.

1. The sample can save money.
2. The sample can save time.
3. For given resources, the sample can broaden the scope of the study.
4. Because the research process is sometimes destructive, the sample can save product.
5. If accessing the population is impossible, the sample is the only option.

A sample can be cheaper to obtain than a census if the magnitude of questions asked is similar. For example, if an eight-minute telephone interview is being undertaken, conducting these interviews with a sample of 100 customers rather than with a population of 100,000 customers obviously is less expensive. In addition to the cost savings, the significantly smaller number of interviews usually requires less total time. Thus if there is an urgency about obtaining the results, sampling can provide them more quickly. With the volatility of some markets and the constant barrage of new competition and new ideas, sampling has a strong advantage over a census in terms of research turnaround time.

If the resources allocated to a research project are fixed, more detailed information can be gathered by taking a sample than by conducting a census. With resources concentrated on fewer individuals or items, the study can be broadened in scope to allow for more specialized questions. One organization budgeted $100,000 for a study and opted to take a census instead of a sample by using a mail survey. The researchers mass mailed thousands of copies of a computer card that looked like a major league all-star ballot. The card contained twenty questions that could be answered yes or no by the respondent punching out a perforated hole. The information retrieved amounted to the percentages of respondents who answered yes and no on the twenty questions. For the same amount of money, the company could have taken a random sample from the population and held interactive one-on-one sessions by highly trained interviewers and gathered detailed information regarding the process being studied. By using the money on a sample, the researchers could have spent significantly more time with each respondent, increasing the potential for gathering more useful information.

Some research processes are destructive to the product or item being studied. For example, if light bulbs are being tested to determine how long they burn or if candy bars are being taste tested to determine whether the taste is acceptable, the product is destroyed. If a census were conducted for this type of research, there would be no product to sell. Thus taking a sample is the only realistic option for testing such products.

Sometimes a population is virtually impossible to access for research. For example, some people refuse to answer sensitive questions, and some telephone numbers are unlisted. Some items of interest (like 1957 Chevrolets) are unavailable, because locating all of them is extrememly difficult. For these and other reasons, the population is inaccessible, and sampling is the only option.

Reasons for Taking a Census

Sometimes taking a census makes more sense than using a sample. One reason to take a census is to eliminate the possibility that by chance a randomly selected sample might not be representative of the population. Even when all the proper sampling techniques are implemented, a sample that is nonrepresentative of the population can be selected by chance. For example, if the population of interest is all truck owners in the state of Colorado, a random sample of owners could yield mostly ranchers when in fact many of the truck owners in Colorado are urban dwellers.

A second reason to take a census is that the client (person authorizing and/or underwriting the study) might not have an appreciation for random sampling and feels more comfortable with conducting a census. Both of these reasons for taking a census are based on the assumption that enough time and money are available to conduct such a census.

Frame

frame

Every research study has a target population that consists of the individuals, institutions, or entities that are the object of investigation. The sample is taken from a population list, map, directory, or other source that is being used to represent the population. This list, map, or directory is called the **frame,** which can be school lists, trade association lists, or even lists sold by list brokers. Ideally, there is a one-to-one correspondence between the frame units and the population units. The reality is that often the frame and the target population are different. For example, suppose that the target population is all families living in Detroit. A feasible frame would be the residential pages of the Detroit telephone books. How would the frame differ from the target population? Some families have no phone. Other families have unlisted numbers. Still other families might have moved and/or changed numbers since the directory was printed. Some families even have multiple listings under different names.

Frames can have *overregistration,* in which the frame contains all the target population units plus some additional units. Frames can have *underregistration,* in which the frame contains fewer units than does the target population. Sampling is done from the frame, not the target population. In theory, the target population and the frame are the same. A researcher's goal is to minimize the differences between the frame and the target population.

Random Versus Nonrandom Sampling

There are two main types of sampling: random and nonrandom. In **random sampling** *every unit of the population has the same probability of being selected into the sample.* Random sampling implies that chance enters into the process of selection. For example, most Americans would like to believe that winners of nationwide magazine sweepstakes are selected by some random draw of numbers. Late in the 1960s when the military draft lottery was being used, most people eligible for the draft trusted that a given birthdate was selected by chance as the first date to use to draft people. In both of these situations, members of the population believed that selections were made by chance.

random sampling

In **nonrandom sampling** *every unit of the population does not have the same probability of being selected to the sample.* Members of nonrandom samples are not selected by chance. For example, they might be selected because they are at the right place at the right time or because they know the people conducting the research.

nonrandom sampling

Random sampling is sometimes referred to as *probability sampling,* and nonrandom sampling as *nonprobability sampling.* Because every unit of the population is not equally likely to be selected, assigning a probability of occurrence in nonrandom sampling is impossible. The statistical methods presented and discussed in this text are based on the assumption that the data come from random samples. *Nonrandom sampling methods are not appropriate techniques for gathering data to be analyzed by most of the statistical methodologies presented in this text.* However, several nonrandom sampling techniques are presented in this section, primarily to alert you to their characteristics and limitations.

Random Sampling Techniques

There are four basic random sampling techniques: simple random sampling, stratified random sampling, systematic random sampling, and cluster/area random sampling. Each technique has advantages and disadvantages. Some tech-

TABLE 7.1	91567	42595	27958	30134	04024	86385	29880	99730
A Brief Table of Random Numbers	46503	18584	18845	49618	02304	51038	20655	58727
	34914	63976	88720	82765	34476	17032	87589	40836
	57491	16703	23167	49323	45021	33132	12544	41035
	30405	83946	23792	14422	15059	45799	22716	19792
	09983	74353	68668	30429	70735	25499	16631	35006
	85900	07119	97336	71048	08178	77233	13916	47564

niques are simpler to use, whereas others have the potential for reducing sampling error. Some techniques are less costly than others.

simple random sampling

Simple Random Sampling.   The most elementary random sampling technique is **simple random sampling.** Simple random sampling can be viewed as the basis for the other three random sampling techniques. With simple random sampling, each unit of the frame is numbered from 1 to N (where N is the size of the population). Next, a table of random numbers or a random number generator is used to select n items to the sample. A *random number generator* is usually a computer program that allows computer or calculator output to yield random numbers. Table 7.1 contains a sample of a table of random numbers. Table A.1 contains a full table of random numbers.

These numbers are random in all directions. The spaces in the table are there only for ease of reading the values. For each number any of the ten digits (0–9) is equally likely, so getting the same digit twice or more in a row is possible. For example, from the population frame of companies listed in Table 7.2, let's use simple random sampling to select a sample of six companies.

First, number every member of the population. Select as many digits for each unit sampled as there are in the largest number in the population. For example, if a population has 2,000 members, select four-digit numbers. Because the population in Table 7.2 contains 30 members, only two digits need be

TABLE 7.2	Alaska Airlines	DuPont	LTV
A Population Frame of Thirty Companies	Alcoa	Exxon	Litton
	Amoco	Farah	Mead
	Atlantic Richfield	GTE	Mobil
	Bank of America	General Electric	Occidental Petroleum
	Bell of Pennsylvania	General Mills	Penney
	Chevron	General Dynamics	Philadelphia Electric
	Chrysler	Grumman	Ryder
	Citicorp	IBM	Sears
	Disney	Kmart	Time

			TABLE 7.3
01 Alaska Airlines	11 DuPont	21 LTV	
02 Alcoa	12 Exxon	22 Litton	Numbered Population of
03 Amoco	13 Farah	23 Mead	Thirty Companies
04 Atlantic Richfield	14 GTE	24 Mobil	
05 Bank of America	15 General Electric	25 Occidental Petroleum	
06 Bell Pennsylvania	16 General Mills	26 Penney	
07 Chevron	17 General Dynamics	27 Philadelphia Electric	
08 Chrysler	18 Grumman	28 Ryder	
09 Citicorp	19 IBM	29 Sears	
10 Disney	20 Kmart	30 Time	

selected for each number. The population is numbered from 01 to 30, as shown in Table 7.3.

The object is to sample six companies, so six different two-digit numbers must be selected from the table of random numbers. Because this population contains only thirty companies, all numbers greater than 30 (31−99) must be ignored. If, for example, the number 67 is selected, continue the process until a value between 1 and 30 is obtained. If the same number occurs more than once, proceed to another number. For ease of understanding, start with the first pair of digits in Table 7.1 and proceed across the first row until $n = 6$ different values between 01 and 30 are selected. If additional numbers are needed, proceed down the second row, and so on. Often a researcher will start at some randomly selected location in the table and proceed in a predetermined direction to select numbers.

In the first row of digits in Table 7.1, the first number is 91. This number is out of range so it is cast out. The next two digits are 56. Next is 74, followed by 25, which is the first usable number. Twenty-five is the number associated with Occidental Petroleum, so Occidental Petroleum is the first company selected for the sample. The next number is 95, followed by a 27, which is usable. Twenty-seven is the number for Philadelphia Electric. Continuing the process, the numbers 95 and 83 are passed over. The next usable number is 01, which is the value for Alaska Airlines. Thirty-four is next, followed by 04 and 02, both of which are usable. These numbers are associated with Atlantic Richfield and Alcoa, respectively. Continuing along the first row, the next usable number is 29, which is associated with Sears. As this is the sixth selection, the sample is complete. The following companies comprise the final sample:

Alaska Airlines

Alcoa

Atlantic Richfield

Occidental Petroleum

Philadelphia Electric

Sears

The smaller the population is, the easier simple random sampling becomes. The process of numbering all the members of the population and the selection of items from the population is cumbersome for large populations.

Stratified Random Sampling.   A second type of random sampling is stratified random sampling. In **stratified random sampling,** the population is divided into nonoverlapping subpopulations called *strata*. The researcher then extracts a random sample from each of the subpopulations. The main reason for using stratified random sampling is that it contains the potential for reducing sampling error. Sampling error occurs when, by chance, the sample does not represent the population. With stratified random sampling, the potential to match the sample more closely to the population is greater than with simple random sampling, because portions of the total sample are taken from different population subgroups. However, stratified random sampling is usually more costly than simple random sampling, as each unit of the population must be assigned to a stratum before the random selection process begins.

Strata selection is usually based on available information. Such information may have been gleaned from previous censuses or surveys. Stratification benefits increase as the strata differ more. Internally, a stratum should be relatively homogeneous; externally, strata should contrast with each other. Stratification if often done by using demographic variables, such as gender, socioeconomic class, geographic region, religion, and ethnicity. For example, if a U.S. presidential election poll is to be conducted by a market research firm, what important variables should be stratified? The gender of the respondent might make a difference, because past elections have demonstrated a gender gap in voter preference. That is, men and women have tended to vote differently in national elections. Geographic region also has been an important variable in national elections, since voters are influenced by local cultural values that differ from region to region. Voters in the South voted almost exclusively for Democrats in the past, but recently they have tended to vote for Republican candidates in national elections. Voters in the Rocky Mountain states have supported Republican presidential candidates; in the industrial Northeast, voters have been more inclined toward Democratic candidates.

In FM radio markets, age of listener is an important determinant of the type of programing used by a station. Figure 7.1 contains a stratification by age with three strata, based on the assumption that age makes a difference in preference of programing. This stratification implies that 20–30-year-olds tend to listen to the same type of programing, which is different from that listened to by 30–40-year-olds and 40–50-year-olds. Within each age subgroup (stratum), *homogeneity* or alikeness exists; between each pair of subgroups a difference, or *heterogeneity,* exists.

Suppose a market survey is being done in the state of California to determine the sales potential for a new type of microwavable burrito to be sold in grocery stores. What stratified random samplings might be included? Would this type of burrito appeal more to certain ethnic groups? Is the burrito now

stratified random sampling

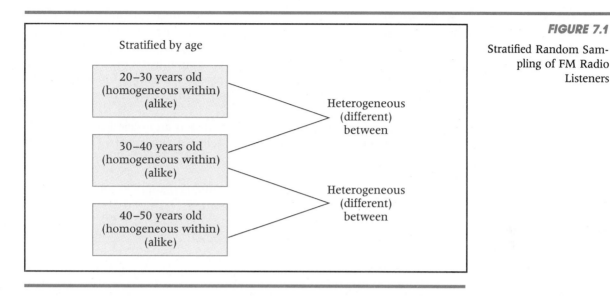

FIGURE 7.1

Stratified Random Sampling of FM Radio Listeners

considered "American" food? Stratifying by ethnicity would ensure that the sample contains enough responses from different ethnic groups to examine this question. Rural, suburban, and urban might be another useful stratification. Age of the shopper could be a third stratification variable. Is there a gender difference in the purchasing of burritos? Should the advertising be aimed at men, women, or both? In thinking of a market strategy—advertising, packaging, pricing, distributing—what variables might make a difference?

Stratified random sampling can be either proportionate or disproportionate. **Proportionate stratified random sampling** occurs *when the percentage of the sample taken from each stratum is proportionate to the percentage that each stratum is within the whole population.* For example, suppose that voters are being surveyed in Boston and that the sample is being stratified by religion with the strata of Catholic, Protestant, Jewish, and others. If Boston's population is 90% Catholic and if a sample of 1,000 voters is being taken, the sample would require inclusion of 900 Catholics in order to achieve proportionate stratification. Any other number of Catholics would be disproportionate stratification. The sample proportion of other religions would also have to follow population percentages. Or consider the city of El Paso, which contains approximately 63% Hispanics. If a researcher is conducting a citywide poll in El Paso and if stratification is by ethnicity, a proportionate stratified random sample should contain 63% Hispanics. Thus an ethnically proportionate stratified sample of 160 residents from El Paso's 500,000 residents should contain approximately 101 Hispanics. Whenever *the proportions of the strata in the sample are different than the proportions of the strata in the population,* **disproportionate stratified random sampling** occurs.

proportionate stratified random sampling

disproportionate stratified random sampling

systematic sampling

Systematic Sampling.   Systematic sampling is a third random sampling technique. Unlike stratified random sampling, systematic sampling is not done in an attempt to reduce sampling error. Rather, **systematic sampling** is used because of its convenience and relative ease of administration. With systematic sampling, every kth item is selected to produce a sample of size n from a population of size N. Systematic sampling has two characteristics.

- The elements of the population are treated as an ordered sequence.
- Elements selected to the sample are selected at a constant interval from the ordered sequence frame.

The value of k can be determined in the following manner. If k is not an integer value, the whole number value should be used.

Determining the Value of k

$$k = \frac{N}{n},$$

where: n = sample size

N = population size

k = size of interval for selection

A few years ago, a management information systems researcher wanted to sample the manufacturers in Texas. He had enough financial support to sample 1,000 companies. The *Directory of Texas Manufacturers* listed approximately 17,000 manufacturers in alphabetical order. Thus N was 17,000, n was 1,000, and k was 17 (17,000/1,000). The researcher selected every 17th company in the directory for his sample.

In selecting every kth value, what value does the researcher begin with? In the study just mentioned, did the researcher begin with the first company listed or the 17th or somewhere in between? A simple random number table should be used to select a value between 1 and k inclusive as a starting point. The second element for the sample is the starting point plus k. In the example, $k = 17$, so the researcher would have gone to a table of random numbers to determine a starting point between 1 and 17. Suppose that he selected the number 5. He would have started with the 5th company, then selected the 22nd (5 + 17), and then the 39th, and so on.

Besides convenience, systematic sampling has other advantages. Because systematic sampling is evenly distributed across the frame, a knowledgeable person can easily determine whether a sampling plan has been followed in a study. However, a problem with systematic sampling can occur if there is periodicity in the data, and the sampling interval falls in syncopation with it. For example, if a list of 150 college students is actually a merged list of five classes with 30 students in each class and if each of the lists of the five classes has been ordered with the names of top students first and bottom students last, systematic sampling of every 30th student could cause selection of all top students, all bottom students, or all mediocre students. That is, there is a cyclical or periodic organization of the original list. Systematic sampling methodology is based on the assumption that the source of population elements is random.

Cluster or Area Sampling. Cluster (or area) sampling is a fourth type of random sampling. **Cluster (or area) sampling** involves dividing the population into nonoverlapping areas or clusters. However, in contrast to stratified random sampling where strata are homogeneous, cluster sampling identifies clusters that are internally heterogeneous. In theory, each cluster contains a wide variety of elements, and the cluster is a miniature, or microcosm, of the population. Examples of clusters are towns, companies, homes, colleges, areas of a city, and geographic regions. Often clusters are naturally occurring groups of the population and are already identified, such as states or Standard Metropolitan Statistical Areas. Although area sampling usually refers to clusters that are areas of the population, such as geographic regions and cities, the terms *cluster sampling* and *area sampling* are used interchangeably in this text.

cluster (or area) sampling

After choosing the clusters, the researcher randomly selects individual elements for the sample from the clusters. One example of business research that makes use of clustering is test marketing of new products. Often in test marketing, the United States is divided into clusters of test market cities, and individual consumers within the test market cities are surveyed.* Figure 7.2

*"Test Markets: Winners and Losers," *Advertising Weekly,* October 3, 1983.

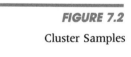

FIGURE 7.2

Cluster Samples

two-stage sampling

shows some U.S. test market cities that are used as clusters to test products. Sometimes the clusters are too large, and a second set of clusters is taken from each original cluster. This technique is called **two-stage sampling.** For example, a researcher could divide the United States into clusters of cities. She could then divide the cities into clusters of blocks and randomly select individual houses from the block clusters. The first stage was selecting the test cities, and the second stage was selecting the blocks.

Cluster or area sampling has several advantages. Two of the foremost advantages are convenience and cost. Clusters are usually convenient to obtain, and the cost of sampling from the entire population is reduced because the scope of the study is reduced to the clusters. The cost per element is usually lower in cluster or area sampling than in stratified sampling, because of lower element listing or locating costs. The time and cost of contacting elements of the population can be reduced, especially if travel is involved, because clustering reduces the distance to the sampled elements. In addition, administration of the sample survey can be simplified. Sometimes cluster or area sampling is the only feasible approach, because the sampling frames of the individual elements of the population are unavailable, prohibiting the use of other random sampling techniques.

Cluster or area sampling also has several disadvantages. If the elements of a cluster are similar, cluster sampling may be statistically less efficient than simple random sampling. In an extreme case—when the elements of a cluster are the same—sampling from the cluster may be no better than sampling a single unit from the cluster. Moreover, the costs and problems of statistical analysis are greater with cluster or area sampling than with simple random sampling.

Nonrandom Sampling

Sampling techniques used to select elements from the population by any mechanism that does not involve a random selection process are called nonrandom sampling techniques. Because chance is not used to select items for the samples, these techniques are nonprobability techniques and are *not desirable for use in gathering data to be analyzed by the methods of inferential statistics presented in this text.* Sampling error cannot be determined objectively for these sampling techniques. Three nonrandom sampling techniques are presented here: convenience sampling, judgmental sampling, and quota sampling.

convenience sampling

Convenience Sampling. In **convenience sampling,** *elements are selected for the sample for the convenience of the researcher.* The researcher tends to choose items that are readily available, nearby, and/or willing to participate. The sample tends to be less variable than the population, because in many environments the extreme elements of the population are not as readily available. The researcher will select more elements from the middle of the population. For example, in conducting door-to-door interviews, a convenience sample of homes might include houses where people are home, houses with no dogs, houses near the street, first-floor apartments, and houses with friendly people. In contrast, a random sample would require the researcher to gather data only from those houses and apartments that have been randomly selected no matter how inconvenient or unfriendly the location is. If a research firm is located in a mall, a convenient sample might be selected by interviewing only those shoppers who pass the shop and look friendly.

Judgment Sampling. **Judgment sampling** occurs when *elements are selected for the sample by the judgment of the researcher*. Researchers often believe that they can obtain a representative sample by using sound judgment, which will result in saving time and money. Sometimes ethical, professional researchers might believe that they can select a more representative sample than the random process will provide. They might be right! Unfortunately, when sampling is done by judgment, calculating the probability that an element is going to be selected for the sample is not possible. The sampling error cannot be determined objectively because probabilities are based on *nonrandom* selection.

judgment sampling

Several other problems are associated with judgment sampling. The researcher tends to make errors of judgment in the same direction. These systematic errors lead to what are called *biases*. For example, a judgment sample might include an overrepresentative number of middle-aged white men. The researcher also is less likely to include extreme elements. For example, if an instructor is selecting students for a sample, he might tend to exclude the oldest and youngest students from the process. Another problem with judgment sampling is that no objective method exists for determining whether one person's judgment is better than another's.

Quota Sampling. A third nonrandom sampling technique is **quota sampling,** which is a similar to stratified random sampling. Certain population subclasses, such as age, gender, or geographic region, are used as strata. However, instead of randomly sampling from each stratum, the researcher uses a nonrandom sampling method to gather data from one stratum until the desired quota of samples is filled. Quotas are described by quota controls, which set the sizes of the sample to be obtained from the subgroups. Often a quota is based on the proportions of the subclasses in the population. In this case, the quota concept is similar to that of proportional stratified sampling.

quota sampling

Quotas often are filled by using available, recent, or applicable elements. For example, instead of randomly interviewing people to obtain a quota of Italian Americans, the researcher would go to the Italian area of the city and interview there until enough responses were obtained to fill the quota. In quota sampling, an interviewer would begin by asking a few filter questions; if the respondent is from a quota that is filled, the interviewer terminates the interview.

Quota sampling can be useful if no frame is available for the population. For example, suppose that a researcher wants to stratify the population into owners of different types of cars but fails to find any lists of Dodge van owners.

Through quota sampling, the researcher would proceed by interviewing all car owners and casting out non-Dodge van owners until the quota of Dodge van owners is filled. Quota sampling is less expensive than most random sampling techniques, because it essentially is a technique of convenience. However, cost may have no meaning, because the quality of nonrandom and random sampling techniques cannot be compared. Another advantage of quota sampling is the speed of data gathering. The researcher does not have to call back or send out a second questionnaire if there is no response. The researcher just moves on to the next one. Preparatory work for quota sampling is minimal.

The main problem with quota sampling is that, when all is said and done, it still is only a *nonrandom* sampling technique. Some researchers have said that, if the quota is filled by *randomly* selecting elements and discarding those that are not from a stratum, quota sampling is essentially a version of stratified random sampling. However, most quota sampling is carried out by the researcher going where the quota can be filled quickly. The object is to gain the benefits of stratification without the high field costs of stratification. Ultimately, it remains a nonprobability sampling method.

Sampling Error

sampling error

Sampling error occurs when the sample is not representative of the population. When random sampling techniques are used to select elements for the sample, sampling error occurs by chance. Many times the statistic computed on the sample is not an accurate estimate of the population parameter, because the sample was not representative of the population. This result is caused by sampling error. With random samples, sampling error can be computed and analyzed.

Nonsampling Errors

nonsampling errors

All errors other than sampling errors are **nonsampling errors.** The many possible nonsampling errors include missing data, recording errors, input processing errors, and analysis errors. Other nonsampling errors have to do with the measurement instrument, such as errors of unclear definitions, defective questionnaires, and poorly conceived concepts. Improper definition of the frame is a nonsampling error. In many cases, finding a frame that perfectly fits the population is impossible. Insofar as it does not fit, a nonsampling error has been committed.

Response errors are also nonsampling errors, such as people who do not know, people who will not say, and people who overstate. Nonsampling errors of recall include telescoping, omission, and errors of detail. **Telescoping error** occurs when *a respondent attributes an event to a wrong time period*. **Omission error** occurs when *a respondent fails to mention past events*. **Detail error** occurs when *a respondent remembers an event incorrectly*. There is virtually no statistical way to measure or control for nonsampling errors. The statistical techniques

telescoping error
omission error
detail error

presented in this text are based on the assumption that none of these nonsampling errors has been committed. The researcher must eliminate these errors through carefully planning and executing the research study.

7.1 Develop a frame for the population of each of the following research projects.

   a. Measuring the job satisfaction of all union employees in a company.

   b. Conducting a telephone survey in Utica, New York, to determine whether there is any interest in having a new hunting and fishing specialty store in the mall.

   c. Interviewing passengers of a major airline about its food service.

   d. Studying the quality control programs of boat manufacturers.

   e. Attempting to measure the corporate culture of cable television companies.

7.2 Make a list of twenty people that you know. Include men and women, various ages, various educational levels, and so on. Number the list and then use the random number list in Table 7.1 to select randomly six people from your list. How representative of the population is the sample? Find the proportion of men in your population and in your sample. How do they compare? Find the proportion of 20-year-olds in your sample and the proportion in the population. How do they compare?

7.3 Use the random numbers in Table 7.1 to select ten of the companies from the thirty companies listed in Table 7.2. Compare the types of companies in your sample to the types in the population. How representative of the population is your sample?

7.4 For each of the following research projects, list three variables for stratification of the sample.

   a. A nationwide study of motels and hotels is being conducted. An attempt will be made to determine the extent of their use of cable TV. A sample of motels and hotels will be taken.

   b. A consumer panel is to be formed by sampling people in Michigan. Members of the panel will be interviewed periodically in an effort to understand current consumer attitudes and behaviors.

   c. A large soft-drink company wants to study the characteristics of the U.S. bottlers of its products, but the company does not want to conduct a census.

   d. The business research bureau of a large university is conducting a project in which the bureau will sample paper manufacturing companies.

7.5 In each of the following cases, the variable represents one way that a sample can be stratified in a study. For each variable, list some strata into which the variable can be divided.

a. Age of respondent (person)

b. Size of company (sales volume)

c. Size of retail outlet (square feet)

d. Geographic location

e. Occupation of respondent (person)

f. Type of business (company)

7.6 A city's phone book lists 100,000 people. If the phone book is the frame for a study, how large would the sample size be if systematic sampling were done on every 200th person?

7.7 If every eleventh item is systematically sampled, producing a sample size of seventy-five items, how large is the population?

7.8 If a company employs 3,500 people and if a random sample of 175 of these employees has been taken by systematic sampling, what is the value of k? The researcher would start the sample selection between what two values? Where could the researcher obtain a frame for this study?

7.9 For each of the following research projects, list at least one area or cluster that could be used in obtaining the sample.

a. A study of road conditions in the state of Missouri.

b. A study of U.S. offshore oil wells.

c. A study of the environmental effects of petrochemical plants west of the Mississippi River.

7.10 Give an example of how judgment sampling could be used in a study to determine how district attorneys feel about attorneys advertising on television.

7.11 Give an example of how convenience sampling could be used in a study of *Fortune 500* executives to measure corporate attitudes toward paternity leave for employees.

7.12 Give an example of how quota sampling could be used to conduct sampling by a company test marketing a new personal computer.

7.2 CENTRAL LIMIT THEOREM AND THE SAMPLING DISTRIBUTION OF $\overline{X}$

How are random samples used in inferential statistics to reach conclusions about a population? Such conclusions can be reached by computing a statistic on a sample and using the statistic to estimate a parameter of the population or to test a particular hypothesized value for the population. One of the most common statistics used in this process is the sample mean.

In order to compute and assign the probability of occurrence of a particular value of a sample mean, the researcher must know the distribution of sample means from the population. Fortunately, a structured way is available to determine the distribution of sample means: the **central limit theorem.**   **central limit theorem**

---

1. If samples of size n are randomly drawn from a population that has a mean of μ and a standard deviation of σ, the sample means, $\bar{X}$, are approximately normally distributed for sufficiently large sample sizes ($n \geq 30$) regardless of the shape of the population distribution. If the population is normally distributed, the sample means are normally distributed for any size sample.

2. The mean of the sample means is the population mean:

    $$\mu_{\bar{x}} = \mu.$$

3. The standard deviation of the sample means is the standard deviation of the population divided by the square root of the sample size:

    $$\sigma_{\bar{x}} = \frac{\sigma}{\sqrt{n}}.$$

Central Limit Theorem

The central limit theorem creates the potential for applying the normal distribution to many problems when sample size is sufficiently large. Sample means that have been computed for random samples drawn from normally distributed populations are normally distributed. However, the real advantage of the central limit theorem is that sample data drawn from populations not normally distributed or from populations of unknown shape also can be analyzed by using the normal distribution, because the sample means are normally distributed for sufficiently large sample sizes. Column 1 of Figure 7.3 shows four different population distributions. Each ensuing column displays the shape of the sample means for a particular sample size. Note in the bottom row for the normally distributed population that the sample means are normally distributed even for $n = 2$. Note also that with the other population distributions, the distribution of the sample means begins to approximate the normal curve as n gets larger. For all four distributions, the distribution of sample means is approximately normal for $n = 30$.

How large must a sample size be for the central limit theorem to apply? The sample size necessary varies according to the shape of the population. However, in this text (as in many others), a sample of *size 30* or larger will suffice. Recall that, if the population is normally distributed, the sample means are normally distributed for sample sizes as small as $n = 1$. Parts 2 and 3 of the central limit theorem also apply to populations that are normally distributed.

FIGURE 7.3

Shapes of the Distributions of Sample Means for Three Sample Sizes Drawn from Four Different Population Distributions

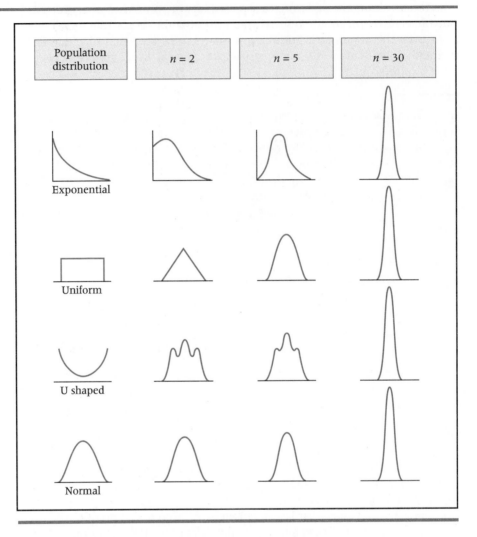

Part 1 of the central limit theorem states that sample means are normally distributed regardless of the shape of the population for large samples and for any sample size with normally distributed populations. Thus sample means can be analyzed by using Z scores. Recall from Chapter 6 that

$$Z = \frac{X - \mu}{\sigma}.$$

If sample means are normally distributed, the Z score formula applied to sample means would be

$$Z = \frac{\overline{X} - \mu_{\bar{x}}}{\sigma_{\bar{x}}}.$$

This result follows the general pattern of Z scores: the difference between the statistic and its mean divided by the statistic's standard deviation. In this formula, the mean of the statistic of interest is $\mu_{\overline{x}}$ and the standard deviation of the statistic of interest is $\sigma_{\overline{x}}$. In order to determine $\mu_{\overline{x}}$, the researcher would have to draw out randomly all possible samples of the given size from the population, compute the sample means, and average them. This task is virtually impossible to accomplish in any realistic period of time. Fortunately, part 2 of the central limit theorem states that $\mu_{\overline{x}}$ equals the population mean, μ, which is easier to access. Likewise, in order to determine directly the value of $\sigma_{\overline{x}}$, the researcher would have to take all possible samples of a given size from a population, compute the sample means, and determine the standard deviation of sample means. This task also is practically impossible. Fortunately, part 3 of the central limit theorem states that $\sigma_{\overline{x}}$ can be computed by using the population standard deviation divided by the square root of the sample size.

As sample size increases, the standard deviation of the sample means gets smaller and smaller, because the population standard deviation is being divided by larger and larger values of the square root of n. The ultimate benefit of the central limit theorem is a practical, useful version of the Z formula for sample means.

$$Z = \frac{\overline{X} - \mu}{\frac{\sigma}{\sqrt{n}}}.$$

Z Formula for Sample Means

When the population is normally distributed and the sample size is 1, this formula for sample means becomes the original Z formula for individual values. The reason is that the mean of one value is that value, and when $n = 1$ the value of $\sigma/\sqrt{n} = \sigma$.

Suppose, for example, that the mean expenditure per customer at a tire store is \$85.00, with a standard deviation of \$9.00. If a random sample of 40 customers is taken, what is the probability that the sample average expenditure per customer will be \$87.00 or more? Because the sample size is greater than 30, the central limit theorem can be used, and the sample means are normally distributed. With $\mu = \$85.00$, $\sigma = \$9.00$, and the Z formula for sample means,

$$Z = \frac{\overline{X} - \mu}{\frac{\sigma}{\sqrt{n}}} = \frac{\$87.00 - \$85.00}{\frac{\$9.00}{\sqrt{40}}} = \frac{\$2.00}{\$1.42} = 1.41.$$

FIGURE 7.4

Graphical Solution to the
Problem with Forty Ran-
dom Customers

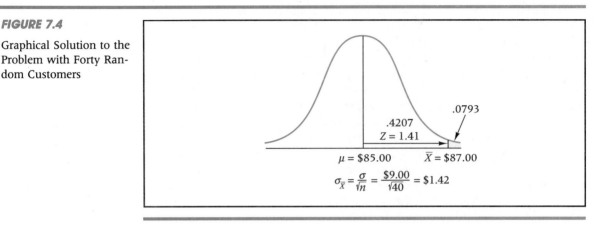

For $Z = 1.41$ in the Z distribution (Table A.5) the probability is .4207. It is the probability of getting a mean between $87.00 and the population mean, $85.00. Solving for the tail of the distribution yields

$$
\begin{array}{r}
.5000 \\
-.4207 \\
\hline
.0793
\end{array}
$$

which is the probability of $\overline{X} \geq \$87.00$. That is, 7.93% of the time, a random sample of 40 customers from this population will yield a mean expenditure of $87.00 or more. Figure 7.4 shows the problem and its solution.

**Demonstration
Problem 7.1**

Suppose that during any hour in a large department store, the average number of shoppers is 448, with a standard deviation of 21 shoppers. What is the probability of randomly selecting 49 different shopping hours, counting the shoppers, and having the sample mean fall between 441 and 446 shoppers?

Solution:

For this problem, $\mu = 448$, $\sigma = 21$, and $n = 49$. The problem is to determine $P(441 \leq \overline{X} \leq 446)$. The following diagram depicts the problem.

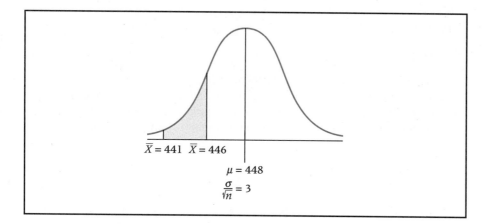

Solve this problem by calculating the Z scores and using Table A.5 to determine the probabilities:

$$Z = \frac{441 - 448}{\dfrac{21}{\sqrt{49}}} = \frac{-7}{3} = -2.33,$$

and

$$Z = \frac{446 - 448}{\dfrac{21}{\sqrt{49}}} = \frac{-2}{3} = -0.67.$$

Z Value	Probability
−2.33	.4901
−0.67	−.2486
	.2415

The probability of a value falling between $Z = -2.33$ and -0.67 is .2415. That is, there is a 24.15% chance of randomly selecting 49 hourly periods for which the sample mean falls between 441 and 446 shoppers.

**Demonstration
Problem 7.2**

In 1989, the highest per capita income in the United States was in Alaska, where it was $21,656. Suppose that a random sample of thirty-two people in Alaska is selected. For a population standard deviation of $6,500, the sample average would be greater than what value 73% of the time?

Solution:

For this problem, $\mu = \$21,656$, $\sigma = \$6,500$, and $n = 32$. More than half the time the sample averages would be greater than the value of interest, so it lies at the lower end of the distribution. The following diagram displays the problem.

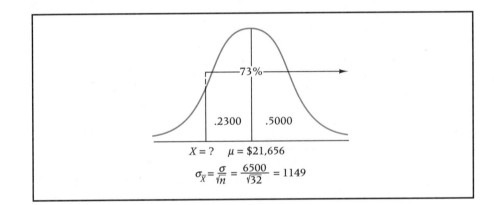

As .7300 of the area lies to the right of $\overline{X}$, .7300 − .5000 = .2300 lies between $\overline{X}$ and the population mean. This value in Table A.5 yields a Z value of −0.61. With this information, the value for $\overline{X}$ can be computed from the Z formula for sample means:

$$Z = \frac{\overline{X} - \mu}{\dfrac{\sigma}{\sqrt{n}}},$$

$$-0.61 = \frac{\overline{X} - 21,656}{\dfrac{6,500}{\sqrt{32}}},$$

$$\overline{X} = 21{,}656 - \frac{(0.61)(6{,}500)}{\sqrt{32}} = \$20{,}955.$$

In Alaska in 1989, if a random sample of 32 residents were drawn from the population, 73% of the time the sample average per capita income would be $20,955 or more.

Sampling from a Finite Population

Demonstration Problems 7.1 and 7.2 were based on the assumption that the population was infinitely or extremely large. In cases of a finite population, a statistical adjustment can be made to the Z formula for sample means. The adjustment is called the **finite correction factor:** $\sqrt{(N - n)/(N - 1)}$, and it operates on the standard deviation of sample means, $\sigma_{\overline{x}}$. Following is the Z formula for sample means when samples are drawn from finite populations.

finite correction factor

$$Z = \frac{\overline{X} - \mu}{\dfrac{\sigma}{\sqrt{n}}\sqrt{\dfrac{N - n}{N - 1}}}.$$

Z Formula for Sample Means When There is a Finite Population

If a random sample of size 35 were taken from a finite population of only 500, the sample mean would be less likely to deviate from the population mean than would a sample of size 35 taken from an infinite population. For a sample of size 35 taken from a finite population of size 500, the finite correction factor is

$$\sqrt{\frac{500 - 35}{500 - 1}} = \sqrt{\frac{465}{499}} = 0.965.$$

Thus the standard deviation of the mean—sometimes referred to as the standard error of the mean—is adjusted downward using .965. As the size of the finite population gets larger in relation to sample size, the finite correction factor approaches 1. In theory, whenever researchers are working with a finite population, they can use the finite correction factor. A rough rule of thumb for many researchers is that, if the sample size is less than 5% of the finite population size, the finite correction factor does not significantly modify the solution. Table 7.4 contains some illustrative finite correction factors.

TABLE 7.4	Population Size	Sample Size	Value of Correction Factor
Finite Correction Factor for Some Sample Sizes	2,000	30 (<5% N)	0.993
	2,000	100	0.975
	2,000	500	0.866
	500	30	0.971
	500	50	0.950
	500	100	0.895
	200	30	0.924
	200	50	0.868
	200	75	0.793

Demonstration Problem 7.3

A production company's 350 hourly employees average 37.6 years of age, with a standard deviation of 8.3 years. If a random sample of 45 hourly employees is taken, what is the probability that the sample will have an average age of less than 40 years?

Solution:

The population mean is 37.6, with a population standard deviation of 8.3; that is, $\mu = 37.6$ and $\sigma = 8.3$. The sample size is 45, but it is being drawn from a finite population of 350; that is, $n = 45$ and $N = 350$. The sample mean under consideration is 40, or $\bar{X} = 40$. The following diagram depicts the problem on a normal curve.

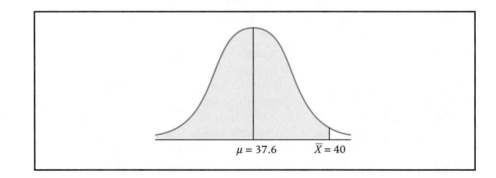

$\mu = 37.6$ $\bar{X} = 40$

Using the Z formula with the finite correction factor gives

$$Z = \frac{40 - 37.6}{\frac{8.3}{\sqrt{45}}\sqrt{\frac{350 - 45}{350 - 1}}} = \frac{2.4}{1.157} = 2.07.$$

This Z value yields a probability (Table A.5) of .4808. Therefore the probability of getting a sample average age of less than 40 years is .4808 + .5000 = .9808. Had the finite correction factor not been used, the Z value would have been 1.94, and the final answer would have been .9738.

**PROBLEMS
Section 7.2**

7.13 A population has a mean of 50 and a standard deviation of 10. If a random sample of 64 is taken, what is the probability that the sample mean is each of the following?

  a. Greater than 52

  b. Less than 51

  c. Less than 47

  d. Between 48.5 and 52.4

  e. Between 50.6 and 51.3

7.14 A population is normally distributed, with a mean of 23.45 and a variance of 14.5. What is the probability of the following?

  a. Taking a sample of size 10 and obtaining a sample mean of 22 or more

  b. Taking a sample of size 4 and getting a sample mean of more than 26

7.15 Suppose that a random sample of size 36 is being drawn from a population with a mean of 278. If 86% of the time the sample mean is less than 280, what is the population standard deviation?

7.16 A random sample of size 81 is being drawn from a population with a standard deviation of 12. If only 18% of the time, a sample mean greater than 300 is obtained, what is the mean of the population?

7.17 Find the probability in each case.

  a. $N = 1{,}000$, $n = 60$, $\mu = 75$, and $\sigma = 6$; $P(\bar{X} < 76.5) = ?$

  b. $N = 90$, $n = 36$, $\mu = 108$, and $\sigma = 3.46$; $P(107 < \bar{X} < 107.7) = ?$

  c. $N = 250$, $n = 100$, $\mu = 35.6$, and $\sigma = 4.89$; $P(\bar{X} \geq 36) = ?$

  d. $N = 5{,}000$, $n = 60$, $\mu = 125$, and $\sigma = 13.4$; $P(\bar{X} \leq 123) = ?$

7.18 Suppose that a subdivision on the southwest side of Denver, Colorado, contains 1,500 houses. The subdivision was built in 1983. A sample of 100 houses is randomly selected and evaluated by an appraiser. If the mean appraised value of a house in this subdivision for all houses is $137,000, with a standard deviation of $8,500, what is the probability that the sample average is greater than $145,000?

7.19 Suppose that the average checkout tab at a large supermarket is $65.12, with a standard deviation of $21.45. Twenty-three percent of the time that a random sample of forty-five customer tabs is examined the sample average should exceed what value?

7.20 A survey of 792 firms conducted by Hewitt Associates found that employers' health costs rose an average of $2,823 in 1990. Assume that the standard deviation of this increase was $883 and that the average of $2,823 applies to all 792 firms. What is the probability of randomly selecting 57 firms and finding the following?

   a. A sample average of $2,900 or less

   b. A sample average of more than $3,000

   c. A sample average of less than $2,500

7.21 The U.S. Department of Commerce reported that the number of Hispanic firms in the United States increased 81% between 1982 and 1987. According to the figures released, the average receipts for a Hispanic firm in the retail trade industry is $109,000. Suppose that a survey of 42 randomly selected Hispanic retailers is conducted and assume a population standard deviation of $31,000.

   a. What is the probability of getting a sample average of more than $120,000?

   b. What is the probability of getting a sample average of less than $100,000?

   c. What is the probability of getting a sample average of between $102,000 and $107,000?

   d. What is the probability of getting a sample average of between $108,000 and $111,000?

   e. If the standard deviation is unknown and the average receipts for 71% of all Hispanic firms are more than $106,000, what is the standard deviation of the population?

7.3   SAMPLING DISTRIBUTION OF $\hat{p}$

Sometimes in analyzing a sample, a researcher will choose to use the sample proportion, denoted $\hat{p}$, instead of the sample mean. Whereas the mean is **sample proportion**   computed by averaging a set of values, the **sample proportion** is computed by dividing the frequency that a given characteristic occurs in a sample by the number of items in the sample.

$$\hat{p} = \frac{X}{n},$$

where: X = number of items in a sample that possess the characteristic
n = number of items in the sample

For example, in a sample of 100 factory workers, 30 workers might belong to the union. The value of $\hat{p}$ for this characteristic, union membership, is $30/100 = 0.30$. Or, in a sample of 500 businesses in suburban malls, 10 are shoe stores. The sample proportion of shoe stores is $10/500 = 0.02$. The sample proportion is a widely used statistic and is usually computed on questions involving *yes* or *no* answers. For example, do you have at least a high school education? Are you predominately right-handed? Are you female? Do you belong to the student accounting association?

How does a researcher use the sample proportion in analysis? The central limit theorem also applies to sample proportions in that the normal distribution approximates the shape of the distribution of sample proportions if $n \cdot P > 5$ and $n \cdot Q > 5$ (P is the population proportion and $Q = 1 - P$). The central limit theorem also states that the mean of sample proportions for all samples of size n randomly drawn from a population is P (the population proportion) and the standard deviation of sample proportions is $\sqrt{(P \cdot Q)/n}$. Sample proportions also have a Z formula.

$$Z = \frac{\hat{p} - P}{\sqrt{\dfrac{P \cdot Q}{n}}},$$

where: $\hat{p}$ = sample proportion
n = sample size
P = population proportion
$Q = 1 - P$

Suppose that 60% of the electrical contractors in a region use a particular brand of wire. What is the probability of taking a random sample of size 120 from these electrical contractors and finding that 0.50 or less use that brand of wire? For this problem,

$$P = 0.60, \qquad \hat{p} = 0.50, \qquad \text{and} \qquad n = 120.$$

FIGURE 7.5

Graphical Solution to the
Electrical Contractor
Problem

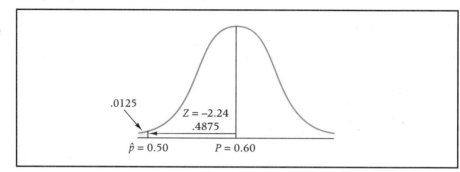

The Z formula yields

$$Z = \frac{0.50 - 0.60}{\sqrt{\dfrac{(0.60)(0.40)}{120}}} = \frac{-0.10}{0.0447} = -2.24.$$

From Table A.5, the probability corresponding to $Z = -2.24$ is .4875. For $Z < -2.24$ (tail of the distribution), the answer is $.5000 - .4875 = .0125$. Figure 7.5 shows the problem and solution graphically.

This answer indicates that a researcher would have difficulty (probability of .0125) finding that 50% of a sample of 120 contractors use a given brand of wire if indeed the population market share for that wire is 0.60. If this sample result actually occurs, either it is a rare chance result, or perhaps the 0.60 proportion does not hold for this population.

**Demonstration
Problem 7.4**

If 10% of a population of parts is defective, what is the probability of randomly selecting eighty parts and finding that twelve or more parts are defective?

Solution:

Here, $P = 0.10$, $\hat{p} = 12/80 = 0.15$, and $n = 80$. Using the Z formula gives

$$Z = \frac{0.15 - 0.10}{\sqrt{\dfrac{(0.10)(0.90)}{80}}} = \frac{0.05}{0.0335} = 1.49.$$

Table A.5 gives a probability of .4319 for a Z value of 1.49, which is the area between the sample proportion, 0.15, and the population proportion, 0.10. The answer to the question is

$$P(\hat{p} \geq 0.15) = .5000 - .4319 = .0681.$$

Thus about 6.81% of the time, twelve or more defective parts would appear in a random sample of eighty parts when the population proportion is 0.10. If this result actually occurred, the 10% proportion for population defects would be open to question. The diagram shows the problem graphically.

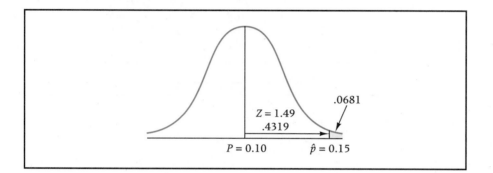

Demonstration Problem 7.5

Thirty-five percent of all American households had a telephone answering machine in 1990. A researcher believes that this proportion may not be true for her region of the country. If she takes a random sample of 500 households and finds that only 100 have an answering machine, what is the probability of getting a sample proportion this small or smaller if the population proportion really is 0.35?

Solution:

In this case $P = 0.35$, $\hat{p} = 100/500 = 0.20$, and $n = 500$. Solving for Z gives

$$Z = \frac{0.20 - 0.35}{\sqrt{\dfrac{(0.35)(0.65)}{500}}} = \frac{-0.15}{0.0213} = -7.04.$$

Almost all the area under the curve lies to the right of this Z value. The probability of getting this sample proportion or a smaller one is virtually zero. That is, the results obtained from this sample are almost too different from the 35% proportion for the researcher to accept the national figure for this region. The following diagram illustrates the problem and solution graphically.

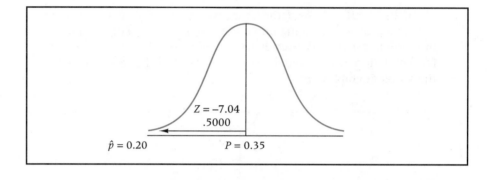

PROBLEMS
Section 7.3

7.22 If the population proportion is 0.25, what is the probability of getting the following sample results from this proportion?

a. $n = 110$ and $\hat{p} \le 0.21$

b. $n = 33$ and $\hat{p} > 0.24$

c. $n = 59$ and $0.24 \le \hat{p} < 0.27$

d. $n = 80$ and $\hat{p} > 0.30$

e. $n = 800$ and $\hat{p} > 0.30$

7.23 If the population proportion is 0.90, what is the probability of getting the following sample results?

a. $n = 75$ and $\hat{p} < 0.89$

b. $n = 40$ and $\hat{p} \le 0.89$

c. $n = 200$ and $\hat{p} \ge 0.85$

d. $n = 1100$ and $\hat{p} > 0.93$

e. $n = 450$ and $0.80 \le \hat{p} \le 0.86$

7.24 Suppose that a population proportion is 0.40 and that 80% of the time you draw a random sample from this population, you get a sample proportion of 0.35 or more. How large a sample were you taking?

7.25 If a population proportion is 0.28 and if the sample size is 140, 30 percent of the time the sample proportion will be less than what value if you are taking random samples?

7.26 Sixty-nine percent of all U.S. households had a VCR in 1990. If 600 households are randomly selected from the population, what is the probability that 400 or more households have a VCR?

7.27 In 1989, Harley-Davidson had the largest market share of superheavyweight motorcycles in the United States, with a little over 59%. Honda had almost 15% of the market. Suppose that a frame of superheavyweight motorcycle owners could be determined. If 200 owners were randomly sampled from this frame, what is the probability that fewer than 110 owned a Harley-Davidson? What is the probability that more than 50 owned a Honda?

7.28 Statistics released by the U.S. Bureau of Labor Statistics in 1989 showed that the employers of approximately 90% of all U.S. workers paid them for time spent on jury duty. Researchers believe that, in a particular industry, the figure is not valid. If 278 workers who have been on jury duty during the past year are randomly selected from that industry, what is the probability that less than 235 of them were paid while on jury duty?

7.29 In the Spring of 1990, the J.C. Penney company in conjunction with Aetna Life and Casualty adopted a program called "Healthy Beginnings" for expectant mothers. During the first three months of pregnancy, women are asked to contact Aetna nurses who help them identify personal habits or diseases that might contribute to birth problems. Aetna sends letters to physicians of high-risk mothers, asking the physicians to monitor them closely. Thirty percent of the women in the program have been diagnosed as high-risk mothers. Suppose that this figure is true for all expectant mothers. What is the probability of randomly sampling 100 expectant mothers and getting each of the following?

a. More than 35 high-risk mothers

b. Less than 20 high-risk mothers

c. Between 20 and 40 high-risk mothers

d. More than 45 high-risk mothers

For part d, explain why this low probability might occur.

SAMPLING DISTRIBUTION OF $\bar{X}_1 - \bar{X}_2$

In certain research designs the sampling plan calls for selecting two different, independent samples. The object might be to determine whether the two samples come from the same population; or, if they come from different populations, to determine the amount of difference in the populations. If the researcher selects the mean as the statistic and if *two* samples are randomly chosen, the researcher has *two* sample means to compare. This type of analysis is particularly useful in business when the researcher is attempting to determine, for example, whether there is a difference in the effectiveness of two brands of toothpaste or the difference in wear of two brands of tires. Research might be conducted to study the difference in the productivity of men and women on an assembly line under certain conditions. An engineer might want to determine differences in the strength of aluminum produced under two different temperatures. Is there a difference in the average cost of a two-bedroom, one-story house between Boston and Seattle? If so, how much is the difference? These and many other interesting questions can be researched by comparing results obtained from two random samples.

How does a researcher approach the analysis of the difference of two samples using sample means? The central limit theorem states that the difference in two sample means, $\bar{X}_1 - \bar{X}_2$, is normally distributed for large sample sizes (both n_1 and $n_2 \geq 30$). The central limit theorem for the difference in sample means also states that

$$\mu_{\bar{X}_1 - \bar{X}_2} = \mu_1 - \mu_2 \quad \text{and} \quad \sigma_{\bar{X}_1 - \bar{X}_2} = \sqrt{\frac{\sigma_1^2}{n_1} + \frac{\sigma_2^2}{n_2}}.$$

Using these expressions leads to a Z formula for the difference in two sample means.

Z Formula for the Difference in Two Sample Means for n_1 and $n_2 \geq 30$	$Z = \dfrac{(\bar{X}_1 - \bar{X}_2) - (\mu_1 - \mu_2)}{\sqrt{\dfrac{\sigma_1^2}{n_1} + \dfrac{\sigma_2^2}{n_2}}},$

where: μ_1 = the mean of population 1
μ_2 = the mean of population 2
n_1 = size of sample 1
n_2 = size of sample 2

This formula makes possible the solution of problems involving two random samples and their means. Suppose that two random samples are drawn from the workers of a large manufacturing company. That is, both samples come from the same population. Company records are used to determine the number of years that each worker has been with the company. The mean number of years is computed for workers in each sample. What is the probability that the difference in the means will be at least five years? Assume that the variance of the population is ten years and that both sample sizes are 49. As the two samples are from the same population, the difference in population means is zero, and the population variances are equal:

$$\mu_1 - \mu_2 = 0, \quad \sigma_1^2 = 10, \quad \text{and} \quad \sigma_2^2 = 10$$

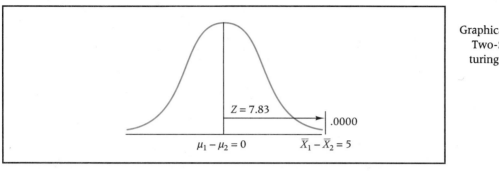

because

$$\sigma_1^2 = \sigma_2^2 = \sigma^2 \qquad \text{(same population = same variance)}$$

and

$$n_1 = n_2 = 49.$$

The Z value is

$$Z = \frac{(\bar{X}_1 - \bar{X}_2) - (\mu_1 - \mu_2)}{\sqrt{\dfrac{\sigma_1^2}{n_1} + \dfrac{\sigma_2^2}{n_2}}} = \frac{5 - 0}{\sqrt{\dfrac{10}{49} + \dfrac{10}{49}}} = \frac{5}{0.6389} = 7.83$$

Figure 7.6 depicts this problem and its solution graphically. Because $Z = 7.83$ is so large, it is not included in the Z table. Thus the probability of obtaining a Z value that large or larger by chance is virtually zero. Therefore the probability of obtaining two means with a difference of five years or more tenure with the firm from this same population is virtually zero.

**Demonstration
Problem 7.6**

Suppose that in January the average natural gas bill for households using natural gas in a northern state is $185, with a standard deviation of $35. Suppose that, for the same month, the average natural gas bill for households using natural gas in a southern state is $91 with a standard deviation of $22. If forty households in the northern state and thirty-two households in the southern state are randomly sampled, what is the probability that the difference in sample averages will be at least $100?

Solution:

In this case, $\mu_1 = 185$, $\mu_2 = 91$, $\sigma_1 = 35$, $\sigma_2 = 22$, $n_1 = 40$, and $n_2 = 32$. The difference in sample means, $\overline{X}_1 - \overline{X}_2$, is 100. The Z formula yields

$$Z = \frac{(\overline{X}_1 - \overline{X}_2) - (\mu_1 - \mu_2)}{\sqrt{\dfrac{\sigma_1^2}{n_1} + \dfrac{\sigma_2^2}{n_2}}} = \frac{100 - (185 - 91)}{\sqrt{\dfrac{35^2}{40} + \dfrac{22^2}{32}}} = \frac{6}{6.764} = 0.89.$$

From Table A.5, the probability of getting a Z value between 0 and 0.89 is .3133. The probability of getting a Z value larger than 0.89 is .5000 − .3133 = .1867. When the difference in the means of the population is $185 − $91 = $94, the difference of $100 or more for the sample means occurs 18.67% of the time. Graphically, the problem and its solution are shown in the following diagram.

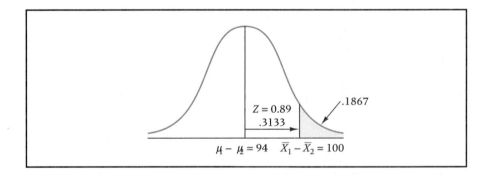

PROBLEMS
Section 7.4

7.30 Assume that two independent random samples of size 50 each are taken from a population that has a variance of 36. What is the probability that the difference in the sample means will be each of the following?

a. Greater than 2

b. Less than −0.5

c. Between 1 and 4

d. Between −2 and 3

7.31 A random sample of size 45 is taken from a population that has a mean of 150 and a standard deviation of 10. Another random sample of size

40 is taken from a second population that has a mean of 120 and a standard deviation of 20. What is the probability that the difference in sample means will be each of the following?

a. >50

b. >40

c. >30

d. >20

7.32 Population A has a mean of 200 and a standard deviation of 27. Population B has a mean of 210 and a standard deviation of 23. A sample of 35 items is taken from population A, and a sample mean of 197 is obtained. A sample of 42 items is taken from population B, and a sample mean of 212 is obtained. What is the probability of getting this much difference—or more—in this direction from these samples of these two populations?

7.33 Figures released by the U.S. Department of Commerce show that the average annual receipts for Hispanic-owned firms in the construction industry is $62,000. The average for Hispanic-owned transportation and public utility companies is $51,000. Assume that the standard deviation of annual receipts in the construction industry is $18,600 and for the transportation and public utility businesses is $14,700. A random sample of thirty-five Hispanic-owned firms in the construction industry is taken, along with a random sample of thirty-two Hispanic-owned transportation and public utility firms. What is the probability that the difference between the average annual receipts for the sampled Hispanic-owned construction firms and the sampled Hispanic-owned transportation and public utility firms is more than $15,000?

7.34 McDonald's Corporation estimates that, on average, one of its restaurants generates about 238 lb of waste every day. Assume that the standard deviation for this waste is 72 lb. Suppose that a random sample of thirty-one McDonald's restaurants west of the Mississippi is taken and that these restaurants generated an average of 252 lb of waste every day. Suppose that a random sample of thirty-five McDonald's restaurants east of the Mississippi is taken and that the restaurants generated an average of 231 pounds of waste every day. If there is no difference in the population means of daily waste between McDonald's restaurants west of the Mississippi and east of the Mississippi, what is the probability of getting a sample difference this large or larger?

SAMPLING DISTRIBUTION OF $\hat{p}_1 - \hat{p}_2$ **7.5**

Sample proportions can be used as the statistic to make inferences about populations from two random samples. Sometimes the measurement being studied is not conducive to computation of means but does lend itself to computation of proportions. Proportions are especially useful in studying market share, proportion of the vote, ethnic makeup of the population, and many other things. When a researcher wants to compare two populations or determine whether two samples come from the same population, the difference in sample proportions, $\hat{p}_1 - \hat{p}_2$, is a useful statistic. This statistic is computed by taking random samples and determining $\hat{p}$ for each sample for a given characteristic and calculating the difference in these sample proportions.

The central limit theorem states that, for large samples (each of $n_1 \cdot \hat{p}_1$, $n_1 \cdot \hat{q}_1$, $n_2 \cdot \hat{p}_2$, and $n_2 \cdot \hat{q}_2 > 5$, where $\hat{q} = 1 - \hat{p}$), the difference in sample proportions is normally distributed with a mean difference of

$$\mu_{\hat{p}_1 - \hat{p}_2} = P_1 - P_2$$

and a standard deviation of the difference of sample proportions of

$$\sigma_{\hat{p}_1 - \hat{p}_2} = \sqrt{\frac{P_1 \cdot Q_1}{n_1} + \frac{P_2 \cdot Q_2}{n_2}}.$$

From this information, a Z formula for the difference in sample proportions can be developed.

Z Formula for the Difference in Two Sample Proportions

$$Z = \frac{(\hat{p}_1 - \hat{p}_2) - (P_1 - P_2)}{\sqrt{\dfrac{P_1 \cdot Q_1}{n_1} + \dfrac{P_2 \cdot Q_2}{n_2}}},$$

where: $\hat{p}_1$ = proportion from sample 1
$\hat{p}_2$ = proportion from sample 2
n_1 = size of sample 1
n_2 = size of sample 2
P_1 = proportion from population 1
P_2 = proportion from population 2
$Q_1 = 1 - P_1$
$Q_2 = 1 - P_2$

A study of unemployment among architects showed that in the spring of 1991 about 30% of the architects in New York state were unemployed, as were about 25% of Massachusett's architects. If these figures are accurate for the populations of architects in each of these states, what is the probability of randomly selecting 180 architects from each state and getting a difference of 7% or more between the unemployed proportion of the sample of New York's architects and the unemployed proportion of the sample of Massachusett's architects?

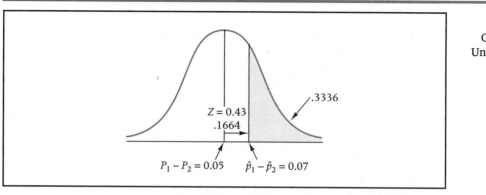

FIGURE 7.7

Graphical Solution to
Unemployed Architects
Problem

Let P_1 = proportion of New York's architects unemployed = 0.30.
Let P_2 = proportion of Massachusett's architects unemployed = 0.25.
Also, n_1 = 180, n_2 = 180, and $\hat{p}_1 - \hat{p}_2$ = 0.07.

What is the probability of getting 0.07 or more? The Z formula for the difference
in two sample proportions gives

$$Z = \frac{(0.07) - (0.30 - 0.25)}{\sqrt{\dfrac{(0.30)(0.70)}{180} + \dfrac{(0.25)(0.75)}{180}}} = \frac{(0.02)}{(0.047)} = 0.43.$$

From Table A.5, the area beyond Z = 0.43 is .5000 − .1664 = .3336. That
is, 33.36% of the time, the difference in sample proportions would be .07 or
more when random samples of size 180 are drawn from these two populations.
Graphically, the problem and its solution are depicted in Figure 7.7.

**Demonstration
Problem 7.7**

In 1989, Goodyear/Kelly-Springfield had 17% of the U.S. replacement
passenger-car tire market based on unit sales. Suppose that in New
England a random sample of 400 owners of recently purchased tires
are contacted, and 75 had bought Goodyear/Kelly-Springfield tires.
Suppose that in Ohio a similar survey of 350 tire purchasers is taken,
and 90 of them purchased Goodyear/Kelly-Springfield tires. What is
the probability of getting a difference this great or greater for the sample
proportions taken from these two states?

Solution:

Both P_1 and P_2 = 0.17 because the population, in theory, is the same. The sample proportion of Goodyear/Kelly-Springfield tire purchasers from New England is $\hat{p}_1$ = 75/400 = 0.1875, and the sample proportion of Goodyear/Kelly-Springfield tire purchasers from Ohio is $\hat{p}_2$ = 90/350 = 0.2571. Also, n_1 = 400 and n_2 = 350. Solve for Z:

$$Z = \frac{(0.1875 - 0.2571) - (0.17 - 0.17)}{\sqrt{\dfrac{(0.17)(0.83)}{400} + \dfrac{(0.17)(0.83)}{350}}} = \frac{-0.0696}{0.0275} = -2.53.$$

This Z value yields an area of $0.5000 - 0.4943 = 0.0057$. The diagram shows the problem and solution graphically.

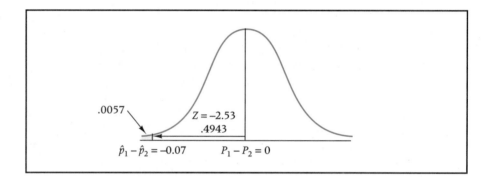

Suppose that these sample proportions had actually been obtained. Because this great a difference in sample proportions is unlikely if the samples come from the same population, the market share for Goodyear/Kelly-Springfield must be different in Ohio than in New England. Examination of the two sample proportions indicates that the market share is higher in Ohio.

PROBLEMS
Section 7.5

7.35 Two random samples are drawn from a population. If the population proportion for a given characteristic is 0.30, what is the probability of getting a difference as great or greater than the following sample proportions?

  a. $\hat{p}_1$ = 0.33 and $\hat{p}_2$ = 0.27 for n_1 = 100 and n_2 = 120
  b. $\hat{p}_1$ = 0.35 and $\hat{p}_2$ = 0.25 for n_1 = 100 and n_2 = 120
  c. $\hat{p}_1$ = 0.35 and $\hat{p}_2$ = 0.25 for n_1 = 1,000 and n_2 = 1,200

7.36 According to a survey, approximately 63% of all clothing purchased in Japan is a domestic brand (Japanese). Suppose that a random sample of 175 rural Japanese clothing purchasers revealed that 80% purchased domestic brand clothing. Suppose that a random sample of 225 urban Japanese clothing purchasers revealed that only 56% purchased domestic clothing. Is it likely that the two samples came from the same Japanese population? Use the Z formula for sample proportions to determine the probability of getting differences this great or greater.

7.37 In a 1991 survey the Roper Organization found that almost three-fourths of the parents said that they take their children out to eat frequently or fairly often. Surveys taken in 1976 showed that less than one-half of the parents took their children out to eat frequently or fairly often. Suppose that a survey of 780 randomly selected parents was taken in 1976 and that 375 of the parents reported taking their children out to eat frequently or fairly often. Suppose that a similar survey of 970 randomly selected parents in 1991 showed that 730 of the parents reported taking their children out to eat frequently or fairly often. What is the probability of getting differences in sample proportions this great or greater if the population figures for 1976 and 1991 were actually 50% and 75%, respectively, as reported.

7.38 A survey conducted by the National Center for Education Statistics showed that 50% of the college graduates who earned a bachelor's degree in 1986 were working in jobs closely related to their field one year later. This figure varied according to the field. For example, only 13% of the history majors were working in their field one year after graduation, but 92% of nursing majors were working in their field one year later.

Suppose that a random sample of 300 engineering graduates and a random sample of 250 accounting graduates is taken in 1991. Suppose also that, in 1992, one year after graduation, 227 of the engineering graduates and 204 of the accounting graduates are working in a field closely related to their major. What is the probability that in these two fields, this much difference or more would be obtained in the sample proportions if there is no difference in the proportions of the populations and the proportion of each is about .80?

QUALITY CONTROL | **7.6**

What Is Quality?

Quality means different things to different people. If someone is asked whether his or her automobile has quality or not, the response would vary according to that person's perspective. One person's view might be that quality means that an automobile will go 75,000 miles without needing any major repair work. Another person perceives automobile quality as comfortable seats and extra electronic gadgetry. Still other purchasers define automobile quality as the presence of many safety features.

There are almost as many definitions of quality as there are people and products. Let's assume that in the marketplace buyer and seller agree on the specifications of a product. One definition of **quality** then is *when a product delivers what is stipulated for it in its specifications.*

quality

From this point of view, quality work occurs when producer delivers what has been specified in the product description, as agreed upon by both buyer and seller. For example, the Lakeland Motor Company in Toledo, Ohio, produces the L27 motor that is used in electrical appliances. If the L27 motor has a specified amount of yield, has specified physical characteristics, and carries a warranty for a specified number of years of maintenance-free service, then a purchased L27 motor that meets these standards has quality.

Most automobile purchasers agree that a Cadillac has quality. If the buyer agreed to purchase a Ford Escort and a Ford Escort is delivered to the buyer in the condition specified, the Ford Escort is also a quality car even though it is not a Cadillac. A VCR in the medium price range can be a quality VCR if it delivers the performance and attributes specified by the producer.

David A. Garvin, an authority on quality control, advocates that quality be defined in at least three dimensions: user based, manufacturing based, and product based.* User-based quality means that the quality of a product is determined by the consumer. If a company produces a product that the consumer is seeking and is pleased with, the product has quality. Thus several years ago when Cabbage Patch dolls were in such great demand, they were quality products according to a user-based quality definition regardless of whether they had defects or whether they were durable.

Manufacturing-based quality is judged by standards set by the producer. Does the product meet the design specifications? Are there defects in the product? Is the manufacturing or production process reducing errors and becoming more efficient?

Product-based quality is measurable in the product. For example, a baseball glove with more stitching has more quality. A hard-disk drive personal computer with more memory has more quality. For a specific type of material, a tire with more tread has more quality.

What Is Quality Control?

quality control

How does a company know whether it is producing a quality product? **Quality control** (or quality assurance) is *the collection of strategies, techniques, and actions taken by an organization to assure themselves that they are producing a quality product.* This process begins at the product planning stage, where measurable

* Garvin, David A., "What Does 'Product Quality' Really Mean," *Sloan Management Review,* 1984, 26(1):25-43.

attributes of the product are determined and specified. Each attribute of the product is a potential contributor to overall product quality. In order to determine whether there is quality control for a product, measurable attributes and specifications must exist, against which the actual attributes of the product can be compared.

Quality control can be undertaken in two distinct ways: after-process control and in-process control. **After-process quality control** involves inspecting the attributes of a finished product to determine whether the product is acceptable, is in need of rework, or is to be rejected and scrapped. The after-process quality control method was the leading quality control technique for American manufacturers for several decades until the 1980s. The emphasis in the after-process method is on *weeding out* defective products before they reach the consumer. The problem with this method is that it does not generate information that can correct in-process problems or raw materials problems. Two main outcomes of the after-process methodology are (1) reporting the number of defects produced during a specific period of time and (2) screening defective products from consumers. Because American companies dominated world markets in many areas for several decades during and after World War II, their managers had little interest in changing from the after-process procedures.

after-process quality control

However, as Japan, other Asian nations, and Western European countries began to compete strongly with U.S. goods in the world market in the late 1970s and 1980s, U.S. companies began to reexamine quality control methods. As a result, many U.S. companies, following the example of Japanese and European manufacturers, developed quality control programs based on in-process control. **In-process quality control** techniques measure product attributes at various intervals throughout the manufacturing process in an effort to pinpoint problem areas. This information allows quality control personnel in conjunction with production personnel to make corrections in operations as products are being made. This intervention in turn opens the door to opportunities for improving the process and the product. Among the leading proponents of in-process quality control has been W. Edwards Deming.

in-process quality control

Total Quality Management

W. Edwards Deming, who directed the Japanese rise to the top in quality management, told them that the achievement of quality is an organic phenomenon that begins with top management's commitment and extends all the way to suppliers on the one hand and consumers on the other hand. His philosophy is that a company's principal purpose is not to make money but to continue to exist and provide jobs. Deming believes that quality control is a long-term total company effort. The effort called for by Deming is **total quality management.** Total quality management involves all members of the organization—from the CEO to the line worker—in improving quality. In addition, the goals and objectives of the organization come under the purview

total quality management

of quality control and can be measured in quality terms. Suppliers, raw materials, worker training, and opportunity for workers to make improvements all are part of total quality management. The antithesis of total quality management is when a company turns quality control exclusively over to a quality control department with total responsibility for improving product quality.

Diagnostic Techniques

A variety of approaches and techniques can be used to investigate quality problems in the search for solutions. One such technique is Pareto analysis.

Pareto analysis

Pareto Analysis.   **Pareto analysis** is a quantitative tallying of the number and types of defects that occur with a product. Analysts use this to produce a vertical bar chart that displays the most common types of defects, ranked in order of occurrence from left to right. The bar chart is called a *Pareto chart*. This chart allows quality control decision makers to separate important defects from trivial defects. It helps the decision makers set priorities for needed quality improvement work.

Suppose, for example, that the number of finished L27 motors being rejected by inspectors for the Lakeland Motor Company has been increasing. Company officials examine the records of 800 of these motors that had at least one defect in an effort to determine what defects were occurring. If a Pareto chart is constructed from these findings, the resulting Pareto chart might look like the one shown in Figure 7.8.

Using this Pareto chart, officials at the Lakeland Motor Company would likely begin examining those parts of the production process that involve the

FIGURE 7.8

Pareto Chart

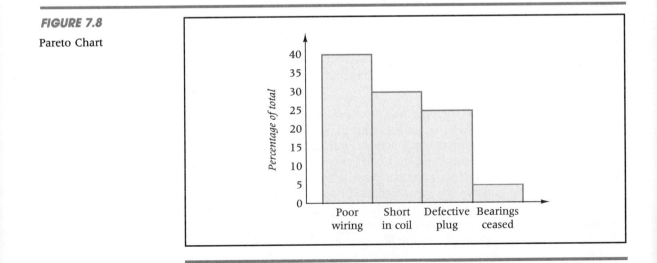

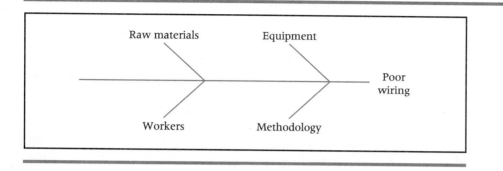

FIGURE 7.9

Fishbone Diagram

wiring, the coil, and the plug in that order. They now can begin to formulate a logical plan that should result in increased productivity and quality by reducing the number of defects.

Fishbone Diagram.   Another diagnostic technique is the fishbone, or Ishikawa, diagram. The **fishbone diagram** displays potential cause-and-effect relationships for quality problems. Each diagram represents possible causes of one problem. The problem is depicted at the front of the diagram, like the fish's head. Different possible causes of the problem are listed on each branch of the skeleton.

    Suppose the officials at Lakeland Motor Company want to construct a fishbone diagram for the poor wiring problem with the electric motors. The possible causes of poor wiring include raw materials, faulty or maladjusted equipment, workers, and methodology. Figure 7.9 shows a fishbone diagram for this problem and these potential causes.

Quality Circles.   Another helpful technique used to locate and solve quality problems is the quality circle. In virtually any business, quality circles can be used to identify, analyze, and solve production and quality problems. A **quality circle** is a small group of workers consisting of supervisors and six to ten employees who meet regularly to consider quality issues in their department or area of the business.

    Quality circles need to be *safe* places, where employees believe that they will not be penalized for any ideas shared. Each person is to be respected as an integral, important part of the team. Because employees may hold negative attitudes based on similar meetings in the past, a few meetings may be necessary before a quality circle becomes effective. Eventually, if the participants realize that the quality circle is a serious, useful endeavor, they may begin to offer information about specific items in the production process that need attention.

    Quality circles can elevate production workers from a level of "just installing their part" to a level of "analyst." The circles have the potential for generating communication, cooperation, and teamwork and have enjoyed

fishbone diagram

quality circle

great success in Japan. In the United States, the concept of quality circles has been introduced in various types of businesses, ranging from hospitals to chemical production facilities.

Just-in-Time Systems.   Another technique used to improve quality control is the just-in-time system for inventory, which focuses on raw materials, subparts, and suppliers. Ideally, a **just-in-time inventory system** means that no extra raw materials or inventory of parts are stored for production. Necessary supplies and parts needed for production arrive "just in time." The advantage of this system is that holding costs, personnel, and space needed to manage inventory are reduced. Even within the production process, as subparts are assembled and merged, the just-in-time philosophy can be applied to smooth the process and eliminate bottlenecks.

just-in-time inventory system

A production facility is unlikely to become 100% just in time. One of the residual effects of installing a just-in-time system throughout the production process is that, as the inventory "fat" is trimmed from the production process, the pressure of the system to produce often discloses problems that had gone undetected. For example, one subpart being made on two machines cannot be produced in enough quantity to supply the next step. Installation of the just-in-time system shows that this station is a bottleneck. The company might choose to add another machine to produce more subparts, change the production schedule, or develop another strategy. As the bottleneck is loosened and the problem is corrected, other areas of weakness may emerge. Thus the residual effect of a just-in-time inventory system can be the opportunity for production managers to work their way methodically through a maze of previously unidentified problems that otherwise would not normally manifest themselves.

A just-in-time inventory system changes the relationship between suppliers and producers. Most companies using this system have fewer suppliers than they did before installing the system. The tendency is for manufacturers to give suppliers longer contracts under the just-in-time system. However, the suppliers are expected to produce raw materials and subparts to a specified quality and to deliver the goods as near to just-in-time as possible. Just-in-time suppliers may even build production or warehouse facilities next to the producer's. In the just-in-time system, the suppliers become part of total quality management.

Control Charts

Variation exists for virtually any product or service. Among the reasons for product variation are differences in the quality of raw materials, workers, and the environment. For example small variations can be caused by unnoticable events, such as a passing truck that emits vibrations or dust that affects machine operation. Variations need to be measured, recorded, and studied so that out-of-control conditions can be identified and corrections made in the process. The construction of control charts is a means that can be used to accomplish these ends.

W. A. Shewhart is credited with developing **control charts** in the 1920s.
Each control chart has a centerline, an upper control limit, and a lower control
limit. Data are recorded on the control chart, and, if a data point falls above
the upper control limit or below the lower control limit, the attribute being
measured is out-of-control. There are two general types of control charts: (1)
control charts for measurements and (2) control charts for compliance items.
Here, two types of control charts for measurements, the $\overline{X}$ and R charts, and
one type of control chart for compliance items, the p chart, are discussed.

$\overline{X}$ Charts. An $\overline{X}$ **chart** is a graph of sample means computed for a series of
small random samples over a period of time. These means are average mea-
surements of some product characteristic. For example, the measurement could
be the volume of fluid in a 12-oz soft-drink bottle, the thickness of a piece of
sheet metal, or the actual width of a 2 in. $\times$ 4 in. piece of lumber.

The $\overline{X}$ chart graphs these sample means against a centerline. The centerline
is the average of the sample means, $\overline{\overline{X}}$. The $\overline{X}$ chart has an upper control limit,
UCL, three standard deviations of means above the centerline. The lower
boundary of the $\overline{X}$ chart, called the lower control limit, LCL, is three standard
deviations of means below the centerline. Recall the empirical rule presented
in Chapter 3, which states that if data are normally distributed, approximately
99.7% of all values will fall within three standard deviations of the mean.
Because the shape of the sampling distribution of $\overline{X}$ is normal for large sample
sizes regardless of the population shape, the empirical rule applies. However,
because small samples are often used, an approximation of the three standard
deviations of means is used to determine UCL and LCL. Instead of a calculated
$3\sigma_{\overline{x}}$, $\overline{X}$ control charts are based on $A_1\overline{R}$, where $\overline{R}$ is the average value of the
range for all samples and A_1 is a value obtained from Table A.9. The following
steps produce an $\overline{X}$ chart.

1. Decide on the quality to be measured.
2. Determine a sample.
3. Gather twenty to thirty samples under controlled conditions.
4. Compute the sample average, $\overline{X}$, for each sample.
5. Compute the sample range, R, for each sample.
6. Determine the average sample mean for all samples, $\overline{\overline{X}}$, as follows:

$$\overline{\overline{X}} = \frac{\Sigma \overline{X}}{k},$$

where: k is the number of samples.

7. Determine the average sample range for all samples, $\overline{R}$, as follows:

$$\overline{R} = \frac{\Sigma R}{k}.$$

8. Using the size of the samples, n_i, determine the value of A_1 from Table A.9.

9. Construct the centerline, the upper control limit, and the lower control limit:

$\overline{\overline{X}}$ is the centerline;

$\overline{\overline{X}} + A_1\overline{R}$ is the UCL;

$\overline{\overline{X}} - A_1\overline{R}$ is the LCL.

Demonstration Problem 7.8

A manufacturing facility is producing combs. The length specified for the combs is 5 in. Every hour for eight hours, six combs are sampled and their lengths are measured and recorded. Use the resulting data and construct an $\overline{X}$ chart.

Sample 1	Sample 2	Sample 3	Sample 4
5.13	4.96	5.21	5.02
4.92	4.98	4.87	5.09
5.01	4.95	5.02	4.99
4.88	4.96	5.08	5.02
5.05	5.01	5.12	5.03
4.97	4.89	5.04	5.01

Sample 5	Sample 6	Sample 7	Sample 8
5.12	4.98	4.99	4.96
5.08	5.02	5.00	5.01
5.09	4.97	5.00	5.02
5.13	4.99	5.02	5.05
5.06	4.98	5.01	5.04
5.13	4.99	5.01	5.02

Solution:

Compute the value of $\overline{X}$ for each sample and average these values, resulting in $\overline{\overline{X}}$:

$$\overline{\overline{X}} = \frac{\overline{X}_1 + \overline{X}_2 + \overline{X}_3 + \overline{X}_4 + \overline{X}_5 + \overline{X}_6 + \overline{X}_7 + \overline{X}_8}{8}$$

$$= \frac{\begin{array}{c}4.9933 + 4.9583 + 5.0566 + 5.0266 + \\ 5.1016 + 4.9883 + 5.0050 + 5.0166\end{array}}{8}$$

$$= 5.0183 \quad \text{(the centerline).}$$

Compute the values of R and average them, resulting in $\overline{R}$:

$$\overline{R} = \frac{R_1 + R_2 + R_3 + R_4 + R_5 + R_6 + R_7 + R_8}{8}$$

$$= \frac{0.25 + 0.12 + 0.34 + 0.10 + 0.07 + 0.05 + 0.03 + 0.09}{8}$$

$$= .1313.$$

Determine the value of A_1 by using $n_i = 6$ (the size of the sample) from Table A.9: $A_1 = 0.483$. The UCL is

$$\overline{\overline{X}} + A_1\overline{R} = 5.0183 + (.483)(.1313) = 5.0183 + .0634 = 5.0817.$$

The LCL is

$$\overline{\overline{X}} - A_1\overline{R} = 5.0183 - (.483)(.1313) = 5.0183 - .0634 = 4.9549.$$

The following graph depicts the $\overline{X}$ control chart. Note from the $\overline{X}$ chart that the sample mean for sample 5 falls above the UCL. This result signals that sample 5 is out of control and alerts the production supervisor to initiate a further investigation of combs produced during that time period. All other samples lie within the control limits.

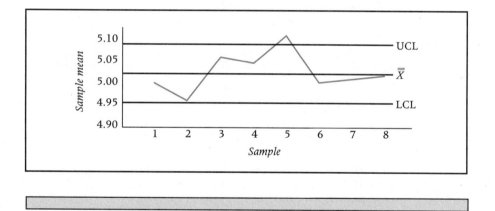

R Charts. An **R chart** is a plot of the sample ranges and often is used in conjunction with an $\overline{X}$ chart. Whereas $\overline{X}$ charts are used to plot the central tendency values, $\overline{X}$, for each sample, R charts are used to plot the variation of each sample as measured by the sample range. The centerline of an R chart is the average range, $\overline{R}$. Lower control limits (LCLs) are determined by $D_3\overline{R}$, where D_3 is a weight applied to $\overline{R}$, reflecting sample size. The value of D_3 can be obtained from Table A.9. Upper control limits, UCLs, are determined by $D_4\overline{R}$, where D_4 is a value obtained from Table A.9, which also reflects sample size. The following steps lead to an R chart.

R chart

1. Decide on the quality to be measured.
2. Determine a sample

3. Gather twenty to thirty samples under controlled conditions.
4. Compute the sample range, R, for each sample.
5. Determine the average sample range for all samples, $\bar{R}$, as follows:

$$\bar{R} = \frac{\Sigma R_j}{k},$$

where: k = the number of samples.

6. Using the size of the samples, n_i, find the values of D_3 and D_4 in Table A.9.
7. Construct the centerline and control limits:

Centerline = $\bar{R}$

LCL = $D_3 \bar{R}$

UCL = $D_4 \bar{R}$

Demonstration Problem 7.9

Construct an $\bar{R}$ chart for the eight samples of Demonstration Problem 7.8, where n_i = 6 combs.

Solution:

Shown are the data from the eight samples and the computed sample ranges.

Sample 1	Sample 2	Sample 3	Sample 4
5.13	4.96	5.21	5.02
4.92	4.98	4.87	5.09
5.01	4.95	5.02	4.99
4.88	4.96	5.08	5.02
5.05	5.01	5.12	5.03
4.97	4.89	5.04	5.01
$R_1 = 0.25$	$R_2 = 0.12$	$R_3 = 0.34$	$R_4 = 0.10$
Sample 5	**Sample 6**	**Sample 7**	**Sample 8**
5.12	4.98	4.99	4.96
5.08	5.02	5.00	5.01
5.09	4.97	5.00	5.02
5.13	4.99	5.02	5.05
5.06	4.98	5.01	5.04
5.13	4.99	5.01	5.02
$R_5 = 0.07$	$R_6 = 0.05$	$R_7 = 0.03$	$R_8 = 0.09$

$$\bar{R} = \frac{0.25 + 0.12 + 0.34 + 0.10 + 0.07 + 0.05 + 0.03 + 0.09}{8}$$

$$= 0.1313.$$

For $n_i = 6$, $D_3 = 0$ and $D_4 = 2.004$ (from Table A.9) and

Centerline, $\bar{R} = 0.1313$
LCL $= D_3\bar{R} = (0)(0.1313) = 0$
UCL $= D_4\bar{R} = (2.004)(0.1313) = 0.2631$

The following graph shows this $\bar{R}$ chart. Note that the range for sample 3 is out of control (beyond the UCL). The range of values in sample 3 appears to be unacceptable. Further investigation of the population from which this sample was drawn is warranted.

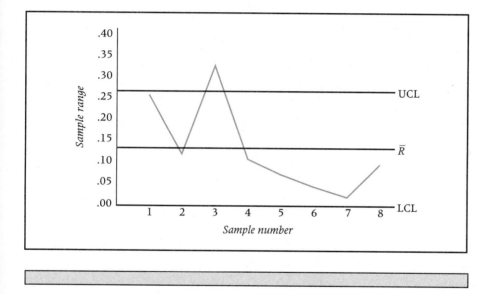

P Charts. When product attributes are measurable, $\bar{X}$ charts and R charts can be formulated from the data. Sometimes, however, product inspection yields no measurement—only a *yes* or *no* type of conclusion based on whether the item complies with the specifications. For this type of data, no measure is available from which to average or determine the range. However, attribute compliance can be depicted graphically by a P chart. A **P chart** graphs the proportions of sample items in noncompliance for multiple samples.

P chart

For example, suppose that the Lakeland Motor Company officials sample forty motors three times a week for a month. For each group of forty motors, they determine the proportion of the sample group that does not comply with the specifications. They then plot these sample proportions, $\hat{p}$, on a P chart in order to identify trends or samples with unacceptably high proportions of noncomformance. Other P-chart applications include determining whether a gallon of paint has been manufactured with acceptable texture, a pane of glass contains cracks, or a tire has a defective tread.

Like the $\bar{X}$ chart and the R chart, a P chart contains a centerline. The centerline is the average of the sample proportions. Upper and lower control limits are computed from the average of the sample proportions ± 3 standard deviations of proportions. The following are the steps for constructing a P chart.

1. Decide on the quality to be measured.
2. Determine a sample.
3. Gather twenty to thirty samples under controlled conditions.
4. Compute the sample proportion:

$$\hat{p} = \frac{n_{non}}{n},$$

where: n_{non} = the number of items in the sample in noncompliance
       n = the number of items in the sample

5. Compute the average proportion:

$$P = \frac{\Sigma \hat{p}}{k},$$

where: $\hat{p}$ = the sample proportion
       k = the number of samples

6. Determine the centerline, UCL, and LCL, when $Q = 1 - P$:

Centerline $= P$
$UCL = P + 3\sqrt{(P \cdot Q)/n}$
$LCL = P - 3\sqrt{(P \cdot Q)/n}$

Demonstration Problem 7.10

A company produces bond paper and, at regular intervals, samples of fifty sheets of paper are inspected. Suppose that seven random samples of fifty sheets of paper each are taken during a certain period of time, with the following number of sheets in noncompliance per sample. Construct a P chart from these data.

Sample	n	Number Out of Compliance
1	50	4
2	50	3
3	50	1
4	50	0
5	50	5
6	50	2
7	50	3

Solution:

From the data, $n = 50$. The values of $\hat{p}$ are

Sample	$\hat{p}$ *(Out of Compliance)*
1	$4/50 = 0.08$
2	$3/50 = 0.06$
3	$1/50 = 0.02$
4	$0/50 = 0.00$
5	$5/50 = 0.10$
6	$2/50 = 0.04$
7	$3/50 = 0.06$

The value of P is obtained by averaging these $\hat{p}$ values:

$$P = \frac{\hat{p}_1 + \hat{p}_2 + \hat{p}_3 + \hat{p}_4 + \hat{p}_5 + \hat{p}_6 + \hat{p}_7}{k}$$

$$= \frac{0.08 + 0.06 + 0.02 + 0.00 + 0.10 + 0.04 + 0.06}{7} = 0.0514.$$

The centerline is $P = 0.0514$.
The upper control limit (UCL) is

$$P + 3\sqrt{\frac{P \cdot Q}{n}} = 0.0514 + 3\sqrt{\frac{(0.0514)(0.9486)}{50}} = 0.1451.$$

The lower control limit (LCL) is

$$P - 3\sqrt{\frac{P \cdot Q}{n}} = 0.0514 - 3\sqrt{\frac{(0.0514)(0.9486)}{50}} = -0.0423.$$

To have -0.0423 nonconformance items is impossible, so the lower control limit is 0. The following is the P chart for this problem. Note that all seven proportions lie within the quality control limits.

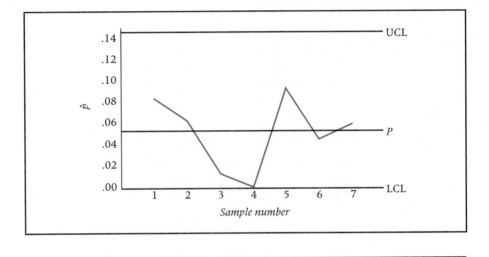

**PROBLEMS
Section 7.6**

7.39 The following data were gathered from five random samples:

Sample 1	Sample 2	Sample 3	Sample 4	Sample 5
25	22	30	32	25
23	21	23	26	23
29	24	22	27	29
31	25	26	28	27
26	23	28	25	27
28	26	27	25	26
27	29	21	31	24

Use these data to construct an $\bar{X}$ chart and an R chart.

7.40 Use the following data, which were gathered from seven random samples of size four each, to construct an $\overline{X}$ chart and an R chart:

Sample 1	Sample 2
4.1	3.6
5.2	4.3
3.9	3.9
5.0	4.6

Sample 3	Sample 4
4.0	4.6
4.8	4.8
5.1	4.7
5.3	4.7

Sample 5	Sample 6	Sample 7
3.9	5.1	4.6
3.8	4.7	4.4
4.6	4.8	4.0
4.9	4.3	4.5

7.41 The quality control inspection team at a manufacturing facility gathered ten different random samples of an item being produced. The team's inspection determined whether the items were in compliance or out of compliance with the specifications. Each sample contained 100 inspected items. Construct a P chart from the following data:

Sample	Size	Number Out of Compliance
1	100	2
2	100	7
3	100	4
4	100	3
5	100	3
6	100	5
7	100	2
8	100	0
9	100	1
10	100	6

7.42 A manufacturing firm, as a part of its quality control effort, randomly sampled seven groups of size forty items. Construct a *P* chart from the following data, which reflect the results of the firm's effort:

Sample	Size	Number Out of Compliance
1	40	1
2	40	0
3	40	1
4	40	3
5	40	2
6	40	5
7	40	2

CHAPTER SUMMARY

For much business research, successfully conducting a census is virtually impossible, and the sample presents a feasible alternative. Other reasons for sampling include cost reduction, potential for broadening the scope of the study, and loss reduction when the testing process destroys the product.

In order to take a sample, a population has to be identified. Often, the researcher has no exact roster or list of the population and so must find some way to identify the population as closely as possible. The final list or directory used to represent the population and from which the sample is drawn is called the frame.

The two main types of sampling are random and nonrandom. Random sampling occurs when each unit of the population has the same probability of being selected for the sample. Nonrandom sampling is any sampling that is not random. The four main types of random sampling discussed were simple random sampling, stratified sampling, systematic sampling, and cluster or area sampling.

In simple random sampling, every unit of the population is numbered. A table of random numbers or a random number generator is used to select *n* units from the population for the sample. Stratified random sampling uses the researcher's prior knowledge of the population to stratify the population into subgroups. Each subgroup is internally homogeneous but different from the others. Stratified random sampling is an attempt to reduce sampling error and ensure that at least some of each of the subgroups appear in the sample. After the strata have been identified, units are randomly sampled from each stratum. If the proportions of units selected from each subgroup for the sample are the

W. Edwards Deming grew up in Wyoming and earned a Bachelor's degree at the University of Wyoming. He received a Master's degree from the University of Colorado in mathematics and physics and later a PhD in mathematical physics from Yale University. Deming had to reconcile his fascination with mathematical systems and his farm background of asking why and why not questions. He discovered that the science of statistics best suited his interests.

After Yale, he went to work for Bell Laboratories, where he studied under W. A. Shewhart, the physicist and statistician who pioneered the technique of statistical process control. In 1946, Deming left his job as a statistician with the U.S. Bureau of the Census to start his own consulting business. He always returned to Shewhart's methods of process control, but, at that time, U.S. industry was operating at near capacity and had no interest in Deming's theories.

Deming first observed the Japanese economy in 1947 as an advisor in sampling techniques to the Supreme Command of Allied Powers in Tokyo. In 1950, a group of Japanese scientists and engineers invited him to conduct seminars on statistical control. So Deming returned to Japan to help reconstruct its industrial base. He told the Japanese that if they would rebuild by using his methods, they could achieve world dominance. He succeeded so well that the Japanese revered him as a national hero. In 1951, they named a special medal in his honor. During the next three decades, Deming taught in Paris and London and taught and consulted in Germany, Mexico, Turkey, and Argentina. Deming received little respect in the United States because of the lack of competition for U.S. products.

In 1980, an NBC television documentary named Deming the father of the postwar Japanese economic miracle. Ford's top executives were watching the program; they contacted Deming and the long-awaited American showcase for Deming's methods began. Now in his early 90s, Deming is an active consultant, teacher, and speaker. He is considered by some to be the philosophical master of quality.

Source: Adapted from Katz, Donald R., "Coming Home," *Business Month*, October 1988, pp. 57–62.

same as the proportions of the subgroups in the population, the process is called proportionate stratified sampling. If not, it is called disproportionate stratified sampling.

A third random sampling technique is systematic sampling. With systematic sampling, every *k*th item of the population is sampled until *n* units have been selected. Systematic sampling is used because of its convenience and ease of administration.

The fourth random sampling technique is cluster or area sampling. This technique involves subdividing the population into nonoverlapping clusters or areas. Each cluster or area is a microcosm of the population and is heterogenous within. Individual units are then randomly selected from the clusters or areas to get the final sample. Cluster or area sampling is usually done to reduce costs. If a set of second clusters or areas is selected from the first set, the method is called two-stage sampling.

Three types of nonrandom sampling were discussed: convenience, judgment, and quota. In convenience sampling the researcher selects units from the population to be in the sample for convenience. In judgment sampling, units are selected according to the judgment of the researcher. Quota sampling is similar to stratified sampling, with the researcher identifying subclasses or strata. However, the researcher selects units from each stratum by some nonrandom technique until a specified quota from each stratum is filled.

Sampling error occurs when the sample does not represent the population. With random sampling, sampling error occurs by chance. Nonsampling errors are all other research and analysis errors that occur in a study. They include recording errors, input errors, missing data, and incorrectly defining the frame.

According to the central limit theorem, if a population is normally distributed, the sample means for samples taken from that population also are normally distributed regardless of sample size. The central limit theorem also says that if the sample sizes are large ($n \geq 30$), the sample mean is approximately normally distributed regardless of the shape of the population. This is an extremely useful theorem, because it allows researchers to analyze sample data by using the normal distribution for virtually any type of study in which means are an appropriate statistic, so long as the sample size is large enough. The central limit theorem states that sample proportions, the difference in two sample means, and the difference in two sample proportions are normally distributed for large sample sizes.

A quality product is one that delivers to the customer those attributes that have been agreed upon by the buyer and seller in the product's specifications. Quality control is the collection of strategies, techniques, and actions that an organization can use to ensure production of a quality product. For decades, U.S. companies used after-process quality control, which essentially consisted of inspectors determining whether a product complied with the specifications. During 1980s, U.S. companies joined businesses from Western Europe and Asia in instituting in-process control. In-process quality control affords the producer the opportunity to determine weaknesses and flaws in the production process that can then be overcome to increase product quality.

Several diagnostic techniques can be used in process to improve quality, including Pareto analysis, the fishbone diagram, quality circles, and just-in-time inventory systems. Pareto analysis begins with a tally of the numbers and types of product defects. A Pareto chart constructed from this information depicts a hierarchy of defects. From this information, quality experts can assign priorities to needed quality improvements. The fishbone diagram displays cause-and-effect relationships for quality problems. Each fishbone represents the possible causes for a given problem. Quality circles are small groups of workers and supervisors who meet regularly to discuss process problems and suggest possible solutions. In just-in-time inventory systems, a producer attempts to reduce inventory by having raw materials or subparts delivered just in time for production.

Control charts can be used to measure and depict the variation between items produced. The three types of control charts are $\overline{X}$ charts, R charts, and P charts. The $\overline{X}$ charts and R charts are control charts for measurements, and P charts are control charts for compliance of items. The $\overline{X}$ chart is used to graph sample means for a series of samples against the mean of the sample means, $\overline{\overline{X}}$. Using this chart, the analyst can determine whether a sample or a batch is averaging a measurement that is out-of-control from specified values. An R chart can be used to determine whether the deviation of a sample as measured by the range is unacceptable. A P chart is used to plot the proportion of samples out of compliance with specifications against an average proportion of items out of compliance with specifications. It facilitates the discovery of samples when an inordinately high or low number of items are out of compliance with specifications.

Key Words

Frame
Random sampling
Nonrandom sampling
Simple random sampling
Stratified random sampling
Proportionate stratified random
  sampling
Disproportionate stratified random
  sampling
Systematic sampling
Cluster (or area) sampling
Two-stage sampling
Convenience sampling
Judgment sampling
Quota sampling
Sampling error
Nonsampling errors
Telescoping error

Omission error
Detail error
Central limit theorem
Finite correction factor
Sample proportion
Quality
Quality control
After-process quality control
In-process quality control
Total quality management
Pareto analysis
Fishbone diagram
Quality circle
Just-in-time inventory system
Control charts
$\overline{X}$ chart
R chart
P chart

USING THE COMPUTER

You can use Minitab to generate random numbers. The basic Minitab command for accomplishing this is **RANDOM**. This command in conjunction with a subcommand can generate random numbers from the following distributions: binomial, chi-square, F, normal, Poisson, t, and uniform. The binomial distribution, the normal distribution, and the Poisson distribution are the only ones that have been presented in the text so far. Hence the focus here is on generating random numbers from these three distributions.

To generate random numbers, type the **RANDOM** command after the Minitab prompt:

MTB > RANDOM

The **RANDOM** command requires two other items of information: the number of values to be generated and the location where the random values are to be stored. For example, if you want to generate fifty random numbers and store them in column 1, the command is

MTB > RANDOM 50 C1

If the **RANDOM** command is not followed by a subcommand, Minitab will default to the normal distribution with a mean of zero and a standard deviation of 1 (the Z distribution). To obtain random numbers generated from any other distribution, you must use a subcommand. To obtain a subcommand prompt, end the **RANDOM** command with a semicolon. Minitab will then issue a subcommand prompt, **SUBC**>.

To obtain random numbers from a binomial distribution, type **BINOMIAL** after the subcommand prompt. The **BINOMIAL** subcommand is followed by the n value of the binomial distribution and the p value of the distribution. The p value should include the decimal point. For example, to generate fifty random numbers from a binomial distribution of $n = 20$ and $p = 0.40$ and then store the numbers in column 2 use the commands:

MTB > RANDOM 50 C2;
SUBC > BINOMIAL 20.40.

Note that the subcommand information is followed by a period. The period tells Minitab that you are through with subcommand prompts and are ready to return to a Minitab prompt. The random numbers will not appear on your screen. They are compiled in a column, so you must print the column in order to display them.

To generate numbers from a normal distribution or by the Poisson distribution, use the RANDOM command to tell Minitab how many numbers are being generated and where to store the numbers. Follow that Minitab command with a semicolon, and a subcommand prompt will appear. To generate random numbers from a normal distribution, use the subcommand NORMAL followed by the value of the mean and the standard deviation of the population. For example, if you want to generate 40 random numbers from a normal distribution that has a mean of 250 and a standard deviation of 60 and store them in column 3, use the commands:

```
MTB > RANDOM 40 C3;
SUBC > NORMAL 250 60.
```

Use the subcommand, POISSON, to generate values from a Poisson distribution. The POISSON command is followed by only one parameter, λ. To generate 35 values from a Poisson distribution with a lambda of 1.60 and store the values in column 4, use the commands:

```
MTB > RANDOM 35 C4;
SUBC > POISSON 1.60.
```

In each case, you need to use the PRINT command to display the values on the screen. In this case,

```
MTB > PRINT C4
```

If you want to generate multiple columns at one time, in place of the column location in the RANDOM command, insert the column location of the first set of numbers, then a dash ($-$), and then the column location of the last values stored. For example, if you want to generate ten columns of 50 random numbers each from a normal distribution with a mean of 100 and a standard deviation of 15, the commands are

```
MTB > RANDOM 50 C1-C10;
SUBC > NORMAL 100 15.
```

Using Minitab to Produce Quality Control Charts

Minitab has the capability to generate $\overline{X}$ charts, R charts, and P charts. There is a specific Minitab command for each chart. In each case, after inputting data, you need to use only one command to produce the control chart. The output consists of a graph with the centerline, the upper control limit, and the lower control limit. The $\overline{X}$ charts and R charts are set up the same way, so they are discussed together.

For both the $\overline{X}$ chart and the R chart the sample data from *all* the samples to be included in the chart are input with the **SET** command into *one* column. Make certain that the data from each sample are entered together, followed by the data from the next sample, and so on. After the data are entered into a column, use the **XBARCHART** Minitab command to produce an $\overline{X}$ chart. This command requires two pieces of information: the column location of the data and the number of values in each sample. For example, if the data are in column 1 and there are 40 values in each sample, the command to produce an $\overline{X}$ chart is

    MTB > XBARCHART C1 40

Suppose that you want to work Demonstration Problem 7.8 and produce the same $\overline{X}$ chart. The Minitab commands required to accomplish this are

    MTB > SET C1
    DATA > 5.13 4.92 5.01 4.88 5.05 4.97 4.96 4.98 4.95 4.96 5.01 4.89
    DATA > 5.21 4.87 5.02 5.08 5.12 5.04 5.02 5.09 4.99 5.02 5.03 5.01
    DATA > 5.12 5.08 5.09 5.13 5.06 5.13 4.98 5.02 4.97 4.99 4.98 4.99
    DATA > 4.99 5.00 5.00 5.02 5.01 5.01 4.96 5.01 5.02 5.05 5.04 5.02
    DATA > end
    MTB > XBARCHART C1 6

The output from these commands is nearly identical to the $\overline{X}$ chart shown in the text. The value of $\overline{X} = 5.018$ is given, along with the UCL and LCL.

The R chart is produced exactly the same way as the $\overline{X}$ chart, except that the command is different. The Minitab command that you use to generate an R chart is **RCHART**. This command, like the **XBARCHART**, command requires the column location of the data and the number of items per sample:

    MTB > RCHART C n

To produce the R chart from Demonstration Problem 7.9, enter the same data as for $\overline{X}$ chart. Then use the command:

    MTB > RCHART C1 6

The output is an R chart that looks essentially like the one in the text.

Minitab can produce a P chart if you use the command, **PCHART**. However, you enter the data differently than for the $\overline{X}$ and R charts. With P charts, the number of items in noncompliance for each sample is **SET** into one column. In another column, the number of items inspected per sample is **SET**. Then give the **PCHART** command, followed by the column in which the number of noncompliance items is stored and then the column containing the number of items per sample. For example, if the number of noncompliance items for four samples are 6, 7, 3, and 4, respectively, and if the sizes of these four samples are 60, 75, 20, and 30, respectively, the commands to produce a *P* chart are

```
MTB  > SET C1
DATA > 6  7  3  4
DATA > end
MTB  > SET C2
DATA > 60  75  20  30
DATA > end
MTB  > PCHART C1 C2
```

The output is similar to that of the $\overline{X}$ and *R* charts.

To reproduce the *P* chart for Demonstration Problem 7.10, use the commands:

```
MTB  > SET C1
DATA > 4  3  1  0  5  2  3
DATA > end
MTB  > SET C2
DATA > 50  50  50  50  50  50  50
DATA > end
MTB  > PCHART C1 C2
```

SUPPLEMENTARY PROBLEMS

7.43 Suppose that you work for a large firm that has 20,000 employees. The CEO calls you in and asks you to determine employee attitudes toward the company. She is willing to commit $100,000 to this project. What are the advantages of taking a sample versus conducting a census? What are the trade-offs?

7.44 Determine a possible frame for conducting random sampling in each of the following studies.

a. The average amount of overtime per week for production workers in a plastics company in Pennsylvania

b. The average number of employees in all Alpha/Beta supermarkets in California

c. A survey of commercial lobster catchers in the state of Maine.

7.45 Use Table A.1 to select 20 three-digit random numbers. Did any of the numbers occur more than once? How can this happen? Do a stem-and-leaf plot of the numbers with the stem being the left digit. Did the numbers seem to be equally distributed or were they bunched together?

7.46 A company has 1,250 employees, and you want to take a simple random sample of $n = 60$ employees. Explain how you would go about selecting this sample using the table of random numbers. Are there numbers that you cannot use? Explain.

7.47 Suppose that the age distribution in a city is as follows:

Under 18	22%
18–25	18%
26–50	36%
51–65	10%
Over 65	14%

A researcher is conducting a proportionate stratified random sampling plan with a sample size of 250. Approximately how many people should he sample from each stratum?

7.48 Give a variable that could be used to stratify the population for the following studies. List at least four subcategories for each variable.

a. A political party wants to conduct a poll prior to an election for the office of U.S. Senator in Minnesota.

b. A soft-drink company wants to take a sample of soft-drink purchases in an effort to estimate market share.

c. A retail outlet desires to interview customers over a one-week period.

d. An eye glasses manufacturer and retailer wants to determine the demand for prescription eye glasses in its marketing region.

7.49 A directory of personal computer retail outlets in the United States contains 12,080 alphabetized entries. Explain how systematic sampling could be used to select a sample of 300 outlets.

7.50 A researcher is conducting a study of a *Fortune 500* company that has factories, distribution centers, and retail outlets across the country. How can she use cluster or area sampling to take a random sample of employees of this firm?

7.51 Suppose that you are sending out questionnaires to a randomly selected sample of 100 managers. The frame for this study is the membership list of the American Managers Association. The questionnaire contains demographic questions about the company and its top manager. In addition, it asks questions about the manager's leadership style. Research assistants are to score and enter the responses into the computer as soon as they are received. You are to conduct a statistical analysis of the data. Name and describe four nonsampling errors that could occur in this study.

7.52 The average cost of a one-bedroom apartment in a town is $450 per month. What is the probability of randomly selecting a sample of fifty apartments in this town and getting a sample mean of less than $430 if the population standard deviation is $100?

7.53 Suppose that the average client charge per hour for lawyers in the state of Iowa for out-of-court work is $125. Suppose further that a random telephone sample of thirty-two lawyers in Iowa is taken and that the sample average charge per hour for out-of-court work is $110. If the population variance is $525, what is the probability of getting a sample mean this large or larger? What is the probability of getting a sample mean larger than $135 per hour? What is the probability of getting a sample mean of between $120 and $130 per hour?

7.54 According to *Corporate Travel Magazine*, an out-of-town business person spends an average of $248 per day in Washington, D.C. This cost includes hotel, meals, car rental, and incidentals. A survey of sixty-five randomly selected business people who have been to Washington, D.C., on business recently is taken. For the population mean of $248 per day, what is the probability of getting a sample average of more than $240 per day if the population standard deviation is $47?

7.55 The Aluminum Association reports that the average American used 56.8 lb of aluminum in 1989. Suppose that the association wants to determine whether aluminum usage in 1992 is the same. A random sample of fifty-one households is monitored for one year to determine aluminum usage. If the population standard deviation of annual usage is 12.3 lb, what is the probability that the sample mean for 1992 will be each of the following?

   a. More than 60 lb if the 1989 population mean still holds
   b. More than 58 lb if the 1989 population mean still holds
   c. Between 56 and 57 lb if the 1989 population mean still holds
   d. Less than 55 lb if the 1989 population mean still holds
   e. Less than 50 lb if the 1989 population mean still holds

7.56 Candidate Jones believes that she will receive 0.55 of the total votes cast in her county. However, in an attempt to validate this figure, she has her pollster contact a random sample of 600 registered voters in the county. The poll results in 298 of the voters saying that they are committed to voting for her. If she actually has 0.55 of the total vote, what is the probability of getting a sample proportion this small or smaller? Do you think she actually has 55% of the vote? Why or why not?

7.57 In a particular area of the Northeast, an estimated 75% of the homes use heating oil as the principal heating fuel during the winter. A random telephone survey of 150 homes is taken in an attempt to determine whether this figure is correct. Suppose that 120 of the 150 homes surveyed replied that they use heating oil as the principal heating fuel. What is the probability of getting a sample proportion this large or larger if the population estimate is true?

7.58 In 1990, 55% of all college students were women according to estimates by the National Center for Education Statistics. Suppose that a national list of 1990 college students were available and that the student's gender was recorded.

a. If a random sample of 820 students is taken, what is the probability that less than 400 are women?

b. If a random sample of 388 students is taken, what is the probability that more than 65% are women?

c. If a random sample of 1,253 students is taken, what is the probability that between 640 and 680 students are women?

7.59 According to a survey by the employee benefits consulting firm of Hewitt Associates, 9% of all U.S. employers provide child-care centers. Eighty-nine percent have dependent-care spending accounts for employees and 41% have resource and referral services for child care. Assume that the figures obtained by Hewitt Associates are correct for all U.S. employers and that a random sample of eighty-four U.S. employers is taken.

a. What is the probability that less than 5% of the sample have child-care centers?

b. What is the probability that more than 15% of the sample have child-care centers?

c. What is the probability that less than 70% of the sample have dependent-care spending accounts for employees?

d. What is the probability that between 35% and 50% of the sample have resource and referral services for child care?

7.60 The average monthly rent for an apartment in city A is $510, with a standard deviation of $90. The average monthly rent for an apartment in city B is $480, with a standard deviation of $110. What is the probability of selecting a random sample of 60 apartments from city A and 55 apartments from city B and having a difference of $40 or more in the sample means?

7.61 Suppose that the average cost per hour for legal out-of-court work in Minnesota is $120 per hour, with a standard deviation of $18. For the Iowa population data in Problem 7.53, what is the probability of getting a sample difference of $10 or more, with Iowa being more expensive, if random samples of size 50 are taken from each state?

7.62 A certain automobile costs an average of $14,755 in the Pacific Northwest. The standard deviation of these prices is $650. Suppose that a random sample of thirty dealerships in Oregon and thirty dealerships in Washington are taken, and their managers are asked what they charge for this automobile. The sample mean for the Oregon sample is $15,098 and for the Washington sample is $14,600. What is the probability of getting a difference this great or greater from these sample means, with Oregon being more expensive if they actually come from the same population?

7.63 A sample of fifty-five Hispanic-owned firms in the service industry resulted in a sample average of annual receipts of $33,000. A sample of forty-seven Hispanic-owned firms in the finance, insurance, and real estate industry produced average annual receipts of $39,000. If the standard deviation of the population of annual receipts for the service industry firms is $9,850 and for the finance, insurance, and real estate firms is $10,090, what is the probability of getting a difference of $6,000 or more in the sample means, with the service industry being less, if there is no difference in the population means for these two industries?

7.64 In the New York City area, is there a difference in the size of food stores in the inner city and in middle-class areas? A random sample of thirty-three inner-city stores revealed an average size of 6,500 sq ft. Assume that the population standard deviation for these stores is 2,100 sq ft. A random sample of forty middle-class stores revealed an average size of 24,000 sq ft. Assume that the population standard deviation for these stores is 5,990 sq ft. Use these data to determine the probability of getting sample means this different or more (17,500 or more), with middle-class food stores being larger, if there is no difference in the population means between inner-city and middle-class food stores in New York City.

7.65 According to a survey of employed mothers of children under age 5 nearly 41% of all primary child-care arrangements in 1977 were in another home. By 1987, this figure had dropped to about 36%. If a random sample of 200 mothers had been taken in 1977 and a random sample of 245 mothers had been taken in 1987, what is the probability that the difference in sample proportions would be more than 12%, with 1977 figures being higher?

7.66 Suppose that a survey in 1991 shows that the figure given for 1987 in Problem 7.65 has remained the same (still 36%). What is the probability of sampling 200 mothers in 1991 along with the 245 in 1987 and getting a difference of sample proportions of more than 12%, with 1987 figures being higher?

7.67 Suppose that, in a sample of 500 Midwest homeowners, 200 believe that their house would sell for more today than it would have last year. Suppose that, in a sample of 400 homeowners in the West, 176 believe that their home would sell for more today than a year ago. If these people came from the same population (no difference between opinions of westerners and midwesterners), what is the probability of getting a difference in sample proportions this great or greater (.04 or more), with the West proportion being greater? Let $P = .42$.

7.68 According to the U.S. Bureau of Labor Statistics, 20% of all people aged 16 or older do volunteer work. Women volunteer slightly more than men, with 22% of women volunteering and 19% of men volunteering. Suppose that you wanted to determine whether the 3% difference in the proportion of volunteering rates held for the city in which you live. For this 3% difference, what is the probability of randomly sampling 140 women aged 16 and older and 118 men aged 16 and older and discovering that 35 of the women and 21 of the men do volunteer work in this city? Solve for this sample difference or more, with women being higher.

7.69 A survey conducted by Survey Sampling of Fairfield, Connecticut, showed that more than 28% of all U.S. households had unlisted telephone numbers as of 1990. The city with the greatest proportion of unlisted numbers was Los Angeles, with almost 60%. Las Vegas, Nevada was second with about 1.6% less. Suppose that a survey of 565 Los Angeles households showed that 344 had unlisted telephone numbers and that a survey of 381 Las Vegas households showed that 217 households had unlisted numbers. What is the probability of getting this sample result difference or greater, with Los Angeles having the higher proportion?

7.70 A fruit juice company sells a glass container filled with 24 oz of cranapple juice. Inspectors are concerned about the consistency of volume of fill in these containers. Every two hours for three days of production, a sample of five containers is randomly selected and the volume of fill is measured. The results are as follows:

Sample 1	Sample 2	Sample 3	Sample 4
24.05	24.01	24.03	23.98
24.01	24.02	23.95	24.00
24.02	24.10	24.00	24.01
23.99	24.03	24.01	24.01
24.04	24.08	23.99	24.00

Sample 5	Sample 6	Sample 7	Sample 8
23.97	24.02	24.01	24.08
23.99	24.05	24.00	24.03
24.02	24.01	24.00	24.00
24.01	24.00	23.97	24.05
24.00	24.01	24.02	24.01

Sample 9	Sample 10	Sample 11	Sample 12
24.00	24.00	24.01	24.00
24.02	24.01	23.99	24.05
24.03	24.00	24.02	24.04
24.01	24.00	24.03	24.02
24.01	24.00	24.01	24.00

Use this information to construct $\overline{X}$ and R charts and comment on any samples that are out of compliance.

7.71 A bottled-water company has been randomly inspecting bottles of water to determine whether they are acceptable for delivery and sale. The inspectors are looking at water quality, bottle condition, and seal tightness. A series of ten random samples of fifty bottles each has been taken. Some bottles have been rejected. Use the following information on the number of bottles from each batch that were rejected as out of compliance to construct a *P* chart:

Sample	n	Number Out of Compliance
1	50	3
2	50	11
3	50	7
4	50	2
5	50	5
6	50	8
7	50	0
8	50	9
9	50	1
10	50	6

CONFIDENCE INTERVALS: LARGE SAMPLES

8

CHAPTER LEARNING OBJECTIVES

The overall objective of Chapter 8 is to help you understand estimating parameters for situations in which the sample size is large and the formulas are derived from the central limit theorem, thereby enabling you to

1. Estimate a population mean from a sample mean.
2. Estimate a population proportion from a sample proportion.
3. Estimate the difference in two population means from the difference in two sample means.
4. Estimate the difference in two population proportions from the difference in two sample proportions.
5. Estimate the minimum sample size necessary to achieve given statistical goals.

The Valencia Department store in Phoenix, Arizona, has been investing a significant amount of revenue in an advertising program that management believes will increase traffic through its largest store in a large suburban mall. The CEO has just realized that increased traffic is only one indicator of a successful advertising program. The CEO meets with one of the senior managers, Larry Robinson, and assigns him the task of determining other measures of success for the advertising campaign. She also charges Robinson with the task of estimating those measures of success of the advertising campaign for the population of Valencia shoppers.

Larry Robinson and a small team of other management officials meet and decide that length of time in the store per visit and dollar amount spent per visit per customer also are useful measurements of advertising success. They agree that, because gathering these measurements on the population of shoppers is impossible, they will take samples and estimate population measures from sample data.

**Managerial
Questions**

- How will they determine their sample?
- How will they measure these variables?
- How large a sample is sufficient to gather the required information?
- How are sample data taken and population values estimated from the sample data?
- Is there potential error in this process?
- Are there other useful variables that they could measure?

The central limit theorem presented in Chapter 7 states that certain statistics of interest, such as the sample mean, the sample proportion, the difference in two sample means, and the difference in two sample proportions, are normally distributed for large sample sizes regardless of the shape of the population. A Z formula for each statistic was developed and discussed. These Z formulas have the potential for use in parametric estimation, hypothesis testing, and determination of sample size. This chapter describes how these Z formulas for large statistics can be manipulated algebraically into a format that can be used to estimate population parameters and to determine the size of samples necessary to conduct research.

ESTIMATING THE POPULATION MEAN | *8.1*

On many occasions estimating the population mean is useful in business research. For example, the manager of human resources in a company might want to estimate the average number of days of work an employee misses per year because of illness. If the firm has thousands of employees, direct calculation of a population mean such as this may be practically impossible. Instead, a random sample of employees can be taken, and mean number of sick days for the sample can be used to estimate the population mean. Suppose that another company has developed a new process for prolonging the shelf life of a loaf of bread. The company wants to be able to date each loaf for freshness, but company officials do not know exactly how long the bread will stay fresh. By taking a random sample and determining the mean shelf life for the sample, they can estimate the average shelf life for the population of bread.

How does the process of estimating population means from sample means begin? As a result of the central limit theorem, the following Z formula for sample means can be used when sample sizes are large, regardless of the shape of the population distribution or for smaller sizes if the population is normally distributed:

$$Z = \frac{\overline{X} - \mu}{\frac{\sigma}{\sqrt{n}}}.$$

Rearranging this formula algebraically to solve for μ gives

$$\mu = \overline{X} - Z\frac{\sigma}{\sqrt{n}}.$$

Because a sample mean can be greater than or less than the population mean, Z can be positive or negative. Thus the preceding expression takes the form:

$$\overline{X} \pm Z\frac{\sigma}{\sqrt{n}}.$$

The value of the population mean, μ, lies somewhere within this range. Rewriting this expression yields the confidence interval formula for estimating μ with large size samples.

(8.1)
$$\overline{X} - Z\frac{\sigma}{\sqrt{n}} \leq \mu \leq \overline{X} + Z\frac{\sigma}{\sqrt{n}}.$$

Confidence
Interval to
Estimate μ

The vice president of operations for a new cellular telephone company is in the process of developing a strategic management plan. He believes that the ability to estimate the length of the average phone call on the system is important. Because thousands of calls have been placed on the system, averaging all the calls is virtually impossible. Therefore he takes a random sample of sixty calls from company records and finds that the mean sample length for a call is 4.26 min. Past history for these types of calls has shown that the population standard deviation for call length is about 1.1 min. Using Formula 8.1, he estimates the population mean call length:

$$\overline{X} = 4.26, \qquad \sigma = 1.1, \qquad \text{and} \qquad n = 60.$$

$$\overline{X} - Z\frac{\sigma}{\sqrt{n}} \le \mu \le \overline{X} + Z\frac{\sigma}{\sqrt{n}};$$

$$4.26 - Z\frac{1.1}{\sqrt{60}} \le \mu \le 4.26 + Z\frac{1.1}{\sqrt{60}}.$$

point estimate

interval estimate

If he wants to produce a single number estimate of the value of μ, he can use the sample mean, $\overline{X} = 4.26$, calls. In this instance, the sample mean is called a point estimate of the population mean. A **point estimate** is *when a statistic taken from the sample is used to estimate a population parameter.* In this case, the value of the sample mean may be the best available estimate of the population mean. However, the company vice president realizes that if he were to randomly sample another sixty telephone calls, this second sample mean likely would be different from the first, and hence the point estimate would change. In fact, for every sample taken, the likelihood is strong that the point estimate *will* change. Thus estimating a population parameter with an interval estimate often is preferable. The **interval estimate** *is a range of values within which the analyst can declare with some confidence that the population parameter will fall.* Confidence intervals can be two sided or one sided. This text presents only two-sided confidence intervals. Formula 8.1 yields confidence intervals to estimate a population mean for large samples.

Note that, when Formula 8.1 was applied to the cellular telephone problem, no value for Z was entered into the formula. The value of Z is determined by the level of confidence desired. To have 100% confidence that the population mean actually falls into a computed confidence interval is virtually impossible. The researcher must select a desired level of confidence, some of the more common of which are 90%, 95%, 98%, and 99%. Why would a researcher not just select the highest confidence and always use that level? The reason is that trade-offs between sample size, interval width, and level of confidence must be considered. For example, as the level of confidence is increased, the interval gets wider, provided the sample size and standard deviation remain constant.

For the cellular telephone problem, suppose that the vice president decided on a 95% confidence interval for the results. Figure 8.1 shows a normal distribution of sample means about the population mean. When using a 95%

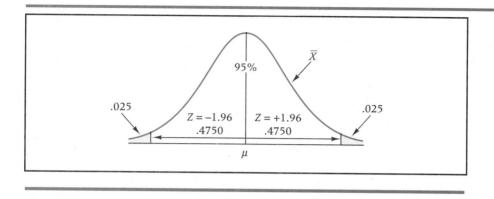

FIGURE 8.1

Distribution of Sample Means for 95% Confidence

level of confidence, he is selecting an interval centered on μ within which 95% of all sample mean values will fall.

Because the distribution is symmetric and the interval is equal on each side of the population mean, $(1/2)/(95\%)$ or .4750 of the area falls on each side of the mean. Table A.5 yields a Z value of 1.96 for this portion of the normal curve. Thus the Z value for a 95% confidence interval is always 1.96. In other words, of all the possible $\overline{X}$ values along the horizontal axis of the diagram, 95% of them should fall within a Z score of 1.96 from the population mean.

The vice president can now complete the cellular telephone problem. To determine a 95% confidence interval for $\overline{X} = 4.26$, $\sigma = 1.1$, $n = 60$, and $Z = 1.96$, he estimates the average call length by including the value of Z in the formula:

$$4.26 - 1.96\frac{1.1}{\sqrt{60}} \leq \mu \leq 4.26 + 1.96\frac{1.1}{\sqrt{60}};$$
$$4.26 - 0.28 \leq \mu \leq 4.26 + 0.28;$$
$$3.98 \leq \mu \leq 4.54.$$

The vice president of the cellular telephone company can be 95% confident that the average length of a call for the population is between 3.98 and 4.54 min.

What does being 95% confident that the population mean is in an interval actually indicate? It indicates that, if the company vice president were to randomly select 100 samples of sixty calls and use the results of each sample to construct a 95% confidence interval, approximately 95 of the 100 intervals would contain the population mean. It also indicates that 5% of the intervals would not contain the population mean. The company vice president is likely to take only a single sample and compute the confidence interval from that sample information. That interval either contains the population mean or it does not. The odds are in his favor.

FIGURE 8.2

Twenty 95% Confidence
Intervals of μ

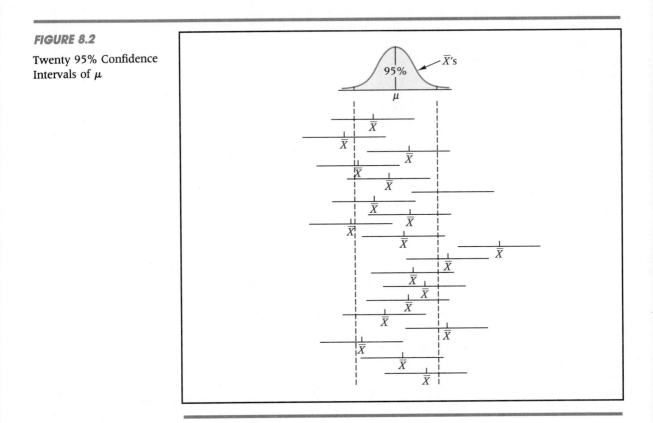

Figure 8.2 depicts the meaning of a 95% confidence interval for the mean. Note that if 20 random samples are taken from the population, 19 of the 20 will likely contain the population mean if a 95% confidence interval is used (19/20 = 95%). If a 90% confidence interval is constructed, only 18 of the 20 intervals are likely to contain the population mean.

Demonstration Problem 8.1

survey was taken of U.S. companies who do business with firms in India. One of the questions on the survey was: Approximately how many years has your company been trading with firms in India? A random sample of forty-four responses to this question yielded a mean of 10.455 years. Suppose that the population standard deviation for this question is 7.7 years. Using this information, construct a 90%

confidence interval for the mean number of years that a company has been trading in India for the population of U.S. companies trading in India.

Solution:

Here, $n = 44$, $\overline{X} = 10.455$, and $\sigma = 7.7$. To determine the value of Z, divide the 90% confidence in half. The Z distribution of $\overline{X}$ around μ contains .4500 of the area on each side of μ, or $(1/2)(90\%)$. Table A.5 yields a Z value of 1.645 for the area of .4500 (interpolating between .4495 and .4505). The confidence interval is

$$\overline{X} - Z\frac{\sigma}{\sqrt{n}} \leq \mu \leq \overline{X} + Z\frac{\sigma}{\sqrt{n}};$$

$$10.455 - 1.645\frac{7.7}{\sqrt{44}} \leq \mu \leq 10.455 + 1.645\frac{7.7}{\sqrt{44}};$$

$$10.455 - 1.91 \leq \mu \leq 10.455 + 1.91;$$

$$8.545 \leq \mu \leq 12.365.$$

That is, the analyst is 90% confident that, if a census of all U.S. companies trading in India were taken at the time of this survey, the actual population mean number of years a company would have been trading in India would lie between 8.545 and 12.365.

Finite Correction Factor

Recall from Chapter 7 that, if the sample is taken from a finite population, a finite correction factor may be used to increase the accuracy of the solution. In the case of interval estimation, the finite correction factor is used to reduce the width of the interval. As stated in Chapter 7, if the sample size is less than 5% of the population, the finite correction factor does not significantly alter the solution. Formula 8.1 is modified to include the finite correction factor.

| (8.2) | $$\overline{X} - Z\frac{\sigma}{\sqrt{n}}\sqrt{\frac{N-n}{N-1}} \leq \mu \leq \overline{X} + Z\frac{\sigma}{\sqrt{n}}\sqrt{\frac{N-n}{N-1}}.$$ | **Formula for Confidence Interval to Estimate μ Using the Finite Correction Factor** |

Demonstration Problem 8.2

A study is being conducted in a company that has 800 engineers. A random sample of 50 of these engineers reveals that the average sample age is 34.3 years. Historically, the population standard deviation of age of the company's engineers is approximately 8 years. Construct a 98% confidence interval to estimate the average age of all the engineers in this company.

Solution:

This problem has a finite population. The sample size, 50, is greater than 5% of the population, so the finite correction factor may be helpful. In this case $N = 800$, $n = 50$, $\overline{X} = 34.3$, and $\sigma = 8$. The Z value for a 98% confidence interval is 2.33 (.98 divided into two equal parts yields .4900; the Z value is obtained from Table A.5 by using .4900). Substituting into Formula 8.2 and solving for the confidence interval gives

$$34.3 - 2.33\frac{8}{\sqrt{50}}\sqrt{\frac{750}{799}} \leq \mu \leq 34.3 + 2.33\frac{8}{\sqrt{50}}\sqrt{\frac{750}{799}};$$

$$34.3 - 2.554 \leq \mu \leq 34.3 + 2.554;$$

$$31.75 \leq \mu \leq 36.85.$$

Without the finite correction factor, the result would have been

$$34.3 - 2.64 \leq \mu \leq 34.3 + 2.64;$$

$$31.66 \leq \mu \leq 36.94.$$

The finite correction factor takes into account the fact that the population contains only 800 instead of being infinitely large. The sample, $n = 50$, is a greater proportion of the 800 than it would have been of a larger population, and thus the width of the confidence interval is reduced.

Confidence Interval to Estimate μ When σ Is Unknown

In the formulas and problems presented so far in this section, the population standard deviation was known. Estimating the population mean when the population standard deviation is known may seem strange. Sometimes the population standard deviation is estimated from past records or from industry standards. However, the reality is that in many instances, the population standard deviation is unknown. For example, in the cellular telephone example, the company is new and the average length of a call is unknown. The likelihood is high that the population standard deviation also is unknown. So how does the researcher get around this dilemma?

When sample sizes are large ($n \geq 30$), the sample standard deviation is a good estimate of the population standard deviation and can be used as an acceptable approximation of the population standard deviation in the Z formula for a mean. Because formulas based on the central limit theorem require large samples for nonnormal populations, it makes sense to modify Formula 8.1 in order to use the sample standard deviation, S. Beware, however, not to use this modified formula for small samples when the population standard deviation is unknown, even when the population is normally distributed. Chapter 10 presents techniques to handle the case of the small sample when the population standard deviation is unknown and X is normally distributed.

$$\overline{X} - Z\frac{S}{\sqrt{n}} \leq \mu \leq \overline{X} + Z\frac{S}{\sqrt{n}}.$$

Confidence Interval to Estimate μ When Population Standard Deviation Is Unknown and n Is Large

Demonstration Problem 8.3

Suppose that a U.S. car rental firm wants to estimate the average number of miles traveled per day by each of its cars rented in California. A random sample of 110 cars rented in California reveals that the sample mean travel distance per day is 85.5 miles, with a sample standard deviation of 19.3 miles. Compute a 99% confidence interval to estimate μ.

Solution:

Here, $n = 110, \overline{X} = 85.5$, and $S = 19.3$. For a 99% level of confidence, a Z value of 2.575 is obtained. The confidence interval is

$$\overline{X} - Z\frac{S}{\sqrt{n}} \leq \mu \leq \overline{X} + Z\frac{S}{\sqrt{n}};$$

$$85.5 - 2.575\frac{19.3}{\sqrt{110}} \leq \mu \leq 85.5 + 2.575\frac{19.3}{\sqrt{110}};$$

$$85.5 - 4.7 \leq \mu \leq 85.5 + 4.7;$$

$$80.8 \leq \mu \leq 90.2.$$

Table 8.1 contains some of the more common levels of confidence and their associated Z values.

	Confidence Level	Z Value
TABLE 8.1		
Values of Z for Some of the More Common Levels of Confidence	90%	1.645
	95%	1.96
	98%	2.33
	99%	2.575

**PROBLEMS
Section 8.1**

8.1 For a random sample of 36 items and a sample mean of 211, compute a 95% confidence interval for μ if the population standard deviation is 23.

8.2 A random sample of 81 items is taken producing a sample mean of 47 and a sample standard deviation of 5.89. Construct a 90% confidence interval to estimate the population mean.

8.3 Suppose that X is normally distributed in the population. If a random sample of size 15 is taken from the population, producing a sample mean of 8.67, what is the confidence interval to estimate μ? Assume that the population variance is 6.12 and that an 80% level of confidence is desired.

8.4 A random sample of size 70 is taken from a population that has a variance of 49. The sample mean is 90.4. What is the point estimate of μ? Construct a 94% confidence interval for μ.

8.5 A random sample of size 39 is taken from a population of 200 members. The sample mean is 66 and the sample standard deviation is 11. Construct a 96% confidence interval to estimate the population mean. What is the point estimate of the population mean?

8.6 A candy company fills a 20 oz package of Halloween candy with individually wrapped pieces of candy. The number of pieces of candy per package varies, because the package is sold by weight. The company wants to estimate the number of pieces per package. Inspectors randomly sample 120 packages of this candy and count the number of pieces in each package. They find that the sample mean number of pieces is 18.72, with a sample variance of 0.763. What is the point estimate of the number of pieces per package? Construct a 99% confidence interval to estimate the mean number of pieces per package for the population.

8.7 A small lawnmower company produced 1,500 lawnmowers in 1980. In an effort to determine how maintenance free these units were, the company decided to conduct a multiyear study of the 1980 lawnmowers. A sample of 200 owners of these lawnmowers was randomly drawn from company records and contacted. The owners were given an 800 number and asked to call the company when the first major repair was required for the lawnmowers. Owners who no longer used the lawnmower to cut their grass were disqualified. After many years, 187 of the owners had reported. The other 13 disqualified themselves. The average number of years until the first major repair was 5.3 for the 187 owners reporting, and the sample standard deviation was 1.28 years. If the company wants to advertise an average number of years of repair-free lawnmowing for this lawnmower, what is the point estimate? Construct a 95% confidence interval for the average number of years until the first major repair.

8.8 The average total dollar purchase at a convenience store is less than that at a supermarket. Despite smaller ticket purchases, convenience stores can still be profitable because of the size of operation, volume of business, and the markup. A researcher is interested in estimating the average purchase amount for convenience stores in suburban Long Island. To do so, she randomly sampled thirty-two purchases from several convenience stores in suburban Long Island and tabulated the amounts to the nearest dollar. Use the following data to construct a 90% confidence interval for the population average amount of purchase:

$ 2	$11	$8	$ 7
5	4	2	1
14	7	6	3
4	1	3	6
9	3	3	6
10	8	5	4
7	2	3	6
8	4	7	12

8.9 A community health association is interested in estimating the average number of maternity days women stay in the local hospital. A random sample is taken of thirty-six women who had babies in the hospital during the past year. The following numbers of maternity days each woman was in the hospital are rounded to the nearest day.

3	3	4	3	2	5	3	1	4	3	4	2
3	5	3	2	4	3	2	4	1	6	3	4
3	3	5	2	3	2	3	5	4	3	5	4

Use these data to construct a 98% confidence interval to estimate the average maternity stay in the hospital for all women who have babies in this hospital.

8.10 Suppose that the National Homeowners Association wants to estimate the current average mortgage interest rate. Using a master list, the Association's analyst randomly selects forty-eight national mortgage lenders and surveys the lenders' rates by telephone interview. The survey results in a sample average mortgage rate of 9.68%, with a standard deviation of 0.28%. Use this information to determine the following.

a. The point estimate for the current national average mortgage interest rate

b. A 98% confidence interval to estimate the current national average mortgage interest rate

8.11 A meat processing company in the Midwest produces and markets a package of eight small sausage sandwiches. The product is nationally distributed, and the company is interested in knowing the average retail price charged for this item in stores across the country. The company cannot justify a national census to generate this information. The company information system produces a list of all retailers who carry the product. A researcher for the company contacts thirty-six of these retailers and ascertains the selling prices for the product. Use the following price data to determine a point estimate for the national retail price of the product. Construct a 90% confidence interval to estimate this price:

$2.23	$2.11	$2.12	$2.20	$2.17	$2.10
2.16	2.31	1.98	2.17	2.14	1.82
2.12	2.07	2.17	2.30	2.29	2.19
2.01	2.24	2.18	2.18	2.32	2.02
1.99	1.87	2.09	2.22	2.15	2.19
2.23	2.10	2.08	2.05	2.16	2.26

8.2   ESTIMATING THE POPULATION PROPORTION

Business decision makers and researchers often need to be able to estimate the population proportion. For most businesses, estimating market share (their proportion of the market) is important, because many company decisions evolve from market share information. Political pollsters are interested in estimating the proportion of the vote that their candidates will receive. Companies spend thousands of dollars estimating the proportion of produced goods that are defective. Market segmentation opportunities come from a knowledge of the proportion of various demographic characteristics among potential customers or clients.

Methods similar to those in Section 8.1 can be used to estimate the population proportion. The central limit theorem for sample proportions led to the following formula in Chapter 7:

$$Z = \frac{\hat{p} - P}{\sqrt{\dfrac{P \cdot Q}{n}}},$$

where: $Q = 1 - P$.

Recall that this formula can be applied only when $n \cdot P$ and $n \cdot Q$ are greater than 5.

Algebraically manipulating this formula to estimate P involves solving for P. However, P is in both the numerator and the denominator, so solving for P would involve using quadratic equations, which is unsatisfactory. For this reason—for confidence interval purposes only—$\hat{p}$ is substituted for P in the denominator, yielding

$$Z = \frac{\hat{p} - P}{\sqrt{\dfrac{\hat{p}\hat{q}}{n}}},$$

where: $\hat{q} = 1 - \hat{p}$.

Solving for P results in the confidence interval.

$$\hat{p} - Z\sqrt{\frac{\hat{p}\hat{q}}{n}} \leq P \leq \hat{p} + Z\sqrt{\frac{\hat{p}\hat{q}}{n}},$$

where: $\hat{p}$ = sample proportion
$\hat{q} = 1 - \hat{p}$
P = population proportion
n = sample size

Confidence Interval to Estimate *P*

In 1988, a study of eighty-seven randomly selected companies with a telemarketing operation was completed. The study revealed that 39% of the sampled companies had used telemarketing to assist them in order processing. Using this information, how could a researcher estimate the *population* proportion of telemarketing companies who use their telemarketing operation to assist them in order processing?

The sample proportion, $\hat{p} = 0.39$, is the *point estimate* of the population proportion, P. For $n = 87$ and $\hat{p} = 0.39$, a 95% confidence interval can be computed to determine an interval estimation of P. The Z value for 95% confidence is 1.96. The value of $\hat{q} = 1 - \hat{p} = 1 - 0.39 = 0.61$. The confidence interval estimate is

$$0.39 - 1.96\sqrt{\frac{(0.39)(0.61)}{87}} \le P \le 0.39 + 1.96\sqrt{\frac{(0.39)(0.61)}{87}};$$

$$0.39 - 0.10 \le P \le 0.39 + 0.10$$

$$0.29 \le P \le 0.49.$$

This interval suggests that the population proportion of telemarketing firms who use their operation to assist order processing is somewhere between 0.29 and 0.49. This result has a 95% level of confidence.

Demonstration Problem 8.4

A clothing company produces men's jeans. The jeans are made and sold with either a regular cut or a boot cut. In an effort to estimate the proportion of their men's jeans market in Oklahoma City that is for boot-cut jeans, the analyst takes a random sample of 212 jeans sales from the company's two Oklahoma City retail outlets. Only thirty-four of the sales were for boot-cut jeans. Construct a 90% confidence interval to estimate the proportion of the population who prefer boot-cut jeans.

Solution:

The sample size is 212, and the number preferring boot-cut jeans is 34. The sample proportion is $\hat{p} = 34/212 = 0.16$. A point estimate for boot-cut jeans in the population is 0.16 or 16%. The Z value for a 90% level of confidence is 1.645, and the value of $\hat{q} = 1 - \hat{p} = 1 - 0.16 = 0.84$. The confidence interval estimate is

$$0.16 - 1.645\sqrt{\frac{(0.16)(0.84)}{212}} \le P \le 0.16 + 1.645\sqrt{\frac{(0.16)(0.84)}{212}};$$

$$0.16 - 0.04 \le P \le 0.16 + 0.04;$$

$$0.12 \le P \le 0.20.$$

The analyst estimates that the population proportion of boot-cut jeans purchases is between 0.12 and 0.20. The level of confidence in this result is 90%.

Demonstration Problem 8.5

A national accrediting agency would like to know the proportion of all business graduate students who have a degree in engineering. As a frame for this population, the agency decides to use all students who take the GMAT. Interviewers go to locations where the GMAT is given and obtain a random sample of 635 people who are taking the GMAT. Of those people interviewed, 172 respond that they have at least one degree in engineering or that they are seniors in an engineering program. Use this information to construct a 92% confidence interval for P.

Solution:

The sample size is 635. The sample proportion is $\hat{p} = 172/635 = 0.27$. The value of $\hat{q}$ is $1 - 0.27 = 0.73$, and $Z = 1.75$. Computing the confidence interval yields

$$0.27 - 1.75\sqrt{\frac{(0.27)(0.73)}{635}} \le P \le 0.27 + 1.75\sqrt{\frac{(0.27)(0.73)}{635}};$$
$$0.27 - 0.03 \le P \le 0.27 + 0.03;$$
$$0.24 \le P \le 0.30.$$

The agency's analyst estimates that between 24% and 30% of all graduate business majors are or will be engineers.

**PROBLEMS
Section 8.2**

8.12 Use the information about each of the following samples to compute the confidence interval to estimate P.

  a. $n = 44$ and $\hat{p} = 0.51$; compute a 99% confidence interval.

  b. $n = 300$ and $\hat{p} = 0.82$; compute a 95% confidence interval.

  c. $n = 1{,}150$ and $\hat{p} = 0.48$; compute a 90% confidence interval.

  d. $n = 95$ and $\hat{p} = 0.32$; compute an 88% confidence interval.

8.13 Use the following sample information to calculate the confidence interval to estimate the population proportion. Let x be the number of items in the sample possessing the characteristic of interest.

  a. $n = 116$ and $x = 57$, with 99% confidence.

  b. $n = 800$ and $x = 479$, with 97% confidence.

  c. $n = 240$ and $x = 106$, with 85% confidence.

  d. $n = 60$ and $x = 21$, with 90% confidence.

8.14 Suppose that a random sample of eighty-five items has been taken from a population and forty of the items contain the characteristic of interest. Use this information to calculate a 90% confidence interval to estimate the proportion of the population that possesses the characteristic of interest. Calculate a 95% confidence interval. Calculate a 99% confidence interval. As the level of confidence changed and the other sample information stayed constant, what happened to the confidence interval?

8.15 In a random sample of 75 blood donors, 29 had type O+ blood. Use this information to estimate the proportion of the population who have type O+ blood. What is the point estimate? Use a 99% level of confidence to compute the confidence interval. If the same sample proportion had been obtained from a sample of 750 donors, what would happen to the confidence interval if the level of confidence is still 99%?

8.16 Suppose that the marketing people at Walt Disney, Inc., want to know if men or women take children under the age of eight to see an animated movie. Suppose that a random sample of groups of small children at various theaters revealed that, of the 136 groups selected, 101 were brought primarily by women. Use this information to establish a 95% confidence interval to estimate the proportion of the population of these groups brought to the movie by men. How could Walt Disney, Inc., use this information?

8.17 What proportion of pizza restaurants that are primarily for walk-in business have a salad bar? Suppose that, in an effort to determine this figure, a random sample of 1,250 of these restaurants across the U.S. based on the Yellow Pages is called. If 997 of the restaurants sampled have a salad bar, what is the 98% confidence interval for the population pro-p ortion?

8.18 The highway department wants to estimate the proportion of vehicles on Interstate 25 between the hours of midnight and 5:00 A.M. that are eighteen-wheel tractor trailers. The estimate can be used to determine highway repair and construction considerations and in highway patrol planning. Suppose researchers for the highway department counted vehicles at different locations on the interstate for several nights during this time period. Of the 3,481 vehicles counted, 927 were eighteen wheelers.

   a. Determine the point estimate for the proportion of vehicles traveling Interstate 25 during this time period that are eighteen wheelers.

   b. Construct a 99% confidence interval for the proportion of vehicles on Interstate 25 during this time period that are eighteen wheelers.

8.19 What proportion of commercial airline pilots are older than age forty? Suppose that a researcher has access to a list of all pilots who are members of the Commercial Airline Pilots Association. If this list is used as a frame for the study, she can randomly select a sample of pilots, contact them, and ascertain their ages. From eighty-nine of these pilots so selected, she learns that forty-eight of them are older than age forty. Construct an 85% confidence interval to estimate the population proportion of commercial airline pilots who are older than age forty.

ESTIMATING THE DIFFERENCE IN TWO POPULATION MEANS | 8.3

Sometimes being able to estimate the difference in the means of two popula
is valuable. How much does the size or weight or age of two populations di
By how much does the effectiveness of two products differ? Is there a differei
in mean results using two different methods? The answers to these questio.
are often difficult to obtain through census techniques. The alternative is t
take a random sample from each of the two populations and study the differenc
in the sample means.

The central limit theorem yields a formula for the difference in sample
means when the sample sizes are large or when the populations are normally
distributed:

$$Z = \frac{(\overline{X}_1 - \overline{X}_2) - (\mu_1 - \mu_2)}{\sqrt{\dfrac{\sigma_1^2}{n_1} + \dfrac{\sigma_2^2}{n_2}}}.$$

Algebraically, this formula can be manipulated to produce a formula for constructing confidence intervals for the difference in two population means.

(8.3) $$(\overline{X}_1 - \overline{X}_2) - Z\sqrt{\frac{\sigma_1^2}{n_1} + \frac{\sigma_2^2}{n_2}} \leq \mu_1 - \mu_2 \leq (\overline{X}_1 - \overline{X}_2) + Z\sqrt{\frac{\sigma_1^2}{n_1} + \frac{\sigma_2^2}{n_2}}.$$

Confidence Interval to Estimate $\mu_1 - \mu_2$

As noted in Section 8.1, sample standard deviations are good approxi-
mations of population standard deviations if the sample sizes are large enough.
As Formula 8.3 is based on the central limit theorem for large samples, it can
be modified to use sample standard deviations instead of the population values
as an approximation of the confidence interval to estimate, $\mu_1 - \mu_2$:

$$(\overline{X}_1 - \overline{X}_2) - Z\sqrt{\frac{S_1^2}{n_1} + \frac{S_2^2}{n_2}} \leq \mu_1 - \mu_2 \leq (\overline{X}_1 - \overline{X}_2) + Z\sqrt{\frac{S_1^2}{n_1} + \frac{S_2^2}{n_2}}.$$

Confidence Interval to Estimate $\mu_1 - \mu_2$ **When** n_1 **and** n_2 **Are Large and** σ^1, σ^2 **Are Unknown**

Demonstration Problem 8.6

A study of coupon shoppers was undertaken by D'Arcy Masius Benton & Bowles, a New York-based advertising agency in 1990. The results showed that the typical coupon shopper was a middle-aged married working woman with a household income of $29,000. The study also showed that the average coupon shopper saved $6.00 off the weekly grocery bill using coupons. Low-income families did not use coupons as much as middle-income families, because they are not exposed to as many coupons through magazines, newspapers, and other sources.

Suppose that another study is conducted to estimate the difference between middle-income shoppers and low-income shoppers in terms of the average amount saved from grocery bills per week. Random samples of sixty middle-income shoppers and eighty low-income shoppers are taken, and their purchases are monitored for one week. The average amounts saved with coupons, as well as sample sizes and sample standard deviations, are as follows:

Middle-Income Shoppers	Low-Income Shoppers
$n_1 = 60$	$n_2 = 80$
$\overline{X}_1 = \$5.84$	$\overline{X}_2 = \$2.67$
$S_1 = \$1.41$	$S_2 = \$0.54$

Use this information to construct a 98% confidence interval to estimate the difference between the mean amount saved using coupons by middle-income shoppers and the mean amount saved using coupons by low-income shoppers.

Solution:

$$(5.84 - 2.67) - 2.33\sqrt{\frac{1.41^2}{60} + \frac{0.54^2}{80}} \leq \mu_1 - \mu_2$$

$$\leq (5.84 - 2.67) + 2.33\sqrt{\frac{1.41^2}{60} + \frac{0.54^2}{80}};$$

$3.17 - 0.45 \leq \mu_1 - \mu_2 \leq 3.17 + 0.45;$

$2.72 \leq \mu_1 - \mu_2 \leq 3.62.$

There is a 98% confidence that the actual difference in the population mean coupon savings per week between middle-income and low-income families is between $2.72 and $3.62. That is, the difference could be as little as $2.72 or as great as $3.62. Note that a zero difference in the population means of these two groups is unlikely, because zero does not fall in the 98% range.

Demonstration Problem 8.7

A consumer test group wants to determine the difference in gasoline mileage of cars using regular unleaded gas and cars using premium unleaded gas. Researchers for the group divided a fleet of 100 of the same make of cars in half and tested each car on one tank of gas. Fifty of the cars were filled with regular unleaded gas, and 50 were filled with premium unleaded gas. The sample average for the regular gasoline group was 21.45 mpg, with a standard deviation of 3.46 mpg. The sample average for the premium gasoline group was 24.6 mpg, with a standard deviation of 2.99 mpg. Construct a 95% confidence interval to estimate the difference in the mean gas mileage between the cars using regular gasoline and the cars using premium gasoline.

Solution:

The Z value for a 95% confidence interval is 1.96. The other sample information is:

Regular	Premium
$n_r = 50$	$n_p = 50$
$\overline{X}_r = 21.45$	$\overline{X}_p = 24.6$
$S_r = 3.46$	$S_p = 2.99$

Based on this information, the confidence interval is

$$(21.45 - 24.6) - 1.96\sqrt{\frac{3.46^2}{50} + \frac{2.99^2}{50}} \leq \mu_1 - \mu_2$$

$$\leq (21.45 - 24.6) + 1.96\sqrt{\frac{3.46^2}{50} + \frac{2.99^2}{50}};$$

$$-3.15 - 1.27 \leq \mu_1 - \mu_2 \leq -3.15 + 1.27;$$

$$-4.42 \leq \mu_1 - \mu_2 \leq -1.88.$$

Designating one group as group 1 and another group as group 2 is an arbitrary decision. If the two groups in Demonstration Problem 8.7 had been reversed, the confidence interval would be the same, except that the signs would be reversed and the inequalities would be switched. Thus the researcher must interpret the confidence interval in light of the sample information. For the confidence interval in the gasoline mileage problem, the population difference in mean mileage between regular and premium could be as much as -4.40 mpg. This result means that the premium gasoline could have an average difference of 4.4 mpg more than regular gasoline. The other side of the interval shows that, based on the sample information, the difference in favor of premium gasoline could be as little as 1.9 mpg more. The confidence interval does not contain the value of zero, which indicates that no difference in the population average mileage between regular and premium gasoline is unlikely. If both signs are the same in a confidence interval for the difference between two means, the entire interval indicates the same direction of difference, and the values tell the magnitude of difference. If the signs of the confidence interval for the difference of the sample means are different, the interval includes zero, and no significant difference in population means is possible.

**PROBLEMS
Section 8.3**

8.20 Use the following sample information to determine an 85% confidence interval for the difference in means for population A and population B:

Sample A	Sample B
$n_A = 110$	$n_B = 100$
$\bar{X}_A = 47.2$	$\bar{X}_B = 53.4$
$S_A = 4.1$	$S_B = 4.0$

8.21 Use the following sample information to construct a 90% confidence interval for the difference in the two population means:

Sample 1	Sample 2
$n_1 = 32$	$n_2 = 31$
$\bar{X}_1 = 70.4$	$\bar{X}_2 = 68.7$
$S_1 = 5.76$	$S_2 = 6.1$

8.22 Suppose that you own a plumbing repair business and employ fifteen plumbers. You are interested in estimating the difference in the average number of calls completed per day between two of the plumbers. A random sample of forty days of plumber A's work results in a sample average of 5.3 calls, with a variance of 1.99. A random sample of thirty-seven days of plumber B's work results in a sample mean of 6.5 calls, with a variance of 2.36. Use this information and a 95% level of confidence to estimate the difference in population mean daily efforts between plumber A and plumber B. Interpret the results. Is there a possibility that, for these populations of days, there is no difference in the average number of calls completed between plumber A and plumber B?

8.23 Suppose that you are curious about whether there is a difference in the average number of runs scored by a National League team and an American League team in a major league baseball game, and, if there is a difference, how much the difference is. To determine the answer, you randomly sample fifty American League games, pick a team, and record the number of runs it scored. You then calculate a sample mean of 3.82 runs per game, with a standard deviation of 1.46 for the American League sample. With a sample of sixty National League games, you get a sample mean of 3.62 runs per game, with a standard deviation of 1.29. Use a 98% confidence interval to estimate the difference in population means between the two leagues. What is the point estimate? Based on this experiment, is the evidence conclusive that one league averages more runs per game? Why or why not?

8.24 Suppose that a market analyst wants to determine the difference in the average price of a gallon of whole milk in Seattle and Atlanta. To accomplish this, he takes a telephone survey of thirty-one randomly selected consumers in Seattle. He first asks whether they have purchased a gallon of milk during the past two weeks. If they say no, he continues to select consumers until $n = 31$. If they say yes, he asks them to say how much they paid for the milk. The analyst undertakes a similar survey in Atlanta with thirty-one respondents. Using the resulting sample information that follows, compute a 99% confidence interval to estimate the difference in the mean price of a gallon of milk between the two cities:

Seattle			Atlanta		
$2.55	$2.36	$2.43	$2.25	$2.40	$2.39
2.67	2.54	2.43	2.30	2.33	2.40
2.50	2.54	2.38	2.19	2.29	2.23
2.61	2.80	2.49	2.41	2.18	2.29
3.10	2.61	2.57	2.39	2.59	2.53
2.86	2.56	2.71	2.26	2.38	2.19
2.50	2.64	2.97	2.19	2.25	2.45
2.47	2.72	2.65	2.42	2.61	2.33
2.76	2.73	2.80	2.60	2.25	2.51
2.65	2.83	2.69	2.38	2.29	2.36
		2.71			2.44

8.25 What is the difference between the average salaries of architects who have reached partnership status and architects who are not partners? A researcher obtains a frame list of architects through the American Institute of Architects. She then interviews thirty-seven architects who have reached the level of partner. The average salary for this sample is $62,000, with a sample standard deviation of $5,590. She randomly selects forty-four architects who have not reached the level of partner. The average salary for this sample is $39,000, with a sample standard deviation of $8,025. Use this information to determine a point estimate for the difference of average salaries between architects who are partners and architects who are not. Construct a 90% confidence interval to estimate this difference.

8.4 ESTIMATING THE DIFFERENCE IN TWO POPULATION PROPORTIONS

In business research determining the difference in proportions for two populations sometimes is useful. For example, suppose that music industry officials want to target purchasers of classical music albums better. They might be interested in estimating the difference in the proportion of college-educated music consumers who purchase classical music and the proportion of non-college-educated music consumers who purchase classical music. Health administrators might want to estimate the difference between the proportion of patients at public hospitals who are medicare patients and the proportion of private hospital patients who are medicare patients. Airline industry management might be interested in knowing the difference between the proportion of flyers who fly first class on domestic flights and the proportion who fly first class on intercontinental flights.

In many cases, computing population proportions and comparing them is difficult. For this reason, a random sample is taken from each population, and the sample proportions are computed and compared. The following formula was developed from the central limit theorem in Chapter 7 for the difference in two sample proportions. It applies to large samples only when $n_1 \cdot \hat{p}_1, n_1 \cdot \hat{q}_1, n_2 \cdot \hat{p}_2$, and $n_2 \cdot \hat{q}_2$ all are greater than 5.

$$Z = \frac{(\hat{p}_1 - \hat{p}_2) - (P_1 - P_2)}{\sqrt{\frac{P_1 Q_1}{n_1} + \frac{P_2 Q_2}{n_2}}}.$$

This formula can be used to estimate $P_1 - P_2$, but, for reasons similar to those presented in Section 8.2, the sample proportions must be used instead of the population proportions in the denominator. That is,

$$Z = \frac{(\hat{p}_1 - \hat{p}_2) - (P_1 - P_2)}{\sqrt{\dfrac{\hat{p}_1\hat{q}_1}{n_1} + \dfrac{\hat{p}_2\hat{q}_2}{n_2}}}.$$

Solving this equation for $P_1 - P_2$ produces the formula for constructing confidence intervals for $P_1 - P_2$.

$$(\hat{p}_1 - \hat{p}_2) - Z\sqrt{\frac{\hat{p}_1\hat{q}_1}{n_1} + \frac{\hat{p}_2\hat{q}_2}{n_2}} \le P_1 - P_2 \le (\hat{p}_1 - \hat{p}_2) + Z\sqrt{\frac{\hat{p}_1\hat{q}_1}{n_1} + \frac{\hat{p}_2\hat{q}_2}{n_2}}$$

Confidence Interval to Estimate $P_1 - P_2$

(8.4)

Demonstration Problem 8.8

There seems to be a trend away from single practitioner physicians. Does this trend hold true for dentists also? Suppose that you want to estimate the difference in proportion of physicians who still practice alone and the proportion of dentists who practice alone. You obtain a list of physicians through the American Medical Association and a list of dentists through the American Dental Association. A random sample of 134 physicians reveals that only 16 are in private practice. A random sample of 181 dentists reveals that 96 practice alone. Construct a 95% confidence interval to estimate the difference in proportions of physicians who practice alone and dentists who practice alone.

Solution:

random sample

Here, $n_1 = 134$, $\hat{p}_1 = 16/134 = 0.12$, $n_2 = 181$, and $\hat{p}_2 = 96/181 = 0.53$. The Z value for 95% confidence is 1.96. Substituting into Formula 8.4 gives

$$(0.12 - 0.53) - 1.96\sqrt{\frac{(0.12)(0.88)}{134} + \frac{(0.53)(0.47)}{181}} \le P_1 - P_2$$

$$\le (0.12 - 0.53) + 1.96\sqrt{\frac{(0.12)(0.88)}{134} + \frac{(0.53)(0.47)}{181}};$$

$$-0.41 - 0.09 \le P_1 - P_2 \le -0.41 + 0.09;$$
$$-0.50 \le P_1 - P_2 \le -0.32.$$

You are 95% confident that the difference in population proportions lies between -0.50 and -0.32. That is, from 32% to 50% more dentists than physicians practice alone.

Demonstration Problem 8.9

In an attempt to target its clientele, management of a supermarket chain wants to determine the difference between the proportion of morning shoppers who are men and the proportion of after 5 P.M. shoppers who are men. Over a period of two weeks, the chain's researchers conduct a systematic random sample survey of 400 morning shoppers, which reveals that 352 were women and 48 were men. During this same period, a systematic random sample of 480 after 5 P.M. shoppers reveals that 293 were women and 187 were men. Construct a 98% confidence interval to estimate the difference in the population proportions of men.

Solution:

The sample information is as follows:

Morning Shoppers	After 5 P.M. Shoppers
$n_1 = 400$	$n_2 = 480$
$x_1 = 48$ men	$x_2 = 187$ men
$\hat{p}_1 = 0.12$	$\hat{p}_2 = 0.39$
$\hat{q}_1 = 0.88$	$\hat{q}_2 = 0.61$

For a 98% level of confidence, $Z = 2.33$. Using Formula 8.4 yields

$$(0.12 - 0.39) - 2.33 \sqrt{\frac{(0.12)(0.88)}{400} + \frac{(0.39)(0.61)}{480}} \leq P_1 - P_2$$

$$\leq (0.12 - 0.39) + 2.33 \sqrt{\frac{(0.12)(0.88)}{400} + \frac{(0.39)(0.61)}{480}};$$

$$-0.27 - 0.064 \leq P_1 - P_2 \leq -0.27 + 0.064;$$

$$-0.334 \leq P_1 - P_2 \leq -0.206.$$

There is a 98% level of confidence that the difference in population proportions is between -0.334 and -0.206. Because the after 5 P.M. shopper proportion was subtracted from the morning shoppers, the negative signs in the interval indicate a higher proportion of men in the after 5 P.M. shoppers than in the morning shoppers. Thus the confidence level is 98% that the difference in proportions is at least 0.206 and may be as much as 0.334.

8.26 In each of the following cases, calculate a confidence interval to estimate $P_1 - P_2$.

   a. $n_1 = 85$, $n_2 = 90$, $\hat{p}_1 = 0.75$, $\hat{p}_2 = 0.67$;
    level of confidence = 90%.

   b. $n_1 = 300$, $n_2 = 300$, $\hat{p}_1 = 0.45$, $\hat{p}_2 = 0.49$;
    level of confidence = 98%.

   c. $n_1 = 1{,}100$, $n_2 = 1{,}300$, $\hat{p}_1 = 0.19$, $\hat{p}_2 = 0.17$;
    level of confidence = 95%.

   d. $n_1 = 140$, $n_2 = 150$, $\hat{p}_1 = 0.56$, $\hat{p}_2 = 0.50$;
    level of confidence = 99%.

8.27 For each of the following cases, construct a confidence interval to estimate $P_1 - P_2$ from the information given.

   a. $n_1 = 200$, $n_2 = 300$, $x_1 = 174$, $x_2 = 189$;
    level of confidence = 86%.

   b. $n_1 = 430$, $n_2 = 399$, $x_1 = 275$, $x_2 = 275$;
    level of confidence = 85%.

   c. $n_1 = 49$, $n_2 = 64$, $x_1 = 25$, $x_2 = 35$;
    level of confidence = 95%.

   d. $n_1 = 1{,}500$, $n_2 = 1{,}500$, $x_1 = 1{,}050$, $x_2 = 1{,}100$;
    level of confidence = 80%.

8.28 A large production facility uses two machines to produce a key part for its main product. Inspectors have expressed concern about the quality of the finished product. Quality control investigation has revealed that the key part made by the two machines is defective at times. The inspectors randomly sample thirty-five units of the key part from each machine. Of those produced by machine A, five were defective. Seven of the thirty-five sampled parts from machine B were defective. The production manager is interested in estimating the difference in proportions of the populations of parts that are defective between machine A and machine B. From the sample information, compute a 98% confidence interval for this difference.

8.29 The Democratic Party in Virginia has candidates in the races for both Governor and Lieutenant Governor. The Party hired a pollster to estimate the difference in the proportions of votes likely to be cast for the two candidates. The following data are results of a randomly conducted survey:

Democratic Party Candidates	
Governor	Lieutenant Governor
$n_1 = 650$ voters	$n_2 = 650$ voters
$x_1 = 330$ in favor	$x_2 = 300$ in favor

Compute a 95% confidence interval for $P_1 - P_2$.

8.30 A national nutrition organization believes that geographic location is an important variable in the tendency of a family to eat fish. Its directors decide to estimate the difference in the proportions of families living on the coast who have fish in their diets and families situated in the Midwest who have fish in their diets. To determine this difference, the organization's researchers randomly contact 480 families in Boston and 505 families in Minneapolis/St. Paul. The responding family members are asked whether fish is served at least once a week in their homes. In the Boston sample, 427 families replied "yes." Only 212 of the Minneapolis/St. Paul familes replied "yes." Use this information to compute a 90% confidence interval to estimate the difference in population proportions.

8.31 A film manufacturing company is interested in the proportion of 35-mm camera users who use primarily 100 ASA film (oriented more toward outdoor than indoor use). The company believes that the proportion of 100 ASA users is higher in July than in January, and their sales records show that to be true. Suppose that the company's analysts randomly call 900 camera owners who have a 35-mm camera and determine that 647 of these owners use primarily 100 ASA film in July. The analysts then ask an independent sample of 900 35-mm camera owners which ASA type film they use the most in January, and only 380 report using 100 ASA the most. Calculate an 80% confidence interval for the difference in the proportion of 100 ASA film users in July and the proportion of 100 ASA users in January.

8.32 What is the difference in the proportion of all ships carrying imported goods to Long Beach, California, that are U.S. owned and the proportion of all ships carrying imported goods to Baltimore, Maryland, that are U.S. owned? A sample of fifty-six ships docked in Long Beach harbor are examined, and eighteen are registered to American owners. A sample of thirty-eight ships docked in Baltimore harbor are examined, and fourteen are registered to American owners. Construct a 90% confidence interval to estimate the difference in these two proportions of U.S. owned ships. Comment on the meaning of the interval.

ESTIMATING SAMPLE SIZE

In most business research that uses sample statistics to infer about the population, being able to estimate the size of sample necessary to accomplish the purposes of the study is important. The need for **sample size estimation** is the same for the large corporation investing tens of thousands of dollars in a massive study of consumer preference and for students undertaking a small case study and wanting to send questionnaires to local business people. In either case, such things as level of confidence, sampling error, and width of estimation interval are closely tied to sample size. If the large corporation is undertaking a market study, should they sample 40 people or 4,000 people? The question is an important one. In most cases, because of cost considerations, researchers do not want to sample any more units or individuals than necessary.

sample size estimation

Sample Size When Estimating μ

In research studies when μ is being estimated, the size of sample can be determined by using the Z formula for sample means to solve for n:

$$Z = \frac{\overline{X} - \mu}{\frac{\sigma}{\sqrt{n}}}.$$

The difference between $\overline{X}$ and μ is the error of estimation resulting from the sampling process. Let $E = (\overline{X} - \mu) =$ the **error of estimation.** Substituting E into the preceding formula yields

error of estimation

$$Z = \frac{E}{\frac{\sigma}{\sqrt{n}}}.$$

Solving for n produces the sample size.

(8.5)
$$n = \frac{Z^2\sigma^2}{E^2}.$$

Sample Size When Estimating μ

Using Formula 8.5, the researcher can estimate the sample size needed to achieve the goals of the study before gathering data. For example, suppose that a researcher wants to estimate the average monthly expenditure on bread by a family in Chicago. She wants to be 90% confident of her results. How much error is she willing to tolerate in the results? Suppose that she wants the estimate to be within $1.00 of the actual figure. What is the value of σ? Sometimes, σ is available from similar previous studies. If it is not available, the following estimate is usually acceptable:

$$\sigma \approx \frac{1}{4} \text{ range}$$

This estimate is derived from the empirical rule (Chapter 3), which states that approximately 95% of the values in a normal distribution fall with $\pm 2\sigma$ of the mean, giving a span or range within which most of the values fall. In the bread problem suppose that the standard deviation of average monthly bread purchases is $4.00. What is the sample size estimation for this problem? The value of Z for a 90% level of confidence is 1.645. Using Formula 8.5 with $E = \$1.00$, $\sigma = \$4.00$, and $Z = 1.645$ gives

$$n = \frac{Z^2 \sigma^2}{E^2} = \frac{(1.645)^2(4)^2}{1^2} = 43.30.$$

That is, at least $n = 43.3$ must be randomly sampled to attain a 90% level of confidence and produce an error within $1.00 for a standard deviation of $4.00. Sampling 43.3 units is impossible, so this result should be rounded up to $n = 44$: 44 units must be sampled to meet these standards.

Demonstration Problem 8.10

Suppose that you want to estimate the average age of all 727 airplanes now in active domestic U.S. service. You want to be 95% confident, and you want your estimate to be within two years of the actual figure. The 727 was first placed in service thirty years ago, but you believe that no active 727s in the U.S. domestic fleet are more than twenty-five years old. How large a sample size should you take?

Solution:

Here, $E = $ two years, the Z value for 95% is 1.96, and σ is unknown, so it must be estimated by using $\sigma \approx (1/4) \cdot$ (range). As the range of ages is 0 to 25 years, $\sigma = (1/4)(25) = 6.25$. Use Formula 8.5:

$$n = \frac{Z^2 \sigma^2}{E^2} = \frac{(1.96)^2(6.25)^2}{2^2} = 37.52.$$

Because you cannot sample 37.52 units, the required sample size is 38. If you randomly sample 38 units you have an opportunity to estimate the average age of active 727s within two years and be 95%

confident of the results. If you want to be within one year for the estimate ($E = 1$), the sample size estimate changes to

$$n = \frac{Z^2 \sigma^2}{E^2} = \frac{(1.96)^2 (6.25)^2}{1^2} = 150.1.$$

Note that cutting the error by a factor of ½ increases the required sample size by a factor of 4. The reason is the squaring factor in Formula 8.5. If you want to reduce the error to one-half of what you used before, you must be willing to incur the cost of a sample that is four times larger, for the same level of confidence.

Determining Sample Size When Estimating *P*

Determining the sample size required to estimate the population proportion, *P*, also is possible. The process begins with the *Z* formula for sample proportions:

$$Z = \frac{\hat{p} - P}{\sqrt{\dfrac{P \cdot Q}{n}}},$$

where: $Q = 1 - P$.

As various samples are taken from the population, $\hat{p}$ will rarely equal the population proportion, *P*, resulting in an error of estimation. That is, the difference between $\hat{p}$ and *P* is the error of estimation. Let $E = \hat{p} - P$:

$$Z = \frac{E}{\sqrt{\dfrac{P \cdot Q}{n}}}.$$

Solving for *n* yields the sample size.

(8.6)	$$n = \frac{Z^2 P \cdot Q}{E^2},$$	**Sample Size When Estimating *P***

where: P = population proportion
   $Q = 1 - P$
   E = error of estimation
   n = sample size

How can the value of *n* be determined prior to a study if the formula requires the value of *P* and the study is being done to estimate *P*? Although the actual value of *P* is not known prior to the study, similar studies might

	P	P · Q
	0.5	0.25
	0.4	0.24
	0.3	0.21
	0.2	0.16
	0.1	0.09

TABLE 8.2

$P \cdot Q$ for Various
Selected Values of P

have generated a good approximation for P. If no previous value is available for use in estimating P, some possible P values, as shown in Table 8.2, might be considered.

Note that, as $P \cdot Q$ is in the numerator of the sample size formula, $P = 0.5$ or near 0.5 will result in the largest sample sizes. Often *if P is unknown, researchers use 0.5 as an estimate of P* in Formula 8.6. This selection results in the largest sample size that could be determined from Formula 8.6 for a given Z value and a given error value.

**Demonstration
Problem 8.11**

Suppose that you want to estimate the proportion of business managers that are left-handed. You want to be 98% confident of your finding, and you want to be within 0.03 of the true value. How large a sample size should you take? Assume that about 10% of the general public is left-handed.

Solution:

Here, $E = 0.03$, $P = 0.10$ (from the general public), and a 98% confidence level produces a Z value of 2.33. Solving for n yields

$$n = \frac{Z^2 P \cdot Q}{E^2} = \frac{(2.33)^2(0.10)(0.90)}{(0.03)^2} = 542.89.$$

You would have to sample at least 543 managers to be 98% confident of the results and maintain a maximum 3% error.

**Demonstration
Problem 8.12**

Suppose that a company is conducting an analysis of soft-drink consumers in which it randomly selects cola drinkers and asks each consumer if he or she prefers brand X. From this information, the company hopes to estimate brand X's market share. The company wants to be 90% confident of the results and be within 0.05 of the actual market share proportion. Assume that the company has no knowledge of brand X's market share. How large a sample size should it take?

Solution:

Here, $E = 0.05$, and Z for 90% is 1.645. With no historical proportion for this study, the company should use $P = 0.50$ to determine sample size. Solving for n gives

$$n = \frac{Z^2 P \cdot Q}{E^2} = \frac{(1.645)^2(0.50)(0.50)}{(0.05)^2} = 270.6$$

The company should sample 271 consumers.

Determining Sample Size When Estimating $\mu_1 - \mu_2$

When taking two random samples and using the difference in sample means to estimate the difference in population means, a researcher should have an idea of how large the sample sizes need to be. The sample size formula presented in this section is derived from the Z formula for the difference in sample means:

$$Z = \frac{(\overline{X}_1 - \overline{X}_2) - (\mu_1 - \mu_2)}{\sqrt{\dfrac{\sigma_1^2}{n_1} + \dfrac{\sigma_2^2}{n_2}}}.$$

Solving for the value of n in this formula does not look promising. The equation has nine variables, including two different values of n. However, making some assumptions can generate a workable sample size formula. The first is that the variances of the two populations are the same: $\sigma_1^2 = \sigma_2^2 = \sigma^2$. The second is that the sample size for each sample is the same: $n_1 = n_2 = n$. The difference between $\overline{X}_1 - \overline{X}_2$ and $\mu_1 - \mu_2$ is the error of the estimation, or

$$E = (\overline{X}_1 - \overline{X}_2) - (\mu_1 - \mu_2).$$

Incorporating these assumptions into the Z formula yields

$$Z = \frac{E}{\sqrt{\dfrac{\sigma^2}{n} + \dfrac{\sigma^2}{n}}} = \frac{E}{\sqrt{\dfrac{2\sigma^2}{n}}} = \frac{E}{\sqrt{\dfrac{2}{n}}\,\sigma}.$$

Solving for n produces the sample size.

Sample Size When Estimating $\mu_1 - \mu_2$	$n = \dfrac{2Z^2\sigma^2}{E^2}.$	(8.7)

Note that Formula 8.7 is the same as Formula 8.5 for single means, except that the numerator contains a 2. The necessary sample sizes for comparing two sample means are *each* twice as large as the required sample size for estimating single sample means. Because Formula 8.7 is based on the assumption that the two sample sizes are the same, only one sample size answer is given. However, in business research sample sizes often are unequal. As a result, sample size formulas often are used as minimum rules of thumb. For example, if Formula 8.7 indicated that a sample size of 80 is required, the researcher has the option of sampling 85 from one population and 100 from the other. In practical terms, the impact of the formula is that the researcher does not need to sample 500 or 1,000 from each population in order to achieve the level of confidence required within a given amount of error. Remember that, usually, the larger the sample, the more it costs. Thus *sample size formulas can be effective aids in ensuring that a research project's goals are met and that the cost of sampling is minimized.*

Demonstration Problem 8.13

A college admissions officer wants to estimate the difference in the average GMAT scores of men and women. She plans to take a random sample of men and a random sample of women who have taken the GMAT at the same time. She wants to be within 10 points of the true difference in the mean scores of men and women and 95% confident of her results. Past GMAT test results indicate that the standard deviation of GMAT scores is about 105 points. How large should the sample sizes be?

Solution:

Here, $E = 10$, $Z = 1.96$, and $\sigma = 105$. Solving for n gives

$$n = \frac{2Z^2\sigma^2}{E^2} = \frac{2(1.96)^2(105)^2}{(10)^2} = 847.1.$$

She needs to randomly sample at least 848 men and 848 women to achieve an error within 10 points and a 95% level of confidence.

**Demonstration
Problem 8.14**

The admission price of going to a movie or a professional sporting event is just part of the total cost. Sometimes there is a parking fee, and families often spend as much on food and beverages at the event as they spend for admission. A researcher wants to estimate the difference between the average amount a family spends on food and beverages while they are at a theater to watch a first-run movie and the average amount it spends on food and beverages while at a professional sports event. How many families should be randomly interviewed for each sample if the researcher wants to be 98% confident of the results and within $3.00 of the true difference? The researcher assumes that the standard deviation of food and beverage consumption at one of these events is about $5.00.

Solution:

Here, $E = 3$, $\sigma = 5$, and $Z_{0.98} = 2.33$. Using Formula 8.7 yields

$$n = \frac{2Z^2\sigma^2}{E^2} = \frac{2(2.33)^2(5)^2}{3^2} = 30.16.$$

Each sample should contain at least 31 families.

**PROBLEMS
Section 8.5**

8.33 Determine the sample size necessary to estimate μ with the following conditions.

   a. 99% level of confidence, a standard deviation of 15, and an error within 4

   b. 85% level of confidence, a standard deviation of 4.25, and an error within 1

   c. 80% level of confidence, a variance of 900, and an error within 5

8.34 Determine the sample size necessary to estimate P with the following conditions.

   a. 90% level of confidence, P of approximately 0.65, and an error within 0.03

   b. 96% level of confidence, P unknown, and an error within 0.05

   c. 95% level of confidence, P unknown, and an error within 0.10

8.35 Determine the sample size necessary to estimate $\mu_1 - \mu_2$ with the following conditions.

    a. 98% level of confidence, standard deviation of 20.4, and an error within 7.3

    b. 88% level of confidence, variance of 2,000, and an error within 15

    c. 92% level of confidence, variance of 140, and an error within 3

8.36 A bank officer wants to determine the amount of the average total monthly deposits per customer at the bank. He believes that an estimate of this average amount using a confidence interval is sufficient. How large a sample should he take to be within $200 of the actual average with 99% confidence? He assumes that the standard deviation of total monthly deposits for all customers is about $1,000.

8.37 Suppose that you have been following a particular airline stock for many years. You are interested in determining the average daily price of this stock over ten years, and you have access to the stock reports for these years. However, you do not want to average all the daily prices over ten years because of the more than 2,500 data points, so you decide to take a random sample of them and estimate the average. You want to be 90% confident of your results, you want the estimate to be within $2.00 of the true average, and you believe that the standard deviation of the price of this stock is about $12.50 over this period of time. How large a sample should you take?

8.38 A group of investors wants to develop a chain of fast-food restaurants. In determining potential costs for each facility, they must consider, among other expenses, the average monthly electric bill. They decide to sample some fast-food restaurants presently operating in an effort to estimate the monthly cost of electricity. They want to be 90% confident of their results and want to be within $100 of the correct figure. They estimate that such bills range from $600 to $2,500. How large a sample should they take?

8.39 Suppose that a production facility purchases a particular component part in large lots from a supplier. The production manager wants to estimate the proportion of defective parts received from this supplier. She believes that the proportion of defects is no more than 0.20 and wants to be within 0.02 of the true proportion of defects with a 90% level of confidence. How large a sample should she take?

8.40 What proportion of secretaries of *Fortune 500* companies has a personal computer at his or her work station? You want to answer this question by conducting a random survey. How large a sample should you take if you want to be 95% confident of the results and within 0.05 of the population proportion with the estimate? Assume that no one has any idea of what the proportion actually is.

8.41 What proportion of shoppers at a large appliance store actually make a large ticket purchase? To estimate this proportion within 10% and be

95% confident of the results, how large a sample should you take? Assume that no more than 50% of all shoppers actually make a large-ticket purchase.

8.42 A researcher wants to estimate the difference between the average price of a 21-in. black and white television and the average price of a 21-in. color television set. He believes that the standard deviation of the price of a 21-in. television set is about $100. He wants to be 99% confident of his results and within $20 of the true difference. How large a sample should he take for each type of television set?

8.43 The trucking industry has some large corporate firms and some independent truckers. Suppose that, in setting standards, national transportation officials would like to estimate the difference between the average number of miles driven per day by large-firm truckers and independent truckers. They would like to be within ten miles of the true difference with a confidence level of 99%. How many truckers should be randomly sampled from each group if the standard deviation of daily truck runs seems to be about seventy-five miles?

8.44 A nonprofit fund-raising group wants to estimate the difference in the mean annual amount contributed per person by employees of production firms and service firms to one of its largest funds. To obtain this estimate the fund-raising group is going to randomly sample workers from each industry and determine from the records how much each person contributed to the large fund. The fund-raising group wants to be 95% confident of its results and within $25 of the actual difference between the average contribution of each industry. The group estimates that, in any industry, the range of annual individual contributions varies from $10 to $1,500. How large a sample should the fund-raising group take in each industry?

CHAPTER SUMMARY

Information was presented about how to estimate population parameters from sample statistics using confidence intervals and about how to determine the size of a sample. These techniques are valid only for large sample statistics, and the formulas used are derived from the Z formulas of the four types of sampling statistics discussed in Chapter 7. These include the sample mean, the sample proportion, the difference in two sample means, and the difference in two sample proportions.

At times in business research a product is new and/or untested or information about the population is unknown. In such cases gathering data from a sample and making estimates about the population is useful and can be done with a point estimate or an interval estimate. A point estimate is the use of a statistic from the sample as an estimate for a parameter of the population. The problem with point estimates is that they are likely to change with every sample taken. An interval estimate is a range of values computed from the sample within which the researcher believes the population parameter lies with some confidence. Certain levels of confidence seem to be used more than others: 95%, 90%, 98%, and 99%. A 95% level of confidence, for example, means that if the interval were computed on 100 random samples, it is likely that 95 of the intervals would include the population parameter and 5 would not. If the level of confidence is increased, the width of the interval increases if all other factors are held constant. An interval width can be decreased either by reducing the level of confidence or by increasing the sample size. In estimating the population mean or the difference in two population means when sample size is large, it is permissible to use the sample standard deviation as an approximation for the population standard deviation when the population standard deviation is unknown.

The formulas in Chapter 7 resulting from the central limit theorem can be manipulated to produce formulas for estimating sample size. Determining the sample size necessary to estimate a population mean, if the population standard deviation is unavailable, can be based on an estimate of one-fourth the range as the population standard deviation. Estimating the population proportion calls for the value of the population proportion. The population proportion is the parameter to be estimated, so it is unknown. A value of the population proportion from a similar study can be used in sample size determination. If none is available, using a value of 0.50 will result in the largest sample size estimation for that problem if other variables are held constant. Determining the sample sizes necessary to estimate the difference in two population means requires the assumption that the population standard deviations are the same and that the sample sizes are the same. Sample size determination is used mostly to provide a ballpark figure to give researchers some guidance. Costs are associated with research, and larger samples sizes usually result in greater costs.

Key Words

Point estimate	Sample size estimation
Interval estimate	Error of estimation

USING THE COMPUTER

You can use Minitab to construct confidence intervals for single means and the difference in two means. The Minitab commands for estimating single population means are ZINTERVAL and TINTERVAL. ZINTERVAL is the command used when the population standard deviation is known. **TINTER-VAL** should be used when the population standard deviation is unknown. In either case, you must know the raw data from the sample and load them into a column location.

Suppose that thirty-two students of a local university are randomly selected and asked their age. Table 8.3 shows the responses. How can you use Minitab to construct a confidence interval for the population mean age of the students from these data? First, you must load the data into a column location, using either the **SET** or **READ** command. If you use the **READ** command, the data must be loaded either into one column (one data piece per line) or into several columns and later stacked into one column. Suppose that you know or have estimated that the population standard deviation of age for the university's students is six years. Because you know the standard deviation, you use the Minitab command **ZINTERVAL**. After reading the data into a column, you enter the **ZINTERVAL** command and then the level of confidence, the value of the population standard deviation, and the location of the data. For example, if you want to be 90% confident, the population standard deviation is 6, and the data are stored in column 1, the command is

MTB > ZINTERVAL 90 6 C1

Including the % sign with the level of confidence in the command is permissible but not necessary. If you do not specify a level of confidence, Minitab will default to the 95% level. Using this command to analyze the age data produces the following output:

THE ASSUMED SIGMA = 6.00

	N	MEAN	STDEV	SE MEAN	90.0 PERCENT C.I.
C1	32	22.66	5.33	1.06	(20.91, 24.40)

The 90% confidence interval to estimate the average age of a student at the university is $20.91 \le \mu \le 24.40$.

Suppose that you do not know the population standard deviation and must use the sample standard deviation as an approximation for it in the calculations. Then you must use the Minitab command, **TINTERVAL**, to construct the confidence interval to estimate the population mean. Following the **TINTERVAL** command you insert only the level of desired confidence and

21	19	19	20	18	24	21	19
27	18	22	21	19	29	32	19
22	18	29	29	35	20	19	22
39	19	18	25	22	20	21	19

TABLE 8.3

Ages of 32 Randomly Selected Students

the location of the data. If you do not specify a level of confidence, this command will also default to the 95% level of confidence. For the university student age data and a 90% level of confidence, the **TINTERVAL** command is

MTB > TINTERVAL 90 C1

Using this command on the age data produces:

```
       N    MEAN    STDEV    SE MEAN    90.0 PERCENT C.I.
C1    32    22.656   5.332     0.943   (   20.058, 24.255)
```

The command, **TINTERVAL**, causes Minitab to compute the sample standard deviation and use it in the interval calculations.

You can construct confidence intervals for several columns simultaneously by using the location of the first column where data are stored, a dash, and the location where the last column of data is stored. Suppose, for example, that age data from four universities are stored in columns 1–4. Using either **ZINTERVAL** or **TINTERVAL**, you can construct four confidence intervals with:

MTB > ZINTERVAL 90 6 C1-C4

or

MTB > TINTERVAL 90 C1-C4

You can use Minitab to estimate the difference in two population means by using the command **TWOSAMPLE**. However, you can use this command only when you do not know the population standard deviations. Minitab has no provision for entering known population standard deviations in the two sample situation. Following the **TWOSAMPLE** command, enter the level of the desired confidence and each of the columns where the two samples of data are located. If you do not specify a level of confidence, Minitab defaults to 95% confidence.

Suppose that you have gathered the ages of 31 students at a second university. Table 8.4 presents them along with the ages gathered from the first

TABLE 8.4	Thirty-Two Students from the First University							Thirty-One Students from the Second University							
Ages of Randomly Selected Students	21	19	19	20	18	24	21	19	20	17	18	19	18	22	19	18
	27	18	22	21	19	29	32	19	21	23	19	18	22	25	20	19
	22	18	29	29	35	20	19	22	19	21	18	19	28	26	20	19
	39	19	18	25	22	20	21	19	20	20	24	17	18	18	19	

group. If you store the two samples of data in columns 1 and 2 and desire a 99% level of confidence, the Minitab command is:

MTB > TWOSAMPLE 99 C1 C2

The output for this command is:

```
TWOSAMPLE T FOR C1 VS C2
      N    MEAN   STDEV   SE MEAN
C1   32   22.66   5.33    0.94
C2   31   20.13   2.67    0.48

99 PCT CI FOR MU C1 − MU C2: (−0.32, 5.37)

TEST MU C1 = MU C2 (VS NE): T=2.39 P=0.021 DF=45
```

The confidence interval for the difference in mean ages of students at these two universities is $-0.32 \leq \mu_1 - \mu_2 \leq 5.37$.

SUPPLEMENTARY PROBLEMS

8.45 Use the following information to construct the confidence intervals specified to estimate μ.
  a. 95% confidence; $\overline{X} = 25$, $\sigma = 3.5$, and $n = 60$
  b. 98% confidence; $\overline{X} = 119.6$, $S = 23.89$, and $n = 75$
  c. 90% confidence; $\overline{X} = 3.419$, $S = 0.974$, and $n = 32$
  d. 80% confidence; $\overline{X} = 56.7$, $\sigma = 12.1$, $N = 500$, and $n = 47$

8.46 Use the following information to construct the confidence intervals specified to estimate P.
  a. 94% confidence; $\hat{p} = 0.37$ and $n = 50$
  b. 88% confidence; $\hat{p} = 0.80$ and $n = 660$
  c. 85% confidence; $x = 479$ and $n = 1,100$
  d. 90% confidence; $x = 85$ and $n = 130$

8.47 Use the following information to construct the confidence intervals specified to estimate $\mu_1 - \mu_2$.
  a. $n_1 = 39$, $\overline{X}_1 = 50$, and $S_1 = 6.79$; $n_2 = 45$, $\overline{X}_2 = 55$, and $S_2 = 8.0$; 98% confidence
  b. $n_1 = 87$, $\overline{X}_1 = 1,157$, and $\sigma_1 = 200$; $n_2 = 101$, $\overline{X}_2 = 1,203$, and $\sigma_2 = 210$; 92% confidence

8.48 Use the following information to construct the confidence intervals specified to estimate $P_1 - P_2$.

a. $n_1 = 550$ and $\hat{p}_1 = 0.37$; $n_2 = 600$ and $\hat{p}_2 = 0.38$; 99% confidence

b. $n_1 = 1,300$ and $\hat{p}_1 = 0.52$; $n_2 = 1,250$ and $\hat{p}_2 = 0.48$; 95% confidence

c. $n_1 = 130$ and $x_1 = 58$; $n_2 = 125$ and $x_2 = 61$; 75% confidence

d. $n_1 = 436$ and $x_1 = 252$; $n_2 = 440$ and $x_2 = 212$; 92% confidence

8.49 Determine the sample size necessary to estimate μ for the following information.

a. $\sigma = 36$ and $E = 5$ at 95% confidence

b. $\sigma = 4.13$ and $E = 1$ at 99% confidence

c. Values range from 80 to 500, error is to be within 10, and the confidence level is 90%.

d. Values range from 50 to 108, error is to be within 3, and the confidence level is 88%.

8.50 Determine the sample size necessary to estimate P for the following information.

a. $E = 0.02$, P is approximately 0.40, and confidence level is 96%.

b. Error is to be within 0.04, P is unknown, and confidence level is 95%.

c. Error is to be within 5%, P is approximately 55%, and confidence level is 90%.

d. $E = 0.01$, P is unknown, and confidence level is 99%.

8.51 Determine the sample size necessary to estimate $\mu_1 - \mu_2$ for the following information.

a. $E = 12$, $\sigma = 48$, and 98% confidence

b. $E = 1.28$, $\sigma = 11.6$, and 88% confidence

c. Error is to be within 3.3, standard deviation of population is approximately 15, and confidence level is 90%.

d. Error is to be within 40, standard deviation of the population is approximately 300, and confidence level is 95%.

8.52 A random sample of small-business managers was given a leadership-style questionnaire. The results were scaled so that each manager received a score for initiative. Suppose that the following data are a random sample of these scores:

37	42	40	39	38	31	40	37	35	45	30	33	35
44	36	37	39	33	39	40	41	33	35	36	41	33
37	38	40	42	44	35	36	33	38	32	30	37	42

Use these data to construct a 90% confidence interval to estimate the average score on initiative for all small-business managers.

8.53 A national survey on telemarketing was undertaken. One of the questions asked was: How long has your organization had a telemarketing operation? Suppose that the following data represent some of the answers received to this question. Suppose further that only 300 telemarketing firms comprised the population when this survey was taken. Use the following data to compute a 98% confidence interval to estimate the average number of years a telemarketing organization had had a telemarketing operation:

3	3	4	1	4	5	3	3	4	6	2	7	4	8	2
3	8	9	3	12	5	3	7	4	5	1	2	1	5	3
7	1	4	6	14	10	9	3	2	1	4	3	6	1	3
7	5	11	2	4	3	6	1	3	6	5	9	3	12	2

8.54 A survey of seventy-seven commercial airline flights of under two hours resulted in a sample average late time for a flight of 2.48 min. The sample standard deviation was 12 min. Construct a 95% confidence interval for the average time that a commercial flight of under two hours is late. What is the point estimate? What does the interval tell about whether the average flight is late?

8.55 What is the average length of a company's policy book? Suppose that policy books are sampled from forty-five medium-sized companies. The average number of pages in the sample books is 213 with a sample standard deviation of 48. Use this information to construct a 98% confidence interval to estimate the mean number of pages for the population of medium-sized company policy books.

8.56 The price of a head of lettuce varies greatly with the season and the geographic location of a store. During February a researcher contacts a random sample of thirty-nine grocery stores across the United States and asks the produce manager of each to state the current price charged for a head of lettuce. Using the researcher's results that follow, construct a 99% confidence interval to estimate the mean price of a head of lettuce in February in the United States:

$1.59	$1.25	$1.65	$1.40	$0.89	$1.19
1.50	1.49	1.30	1.39	1.29	1.60
0.99	1.29	1.19	1.20	1.50	1.49
1.29	1.35	1.10	0.89	1.10	1.39
1.39	1.50	1.50	1.55	1.20	1.15
0.99	1.00	1.30	1.25	1.10	1.00
1.55	1.29	1.39			

8.57 A national survey of companies included a question that asked whether the company had at least one bilingual telephone operator. The sample results of 90 companies are as follows (y denotes that the company does have at least one bilingual operator; n denotes that it does not):

```
n  n  n  n  y  n  y  n  n  y  n  n  n  y  y
n  n  n  n  n  y  n  y  n  y  n  y  y  y  n
y  n  n  n  y  n  n  y  n  n  n  n  n  n  n
y  n  y  y  n  n  y  n  y  n  n  y  y  n  n
n  n  n  y  n  n  n  n  y  n  n  n  y  y  y
n  n  y  n  n  n  n  n  n  y  y  n  n  y  n
```

Use this information to estimate the proportion of the population that does have a least one bilingual operator with 95% confidence.

8.58 A regional survey of 560 companies asked the vice president of operations how satisfied he or she was with the software support being received from the computer staff of the company. Suppose that 33% of the 560 vice presidents said that they were satisfied. Construct a 99% confidence interval for the proportion of the population of vice presidents who would have said that they were satisfied if a census had been taken.

8.59 A national survey of insurance offices was taken, resulting in a random sample of 245 companies. Of these 245 companies, 189 responded that they were going to purchase new software for their offices in the next year. Construct a 90% confidence interval to estimate the population proportion of insurance offices that intend to purchase new software during the next year.

8.60 In 1991, a survey was conducted by the Employee Benefit Organization and the Gallup Organization on health care in America. Fifty-six percent of the people in the survey characterized the nation's health-care system as "fair" or "poor." Suppose that an organization in Canada decided to conduct a similar survey concerning the Canadian health-care system, and a random sample of 468 Canadians produced only 105 people who responded that their health-care system is "fair" or "poor." Use this information to construct a 90% confidence interval to estimate the proportion of Canadians who believe that their health-care system is only "fair" or "poor."

8.61 Is the environment a major issue with Americans? To answer that question, a researcher conducts a survey of 1,255 randomly selected Americans. If 714 of the sampled people replied that the environment is a major issue with them, construct a 95% confidence interval to estimate the proportion of Americans who feel that the environment is a major issue with them. What is the point estimate of this proportion?

8.62 A study was conducted to develop a scale to measure stress in the workplace. Respondents were asked to rate twenty-six distinct work events. Each event was to be compared to the stress of the first week on the job, which was awarded an arbitrary score of 500. Sixty professional men and forty-one professional women participated in the study. One of the stress events was "lack of support from the boss." The men rated this event with a sample average of 631. The women rated this event with a sample average of 848. Suppose that the sample standard deviations for men and for women both were about 100. Construct a 95% confidence interval to estimate the difference in the population mean scores on this event for men and women.

8.63 A survey of local government workers across the United States is undertaken to measure such things as job satisfaction and need for self-actualization. Suppose that one group of 800 workers produces a mean self-actualization need score of 4.47, with a standard deviation of 0.28. Suppose that a second group of 840 workers produces a mean self-actualization score of 3.08, with a standard deviation of 0.49. The self-actualization need scores were taken from a Likert-type scale with scores from 1 to 5, with 5 being the greatest need for self-actualization. Construct a 96% confidence interval to estimate the difference in population mean scores on this scale.

8.64 Suppose that students at two different universities were asked how many years of work experience they presently have in the field in which they are majoring. One of the universities is a commuter school that attracts older students who are likely to have more work experience, and the other university is one that more students attend full time. The following represent work experience figures for a random sample of students at each university:

				Commuter University					
2	0	4	2	3	5	2	3	13	4
6	3	5	2	7	5	3	4	5	10
15	10	6	2	4	8	9	11	2	5
9	3	2	5	7	4	12	4	2	1

				Full-time University					
0	1	1	0	2	1	0	3	1	0
1	0	0	0	2	1	1	2	4	1
4	2	0	0	0	1	0	2	3	2
1	1	1	0	1	2	0	4	3	2

Use the data to construct a 99% confidence interval to estimate the difference in average number of years of work experience between students attending these two universities.

8.65 Executives often spend many hours in meetings, leaving them with relatively little time to manage their individual areas of operation. What is the difference in mean time spent by executives of the aerospace industry in meetings and the mean time spent by executives of the automobile industry in meetings? Suppose that random samples of thirty-three aerospace executives and thirty-five automobile executives are monitored for a week to determine how much time they spend in meetings. The results are as follows:

Aerospace	Automobile
$n_1 = 33$	$n_2 = 35$
$\overline{X}_1 = 12.4$ hr	$\overline{X}_2 = 4.6$ hr
$S_1 = 2.9$ hr	$S_2 = 1.8$ hr

Use the data obtained to estimate the difference in the mean time per week executives in these two industries spend in meetings. Use a 99% level of confidence.

8.66 Is there a difference in the average time devoted to commercials on an all-talk AM radio station and a rock-oriented FM radio station within the same city? Fifty-one hours of air play are sampled from all-talk AM radio stations and forty-two hours of air play are sampled from rock-oriented FM radio stations. The number of minutes per hour of commercials is measured for each hour for each type of station. The results are as follows:

All Talk	Rock Oriented
$n_1 = 51$	$n_2 = 42$
$\overline{X}_1 = 23.6$ min	$\overline{X}_2 = 18.9$ min
$S_1 = 2.1$ min	$S_2 = 3.4$ min

Use these data to construct a 90% confidence interval to estimate the difference in minutes of airtime for commercials on these two types of stations.

8.67 One of the important aspects of a store's image is the perceived quality of its merchandise. Other factors include merchandise pricing, assortment of products, convenience of location, and service. Suppose that image perceptions of shoppers of specialty stores and shoppers of discount stores are being compared. A random sample of shoppers is taken at each type of store, and the shoppers are asked whether the quality of merchandise is a determining factor in their perception of the store's image. Some 75% of the 350 shoppers at the specialty stores say "yes" and only 52% of the 500 shoppers at the discount store say "yes." Construct a 90% confidence interval for the difference in population proportions.

8.68 Suppose that a random survey of 2,354 workers in industry A is taken and that 890 of these workers belong to a health maintenance organization (HMO). Suppose that a random survey of 1,875 workers in industry B showed that 908 workers belong to an HMO. Construct a 99% confidence interval to estimate the difference in population proportions of workers who belong to HMOs in these two industries.

8.69 Do a higher percentage of people who are eating at a steak restaurant have a salad with their dinner than people who are eating at an Italian restaurant? A survey of 236 diners at a steak restaurant showed that 200 of them had a salad with their dinner. A similar survey of 165 diners at an Italian restaurant revealed that 113 had a salad with their dinner. Using this information, construct a 98% confidence interval to estimate the difference in the population proportions of people who eat salads with their dinner at these two types of restaurants.

8.70 Is there a difference in the proportion of construction workers who are under thirty-five years of age and the proportion of telephone repair people who are under thirty-five years of age? Suppose that a study is conducted in Minneapolis of a random sample of 338 construction workers and 281 telephone repair people. The sample of construction workers included 297 people under thirty-five years of age, and the sample of telephone repair people included 192 people under that age. Use these data to construct a 90% confidence interval to estimate the difference in proportions of people under thirty-five years of age in construction workers and telephone repair people.

8.71 In an effort to cut costs, many U.S. retailers have reduced the number of clerks available to help customers in store showrooms. Has this reduction had an impact on consumer ratings of retailers' service? A survey of 546 randomly selected customers of a large department store chain conducted in 1980 revealed that 421 thought that service at the company's stores was good or excellent. A survey of 483 of this chain's customers in 1990 showed that only 218 thought that the stores' service was good or excellent. Construct a 95% confidence interval to estimate the difference in 1980 and 1990 proportions of customers who thought that the stores' service was good or excellent.

8.72 A national beauty salon chain wants to estimate the number of times per year that a woman has her hair done at a beauty salon if she uses one at least once a year. The chain's researcher estimates that, of those women who use a beauty salon at least once a year, the standard deviation of number of times of usage is approximately six. The national chain wants the estimate to be within one time of the actual mean value. How large a sample should the researcher take in order to obtain a 98% confidence level?

8.73 An entrepreneur wants to open an appliance service repair shop. She would like to know about what the average home repair bill is, including the charge for the service call for appliance repair in the area. She wants the estimate to be within $20 of the actual figure. She believes that the range of such bills is between $30 and $600. How large a sample size should the entrepreneur take if she wants to be 95% confident of the results?

8.74 A research firm has been asked to determine the proportion of all restaurants in the state of Ohio that serve alcoholic beverages. The firm wants to be 98% confident of its results but has no idea of what the actual proportion is. The firm would like to report an error of no more than 0.05. How large a sample should it take?

8.75 Suppose that you want to estimate the proportion of foreign cars being driven in Kansas City, Missouri, at rush hour by standing on the corner of I-70 and I-470 and counting cars. You believe that the figure is no higher than 0.40. If you want to be within 0.03 of the actual proportion, how many cars should you randomly sample? Use a 90% level of confidence.

8.76 Suppose that you want to estimate the difference between the amount spent on the average interstate bus ticket and the average interstate airplane ticket in the United States. You want to be 95% confident of your results and no more than $20 off on your estimate. If the standard deviation of all these tickets is $100, what sample size should you take from each group? The sample size formula used in this text for estimating the difference in two population means is based on the assumption that each population has the same standard deviation. Does this assumption hold for airplane and bus tickets? Why or why not?

8.77 A convention center wants to estimate the difference between the mean price of a standard folding chair and the mean price of a folding chair with cloth padding. The executive director is willing to call around the United States to different furniture outlets to obtain sample prices in an effort to estimate this difference. He wants to be 90% confident of the results and within $1.00 of the true difference. Suppose that the standard deviation of prices on folding chairs is only $4.50. How large a sample size of outlets should he sample for each type of chair?

HYPOTHESIS TESTING: LARGE SAMPLES

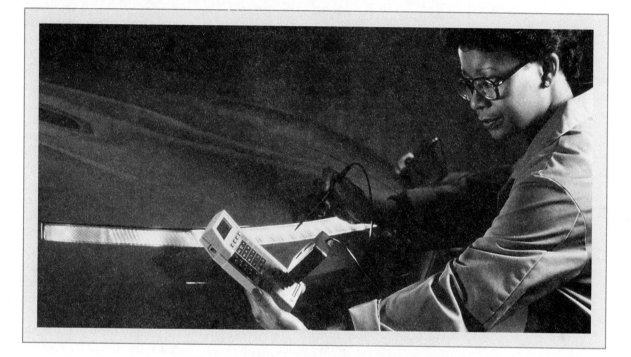

CHAPTER LEARNING OBJECTIVES

The main objective of Chapter 9 is to help you to learn how to test hypotheses by using statistics for large samples, specifically enabling you to

1. Understand the logic of hypothesis testing, and know how to establish null and alternate hypotheses.
2. Understand Type I and Type II errors, and know how to solve for Type II errors.
3. Use large samples to test hypotheses about a single population mean and a single population proportion.
4. Use large samples to test hypotheses about the differences in two population means and in two population proportions.

TESTING A LAYOFF PROJECTION

Julie Warner is the promotions manager for the chamber of commerce of a large city in the industrial Midwest. She spends much of her time promoting the city as a growing, attractive place for companies and individuals to settle. However, just recently she read in a Small Business Service Bureau report that 10% of surveyed owners plan to lay off workers this year. Warner is disturbed by this report and wants to test the 10% figure for her city. She is a promoter, not a statistician, and does not know where to begin.

Managerial Questions

- Under what logic does Warner test the 10% figure?
- Can she use a sample to make the test?
- What type of calculations would she do to test the 10% figure?
- What percent would she have to obtain to reject the Small Business Service Bureau's survey figure as true for her city?
- What is the probability that Warner would draw the wrong conclusion by chance?

The concept of hypothesis testing lies at the very heart of inferential statistics, and the use of statistics to "prove" or "disprove" claims hinges on it. Applications of statistical hypothesis testing run the gamut from determining whether a production line process is out of control to providing conclusive evidence that a new medicine is significantly more effective than the old. Statistics can be taken to court and hypothesis testing used in the legal system to provide evidence in civil suits. Hypotheses are tested in virtually all areas of life, including education, psychology, marketing, science, law, and medicine. How does the hypothesis testing process begin?

9.1   INTRODUCTION TO HYPOTHESIS TESTING

hypothesis testing

indirect proof

Hypothesis testing is derived from the mathematical notion of indirect proof. As many of you know from a geometry course, in situations where proving something directly is not practical, the indirect proof is a useful tool. In statistics with an indirect proof, the researcher defines the potential outcomes so that only X or Y can be true but not both (mutually exclusive and collectively exhaustive). If the researcher can prove that X is not true, then Y is true by default. Figure 9.1 conceptually demonstrates this process.

In statistical hypothesis testing, two hypotheses that include all possible outcomes are set up. The two hypotheses are mutually exclusive and collec-

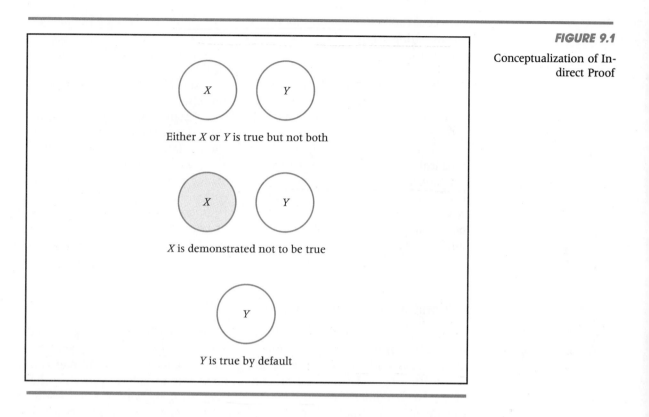

FIGURE 9.1

Conceptualization of In-
direct Proof

tively exhaustive. As with the indirect proof, either one hypothesis is true or the other is true but not both. The idea is that statisticians can "prove" that a hypothesis is true by rejecting the other hypothesis.

Steps in Testing Hypotheses

Most researchers take the following steps when testing hypotheses:

1. Establish hypotheses.
2. Determine alpha.
3. Determine the appropriate statistical test.
4. Establish critical values.
5. Gather data.
6. Analyze the data.
7. Reach a conclusion.

The first step in establishing statistical hypotheses involves determining a null hypothesis and an alternative hypothesis. After stating the hypotheses, the researcher can determine the amount of risk, or alpha. Alpha is the probability of committing a Type I error and is discussed later. Next, the researcher selects a statistical test. This selection involves matching the level of data collected and the type of statistic being analyzed with the statistical tests available. In this chapter and Chapters 10 and 12, various statistical tests are presented, along with their applicability to specific situations.

Critical values are determined by the type of statistical test being used (t, Z, F for example) and the value of alpha. These values are obtained from tables and are used as standards against which gathered data are compared to reach statistical conclusions. The researcher should *not* gather data before taking the first four hypothesis testing steps. Too often, the researcher gathers the data first and then tries to determine what to do with it. Analyzing the data involves applying the selected test statistic to the data gathered. After analyzing the data the researcher can draw a conclusion about rejecting or failing to reject the null hypothesis. The hypothesis test is not complete until the researcher makes a decision about the null hypothesis.

Null and Alternative Hypotheses

null hypothesis

alternative hypothesis

The first step in testing a hypothesis is to establish a **null hypothesis** and an **alternative hypothesis.** The null hypothesis is represented by H_0 and the alternative hypothesis by H_a. Establishing null and alternative hypotheses can be a frustrating and confusing process. A good rule to follow is to view the alternative hypothesis as the hypothesis *upon which the burden of proof falls*. Usually, it is the hypothesis that the researcher is most interested in demonstrating to be true. The null hypothesis is *a statement that the alternative hypothesis is not true.* For example, if a researcher is interested in testing to determine whether a newly developed drug is significantly more effective than aspirin in treating headaches, the hypotheses might be

$$H_0: \text{New drug} \leq \text{aspirin}$$
$$H_a: \text{New drug} > \text{aspirin}$$

In this example, the assumption stated in the null hypothesis is that the new drug is no better than the old and indeed might be worse. The alternative to this assumption, or the alternative hypothesis, is that the new drug *is* more effective than aspirin. In order to test the hypotheses, a sample is taken and data are gathered. If the data show that the null hypothesis is false, the alternative hypothesis is accepted by default: The new drug has been shown to be more effective.

In the process of hypothesis testing, the null hypothesis initially is assumed to be true. The data are gathered and examined to determine whether the evidence is strong enough away from the null hypothesis to reject it. When the researcher is testing an industry standard or a widely accepted value, the standard or accepted value is assumed true in the null hypothesis. *Null* in this sense means that nothing is new, or there is no new value or standard. The burden is then placed on the researcher to demonstrate through gathered data that the null hypothesis is false. This task is analogous to the courtroom ideal of innocent until proven guilty. In the courtroom the accused is assumed to be innocent before the trial (null assumed true). Evidence is presented during the trial (data are gathered). If there is enough evidence against innocence, the accused is found guilty (reject the null hypothesis). If there is not enough evidence to prove the accused guilty, the prosecutors have failed to prove the accused guilty. However, they have not "proven" the accused innocent.

Suppose that a company markets a soft drink with a label of 12 fluid ounces on the can. Suppose further that a consumer advocate believes that the company is, on average, filling cans with less than 12 oz. If the consumer advocate desires to test this belief, she would assume that the cans contain at least 12 fluid ounces (null hypothesis). The alternative hypothesis would be that they contain less than 12 oz. Thus

mean

$$H_0: \mu \geq 12 \text{ oz}$$ *company telling the truth*
$$H_a: \mu < 12 \text{ oz}$$ *or false*

The assumption is that the company is telling the truth in its labeling. The consumer advocate must gather evidence to contradict that assumption. The new theory or idea should always be the alternative hypothesis. The null hypothesis is that the new theory is not true, that nothing has changed from before, that the status quo is unchanged.

Acceptance and Rejection Regions

After establishing the null and alternative hypotheses, the researcher can set up decision rules to determine whether the null hypothesis is going to be rejected or not. In the soft-drink can example, how much fill would a researcher have to find in 12-oz cans in order to reject the null hypothesis? Common sense says that expecting all cans to be filled with exactly 12 oz of fluid is unrealistic. More reasonable is to expect that the cans *average* 12 fluid ounces. In this way the hypotheses are structured around the mean value, not individual fills.

Suppose that the company's label claim is being tested by a consumer advocate who takes a sample of n cans. How much fluid should the sample cans average for the consumer advocate to reject the labeling of the company? Would the null be rejected if a sample mean of 11.99 oz is obtained? In testing a hypothesis, the researcher should establish a **rejection region** after determining the null and alternative hypotheses. Figure 9.2 shows a normal distribution with the mean in the middle and a rejection region from the soft-drink can example in the lower tail. In this case, the mean of the distribution is 12 oz. The rejection region is established in the lower tail of the distribution,

rejection region

FIGURE 9.2

Rejection and Accep-
tance Regions

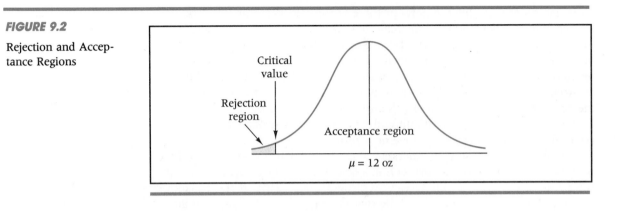

because the only way to reject a null hypothesis of H_0: $\mu \geq 12$ oz is to get a result in the region of $\mu < 12$ oz. The rejection region is in the direction *away* from the null hypothesis.

The rejection region is divided from the rest of the distribution by a point **critical value**   called the **critical value.** If results obtained from the data yield a computed value in the rejection region beyond the critical value (in this case, *less than* the critical value), the null hypothesis is rejected. The rest of the distribution, **acceptance region**   which is not in the rejection region, is called the **acceptance region.**

Type I and Type II Errors

Occasionally, the sample data gathered in the research process lead to a decision **Type I error**   to reject a null hypothesis when actually it is true. A **Type I error** is committed *when a true null hypothesis is rejected.* In drawing random samples from a population, the possibility of selecting a sample from the fringe of the distribution by chance always exists. In the case of the soft-drink can example, the researcher could randomly select fifty of the cans with the smallest amounts of fluid, causing rejection of the null hypothesis even when the company actually is filling the cans with an average of 12 oz. In that case, the researcher would incorrectly conclude that the company is not filling the cans with an average of 12 oz and commit a Type I error.

alpha (α)   **Alpha (α),** or the **level of significance,** is the probability of committing **level of significance**   a Type I error. Alpha is the proportion of the area of the curve occupied by the rejection region. The most commonly used values of alpha are .01, .05, .001, and .10. Recall that determination of alpha is step 2 in the hypothesis testing procedure. It is sometimes referred to as the amount of *risk* taken in an experiment. The larger the area of the rejection region, the greater is the risk of committing a Type I error.

Type II error   A **Type II error** is committed by *failing to reject a false null hypothesis.* In some instances the null hypothesis is not true, but the data gathered yield a computed value that falls in the acceptance region. For example, suppose that the consumer advocate is testing a null hypothesis of $\mu = 12$ oz, and the soft-drink company actually is filling the cans with an average of 11.85 oz. She could select a random batch of cans from this distribution of fills and get a sample average of 11.95 oz. If the mean of 11.95 falls in the acceptance region of the null hypothesis, she incorrectly determines that the null hypothesis is true.

The probability of committing a Type II error is represented by **beta (β).** The value of beta varies within an experiment, depending on various alternative values of the parameter (mean). Whereas alpha is determined before the experiment, beta is computed using alpha, the hypothesized parameter, and various theoretical alternatives to the null hypothesis.

beta (β)

Power is equal to $1 - \beta$. It is the probability of a test rejecting the null hypothesis when the null hypothesis is false. Figure 9.3 shows the relationship between α, β, and power.

power

One-Tailed and Two-Tailed Tests

If the consumer advocate wants to determine whether buyers of 12-oz cans of soft drink produced by a company are getting cheated, she probably is concerned only if the consumer is receiving, on average, *less* than 12 oz of fluid. If the cans average more than 12 oz of fluid, the consumer advocate is not concerned, because it is not a disadvantage to the consumer. She is worried only about underfills. The hypothesis set up by the consumer advocate to be tested would produce a **one-tailed test.** Anytime that hypotheses are established so that the alternative hypothesis is directional (less than or greater

one-tailed test

FIGURE 9.3

Alpha, Beta, and Power

		State of nature	
		Null true	Null false
Action	Fail to reject null	Correct decision	Type II error (β)
	Reject null	Type I error (α)	Correct decision (power)

than), the test is one-tailed. The one-tailed hypotheses for the 12-oz soft-drink can example are

$$H_0: \mu \geq 12 \text{ oz}$$
$$H_a: \mu < 12 \text{ oz}$$

With a one-tailed test, α is concentrated at one end of the sampling distribution. Figure 9.4 shows the sampling distribution for the soft-drink can example.

Setting up the null and alternative hypotheses is more difficult with one-tailed tests, because the direction of the inequality must be determined. In order to use a one-tailed test, the researcher must have some knowledge of the subject matter being studied ahead of time in order to determine the direction of the hypotheses.

two-tailed test   A **two-tailed test** is nondirectional. In a two-tailed test, the null hypothesis has an equals sign, and the alternative hypothesis has a does not equal sign. A two-tailed test is used either when the researcher has no idea which direction the study will go or when the researcher is interested in testing both directions. If a new technique, theory, or product is being developed, a two-tailed test might be used, because the researcher does not have enough knowledge of the phenomena to perform a directional test. At other times, a two-tailed test can be used, because the researcher is interested in both ends of the distribution.

For example, if a machine shop is trying to produce 3-in. nails, quality controllers are concerned about nails that are too long *or* too short. Thus a significant variation from the mean in either direction could cause the quality controller to reject the batch. An example of a two-tailed test with the nails might be

$$H_0: \mu = 3 \text{ in.}$$
$$H_a: \mu \neq 3 \text{ in.}$$

FIGURE 9.4

A Sampling Distribution
with Alpha

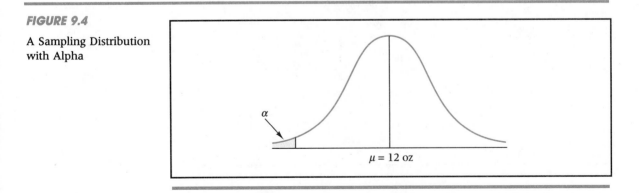

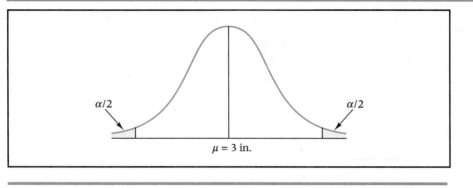

FIGURE 9.5

Rejection Regions for a
Two-Tailed Test

In this case, α is divided in half, and $\alpha/2$ is the probability of having the mean fall in the rejection region at either end of the distribution by chance, as depicted in Figure 9.5.

For any value of alpha, a two-tailed test causes the critical value to be farther from the center of the distribution than a one-tailed test, because the two-tailed test splits the α and results in a smaller area in the tail and a larger magnitude of the Z_c value.*

TESTING HYPOTHESES ABOUT A SINGLE MEAN   *9.2*

One of the most basic hypothesis tests that can be made is a test about a population mean. A researcher might be interested in testing to determine whether an established or accepted mean value for an industry is still true. Or a researcher might be interested in testing a mean value for a new theory or product. The test of a single population mean can be used to accomplish either objective. A formula can be used to test hypotheses about a single population mean if the sample size is large ($n \geq 30$). The same formula can also be used for small samples ($n < 30$) if X is normally distributed *and* σ is known.

(9.1)

$$Z = \frac{\overline{X} - \mu}{\frac{\sigma}{\sqrt{n}}}.$$

Z Test for a Single Mean

*From here on, Z_c denotes the critical value of Z.

Suppose, for example, that at a large university the administration has generally assumed that the average age of a student is no more than 20 years. However, lately the students have appeared to be somewhat older than before, and some administrators believe that the average age now might be older. If the administration decided to test this notion, the null and alternative hypotheses for this problem would be

$$H_0: \ \mu \leq 20 \ \text{yr}$$
$$H_a: \ \mu > 20 \ \text{yr}$$

The null hypothesis is that the mean age is still the same as it was ($\mu \leq 20$). The alternative hypothesis is that the average age is older than twenty years. Assume that the administrators selected $\alpha = .05$ and the Z statistic to test sample means for large samples for the test. Figure 9.6 shows a diagram of the problem, with its rejection region and critical Z value. This test is one-tailed, with the rejection region in the upper tail.

The Z_c value for .05 is 1.645. Alpha is the area in the tail of the Z distribution in this problem. Table A.5 (the Z table) contains Z values for areas between the mean and the critical value. Thus $\alpha = .05$ must be subtracted from .5000 to obtain the value of .4500 for which $Z_c = 1.645$. Suppose that fifty students are chosen at random from enrollment records, along with their ages. Table 9.1 shows ages of the fifty students.

The administration assumes that the population standard deviation for the ages of these university students is 3.6 years. Using statistical formulas and sample data, a *calculated* value of Z will be computed and compared to the *critical* value of Z (table value) to determine if the null hypothesis is rejected or not. A *calculated* Z value (Formula 9.1) of greater than 1.645 must be attained in order for the results to be in the rejection region. If the calculated value is not greater than 1.645, the administration fails to reject the null hypothesis. The sample mean for the data in Table 9.1 is 20.76. For $\sigma = 3.6$, the resulting calculated Z value is

---

FIGURE 9.6

Critical Value and Rejection Region for Age Problem

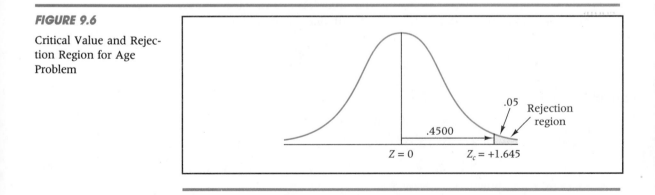

$Z = 0$ $Z_c = +1.645$

21	24	20	21	37	18	21	19	32	21
26	19	18	19	18	19	18	18	24	22
20	20	21	21	19	21	20	18	18	19
18	19	24	17	20	27	23	18	22	24
19	20	19	20	17	22	19	20	19	19

TABLE 9.1

Ages of Fifty University Students

$$Z = \frac{\bar{X} - \mu}{\frac{\sigma}{\sqrt{n}}} = \frac{20.76 - 20}{\frac{3.6}{\sqrt{50}}} = \frac{0.76}{0.51} = 1.49.$$

This calculated value falls inside the acceptance region in Figure 9.6, so the null hypothesis is not rejected. Although an average of 20.76 years of age was attained from a random sample of fifty students, there is not enough evidence to statistically reject a hypothesized value of $\mu \leq 20$. The sample mean value of 20.76 years may be viewed as a mere chance variation of fifty students from a population with a mean of 20 years of age.

Using a Sample Standard Deviation

In many real-life situations, the population value for the standard deviation is unavailable. With large sample sizes ($n \geq 30$) use of the sample standard deviation as a good approximate substitute for the population standard deviation, σ, is permitted.

(9.2)	$$Z = \frac{\bar{X} - \mu}{\frac{S}{\sqrt{n}}}.$$	**Z Formula to Test a Mean with σ Unknown—Large Samples Only**

Formula 9.2 can be used only for *large* sample sizes, regardless of the shape of the distribution of X. In the college students' ages example, the sample standard deviation was 3.634. This approximation of σ could have been used to calculate the Z value.

Testing the Mean with a Finite Population

If the hypothesis test for the population mean is being conducted with a known finite population, the population information can be incorporated into the hypothesis testing formula. Doing so can increase the potential for rejecting the null hypothesis. Formula 9.1 can be amended to include the population information.

Formula to Test Hypotheses About μ with a Finite Population

$$Z = \frac{\overline{X} - \mu}{\dfrac{\sigma}{\sqrt{n}}\sqrt{\dfrac{N - n}{N - 1}}}.$$

In the ages of university students example, suppose that only 250 students were enrolled in the entire university. The calculated Z value would change to

$$Z = \frac{\overline{X} - \mu}{\dfrac{\sigma}{\sqrt{n}}\sqrt{\dfrac{N - n}{N - 1}}} = \frac{20.76 - 20}{\dfrac{3.6}{\sqrt{50}}\sqrt{\dfrac{250 - 50}{250 - 1}}} = \frac{0.76}{0.46} = 1.65.$$

Using the finite correction factor, the calculated Z value increased from 1.49 to 1.65. The decision to fail to reject the null hypothesis changes with this new information to a decision to reject the null hypothesis. Thus, on occasion, the finite correction factor can make the difference between rejecting and failing to reject the null hypothesis.

Alternative Methods of Testing Hypotheses

Two other methods of testing hypotheses are the critical value method and the probability method. All three methods of testing lead to the same conclusion with regard to rejection or failure to reject the null hypothesis. Each of these other two methodologies is explained here.

Critical Value Method.   One alternative method of testing hypotheses is the
critical value method   **critical value method.** In the preceding example, the null hypothesis was not rejected, because the computed value of Z did not fall into the rejection zone. What mean age would it take to cause the calculated Z value to fall into the rejection zone? The critical value method determines the critical mean value required for Z to be in the rejection region and uses it to test the hypotheses.

This method also uses Formula 9.1. However, instead of a calculated Z, a critical $\overline{X}$ value, $\overline{X}_c$, is determined. The critical table value of Z_c is inserted into the formula, along with μ and σ. Thus

$$Z_c = \frac{\overline{X}_c - \mu}{\dfrac{\sigma}{\sqrt{n}}}.$$

Substituting values from the preceding example gives

$$1.645 = \frac{\overline{X}_c - 20}{\frac{3.6}{\sqrt{50}}},$$

or

$$\overline{X}_c = 20 + 1.645 \frac{3.6}{\sqrt{50}} = 20 + 0.8375 = 20.8375.$$

Figure 9.7 depicts graphically the acceptance and rejection regions in terms of means instead of Z scores.

With the critical value method, most of the computational work is done ahead of time. In this case, before the sample means are computed, the analyst knows that a sample mean value of greater than 20.8375 years must be attained in order to reject the population mean. Because the sample mean for this problem was only 20.76, the analyst fails to reject the null hypothesis. This method is particularly attractive in industrial settings where standards can be set ahead of time and then quality control technicians can gather data and compare actual measurements of products to specifications. .

Probability Method. A third way to make decisions in hypothesis testing problems is by using the **probability method.** In this method, instead of comparing the computed statistic (Z value) with a table value to determine whether the value falls into the rejection region, the researcher determines a *probability* for the computed value and compares that probability to *alpha*.

For example, in the university students' ages example, the computed value of Z was 1.49. The Z table, Table A.5, lists the probability of a value this large

probability method

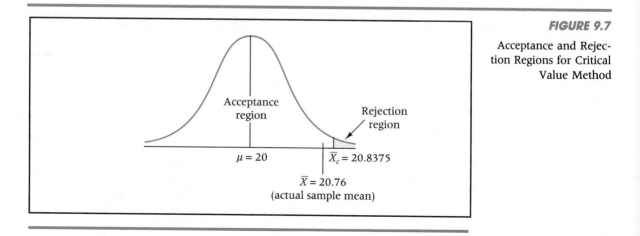

FIGURE 9.7

Acceptance and Rejection Regions for Critical Value Method

Acceptance region

Rejection region

$\mu = 20$

$\overline{X}_c = 20.8375$

$\overline{X} = 20.76$
(actual sample mean)

or larger occurring by chance as .0681 (.5000 − .4319). As this probability is greater than α, the null hypothesis is accepted. Figure 9.6 shows that only 5% of the area lies beyond the critical value in the rejection region. The computed Z value for this problem falls at a point on the graph where 6.81% of the values lie beyond it. Therefore the computed value falls short of the rejection region. *In order to reject the null hypothesis with the probability method, the probability of the computed value must be less than α for a one-tailed test or less than $\alpha/2$ for a two-tailed test.*

This method of decision making for hypothesis testing is particularly useful when a computer software package is used to analyze data. Computer statistical packages normally yield both a computed Z value and the probability of that value occurring by chance. The user merely needs to compare the probability to α for one-tailed tests or $\alpha/2$ for two-tailed tests to reach a conclusion about rejecting or failing to reject the null hypothesis.

Demonstration Problem 9.1

Based on surveys, researchers have claimed that the average amount of leisure time per week for American men is 41.0 hours. You want to test this figure so you randomly select eighty-four working American men and have them keep a log of their time for a representative week. Suppose that the sample average turns out to be 38.7 hours of leisure time with a sample standard deviation of 12 hours. Based on this sample information, would you reject or fail to reject the claim that the average amount of leisure time for an American working man is 41.0 hours? Use a level of significance of .05.

Solution:

The sample information is $\overline{X} = 38.7$ hr, $S = 12$ hr, $n = 84$, and $\alpha = .05$. The hypotheses for this problem are

$$H_0: \mu = 41 \text{ hr}$$
$$H_a: \mu \neq 41 \text{ hr}$$

This is a two-tailed test, because you are testing to reject or not reject the population average amount of leisure time of 41 hr. You are *not* testing that $\mu > 41$ or that $\mu < 41$. The two-tailed test requires that you split α and find a table Z_c associated with an area of .0250. The Z value from the table is

$$Z_{.025} = 1.96.$$

The following diagram shows the rejection regions for this problem.

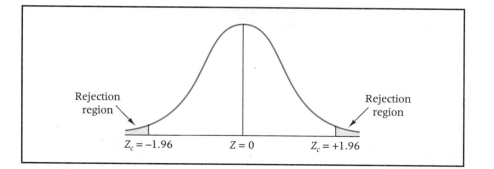

Solving for Z yields

$$Z = \frac{\bar{X} - \mu}{\dfrac{S}{\sqrt{n}}} = \frac{38.7 - 41.0}{\dfrac{12}{\sqrt{84}}} = -1.76.$$

As the calculated $Z = -1.76$ is not far enough out' to reach the rejection region ($Z_c = -1.96$), you fail to reject the null hypothesis. Even though the sample of eighty-four men produced a sample mean different from 41 hours, there is not enough evidence to reject the claim from this sample.

The probability method can also be used to solve this problem. Locate the calculated sample Z value, $Z = -1.76$, in the Z table (Table A.5) and find the corresponding probability value of .0392. Alpha is .05 but must be divided in half, because this problem has a two-tailed hypothesis test. Thus a probability of less than .025 must be obtained from the calculated Z value before the null hypothesis can be rejected. Because the probability of the Z value for this problem is only .0392, you fail to reject the null hypothesis. This conclusion is the same as that reached using the table Z method.

You can also use the critical value method to solve this problem, utilizing the hypothesized value of the mean, the standard deviation, and the table value of Z_c. With these values, the critical value of $\bar{X}$ is

$$\bar{X}_c = \mu \pm Z_c \frac{S}{\sqrt{n}} = 41 \pm (1.96)\frac{12}{\sqrt{84}}$$
$$= 38.43 \quad \text{and} \quad 43.57.$$

The sample mean would have to be less than 38.43 or greater than 43.57 for you to reject the null hypothesis. The obtained sample mean for this problem is 38.70, which is not less than 38.43. Thus your conclusion is not to reject the null hypothesis. This conclusion is consistent with the probability method and the calculated Z method, as it should be, because all three methods should produce the same final conclusion.

**PROBLEMS
Section 9.2**

9.1 **a.** Use the data given to test the following hypotheses:

$$H_0: \mu = 25 \qquad H_a: \mu \neq 25$$
$$\overline{X} = 28.1, \qquad n = 57, \qquad S = 8.46, \qquad \text{and} \qquad \alpha = .01$$

b. If you had used the critical value method, what would be the critical sample mean values?

9.2 Use the data given to test the following hypotheses:

$$H_0: \mu \geq 7.48 \qquad H_a: \mu < 7.48$$
$$\overline{X} = 6.91, \qquad n = 96, \qquad S = 1.21, \qquad \text{and} \qquad \alpha = .01$$

9.3 **a.** Use the data given to test the following hypotheses:

$$H_0: \mu \leq 1200 \qquad H_a: \mu > 1200$$
$$\overline{X} = 1,215, \qquad n = 113, \qquad S = 100, \qquad \text{and} \qquad \alpha = .10$$

b. Use the probability method to obtain the results.
c. Solve for the critical value required to reject the mean.

9.4 A survey of working men found that the average Soviet man spends about fifty-four hours per week earning a living. Suppose that a researcher wants to test this survey result by taking a survey of his own. Working with the Soviet government, he is able to randomly sample thirty-two Soviet men. The following data represent their responses to the question of how much time per week they spend earning a living:

57	51	44	60	49	55	53	51
53	57	58	48	50	61	67	49
55	60	48	40	47	55	52	51
50	50	61	53	48	59	55	56

Use these data to determine whether the claim of fifty-four hours per week should be rejected by the researcher's survey results. Use $\alpha = .02$.

9.5 A 1990 survey showed that the average check at Perkins Family Restaurants is $4.70. A competitor has just opened a family restaurant and wants to demonstrate that the average check at her restaurant is less than that at Perkins's. To demonstrate that she is correct, the owner of the new restaurant takes a random sample of fifty-four checks and determines that the sample average check is $4.58. The standard deviation of the checks is $0.86. Using $\alpha = .05$, she tests to determine whether her restaurant check average is significantly lower than $4.70. Use the critical value method to determine the sample average that she would need to obtain to reject the null hypothesis and determine whether the null hypothesis would be rejected.

9.6 The average tuition at a four-year private college is $9,391, with a standard deviation of $2,450. A researcher has a theory that the average tuition at a four-year private college is actually higher than that, and he sets out to demonstrate that the theory is true by randomly sampling forty private colleges. Suppose that the sample of private colleges produces a sample average tuition of $10,140 and that there are only 650 private colleges in the population. Use $\alpha = .10$ to test the researcher's theory.

9.7 A survey of female college graduates showed that the average yearly cash income for these women is more than $35,500. In the part of the United States where you live, this average does not seem possible, so you decide to test this claim. You randomly select forty-eight working women who are college graduates. The sample average income for these women is $33,900, with a standard deviation of $6,570. Is there enough evidence from this sample data to reject the national claim for your area as being too high? Use $\alpha = .10$.

9.8 A manufacturing firm has been averaging 18.2 orders per week for several years. However, the 1990–1991 recession appears to have slowed orders. Suppose that the firm's production manager randomly samples thirty-two weeks between 1990 and 1992 and finds a sample mean of 15.6 orders, with a sample standard deviation of 2.3 orders. Test to determine whether the average number of orders is down from the past by using $\alpha = .10$.

9.9 A study conducted by Runzheimer International showed that Paris is the most expensive place to live of the twelve European Community cities. Paris ranks second in housing expense, with a rental unit of six to nine rooms costing an average of $4292 a month. Suppose that a company's CEO believes that this figure is too high and decides to conduct her own survey. Her assistant contacts the owners of fifty-five randomly selected rental units of six to nine rooms and finds that the sample average cost is $4,008, with a standard deviation of $386. Based on the sample results and using $\alpha = .01$, test to determine whether the figure published by Runzheimer International is too high.

9.3   TESTING HYPOTHESES ABOUT A PROPORTION

The formula for proportions based on the central limit theorem makes possible the testing of hypotheses about the population proportion in a manner similar to that of the formula used to test sample means. A proportion is a value between 0 and 1 that expresses the part of the whole that possesses a given characteristic. For example, approximately 0.10 of the population are left-handed. Whereas means are computed by averaging measurements, proportions are calculated by counting or tallying the number of items in a population that possess a characteristic and then dividing that number by the total. Recall that $\hat{p}$ denotes a sample proportion and that P denotes the population proportion.

The central limit theorem applied to sample proportions states that $\hat{p}$ values are normally distributed, with a mean of P and a standard deviation of $\sqrt{P \cdot Q / n}$, when $N \cdot P$ and $N \cdot Q$ are greater than 5. A Z test is used to test hypotheses about P.

Z Test of Population Proportion

$$Z = \frac{\hat{p} - P}{\sqrt{\dfrac{P \cdot Q}{n}}},$$

where: $\hat{p}$ = sample proportion
P = population proportion
$Q = 1 - P$

For example, 10% of all people are generally believed to write predominantly with the left hand. Suppose that a researcher wants to test this belief. The null and alternate hypotheses are

$$H_0: P = 0.10$$
$$H_a: P \neq 0.10$$

This test is a two-tailed test, because the hypothesis being tested is whether the proportion of left-handedness is .10. No effort is being made to hypothesize that the figure is greater or less than .10. Alpha is selected to be .10. Figure 9.8 shows the distribution, with the rejection regions and Z_c. Because α is divided for a two-tailed test, the table value for an area of $(1/2)(.10) = .05$ is $Z_c = 1.645$.

For the researcher to reject the null hypothesis, the magnitude of the calculated Z value must be greater than 1.645. The researcher randomly selects a sample of 200 people, each person is interviewed for left-handedness, and

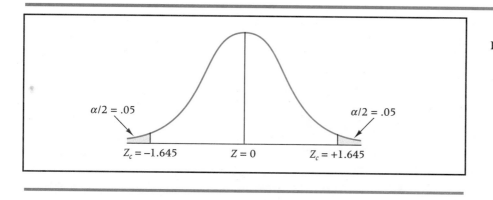

43 people report that they are predominantly left-handed in writing. Calculating the sample proportion gives

$$\hat{p} = \frac{43}{200} = 0.215.$$

The calculated Z value is

$$Z = \frac{\hat{p} - P}{\sqrt{\dfrac{P \cdot Q}{n}}} = \frac{0.215 - 0.100}{\sqrt{\dfrac{0.10(0.90)}{200}}} = \frac{0.115}{0.021} = 5.48.$$

Note that the denominator of the Z formula contains the population proprtion. Although the researcher does not actually know the population proportion, he is testing a population proportion value. Hence he uses the hypothesized population value in the denominator of the formula as well as in the numerator. This method contrasts with the confidence interval formula, where the sample proportion is used in the denominator.

The calculated value of Z falls in the rejection region (calculated $Z = 5.48 >$ table $Z_c = +1.645$), so the researcher rejects the null hypothesis. He concludes that the proportion of left-handed writers in the population from which the sample of 200 was drawn is not 0.10. With $\alpha = .10$, the risk of committing a Type I error in this example is 0.10.

The calculated value of $Z = 5.48$ is outside the range of values for virtually all Z tables. Thus if the researcher were using the probability method to arrive at a decision about the null hypothesis, the probability would be .0000, and he would reject the null hypothesis.

Suppose that he wanted to use the critical value method. He would enter the table value of $Z_c = 1.645$ in the Z formula for single sample proportions, along with the hypothesized population proportion and n, and solve for the critical value of $\hat{p}$, $\hat{p}_c$. The result is

FIGURE 9.9

Distribution Using Critical Value Method for Left-Handedness Example

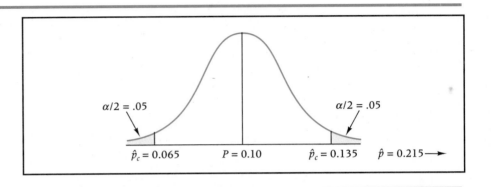

$$Z_c = \frac{\hat{p}_c - P}{\sqrt{\dfrac{P \cdot Q}{n}}},$$

$$\pm 1.645 = \frac{\hat{p}_c - 0.10}{\sqrt{\dfrac{(0.10)(0.90)}{200}}}$$

and

$$\hat{p}_c = 0.10 \pm 1.645 \sqrt{\frac{(0.10)(0.90)}{200}} = 0.10 \pm 0.035$$

$$= +0.065 \text{ and } +0.135.$$

Examination of the sample proportion, $\hat{p} = 0.215$, and Figure 9.9 clearly shows that the sample proportion lies in the rejection region. Thus the critical value method yields the same conclusion as the other two methods.

Demonstration Problem 9.2

A survey of the morning beverage market has shown that the primary breakfast beverage for 17% of Americans is milk. A milk producer in Wisconsin, where milk is plentiful, believes that the figure is higher for Wisconsin. To test this idea, she contacts a random sample of 550 Wisconsin residents and asks which primary beverage they consumed for breakfast that day. Suppose that 115 replied that milk was the primary beverage. Using a level of significance of .05, test the idea that the milk figure is higher for Wisconsin.

Solution:

The milk producer's theory is that a higher proportion of Wisconsin residents drink milk for breakfast than the national proportion, which is the alternative hypothesis. The null hypothesis is that the proportion in Wisconsin does not differ from the national average and perhaps is less than the national average. That is, the hypotheses for this problem are

$$H_0: P \le 0.17$$
$$H_a: P > 0.17$$

This is a one-tailed test, and the table Z_c value is $Z_{.05} = +1.645$. The sample results have to yield a calculated Z value greater than 1.645 in order for the milk producer to reject the null hypothesis. The following diagram displays Z_c and the rejection region for this problem.

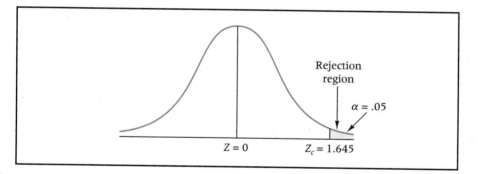

Then

$$\hat{p} = \frac{115}{550} = 0.209,$$

and

$$Z = \frac{\hat{p} - P}{\sqrt{\dfrac{P \cdot Q}{n}}} = \frac{0.209 - 0.17}{\sqrt{\dfrac{(0.17)(0.83)}{550}}} = \frac{0.039}{0.016} = 2.44.$$

As $Z = 2.44$ falls beyond $Z_c = 1.645$ in the rejection region, the milk producer rejects the null hypothesis. Based on this random sample, the producer is ready to conclude that a higher proportion of Wisconsin residents drink milk as the primary beverage for breakfast than the national proportion.

The probability of obtaining a $Z \ge 2.44$ by chance is .0073. As this probability is less than $\alpha = .05$, the null hypothesis is also rejected with the probability method.

A critical proportion can be solved for by

$$Z_c = \frac{\hat{p}_c - P}{\sqrt{\dfrac{P \cdot Q}{n}}};$$

$$1.645 = \frac{\hat{p}_c - 0.17}{\sqrt{\dfrac{0.17(0.83)}{550}}};$$

$$\hat{p}_c = 0.17 + 0.026 = 0.196.$$

With the critical value method, a sample proportion greater than 0.196 must be obtained to reject the null hypothesis. The sample proportion for this problem is 0.209, so the null hypothesis is rejected with the critical value method. Thus all three methods yield the same results, as expected.

<hr>

PROBLEMS
Section 9.3

9.10 Suppose that you are testing H_0: $P \le 0.45$ versus H_a: $P > 0.45$. A random sample of 310 people produces a value of $\hat{p} = 0.465$. Use $\alpha = .05$ to test this hypothesis.

9.11 Suppose that you are testing H_0: $P \ge 0.63$ versus H_a: $P < 0.63$. For a random sample of 100 people, $x = 55$, where x denotes the number in the sample that passes the characteristic of interest. Use a .01 level of significance to test this hypothesis.

9.12 Suppose that you are testing H_0: $P = 0.29$ versus H_a: $P \ne 0.29$. A random sample of 740 items shows that 207 have this characteristic. If the probability of committing a Type I error is .05, test the hypothesis. If you had used the critical value method, what would the two critical values be? How do the sample results compare to the critical values? For the probability method, what is the probability of the calculated Z value for this problem?

9.13 A survey taken in the fall of 1990 showed that only 20% of consumers believed that "now is a good time to buy things they want and need." A market analyst believes that this survey is pessimistic but, for hypothesis testing purposes, accepts 20% as the population proportion. Suppose that she takes her own random survey of consumers. Of the 380 consumers surveyed, 87 responded that "now is a good time to buy things they want and need." Use this new sample survey data to test to determine whether the market analyst should reject the fall 1990 survey figure as too low. Use $\alpha = .10$.

9.14 A political census taken in 1988 showed that 89% of all Hispanic elected officials in the United States were Democrats. Suppose that, owing to inroads made by the Republican party in the early 1990s, a Republican state chairman believes that the figure may now be lower and wants to test that theory. He assumes that the proportion of Hispanics is still 0.89 and randomly samples eighty Hispanic officeholders in 1992. Only sixty-four of the eighty are Democrats. Is there enough evidence for the chairman to reject the null hypothesis as being too high? Use $\alpha = .05$.

9.15 As of 1990, some 10% of all the armed forces (Army, Navy, Air Force, and Marines) were women. Suppose that a large marine boot camp is located near you, and you want to determine whether the 10% figure holds for the recruits at that camp. A random sample of 165 recruits at that camp reveals that 12 are women. Use a 10% level of significance to determine whether the proportion of women at the boot camp represented by the sample is significantly different from the national figure.

9.16 The U.S. Census Bureau reported that in 1990 approximately 44% of all Americans were in the 25-to-44 age bracket. Suppose that you live in Southern California and believe that the percentage of people in this age bracket is higher in the area where you live. To test your idea, you randomly sample 390 people from your area and exactly one-half of them are in the 25-to-44 age bracket. Is this enough evidence to reject the Census Bureau's figure as being too low for your area of Southern California? Use $\alpha = .01$. Would your decision have been different had you been conducting a two-tailed test?

9.17 Industry estimates show that the Philips company controls 0.39 of the Western European light-bulb market. You are the marketing vice president of a competing company and your company has just completed an extensive, expensive advertising campaign to shift some of Philips's control of the market to your company. To determine whether this campaign worked, you randomly telephone a mixture of 1,150 Western European homes and businesses and ask which brand of light bulb they purchased the last time they bought a light bulb. Of the participants in your survey, 414 replied that they had bought the Philips brand. For $\alpha = .05$, is this enough evidence to conclude that Philips's share of the market is now less than 0.39? If the vice president had used the critical value methodology, what would be the critical sample proportion value?

9.18 A large manufacturing company investigated the service it has received from suppliers and discovered that, in the past, 32% of all materials shipments have been received late. However, the company recently installed a just-in-time system in which suppliers are more closely linked to the manufacturing process. A random sample of 118 deliveries since the just-in-time system was installed revealed that 22 deliveries were late.

Use this sample information to test whether the proportion of late deliveries has been reduced significantly. Let $\alpha = .05$.

9.19 Suppose that, in 1970, 12% of all businesses classified as small businesses hired a CPA as a consultant to provide accounting guidance. Because of increased government regulation and other requirements, small businesses are feeling more pressure to hire outside professional accounting assistance. As a result, a greater proportion of small businesses seem to hire CPAs as consultants in 1992. To test this theory, suppose that 378 small businesses are randomly sampled from a list provided by the Small Business Administration in Washington, D.C. If 71 of these sampled small businesses use a CPA as a consultant, is there enough evidence to reject the 1970 figure as too low? Assume a 1% level of significance.

9.4 TESTING HYPOTHESES ABOUT THE DIFFERENCE IN TWO MEANS

The difference in two sample means is normally distributed for large sample sizes ($n_1, n_2 \geq 30$), according to the central limit theorem. This characteristic makes possible testing the differences in two population means. The mean of the distribution of two sample means is $\mu_1 - \mu_2$ and the standard deviation is

$$\sigma_{\bar{X}_1 - \bar{X}_2} = \sqrt{\frac{\sigma_1^2}{n_1} + \frac{\sigma_2^2}{n_2}}.$$

A Z formula is used to test the difference in two population means.

Z Formula to Test for the Difference in Two Means

$$Z = \frac{(\bar{X}_1 - \bar{X}_2) - (\mu_1 - \mu_2)}{\sqrt{\frac{\sigma_1^2}{n_1} + \frac{\sigma_2^2}{n_2}}}. \qquad (9.3)$$

In many instances a researcher wants to test the differences in the mean values of two populations. One might be to test the difference between the mean values of men and women on achievement, intelligence, or other characteristics. A consumer organization might want to test two brands of light bulbs to determine whether one burns longer than the other. A company wanting to relocate might want to determine whether there is a significant difference in the average price of a home between Newark, New Jersey, and Cleveland, Ohio.

For example, suppose that a researcher wants to know if there is a difference between the average afternoon high temperature for July in Phoenix, Arizona, and Memphis, Tennessee. The weather records over the years might yield the data in Table 9.2.

Phoenix				Memphis			
108	104	105	103	97	94	100	97
100	112	109	112	93	99	98	103
104	99	107	104	96	96	99	94
98	104	102	113	104	95	93	98
109	108	105	103	99	100	93	89
100	109	112	108	96	98	96	99
102	100	108	105	99	94	104	98
113	106	109	107	96	93	96	99

$$\overline{X}_{\text{Phoenix}} = 105.88$$
$$S_{\text{Phoenix}} = 4.21$$
$$n_1 = 32$$

$$\overline{X}_{\text{Memphis}} = 97.03$$
$$S_{\text{Memphis}} = 3.34$$
$$n_2 = 32$$

TABLE 9.2

July Afternoon High Temperatures in Phoenix and Memphis

The null hypothesis in this type of problem is a hypothesized difference between μ_1 and μ_2. In most of the hypothesis tests about two means, the hypothesized difference is zero. Is there any difference between the two population means? The null and alternative hypotheses for this problem are

$$H_0: \ \mu_1 - \mu_2 = 0$$
$$H_a: \ \mu_1 - \mu_2 \neq 0$$

In this problem, the researcher is testing only to determine whether there is a difference in the average July afternoon high temperatures, so this is a two-tailed test. If the researcher had hypothesized that the average temperature of one city is hotter than the average of the other, it would have been a one-tailed test. However, since this problem is a two-tailed test, if $\alpha = .02$, each of the two rejection regions has an area of .01. Figure 9.10 shows the associated table Z_c value of 2.33, along with the rejection regions.

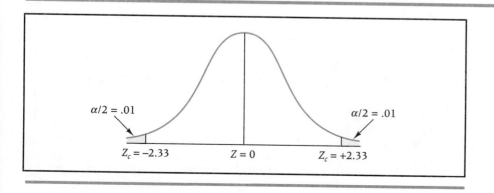

FIGURE 9.10

Critical Values and Rejection Regions for the Temperature Example

$\alpha/2 = .01$

$\alpha/2 = .01$

$Z_c = -2.33$ $Z = 0$ $Z_c = +2.33$

Note that the population variances are not available in this problem. So long as the sample size is large, S^2 is a good approximation of σ^2. Thus the following formula is equivalent to Formula 9.3 for large samples.

Z Formula to Test the Difference in Population Means with σ_1^2, σ_2^2 Unknown and n_1, n_2 Large	$$Z = \frac{(\bar{X}_1 - \bar{X}_2) - (\mu_1 - \mu_2)}{\sqrt{\dfrac{S_1^2}{n_1} + \dfrac{S_2^2}{n_2}}}.$$	**(9.4)**

Formula 9.4 and the statistics gathered from weather records yield a Z value to complete the hypothesis test:

$$Z = \frac{(105.88 - 97.03) - (0)}{\sqrt{\dfrac{4.21^2}{32} + \dfrac{3.34^2}{32}}} = \frac{8.85}{0.95} = 9.32.$$

The calculated value of 9.32 is greater than the 2.33 critical value obtained from the table. The researcher rejects the null hypothesis and can say that there is a significant difference between the average July afternoon high temperature in Phoenix and the average July afternoon high temperature in Memphis. The researcher then examines the sample means and uses common sense to conclude that Phoenix mean high temperatures in July are higher than those for Memphis. Figure 9.11 shows the relationship between the calculated Z and Z_c.

FIGURE 9.11

Location of Calculated Z Value for Temperature Example

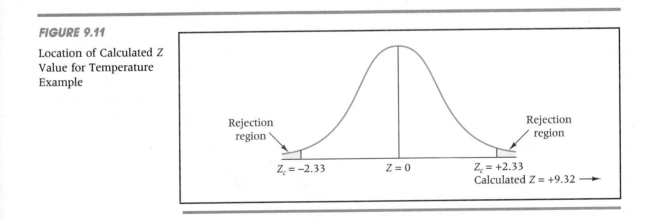

A sample of eighty-seven professional working women showed that the average amount paid into a private pension fund per person was $3,352, with a sample standard deviation of $1,100. A sample of seventy-six professional working men showed that the average amount paid into a private pension fund per person was $5,727, with a sample standard deviation of $1,700. A women's activist group wants to "prove" that women do not pay as much per year as men into private pension funds. They want to use these sample data to demonstrate their point. If they use $\alpha = .001$, will they be able to reject a null hypothesis that women pay the same as or more than men into private pension funds?

Solution:

This test is one-tailed. Because the women's activist group wants to "prove" that women pay less than men into private pension funds, the alternative hypothesis should be $\mu_w - \mu_m < 0$, and the null hypothesis is that women pay the same as or more than men $\mu_w - \mu_m \geq 0$. Alpha is .001. The table Z_c value is $Z_{.001} = -3.08$. The sample data are as follows:

Women	Men
$\overline{X}_1 = \$3,352$	$\overline{X}_2 = \$5,727$
$S_1 = \$1,100$	$S_2 = \$1,700$
$n_1 = 87$	$n_2 = 76$

Solving for Z gives

$$Z = \frac{3,352 - 5,727}{\sqrt{\dfrac{1,100^2}{87} + \dfrac{1,700^2}{76}}} = \frac{-2,375}{227.9} = -10.42.$$

The calculated Z value of -10.42 falls deep in the rejection region, well past the table value of $Z_c = -3.08$. Even with the small $\alpha = .001$, the null hypothesis is rejected. The evidence is substantial that women, on average, pay less than men into private pension funds. The following diagram displays these results:

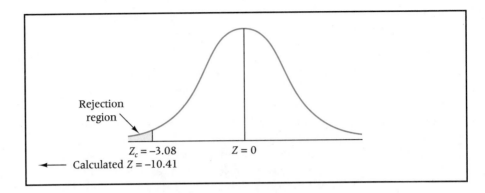

The probability of obtaining a calculated Z value of -10.42 by chance is virtually zero, because the value is beyond the limits of the Z table. By the probability method, the null hypothesis is rejected because the probability is .0000, or less than $\alpha = .001$.

If this problem were worked by the critical value method, what critical value of the difference in the two means would have to be surpassed in order to reject the null hypothesis for a table Z value of -3.08? The answer is

$$(\overline{X}_1 - \overline{X}_2)_c = (\mu_1 - \mu_2) - Z\sqrt{\frac{S_1^2}{n_1} + \frac{S_2^2}{n_2}}$$

$$= 0 - 3.08(227.9) = -701.9.$$

The difference in sample means would need to be at least 701.9 to reject the null hypothesis. The actual sample difference in this problem was $-2,375(3,352 - 5,727)$, which is considerably larger than the critical value of difference. Thus, with the critical value method also, the null hypothesis is rejected.

**PROBLEMS
Section 9.4**

9.20 **a.** Test the null hypothesis of no difference in population means using the following data ($\alpha = .10$):

Sample 1	Sample 2
$\overline{X}_1 = 51.3$	$\overline{X}_2 = 53.2$
$S_1^2 = 52$	$S_2^2 = 60$
$n_1 = 32$	$n_2 = 32$

b. Use the critical value method to find the critical difference in the mean values required to reject the null hypothesis.

9.21 Use the data given to test the following hypotheses ($\alpha = .02$):

$$H_0: \mu_1 - \mu_2 \leq 0 \qquad H_a: \mu_1 - \mu_2 > 0$$

Sample 1			Sample 2		
90	88	80	78	85	82
88	87	91	90	80	76
81	84	84	77	75	79
88	90	91	82	83	88
89	95	97	80	90	74
88	83	94	81	75	76
81	83	88	83	88	77
87	87	93	86	90	75
88	84	83	80	80	74
95	93	97	89	84	79

9.22 Use the following data to test the alternative hypothesis that sample 1 comes from a population with a smaller average than the population from which sample 2 comes:

Sample 1	Sample 2
$n_1 = 45$	$n_2 = 51$
$\overline{X}_1 = 201$	$\overline{X}_2 = 203$
$S_1 = 8$	$S_2 = 9$

Use the probability method and a risk of 5% of committing a Type I error.

9.23 The Trade Show Bureau conducted a survey to determine why people go to trade shows. The respondents were asked to rate a series of reasons on a scale from 1 to 5, with 1 representing little importance and 5 representing great importance. One of the reasons suggested was general curiosity. The average response to this reason from the computers/electronics industry people was 2.2. The average response from people in the food/beverage industry was 3.1. Suppose that these averages were obtained from a random sample of fifty people from each industry and that the standard deviation of responses in each group to this question was about 1.00. Use $\alpha = .01$ to determine whether there is a significant difference between people in these two industries on this question.

9.24 Is there a difference between the average salary of a legal secretary and a medical secretary? In an effort to answer that question, a researcher takes a random sample of thirty-three legal secretaries across the United States, resulting in a sample average salary of $23,100, with a standard deviation of $1,550. The researcher then takes a random sample of thirty-five medical secretaries across the nation, which yields an average salary of $18,500, with a standard deviation of $2,100. Use $\alpha = .01$ to test this question.

9.25 A company in Philadelphia occasionally sends members of its management team to visit its two production facilities in Burlington, Vermont, and Springfield, Massachusetts. The company believes that the per diem cost is significantly higher in Burlington than in Springfield. To test this belief, an analyst takes the records of thirty-one business trips by managers to Burlington. The average per diem expense was $95, with a standard deviation of $14. The analyst then takes a random sample of thirty-four business trips by managers to Springfield. The average per diem expenses for the sample was $92, with a standard deviation of $12. Use $\alpha = .10$ and test to determine whether the per diem cost in Burlington is significantly higher than that in Springfield.

9.26 A company's auditor believes that the per diem cost in Baton Rouge, Louisiana, has risen significantly between 1982 and 1988. To test this belief the auditor samples fifty-one business trips from the company's records for 1982; the sample average was $79 per day, with a sample standard deviation of $8.50. The auditor selects a second random sample of forty-seven business trips from the company's records for 1988; the sample average was $81 per day, with a standard deviation of $5.60. If he used a risk of committing a Type I error of .02, did the auditor find that the per diem average expense in Baton Rouge has gone up significantly?

9.27 Employee suggestions can provide useful and insightful ideas for management. Some companies solicit and receive employee suggestions more than others, and company culture influences the use of employee suggestions. Japanese companies reportedly receive and use significantly more employee suggestions than American companies do. Suppose that a study is conducted to determine whether there is a significant difference between the mean number of suggestions a month per employee for the Canon Corporation and the Pioneer Electronic Corporation. One study reported that the average number of suggestions per month was 5.8 at Canon and 5.0 at Pioneer. Suppose that these figures were obtained from random samples of thirty-six and forty-five employees, respectively. If the standard deviations of suggestions per employee are 1.7 and 1.4, respectively, for Canon and Pioneer, is there a significant difference in the population means? Use $\alpha = .05$.

9.28 Two processes in a manufacturing line are performed manually: operation A and operation B. A random sample of fifty different assemblies using operation A shows that the sample average time per assembly is 8.05

min, with a standard deviation of 1.36 min. A random sample of thirty-eight different assemblies using operation B shows that the sample average time per assembly is 7.26 min, with a standard deviation of 1.06 min. For $\alpha = .10$, is there enough evidence in these samples to declare that operation A takes significantly longer than operation B to perform?

TESTING HYPOTHESES ABOUT THE DIFFERENCE IN TWO PROPORTIONS | 9.5

The difference in two population proportions can also be tested using a Z formula. The central limit theorem applies to the difference in two sample proportions when sample sizes are large. The resulting formula is

$$Z = \frac{(\hat{p}_1 - \hat{p}_2) - (P_1 - P_2)}{\sqrt{\dfrac{P_1 \cdot Q_1}{n_1} + \dfrac{P_2 \cdot Q_2}{n_2}}},$$

(9.5)

where: $\hat{p}$ = sample proportion

P = population proportion

$Q = 1 - P$

Most of the time the null hypothesis is a zero difference in the two proportions, or $P_1 - P_2 = 0$. However, the population proportions are not known, so Formula 9.5 cannot be utilized. But a formula in which a pooled value obtained from the sample proportions replaces the population proportions in the denominator of Formula 9.5 can be used.

$$Z = \frac{(\hat{p}_1 - \hat{p}_2) - (P_1 - P_2)}{\sqrt{(\bar{P} \cdot \bar{Q})\left(\dfrac{1}{n_1} + \dfrac{1}{n_2}\right)}},$$

Z Formula to Test the Difference in Population Proportions

where: $\bar{P} = \dfrac{x_1 + x_2}{n_1 + n_2} = \dfrac{n_1 \hat{p}_1 + n_2 \hat{p}_2}{n_1 + n_2}$

$\bar{Q} = 1 - \bar{P}$

Testing the difference in two population proportions is useful whenever the researcher is interested in comparing the proportion of one population possessing a certain characteristic with the proportion of a second population that possesses the same characteristic. For example, a researcher might be interested in determining whether the proportion of the population of Boston who are Catholic is different from the proportion of the population of Buffalo who are Catholic.

Another researcher might be interested in determining whether the proportion of people driving new cars (less than one year old) in Houston is different from the proportion in Denver. A study could be conducted using a random sample of Houston drivers and a random sample of Denver drivers to test this idea.

As an example of a test between two proportions, suppose that a political analyst wants to determine whether the proportion of young voters (aged 21–29) in America who voted for President Bush is less than the proportion of older voters (aged 65 and older) who voted for President Bush. The theory is that a higher proportion of older voters than younger voters voted for Mr. Bush.

$$H_0: P_1 - P_2 \geq 0$$
$$H_a: P_1 - P_2 < 0$$

where: P_1 = proportion of young voters for Bush
P_2 = proportion of old voters for Bush

Note that the alternative hypothesis is the one that the political analyst wants to "prove." If $\alpha = .10$ and a one-tailed test is used, the resulting critical table Z_c value is -1.28. Figure 9.12 shows the rejection region. A random sample of voters might produce the statistics shown in Table 9.3.

The sample proportions are

$$\hat{p}_1 = \frac{210}{440} = 0.477, \quad \text{and} \quad \hat{p}_2 = \frac{205}{378} = 0.542.$$

FIGURE 9.12

Rejection Region for
Voter Example

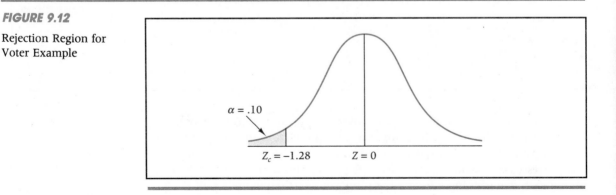

	Age 21–29	Age 65 and Older	TABLE 9.3
Number in sample	$n_1 = 440$	$n_2 = 378$	Number of People from Samples of Two Different Age Brackets Who Voted for President Bush
Voted for Bush	$x_1 = 210$	$x_2 = 205$	

Then $\bar{P}$ can be calculated as

$$\bar{P} = \frac{x_1 + x_2}{n_1 + n_2} = \frac{210 + 205}{440 + 378} = 0.507.$$

If the raw data are unavailable and only the sample proportions and sample sizes are known, then $\bar{P}$ can be obtained by

$$\bar{P} = \frac{n_1\hat{p}_1 + n_2\hat{p}_2}{n_1 + n_2} = \frac{440(0.477) + 378(0.542)}{440 + 378}$$

$$= \frac{210 + 205}{440 + 378} = \frac{415}{818} = 0.507.$$

The calculated Z value is

$$Z = \frac{(0.477 - 0.542) - 0}{\sqrt{(0.507)(0.493)\left(\dfrac{1}{440} + \dfrac{1}{378}\right)}} = -1.85.$$

This value lies in the rejection region. Thus the analyst rejects the null hypothesis. There is enough evidence to declare that older voters favor Mr. Bush more than younger voters based on these samples.

Demonstration Problem 9.4

A study of female entrepreneurs was conducted to determine their definition of success. The women were offered optional choices such as happiness/self-fulfillment, sales/profit, and achievement/challenge. The women were divided into groups according to the gross sales of their businesses. A significantly higher proportion of female entrepreneurs in the $100,000 to $500,000 category than in the less than $100,000 category seemed to rate sales/profit as a definition of success. Suppose that you decided to test this result by taking a survey of your own and identified female entrepreneurs by gross sales. You interview 100 female entrepreneurs with gross sales of less than $100,000, and 24 of them define sales/profit as success. You then interview 95 female entrepreneurs with gross sales of $100,000 to $500,000, and 39 say that sales/profit is a definition of success to them. Use this information to test to determine whether there is a significant difference in the proportions of the two groups that define success as sales/profit. Use $\alpha = .01$.

Solution:

You are testing to determine whether there is a difference between two groups of entrepreneurs, so a two-tailed test is required. With $\alpha = .01$, you obtain a table Z_c value for $(1/2)(.01) = .005$ and $Z_{.005} = 2.575$. The hypotheses are

$$H_0: P_1 - P_2 = 0$$
$$H_a: P_1 - P_2 \neq 0$$

The following graph depicts the rejection region and the Z_c values.

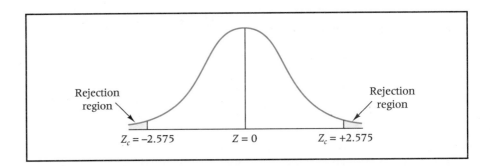

Rejection region   Rejection region

$Z_c = -2.575$ $Z = 0$ $Z_c = +2.575$

The sample information is

	Less Than $100,000	$100,000 to $500,000
	$n_1 = 100$	$n_2 = 95$
	$x_1 = 24$	$x_2 = 39$
	$\hat{p}_1 = \dfrac{24}{100} = 0.24$	$\hat{p}_2 = \dfrac{39}{95} = 0.41$

where: $\bar{P} = \dfrac{x_1 + x_2}{n_1 + n_2} = \dfrac{24 + 39}{100 + 95} = \dfrac{63}{195} = 0.323$

x = the number of entrepreneurs who define sales/profits as success

The calculated Z value is

$$Z = \frac{(\hat{p}_1 - \hat{p}_2) - (P_1 - P_2)}{\sqrt{(\bar{P} \cdot \bar{Q})\left(\dfrac{1}{n_1} + \dfrac{1}{n_2}\right)}} = \frac{(0.24 - 0.41) - 0}{\sqrt{(0.323)(0.677)\left(\dfrac{1}{100} + \dfrac{1}{95}\right)}}$$

$$= \frac{-0.17}{0.067} = -2.54.$$

Although this calculated value is near the rejection region, it lies in the acceptance region. The null hypothesis is not rejected. That is, there is not enough evidence here to reject the null hypothesis and declare that the responses to the question by the two groups are any different statistically. Note that α was small and that a two-tailed test was conducted. If a one-tailed test had been used, Z_c would have been $Z_{.01} = 2.33$, and the null hypothesis would have been rejected. If α had been .05, the Z_c would have been $Z_{.025} = 1.96$, and the null hypothesis would have been rejected. This result underscores the crucial nature of selecting alpha and determining whether to use a one-tailed or two-tailed test in hypothesis testing.

**PROBLEMS
Section 9.5**

9.29 Use the sample information given and a 5% level of significance, and test the following hypotheses:

$$H_0: P_1 - P_2 = 0 \qquad H_a: P_1 - P_2 \neq 0$$

Sample 1	Sample 2
$n_1 = 368$	$n_2 = 405$
$x_1 = 175$	$x_2 = 182$

Note that x is the number in the sample possessing the characteristic of interest.

9.30 Use the sample information given to test the following hypotheses $(\alpha = .10)$:

$$H_0: P_1 - P_2 \leq 0 \qquad H_a: P_1 - P_2 > 0$$

Sample 1	Sample 2
$n_1 = 649$	$n_2 = 558$
$\hat{p}_1 = 0.38$	$\hat{p}_2 = 0.25$

9.31 Use the sample data given to test the following hypotheses (with a 1% risk of committing a Type I error):

$$H_0: P_1 - P_2 \geq 0 \qquad H_a: P_1 - P_2 < 0$$

Sample 1	Sample 2
$n_1 = 1,250$	$n_2 = 1,352$
$x_1 = 568$	$x_2 = 703$

9.32 Early in 1990, a consumer comfort poll showed that about 53% of all consumers felt that prices were going up. Suppose that an economist decides to conduct a similar poll and wants to compare the consumer attitudes about the economy of those who live in the Southeastern United States and those who live in the Northwest. To do so she conducts a telephone poll of 1,200 people in the Southeast and 1,100 people in the Northwest. At this time, she has no idea about which group of people, if either, will have a more positive or negative view of the economy. Thus she decides to conduct a two-tailed test, using $\alpha = .05$. She asks the random sample of people from each region whether they agree that prices are going up. In the Southeast 705 people agree with that statement and in the Northwest 623 people agree with the statement. Test to determine whether there is a significant difference in the proportions of these two regions who agree with the statement about the economy.

9.33 In times of slow business activity, small businesses utilize job cuts to maintain a positive balance sheet. During a 1989 slowdown, there was evidence that the number of job cuts by small businesses varied by industry. For example, 30% of the small businesses in the construction industry cut jobs, whereas only 11% of the small businesses in the finance industry cut jobs during that period. Suppose that the economy is currently in a slow business period. Suppose further that 128 small-business firms in the agricultural industry and 157 small-business firms in the retail industry are randomly selected. Of the sampled small businesses 18% and 16%, respectively, have cut jobs. Is there enough information to declare that a significantly higher proportion of agricultural industry than retail industry small-business firms cut jobs? Use $\alpha = .10$.

9.34 Companies that have recently developed new products were asked to rate which activities are most difficult to accomplish with new products. Questions include such things as assessing market potential, market testing, finalizing the design, developing a business plan, and the like. A researcher wants to conduct a similar study to compare the results between two industries: the computer hardware industry and the banking industry. He takes a random sample of fifty-six computer firms and eighty-nine banks. The researcher asks whether market testing is the most difficult activity to accomplish in developing a new product. Some 48% of the sampled computer companies and 56% of the sampled banks respond that it is the most difficult activity. Use a level of significance of .20 to test whether there is a significant difference in the responses from these two industries to the question.

9.35 In a study in 1970, women were asked whether most men are basically selfish and self-centered and 32% agreed. In 1990, women were asked the same question and 42% agreed. The survey in 1970 was conducted with 349 women and the survey in 1990 was conducted with 268 women. Is enough evidence available from these sample data to declare that a significantly higher proportion of women in 1990 than in 1970 believed men to be basically selfish and self-centered? Use a 5% chance of making a Type I error.

9.36 Between 1986 and 1989, gasoline companies who bought their fuel from wholesalers rather than major oil companies saw their sales decline, according to a survey by the Energy Information Administration. Gasoline companies purchasing from wholesalers accounted for 0.54 of the market in 1986 but only 0.47 of the market in 1989. Suppose that a random sample of 1,150 gasoline stations in 1986 showed that 594 of them bought their gasoline from wholesalers and that a random sample of 1,200 gasoline stations in 1989 showed that 564 bought their gasoline from wholesalers. Use $\alpha = .05$ to test whether there was a significantly smaller proportion of gasoline stations that bought gas from wholesalers in 1989 than in 1986, based on the sample data.

9.37 Two different surveys showed that Minute Maid and Tropicana were running almost a dead heat in the race for the orange juice market. Tropicana has a larger share of the ready-to-serve orange juice market, but Minute Maid is the stronger of the two in the frozen concentrate market. Two surveys were conducted in 1990 to determine market share in the orange juice arena. A survey by Nielsen showed that Tropicana held 21.4% of the market. A survey by Information Resources showed that Tropicana held 22.0% of the market. Suppose that each of these surveys was conducted by asking 1,500 different orange juice consumers what brand of orange juice they preferred. Is there a significant difference in the proportions obtained by Nielsen and Information Resources for the market share held by Tropicana? Use $\alpha = .01$.

9.6   SOLVING FOR TYPE II ERRORS

Determining the probability of committing a Type II error is more complex than finding the probability of committing a Type I error. The probability of committing a Type I error either is given in a problem or is stated by the researcher before proceeding with the study. A Type II error, β, varies with possible values of the alternative parameter. For example, suppose that a researcher is conducting a statistical test on the following hypotheses:

$$H_0: \mu \geq 12 \text{ oz}$$
$$H_a: \mu < 12 \text{ oz}$$

A Type II error can be committed only when the researcher fails to reject the null hypothesis and the null hypothesis is false. In these hypotheses, if the null hypothesis, $\mu \geq 12$ oz is false, what is the true value for the population mean? Is the mean really 11.99 oz or 11.90 oz or 11.5 oz or 10 oz? For each of these possible values of the population mean, the researcher can compute the probability of committing a Type II error. Often, when the null hypothesis is false, the value of the alternative mean is unknown, so the researcher will compute the probability of committing Type II errors for several possible values. How can the probability of committing a Type II error be computed for a *specific* alternative value of the mean?

Suppose that, in testing the hypotheses above, a sample of 60 cans of beverage yields a sample mean of 11.985 oz, with a standard deviation of 0.10 oz. For $\alpha = .05$ and a one-tailed test, the table Z value is -1.645. The calculated Z value is

$$Z = \frac{11.985 - 12.00}{\frac{0.10}{\sqrt{60}}} = -1.16.$$

From this calculated value of Z, the researcher determines not to reject the null hypothesis. By not rejecting the null hypothesis, the researcher either made a correct decision or committed a Type II error. What is the probability of committing a Type II error in this problem if the population mean actually is 11.99?

The first step in determining the probability of a Type II error is to calculate a critical value for the mean, $\overline{X}_c$. This value is used in testing the null hypothesis by the critical value method as the cutoff for the acceptance region. For any sample mean obtained that is less than $\overline{X}_c$ (or greater for an upper tail rejection region), the null hypothesis is rejected. Any sample mean greater than $\overline{X}_c$ (or less for an upper tail rejection region) causes the researcher to accept the null hypothesis. Solving for the critical value of the mean gives

$$Z_c = \frac{\overline{X}_c - \mu}{\dfrac{S}{\sqrt{n}}};$$

$$-1.645 = \frac{\overline{X}_c - 12}{\dfrac{0.10}{\sqrt{60}}};$$

$$\overline{X}_c = 11.979.$$

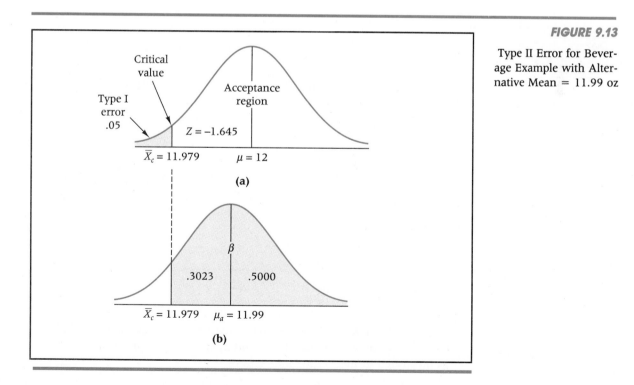

FIGURE 9.13

Type II Error for Beverage Example with Alternative Mean = 11.99 oz

Figure 9.13(a) shows the distribution of values if the null hypothesis were true. It contains a critical value of the mean, $\overline{X}_c = 11.979$ oz, below which the null hypothesis will be rejected. Figure 9.13(b) shows the distribution if the alternative mean, $\mu_a = 11.99$ oz, were true. How often will the researcher accept the top distribution as true, when, in reality, the bottom distribution is true? If the null hypothesis is false, the null hypothesis will be incorrectly accepted whenever μ falls in the acceptance region, $\overline{X}_c \geq 11.979$ oz. If μ actually equals 11.99 oz, what is the probability of failing to reject $\mu = 12$ oz when 11.979 oz is the critical value? The researcher calculates this probability by extending the critical value ($\overline{X}_c = 11.979$ oz) from distribution (a) to distribution (b) and solving for the area to the right of $\overline{X}_c = 11.979$:

$$Z_c = \frac{\overline{X}_c - \mu_a}{\frac{S}{\sqrt{n}}} = \frac{11.979 - 11.99}{\frac{0.10}{\sqrt{60}}} = -0.85.$$

This value of Z yields an area of .3023. The probability of committing a Type II error is all the area to the right of $\overline{X}_c = 11.979$ in distribution (b), or $.3023 + .5000 = .8023$. Hence there is an 80.23% chance of committing a Type II error if the alternative mean is 11.99 oz.

Demonstration Problem 9.5

Recompute the probability of committing a Type II error for the beverage example if the alternative mean is 11.96 oz.

Solution:

Everything in distribution (a) stays the same: The null hypothesized mean is still 12 oz, the critical value is still 11.979 oz, and $n = 60$. However, distribution (b) changes with $\mu_a = 11.96$ oz, as the following diagram shows. The Z formula used to solve for the area of distribution (b), $\mu_a = 11.96$, to the right of 11.979 is

$$Z = \frac{\overline{X}_c - \mu_a}{\frac{S}{\sqrt{n}}} = \frac{11.979 - 11.96}{\frac{0.10}{\sqrt{60}}} = 1.47.$$

From Table A.5 only .0708 of the area lies to the right of the critical value. Thus the probability of committing a Type II error is only .0708 as illustrated in the following diagram.

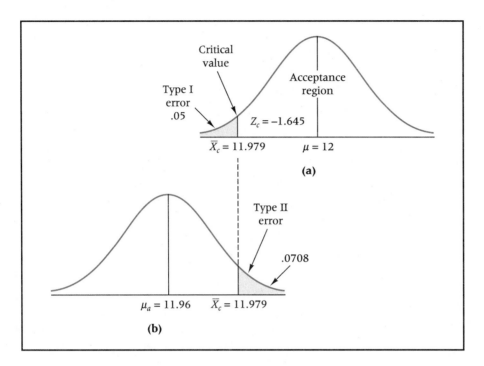

(a)

(b)

Demonstration Problem 9.6

Suppose that you are conducting a two-tailed hypothesis test of proportions. The null hypothesis is that the population proportion is .40. The alternative hypothesis is that the population proportion is not .40. A random sample of 250 produces a sample proportion of .44. Using alpha of .05, the table Z value for $\alpha/2$ is 1.96. The calculated Z from the sample information is

$$Z = \frac{\hat{p} - P}{\sqrt{\dfrac{P \cdot Q}{n}}} = \frac{0.44 - 0.40}{0.031} = 1.29.$$

Thus the null hypothesis is not rejected. Either a correct decision has been made, or a Type II error has been committed. Suppose the alternative population proportion really is 0.36, what is the probability of committing a Type II error?

Solution:

Solve for the critical value of the proportion

$$Z_c = \frac{\hat{p}_c - P}{\sqrt{\dfrac{P \cdot Q}{n}}};$$

$$\pm 1.96 = \frac{\hat{p}_c - 0.40}{\sqrt{\dfrac{(0.40)(0.60)}{250}}};$$

$$\hat{p}_c = 0.40 \pm 0.06.$$

The critical values are 0.34 on the lower end and 0.46 on the upper end. The alternative population proportion is 0.36. The following diagram illustrates these results and the remainder of the solution to this problem.

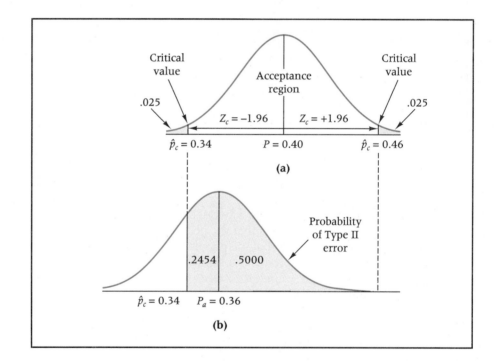

Solving for the area between $\hat{p}_c = 0.34$ and $P_a = 0.36$ yields

$$Z = \frac{0.34 - 0.36}{\sqrt{\dfrac{(0.36)(0.64)}{250}}} = 0.66$$

The area associated with $Z = 0.66$ is .2454. The probability of committing a Type II error is $.5000 + .2454 = .7454$.

The area associated with $Z = 0.66$ is .2454. The probability of committing a Type II error is $.5000 + .2454 = .7454$.

With two-tailed tests, both tails of the distribution contain rejection regions. If the null hypothesis is false, obtaining a calculated statistic falling in the tails results in the correct decision: to reject the null hypothesis. In this case, the probability of committing a Type II error exists only for the area between the two critical values (the acceptance region). However, the right critical value is so far away from the alternative mean that the area between the right critical value and the mean essentially is .5000. Had there been any area past the upper critical value of $\hat{p}_c$ (0.46), it would have been subtracted from .5000, slightly reducing the value of .7454.

Some Observations About Type II Errors

Type II errors are committed only when the researcher fails to reject the null hypothesis but the alternative hypothesis is true. If the alternative mean or proportion is close to the hypothesized value, the probability of committing a Type II error is high. If the alternative value is relatively far away from the hypothesized value, as in the problem with $\mu = 12$ oz and $\mu_a = 11.96$ oz, the probability of committing a Type II error is small. The implication is that when a value is being tested as a null hypothesis against a true alternative value that is relatively far away, the sample statistic obtained is likely to show clearly which hypothesis is true. For example, suppose that a researcher is testing to determine whether a company really is filling two-liter bottles of cola with an average of two-liters. If the company decides to underfill the bottles by filling them with only one-liter, a sample of fifty bottles is likely to average a quantity near the one-liter fill rather than near the two-liter fill. Committing a Type II error is highly unlikely. Even a customer can probably see by looking at the bottles on the shelf that they are underfilled. However, if the company fills two-liter bottles with 1.99 liters, the bottle fills are close in volume to those filled with 2.00 liters. In this case, the probability of committing a Type II error is much greater. A customer probably cannot catch the underfill just by looking.

In general, if the alternative value is relatively far from the hypothesized value, the probability of committing a Type II error is smaller than it is when the alternative value is close to the hypothesized value. The probability of committing a Type II error decreases as alternative values of the hypothesized parameter move farther away from the hypothesized value.

**PROBLEMS
Section 9.6**

9.38 Suppose that a null hypothesis is that the population mean is greater than or equal to 100. Suppose further that a random sample of 48 items is taken and the sample standard deviation is 14. For each of the following

α values, compute the probability of committing a Type II error if the population mean actually is 99.

a. $\alpha = .10$

b. $\alpha = .05$

c. $\alpha = .01$

d. Based on the answers to (a), (b), and (c), what happens to the value of β as α gets smaller?

9.39 For Problem 9.38, use $\alpha = .05$ and solve for the probability of committing a Type II error for the following possible true alternative means.

a. $\mu_a = 98.5$

b. $\mu_a = 98$

c. $\mu_a = 97$

d. $\mu_a = 96$

e. What happens to the probability of committing a Type II error as the alternative value of the mean gets farther from the null hypothesized value of 100?

9.40 Suppose that a hypothesis states that the mean is exactly 50. If a random sample of thirty-five items is taken to test this hypothesis, what is the value of β if the standard deviation is 7 and the alternative mean is 53? Use $\alpha = .01$.

9.41 A null hypothesis is that $P \geq 0.65$. To test this hypothesis, a random sample of size 360 is taken. What is the probability of committing a Type II error if $\alpha = .05$ and the alternative proportion is

a. $P_a = 0.60$.

b. $P_a = 0.55$.

c. $P_a = 0.50$.

9.42 A two-sample means test is being conducted to determine whether there is a significant difference in the means of two populations. The null and alternative hypotheses are

$$H_0: \ \mu_1 - \mu_2 = 0 \qquad H_a: \ \mu_1 - \mu_2 \neq 0$$

Use $\alpha = .01$. Two samples of size 50 each are taken, and the population standard deviations are both about 30. What is the probability of committing a Type II error if the alternative difference in the two means actually is 15?

9.43 The New York Stock Exchange recently reported that the average age of a female shareholder is 44 years. A broker in Chicago wants to know whether this figure is accurate for the female shareholders in Chicago. The broker secures a master list of shareholders in Chicago and takes a random sample of fifty-eight women. Suppose that the average age for shareholders in the sample is 45.1 years, with a standard deviation of 8.7 years. Test to determine whether the broker's sample data differ significantly enough from the 44-year figure released by the New York Stock Exchange to declare that Chicago female shareholders are different in age from female shareholders in general. Use $\alpha = .05$. If there is no significant difference, what is the broker's probability of committing a Type II error if the average age of a female Chicago shareholder is actually 46 years? What is the broker's probability of committing a Type II error if the average age of a female Chicago shareholder actually is 47 years?

9.44 Figures released by InfoCorp show that Canon manufactured 64% of the low-end laser printers during the first quarter of 1991. Suppose that the company conducted a nationwide random sample telephone survey of a variety of offices in the spring of 1992. Of 463 contacted who had just purchased a low-end laser printer, 291 had purchased a Canon. Is this enough evidence to reject the 64% market share figure released in 1991 as too high? Use a 10% level of significance. If the company fails to reject the null hypothesis and if the market share actually is 63%, what is the probability of committing a Type II error? What is the probability of committing a Type II error if the market share actually is 60%? What is the probability of committing a Type II error if the market share actually is 55%?

CHAPTER SUMMARY

Hypothesis testing is a mechanism for utilizing inferential statistics. The process begins with the selection of a null hypothesis and an alternative hypothesis. The null and alternative hypotheses are structured so that either one or the other is true but not both. By examining the sampled data, the researcher either rejects or does not reject the null hypothesis. If the null hypothesis is rejected, the alternative hypothesis is accepted by default.

The hypothesis testing process is somewhat analogous to an indirect proof. Often the researcher wants to prove that the alternative hypothesis is true but cannot do so directly. In testing hypotheses, the researcher assumes that the null hypothesis is true. If the sample data are significantly in opposition to the null hypothesis, the researcher rejects the null hypothesis and accepts the alternative hypothesis by default. Thus the alternative hypothesis has been "proven" indirectly.

Hypothesis tests can be one-tailed or two-tailed. Two-tailed tests always utilize $=$ and $\neq$ in the null and alternative hypotheses. These tests are non-directional in that significant deviations from the hypothesized value either greater than or less than the value fall in rejection regions. The one-tailed test is directional, and the hypotheses contain $<$ or $>$ signs. In these tests, only one end or tail of the distribution contains a rejection region. In a one-tailed test, the researcher is interested only in deviations from the hypothesized value that are either greater than or less than the value but not both.

When a researcher makes a decision about the null hypothesis, it can involve an error. If the null hypothesis is true, the researcher can make a Type I error by rejecting the null hypothesis. The probability of making a Type I error is alpha (α). Alpha is usually set by the researcher when establishing the hypotheses. Another expression sometimes used for the value of α is level of significance.

If the null hypothesis is false and the researcher fails to reject the null hypothesis, a Type II error has been committed. Beta (β) is the probability of committing a Type II error. Type II errors must be computed from the hypothesized value of the parameter, α, and a specific alternative value of the parameter being examined. There are as many possible Type II errors in a problem as there are possible alternative statistical values.

If a null hypothesis is true and the researcher fails to reject it, no error has been committed, and the researcher has made a correct decision. Similarly, if a null hypothesis is false and it is rejected, no error has been committed. Power $(1 - \beta)$ is the probability of a statistical test rejecting the null hypothesis when the null hypothesis is false.

Large sample tests of hypothesis using the Z distribution for analysis include the analysis of single means, single proportions, difference in two means, and difference in two proportions. Three different analytic approaches were presented: (1) standard method, (2) critical value method, and (3) probability method. Chapter 10 presents techniques for analyzing hypothesis tests involving small samples.

Key Words

Hypothesis testing	Level of significance
Indirect proof	Type II error
Null hypothesis	Beta (β)
Alternative hypothesis	Power
Rejection region	One-tailed test
Critical value	Two-tailed test
Acceptance region	Critical value method
Type I error	Probability method
Alpha (α)	

USING THE COMPUTER

Minitab contains sufficient commands to enable you to solve hypothesis testing problems for single means when you know the population standard deviation and have the raw data available. Minitab does *not* have the direct capability to work hypothesis testing problems about two sample means when the standard deviations are known, to test hypotheses about proportions, or determine Type II error probabilities. The command that you use to solve problems from Chapter 9 is ZTEST, which is used to test hypotheses about single means. Chapter 10 contains a Minitab command that you can use to compare two sample means. However, the test for this type of analysis is a *t* test, which are used in situations when you do not know the standard deviations.

Single Sample Mean

The ZTEST command analyzes hypotheses about a single sample mean when you have the raw data and know the population standard deviation. Begin by loading the sample data into a column, using either the READ or SET command. Because it is single sample data, the SET command is preferred. Next, use the ZTEST command and then a specified hypothesized value of μ, the population standard deviation, and the column where the data are to be stored. For example, if data are stored in column 4, the hypothesized value of the population mean is 20, and the population standard deviation is 3.6, the command is

MTB > ZTEST 20 3.6 C4

The subcommand, ALTERNATIVE, is used to specify a one-tailed or two-tailed test and, for a one-tailed test, the tail of the rejection region. The following options for this subcommand are available:

SUBC > ALTERNATIVE 0.   (for two-tailed tests)
SUBC > ALTERNATIVE +1.   (one-tailed test—upper tail)
SUBC > ALTERNATIVE −1.   (one-tailed test—lower tail)

Minitab will default to the two-tailed option if you do not specify an ALTERNATIVE. In order to use a subcommand, you must end the Minitab command being used with a semicolon (;). For example,

MTB > ZTEST 20 3.6 C4;
SUBC > ALTERNATIVE +1.

Minitab will continue to produce subcommand prompts until you end the subcommand with a period. Thus you should end the subcommand ALTERNATIVE with a period.

Working an Example with Minitab

You can work the example presented in Section 9.2 with Minitab by using the following commands:

```
MTB > SET C4
DATA> 21 24 20 21 37 18 21 19 32 21
DATA> 26 19 18 19 18 19 18 18 24 22
DATA> 20 20 21 21 19 21 20 18 18 19
DATA> 18 19 24 17 20 27 23 18 22 24
DATA> 19 20 19 20 17 22 19 20 19 19
DATA> end
MTB > ZTEST 20 3.6 C4;
SUBC > ALTERNATIVE +1.
```

The resulting Minitab output is

```
TEST OF MU = 20.000 VS MU G.T. 20.000
THE ASSUMED SIGMA = 3.60
```

	N	MEAN	STDEV	SE MEAN	Z	P VALUE
C4	50	20.760	3.634	0.509	1.49	0.068

The calculated Z value is 1.49. A Z of 1.49 has a one-tailed test probability of .068 of occurring by chance even when $\mu = 20$. As $.068 > .05$, by the probability method, the null hypothesis is accepted.

SUPPLEMENTARY PROBLEMS

9.45 Test the following hypotheses with the sample information given.

a. H_0: $\mu = 33$ H_a: $\mu \neq 33$
$\overline{X} = 31.2$ $S = 5.6$ $n = 50$ $\alpha = .05$

b. H_0: $\mu \leq 164$ H_a: $\mu > 164$
$\overline{X} = 169$ $S = 24.3$ $n = 31$ $\alpha = .10$

c. H_0: $\mu = 5.83$ H_a: $\mu \neq 5.83$
$\overline{X} = 6.71$ $S^2 = 4.20$ $n = 64$ $\alpha = .01$

d. H_0: $\mu \geq 27$ H_a: $\mu < 27$
$\overline{X} = 26.4$ $S^2 = 1.5$ $n = 31$ $\alpha = .01$

e. H_0: $\mu \leq 121$ H_a: $\mu > 121$
$\overline{X} = 123.4$ $\sigma^2 = 6.3$ $n = 14$ $\alpha = .05$ Assume that X is normally distributed.

9.46 Test the following hypotheses with the sample information given.

a. H_0: $P \geq 0.48$ H_a: $P < 0.48$
$\hat{p} = 0.43$ $n = 110$ $\alpha = .05$

b. H_0: $P \leq 0.67$ H_a: $P > 0.67$
$\hat{p} = 0.75$ $n = 562$ $\alpha = .01$

c. H_0: $P = 0.35$ H_a: $P \neq 0.35$
    $x = 513$ $n = 1,350$ $\alpha = .10$

d. H_0: $P \leq 0.20$ H_a: $P > 0.20$
    $x = 163$ $n = 740$ $\alpha = .005$

e. H_0: $P = 0.50$ H_a: $P \neq 0.50$
    $x = 42$ $n = 70$ $\alpha = .02$

9.47 Test the following hypotheses with the sample information given.

a. H_0: $\mu_1 - \mu_2 = 0$ H_a: $\mu_1 - \mu_2 \neq 0$ $\alpha = .05$

Sample 1	*Sample 2*
$n_1 = 120$	$n_2 = 125$
$\overline{X}_1 = 56.26$	$\overline{X}_2 = 58.4$
$S_1^2 = 210$	$S_2^2 = 195$

b. H_0: $\mu_1 - \mu_2 \geq 0$ H_a: $\mu_1 - \mu_2 < 0$ $\alpha = .05$

Sample 1	*Sample 2*
$n_1 = 40$	$n_2 = 40$
$\overline{X}_1 = 131.3$	$\overline{X}_2 = 135.2$
$S_1^2 = 858$	$S_2^2 = 861$

c. H_0: $\mu_1 - \mu_2 = 0$ H_a: $\mu_1 - \mu_2 \neq 0$ $\alpha = .01$

Sample 1	*Sample 2*
$n_1 = 84$	$n_2 = 90$
$\overline{X}_1 = 9.64$	$\overline{X}_2 = 8.01$
$S_1 = 1.245$	$S_2 = 1.304$

d. H_0: $\mu_1 - \mu_2 \geq 0$ H_a: $\mu_1 - \mu_2 < 0$ $\alpha = .01$

Sample 1	*Sample 2*
$n_1 = 35$	$n_2 = 32$
$\overline{X}_1 = 458.6$	$\overline{X}_2 = 479.1$
$S_1 = 104.1$	$S_2 = 106.7$

9.48 Test the following hypotheses with the sample information given.

　　a. $H_0: P_1 - P_2 \geq 0$　　$H_a: P_1 - P_2 < 0$　　$\alpha = .05$

Sample 1	Sample 2
$n_1 = 540$	$n_2 = 550$
$\hat{p}_1 = 0.62$	$\hat{p}_2 = 0.64$

　　b. $H_0: P_1 - P_2 \leq 0$　　$H_a: P_1 - P_2 > 0$　　$\alpha = .10$

Sample 1	Sample 2
$n_1 = 225$	$n_2 = 200$
$\hat{p}_1 = 0.38$	$\hat{p}_2 = 0.30$

　　c. $H_0: P_1 - P_2 = 0$　　$H_a: P_1 - P_2 \neq 0$　　$\alpha = .05$

Sample 1	Sample 2
$n_1 = 1,100$	$n_2 = 1,100$
$\hat{p}_1 = 0.48$	$\hat{p}_2 = 0.52$

　　d. $H_0: P_1 - P_2 = 0$　　$H_a: P_1 - P_2 \neq 0$　　$\alpha = .20$

Sample 1	Sample 2
$n_1 = 190$	$n_2 = 188$
$x_1 = 34$	$x_2 = 55$

　　e. $H_0: P_1 - P_2 \leq 0$　　$H_a: P_1 - P_2 > 0$　　$\alpha = .01$

Sample 1	Sample 2
$n_1 = 1,350$	$n_2 = 1,450$
$x_1 = 1,010$	$x_2 = 1,015$

9.49 A national publication reported that a college student living away from home spends, on average, no more than $15 per month on laundry. You believe that this figure is too low and want to disprove this claim. To conduct the test, you randomly select thirty-five college students and ask them to keep track of the amount of money they spend during a given month for laundry. The sample produces an average expenditure on laundry of $19.34, with a standard deviation of $4.52. Use these sample data to conduct the hypothesis test. Assume that you are willing to take a 10% risk of making a Type I error.

9.50 The average cost per square foot for office rental space in Philadelphia is said to be $25.25 per year. A large real estate company wants to confirm this figure. The firm conducts a telephone survey of ninety-five offices in the Philadelphia area and asks the office managers how much they pay in rent per square foot. Suppose that the sample average is $24.50 and the population variance is $26.14 for this rental space.

   a. Conduct a hypothesis test using $\alpha = .05$ to determine whether the original cost per square foot should be rejected by the sample data.

   b. Suppose that the average cost per square foot for office rental space in Philadelphia actually is $24.00. What is the probability of committing a Type II error?

9.51 Often problems using percentages convert to hypothesis tests about proportions. However, sometimes percentages are used as measurements that are averaged; in these instances, the percentage averages are used to conduct hypothesis tests about means. For example, a 1990 survey of state and city pension funds showed that the average expected earnings for pension fund investments for the state of Minnesota was 8.5%. Suppose that an independent survey is conducted to test this figure and a random sample of forty-one state and city pension funds produced a sample mean earnings of 8.12%, with a standard deviation of 1.39%.

   a. Use $\alpha = .01$ to test whether the average expected earnings for the state of Minnesota really was 8.5%.

   b. Calculate the probability of committing a Type II error if the actual figure is 8.3%.

9.52 A life insurance salesperson claims that the average worker in the city of Cincinnati has no more than $25,000 of personal life insurance. To test this claim, you randomly sample 100 workers from the city of Cincinnati. You find that this sample of workers has an average of $26,650 of personal life insurance and that the standard deviation is $12,000.

   a. Determine whether there is enough evidence to reject the null hypothesis posed by the salesperson. Assume that the probability of committing a Type I error is .05.

   b. If the actual average for this population is $30,000, what is the probability of committing a Type II error?

9.53 According to Zero Population Growth, the average urban American uses 3.3 lb of food per day. Is this figure accurate for rural Americans? Suppose that sixty-four rural Americans are identified by a random procedure and that their average consumption per day is 3.45 lb of food. Assume a population variance of 1.31 lb of food per day. Use a 5% level of significance to determine whether the Zero Population Growth figure for urban Americans also is true for rural Americans, based on the sample data.

9.54 Studies have shown that at least 70% of all American adults visit a shopping mall one or more times per week. Suppose that you operate a chain of malls across the country, and you want to conduct a test of this figure in a Denver mall. You hire a researcher who uses direct random digit dialing to residences in Denver. The researcher asks an adult at the residence whether he or she has been to a mall during the past week. Of the 420 adults interviewed, 275 had been to a mall in the past week.

  a. Is this enough evidence to reject the claim of 70% as too high? Use $\alpha = .01$.

  b. Suppose that the true population proportion is 0.68. What is the probability of committing a Type II error?

9.55 Computer crime has been a growing problem for the past decade. The types of computer crime include money theft, theft of services, alteration of data, damage to software, theft of information to programs, and trespass. A national study showed that 12% of all computer crime involved alteration of data. You want to test this claim and randomly select the records from 168 computer crime cases across the United States.

  a. If 28 of the cases involved alteration of data, is there enough evidence contrary to the claim of 0.12 to reject it? Use $\alpha = .05$ to test this claim.

  b. If the true proportion is 0.17, what is the probability of committing a Type II error?

9.56 According to one survey, Compaq computers held nearly 8% of the laptop and notebook computer market. Suppose that Compaq executives believe that this figure is too low for the Southwest. They have a random sample taken of laptop and notebook purchases in the Southwest and find that, of 428 purchases, 43 are Compaq computers.

  a. Is this enough evidence to declare that Compaq has a significantly higher market share in the Southwest than nationally?

  b. Is this a one-tailed or two-tailed test? Use a level of significance of 5%.

  c. If the actual figure is 13%, what is the probability of committing a Type II error?

9.57 In 1988, 14% of all prerecorded music shoppers were in the 25–29-year-old age group. A woman is interested in opening a prerecorded music shop on the north side of Phoenix and is trying to determine the age distribution of potential customers. She goes to the nearest mall, stands outside a prerecorded music store, and asks the age of the store's customers as they exit. Of the 80 people interviewed, only 10 are in the 25–

29 age group. If the woman uses $\alpha = .01$, does she have enough information to reject the hypothesis that 14% of all prerecorded music shoppers are in this age group?

9.58 Brokers generally agree that bonds are a better investment during times of low interest rates than during times of high interest rates. A survey of executives during a time of low interest rates showed that 57% of them had some retirement funds invested in bonds. Assume that this percentage is constant for bond market investment by executives with retirement funds. Suppose that interest rates have risen lately and that the proportion of executives with retirement investment money in the bond market may have dropped. To test this idea, a researcher randomly samples 210 executives who have retirement funds. Of these, 93 now have retirement funds invested in bonds. For $\alpha = .10$, is this enough evidence to declare that the proportion of executives with retirement fund investments in the bond market is significantly lower than 0.57?

9.59 The average nightly rate for a room at a hotel that is less than three-years-old is believed to be more than the average nightly rate of an older hotel. To test this notion, a market analyst establishes a null hypothesis of no difference in rates, along with an alternative hypothesis that rooms at the newer hotels have higher rates. A random sample of forty-five of the newer hotels reveals a sample average of $69 per night, with a standard deviation of $8.50. A random sample of fifty of the older hotels reveals a sample average of $59 per night, with a standard deviation of $8.10. Use $\alpha = .05$ to test the hypotheses.

9.60 Is there any difference in the average salaries of accounting clerks and data entry operators? To test this question, a personnel manager takes a random sample of sixty-three accounting clerks; the sample average salary is $15,800, with a standard deviation of $1,200. She takes a second random sample of fifty-six data entry operators; the sample average salary is $15,200, with a standard deviation of $1,050. For $\alpha = .10$, does she have enough evidence to declare that there is a difference in the population average salaries for these two groups?

9.61 According to one survey, the average office rental rate apparently is higher in Chicago than in Houston. Suppose that an analyst wanted to "prove" that this difference is true. He takes random samples of thirty-five office managers in each of Chicago and Houston, which result in the following data:

Chicago	Houston
$\overline{X}_C = \$30.77$	$\overline{X}_H = \$15.00$
$S_C = \$5.98$	$S_H = \$3.90$

Use these data and $\alpha = .05$ to test whether the average rental rate for office space is significantly higher in Chicago than it is in Houston.

9.62 Various types of retail outlets sell toys during the Christmas season. Among them are the specialty shop toy stores, the large discount toy stores, and other retailers who carry toys as only one part of their stock of goods. Is there any difference in the dollar amount of a customer purchase at a large discount toy store and a toy specialty shop if they carry relatively comparable types of toys? Suppose that in December a random sample of sixty sales slips is selected from a large discount toy outlet and a random sample of forty sales slips is selected from a toy specialty shop. The data gathered from these samples are as follows:

Large Discount Toy Store	Specialty Toy Store
$\bar{X}_d = \$47.20$	$\bar{X}_s = \$27.40$
$S_d = \$12.45$	$S_s = \$9.82$

Use $\alpha = .01$ and the data to determine whether there is a significant difference in the average size of purchases at these stores.

9.63 A tree nursery has been experimenting with fertilizer to increase the growth of seedlings. A sample of 35 two-year-old pine trees is grown for three more years with a cake of fertilizer buried in the soil near the trees' roots. A second sample of 35 two-year-old pine trees is grown for three more under identical conditions—soil, temperature, water—as the first group, except that it is not fertilized. Tree growth is measured over the three-year period with the following results:

Trees with Fertilizer	Trees without Fertilizer
$n_1 = 35$	$n_2 = 35$
$\bar{X}_1 = 38.4$ in.	$\bar{X}_2 = 23.1$ in.
$S_1 = 9.8$ in.	$S_2 = 7.4$ in.

Do the data support the theory that the population of trees with the cake of fertilizer grow significantly larger during the period that they are fertilized than the nonfertilized trees? Use $\alpha = .01$.

9.64 The General Electric Corporation has held a large share of the U.S. health diagnostic equipment market for many decades. One relatively new piece of diagnostic equipment is a computed tomography (CT) machine, which is used to construct body images. In 1986, General Electric held nearly 50% of the market share of CT sales. Some industry analysts believe that GE's proportion of CT sales has slipped since then because of international competition. Suppose that you want to test whether GE's share of CT sales is significantly lower than it was in 1986. Suppose further that a random sample of 450 CT sales in 1986 produced 212 GE purchases and that a random sample of 390 CT sales in 1991 produced 171 GE purchases. Use this information and $\alpha = .05$ to determine whether GE's proportion of the CT market in 1991 is significantly less than its proportion in 1986.

9.65 One newspaper article quoted a survey that demonstrated how the Shell Oil Company holds different percentages of market share in different cities for the sale of premium gasoline. The study stated that Shell held a 15% to 16% share of the market of premium gasoline in the Baltimore and Washington, D.C., areas. It appears that, because of the proximity of these two areas, there is no difference in market share. To test this supposition, a market analyst samples 235 motorists in Baltimore and 215 motorists in Washington, D.C., who use premium gasoline. The results show that 35 of the motorists in Baltimore and 34 of the motorists in Washington purchase Shell gasoline. Determine whether there is a significant difference in the proportions of consumers of premium gasoline who purchase the Shell brand in these two cities. Use $\alpha = .10$.

9.66 The cold cereal market is dominated by several well-known companies, including General Mills, Quaker Oats, C.W. Post, Nabisco Brands, and Kellogg. Surveys show that the cold cereal market shares of Ralston Purina and Nabisco Brands are no more than a percentage point apart. Suppose that a survey is conducted in North Carolina to determine whether there is a difference in cold cereal market share between these two companies, and the following data are gathered:

Ralston Purina	Nabisco Brands
$n_R = 840$	$n_N = 900$
$x_R = 50$	$x_N = 45$

Use $\alpha = .10$ to determine whether there is a significant difference in market proportions for these two companies in North Carolina.

9.67 A survey was conducted to determine the extent to which Americans order take-out food. Sixty-two percent of all hamburgers were take out, followed by 56% of pizza, 33% of fried chicken, 26% of salad, and 22% of Chinese food. A market researcher theorizes that in the Midwest the percentage of take-out food is smaller than in Southern California. To test this theory, he selects a McDonald's restaurant in Des Moines, Iowa, and one in Anaheim, California. The researcher records the number of hamburgers purchased and whether they are take out or not. The results show that 54% of the 390 hamburgers purchased in Des Moines were take out. However, in Anaheim, 71% of the 526 hamburgers purchased were take out. Use $\alpha = .01$ to test whether the figure in Des Moines is significantly lower than that in Anaheim.

9.68 A manufacturer has two machines that are used to drill holes in a piece of sheet metal used in engine construction. The workers who attach the sheet metal to the engine become inspectors in that they reject sheets that have been so poorly drilled that they cannot mount the sheets. The production manager is interested in knowing whether one machine produces more defective drillings than the other machine. As an experiment, employees mark the sheets so that the manager can determine which machine was used to drill the holes. A random sample of 191 sheets of metal drilled by machine 1 is taken, and 38 of the sheets are defective. A random sample of 202 sheets of metal drilled by machine 2 is taken, and 21 of the sheets are defective. Use $\alpha = .05$ to determine whether there is a significant difference in the proportion of sheets drilled with defective holes between machine 1 and machine 2.

9.69 As of May 15, 1991, approximately .68 of the first-year MBA students at major universities were able to secure summer internships with companies. Just prior to the summer of 1992, of a random sample of 123 first-year MBA students at major universities 88 say that they have secured a summer internship with a company. Use this information to test whether the .68 figure for 1991 is too low for 1992, based on the sample data. Use $\alpha = .05$. If the figure for the summer of 1992 really is .75, what is the probability of committing a Type II error? If the figure for the summer of 1992 really is .80, what is the probability of committing a Type II error?

9.70 According to the U.S. Bureau of Labor Statistics, the average price of a half gallon of milk in the north central United States was $1.43 in 1990. You want to test whether the figure is now significantly higher. Suppose that the population standard deviation for the price of a half gallon of milk is $0.12 and that the price of a half gallon of milk is ascertained from forty-five randomly selected stores in the north central United States. Let $\alpha = .10$.

     a. What is the probability of committing a Type II error if the population mean figure now is $1.45?

     b. What is the probability of committing a Type II error if the population mean figure now is $1.48?

     c. What is the probability of committing a Type II error if the population mean figure now is $1.48 but $\alpha = .01$?

SMALL SAMPLE STATISTICS: HYPOTHESIS TESTS AND CONFIDENCE INTERVALS

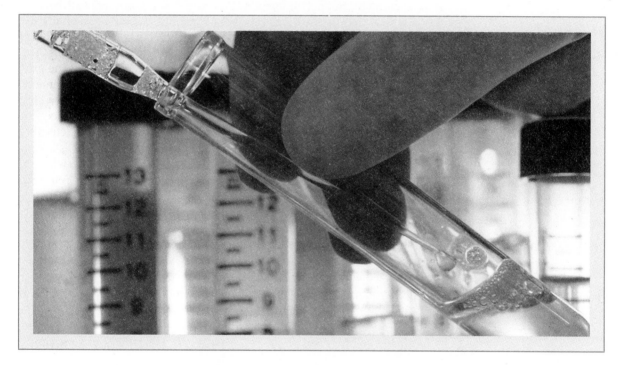

CHAPTER LEARNING OBJECTIVES

The overall learning objective of Chapter 10 is to help you to learn to apply statistical techniques with small sample sizes, specifically enabling you to

1. Understand the difference between the t distribution and the Z distribution.
2. Test hypotheses and establish confidence intervals for single means when sample size is small and the standard deviation or variance is unknown.
3. Test hypotheses and establish confidence intervals for two sample means when sample sizes are small and the standard deviations or variances are unknown.
4. Test hypotheses and establish confidence intervals for the mean difference in two related measures.
5. Test hypotheses about the difference of the means for more than two samples.

**JEFF LONG SURVEYS
COUPON USERS**

The Discount Food Market is a large national food retailer with head-quarters in Knoxville, Tennessee. The company targets its stores to low-income Americans. The management of the Discount Food Market company realizes that a high percentage of its customers use coupons, and the company wants to capitalize on this use. Management read of a survey by D'Arcy Masius Benton & Bowles that found that the typical coupon shopper reduced a $74.00 per week grocery bill by $6.00 with coupons. The Vice President of Operations for the Discount company assigned Jeff Long the task of gathering data from its stores in Milwaukee and Pittsburgh to determine the extent of customer coupon use in those cities. Long understands that, because of cost and time constraints, the samples will be small and information about population parameters will be unknown. He believes that weekly customer grocery bills and coupon use are normally distributed.

**Managerial
Questions**

- Are the average grocery bill and coupon use for Discount's customers different from those in the national survey?
- Is there a difference in the results of the Pittsburgh survey and the Milwaukee survey?
- What is an estimate of the average grocery bill and the average coupon reduction for Discount's survey?
- What is the estimate of the difference between the average grocery bill of a customer in Pittsburgh and a customer in Milwaukee?
- What is the estimate of the difference between the average grocery bill reduction by coupons for a customer in Pittsburgh and a customer in Milwaukee?

The samples used to construct confidence intervals in Chapter 8 and to test hypotheses in Chapter 9 were large samples. Those tests were based on the central limit theorem, which states that the sample mean and the difference in sample means are normally distributed if sample size is large and the population standard deviation is known. An additional feature of large sample statistics is that, when the population standard deviation is unknown, the sample standard deviation is an acceptable estimate, and the distribution of sample means and the difference in sample means are approximately normal. In both cases, $n \geq 30$ is generally considered a lower limit for large sample size.

INTRODUCTION TO SMALL SAMPLE ANALYSIS | **10.1**

However, in many real-life situations, sample sizes of less than thirty are the norm. For example, a researcher is interested in studying the average flying time of a DC-10 from New York to Los Angeles, but a sample of only twenty-one flights is available. Another researcher is studying the impact of movie video advertisements on consumers, but the group used in the study contains only eleven people. In both studies, the central limit theorem is not appropriate because of the small sample sizes, and alternate techniques are required.

If the population is known to be normally distributed and the population standard deviation is known, the sample means are normally distributed regardless of sample size. Thus, by assuming that the *population* is normally distributed (many phenomena are normally distributed) and that the population standard deviation is known, a researcher could theoretically continue to use the techniques presented in Chapters 8 and 9 for hypothesis testing and confidence interval estimation, even with small samples. These formulas for sample means are

$$ Z = \frac{\overline{X} - \mu}{\frac{\sigma}{\sqrt{n}}} \quad \text{and} \quad \overline{X} - Z\frac{\sigma}{\sqrt{n}} \leq \mu \leq \overline{X} + Z\frac{\sigma}{\sqrt{n}}. $$

In many research situations, the population standard deviation is not known and must be estimated by using the sample standard deviation. In these situations, S is substituted into the preceding formula:

$$ Z = \frac{\overline{X} - \mu}{\frac{S}{\sqrt{n}}} \quad \text{and} \quad \overline{X} - Z\frac{S}{\sqrt{n}} \leq \mu \leq \overline{X} + Z\frac{S}{\sqrt{n}}. $$

However, the sample standard deviation, S, is only a good approximation for the population standard deviation, σ, for large samples. These Z formulas that use S, therefore, are not applicable to small sample analysis. This problem was considered and solved by a British statistician, William S. Gosset.

The *t* Test

Gosset learned that the expression

$$ Z = \frac{\overline{X} - \mu}{\frac{S}{\sqrt{n}}} $$

does not necessarily yield a normal distribution for small sample sizes, even if the population is normally distributed, because the population standard de-

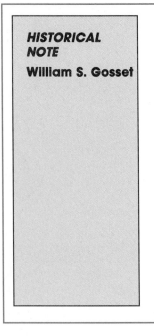

HISTORICAL NOTE

William S. Gosset

William S. Gosset was born in 1876 in Canterbury, England. He studied chemistry and mathematics and in 1899 went to work for the Guinness Brewery in Dublin, Ireland. Gosset was involved in quality control with the brewery, studying variables such as raw materials and temperature. Because of the circumstances of his experiments, Gosset conducted many studies with small samples. He discovered that using the standard Z test with a *sample* standard deviation produced inexact and incorrect distributions for small sample sizes. This led to his development of the distribution of the sample standard deviation and the t test.

Gosset was a student and close personal friend of Karl Pearson. When Gosset's first work on the t test was published, he used the pen name "student." As a result, the t test is sometimes referred to as the "student's t test." Gosset's contribution was significant because it led to more exact statistical tests, which some say marked the beginning of the modern era in mathematical statistics.

Source: Adapted from Dudycha, Arthur L., and Linda W. Dudycha, "Behavioral Statistics: An Historical Perspective," in *Statistical Issues: A Reader for the Behavioral Sciences*, edited by Roger Kirk (Monterey, Calif.: Brooks/Cole, 1972).

t distribution

viation is unknown. Gosset developed a distribution that does describe the sample data when the population is normally distributed. It is called the **t distribution.** The formula used to test hypotheses about a single sample mean when the standard deviation of the population is unknown, the sample size is small, and the population is normally distributed is

$$t = \frac{\overline{X} - \mu}{\dfrac{S}{\sqrt{n}}}.$$

This formula is essentially the same as the Z formula, but the distribution table values are not. The t distribution values are contained in Table A.6 and, for convenience, inside the back cover of the text.

The t distribution actually is a series of distributions, because every sample size has a different distribution, thereby creating the potential for many t tables. In order to make these t values more manageable, only select key values are presented; each line in the table represents a different t distribution. The assumption underlying the use of the techniques discussed in this chapter for small sample sizes is that the population is normally distributed. If the population distribution is not normal or is unknown, nonparametric techniques presented in Chapter 12 should be used.

Characteristics of the *t* Distribution

Figure 10.1 displays two *t* distributions superimposed on a normal distribution. Like the normal curve, *t* distributions are symmetric, unimodal, and a family of curves. The *t* distributions are flatter in the middle and have more area in their tails than the normal distribution. In terms of hypothesis testing, for a given α value, the critical values (in the tails) are farther from the mean statistic than critical values are with the normal curve.

An examination of *t* distribution values reveals that the *t* distribution approaches the normal curve as *n* gets large. Some researchers prefer to use the *t* distribution anytime the population variance or standard deviation is unknown, regardless of sample size. However, in this text, the *t* distribution is reserved for use with small sample size problems ($n < 30$), because, as *n* nears size 30, the *t* table values approach the *Z* table values.

Reading the *t* Distribution Table

To find a value in the *t* distribution table requires knowing the sample size. The *t* distribution table is a compilation of many *t* distributions, with each line of the table representing a different sample size. However, the sample size must first be converted to **degrees of freedom (df)** before a table value can be determined. The formula to compute degrees of freedom varies according to which *t* test is being performed, so a df formula is given for each *t* test. The concept of degrees of freedom is difficult and beyond the scope of this text. A brief explanation is that *t* tests are used because the population variance or standard deviation, which is part of the *Z* formula, is unknown and must be estimated by a sample standard deviation or variance. For every parameter (such as variance or standard deviation) of a statistical test formula that is unknown and must be estimated by a statistic (sample variance or standard deviation) in the formula, one degree of freedom is lost.

In Table A.6 the degrees of freedom are located in the left column. Across the top of the table are a few selected values of α ranging from .10 to .005. The *t* value is located at the intersection of the df value and the selected α

degrees of freedom (df)

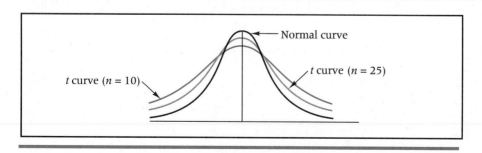

FIGURE 10.1

Comparison of Two *t* Distributions to the Normal Curve

TABLE 10.1	*Degrees of Freedom*	$t_{.100}$	$t_{.050}$	$t_{.025}$	$t_{.010}$	$t_{.005}$
t Distribution						
	.					
	.					
	.					
	23					
	24		1.711			
	25					
	.					
	.					
	.					

value. For example, if the degrees of freedom for a given *t* statistic are 24 and the desired alpha value is .05, the *t* value is 1.711, as shown in Table 10.1.

10.2   SMALL SAMPLE STATISTICS ABOUT μ

Hypothesis Testing

Probably the simplest *t* test is the test of hypotheses about a single population mean, μ. Occasionally, a researcher wants to determine whether some hypothesized value is the population mean. For example, a production manager might want to know whether a sheet metal machine is producing a part that meets the desired specification of a hole punched exactly 0.35 cm in diameter. Is the machine actually producing holes that average 0.35 cm in diameter, or is the machine producing holes of some other size?

Or a consumer group might want to determine whether the life of company X's light bulbs is actually 1,200 lumin-hours as promised in the labeling or is less than 1,200 lumin-hours. The *t* test for single population means is appropriate in these two situations. In general, this *t* test is applicable whenever the researcher is drawing a single random sample to test the value of a population mean, μ, when using small samples and the population standard deviation is unknown.

t Test for μ	$$t = \frac{\overline{X} - \mu}{\frac{s}{\sqrt{n}}};$$ degrees of freedom (df) $= n - 1$.	**(10.1)**

The U.S. Farmers' Production Company builds large harvesters. In order for it to be properly balanced when operating, a 25-lb plate is installed on the side of the harvester. The machine that produces these plates is set to yield plates that average 25 lb. The distribution of plates produced from the machine is normal. However, the shop foreman is worried that the machine is out of adjustment and is producing plates that do not average 25 lb. To test this idea, he randomly selects twenty of the plates produced the day before and weighs them. Table 10.2 shows the weights obtained.

The test is to determine whether the machine is out of control, and the shop foreman has not specified whether he believes that the machine is producing plates that are too heavy or too light. Thus a two-tailed test is appropriate. The hypotheses are

$$H_0: \ \mu = 25 \text{ lb}$$
$$H_a: \ \mu \neq 25 \text{ lb}$$

An α of .05 is used. Figure 10.2 shows the rejection regions.

Computation of the test statistic yields

$$t = \frac{\overline{X} - \mu}{\dfrac{S}{\sqrt{n}}} = \frac{25.51 - 25.0}{\dfrac{2.1933}{\sqrt{20}}} = 1.04 \qquad \text{(Calculated } t\text{)}.$$

Since $n = 20$, the degrees of freedom for this test are 19 $(20 - 1)$. The t distribution table is a one-tailed table. This test is two-tailed, so alpha must be

22.6	22.2	23.2	27.4	24.5	**TABLE 10.2**
27.0	26.6	28.1	26.9	24.9	
26.2	25.3	23.1	24.2	26.1	Weights in Pounds of a Sample of Twenty Plates
25.8	30.4	28.6	23.5	23.6	

$$\overline{X} = 25.51 \text{ lb}, \quad S = 2.1933 \text{ lb}, \quad \text{and} \quad n = 20.$$

FIGURE 10.2

Rejection Regions for the Machine Plate Example

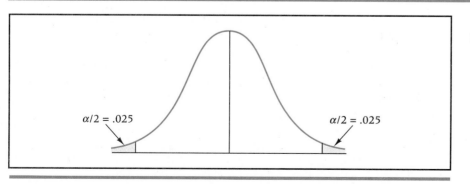

$\alpha/2 = .025$ $\alpha/2 = .025$

FIGURE 10.3

Graph of Calculated and
Critical t Values for the
Machine Plate Example

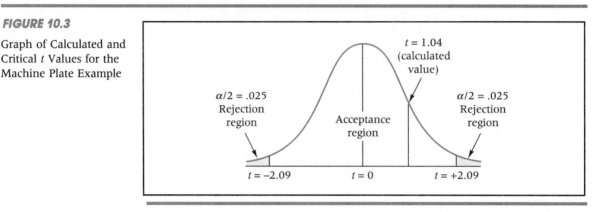

split, which yields $\alpha/2 = .025$, the value in each tail. When conducting a two-tailed test, to obtain the table t value, always split alpha and use $\alpha/2$. The table t value for this example is 2.093. Table values such as this one are often written in the form:

$$t_{.025,19} = 2.093.$$

The subscripts denote to other researchers the alpha value (for two-tailed tests, $\alpha/2$) and the number of degrees of freedom used. Figure 10.3 depicts the t distribution for this example, along with the critical values, the calculated t value, and the rejection regions. In this case, the decision rule is to reject the null hypothesis if the calculated value of t is less than -2.093 or greater than $+2.093$ (in the tails of the distribution). Because the calculated value is $+1.04$, the null hypothesis is not rejected. There is not enough evidence in this sample to reject the hypothesis that the population mean is 25 lb.

**Demonstration
Problem 10.1**

One 1990 estimate of the value of U.S. farmland was $686 per acre. Suppose that a researcher believes that this value has increased since then. To test this belief, she randomly samples twenty-three farms across the country and determines the selling price per acre of these farms. The data for each farm are shown (in dollars per acre). The researcher uses $\alpha = .05$ to test the theory that farmland is now worth more than $686 per acre.

750	800	680	910	845	790
1100	950	735	600	800	850
845	900	1150	1000	780	900
900	850	990	1200	850	

Solution:

The hypothesis that the average value of U.S. farmland is now more than $686 is a new theory or idea. It is what the researcher is trying to "prove." Therefore it should be the alternative hypothesis. The null hypothesis is that the average value of farmland is still $686 or actually may be less than $686 per acre. Thus

$$H_0: \mu \le \$686$$
$$H_a: \mu > \$686$$

With twenty-three data points, df = $n - 1$ = 22. This test is one-tailed, and the table t value is

$$t_{.05,22} = 1.717.$$

The sample mean is $877.17, and the sample standard deviation is $142.92. The computed t value is

$$t = \frac{\overline{X} - \mu}{\frac{S}{\sqrt{n}}} = \frac{877.17 - 686}{\frac{142.92}{\sqrt{23}}} = 6.41.$$

The computed t value of 6.41 is greater than the table t value of 1.717, so the researcher rejects the null hypothesis. She accepts the alternative hypothesis and concludes that the average value of U.S. farmland is now greater than $686 per acre. The following graph pictorially represents this analysis.

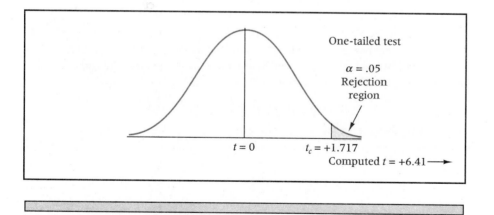

One-tailed test

$\alpha = .05$
Rejection
region

$t = 0$ $t_c = +1.717$
              Computed $t = +6.41 \longrightarrow$

Confidence Intervals

Formula 10.1 can be manipulated algebraically to produce a formula for estimating the population mean using small samples when σ is unknown and the population is normally distributed.

Confidence Interval to Estimate μ: Small Samples and Population Standard Deviation Unknown	$$\bar{X} \pm t\frac{S}{\sqrt{n}};$$ $$\bar{X} - t\frac{S}{\sqrt{n}} \le \mu \le \bar{X} + t\frac{S}{\sqrt{n}};$$ $$\text{df} = n - 1.$$	**(10.2)**

Formula 10.2 can be used in a manner similar to methods presented in Chapter 8 for constructing a confidence interval to estimate μ. For example, in the aerospace industry some companies allow their employees to accumulate extra working hours beyond their forty-hour week. These extra hours sometimes are referred to as *green* time or *comp* time. Many managers work longer than the eight-hour workday, preparing proposals, overseeing crucial tasks, and taking care of paperwork. Recognition of such overtime is important. Most managers are not paid extra for this work, but a record is kept of this time and occasionally the manager is allowed to use some of this comp time as extra leave or vacation time.

Suppose that a researcher wants to estimate the average amount of comp time accumulated per week for managers in the aerospace industry. He randomly samples eighteen managers and measures the amount of extra time they work during a specific week and obtains the results shown (in hours).

6	21	17	20	7	0	8	16	29
3	8	12	11	9	21	25	15	16

He constructs a 90% confidence interval to estimate the average amount of extra time per week worked by a manager in the aerospace industry. The sample size is 18, so df = 17. A 90% level of confidence results in $\alpha/2$ = .05 area in each tail. The table t value is

$$t_{.05,17} = 1.740.$$

The sample mean is 13.56 hr, and the sample standard deviation is 7.8 hr. The confidence interval is computed from this information as

$$\bar{X} \pm t\frac{S}{\sqrt{n}};$$

$$13.56 \pm 1.740 \frac{7.8}{\sqrt{18}} = 13.56 \pm 3.20;$$

$$10.36 \le \mu \le 16.76.$$

The point estimate for this problem is 13.56 hr, with an error of ± 3.20 hr. The researcher is 90% confident that the average amount of comp time accumulated by a manager per week in this industry is between 10.36 hours and 16.76 hours.

The owner of a large equipment rental company wants to make a rather quick estimate of the average number of days a ditchdigger piece of equipment is rented out per person per time. The company has records of all rentals, but the amount of time required to conduct an audit of *all* accounts would be prohibitive. She decides to take a random sample of rental invoices. Fourteen different rentals of ditchdiggers are randomly selected from the files, yielding the following data. The owner uses these data to construct a 99% confidence interval to estimate the average number of days that a ditchdigger is rented.

$$3 \quad 1 \quad 3 \quad 2 \quad 5 \quad 1 \quad 2 \quad 1 \quad 4 \quad 2 \quad 1 \quad 3 \quad 1 \quad 1$$

Solution:

As $n = 14$, the df $= 13$. The 99% level of confidence results in $\alpha = .005$ area in each tail of the distribution. The table t value is

$$t_{.005,13} = 3.012.$$

The sample mean is 2.14, and the sample standard deviation is 1.29. The confidence interval is

$$\overline{X} \pm t\frac{S}{\sqrt{n}};$$

$$2.14 \pm 3.012\frac{1.29}{\sqrt{14}} = 2.14 \pm 1.04;$$

$$1.10 \leq \mu \leq 3.18.$$

A point estimate of the average length of time per rental is 2.14 days, with an error of ± 1.04. With a 99% level of confidence, the company's owner can estimate that the average length of time per rental is between 1.10 days and 3.18 days. Combining this figure with variables such as frequency of rental per year can help the owner estimate potential profit or loss per year for such a piece of equipment.

**PROBLEMS
Section 10.2**

10.1 A random sample of size 20 is taken, resulting in a sample mean of 16.45 and a sample standard deviation of 3.59. Assume that X is normally distributed and use this information and $\alpha = .05$ to test the following hypotheses:

$$H_0: \mu = 16 \qquad H_a: \mu \neq 16$$

10.2 A random sample of 8 items is taken, with $\overline{X} = 58.42$ and $S^2 = 25.68$. Use these data to test the following hypotheses, assuming that you want to take only a 1% risk of committing a Type I error and that X is normally distributed:

$$H_0: \mu \geq 60 \qquad H_a: \mu < 60$$

10.3 The following data were gathered from a random sample of 11 items:

1200   1175   1080   1275   1201   1387
1090   1280   1400   1287   1225

Use these data and a 5% level to test the following hypotheses of significance, assuming that the data come from a normally distributed population:

$$H_0: \mu \leq 1160 \qquad H_a: \mu > 1160$$

10.4 The following data (in lb), which were randomly selected from a normally distributed population of values, represent measurements of a machine part that is supposed to weigh, on average, 8.3 lb:

8.1   8.4   8.3   8.2   8.5   8.6   8.4   8.3   8.4   8.2
8.8   8.2   8.2   8.3   8.1   8.3   8.4   8.5   8.5   8.7

Use these data and $\alpha = .01$ to test the hypothesis that the parts average 8.3 lb.

10.5 Suppose that the following data are randomly selected from a population of normally distributed values:

40   51   43   48   44   57   54
39   42   48   45   39   43

Construct a 95% confidence interval to estimate the population mean value.

10.6 If a random sample of twenty-seven items produces $\overline{X} = 128.4$ and $S = 20.6$, what is the 98% confidence interval for μ? Assume that X is normally distributed for the population. What is the point estimate?

10.7 A random sample of fifteen items is taken producing a sample mean of 2.364, with a sample variance of 0.81. Assume that X is normally distributed and construct a 90% confidence interval for the population mean.

10.8 Use the following data to construct a 99% confidence interval for μ:

16.4	17.1	17.0	15.6	16.2
14.8	16.0	15.6	17.3	17.4
15.6	15.7	17.2	16.6	16.0
15.3	15.4	16.0	15.8	17.2
14.6	15.5	14.9	16.7	16.3

Assume that X is normally distributed. What is the point estimate for μ?

10.9 Suppose that you want to determine the market opportunities of advertising for small businesses. A recent survey showed that companies with annual revenues of less than $1,000,000 expend, on average, approximately $158,000 per year on advertising. You believe that this figure is too high. To test your belief, you conduct a random survey of twenty-two companies having annual revenues of less than $1,000,000. The results are a sample average of $140,000, with a sample standard deviation of $39,000. Determine whether the $158,000 figure is too high for $\alpha = .01$. Assume that advertising revenues are normally distributed.

10.10 Use the sample information from Problem 10.9 to construct a 98% confidence interval to estimate the average advertising revenue for a business with less than $1,000,000 annual sales.

10.11 A university counseling center offers GMAT review courses five times a year. The director of the center wants to take the attendance figures for the last five sessions and compute an estimate for a population mean attendance if the review courses were to go on as they are for a long time. The attendance figures for the last five sessions were 21, 29, 16, 13, and 22. The director assumes that attendance is normally distributed, uses a 95% level of confidence, and applies the t test confidence interval formula. What is the estimated population mean attendance value obtained?

10.12 The director of the counseling center in Problem 10.11 had publicly predicted that the average attendance would be at least twenty-three people. Is there enough evidence in the data to reject that claim as too high if $\alpha = .10$?

10.13 In 1990, some fast-food chains offered a lower priced combination meal in an effort to attract budget-conscious shoppers. One chain test marketed an offer of a burger, fries, and a drink for $1.71. The weekly sales volume for these meals was impressive. Suppose that the company wants to estimate the average amount its customers spend on a meal at their restaurant while this offer was in effect. An analyst gathers data from twenty-eight randomly selected customers. The following data represent the sample meal totals:

$3.21	$5.40	$3.50	$4.39	$5.60	$8.65	$5.02
4.20	1.25	7.64	3.28	5.57	3.26	3.80
5.46	9.87	4.67	5.86	3.73	4.08	5.47
4.49	5.19	5.82	7.62	4.83	8.42	9.10

Use these data to construct a 90% confidence interval to estimate the population mean value. Assume that the amounts spent are normally distributed.

10.14 National TV news reported that the average price for a gallon of self-serve regular unleaded gasoline is $1.38. You believe that in your area of the country this figure is too low. You decide to test this claim for your part of the United States by randomly calling gasoline stations. Your random survey of twenty-five stations produces the following prices:

$1.40	$1.48	$1.32	$1.39	$1.47
1.44	1.53	1.40	1.37	1.38
1.40	1.45	1.42	1.52	1.33
1.48	1.48	1.53	1.42	1.44
1.50	1.52	1.53	1.42	1.41

Assume that the average figure for the United States holds for your region and that gasoline prices for a region are normally distributed. Do the data you obtained provide enough evidence to reject the claim? Use a 1% level of significance.

10.15 The average age of first-time brides reportedly has increased during the past two decades. By late in the 1980s, the average age of a first-time bride was about 24. Suppose that you want to test this figure, because you believe that the average age is younger than that now. You take a random sample of ages of nineteen first-time brides this year and obtain the following data:

22	17	24	26	25	28	21	19	35	32
28	22	21	19	20	18	19	22	24	

According to these data, is there enough evidence to reject the claim for the late 1980s as too high for this year? Assume that ages of first-time brides are normally distributed and use $\alpha = .10$.

10.16 The marketing director of a large department store wants to estimate the average number of customers who enter the store every five minutes. She has a research assistant randomly select five-minute intervals and count the number of arrivals at the store. The assistant obtains the figures: 58, 32, 41, 47, 56, 80, 45, 29, 32, and 78. The analyst assumes that the number of arrivals is normally distributed. Using these data the analyst computes a 95% confidence interval to estimate the mean value for all five-minute intervals. What interval values does she get?

10.17 An information systems manager for a large corporation is attempting to write a computer program to predict the travel costs for sending employees to various places in the United States. Part of the process involves estimating the parameters for certain variables. One of the variables is the average cost of a hotel room for single occupancy per day. To estimate it, the information systems manager gathers sample data from many cities. The following costs are for a single occupancy room per day for various hotels in Dallas. Assuming the costs are normally distributed, use these data to construct a 98% confidence interval to estimate the average per day cost of a single occupancy room in Dallas:

$ 85	$119
115	145
110	95
112	75
92	105
105	125
115	118

SMALL SAMPLE STATISTICS ABOUT $\mu_1 - \mu_2$ | **10.3**

Hypothesis Testing

In business research, to be able to test hypotheses about certain measurements of two populations to determine whether they are alike or different often is useful. For example, do men and women react differently to advertising stimuli? Is the average age of a diet cola consumer different from the average age of a regular cola consumer? Do brand A tires wear longer than brand B tires?

The hypothesis test presented in this section is a test that compares the means of two samples to determine whether the means of the two populations from which the samples come are alike or different. This technique is for small samples (n_1, $n_2 < 30$), unknown population variances, and **independent samples** (not related in any way). An assumption underlying this technique

independent samples

is that the measurement or characteristic being studied is normally distributed for both populations. In Chapter 9, the difference in large sample means was analyzed by

$$Z = \frac{(\bar{X}_1 - \bar{X}_2) - (\mu_1 - \mu_2)}{\sqrt{\dfrac{\sigma_1^2}{n_1} + \dfrac{\sigma_2^2}{n_2}}}.$$

If $\sigma_1^2 = \sigma_2^2$, the preceding formula algebraically reduces to

$$Z = \frac{(\bar{X}_1 - \bar{X}_2) - (\mu_1 - \mu_2)}{\sigma\sqrt{\dfrac{1}{n_1} + \dfrac{1}{n_2}}}.$$

If σ is unknown, it can be estimated by *pooling* the two sample variances and computing a pooled sample standard deviation:

$$\sigma \approx S = \sqrt{\frac{S_1^2(n_1 - 1) + S_2^2(n_2 - 1)}{n_1 + n_2 - 2}}.$$

Substituting this expression for σ and changing Z to t produces a formula to test the difference in means.

---

t Formula to Test the Difference in Means Assuming $\sigma_1^2 = \sigma_2^2$

$$t = \frac{(\bar{X}_1 - \bar{X}_2) - (\mu_1 - \mu_2)}{\sqrt{\dfrac{S_1^2(n_1 - 1) + S_2^2(n_2 - 1)}{n_1 + n_2 - 2}}\sqrt{\dfrac{1}{n_1} + \dfrac{1}{n_2}}}, \qquad (10.3)$$

where: $df = n_1 + n_2 - 2$

The important assumption underlying Formula 10.3 is that the population variances are equal: $\sigma_1^2 = \sigma_2^2$. If this assumption is not valid, Formula 10.3 cannot be used and other techniques are available (see Appendix D).

At the Hernandez Manufacturing Company, an application of the test of the difference in small sample means arises. New employees are expected to attend a three-day seminar to learn about the company. At the end of the seminar, they are tested to measure their knowledge about the company. The traditional training method has been lecture and a question and answer session. Management has decided to experiment with a different training procedure, which processes new employees in two days by using videocassettes and having no question and answer session. If this procedure works, it could save the company thousands of dollars over a period of several years. However, there is some concern about the effectiveness of the two-day method.

To test the difference in the two methods, a group of fifteen newly hired employees is randomly selected to take the three-day seminar (method A), and a second group of twelve new employees is randomly selected to utilize the two-day videocassette method (method B). Table 10.3 shows the test scores of the two groups. Using $\alpha = .05$, management wants to determine whether there is a significant difference in the mean scores of the two groups. It assumes that the scores for this test are normally distributed and that the population variances are approximately equal.

The hypotheses for this example are

$$H_0: \mu_1 - \mu_2 = 0$$
$$H_a: \mu_1 - \mu_2 \neq 0$$

The sample means and variances, respectively, are

$$\overline{X}_1 = 47.73 \qquad \overline{X}_2 = 56.5$$
$$S_1^2 = 19.495 \qquad S_2^2 = 18.273$$
$$n_1 = 15 \qquad n_2 = 12$$

Because the hypotheses are $=$ and $\neq$, this test is two-tailed. The degrees of freedom are 25 ($15 + 12 - 2 = 25$) and alpha is .05. The t table requires an alpha value for one tail only, and, as this test is two-tailed, alpha is split from .05 to .025 to obtain the table t value: $t_{.025,25} = \pm 2.060$.

The calculated value of t is

$$t = \frac{(47.73 - 56.50) - 0}{\sqrt{\frac{(19.495)(14) + (18.273)(11)}{(15 + 12 - 2)}} \sqrt{\frac{1}{15} + \frac{1}{12}}} = -5.20.$$

Because the calculated value, $t = -5.20$ is less than the lower critical table value, $t = -2.06$, the calculated value of t falls in the rejection region. The null hypothesis is rejected. There *is* a significant difference in the mean scores of the two tests.

Figure 10.4 shows the critical areas, the calculated t value, and the decision for this example. Note that the computed t value is -5.20, which is enough to cause the managers of the Hernandez Manufacturing Company to reject the null hypothesis. Their conclusion is that there is a significant difference in the effectiveness of the training methods. Upon examining the sample means, they

Training Method A					Training Method B					
56	50	52	44	52	59	54	55	65		
47	47	53	45	48	52	57	64	53		
42	51	42	43	44	53	56	53	57		

TABLE 10.3

Test Scores for New Employees After Training

FIGURE 10.4

t Values for the Hernandez Manufacturing Company Example

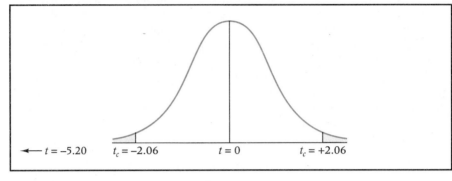

select Method B, because the average score for this group was more than eight points higher than that for the group trained with Method A.

Which group is group 1 and which is group 2 is an arbitrary decision. If the two samples had been designated in reverse, the calculated *t* value would have been $t = +5.20$ (same magnitude but different sign), and the decision would have been the same.

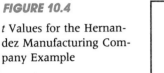

Demonstration Problem 10.3

According to a 1990 survey of work time in eight different countries, Soviet men have the dubious honor of working longer hours each week than men from Japan, the United States, Finland, Hungary, Norway, Denmark, and Sweden. Although Soviet men averaged fifty-four hours of work per week, Japanese men averaged fifty-two hours. Suppose that an analyst believes that this relationship has changed during the past two years and that Soviet men actually work shorter work weeks than Japanese men do. He randomly selects a small sample of working men from each country, resulting in the following data. The analyst uses $\alpha = .01$ to test the theory that Soviet men now work shorter weeks than Japanese men do. He assumes that work week hours are normally distributed and that the variances of the populations are approximately the same.

Soviet Men	Japanese Men
$\bar{X}_S = 49.3$ hr	$\bar{X}_J = 51.7$ hr
$S_S = 4.12$ hr	$S_J = 3.98$ hr
$n_S = 14$	$n_J = 15$

Solution:

Because the analyst is testing the theory that Soviet men may now work shorter weeks than Japanese men do and because previous research has indicated that the opposite is true, he postulates as an alternative hypothesis what he wants to prove: Soviet men work shorter weeks than Japanese men do. The null hypothesis is that the previous survey results are still true: Soviet men work more hours per week than Japanese men do. Thus

$$H_0: \; \mu_S - \mu_J \geq 0$$
$$H_a: \; \mu_S - \mu_J < 0$$

This test is one-tailed, with $\alpha = .01$. The degrees of freedom are $n_S + n_J - 2 = 14 + 15 - 2 = 27$. The table t value is $t_{.01,27} = -2.473$, and the calculated value of t is

$$t = \frac{(49.3 - 51.7) - 0}{\sqrt{\dfrac{4.12^2(13) + 3.98^2(14)}{14 + 15 - 2}} \sqrt{\dfrac{1}{14} + \dfrac{1}{15}}} = \frac{-2.4}{1.5} = -1.60.$$

The calculated value falls short of the critical t value and lies in the acceptance region. Therefore the analyst does not reject the null hypothesis. There is not enough evidence to declare that Soviet men, on average, work shorter weeks than Japanese men do. The following graph depicts the t values for this problem.

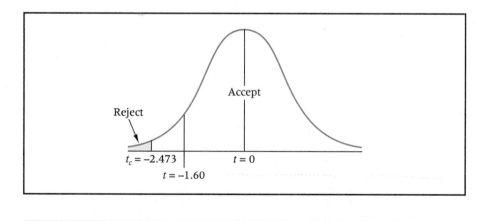

Confidence Intervals

Confidence interval formulas can be derived to estimate the difference in the population means for small samples when the population variances are unknown. The focus in this section is only on confidence intervals when approximately equal population variances and normally distributed populations can be assumed.

Confidence Interval to Estimate $\mu_1 - \mu_2$ with Small Sample Sizes Assuming That the Population Variances Are Unknown and Equal	$$(\bar{X}_1 - \bar{X}_2) \pm t \sqrt{\frac{S_1^2(n_1 - 1) + S_2^2(n_2 - 1)}{n_1 + n_2 - 2}} \sqrt{\frac{1}{n_1} + \frac{1}{n_2}}; \qquad (10.4)$$ $$df = n_1 + n_2 - 2.$$

A record company executive is interested in estimating the difference in the average play length of rock and roll singles and country and western singles. To do so she randomly selects ten country and western singles along with nine rock and roll singles. The play lengths (in minutes) of the selected singles are shown in Table 10.4. Calculate a 99% confidence interval to estimate the difference in population means for these two types of recordings. Assume that play-length times are normally distributed for both types of single records.

The table t value for a 99% level of confidence and 17 degrees of freedom is $t_{.005,17} = 2.898$. The confidence interval is

TABLE 10.4	*Country and Western*	*Rock and Roll*
Length of Single Records for Country and Western and Rock and Roll Records	3.80	3.88
	3.30	4.13
	3.43	4.11
	3.30	3.98
	3.03	3.98
	4.18	3.93
	3.18	3.92
	3.83	3.98
	3.22	4.67
	3.38	
	$n_{cw} = 10$	$n_{rr} = 9$
	$X_{cw} = 3.465$	$X_{rr} = 4.064$
	$S_{cw} = .3575$	$S_{rr} = .2417$
	$df = 10 + 9 - 2 = 17$	

$$(3.465 - 4.064) \pm 2.898 \sqrt{\frac{(0.3575)^2(9) + (0.2417)^2(8)}{10 + 9 - 2}} \sqrt{\frac{1}{10} + \frac{1}{9}};$$

$-0.599 \pm 0.411;$

$-1.010 \leq \mu_1 - \mu_2 \leq -0.188.$

The record company executive is 99% confident that the true difference in population average lengths of play lies between -1.01 minutes and -0.188 minutes. Zero does not lie in this interval, so she could conclude that there is a significant difference in the average length of single play time between country and western and rock and roll recordings. Examination of the sample results indicates that rock and roll single recordings are longer.

Demonstration Problem 10.4

A coffee manufacturer is interested in estimating the difference in the average daily coffee consumption of regular coffee drinkers and decaffeinated coffee drinkers. Its researcher randomly selects thirteen regular coffee drinkers and asks how many cups of coffee per day they drink. He randomly locates fifteen decaffeinated coffee drinkers and asks how many cups of coffee per day they drink. The average for the regular coffee drinkers is 4.35 cups, with a standard deviation of 1.20 cups. The average for the decaffeinated coffee drinkers is 6.84 cups, with a standard deviation of 1.42 cups. The researcher assumes, for each population, that the per day consumption is normally distributed, and he constructs a 95% confidence interval to estimate the difference in the averages of the two populations.

Solution:

The table t value for this problem is $t_{.025,26} = 2.056$. The confidence interval estimate is

$$(4.35 - 6.84) \pm 2.056 \sqrt{\frac{(1.20)^2(12) + (1.42)^2(14)}{13 + 15 - 2}} \sqrt{\frac{1}{13} + \frac{1}{15}};$$

$-2.49 \pm 1.03;$

$-3.52 \leq \mu_1 - \mu_2 \leq -1.46.$

The researcher is 95% confident that the difference in population average daily consumption of cups of coffee between regular and decaffeinated coffee drinkers is between 1.46 cups and 3.52 cups. The point estimate for the difference in population means is 2.49 cups, with an error of 1.03 cups.

10.18 Use the data given to test the following hypotheses:

$$H_0: \quad \mu_1 - \mu_2 \geq 0 \qquad H_a: \quad \mu_1 - \mu_2 < 0$$

Sample 1	Sample 2
$n_1 = 8$	$n_2 = 11$
$\overline{X}_1 = 24.56$	$\overline{X}_2 = 26.42$
$S_1^2 = 12.4$	$S_2^2 = 15.8$

Use a 1% level of significance, and assume that X is normally distributed.

10.19 Use the following data and $\alpha = .10$ to test the stated hypotheses. Assume that X is normally distributed in the populations and that the variances of the populations are approximately equal.

$$H_0: \quad \mu_1 - \mu_2 = 0 \qquad H_a: \quad \mu_1 - \mu_2 \neq 0$$

Sample 1	Sample 2
$n_1 = 20$	$n_2 = 20$
$\overline{X}_1 = 118$	$\overline{X}_2 = 113$
$S_1 = 23.9$	$S_2 = 21.6$

10.20 Suppose that for years the mean of population 1 has been accepted as the same as the mean of population 2 but that now population 1 is believed to have a greater mean than population 2. Letting $\alpha = .05$ and assuming that the populations have equal variances and that X is approximately normally distributed, use the following data to test this idea:

Sample 1		Sample 2	
43.6	45.7	40.1	36.4
44.0	49.1	42.2	42.3
45.2	45.6	43.1	38.8
40.8	46.5	37.5	43.3
48.3	45.0	41.0	40.2

10.21 Suppose that you want to determine whether the average values for populations 1 and 2 are different, and you randomly gather the following data.

Sample 1						Sample 2					
2	10	7	8	2	5	10	12	8	7	9	11
9	1	8	0	2	8	9	8	9	10	11	10
11	2	4	5	3	9	11	10	7	8	10	10

Test your conjecture, using a probability of committing a Type I error of .10. Assume that the population variances are the same and that X is normally distributed in the populations.

10.22 Using the sample data given, construct a 95% confidence interval to estimate the difference in the population means. Assume that the population variances are approximately equal and that X is normally distributed.

Sample 1			Sample 2		
109	105	111	112	108	113
98	99	102	107	114	99
101	110	107	106	110	103
105			112	104	108

10.23 Using the sample data shown, construct a 99% confidence interval to estimate the difference in the population means. Assume that the population variances are approximately equal and that X is normally distributed.

Sample 1		Sample 2	
1.29	2.33	1.09	1.18
1.00	1.87	1.56	1.03
2.03	2.45	1.93	1.65
2.05	1.96	1.34	1.60
1.31	1.27	1.07	1.02
2.31	2.08	1.07	

10.24 Using the sample data given, construct a 90% confidence interval to estimate the difference in the population means. Assume that the population variances are approximately equal and that X is normally distributed.

Sample 1	Sample 2
$n_1 = 17$	$n_2 = 14$
$\overline{X}_1 = 64.5$	$\overline{X}_2 = 57.8$
$S_1 = 12.4$	$S_2 = 11.9$

10.25 Using the sample data given, construct a 99% confidence interval to estimate the difference in the population means. Assume that the population variances are approximately equal and that X is normally distributed.

Sample 1	Sample 2
$n_1 = 25$	$n_2 = 28$
$\overline{X}_1 = 563$	$\overline{X}_2 = 674$
$S_1^2 = 99.3$	$S_2^2 = 103.6$

10.26 The 1980s housing price boom in the United States occurred mainly on the East and West Coasts. Housing prices in the Midwest remained relatively stable throughout this time period. Suppose that a realtor is interested in comparing the asking prices of midrange homes in Peoria, Illinois, and Evansville, Indiana. The realtor conducts a small telephone survey in the two cities, asking the prices of midrange homes. A random sample of twenty-one listings in Peoria resulted in a sample average price of $66,900, with a standard deviation of $2,300. A random sample of twenty-six listings in Evansville resulted in a sample average price of $64,000, with a standard deviation of $1,750. The realtor assumes that prices of midrange homes are normally distributed and that the variance of prices in the two cities is about the same. What would he obtain for a 90% confidence interval for the difference in mean prices of midrange homes between Peoria and Evansville?

10.27 Test whether there is any difference in the mean prices of midrange homes of the two cities in Problem 10.26 for $\alpha = .05$.

10.28 In 1977, the median age of all brides was 23; in 1987, it was 26. The mean ages for these brides is older, because the mean is influenced by extreme values: Women can marry until they die, but there is a minimum age when most marry. Suppose that you had a random sample of the ages of twenty-six brides who married in 1977. The average age for this group of brides was 23.65 years, with a standard deviation of

6.7 years. Suppose that you also had a random sample of the ages of nineteen brides who married in 1987. The sample age for brides in this group was 27.1 years, with a standard deviation of 5.4 years. Use these sample data to determine whether there is a significant difference in the mean ages of brides between 1977 and 1987. Assume that the ages of brides are normally distributed in each year, that the variances of the data for the two years are similar, and that the probability of committing a Type I error is .10.

10.29 Suppose that you are interested in estimating the difference in the average age of first-time grooms for 1987 and 1992. A random sample of seventeen men who married in 1987 are located, and the sample average age of the grooms was 25.7 years, with a variance of 22.2 years. A sample of twenty men who married in 1992 resulted in a sample mean age of 26.1 years, with a variance of 23.0 years. Construct a 98% confidence interval to estimate the difference in population means for these two years. Assume that age at the time of first marriage for grooms is normally distributed and that the population variances are approximately equal.

10.30 A study was made to compare the costs of supporting a family of four Americans for a year in different foreign cities. The lifestyle of living in the United States on an annual income of $75,000 was the standard against which living in foreign cities was compared. A comparable living standard in Toronto and Mexico City was attained for about $64,000. Suppose that an executive wants to determine whether there is any difference in the average annual cost of supporting her family of four in the manner to which they are accustomed between Toronto and Mexico City. She uses the following data, randomly gathered from eleven families in each city, and an alpha of .01 to test this difference. She assumes that the annual cost is normally distributed and that the population variances are equal. What does the executive find?

Toronto	Mexico City
$69,000	$65,000
64,500	64,000
67,500	66,000
64,500	64,900
66,700	62,000
68,000	60,500
65,000	62,500
69,000	63,000
71,000	64,500
68,500	63,500
67,500	62,400

10.31 Use the data in Problem 10.30 to construct a 95% confidence interval to estimate the difference in average costs between the two cities.

10.32 Advertising and sales promotion spending varies by company size. In an effort to determine whether very large companies spend significantly more than large companies, an account manager takes a survey. Suppose that he interviews representatives of nineteen companies with sales volumes of more than $1 billion and finds that the sample average annual advertising and sales promotion expenditure is $2.303 million. Suppose that he then interviews representatives of fifteen companies with sales volumes of $500 million to $1 billion dollars and finds that the sample average annual expenditure on advertising and sales promotion is $2.225 million. He assumes that the standard deviation of expenditures for advertising and sales promotion for both sizes of company is $0.350 million. He uses $\alpha = .05$ to determine whether the larger companies (>$1 billion) expend significantly more dollars, on average, than do the smaller companies. He further assumes that advertising and sales expenditures are normally distributed. What does he find?

10.33 What is the difference in the average amount of time that a high school student and an adult spend watching television per week? Suppose that you want to construct a 90% confidence interval to estimate this difference and have gathered the following data (in hours of viewing time):

High School Student				Adult			
11	15	9	22	6	8	12	7
15	17	11	8	10	9	6	9
12	16	13	17	7	3	11	9

Assume that the population variances are equal and that X is normally distributed. Estimate the difference in mean hours of television viewing time.

10.4   **SMALL SAMPLE STATISTICS FOR TWO RELATED SAMPLES**

Hypothesis Testing

In the preceding section, hypotheses were tested about the difference in two population means when the samples were *independent*. In this section, a method is presented to analyze **related samples** (also called dependent samples).

related samples

Some researchers refer to this test as the **matched-pairs test.** Others call it the *t test for related measures* or the *correlated t test.*

matched-pairs test

What are some types of situations in which the two samples being studied are related or dependent? Let's begin with the before-and-after study. Sometimes as an experimental control mechanism, the same person or object is measured both before and after a treatment. Certainly, the after measurement is *not* independent of the before measurement, because the measurements are taken on the same person or object in both cases. Table 10.5 presents a hypothetical study in which people were asked to rate the music of a rock band before and after one week of viewing a four-minute videocassette of the band twice a day. The before scores are one sample and the after scores are a second sample, but each pair of scores is related, because the two measurements apply to the same person. The before-and-after scores are not as likely to vary from each other as much as those scores gathered from independent samples, because individuals bring their biases about rock music to the study. These individual biases affect both the before-and-after scores in the same way, because each pair of scores is measured on the same person.

Other examples of related measures samples include studies in which twins, siblings, or spouses are matched and placed in two different groups. For example, a fashion merchandiser might be interested in comparing men's and women's perceptions of women's clothing. If the men and women selected for the study are spouses or siblings, a built-in relatedness to the measurements of the two groups in the study is likely. Their scores are more likely to be alike or related than those of randomly chosen independent groups of men and women because of similar backgrounds or tastes.

The researcher must determine whether the two samples being studied are related or independent. Use of the techniques in Section 10.3 to analyze related group data instead of the techniques in this section can result in a loss of power and an increase in Type II errors. The approach to analyzing two *related* samples is different from the techniques used to analyze independent samples. The matched-pairs test requires that the two samples be the same size and that the individual related scores are matched.

Individual	Before	After
1	32	39
2	11	15
3	21	35
4	17	13
5	30	41
6	38	39
7	14	22

TABLE 10.5

Rating of a Rock Band (on a scale from 0 to 50)

| *t* Formula to Test the Difference in Two Related Samples | $$t = \frac{\bar{d} - D}{\frac{S_d}{\sqrt{n}}};$$ $$df = n - 1;$$ | **(10.5)** |

where: n = number of pairs
d = sample difference in pairs
D = mean population difference
S_d = standard deviation of sample difference
$\bar{d}$ = mean sample difference

The t test for related measures uses the sample difference, d, between individual matched sample values as the basic measurement of analysis instead of individual sample values. Analysis of the d values effectively converts the problem from a two-sample problem to a single sample of differences, which is an adaptation of the single-sample means formula. This test utilizes the sample mean of differences, $\bar{d}$, and the standard deviation of differences, S_d. An assumption for this test in the analysis of small samples is that the data from the two populations are normally distributed. If this assumption is not true, a nonparametric alternative to this test should be used. Nonparametric techniques are presented in Chapter 12.

| Formulas for $\bar{d}$ and S_d | $$\bar{d} = \frac{\Sigma d}{n};$$ $$S_d = \sqrt{\frac{\Sigma(d - \bar{d})^2}{n - 1}} = \sqrt{\frac{\Sigma d^2 - \frac{(\Sigma d)^2}{n}}{n - 1}}.$$ |

Analyzing data by this method involves calculating a t value with Formula 10.5 and comparing it to a critical t value obtained from the table. The critical t value is obtained from the t distribution table in the usual way, except that, in the degrees of freedom $(n - 1)$, n is the number of matched pairs of scores.

Demonstration Problem 10.5

A drilling company executive is interested in determining whether there is a significant difference in U.S. oil-drilling activity from one year to the next. He has data for rig activity for September 1988 and

1989 gathered from seven states, as shown. These data are related, because the two samples (1988 and 1989) are taken from the same seven states.

State	September 1988	September 1989
Texas	297	295
Oklahoma	134	136
Louisiana	134	136
California	52	52
Kansas	40	38
Wyoming	57	51
New Mexico	31	28

Solution:

Because the test is to determine whether there is a significant difference between the two years and not the direction of change, the hypothesis is two-tailed. Assume that $\alpha = .01$.

$$H_0: \ D = 0$$
$$H_a: \ D \neq 0$$

Because $\alpha = .01$ and this test is two-tailed, $\alpha/2 = .005$ is used to obtain the table t value. With seven pairs of data, $n = 7$, df $= n - 1 = 6$. The table t value is $t_{.005,6} = \pm 3.707$. The calculated t value is obtained in the following manner.

State	1988	1989	d
Texas	297	295	2
Oklahoma	134	136	-2
Louisiana	134	136	-2
California	52	52	0
Kansas	40	38	2
Wyoming	57	51	6
New Mexico	31	28	3

$$\bar{d} = 1.286, \qquad S_d = 2.87, \qquad \text{and} \qquad n = 7.$$

$$\text{Calculated } t = \frac{1.286 - 0}{\dfrac{2.87}{\sqrt{7}}} = 1.19.$$

As the calculated t value is less than the critical table t value in the upper tail, it falls into the acceptance region. There is not enough evidence from the data to declare a significant difference in the average rig count between 1988 and 1989. The following graph depicts the rejection regions, the critical values of t, and the computed value of t for this problem.

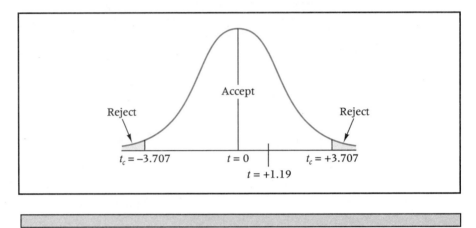

If Demonstration Problem 10.5 had been analyzed by the use of Formula 10.3 for independent samples, a calculated t value of only 0.025 would have been obtained. That analysis would have required solving for the sample means and variances as shown in Table 10.6.

The result ($t = 0.25$) obtained by using the t formula for two independent samples is far removed from the calculated value of $t = 1.19$ obtained using the t test for related measures. Thus recognizing related measures situations and analyzing them with the proper formula is imperative.

Demonstration Problem 10.6

Suppose that you want to conduct a study to compare the speed of typing on a word processor to that on an electric typewriter. You believe that word processing is faster than electric typewriting. In an

TABLE 10.6		1988 Rigs	1989 Rigs
Means and Variances of 1988 and 1989 Oil Rig Sample Data		$\overline{X}_1 = 106.43$ $S_1^2 = 8,890.95$	$\overline{X}_2 = 105.14$ $S_2^2 = 9,027.48$

effort to test this, you randomly select twelve secretaries who are familiar with an electric typewriter and who know a particular word processing system. Each secretary is given the same passage to type, types the passage on an electric typewriter, and then types the passage on a word processor. The typing speeds computed in words per minute are shown in the following table. Use a 1% level of significance to test to determine whether word processing is faster than electric typewriting.

Secretary	Word Processor	Electric Typewriter
1	62	51
2	49	43
3	70	55
4	65	62
5	49	51
6	96	78
7	66	62
8	63	49
9	69	65
10	88	78
11	59	54
12	41	38

Solution:

Because the group of secretaries being measured on electric typewriters is the same group that is being studied on word processors, this is a related groups study. The hypotheses are one-tailed:

$$H_0: \ D \leq 0$$
$$H_a: \ D > 0$$

What you want to "prove" is that word processing is faster than electric typewriters. Faster produces more words per minute, so you want the population difference to be positive. This result is the alternative hypothesis. The null hypothesis is that word processors are no faster than electric typewriters and may even be slower. The degrees of freedom are $n - 1 = 12 - 1 = 11$. For $\alpha = .01$, the table t value is $t_{.01,11} = 2.718$. The matched-pair differences are:

Secretary	Word Processor	Electric Typewriter	d
1	62	51	11
2	49	43	6
3	70	55	15
4	65	62	3
5	49	51	−2
6	96	78	18
7	66	62	4
8	63	49	14
9	69	65	4
10	88	78	10
11	59	54	5
12	41	38	3

$$\bar{d} = 7.583, \quad \text{and} \quad S_d = 5.961.$$

The calculated t value is

$$t = \frac{7.583 - 0}{\dfrac{5.961}{\sqrt{12}}} = 4.41.$$

With the calculated t value being greater than the critical table t value, you should reject the null hypothesis. There is enough evidence for you to conclude that the average difference in words per minute between word processing and electric typewriting is significantly greater than zero. Use of the word processor is significantly faster than use of the electric typewriter. The following graph depicts the calculated value, the rejection region, and the critical t value for this problem.

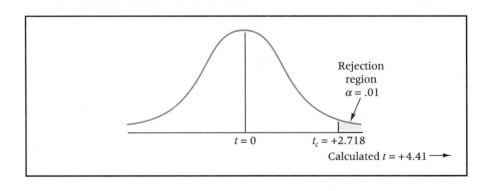

Confidence Intervals

Sometimes a researcher is interested in estimating the mean difference in two populations for related samples. A confidence interval for D, the mean population difference of two related samples, can be constructed by algebraically rearranging Formula 10.5, which was used to test hypotheses about D. Again the assumption is that, for small sample sizes, the population values are normally distributed.

(10.6)	$$\bar{d} \pm t\frac{S_d}{\sqrt{n}};$$ $$\bar{d} - t\frac{S_d}{\sqrt{n}} \le D \le \bar{d} + t\frac{S_d}{\sqrt{n}};$$ $$df = n - 1.$$	**Confidence Interval Formula to Estimate the Difference in Related Samples**

The following housing industry example demonstrates the application of Formula 10.6. The sale of new houses apparently fluctuates seasonally. Superimposed on the seasonality are economic and business cycles that also influence the sale of new houses. In certain parts of the country, new-house sales increase in the spring and early summer and drop off in the fall. Suppose that a national real estate association wants to estimate the average difference in the number of new-house sales per company in Indianapolis between 1990 and 1991. To do so, the association randomly selects eighteen real estate firms in the Indianapolis area and obtains their new-house sales figures for May 1990 and May 1991. The numbers of sales per company are shown in Table 10.7. Using these data, the association's analyst estimates the average difference in the number of sales per real estate company in Indianapolis for May 1990 and May 1991 and constructs a 99% confidence interval.

The number of pairs, n, is 18, and the degrees of freedom are 17. For a 99% level of confidence and these degrees of freedom, the table t value is $t_{.005,17} = 2.898$. The values for d, $\bar{d}$, and S_d are shown in Table 10.8.

The point estimate of the difference is $\bar{d} = -3.39$. The 99% confidence interval is

$$\bar{d} \pm t\frac{S_d}{\sqrt{n}};$$

$$-3.39 \pm 2.898\frac{3.27}{\sqrt{18}} = -3.39 \pm 2.23;$$

$$-5.62 \le D \le -1.16.$$

TABLE 10.7	Realtor	May 1990	May 1991
Number of New-House Sales in Indianapolis	1	8	11
	2	19	30
	3	5	6
	4	9	13
	5	3	5
	6	0	4
	7	13	15
	8	11	17
	9	9	12
	10	5	12
	11	8	6
	12	2	5
	13	11	10
	14	14	22
	15	7	8
	16	12	15
	17	6	12
	18	10	10

TABLE 10.8	Realtor	May 1990	May 1991	d
Differences in Number of New-House Sales, 1990–1991	1	8	11	-3
	2	19	30	-11
	3	5	6	-1
	4	9	13	-4
	5	3	5	-2
	6	0	4	-4
	7	13	15	-2
	8	11	17	-6
	9	9	12	-3
	10	5	12	-7
	11	8	6	$+2$
	12	2	5	-3
	13	11	10	$+1$
	14	14	22	-8
	15	7	8	-1
	16	12	15	-3
	17	6	12	-6
	18	10	10	0

$$\bar{d} = -3.39, \quad \text{and} \quad S_d = 3.27.$$

The analyst estimates with a 99% level of confidence that the average difference in new-house sales for a real estate company in Indianapolis between 1990 and 1991 is somewhere between -5.62 and -1.16 houses. Because 1991 sales were subtracted from 1990 sales, the minus signs indicate more sales in 1991 than in 1990. Note that both ends of the confidence interval contain negatives. This result means that the analyst can be 99% confident that zero difference is not the average difference. If the analyst were using this confidence interval to test the hypothesis that there is no signficant mean difference in average new-house sales per company in Indianapolis between May 1990 and May 1991, the null hypothesis would be rejected for $\alpha = .01$. The point estimate for this example is -3.39 houses, with an error of 2.23 houses.

> **Demonstration Problem 10.7**

Use the data presented at the beginning of this section to construct a 95% confidence interval to estimate the average difference between before-and-after scores with the music video treatment.

Solution:

With seven pairs of scores, df $= 6$. For a 95% confidence interval, the table t value is $t_{.025,6} = 2.447$. The data and the d values are:

Individual	Before	After	d
1	32	39	-7
2	11	15	-4
3	21	35	-14
4	17	13	$+4$
5	30	41	-11
6	38	39	-1
7	14	22	-8

$$\bar{d} = -5.86 \quad \text{and} \quad S_d = 6.09.$$

The 95% confidence interval for the data is

$$-5.86 \pm 2.447 \frac{6.09}{\sqrt{7}} = -5.86 \pm 5.63;$$

$$-11.49 \leq D \leq -0.23.$$

With 95% confidence, we estimate that the scores increased from before to after. The point estimate of the gain is 5.86 points, with an error of 5.63 points. The gain may have been as little as 0.23 point or as great as 11.49 points.

**PROBLEMS
Section 10.4**

10.34 Use the data given to test the following hypotheses. Assume that the data are normally distributed in the population.

H_0: $D = 0$ H_a: $D \neq 0$
$n = 14$, $\bar{d} = 5.334$, $S_d = 6.732$,   and $\alpha = .05$.

10.35 Use the data given to test the following hypotheses. Assume that the data are normally distributed in the population.

H_0: $D \geq 0$ H_a: $D < 0$
$n = 29$, $\bar{d} = -1.053$, $S_d = 7.621$,   and $\alpha = .10$.

10.36 Use the data given and a 1% level of significance to test the following hypotheses. Assume that the data are normally distributed in the population.

H_0: $D \leq 0$ H_a: $D > 0$

Pair	Sample 1	Sample 2
1	38	22
2	27	28
3	30	21
4	41	38
5	36	38
6	38	26
7	33	19
8	35	31
9	44	35

10.37 Use the data given to test the following hypotheses ($\alpha = .01$). Assume that the data are normally distributed in the population.

H_0: $D = 0$ H_a: $D \neq 0$

Individual	Before	After
1	107	102
2	99	98
3	110	100
4	113	108
5	96	89
6	98	101
7	100	99
8	102	102
9	107	105
10	109	110
11	104	102
12	99	96
13	101	100

10.38 Construct a 98% confidence interval to estimate D from the following sample information. Assume that the data are normally distributed in the population.

$$\bar{d} = 40.56, \quad S_d = 26.58, \quad \text{and} \quad n = 22.$$

10.39 Construct a 90% confidence interval to estimate D from the following sample information. Assume that the data are normally distributed in the population.

$$\bar{d} = -10.43, \quad S_d = 13.97, \quad \text{and} \quad n = 8.$$

10.40 Construct a 95% confidence interval to estimate D from the following sample information. Assume that the data are normally distributed in the population.

Client	Before	After
1	32	40
2	28	25
3	35	36
4	32	32
5	26	29
6	25	31
7	37	39
8	16	30
9	35	31

10.41 Construct an 80% confidence interval to estimate D from the following data. Assume that the data are normally distributed in the population.

Salesperson	1991	1992
Edwards	983	968
Jamieson	701	723
Gonzalez	1003	996
Green	678	721
Robertson	899	930
Miles	602	578
DeKalb	752	765

10.42 A company vice president has been concerned about the physical fitness of her employees. The rate of absenteeism because of illness has been increasing. In an attempt to combat the poor physical state of employees and in an effort to persuade employees that the company is interested in them, the vice president hired a part-time aerobics instructor to offer fitness classes at work. Participants were given a fitness test at the beginning of the program and tested on several measures. After three months of the program, the participants were retested. Times for the 1,500-m run are shown for five of the participants, both before and after the three-month program. Use a 1% level of significance to determine whether the times for the 1,500-m run are significantly faster after the three-month aerobic program. Assume that the times for the 1,500-m run are normally distributed.

Participant	Before	After
1	12.36	10.90
2	13.12	11.04
3	10.37	8.12
4	15.98	12.48
5	12.77	9.24

10.43 Eight people trying to get accepted by graduate schools of business have scored low on the GMAT. In an effort to raise their scores, they took an intensive forty-hour GMAT review course. After the course, the eight students took the GMAT again. The average difference for these eight students was a gain of 20 points. The standard deviation of the differences for them was 8.5 points. Assuming that the GMAT scores are normally distributed, use an alpha of .05 to determine whether the GMAT review course significantly increases GMAT scores.

10.44 During the fall of 1990, the U.S. economy seemed to slow. Some retailers claimed that consumers were spending less money on disposable goods. In an effort to ascertain if that were true, a research firm randomly identified twenty-five families. Interviewers asked the families to determine from check stubs and other records their disposable income for October 1990 and October 1989. The sample difference in disposable income for these two years was − $156. That is, in 1990 these families had less disposable income than in 1989. The variance for this sample difference was $1,916. Construct a 99% confidence interval to estimate the average difference for the population from which the twenty-five families were drawn. Interpret the interval. Assume that disposable income was normally distributed in the population for these years.

10.45 The vice president for marketing brought to the attention of sales managers that most of the company's manufacturer representatives contacted clients and maintained client relationships in a disorganized, haphazard manner. The sales managers brought the reps in for a three-day seminar and training session on how to use an *organizer* to schedule visits and recall pertinent information about each client more effectively. Sales reps were taught how to schedule visits most effectively in order to maximize their efforts. Sales managers were given data on the number of site visits by sales reps on a randomly selected day both before and after the seminar. Use the following data to test whether there were significantly more site visits after the seminar ($\alpha = .05$). Assume that the number of site visits are normally distributed.

Rep	Before	After
1	2	4
2	4	5
3	1	3
4	3	3
5	4	3
6	2	5
7	2	6
8	3	4
9	1	5

10.46 Eleven employees were put under the care of the company nurse because of high cholesterol readings. The nurse lectured them on the dangers of this condition and put them on a new diet. Shown are the cholesterol readings of the eleven employees both before the new diet and one month after use of the diet began. Construct a 98% confidence interval to estimate the population mean difference of cholesterol readings for people who are involved in this program. Assume that cholesterol readings are normally distributed in the population.

Employee	Before	After
1	255	197
2	230	225
3	290	215
4	242	215
5	300	240
6	250	235
7	215	190
8	230	240
9	225	200
10	219	203
11	236	223

10.47 A nationally known supermarket has decided to promote its own brand of soft drinks on TV for two weeks. Before the ad campaign, the company randomly selected twenty-one of its stores around the United States to be part of a study to measure the campaign's effectiveness. During a specified half-hour period on a certain Monday morning, all the stores in the sample were to count the number of cans of its own brand of soft drink sold. After the campaign, a similar count was made. The average difference was an increase of seventy-five cans, with a standard deviation of difference of thirty cans. Using this information, construct a 90% confidence interval to estimate the population average difference in soft drink can sales for this company's brand before and after the ad campaign. Assume that soft drink can sales for the company's brand are normally distributed in the population.

10.48 Most consumers who purchase washing machines are aware of the color options, such as white, almond, and light green, and that any color besides white usually costs a few dollars extra. Suppose that you want to estimate the average difference between the selling prices of white washing machines and color washing machines. You randomly select several brands and appliance retailers from across the United States and obtain the following prices for washing machines. Use this information to construct a 95% confidence interval for the average difference in price of a white washing machine and a washing machine of another color. Interpret the interval. Assume that the prices for white and color washing machines are normally distributed in the population.

Brand	White	Color
A	$450	$465
B	575	600
C	500	500
D	615	630
E	550	565
F	485	510

10.49 Is there a significant difference in the gasoline mileage of a car for regular unleaded and premium unleaded? To test this question, a researcher randomly selected fifteen drivers for a study. They were to drive their cars for one month on regular unleaded and for one month on premium unleaded gasoline. The participants drove their own cars for this experiment. The average sample difference was 2.85 miles in favor of the premium unleaded, and the sample standard deviation of difference was 1.9 miles. For $\alpha = .01$, is this enough evidence for the researcher to conclude that there is a significant difference in the car mileage between regular unleaded and premium unleaded gasoline? Assume that gasoline mileage figures are normally distributed in the population.

HYPOTHESIS TESTS ABOUT MORE THAN TWO MEANS: ONE-WAY ANALYSIS OF VARIANCE | 10.5

Thus far hypotheses have been tested about a single mean by taking a random sample from the population and about the difference of two means by taking two samples and testing the sample means. What happens when a researcher wants to test the difference in the means of three or more groups? This section presents a technique that can be used to analyze data from three or more groups.

For example, a company that owns several thousand convenience stores across the United States is interested in determining where to locate bread in the store to optimize bread sales. In terms of the total number of loaves sold per day does location really make any difference? To study this question, the company's market analyst randomly selects nineteen stores from across the United States. She randomly assigns bread to one of four locations in the store:

1. in the front of the store near the door
2. beside the checkout counter
3. in the middle of the food section
4. beside the freezer near the milk

She asks the store managers to count the number of loaves of bread sold during a designated time period on a particular day. Table 10.9 contains the data from each store. Is there a difference in the average number of loaves of bread sold according to where the bread is located in the store?

Is it possible to analyze these four samples by using a t test for the difference in two sample means? These four samples would require $_4C_2 = 6$ individual t tests to accomplish the analysis of two groups at a time. Recall that, if $\alpha = .05$ for a particular test, there is a 5% chance of rejecting a true null hypothesis. If enough tests are done, eventually one or more null hypotheses will be falsely rejected by chance. Thus the $\alpha = .05$ is valid only for one t test. In this problem, with six t tests, the error rate compounds, so that when the analyst is finished with the problem, there is a much greater than .05 chance of committing a Type I error. Fortunately, a technique has been developed which analyzes all the sample means at one time and thus precludes the build-up of error rate.

analysis of variance (ANOVA) This technique is called **analysis of variance (ANOVA).**

completely random- ized design *One-way* ANOVA is used to analyze a particular type of experimental design called the **completely randomized design.** A completely randomized design contains only one variable that is being manipulated or controlled. This variable

independent variable is called an **independent variable** and is sometimes referred to as the *treatment* or *factor.* In the bread location example the independent variable or treatment is the location of bread in the store. Within this independent variable are multiple treatment levels.

TABLE 10.9

Number of Loaves of Bread Sold at Four Store Locations

1	2	3	4
5	2	8	3
7	3	4	5
4	5	6	3
2	4	7	4
	6	9	2
		8	

The **treatment levels** for this example are the four specific locations of the bread being studied. Some of this nomenclature comes from psychological research where, for example, an independent variable or treatment might be an injection of a particular drug. The levels of treatment would be the various dosages studied. The completely randomized design is one of the simplest of the experimental designs. Many other experimental designs also are analyzed by ANOVA, but they are beyond the scope of this text.

One-Way Analysis of Variance

The hypotheses tested in a one-way ANOVA are

H_0: $\mu_1 = \mu_2 = \mu_3 = \ldots = \mu_j$
H_a: At least one of the means is different from
     the others

The null hypothesis states that the population means for all treatment levels are the same. The way the alternative hypothesis is stated, if even one of the population means is different from the others, the null hypothesis is rejected.

Testing these hypotheses by using one-way ANOVA is accomplished by breaking the total variance of the data into two variances: (1) the variance resulting from the treatment and (2) the error variance, or that portion of the total variance unexplained by the treatment. As part of this process, the total sum of squares of deviation of values around the mean can be divided into two additive and independent parts. That is,

Total sum of squares = Error sum of squares + Treatment sum of squares

$$\sum_1^k \sum_1^n (X_{ij} - \overline{X}_{..})^2 = \sum_1^k \sum_1^n (X_{ij} - \overline{X}_{.j})^2 + \sum_1^k n_j (\overline{X}_{.j} - \overline{X}_{..})^2$$

where: n = number of rows
     k = number of columns
     n_j = number of values in a given column
     $\overline{X}_{..}$ = grand mean
     $\overline{X}_{.j}$ = mean of a column
     X_{ij} = individual value

The formulas to accomplish one-way analysis of variance are developed from this relationship. The double summation sign indicates that the values are summed across the row and then down the columns. Simplified versions of this formula are presented later in the section. Basically, ANOVA compares

FIGURE 10.5

Locations of Values from
the Four Treatment
Groups

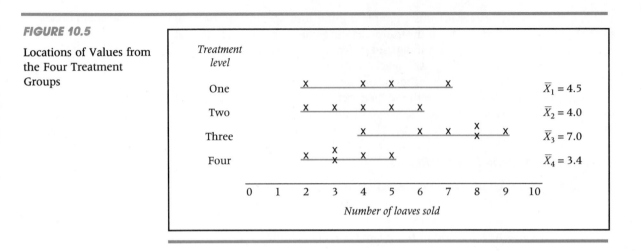

the relative sizes of the variation *between* treatments to the *error* variation. If
there is a significant difference in treatments, the *treatment* variation should be
large relative to the *error* variation.

Figure 10.5 displays the data from the bread location problem in terms of
treatment level. Note the variation of values (**x**) *within* each treatment level.
Now examine the variation *between* levels one through four (the difference in
the location of the line segment). In particular, note that treatment level three
values seem to be located differently from the other three levels. This difference
also is underscored by the mean values for each treatment level: $\overline{X}_1 = 4.5$;
$\overline{X}_2 = 4.0$; $\overline{X}_3 = 7.0$; and $\overline{X}_4 = 3.4$. Analysis of variance is used to determine
statistically whether the variance between the treatment level means is greater
than the variances within levels.

Several important assumptions underlie analysis of variance.*

1. Observations are drawn from normally distributed populations.
2. Observations represent random samples from the populations.
3. Variances of the populations are equal.

The three variances identified—total variance, treatment variance, and
error variance—are used to compute an ANOVA. The following formulas are
used to compute a one-way analysis of variance. The term SS represents sum
of squares, and the term MS represents mean square.

*Kirk, Roger, *Experimental Design: Procedures for the Behavioral Sciences* (Belmont, Calif.: Brooks/
Cole, 1968).

$$SS_{treat} = \sum_{j=1}^{k} \frac{T_j^2}{n_j} - \frac{T^2}{N};$$

$$SS_{error} = \sum_{j=1}^{k}\sum_{i=1}^{n} x_{ij}^2 - \sum_{j=1}^{k} \frac{T_j^2}{n_j};$$

$$SS_{total} = \sum_{j=1}^{k}\sum_{i=1}^{n} x_{ij}^2 - \frac{T^2}{N};$$

$$MS_{treat} = \frac{SS_{treat}}{df_{treat}};$$

Formulas to Compute a One-Way ANOVA

where: T_j is the total for each column

T is the grand total of all values

$\sum_{j=1}^{k}\sum_{i=1}^{n} x_{ij}^2$ is each individual value squared and then summed

$$MS_{error} = \frac{SS_{error}}{df_{error}};$$

$$F = \frac{MS_{treat}}{MS_{error}};$$

where: $df_{treat} = n_j - 1$

nj = number of columns

$df_{error} = N - n_j$

$df_{total} = N - 1$

An F value is the ratio of two variances. In analysis of variance, the F value is determined by dividing the treatment variance ($MS_{treatment}$) by the error variance (MS_{error}). MS stands for Mean Square and is computed by dividing the sum of squares of deviation (SS) by the degrees of freedom (df). Performing these calculations for the bread location example yields:

1	2	3	4
5	2	8	3
7	3	4	5
4	5	6	3
2	4	7	4
	6	9	2
		8	

T_j: $T_1 = 18$, $T_2 = 20$, $T_3 = 42$, $T_4 = 17$,   and $T = 97$.

n_j: $n_1 = 4$, $n_2 = 5$, $n_3 = 6$, $n_4 = 5$,   and $N = 20$.

$$\sum_{j=1}^{k}\sum_{i=1}^{n} x_{ij}^2 = 5^2 + 7^2 + 4^2 + 2^2 + 2^2 + 3^2 + 5^2 + 4^2 + 6^2 + 8^2 + 4^2$$

$$+ 6^2 + 7^2 + 9^2 + 8^2 + 3^2 + 5^2 + 3^2 + 4^2 + 2^2 = 557.$$

$$SS_{treat} = \sum_{j=1}^{k}\frac{T_j^2}{n_j} - \frac{T^2}{N} = \left(\frac{18^2}{4} + \frac{20^2}{5} + \frac{42^2}{6} + \frac{17^2}{5}\right) - \frac{97^2}{20}$$

$$= 512.80 - 470.45 = 42.35;$$

$$SS_{error} = \sum_{j=1}^{k}\sum_{i=1}^{n} x_{ij}^2 - \sum_{j=1}^{k}\frac{T_j}{n_j} = 557 - 512.80 = 44.2;$$

$$SS_{total} = \sum_{j=1}^{k}\sum_{i=1}^{n} x_{ij}^2 - \frac{T^2}{N} = 557 - 470.45 = 86.55;$$

$$df_{treat} = n_j - 1 = 4 - 1 = 3;$$
$$df_{error} = N - n_j = 20 - 4 = 16;$$
$$df_{total} = N - 1 = 20 - 1 = 19;$$

$$MS_{treat} = \frac{SS_{treat}}{df_{treat}} = \frac{42.35}{3} = 14.12;$$

$$MS_{error} = \frac{SS_{error}}{df_{error}} = \frac{44.20}{16} = 2.76;$$

$$F = \frac{MS_{treat}}{MS_{error}} = \frac{14.12}{2.76} = 5.12.$$

From these computations, an analysis of variance chart can be constructed, as shown in Table 10.10. The calculated F value is 5.12. It is compared to a critical table F value to determine whether there is a significant difference in treatments.

Reading the F Distribution Table

F distribution

The **F distribution** is located in Table A.7. Every table value of F is determined from two unique df values: degrees of freedom in the numerator (df_{num}) and degrees of freedom in the denominator (df_{denom}). In order to look up a value in the F distribution table, the researcher must know both degrees of freedom. There are many F distributions, but only two F distributions are included in Table A.7: one for $\alpha = .01$ and one for $\alpha = .05$. Thus, for hypothesis testing

	Source of Variance	SS	df	MS	F
TABLE 10.10					
Analysis of Variance for Bread Location Problem	Treatment	42.35	3	14.12	5.12
	Error	44.20	16	2.76	
	Total	86.55	19		

				Numerator Degrees of Freedom					
		1	*2*	*3*	*4*	*5*	*6*	*7*	*8*	*9*

TABLE 10.11

An Abbreviated *F* Table for α = .05

		1	*2*	*3*	*4*	*5*	*6*	*7*	*8*	*9*
Denominator Degrees of Freedom	· · ·									
	15	4.54	3.68	3.29	3.06	2.90	2.79	2.71	2.64	2.59
	16	4.49	3.63	3.24	3.01	2.85	2.74	2.66	2.59	2.54
	17	4.45	3.59	3.20	2.96	2.81	2.70	2.61	2.55	2.49

with the *F* distribution in this text, only the 5% and 1% levels of significance can be used. However, statistical computer software packages for computing ANOVAs, usually give a probability for the *F* value, which allows a hypothesis testing decision for any alpha, based on the probability method.

In the one-way ANOVA, the df_{num} are the treatment degrees of freedom, $n_j - 1$. The df_{denom} are the error degrees of freedom, $N - n_j$. Table 10.11 contains an abbreviated *F* distribution table for α = .05. For the bread location example, df_{num} = 3 and the df_{denom} = 16. The $F_{.05,3,16}$ from Table 10.11 is 3.24. This value is the critical value of the *F* test. If a calculated *F* value is larger than this critical value, the null hypothesis is rejected. In the case of the bread location example, the calculated *F* value of 5.11 is larger than the table *F* value of 3.24, so the null hypothesis is rejected. All means are not equal, so there is a significant difference in the mean number of loaves sold in various locations within the stores. Figure 10.6 presents a graph of an *F* distribution, showing the critical *F* value for this example and the rejection region. Note that the *F* distribution begins at zero and contains no negative values. The reason is that an *F* value is the ratio of two variances, and variances are always positive.

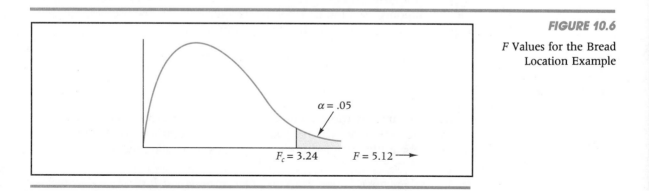

FIGURE 10.6

F Values for the Bread Location Example

Comparison of *F* and *t* Values

Analysis of variance can be used to test hypotheses about the difference in two means. Analysis of data from two samples by both a *t* test and an ANOVA shows that the calculated *F* value equals the calculated *t* value squared:

$$F = t^2, \qquad \text{for df}_{\text{num}} = 1.$$

The *t* test of independent samples actually is a special case of one-way ANOVA when there are only two treatment levels (df$_{\text{num}}$ = 1). The *t* test is computationally simpler than ANOVA for two groups. However, some statistical computer software packages do not contain a *t* test. In these cases, the researcher can perform a one-way ANOVA and then either take the square root of the *F* value to obtain the value of *t* or use the generated probability with the probability method to reach conclusions.

Multiple Comparisons

multiple comparisons

If the null hypothesis is rejected in a one-way ANOVA, at least one of the population means does not equal the others. Another way of stating that is to say that there is an *overall* significant difference. If a significant *F* value is obtained, **multiple comparisons** can be conducted to determine which means, if any, are significantly different from the others. The variety of multiple comparison tests available include the following.*

> Dunn's multiple comparison procedure
> Fisher's least significant difference test
> Tukey's honestly significant difference test
> Scheffe's S method
> Newman–Keuls test
> Duncan's new multiple range test

These tests differ in the way they analyze the means and the manner in which they control error. Tukey's HSD test and Scheffe's S method seem to be the more commonly used multiple comparison techniques. The use of these techniques, however, is beyond the scope of this text.

Demonstration Problem 10.8

A company has three manufacturing plants, and company officials want to determine whether there is a difference in the average age of workers at the three locations. The following data are the ages of five

---

*Kirk, Roger, *Experimental Design: Procedures for the Behavioral Sciences* (Belmont, Calif: Brooks/ Cole, 1968).

randomly selected workers at each plant. Perform a one-way ANOVA to determine whether there is a significant different in the mean ages of the workers at the three plants. Use $\alpha = .01$ and note that the sample sizes are equal.

Employee Age (Treatment Level)		
1	*2*	*3*
29	32	25
27	33	24
30	31	24
27	34	25
28	30	26

T_j: $T_1 = 141$, $T_2 = 160$, $T_3 = 124$,   and $T = 425$.

n_j: $n_1 = 5$, $n_2 = 5$, $n_3 = 5$,   and $N = 15$.

$\sum\sum x_{ij}^2 = 12{,}191$.

$$SS_{treat} = \left(\frac{141^2}{5} + \frac{160^2}{5} + \frac{124^2}{5} \right) - \frac{425^2}{15}$$

$$= 12{,}171.40 - 12{,}041.67 = 129.73;$$

$SS_{error} = 12{,}191 - 12{,}171.40 = 19.60;$

$SS_{total} = 12{,}191 - 12{,}041.67 = 149.33.$

$df_{treat} = 3 - 1 = 2;$

$df_{error} = 15 - 3 = 12;$

$df_{total} = 15 - 1 = 14.$

Source of Variance	*SS*	*df*	*MS*	*F*
Treatment	129.73	2	64.865	39.72
Error	19.60	12	1.633	
Total	149.33	14		

The table F value is $F_{.01,2,12} = 6.93$. The decision is to reject the null hypothesis because the calculated F value of 39.72 is greater than the critical table F value of 6.93. There is a significant difference in the mean ages of workers at the three plants.

The following chart displays the dispersion of the ages of workers from the three samples, along with the mean age for each plant sample. Note the difference in group means. The significant *F* value says that the difference *between* the mean ages is relatively greater than the differences of ages *within* each group.

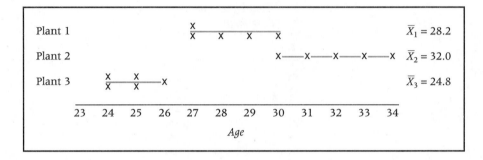

**PROBLEMS
Section 10.5**

10.50 Compute a one-way ANOVA on the following data:

1	2	3
2	5	3
1	3	4
3	6	5
3	4	5
2	5	3
1		5

Determine the computed *F* value. Compare the *F* value with the critical table *F* value and decide whether to reject the null hypothesis. Use $\alpha = .05$.

10.51 Compute a one-way ANOVA on the following data:

1	2	3	4	5
14	10	11	16	14
13	9	12	17	12
10	12	13	14	13
	9	12	16	13
	10		17	12
				14

Determine the computed F value. Compare that F value with the critical table F value and decide whether to reject the null hypothesis. Use $\alpha = .01$.

Compute a one-way ANOVA on the following data:

1	2	3	4
113	120	132	122
121	127	130	118
117	125	129	125
110	129	135	125

Determine the computed F value. Compare it to the critical F value and decide whether to reject the null hypothesis. Use a 1% level of significance.

Compute a one-way ANOVA on the following data:

1	2
27	22
31	27
31	25
29	23
30	26
27	27
28	23

Determine the computed F value. Compare it to the critical table F value and decide whether to reject the null hypothesis. Do a t test for independent measures on the data. Compare the t and F values. Are the results different? Use $\alpha = .05$.

10.54 Suppose that you are using a completely randomized design to study some phenomenon. There are one treatment, five treatment levels, and fifty-four total people in the study. Complete the following ANOVA table:

Source of Variance	SS	df	MS	F
Treatment	583.39			
Error	972.18			
Total	1555.57			

10.55 Suppose that you are using a completely randomized design to study some phenomenon. There are one treatment, three treatment levels, and seventeen total people in the study. Complete the following ANOVA table. Use $\alpha = .05$ to find the table F value and test the null hypothesis using the data.

Source of Variance	SS	df	MS	F
Treatment	29.64			
Error	68.42			
Total				

10.56 A milk company has four machines that fill gallon jugs with milk. The quality control manager is interested in determining whether the average fill for these machines is the same. The following data represent random samples of fill measures (in quarts) for nineteen jugs of milk filled by the different machines. Use $\alpha = .01$ to test the hypotheses.

Machine 1	Machine 2	Machine 3	Machine 4
4.05	3.99	3.97	4.00
4.01	4.02	3.98	4.02
4.02	4.01	3.97	3.99
4.04	3.99	3.95	4.01
	4.00	4.00	
	4.00		

10.57 That the starting salaries of new accounting graduates would differ according to geographic regions of the United States seems logical. A random selection of accounting firms is taken from three geographic regions, and each is asked to state the starting salary for a new accounting graduate who is going to work in auditing. The data obtained are shown. Use a one-way ANOVA to analyze these data. Note that the data can be restated if you desire to make the computations more reasonable (example: $32,500 = 3.25). Use a 1% level of significance.

South	Northeast	West
$28,000	$38,500	$33,000
29,000	37,000	31,000
27,500	36,500	32,500
28,500	35,500	34,000
29,000	37,000	33,500
30,500		

10.58 A management consulting company presents a three-day seminar on project management to various clients. The seminar is basically the same each time it is given. However, sometimes it is presented to high-level management, sometimes to mid-level management, and sometimes to low-level management. The seminar facilitators believe that evaluations of the seminar may vary with the audience. Suppose that the following data are some randomly selected evaluation scores from different levels of management after they have attended the seminar. The ratings are on a scale from 1 to 10, with 10 being the highest. Use a one-way ANOVA to determine whether there is a significant difference in the evaluations according to management level. Assume that $\alpha = .05$.

High Level	Mid Level	Low Level
7	8	5
7	9	6
8	8	5
7	10	7
9	9	4
	10	8
	8	

10.59 Family transportation costs are usually higher than most people believe, because they include car payments, insurance, fuel cost, repairs, parking, and public transportation. Twenty-two randomly selected families from four major cities are asked to use their records to estimate a monthly figure for transportation. Use the data obtained and ANOVA to test whether there is a significant difference in monthly transportation costs for families living in these cities. Assume that $\alpha = .05$.

Atlanta	New York	Los Angeles	Chicago
$650	$250	$850	$540
480	525	700	450
550	300	950	675
600	175	780	550
675	500	600	600
710		900	

CHAPTER SUMMARY

A small sample is one that contains less than thirty values. One of the problems unique to small samples is that the central limit theorem does not apply when the population is not normally distributed; thus there is no guarantee that the sample statistic is normally distributed. This particular problem can be overcome by assuming that all small samples selected for analyses come from a normally distributed population. If a population is normally distributed, the distribution of the sample statistic also will be normal if the standard deviation of the population is known.

A second problem arises in using small samples. If the standard deviation of the population is unknown and the sample standard deviation is used in formulas to estimate it, the resulting computed Z values are not normally distributed. The distributions are flatter and less normal as sample size gets smaller. William S. Gosset discovered this phenomenon and developed a series of t tests that can handle these situations if the population is normally distributed.

This chapter presented three types of t tests: (1) a t test for a single population mean; (2) a t test for two population means where the samples are independent; and (3) a t test for two dependent or related samples. Because the t distribution changes for each sample size, the t table in the Appendix actually is a series of t distributions. Values in the t table are obtained using degrees of freedom. Each of the three t tests presented has its own formula for degrees of freedom.

The t test for single population means is similar to the Z test for single population means, except that the standard deviation of the sample is used and the sample size is small. The calculated t value formula for a single mean is the same as a calculated Z value for the same problem. However, the table t value is different, and so the hypothesis decision for the t test might be different from that reached by a similar Z test. The t test is based on the assumption that the population is normally distributed.

The t test for two population means with independent samples is similar to the Z test. The t test for two means is based on the assumption that the population variances are equal and uses a pooled estimate of the standard deviation computed from a weighted average of the two sample variances. This test also is based on the assumption that both populations are normally distributed.

The t test for the mean difference in two populations is used whenever two related samples are being studied in the analysis. Such is the case when the data are generated from twins, siblings, spouses, or matched objects. It can also manifest itself in situations when the same individual or object is being measured on two different treatments or in before and after designs. The t test for related measures is often more powerful than the t test for population means (independent samples) when applied to related measures problems. It also is based on the assumption of normally distributed populations.

A one-way analysis of variance (ANOVA) can be used to test hypotheses about three or more means. One-way analysis of variance is used to analyze data from a completely randomized design. A completely randomized design has one independent variable or treatment with multiple levels. Analysis of variance produces an F value. Critical F values are presented in Table A.7 for the α value and two measures of degrees of freedom ($\mathrm{df_{num}}$ and $\mathrm{df_{denom}}$). One-way ANOVA F values are the same as a two-tailed t test value for differences of means for independent groups when there are only two samples. In this case F equals t^2.

Key Words

t distribution	Independent variable
Degrees of freedom (df)	Treatment levels
Independent samples	Total variance
Related samples	Treatment variance
Matched-pairs test	Error variance
Analysis of variance (ANOVA)	F distribution
Completely randomized design	Multiple comparisons

USING THE COMPUTER

Minitab contains all the commands necessary to enable you to work the types of problems presented in Chapter 10. The main commands are: **TTEST**, **TINTERVAL**, **TWOSAMPLE**, and **AOVONEWAY**. You use the **TTEST** command to test hypotheses about a single mean and to test hypotheses for related samples. You use **TINTERVAL** to compute confidence intervals for single sample means when the population variance is unknown. You use the **TWO-SAMPLE** command to analyze hypotheses and construct confidence intervals about two population means with independent samples. You use **AOVONE-WAY** to compute one-way analysis of variance tests.

Single Sample Mean

The **TTEST** command analyzes hypotheses about a single sample mean when you do not know the standard deviation of the population. Begin the process by loading the sample data into a column. Usually, the **SET** command is preferred over the **READ** command for this step. Next, use the command **TTEST** to analyze the data that you have loaded. The **TTEST** command requires a hypothesized mean value and the name of the column location of the data. For example, if you are testing to determine whether a sample of students have an average IQ of 100 and have loaded the sample IQs into column 4, the command is

MTB > TTEST 100 C4

You use the subcommand, **ALTERNATIVE**, to specify whether the test is to be a one-tailed or two-tailed test. The following options for this subcommand are available:

SUBC > ALTERNATIVE 0. (gives you a two-tailed test)
SUBC > ALTERNATIVE +1. (one-tailed test—upper tail)
SUBC > ALTERNATIVE −1. (one-tailed test—lower tail)

Minitab will default to the two-tailed option if you do not specify an **ALTERNATIVE**. In order to use this or any subcommand, end the previous Minitab command with a semicolon (**MTB** > **TTEST 100 C4;**). Minitab will continue to produce subcommand prompts until you end the subcommand with a period. Thus ending the subcommand **ALTERNATIVE** with a period (**SUBC** > **ALTERNATIVE 0.**) is advisable.

You can analyze the IQ example in Minitab using a two-tailed test by the following commands:

```
MTB > SET C4
DATA> ------
DATA> ------
DATA> end
MTB > TTEST 100 C4;
SUBC > ALTERNATIVE 0.
```

Minitab automatically prints out these results. They include the sample size, the mean, the standard deviation of the data, the standard error of the mean, the calculated t value, and the probability of that t value occurring by chance if the null hypothesis is true. The following is the Minitab analysis of the data in Table 10.2.

```
MTB > SET C1
DATA> 22.6 22.2 23.2 27.4 24.5
DATA> 27 26.6 28.1 26.9 24.9
DATA> 26.2 25.3 23.1 24.2 26.1
DATA> 25.8 30.4 28.6 23.5 23.6
DATA> END
MTB > TTEST 25 C1;
SUBC > ALTERNATIVE 0.
```

TEST OF MU = 25.000 VS MU N.E. 25.000

	N	MEAN	STDEV	SE MEAN	T	P VALUE
C1	20	25.510	2.193	0.490	1.04	0.31

You use the **TINTERVAL** command to construct confidence intervals for the population mean when you do not know the population standard deviation. Follow the **TINTERVAL** command by entering the desired level of confidence and the column location of the data. For example, if you want to construct a 90% confidence interval for the population mean using data in column 12, the command is

MTB > TINTERVAL 90% C12

The percent sign is optional. If you do not specify a confidence level, Minitab defaults to 95%. Suppose that you want to calculate a 90% confidence interval for the Section 10.2 aerospace manager comp time example data. The Minitab commands are

```
MTB > SET C1
DATA> 6 21 17 20 7 0 8 16 29 3 8 12 11 9 21 25 15 16
DATA> END
MTB > TINTERVAL 90 C1
```

The Minitab output is

```
        N   MEAN   STDEV   SE MEAN    90.0 PERCENT C.I.
C1     18   13.56   7.80     1.84    ( 10.36,   16.75)
```

Two Independent Sample Means

You use the **TWOSAMPLE** command to analyze hypotheses about two independent sample means. It is based on the assumption that the population standard deviations are unknown and must be estimated by using the sample values. The command uses a pooled estimate of the population standard deviation similar to that in Formula 10.3. Begin the process by loading each of the two sample data into separate columns. Next, use the **TWOSAMPLE** command. This command requires only the two columns in which the data are located. For example, if the data from the two samples are located in columns three and four, the command is

```
MTB > TWOSAMPLE C3 C4
```

With the **TWOSAMPLE** command, you have the option of using the *t* test with the pooled variance, which is based on the assumption that the population variances are equal. This version of **TWOSAMPLE** requires the subcommand, **POOLED**, and is equivalent to Formula 10.3. As usual, to access the subcommand prompt, end the Minitab command with a semicolon. If you want to use additional subcommands, such as **ALTERNATIVE** after POOLED, end the POOLED command with a semicolon. When you are through using subcommands, end the last one with a period, which returns you to the Minitab prompt. If you use the **TWOSAMPLE** command without the POOLED subcommand, Minitab uses a formula equivalent to the formula presented in Appendix D for unequal population variances.

The subcommand, **ALTERNATIVE**, allows you to specify a one-tailed or two-tailed test with the same options as those described for the **TTEST** command. Minitab automatically prints out the sample sizes, the means, the standard deviations, the standard errors of the mean, a calculated t value, the probability of that t value occurring by chance (probability method), and the confidence interval. The following is a Minitab analysis of the example used in Section 10.3 comparing the scores of new employees for two different training methods.

Commands

```
MTB > SET C2
DATA> 56 50 52 44 52 47 47 53 45 48 42 51 42 43 44
DATA> END
MTB > SET C3
DATA> 59 54 55 65 52 57 64 53 53 56 53 57
DATA> END
MTB > TWOSAMPLE C2 C3;
SUBC > POOLED;
SUBC > ALTERNATIVE 0.


TWOSAMPLE T FOR C2 VS C3
      N   MEAN  STDEV  SE MEAN
C2   15   47.73  4.42     1.1
C3   12   56.50  4.27     1.2


95 PCT CI FOR MU C1 - MU C2: (-12.2, -5.3)
TTEST MU C1 = MU C2 (VS NE):T= -5.20 P=0.0000 DF=25
```

You construct confidence intervals to estimate the difference in the means of two populations when the variances are unknown with the same **TWOSAMPLE** command. Note in the preceding example that a confidence interval was part of the output. With the command, **TWOSAMPLE**, a confidence interval is always given automatically in the output. As the focus was not on confidence intervals in the example, no confidence level was specified, and Minitab defaulted to a 95% level. Suppose that you want to use Minitab to construct a 99% confidence interval for the example in Section 10.3 for estimating the difference between the mean lengths of country and western single records and rock and roll single records. The commands are

```
MTB > SET C1
DATA> 3.80 3.30 3.43 3.30 3.03 4.18 3.18 3.83 3.22 3.38
DATA> END
MTB > SET C2
DATA> 3.88 4.13 4.11 3.98 3.98 3.93 3.92 3.98 4.67
DATA> END
MTB > TWOSAMPLE 99% C1 C2;
SUBC > POOLED.
```

The output is

```
TWOSAMPLE T FOR C1 VS C2
      N   MEAN   STDEV   SE MEAN
C1   10   3.465   0.357      0.11
C2    9   4.064   0.242     0.081


99 PCT CI FOR MU C1 − MU C2: (−1.01, −0.189)


TTEST MU C1 = MU C2 (VS NE): T= −4.25   P=0.0006   DF= 17
```

Two Related Samples

No Minitab command is available to analyze directly the difference in two related samples. However, as the *t* test for related measures involves a process of combining the two samples into a single sample of differences, you can use Minitab to analyze these types of problems with the command, **TTEST**.

Begin the process by loading the two related samples into separate columns with either the **SET** or **READ** command. Next, create a single new column of differences by using a **LET** command to subtract the two original columns. For example, if you loaded the original data into columns 1 and 2, this command is

```
MTB > LET C3 = C1 − C2
```

As a result, column 3 would contain the data of differences. You now use the **TTEST** command to analyze these differences to determine whether they are significantly different from zero. You would need to supply the **TTEST** command with hypothesized mean difference (usually zero) and the column in which you placed the difference scores. The **TTEST** command might manifest itself as

```
MTB > TTEST 0 C3
```

As before, you have the option of using the subcommand, **ALTERNATIVE**, to specify one-tailed or two-tailed tests and the direction, if the test is one-tailed. The options for **ALTERNATIVE** remain the same.

The following is a Minitab analysis of the rig count example in Section 10.4:

```
MTB > SET C1
DATA> 297 134 134 52 40 57 31
DATA> end
MTB > SET C2
DATA> 295 136 136 52 38 51 28
DATA> end
```

```
MTB  > LET C3 = C1 − C2
MTB  > TTEST 0 C3;
SUBC > ALTERNATIVE 0.
```

TEST of MU = 0.000 VS MU N.E. 0.000

	N	MEAN	STDEV	SE MEAN	T	P VALUE
C3	7	1.286	2.870	1.085	1.19	0.28

You can construct a confidence interval for the difference in two related samples by manipulating the Minitab command, **TINTERVAL**. The procedure is the same as that for testing hypotheses about related samples using **TTEST**. Load the two samples into columns. Use the **LET** command to subtract the two columns and create a third column of differences. Use the **TINTERVAL** command on the third column for the confidence interval estimate. As before, if you do not specify level of confidence, Minitab defaults to 95%. To construct a 99% confidence interval in the difference in the number of new-house sales between 1990 and 1991 in the Section 10.4 example, use the following Minitab commands:

```
MTB  > SET C1
DATA > 8 19 5 9 3 0 13 11 9 5 8 2 11 14 7 12 6 10
DATA > END
MTB  > SET C2
DATA > 11 30 6 13 5 4 15 17 12 12 6 5 10 22 8 15 12 10
DATA > END
MTB  > LET C3 = C1 − C2
MTB  > TINTERVAL 99 C3
```

The output is

	N	MEAN	STDEV	SE MEAN	90.0 PERCENT C.I.
C3	18	−3.389	3.274	0.772	(−5.626, −1.152)

One-Way Analysis of Variance

You can use Minitab to calculate one-way ANOVAs with the command **AOVONEWAY**. Start by loading each sample of data into a different column. The **AOVONEWAY** command requires only a listing of the columns in which you placed the data. For example, if you stored the data in columns 1–5, the **AOVONEWAY** command is:

```
MTB > AOVONEWAY C1 C2 C3 C4 C5
```

You can analyze the bread location example presented in Section 10.5 with Minitab by using the following commands:

```
MTB > SET C1
DATA > 5 7 4 2
DATA > END
MTB > SET C2
DATA > 2 3 5 4 6
DATA > END
MTB > SET C3
DATA > 8 4 6 7 9 8
DATA > END
MTB > SET C4
DATA > 3 5 3 4 2
DATA > END
MTB > AOVONEWAY C1-C4
```

The output is

```
ANALYSIS OF VARIANCE
SOURCE    DF       SS        MS          F        p
FACTOR     3     42.35      14.12       5.11    0.011
ERROR     16     44.20      2.76
TOTAL     19     86.55
```

```
                                      INDIVIDUAL 95 PCT CI'S FOR
                                      MEAN BASED ON POOLED
                                      STDEV
LEVEL    N     MEAN     STDEV   -+---------+---------+---------+-----
C1       4     4.500    2.082       (-------*--------)
C2       5     4.000    1.581       (-------*-------)
C3       6     7.000    1.789                    (------*------)
C4       5     3.400    1.140   (-------*-------)
                                -+---------+---------+---------+-----
POOLED STDEV = 1.662            2.0       4.0       6.0       8.0
```

Note that the output includes the calculated value of F (5.11) and the probability of obtaining an F this large or larger by chance when there is no difference in the treatment levels (0.011). Also, Minitab produces a graph of individual confidence intervals around the sample means. You can visually compare the relative positions of the group means and confidence intervals. Note also that the mean for group 3 (7.000) and the confidence interval for group 3 vary considerably from those of the other groups.

SUPPLEMENTARY PROBLEMS

Test the following hypotheses for the data given. Use $\alpha = .01$ and assume that X is normally distributed in the population.

$$H_0: \mu \le 915 \qquad H_a: \mu > 915$$

947	918	932	951	909
927	914	948	947	919

10.61 Assuming that X is normally distributed, use the following information to compute a 90% confidence interval to estimate μ:

313	320	319	340
325	310	321	329
317	311	307	318

10.62 A random sample of fourteen values yields a mean of 2,155 and a variance of 250,000. Compute a 98% confidence interval to estimate the population mean. Assume that X is normally distributed in the population.

10.63 Test the alternative hypothesis that $\mu > 0$ for the data shown. Assume that X is normally distributed and use $\alpha = .01$.

$$-5 \quad +1 \quad -4 \quad +3 \quad +2 \quad +3 \quad -1 \quad +6 \quad +3 \quad -2 \quad +7$$

10.64 Suppose that a new theory were being espoused that μ is now less than 18. In the past, the average for the population has been greater than or equal to 18. A random sample of 22 yields a sample mean of 17.8, with a sample standard deviation of 1.25. Do these sample data provide enough evidence to support the new theory and reject the old standard if $\alpha = .10$? Assume that X is normally distributed in the population.

10.65 A random sample of fifteen items is selected from a population of normally distributed items. This population is supposed to have a mean of 45. If the sample mean is 43.1 and the sample standard deviation is 12.5, is there enough evidence to reject the null hypothesis for $\alpha = .01$?

10.66 A movie theater has had a poor accounting system. The manager has no idea how many large containers of popcorn are sold per movie showing. She knows that the amounts vary by day of the week and hour of the day. However, she wants to estimate the overall average per movie showing. To do so, she randomly selects twelve movie performances and counts the number of large containers of popcorn sold between one-half hour before the movie showing and fifteen minutes after the movie showing. The sample average was 43.7 containers, with a variance of 228. Construct a 95% confidence interval to estimate the mean number of large containers of popcorn sold during a movie showing. Assume that the number of large containers of popcorn sold per movie is normally distributed in the population.

10.67 A national magazine marketing firm attempts to win subscribers with a mail campaign that involves a contest using magazine stickers. Often when people subscribe to magazines in this manner they sign up for multiple magazine subscriptions. Suppose that the marketing firm wants to estimate the average number of subscriptions per customer of those who purchase at least one subscription. To do so, the marketing firm's researcher randomly selects sixty-five returned contest entries. Twenty-seven contain subscription requests. Of the twenty-seven, the average number of subscriptions is 2.10, with a standard deviation of 0.86. The researcher uses this information to compute a 98% confidence interval to estimate μ and assumes that X is normally distributed. What does he find?

10.68 A study of pollutants showed that certain industrial emissions should not exceed 2.5 parts per million. You believe that a particular company may be exceeding this average. To test this supposition you test the air by randomly taking a sample of nine air tests. The sample average is 3.4 parts per million, with a sample standard deviation of 0.6. Is this enough evidence for you to conclude that the company has been exceeding the safe limit? Use $\alpha = .01$. Assume that emissions are normally distributed.

10.69 In planning both market opportunity and production levels, being able to estimate the size of market can be important. Suppose that a diaper manufacturer wants to know how many diapers a one-month-old baby uses during a twenty-four hour period. To determine this, the manufacturer's analyst randomly selects seventeen parents of one-month-olds and asks them to keep track of diaper usage for twenty-four hours. The results are shown. Construct a 99% confidence interval to estimate the average daily diaper usage of a one-month-old baby. Assume that diaper usage is normally distributed.

12　8　11　9　13　14　10　10　9　13　11　8　11　15　10　7　12

10.70 Test the following hypotheses for the sample data presented. Use $\alpha = .05$, assume that the population variances are equal, and assume that X is normally distributed in the populations.

$$H_0: \mu_1 - \mu_2 = 0 \qquad H_a: \mu_1 - \mu_2 \neq 0$$

Sample 1	Sample 2
1.24	3.49
2.91	1.15
1.84	3.01
1.86	2.24
2.54	2.05
2.04	1.09
1.68	3.64
	1.95

10.71 Use the following information to compute a 99% confidence interval to estimate $\mu_1 - \mu_2$. Assume that $\sigma_1^2 = \sigma_2^2$ and that X is normally distributed in the populations.

Sample 1	Sample 2
11	10
10	9
11	10
12	8
10	10
13	11
9	8
11	7

10.72 Test the following hypotheses with the information given. Use $\alpha = .10$. Assume that the population variances are equal and that X is normally distributed in the populations.

$$H_0: \mu_1 - \mu_2 \geq 0$$
$$H_a: \mu_1 - \mu_2 < 0$$

Sample 1	Sample 2
$\overline{X}_1 = 101.4$	$\overline{X}_2 = 102.9$
$S_1 = 2.6$	$S_2 = 2.8$
$n_1 = 10$	$n_2 = 8$

10.73 Use the information shown to estimate $\mu_1 - \mu_2$ for a 95% confidence interval. Assume equal variance in the populations and that X is normally distributed.

Sample 1	Sample 2
$\overline{X}_1 = 474.6$	$\overline{X}_2 = 485.4$
$S_1 = 29.4$	$S_2 = 27.6$
$n_1 = 17$	$n_2 = 18$

10.74 A national grocery store chain wants to estimate the difference in the average weight of turkeys sold in Detroit and the average weight of turkeys sold in Charlotte. According to the chain's researcher, a random sample of twenty turkeys sold at the chain's stores in Detroit yielded a sample mean of 17.53 lb, with a standard deviation of 3.2 lb. Her random sample of twenty-four turkeys sold at the chain's stores in Charlotte yielded a sample mean of 14.89 lb, with a standard deviation of 2.7 lb. Use a 1% level of significance to determine whether there is a difference in the mean weight of turkeys sold in these two cities. Assume that the population variances are approximately the same and that the weights of turkeys sold in the stores are normally distributed.

10.75 Do boat owners use their boats? Is there a difference in boat usage according to the size of the boat? Suppose that you wanted to estimate the difference between the mean number of days that boat owners of 10–20-ft boats use their boats in July and the mean number of days that owners of 21–40-ft boats use their boats in July. Your survey of boat owners produced the following data. Construct a 98% confidence interval to estimate the difference in mean days for the two types of boats. Assume that boat usage is normally distributed.

10–20-ft boats	21–40-ft boats
12	6
9	4
5	10
17	3
11	5
9	6
13	
7	

10.76 Is there gender discrimination in the nursing profession? The local nurses' association wants to estimate the difference between the average salary of a male nurse and the average salary of a female nurse. Using nursing association directories, one of its members randomly contacts twenty-one female nurses and nineteen male nurses. The results are shown. Construct a 90% confidence interval to estimate the difference in average salaries. Assume that nursing salaries are normally distributed.

Female Nurses	Male Nurses
$\bar{X}_f = \$23,000$	$\bar{X}_m = \$24,900$
$S_f = \$1,800$	$S_m = \$1,500$

10.77 There are two large newspapers in your city. You are interested in knowing whether there is a significant difference in the average number of pages in each newspaper dedicated solely to advertising. You randomly select ten editions of newspaper A and six editions of newspaper B (excluding weekend editions). The data are shown. Use $\alpha = .01$ to test whether there is a significant difference in averages. Assume that the number of pages of advertising per edition is normally distributed and that the population variances are approximately equal.

A	B
17	8
21	11
11	9
19	14
26	10
17	6
15	
19	
22	
16	

10.78 As the prices of heating oil and natural gas increase, consumers become more careful about heating their homes. Researchers want to know how warm homeowners keep their houses in January and how the results between Wisconsin and Tennessee compare. The researchers randomly call twenty-three Wisconsin households between 7 P.M. and 9 P.M. on January 15 and ask the respondent how warm the house is according to the thermostat. The researchers then call nineteen households in Tennessee the same night and ask the same question. The results are as follows:

Wisconsin				Tennessee			
71	71	65	68	73	75	74	71
70	61	67	69	74	73	74	70
75	68	71	73	72	71	69	72
74	68	67	69	74	73	70	72
69	72	67	72	69	70	67	
70	73	72					

For $\alpha = .01$, is the average temperature of a house in Tennessee significantly warmer than a house in Wisconsin on the evening of January 15? Assume that the population variances are equal and that the house temperatures are normally distributed in each population.

10.79 Suppose a large insurance company wants to estimate the difference between the average amount of term life insurance that is purchased per family and the average amount of whole life insurance that is purchased per family. To obtain an estimate, one of the company's actuaries randomly selects twenty-seven families who have term life insurance only and twenty-nine families who have whole life policies only. Each sample is taken from families in which the leading provider is less than 45 years old. Use the data obtained to construct a 95% confidence interval to estimate the difference in means for these two groups. Assume that the amount of insurance is normally distributed.

Term	*Whole Life*
$\bar{X}_t = \$75,000$	$\bar{X}_w = \$45,000$
$S_t = \$22,000$	$S_w = \$15,500$
$n_t = 27$	$n_w = 29$

10.80 Use the following matched-pairs data to test the hypotheses given. Let $\alpha = .01$. Assume that the data come from normally distributed populations and that the difference was determined by subtracting sample 2 values from sample 1 values.

$$\text{H}_0: D \leq 0 \qquad \text{H}_a: D > 0$$

1	*2*
23	22
19	20
21	23
14	10
17	12
22	19
27	23

10.81 Use the following data to construct a 90% confidence interval to estimate D. Assume that the data come from normally distributed populations.

Before	After
1,147	1,130
1,125	1,110
1,119	1,118
1,129	1,107
1,143	1,125
1,126	1,100
1,119	1,111

10.82 Two samples of twenty-nine related values are selected. The sample mean difference is 2.74, with a standard deviation of difference of 1.03. Use this information to construct a 95% confidence interval to estimate the population difference. Assume that the data come from normally distributed populations.

10.83 Use the data given to test the following hypotheses:

H_0: $D = 0$ $\qquad$ H_a: $D \neq 0$

$\bar{d} = 5.37,$ $\qquad$ $S_d = 11.12,$ $\qquad$ $n = 21,$ $\qquad$ and $\qquad$ $\alpha = .10.$

Assume that the data come from normally distributed populations.

10.84 For most people who live in the South, November is a month of relatively low household energy bills because of the mild weather. The high air conditioning bills are gone, and the heating bills are not yet severe. An electric utility company conducts a study to determine whether the utility bills of all-electric houses in the South really do drop significantly in November from utility bills in July. The company's statistician randomly selects fifteen all-electric houses for the study from various parts of the region. The following data show the utility bills for the two months for the households sampled:

July	November	July	November
$185	$ 95	275	150
215	110	220	120
140	65	135	50
190	115	185	90
245	160	210	105
165	80	155	80
200	115	170	70
155	105		

Use these data and a level of significance of .01 to determine whether utility bills really do drop significantly from July to November in the

South. Construct a 98% confidence interval for the difference. Assume that utility bills are normally distributed.

10.85 In manufacturing, does worker productivity drop on Friday? In an effort to determine whether it does, a company's personnel analyst randomly selects from a manufacturing plant five workers who make the same part. He measures their output on Wednesday and again on Friday. The analyst obtains the following results:

Worker	Wednesday Output	Friday Output
1	71	53
2	56	47
3	75	52
4	68	55
5	74	58

The analyst uses $\alpha = .05$ and assumes that productivity is normally distributed. Is there enough evidence to show that productivity drops on Friday?

10.86 A study is conducted to estimate the average difference in bus ridership for a large city during the morning and afternoon rush hours. The transit authority's researcher randomly selects nine buses because of the variety of routes they represent. On a given day she has the number of riders on each bus counted at 7:45 A.M. and at 4:45 P.M., with the following results:

Bus	Morning	Afternoon
1	43	41
2	51	49
3	37	44
4	24	32
5	47	46
6	44	42
7	50	47
8	55	51
9	46	49

Use the data to compute a 90% confidence interval to estimate the population average difference. Assume that ridership is normally distributed.

10.87 One of the new thrusts of quality control management is to examine the process by which the product is produced. This approach also applies to paperwork. In industries where large long-term projects are undertaken, days and even weeks may elapse as a change order makes its way through a maze of approvals before receiving final approval. This process can result in long delays and stretch schedules to the breaking point. Suppose that a quality control consulting group claims that it can significantly reduce the number of days required for such paperwork to receive approval. In an attempt to "prove" its case, the group selects five jobs for which it revises the paperwork system. The following data show the number of days required for a change order to be approved before the group intervened and the number of days required for a change order to be approved after the group instituted a new paperwork system:

Before	After
12	8
7	3
10	8
16	0
8	5

Use $\alpha = .01$ to determine whether there was a significant drop in the number of days required to process paperwork to approve change orders. Assume that in each case the number of days of paperwork is normally distributed.

10.88 What is the average difference between the price of a name brand soup and the price of store brand soup? To obtain an estimate an analyst randomly samples eight stores. Each store sells its own brand and the national name brand. The prices of a can of name brand tomato soup and the store brand of tomato soup are as follows:

Store	Name Brand	Store Brand
1	54¢	49¢
2	55	50
3	59	52
4	53	51
5	54	50
6	61	56
7	51	47
8	53	49

Construct a 90% confidence interval to estimate the average difference. Assume that the prices of tomato soup are normally distributed in each population.

10.89 Compute a one-way ANOVA on the following data. Test F by using $\alpha = .05$.

1	2	3	4
10	9	12	10
12	7	13	10
15	9	14	13
11	6	14	12

10.90 Complete the following ANOVA table:

Source	SS	df	MS	F
Treatment	29.74	2		
Error	41.83	—		
Total		15		

10.91 Compute a one-way ANOVA on the following data ($\alpha = .01$):

1	2	3
7	8	10
6	9	9
9	7	5
5	5	8
7	6	9
8	6	8
5	5	
	6	

10.92 You are asked to analyze a completely randomized design that has six treatment levels and a total of forty-two measurements. Complete the following table, which contains some information from the study:

Source	SS	df	MS	F
Treatment	210			
Error	655			
Total				

10.93 A major automobile manufacturer wants to know whether there is any difference in the average mileage of four different brands of tires (A, B, C, and D), because the manufacturer is trying to select the best supplier in terms of tire durability. The manufacturer selects comparable levels of tires from each company and tests some on comparable cars. The mileage results are as follows:

A	B	C	D
31,000	24,000	30,500	24,500
25,000	25,500	28,000	27,000
28,500	27,000	32,500	26,000
29,000	26,500	28,000	21,000
32,000	25,000	31,000	25,500
27,500	28,000		26,000
	27,500		

Use $\alpha = .05$ to test whether there is a significant difference in the mean mileage of these four brands. Assume that tire mileage is normally distributed.

REGRESSION AND CORRELATION ANALYSIS

11

CHAPTER LEARNING OBJECTIVES

The overall objective of this chapter is to give you an understanding of regression and correlation analysis, specifically enabling you to

1. Compute simple regression analysis.
2. Compute correlation coefficients.
3. Comprehend multiple regression and how it can be used.
4. Appreciate the use of regression in forecasting.

SHAWN WILLIAMS AND THE SITE LOCATION MODEL

Shawn Williams is a quantitative analyst for a large retail chain with headquarters in New York City. He has been assigned the task of developing a mathematical model that can be used to predict potential sales at new retail site locations. Williams begins his search by gathering data on sales and other characteristics for stores presently in operation.

Realizing that stores have varying levels of sales volumes, Williams speculates that perhaps he can determine which store characteristics, if any, are related to sales. Some of the variables he is studying are size of store, size of management team, number of employees, number of competitors within three miles, whether the store is in a large mall or is free-standing, amount of immediate parking space, amount of local advertising, and population density within a five-mile radius. Williams is searching for other important variables.

Managerial Questions

- Which variables, if any, are related to sales in a significant way?
- Which variables best predict sales?
- How does Williams construct a mathematical model that maximizes the information available but is simple enough for management to understand and use?
- Are some variables related to sales in a nonlinear way?
- Are some variables measuring the same thing as other variables and thus are yielding redundant information?

In many business research situations the path to decision making lies in understanding the relationships between two or more variables. For example, in an effort to predict the value of airline stock from day to day, an analyst might find it helpful to determine whether the price of an airline stock is related to the price of West Texas intermediate (WTI) crude oil. In studying the behavior of the bond market, a broker might find it useful to know whether the interest rate of bonds is related to the prime interest rate. In studying the effect of advertising on sales, an account executive might find it useful to know whether there is a strong relationship between advertising dollars and sales dollars for a company. This chapter presents techniques that can be used to determine the strength of a relationship between variables and to construct mathematical models for predicting one variable by other variables.

Two main types of techniques are presented: correlation techniques and regression techniques. **Correlation** is *a measure of the degree of relatedness of two variables.* Correlation is widely used in exploratory research when the objective is to locate variables that might be related in some way to the variable of interest. **Regression** analysis is *the process of constructing a mathematical model*

correlation

regression

or function that can be used to predict or determine one variable by another variable (multiple variables in multiple regression). Whereas correlation attempts to determine the strength of a relationship between variables, regression attempts to determine the functional relationship between the variables. The first part of this chapter focuses on regression analysis and its ramifications.

INTRODUCTION TO SIMPLE REGRESSION ANALYSIS | *11.1*

There are at least three types of models: physical models, analog models, and mathematical models. *Physical* models are exact replicas of the object being modeled. They have the same size and structure as the object. Examples of physical models are the full-size rockets at the entrance to the Johnson Space Center in Houston. *Analog* models are models that are similar to the object being modeled but have different size and structure. Examples of analog models are scale models of trains, jet aircraft, bridges, and buildings. The most abstract of the three models is the *mathematical* model. It is a mathematical expression or equation used to represent the behavior of the phenomenon being studied. As noted in Chapter 5, random arrival rates are often thought to be approximately Poisson distributed. The Poisson formula is sometimes used as part of a mathematical model to represent random arrivals in industries such as banking or retailing. Mathematical models are used in varied business analyses, such as simulating the refining process in a petroleum plant or simulating the transportation and distribution system of an automobile manufacturer. Regression models, such as those presented in this chapter, are mathematical models. These regression models are used to analyze a wide spectrum of variables.

The most elementary regression model is called **simple regression,** which is *bivariate, linear regression.* That is, simple regression involves only two variables: One variable is being predicted by another variable. *The variable being predicted* is called the **dependent variable** and is designated as *Y. The predictor* is called the **independent variable** and is designated as *X.* Although attempting to predict a variable using parabolas, quadratics, logarithmic fits, and other exotic relationships is possible, simple regression is based on a linear fit. The emphasis in this chapter is on simple regression, because most concepts studied under simple regression apply in principle to multiple regression. Multiple regression is covered in Section 11.9.

simple regression

dependent variable
independent variable

An Example

For at least two decades, Americans have been more or less concerned about energy use and the availability of crude oil worldwide. The Persian Gulf War reawakened this concern in many. The United States is the world's greatest energy user. During the past several decades, has the production of crude oil around the world been a function of the energy consumption of the United

States? To assist in the analysis of this question, data released by the Energy Information Administration were gathered for two-year intervals between 1971 and 1988 and are presented in Table 11.1.

Column 2 shows oil production in millions of barrels per day in the world for the even years of 1972 through 1988. Because the objective is to determine whether these production figures can be predicted by U.S. energy consumption, column 1 contains the average amounts of U.S. total energy consumption in quadrillion Btu per year. Note that energy use figures are given for the odd years from 1971 through 1987, whereas production data are for even years. The reason that odd years are used for the energy use data is the theory that U.S. energy consumption for one year may predict the world production figures for the next year. Thus, for example, energy use in 1971 is a predictor of 1972 world oil production. These data are used to develop a linear regression model to predict world production per day for a given year by per day U.S. energy consumption for the previous year. Let's consider the process by which a researcher can develop a regression model to predict world crude oil production by U.S. energy consumption.

Scatter Plot

scatter plot

Usually, the first step in simple regression analysis is to construct a **scatter plot** (or scatter diagram). The independent (predictor) variable normally is scaled along the X axis (abscissa), and the dependent variable (variable being predicted or determined) normally is scaled along the Y axis (ordinate). Graphing the data in this way yields preliminary information about the shape and spread of the data. Beware that one of the ways to "cheat" or mislead with statistics is to plot variables on axes having different scales. However, many real-life regression problems contain data depicted at different scales, and caution should be exercised in interpreting scatter plots.

	U.S. Total Energy Consumption (quadrillion Btu per year)	World Production of Crude Oil (million barrels per day)
TABLE 11.1 Data for Crude Oil Production Problem	68	51
	74	56
	71	57
	76	60
	79	59
	74	53
	71	54
	74	56
	77	58

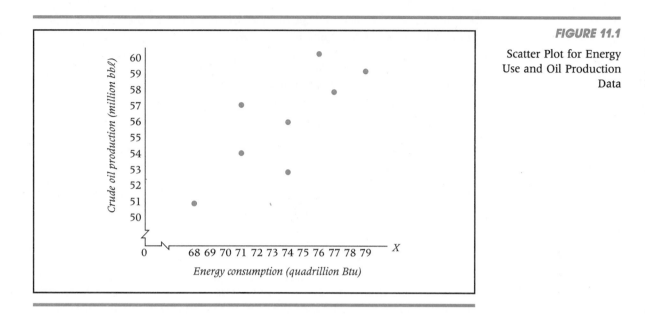

FIGURE 11.1

Scatter Plot for Energy
Use and Oil Production
Data

Figure 11.1 shows a scatter plot of the data in Table 11.1. Try to imagine a line passing through these points. Is there a linear fit? Would a curve fit the data better? The scatter plot gives some idea of how well a regression line fits the data. Later in the chapter, statistical techniques are presented that can be used to determine more precisely how well a regression line fits the data.

DETERMINING THE EQUATION OF THE REGRESSION LINE | 11.2

The first step in determining the equation of the regression line that passes through the sample data is to establish the equation's form. You probably have been exposed to several different types of equations of lines in algebra, finite math, or analytic geometry courses. Recall that among these equations of a line are the two-point form, the point–slope form, and the slope–intercept form. In regression analysis, researchers use the slope–intercept equation of a line. In math courses, the slope–intercept form of the equation of a line often takes the form:

$$Y = mX + b,$$

where: m = slope of the line
b = Y intercept of the line

In statistics, the slope–intercept form of the equation of the regression line through the population points is

$$\hat{Y} = \beta_0 + \beta_1 X,$$

where: $\hat{Y}$ = the predicted value of Y
β_0 = the population Y intercept
β_1 = the population slope

For any specific dependent variable value, Y_i,

$$Y_i = \beta_0 + \beta_1 X + \epsilon_i,$$

where: Y_i = the value of the dependent variable for the ith value
β_0 = the population Y intercept
β_1 = the population slope
ϵ_i = the error of prediction for the ith trial

Unless the points being fitted by the regression equation are in perfect alignment, the regression line will miss at least some of the points. In the preceding equation, ϵ_i represents the error of the regression line in fitting these points. If a point lies on the regression line, $\epsilon_i = 0$.

Virtually all regression analyses of business data involve sample data, not population data. As a result, β_0 and β_1 are unattainable and must be estimated by using the sample statistics, b_0 and b_1. Hence the equation of the regression line contains the sample Y intercept, b_0, and the sample slope, b_1.

Equation of the Simple Regression Line

$$\hat{Y} = b_0 + b_1 X,$$

where: b_1 = the sample slope
b_0 = the sample intercept

---

least squares analysis

In order to determine the equation of the regression line for a sample of data, the researcher must determine the values for b_0 and b_1. This process is sometimes referred to as **least squares analysis.**

Slope of the Regression Line

$$b_1 = \frac{SS_{xy}}{SS_x} = \frac{\Sigma(X - \overline{X})(Y - \overline{Y})}{\Sigma(X - \overline{X})^2} = \frac{\Sigma XY - \dfrac{(\Sigma X)(\Sigma Y)}{n}}{\Sigma X^2 - \dfrac{(\Sigma X)^2}{n}}.$$ **(11.1)**

(11.2) $$b_0 = \bar{Y} - b_1\bar{X} = \frac{\Sigma Y}{n} - b_1\frac{(\Sigma X)}{n}.$$ **Y Intercept of the Regression Line**

Note that the **slope of the regression line** is equal to the ratio of the sum of squares *XY* divided by the sum of squares of *X*. Formulas 11.1 and 11.2 show that the following data are needed from sample information in order to compute the slope and intercept: ΣX, ΣY, ΣX^2, and ΣXY. Table 11.2 contains the results of solving for the slope and intercept and determining the equation of the regression line for the data in Table 11.1.

The least-squares equation of the regression line for this problem is

$$\hat{Y} = 6.052 + 0.677X.$$

The slope of this regression line is 0.677, which means that for every unit of *X* (energy consumption) that is increased, 0.677 of a unit of *Y* (oil production) will increase. The *Y* intercept is the point where the line crosses the *Y* axis. Sometimes in regression analysis, the *Y* intercept is meaningless in terms of the variables studied, because there might never be *X* = 0. In this case, the *Y* intercept would be the amount of crude oil produced even if energy use in the United States were zero.

Superimposing the line representing this equation on the scatter plot indicates how well the regression line fits the data points, as shown in Figure

Consumption X	Production Y	X²	XY
68	51	4,624	3,468
74	56	5,476	4,144
71	57	5,041	4,047
76	60	5,776	4,560
79	59	6,241	4,661
74	53	5,476	3,922
71	54	5,041	3,834
74	56	5,476	4,144
77	58	5,929	4,466
$\Sigma X = 664$	$\Sigma Y = 504$	$\Sigma X^2 = 49,080$	$\Sigma XY = 37,246$

TABLE 11.2

Solving for the Slope and the Y-Intercept of the Line for Crude Oil Problem

$$b_1 = \frac{SS_{xy}}{SS_x} = \frac{\Sigma XY - \frac{(\Sigma X)(\Sigma Y)}{n}}{\Sigma X^2 - \frac{(\Sigma X)^2}{n}} = \frac{(37,246) - \frac{(664)(504)}{9}}{(49,080) - \frac{(664)^2}{9}} = 0.677.$$

$$b_0 = \frac{\Sigma Y}{n} - b_1\frac{\Sigma X}{n} = \frac{(504)}{9} - 0.677\left(\frac{664}{9}\right) = 6.052.$$

FIGURE 11.2

Graph of Regression Line
for Crude Oil Production
Example

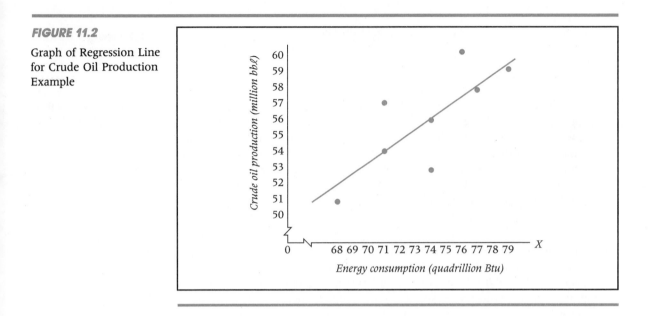

11.2. The next several sections explore mathematical ways that can be used
to test how well the regression line fits the points.

**Demonstration
Problem 11.1**

A specialist in hospital administration stated that the number of FTEs
(full-time employees) in a hospital can be estimated by counting the
number of beds in the hospital (a common measure of hospital size).
A researcher decided to develop a regression model in an attempt to
predict the number of FTEs of a hospital by the number of beds. She
surveyed twelve hospitals and obtained the following data. The data
are presented in sequence, according to the number of beds.

Number of Beds	FTEs	Number of Beds	FTEs
23	69	50	138
29	95	54	178
29	102	64	156
35	118	66	184
42	126	76	176
46	125	78	225

Solution:

The following graph is a scatter diagram of these data. Note the linear appearance of the data.

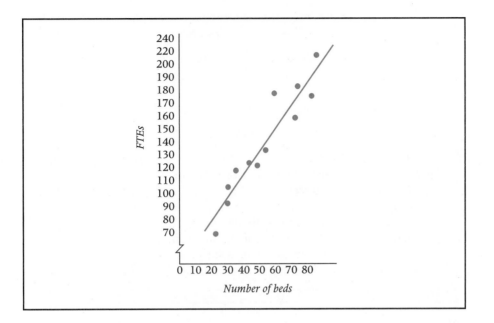

Next, the researcher determines the values of ΣX, ΣY, ΣX^2, and ΣXY.

Hospital	Number of Beds X	FTEs Y	X^2	XY
1	23	69	529	1,587
2	29	95	841	2,755
3	29	102	841	2,958
4	35	118	1,225	4,130
5	42	126	1,764	5,292
6	46	125	2,116	5,750
7	50	138	2,500	6,900
8	54	178	2,916	9,612
9	64	156	4,096	9,984
10	66	184	4,356	12,144
11	76	176	5,776	13,376
12	78	225	6,084	17,550
	$\Sigma X = 592$	$\Sigma Y = 1,692$	$\Sigma X^2 = 33,044$	$\Sigma XY = 92,038$

Next, the researcher solves for the sample slope (b_1) and the sample Y intercept (b_0):

$$b_1 = \frac{SS_{xy}}{SS_x} = \frac{\Sigma XY - \dfrac{(\Sigma X)(\Sigma Y)}{n}}{\Sigma X^2 - \dfrac{(\Sigma X)^2}{n}} = \frac{(92{,}038) - \dfrac{(592)(1{,}692)}{12}}{(33{,}044) - \dfrac{(592)^2}{12}} = 2.232.$$

$$b_0 = \frac{\Sigma Y}{n} - b_1\frac{\Sigma X}{n} = \frac{(1{,}692)}{12} - 2.232\left(\frac{592}{12}\right) = 30.888.$$

The least squares equation of the regression line is

$$\hat{Y} = 30.888 + 2.232X.$$

The slope of the line, $b_1 = 2.232$, means that for every unit of X (every bed) increased, Y (number of FTEs) increases by 2.232. Theoretically, as the Y intercept is 30.888, even if a hospital had no beds, the hospital would still have 30.888 employees to staff it. Even though the Y intercept helps the researcher sketch the graph of the line by being one of the points on the line, it may be meaningless information in terms of the solution. Whether a hospital with no beds is even a hospital, aside from the fact that it has 30.888 employees, is debatable.

**PROBLEMS
Section 11.2**

11.1 Sketch a scatter plot for the following data, and indicate whether there is much of a linear trend in the data:

X	6	11	9	14	5	3
Y	5	2	3	1	7	11

11.2 Sketch a scatter plot for the following data, and determine whether there seems to be a linear relationship between X and Y:

X	36	45	52	20	12	40	63
Y	14	26	35	32	48	18	51

11.3 Determine the equation of the regression line for the following data $(n = 9)$:

$$\Sigma X = 261, \quad \Sigma Y = 148, \quad \Sigma X^2 = 11{,}219,$$
$$\Sigma Y^2 = 3{,}938 \quad \text{and} \quad \Sigma XY = 6{,}596.$$

11.4 Determine the equation of the simple regression line from the following data $(n = 6)$:

$$\Sigma X = 635, \quad \Sigma Y = 129, \quad \Sigma X^2 = 95{,}355,$$
$$\Sigma Y^2 = 3{,}811 \quad \text{and} \quad \Sigma XY = 13{,}818.$$

11.5 Sketch a scatter plot diagram from the following data, and determine the equation of the regression line:

X	12	21	28	8	20
Y	17	15	22	19	24

11.6 Sketch a scatter plot diagram from the data shown and determine the equation of the regression line:

X	140	119	103	91	65	29	24
Y	25	29	46	70	88	112	128

11.7 A corporation owns several companies. The strategic planner for the corporation believes that dollars spent on advertising can to some extent be a predictor of total sales dollars. As an aid in long-term planning, she gathers the following sales and advertising information from several of the companies for 1991 (in $ millions):

Advertising	Sales
12.5	148
3.7	55
21.6	338
60.0	994
37.6	541
6.1	89
16.8	126
41.2	379

Develop the equation of the simple regression line to predict sales from advertising expenditures using these data.

11.8 Investment analysts generally believe that the interest rate on bonds is inversely related to the prime interest rate for loans. That is, bonds perform well when lending rates are down and perform poorly when interests rates are up. Can the bond rate be predicted by the prime interest rate? Use the following data to construct a least squares regression line to predict bond rates by the prime interest rate:

Bond Rate	Prime Interest Rate
5%	16%
12	6
9	8
15	4
7	7

11.9 The U.S. Bureau of Labor Statistics produces the Consumer Price Index (CPI) as an indicator of the cost of goods and services to the consumer. The bureau also produces a CPI–U, which is a consumer price index for all urban consumers (about 80% of the population), and a CPI–W, which is a consumer price index for clerical workers (about 32% of the population). The following are CPI–U and CPI–W values for June 1989 on eight goods and services:

Item	CPI–U	CPI–W
Food, beverages	125.0	124.8
Housing	122.6	120.7
Apparel, upkeep	119.1	117.7
Transportation	115.9	115.9
Medical care	148.7	148.8
Entertainment	126.2	125.5
Other goods	147.7	147.3
Services	131.6	130.5

Use these data to develop a simple regression line to predict the CPI–U from the CPI–W. Discuss the slope and Y intercept in light of the data.

11.10 The Bureau of Economic Analysis of the U.S. Commerce Department produces figures on national income by industry. The following are the figures in \$ billions for the manufacturing industry and the transportation/public utilities industry:

Year	Manufacturing	Transportation/Public Utilities
1960	125.3	35.8
1965	171.6	47.0
1970	215.6	64.4
1975	317.5	101.1
1980	532.1	177.3
1987	718.7	278.7

Determine a simple regression line to predict the national income of manufacturing by the national income of transportation/public utilities.

11.11 That there is a relationship between the number of households in a metropolitan area that have at least one shareholder and the population of the area seems reasonable. That is, the larger the metro area, the more shareholders there are in it. The following are the number of households that contain at least one shareholder for the ten largest metropolitan areas, as provided by the New York Stock Exchange. In addition, the Rand McNally population totals as of 12/31/89 are given for these metro areas.

Metro Area	Households with Shareholder	Metro Population
New York	1,630,000	8,602,100
Los Angeles	1,230,000	8,813,600
Chicago	1,070,000	6,214,400
Detroit	820,000	4,385,400
Philadelphia	720,000	4,934,900
Washington, D.C.	670,000	3,778,200
Boston	620,000	2,849,500
Houston	580,000	3,244,600
Nassau–Suffolk Counties, N.Y.	500,000	2,669,900
Dallas	440,000	2,481,900

a. Construct a scatter plot of the data to predict the number of households with at least one shareholder by the metro area population.
b. Develop the equation of the regression line to predict the number of households with at least one shareholder by the metro area population.

RESIDUAL ANALYSIS

How does a researcher test a regression line to determine mathematically whether the line is a *good* fit of the data? One type of information available is the *historical data* used to construct the equation of the line. In other words, there are actual Y values that correspond to the X values used in constructing the regression line. Why not insert the historical X values into the equation of the sample regression line and get predicted Y values (denoted $\hat{Y}$) and then compare these predicted values to the actual Y values to determine how much error the equation of the regression line produced? Each difference between the actual Y values and the predicted Y values is the error of the regression line at a given point, $Y - \hat{Y}$, and is referred to as the **residual.**

residual

Table 11.3 shows $\hat{Y}$ values and the residuals for each pair of data for the regression model developed in Section 11.1 to predict world crude oil production by U.S. energy use. The predicted values are calculated by inserting an X value into the equation of the regression line and solving for Y. For example, when $X = 68$, $\hat{Y} = 6.052 + 0.677(68) = 52.088$ as displayed in column 3 of Table 11.3. Each of these predicted Y values is subtracted from the actual Y value to determine the error or residual. For example, the first Y value is 51, and the first predicted value is 52.088, resulting in a residual of $51 - 52.088 = -1.088$. The residuals for this problem are displayed in column 4 of Table 11.3.

Note that the sum of the residuals is approximately zero. Except for rounding error, the sum of the residuals always is *zero*. The reason is that a residual is geometrically the vertical distance from the regression line to a data point. The equations used to solve for the slope and intercept place the line geometrically in the middle of all points. That is, vertical distances from the line

TABLE 11.3

Predicted Values and Residuals for Crude Oil Problem

Consumption X	Production Y	Predicted Value $\hat{Y}$	Residual $Y - \hat{Y}$
68	51	52.088	-1.088
74	56	56.150	-0.150
71	57	54.119	2.881
76	60	57.504	2.496
79	59	59.535	-0.535
74	53	56.150	-3.150
71	54	54.119	-0.119
74	56	56.150	-0.150
77	58	58.181	-0.181
			$\Sigma(Y - \hat{Y}) = 0.004$

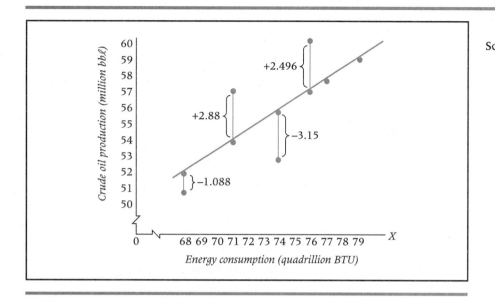

FIGURE 11.3

Scatter Plot with Residu-
als for the Crude Oil
Production Example

to the points will cancel each other and sum to zero. Figure 11.3 displays the scatter plot of the data for the crude oil production example and the residuals.

An examination of the residuals may give the researcher an idea of how well the regression line fits the historical data points. The largest residual for the crude oil example is 3.150, and the smallest is 0.15. As the objective is to predict crude oil production, the regression line produces an error of a little more than three billion barrels for the sixth pair of data. For the second and eighth pairs of data, the model predicted production with almost no error. This result presents the *best* and *worst* cases for residuals. The researcher must examine other residuals to determine how well the regression model fits other data points.

Sometimes residuals are used to locate outliers. **Outliers** are *data points that lie apart from the rest of the points.* Outliers can produce residuals with large magnitudes and are usually easy to identify on scatter plots. Outliers can be the result of misrecorded or miscoded data, or they may simply be data points that do not conform to the same general trend. The equation of the regression line is influenced by every data point used in its calculation in a manner similar to the arithmetic mean. Therefore outliers sometimes can unduly influence the regression line by "pulling" the line toward the outliers. The origin of outliers must be investigated to determine whether they should be retained or whether the regression equation should be recomputed without them.

Residuals are usually plotted against the X axis, which reveals a view of the residuals as X increases. Figure 11.4 presents the residuals plotted against the X axis for the world crude oil production example.

outliers

FIGURE 11.4

Residuals for Crude Oil
Production Example

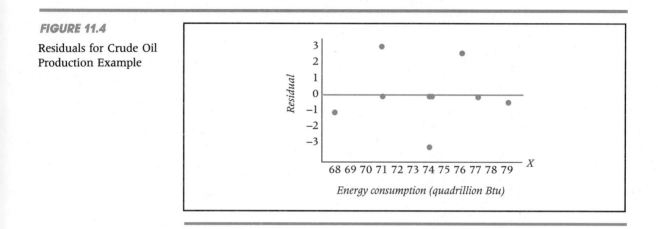

Energy consumption (quadrillion Btu)

Using Residuals to Test the Assumptions of the Regression Model

One of the major uses of residual analysis is to test some of the assumptions underlying regression. The following are the assumptions of simple regression analysis.

1. The model is linear.
2. The error terms have constant variances.
3. The error terms are independent.
4. The error terms are normally distributed.

If a residual plot such as the one shown in Figure 11.5 appears, the assumption that the model is linear does not hold. Note that the residuals are negative for low and high values of X and are positive for middle values of X. The graph of these residuals is parabolic, not linear.

homoscedasticity
heteroscedasticity

The assumption of constant error variance sometimes is called **homoscedasticity.** If the error variances are *not* constant (called **heteroscedasticity**), the residual plots might look like one of the two plots shown in Figure 11.6. Note in Figure 11.6(a) that the error variance is greater for small values of X and smaller for large values of X. The situation is reversed in Figure 11.6(b).

If the error terms are not independent, the residual plots could look like one of the graphs in Figure 11.7. According to these graphs, what is occurring is that—instead of each error term being independent of the one next to it—the value of the residual is a function of the residual value next to it. For example, a large positive residual is next to a large positive residual and a small negative residual is next to a small negative residual.

FIGURE 11.5

Nonlinear Residual Plot

FIGURE 11.6

Nonconstant Error Variance

FIGURE 11.7

Graphs of Nonindependent Error Terms

FIGURE 11.8

Healthy Residual Graph

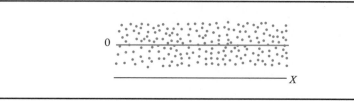

The graph of the residuals from a regression analysis that meets the assumptions—a *healthy residual graph*—might look like the graph in Figure 11.8.

Demonstration Problem 11.2

Compute the residuals for Demonstration Problem 11.1 in which a regression model was developed to predict the number of full-time equivalent workers by the number of beds in a hospital.

Solution:

The data and computed residuals are shown in the following table:

Hospital	Number of Beds X	FTEs Y	Predicted Value $\hat{Y}$	Residuals $Y - \hat{Y}$
1	23	69	82.22	−13.22
2	29	95	95.62	−0.62
3	29	102	95.62	6.38
4	35	118	109.01	8.99
5	42	126	124.63	1.37
6	46	125	133.56	−8.56
7	50	138	142.49	−4.49
8	54	178	151.42	26.58
9	64	156	173.74	−17.74
10	66	184	178.20	5.80
11	76	176	200.52	−24.52
12	78	225	204.98	20.02
			$\Sigma(Y - \hat{Y}) =$	−00.01

Note that the regression model fits these particular data well for hospitals 2 and 5, as indicated by residuals of -0.62 and 1.37 FTEs, respectively. For hospitals 1, 8, 9, 11, and 12, the residuals are relatively large, indicating that the regression model does not fit the data for these hospitals well. The researcher must determine whether a model producing such residuals is acceptable.

**PROBLEMS
Section 11.3**

11.12 Determine the equation of the regression line for the following data, and compute the residuals:

X	15	8	19	12	5
Y	47	36	56	44	21

11.13 Solve for the predicted values of Y and the residuals for the data in Problem 11.5.

11.14 Solve for the predicted values of Y and the residuals for the data in Problem 11.6.

11.15 Solve for the predicted values of Y and the residuals for the data in Problem 11.7.

11.16 Solve for the predicted values of Y and the residuals for the data in Problem 11.8.

11.17 The equation of a regression line is

$$\hat{Y} = -1.646X + 50.506$$

and the data are

X	5	7	11	12	19	25
Y	47	38	32	24	22	10

Solve for the residuals and graph a residual plot. Do these data seem to violate any of the assumptions of regression?

11.18 Wisconsin is an important milk producing state. Some might argue that because of transportation costs, the cost of milk increases with the distance of the market from Wisconsin. Suppose that the milk prices in eight cities are as follows:

Cost of Milk (per gallon)	Distance from Madison (miles)
$2.64	1,245
2.31	425
2.45	1,346
2.52	973
2.19	255
2.55	865
2.40	1,080
2.37	296

Use the prices along with the distance each city is from Madison, Wisconsin, to develop a regression line to predict the price of a gallon of milk by the number of miles the city is from Madison. Use the data and the regression equation to compute residuals for this model. Sketch a graph of the residuals in the order of the X values. Comment on the shape of the residual graph.

11.19 Graph the following residuals, and indicate which of the assumptions underlying regression appear to be in jeopardy based on the graph:

X	$Y - \hat{Y}$
213	−11
216	−5
227	−2
229	−1
237	+6
247	+10
263	+12

11.20 Graph the following residuals, and indicate which of the assumptions underlying regression appear to be in jeopardy, based on the graph:

X	$Y - \hat{Y}$
5	−21
6	+16
8	+14
9	−11
12	−8
13	−7
14	+5
17	−2
18	+1

11.21 Graph the following residuals, and indicate which of the assumptions underlying regression appear to be in jeopardy, based on this graph:

X	$Y - \hat{Y}$
10	+6
11	+3
12	−1
13	−11
14	−3
15	+2
16	+5
17	+8

STANDARD ERROR OF THE ESTIMATE | *11.4*

Residuals represent errors of estimation for individual points. With large samples of data, residual computations become laborious. Even with computers, a researcher sometimes has difficulty working through pages of residuals in an effort to understand the error of the regression model. An alternative way of examining the error of the model is the standard error of the estimate, which provides a single measurement of the regression error.

Because the sum of the residuals is zero, attempting to determine the total amount of error by summing the residuals is fruitless. This zero-sum characteristic of residuals can be avoided by squaring the residuals and then summing them.

Table 11.4 contains the crude oil production data from Table 11.1, along with the residuals and the residuals squared. The *total of the residuals squared* column is called the **sum of squares of error (SSE).**

sum of squares of error (SSE)

TABLE 11.4	Consumption X	Production Y	Residuals $Y - \hat{Y}$	$(Y - \hat{Y})^2$
Determining SSE for the Crude Oil Production Example	68	51	−1.088	1.184
	74	56	−0.150	0.023
	71	57	2.881	8.300
	76	60	2.496	6.230
	79	59	−0.535	0.286
	74	53	−3.150	9.922
	71	54	−0.119	0.014
	74	56	−0.150	0.023
	77	58	−0.181	0.033
	$\Sigma X = 664$	$\Sigma Y = 504$	$\Sigma(Y - \hat{Y}) = 0.004$	$\Sigma(Y - \hat{Y}^2) = 26.015$

Sum of Squares of Error = SSE = 26.015.

SSE

$$SSE = \Sigma(Y - \hat{Y})^2.$$

In theory, infinitely many lines can be fit to a sample of points. However, Formulas 11.1 and 11.2 produce a line of *best fit* for which the SSE is the smallest for any line that can be fit to the sample data. This result is guaranteed, because Formulas 11.1 and 11.2 are derived from calculus to minimize SSE. For this reason, the regression process used in this chapter is called *least squares* regression.

There is a computational version of the formula for computing SSE. This formula is less meaningful in terms of interpretation than $\Sigma(Y - \hat{Y})^2$, but it is usually easier to compute. The computational formula for SSE follows.

Computational Formula for SSE

$$SSE = \Sigma Y^2 - b_0\Sigma Y - b_1\Sigma XY.$$

The sum of squares of error is, in part, a function of the number of pairs of data being used to compute the sum, which lessens the value of SSE as a measurement of error. A more useful measurement of error is the standard error of the estimate. The **standard error of the estimate,** denoted S_e, is *a standard deviation of the error of the regression model* and has a more practical use than SSE. The standard error of the estimate follows.

standard error of the estimate

$$S_e = \sqrt{\frac{SSE}{n-2}}.$$

The standard error of the estimate for the crude oil production example is

$$S_e = \sqrt{\frac{SSE}{n-2}} = \sqrt{\frac{26.015}{7}} = 1.928.$$

How is the standard error of the estimate used? As previously mentioned, the standard error of the estimate is a standard deviation of error. Recall from Chapter 3 that, if data are approximately normally distributed, the empirical rule states that about 68% of all values fall within $\mu \pm 1\sigma$ and that about 95% of all values fall within $\mu \pm 2\sigma$. One of the assumptions listed in Section 11.3 for regression states that the error terms are normally distributed. Because the error terms are normally distributed, S_e is the standard deviation of error, and the average error is zero, approximately 68% of the error values (residuals) should fall within $0 \pm 1S_e$, and 95% of the error values (residuals) should fall within $0 \pm 2S_e$. By having a knowledge of the variables being studied and by examining the value of S_e, the researcher can often make a judgment about the fit of the regression model to the data by using S_e. How can the S_e value for the crude oil production example be interpreted?

The regression model in that example is used to predict the world crude oil production by the U.S. energy consumption rate. Note that the range of the world crude oil data in Table 11.1 is from 51 to 60. The regression model for the data yields an S_e of 1.928 million barrels. An interpretation of S_e is that the estimates produced by this regression model are within 1.928 million barrels of the actual value about 68% of the time and within 3.856 (2 × 1.928) million barrels about 95% of the time. Examination of the residuals reveals that, indeed, six of the nine residuals (67%) fall within one standard error of the estimate (1.928) and 100% of the residuals fall within $2S_e$. Thus the standard error of the estimate provides a single measure of error, which, if the researcher has enough background in the area being analyzed, can be used to determine whether the model is a good fit of the data. In addition, some researchers use the standard error of the estimate to identify outliers. They do so by looking for data that fall outside $\pm 2S_e$ or $\pm 3S_e$.

Demonstration Problem 11.3

Compute the sum of squares of error and the standard error of the estimate for Demonstration Problem 11.1, in which a regression model is developed to predict the number of FTEs at a hospital by the number of beds.

Solution:

Hospital	Number of Beds (X)	FTEs Y	Residuals Y − Ŷ	(Y − Ŷ)²
1	23	69	− 13.22	174.77
2	29	95	− 0.62	0.38
3	29	102	6.38	40.70
4	35	118	8.99	80.82
5	42	126	1.37	1.88
6	46	125	− 8.56	73.27
7	50	138	− 4.49	20.16
8	54	178	26.58	706.50
9	64	156	− 17.74	314.71
10	66	184	5.80	33.64
11	76	176	− 24.52	601.23
12	78	225	20.02	400.80
	$\Sigma X = 592$	$\Sigma Y = 1{,}692$	$\Sigma(Y - \hat{Y}) = -00.01$	$\Sigma(Y - \hat{Y})^2 = 2{,}448.86$

$$\text{SSE} = 2{,}448.86.$$

$$S_e = \sqrt{\frac{\text{SSE}}{n - 2}} = \sqrt{\frac{2{,}448.86}{10}} = 15.65.$$

The standard error of the estimate is 15.65 FTEs. About 68% of the time, this model will predict the number of FTEs of a hospital within 15.65 FTEs. About 95% of the time, this model will predict the number of FTEs within 31.30 FTEs (2×15.65). Is this an acceptable size of error? Hospital administrators probably can best answer that question.

**PROBLEMS
Section 11.4**

11.22 Determine the sum of squares of error (SSE) and the standard error of the estimate (S_e) for Problem 11.5. Determine how many of the residuals computed in Problem 11.13 fall within one standard error of the estimate. If the error terms are normally distributed, approximately how many of these residuals should fall within $\pm 1\ S_e$?

11.23 Determine the SSE and the S_e for Problem 11.6. Use the residuals computed in Problem 11.14 and determine how many of them fall within $\pm 1S_e$ and $\pm 2S_e$? How do these numbers compare to what the empirical rule says should occur if the error terms are normally distributed?

11.24 Determine the SSE and the S_e for Problem 11.7. Think about the variables being analyzed by regression in this problem and comment on the value of S_e.

11.25 Determine the SSE and the S_e for Problem 11.8. Examine the variables being regressed in this problem and comment on the value of S_e.

11.26 Use the data from Problem 11.17 and determine the S_e.

11.27 Determine the SSE and the S_e for Problem 11.18. Comment on the size of S_e for this regression model, which is used to predict the cost of milk.

11.28 Determine the equation of the regression line to predict income from sales using the following 1988 data gathered from *Fortune*. Compute the standard error of the estimate for this model. Does sales volume appear to be a good predictor of a company's income? What are some other variables that might account for income?

Company	Annual Sales (billions)	Annual Income (millions)
General Motors	$121.1	$4,856
Ford Motor	92.4	5,300
Exxon	79.6	5,260
IBM	59.7	5,806
General Electric	49.4	3,386
Mobil	48.2	2,087
Chrysler	35.5	1,050
Texaco	33.5	1,304
DuPont	32.5	2,190

COEFFICIENT OF DETERMINATION | 11.5

coefficient of determination

A widely used measure of fit for regression models is the **coefficient of determination,** or r^2. The coefficient of determination is *the proportion of variability of the dependent variable (Y) accounted for or explained by the independent variable (X).*

Coefficient of Determination (r^2)	$r^2 = 1 - \dfrac{\text{SSE}}{\text{SSY}} = \dfrac{\text{SSE}}{\sum Y^2 - \dfrac{(\sum Y)^2}{n}},$ $0 \le r^2 \le 1,$ (11.3)

where: SSY = sum of squares of Y

The coefficient of determination varies from 0 to 1. An r^2 of zero means that the predictor accounts for none of the variability of the dependent variable and that there is no regression prediction of Y by X. An r^2 of 1 means that there is perfect prediction of Y by X and that 100% of the variability of Y is accounted for by X. Of course, most r^2 values fall between the extremes. The researcher must interpret whether a particular r^2 is high or low, depending upon the use of the model and the context within which the model was developed.

One NASA researcher who uses vehicular weight to predict mission cost would like for the regression models to have an r^2 of .90 or higher. However, a child development researcher who was trying to understand why children have certain understandings about life would be pleased to get an r^2 near .50 in the initial research. In exploratory research where the variables are less understood, lower values of r^2 are likely to be more acceptable than in areas of research where the parameters are more developed and understood.

The dependent variable, Y, being predicted in a regression model has a variation that is measured by the sum of squares of Y (SSY). This variation can be broken into two additive variations: the explained variation, measured by the sum of squares of regression (SSR), and the unexplained variation, measured by the sum of squares of error (SSE). This relationship can be depicted in equation form as

$$\text{SSY} = \text{SSR} + \text{SSE}.$$

If each term in the equation is divided by SSY, the resulting equation is

$$1 = \frac{\text{SSR}}{\text{SSY}} + \frac{\text{SSE}}{\text{SSY}}.$$

The term r^2 is the proportion of Y that is explained by the regression model and represented here as (SSR)/(SSY),

$$1 = r^2 + \frac{\text{SSE}}{\text{SSY}}.$$

Solving for r^2 yields Formula 11.3:

$$r^2 = 1 - \frac{\text{SSE}}{\text{SSY}}.$$

The value of r^2 for the crude oil production example is

$$r^2 = 1 - \frac{\text{SSE}}{\Sigma Y^2 - \frac{(\Sigma Y)^2}{n}} = 1 - \frac{26.015}{28{,}292 - \frac{(504)^2}{9}} = .617.$$

That is, 61.7% of the variability of crude oil production is accounted for or predicted by U.S. energy consumption. This result also means that 38.3% of the variance in crude oil production, Y, is unaccounted for by X or unexplained by the regression model.

> **Demonstration Problem 11.4**

Compute the coefficient of determination (r^2) for Demonstration Problem 11.1, in which a regression model is developed to predict the number of FTEs of a hospital by the number of beds.

Solution:

$$r^2 = 1 - \frac{\text{SSE}}{\Sigma Y^2 - \frac{(\Sigma Y)^2}{n}} = 1 - \frac{2{,}448.86}{260{,}136 - \frac{1692^2}{12}} = .886.$$

This regression model accounts for 88.6% of the variance in FTEs, leaving only an 11.4% unexplained variance.

> **PROBLEMS Section 11.5**

11.29 Compute r^2 for Problem 11.22. Discuss the value of r^2 obtained.

11.30 Compute r^2 for Problem 11.23. Discuss the value of r^2 obtained.

11.31 Compute r^2 for Problem 11.24. Discuss the value of r^2 obtained.

11.32 Compute r^2 for Problem 11.25. Discuss the value of r^2 obtained.

11.33 Compute r^2 for Problem 11.26. Discuss the value of r^2 obtained.

11.34 Predicting the House Appropriation Committee's appropriations to some extent by the president's proposed budget should be possible. How good is the predictability of such a model? The following are proposed fiscal 1992 nondefense appropriations by budget category in \$ billions:

	Bush Budget	House Appropriation
Labor, Health, Education	$56.00	$59.27
Housing, Space, Veterans, Environment	64.90	63.59
Commerce, State, Justice	15.68	15.69
Natural Resources	12.10	13.20
Transportation	14.56	13.63
Treasury, Postal Service	10.80	10.75
Energy, Water	9.83	9.75

Use these data to develop a regression model to predict the House Appropriation Committee's proposed appropriations by President Bush's proposed budget. Compute r^2 for this model and discuss the strength of the model in light of r^2.

11.6   HYPOTHESIS TESTS FOR THE SLOPE OF THE REGRESSION MODEL

A hypothesis test can be conducted on the sample slope of the regression model to determine whether the population slope is significant. This test is another way to determine how well a regression model fits the data. Suppose that a researcher decided that it is not worth the effort to develop a linear regression model to predict Y from X. An alternative approach might be to average the Y values and use $\overline{Y}$ as the predictor of Y for all values of X. For the crude oil production example, instead of using U.S. energy consumption as a predictor, the researcher would use the average value of crude oil production, $\overline{Y}$, for the sample as the predictor. In this case the average value of Y is

$$\overline{Y} = \frac{504}{9} = 56 \text{ million bbl.}$$

Using this result as a model to predict Y, if the amount of U.S. energy consumption is 68 or 76 or 71—or any other number—the predicted value of Y is still 56. Essentially, this approach fits the line of $\overline{Y} = 56$ through the data, which is a horizontal line with a slope of zero. Would a regression analysis offer anything more than the $\overline{Y}$ model? Using this nonregression model (the $\overline{Y}$ model) as a worst case, the researcher can analyze the regression line to determine whether it adds a more significant amount of predictability of Y than does the $\overline{Y}$ model. Because the slope of the $\overline{Y}$ line is zero, one way to determine whether the regression line adds significant predictability is to test the *population* slope of the regression line to find out if the slope is different from zero. As the slope of the regression line diverges from zero, the regression model is adding predictability that the $\overline{Y}$ line is not generating. For this reason, testing the slope of the regression line to determine whether the slope is different from zero is important. If the slope is not different from zero, the regression line is doing nothing more than the $\overline{Y}$ line in predicting Y.

How does the researcher go about testing the slope of the regression line? Why not just examine the calculated slope? For example, the slope of the regression line for the crude oil production data is 0.677. This value obviously is not zero. The problem is that this slope is a *sample* slope obtained from a sample of nine data points. If another sample of crude oil production and U.S. energy consumption measurements were used, a different slope likely would be obtained. Thus the sample slope is a function of the particular sample from which it is obtained. What has to be tested here is the *population* slope. If all the pairs of data points for the population were available, would the slope of that regression line be different from zero? Here the sample slope, b_1, is used as evidence to test whether the population slope is different from zero. The hypotheses for this test are

$$H_0: \beta_1 = 0$$
$$H_a: \beta_1 \neq 0$$

Note that this test is two-tailed. The null hypothesis can be rejected if the slope is either negative or positive. A negative slope indicates an inverse relationship between X and Y. That is, larger values of X are related to smaller values of Y and vice versa. Both negative and positive slopes can be different from zero. To determine whether there is a significant positive relationship between two variables, the hypotheses would be one-tailed, or

$$H_0: \beta_1 \leq 0$$
$$H_a: \beta_1 > 0$$

To test for a significant negative relationship between two variables, the hypotheses also would be one-tailed, or

$$H_0: \beta_1 \geq 0$$
$$H_a: \beta_1 < 0$$

In each case, testing the null hypothesis involves a t test of the slope.

$$t = \frac{b_1 - \beta_1}{S_b},$$

t Test of Slope

where: $S_b = \dfrac{S_e}{\sqrt{SSX}}$

$S_e = \sqrt{\dfrac{SSE}{n-2}}$

$SSX = \Sigma X^2 - \dfrac{(\Sigma X)^2}{n}$

$df = n - 2$

FIGURE 11.9

t Test of Slope from
Crude Oil Production
Example

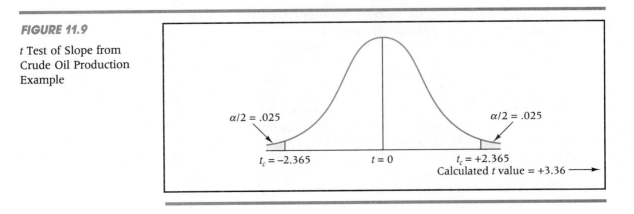

Let's test the slope of the regression line for the crude oil production regression model for $\alpha = .05$. The regression line derived for the data was

$$\hat{Y} = 6.052 + 0.677X.$$

The sample slope is $0.677 = b_1$. The value of S_e is 1.928, $\Sigma X = 664$, $\Sigma X^2 = 49,080$, and $n = 9$. The hypotheses are

$$H_0:\ \beta_1 = 0$$
$$H_a:\ \beta_1 \neq 0$$

The df $= n - 2 = 9 - 2 = 7$. As this test is two-tailed, $\alpha/2 = .025$. The table *t* value is $t_{.025,7} = \pm 2.365$. The calculated *t* value for this sample slope is

$$t = \dfrac{0.677 - 0}{\dfrac{1.928}{\sqrt{49,080 - (664^2/9)}}} = 3.36.$$

As shown in Figure 11.9, the *t* value calculated from the sample slope falls in the rejection region. The null hypothesis that the population slope is zero is rejected. This linear regression model is adding significantly more predictive information to the $\overline{Y}$ model (no regression).

**Demonstration
Problem 11.5**

Test the slope of the regression model developed in Section 11.2 to predict the number of FTEs in a hospital from the number of beds to determine whether there is a significant positive slope. Use $\alpha = .01$.

Solution:

The hypotheses for this problem are

$$H_0: \ \beta_1 \leq 0$$
$$H_a: \ \beta_1 > 0$$

The level of significance is .01. There were 12 pairs of data, so df $= 10$. The critical table t value is $t_{.01,10} = 2.764$. The regression line equation for this problem was

$$\hat{Y} = 30.888 + 2.232X.$$

The sample slope, b_1, is 2.232, $S_e = 15.65$, $\Sigma X = 592$, $\Sigma X^2 = 33{,}044$, and $n = 12$. The calculated t value for the sample slope is

$$t = \frac{2.232 - 0}{\dfrac{15.65}{\sqrt{33{,}044 - (592^2/12)}}} = 8.84.$$

The calculated t value (8.84) falls in the rejection region, because it is greater than the critical table t value of 2.764. The null hypothesis is rejected. The population slope for this regression line is significantly different from zero in the positive direction. This regression model is adding significant predictability over the $\overline{Y}$ model.

Interpreting Computer Output

This chapter has focused on manual computations to this point, but most regression problems are analyzed by using a computer. Analyzing the world crude oil production example by using the computer package Minitab produces the following output:

```
The regression equation is:
Ŷ = 6.0 + 0.677 X
```

Predictor	Coef	t ratio	p
Constant	6.04	0.41	0.697
X	0.677	3.36	0.012

$s = 1.928 \qquad$ R-sq $= 61.7\%$

Analysis of Variance

SOURCE	DF	SS	MS	F	p
Regression	1	41.985	41.985	11.30	0.012
Error	7	26.015	3.716		
Total	8	68.000			

Residuals: $-1.09, -0.15, 2.88, 2.50, -0.54, -3.15, -0.12, -0.15, -0.18$

The regression equation is obvious from the output. The r^2 is 61.7%. The standard error of the estimate appears as $S = 1.928$. The sum of squares of error can be determined by locating SS in the row labeled Error, or SSE $= 26.015$. The residuals can be obtained and printed as shown. The t ratio for the X variable, $t = 3.36$, is the computed t value used to test the slope of the regression model. The value for p to the right of the t ratio is the probability of this t value occurring by chance if the slope of the population is not different from zero. Because the p value is .012, this t ratio is significant at $\alpha = .05$. The F value and its associated p value are a test of the overall regression model. For a simple regression model, this F value equals t^2. For simple regression models, the F value adds nothing to the information that the t value for slopes already reveals. However, for multiple regression models, the F value is more useful. It is explained further in Section 11.9.

PROBLEMS
Section 11.6

11.35 Test the slope of the regression line determined in Problem 11.5. Use $\alpha = .05$.

11.36 Test the slope of the regression line determined in Problem 11.6. Use $\alpha = .01$.

11.37 Test the slope of the regression line determined in Problem 11.7. Use $\alpha = .10$.

11.38 Test the slope of the regression line determined in Problem 11.8. Use a 5% level of significance.

11.7   ESTIMATION

One of the main uses of regression analysis is as a prediction tool. Provided that the regression function is a good model, the researcher can use the regression equation to determine values of the dependent variable from various values of the independent variable. For example, financial brokers would like to have a model with which they could predict the selling price of a particular stock on a certain day by some variable, such as the unemployment rate or the wholesale price index. Marketing managers would like to have a site location model with which they could predict the sales volume of a new location by variables such as population density or number of competitors. The crude oil production example presents a regression model that has the potential to predict world crude oil production by the U.S. energy consumption rate.

A point estimate prediction can be made by taking a particular value of X that is of interest, substituting the value of X into the regression equation, and solving for Y. For example, if the level of energy use in the United States one year is 75 quadrillion Btu, what is the predicted level of world crude oil production per day in millions of barrels for the next year? The regression equation for this example was

$$\hat{Y} = 6.052 + 0.677X.$$

Substituting $X = 75$ into this equation yields a predicted level of 56.83 million barrels per day of crude oil production for the next year.

Confidence Intervals to Estimate the Average Value of Y

Although a point estimate is often of interest to the researcher, the regression line is determined by a sample set of points. If a different sample is taken, a different line will result, yielding a different point estimate. Hence computing a confidence interval for the estimation often is useful. Because for any value of X (independent variable) there can be many values of Y (dependent variable), one type of confidence interval is an estimate of the *average* value of Y for a given X. This average value of Y is denoted $E(Y_x)$—the expected value of Y.

(11.4)
$$\hat{Y} \pm t_{\alpha/2,n-2}S_e\sqrt{\frac{1}{n} + \frac{(X_0 - \bar{X})^2}{\Sigma X^2 - \frac{(\Sigma X)^2}{n}}},$$

Confidence Interval to Estimate $E(Y_x)$ for a Given Value of X

where: X_0 = a particular value of X

Use of this formula can be illustrated with construction of a 95% confidence interval to estimate the average value of Y (crude oil production) for the crude oil production example when X (energy consumption) is 73 quadrillion Btu. This confidence interval utilizes a t value obtained through the degrees of freedom and $\alpha/2$. For a 95% confidence interval, $\alpha = .05$ and $\alpha/2 = .025$. The df $= n - 2 = 9 - 2 = 7$. The table t value is $t_{.025,7} = 2.365$. In addition, other needed values for this problem, which were solved for previously, are

$$S_e = 1.928, \quad \Sigma X = 664, \quad \bar{X} = 73.78, \quad \text{and} \quad \Sigma X^2 = 49,080.$$

For $X_0 = 73$, the value of $\hat{Y} = 55.47$. The computed confidence interval for the average value of Y, $E(Y_{73})$, is

$$55.47 \pm (2.365)(1.928)\sqrt{\frac{1}{9} + \frac{(73 - 73.78)^2}{49,080 - \frac{(664)^2}{9}}} = 55.47 \pm 1.565;$$

$$53.905 \le E(Y_{73}) \le 57.035.$$

X	Confidence Interval	
70	53.442 ± 2.357	51.085 to 55.799
72	54.796 ± 1.741	53.055 to 56.537
74	56.150 ± 1.524	54.626 to 57.674
76	57.504 ± 1.852	55.652 to 59.356
78	58.858 ± 2.521	56.337 to 61.379

TABLE 11.5

Confidence Intervals to Estimate the Average Value of Y for Some X Values in the Crude Oil Production Example

That is, the statement can be made that the average value of Y for X = 73 lies between 53.905 and 57.035 with 95% confidence.

Table 11.5 shows confidence intervals computed for the crude oil production example for several values of X to estimate the average value of Y. Note that, as X values get farther from the mean X value (73.78), the confidence intervals get wider; as the X values get closer to the mean, the confidence interval gets narrower. The reason is that the numerator of the second term under the radical sign approaches zero as the value of X nears the mean and increases as X departs from the mean.

Confidence Intervals to Estimate a Single Value of Y

The second type of confidence interval in regression estimation is an interval to estimate a single value of Y for a given value of X.

Confidence Interval to Estimate Y for a Given Value of X

$$\hat{Y} \pm t_{\alpha/2,n-2}S_e\sqrt{1 + \frac{1}{n} + \frac{(X_0 - \bar{X})^2}{\Sigma X^2 - \frac{(\Sigma X)^2}{n}}},$$ (11.5)

where: X_0 = a particular value of X

Formula 11.5 is virtually the same as Formula 11.4, except for the additional value of 1 under the radical. This additional value widens the confidence interval to estimate a single value of Y from the confidence interval to estimate the average value of Y. This result seems logical, because the average value of Y falls toward the middle of a group of Y values, and the confidence interval to estimate the average need not be as wide as the confidence interval produced by Formula 11.5, which takes into account all the Y values for a given X.

A 95% confidence interval can be computed to estimate the single value of Y for X = 73 from the crude oil production example by using Formula 11.5.

The same values used to construct the confidence interval to estimate the average value of Y are used here:

$$t_{.025,7} = 2.365, \quad S_e = 1.928, \quad \Sigma X = 664,$$
$$\overline{X} = 73.78, \quad \text{and} \quad \Sigma X^2 = 49,080.$$

For $X_0 = 73$, the value of $\hat{Y} = 55.47$. The computed confidence interval for the single value of Y is

$$55.47 \pm (2.365)(1.928)\sqrt{1 + \frac{1}{9} + \frac{(73 - 73.78)^2}{49,080 - \frac{(664)^2}{9}}} = 55.47 \pm 4.821;$$

$$50.649 \le Y \le 60.291.$$

Figure 11.10 displays the confidence intervals for various values of X for both the average Y value and a single Y value. Note that the confidence intervals flare out toward the ends, as the values of X depart from the average X value. Note also that the confidence intervals for a single Y value are always wider than the confidence intervals for the average Y value for any given value of X.

Caution

A regression line is determined from a sample of points. The line, the r^2, the S_e, and the confidence intervals change for different sets of sample points. That is, the linear relationship developed for a set of points does not necessarily hold for values of X outside the domain of those used to establish the model. In the crude oil production example, the domain of X values (U.S. total energy consumption) varied from 68 to 79. The regression model developed from these points may not be valid for years in which the U.S. energy consumption

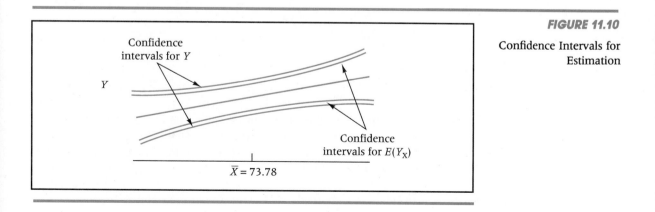

FIGURE 11.10

Confidence Intervals for Estimation

was, say, 20, 100, or 200 quadrillion Btu, because the regression model was not constructed with X values of those magnitudes. However, decision makers sometimes extrapolate regression results to values of X beyond the domain of those used to develop the formulas (often in time-series sales forecasting). Understanding the limitations of this type of use of regression analysis is essential.

Demonstration Problem 11.6

Construct a 95% confidence interval to estimate the average value of Y (FTEs) for Demonstration Problem 11.1 when $X = 40$ beds. Then construct a 95% confidence interval to estimate the single value of Y for $X = 40$ beds.

Solution:

For a 95% confidence interval, $\alpha = .05$; $n = 12$, and df $= 10$. The table t value is $t_{.025,10} = 2.228$; $S_e = 15.65$, $\Sigma X = 592$, $\overline{X} = 49.33$, and $\Sigma X^2 = 33{,}044$. For $X_0 = 40$, $\hat{Y} = 120.17$. The computed confidence interval for the average value of Y is

$$120.17 \pm (2.228)(15.65)\sqrt{\frac{1}{12} + \frac{(40 - 49.33)^2}{33{,}044 - \frac{(592)^2}{12}}}$$

$$= 120.17 \pm 11.35;$$

$$108.82 \le E(Y_{40}) \le 131.52.$$

With 95% confidence, the statement can be made that the average value of Y for $X = 40$ is between 108.82 and 131.52.

The computed confidence interval for the single value of Y is

$$120.17 \pm (2.228)(15.65)\sqrt{1 + \frac{1}{12} + \frac{(40 - 49.33)^2}{33{,}044 - \frac{(592)^2}{12}}}$$

$$= 120.17 \pm 36.67;$$

$$83.5 \le Y \le 156.84.$$

With 95% confidence, the statement can be made that a single value of Y for $X = 40$ is between 83.5 and 156.84. Obviously this interval is much wider than the 95% confidence interval for the average value of Y for $X = 40$.

11.39 Construct a 95% confidence interval for the average value of Y for Problem 11.5. Use $X = 25$.

11.40 Construct a 90% confidence interval for a single value of Y for Problem 11.6; use $X = 100$. Construct a 90% confidence interval for a single value of Y for Problem 11.6; use $X = 130$. Compare the results. Which confidence interval is greater? Why?

11.41 Construct a 98% confidence interval for the average value of Y for Problem 11.7; use $X = 20$. Construct a 98% confidence interval for a single value of Y for Problem 11.7; use $X = 20$. Which is wider? Why?

11.42 Construct a 99% confidence interval for the average bond rate in Problem 11.8 for a prime interest rate of 10%. Discuss the meaning of this confidence interval.

CORRELATION 11.8

Whereas regression analysis involves developing a functional relationship between variables, correlation is the process of determining a measure of the strength of relatedness of variables. For example, do the stocks of two airlines rise and fall in any related manner. Logically, the prices of two stocks in the same industry should be related. For a sample of pairs of data, correlation analysis can yield a numerical value that represents the degree of relatedness of the two stock prices over time. Another example comes from the transportation industry. Is there a correlation between the price of transportation and the weight of the object being shipped? Is there a correlation between price and distance? How strong are the correlations? Pricing decisions can be based in part on shipment costs that are correlated with other variables. In economics and finance, how strong is the correlation between the wholesale price index and the unemployment rate?

Several measures of correlation are available, the selection of which depends mostly on the level of data being analyzed. In this chapter, only one measure of correlation, r, is presented. This measure is applicable only if both variables being analyzed have at least an interval level of data. Chapter 12 presents a correlation measure that can be used when the data are ordinal.

The term r is called the *Pearson product–moment correlation coefficient*. It is named after Karl Pearson (1857–1936), an English statistician who developed several coefficients of correlation along with other significant statistical concepts. The term r is a measure of the linear correlation of two variables. It is a number that varies from -1 to 0 to $+1$, representing the strength of the relationship between the variables. A correlation of $+1$ denotes a perfect positive relationship. A perfect positive correlation means that as one variable increases in size, the other variable also increases. An r value of -1 denotes perfect negative correlation between two sets of numbers. A perfect negative correlation denotes an inverse relationship between two variables. As one variable gets larger, the other gets smaller. A zero value of r means that there is no relationship between the two variables.

Pearson Product–Moment Correlation Coefficient	$$r = \frac{SS_{xy}}{\sqrt{(SSX)(SSY)}} = \frac{\Sigma(X - \bar{X})(Y - \bar{Y})}{\sqrt{\Sigma(X - \bar{X})^2 \, \Sigma(Y - \bar{Y})^2}}$$ $$= \frac{\Sigma XY - \dfrac{(\Sigma X)(\Sigma Y)}{n}}{\sqrt{\left[\Sigma X^2 - \dfrac{(\Sigma X)^2}{n}\right]\left[\Sigma Y^2 - \dfrac{(\Sigma Y)^2}{n}\right]}} \qquad \textbf{(11.6)}$$

Figure 11.11 depicts five different degrees of correlation. Figure 11.11(a) represents strong negative correlation; (b) represents some negative correlation; (c) represents some positive correlation; (d) represents strong positive correlation; and (e) contains no correlation.

FIGURE 11.11

Five Correlations

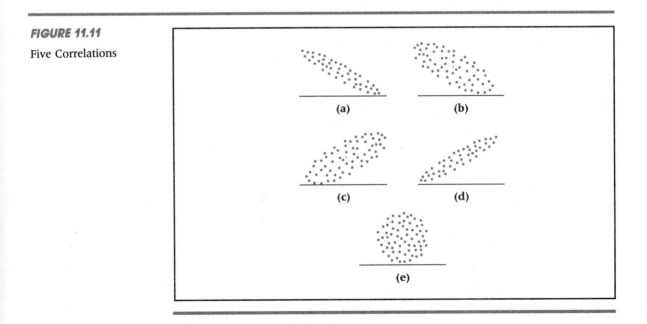

Day	Interest Rate	Futures Index	TABLE 11.6
1	7.43	221	Data for the Economic
2	7.48	222	Example
3	8.00	226	
4	7.75	225	
5	7.60	224	
6	7.63	223	
7	7.68	223	
8	7.67	226	
9	7.59	226	
10	8.07	235	
11	8.03	233	
12	8.00	241	

What is the measure of correlation between the interest rate of federal funds and the commodities futures index? The data in Table 11.6 represent the values for interest rates of federal funds and commodities futures indexes for a sample of twelve days. A correlation coefficient, r, can be computed for these data.

Examination of Formula 11.6 reveals that the following values must be obtained in order to compute r: ΣX, ΣX^2, ΣY, ΣY^2, ΣXY, and n. Unlike regression analysis, in correlation analysis which variable is designated X and which is designated Y does not matter. For this example, the correlation coefficient is computed as shown in Table 11.7. The r value obtained represents a relatively strong positive relationship between interest rates and commodities futures index over this twelve-day period.

Relationship Between r and r^2

Is r, the coefficient of correlation, related to r^2, the coefficient of determination in linear regression? The answer is yes: r^2 equals $(r)^2$. That is, the coefficient of determination is the square of the coefficient of correlation. However, they are used in different contexts: r is used in correlational analysis, and r^2 is used in regression analysis. In the economic example the objective was to determine the correlation between interest rates and commodities futures indexes. The value of r was .815. If this r value is squared, $r^2 = .66$, the result is the proportion of variance of commodities futures indexes accounted for by using interest rate as a predictor in a regression model. Or it is the proportion of variation of interest rates accounted for by using commodities futures indexes as a predictor in a regression model. Earlier in the chapter, a regression model was developed to predict FTEs by number of hospital beds. The r^2 value for that model was .886. Taking the square root of this value yields $r = .941$, which is the correlation between the sample number of beds and FTEs. A word

TABLE 11.7 Computation of r for the Federal Interest Rates and Commodities Futures Indexes

Day	Interest X	Futures Index Y	X^2	Y^2	XY
1	7.43	221	55.205	48,841	1,642.03
2	7.48	222	55.950	49,284	1,660.56
3	8.00	226	64.000	51,076	1,808.00
4	7.75	225	60.063	50,625	1,743.75
5	7.60	224	57.760	50,176	1,702.40
6	7.63	223	58.217	49,729	1,701.49
7	7.68	223	58.982	49,729	1,712.64
8	7.67	226	58.829	51,076	1,733.42
9	7.59	226	57.608	51,076	1,715.34
10	8.07	235	65.125	55,225	1,896.45
11	8.03	233	64.481	54,289	1,870.99
12	8.00	241	64.000	58,081	1,928.00
	$\Sigma X = 92.93$	$\Sigma Y = 2{,}725$	$\Sigma X^2 = 720.220$	$\Sigma Y^2 = 619{,}207$	$\Sigma XY = 21{,}115.07$

$$r = \frac{SS_{xy}}{\sqrt{SSX \cdot SSY}} = \frac{\Sigma XY - \dfrac{(\Sigma X)(\Sigma Y)}{n}}{\sqrt{\left[\Sigma X^2 - \dfrac{(\Sigma X)^2}{n}\right]\left[\Sigma Y^2 - \dfrac{(\Sigma Y)^2}{n}\right]}}$$

$$= \frac{(21{,}115.07) - \dfrac{(92.93)(2725)}{12}}{\sqrt{\left[(720.22) - \dfrac{(92.93)^2}{12}\right]\left[(619{,}207) - \dfrac{(2725)^2}{12}\right]}} = .815.$$

of caution here: Because r^2 is always positive, solving for r by taking $\sqrt{r^2}$ gives the correct magnitude of r but may give the wrong sign. The researcher must examine the sign of the slope of the regression line to determine whether there is a positive or a negative relationship between the variables and assign that sign to the correlation value.

Covariance

Chapter 3 introduced the concept of variance. Recall that the population variance of X was given by

$$\sigma^2 = \frac{\Sigma(X - \overline{X})^2}{n} = \frac{\Sigma X^2 - \dfrac{(\Sigma X)^2}{n}}{n}.$$

covariance   A similar concept is the **covariance,** which is *the variance of X and Y together.* Covariance is given by

$$\sigma_{xy}^2 = \frac{\Sigma(X - \bar{X})(Y - \bar{Y})}{n} = \frac{\Sigma XY - \dfrac{(\Sigma X)(\Sigma Y)}{n}}{n}.$$

The measure of covariance is used by some financial analysts and others as an indicator of relatedness of two variables. Examination of the coefficient of correlation formula reveals that the numerator of the formula contains the numerator of covariance: $\Sigma(X - \bar{X})(Y - \bar{Y})$. If X and Y are positively correlated and X is greater than the mean, Y also will tend to be greater than the mean, and their product will tend to be positive. If X is less than the mean, Y will tend to be less than the mean, again producing a positive product in the numerator. Summing many positive products produces a large positive correlation. Suppose that X and Y are negatively correlated. When X is more than the mean, Y will tend to be less than the mean, producing a negative product. When X is less than the mean, Y will tend to be more than the mean, again producing a negative product. Summing these negatives will tend to produce a large negative, resulting in a negative r value. If there is little or no correlation ($r \approx 0$) and X is greater than the mean, Y may be greater or less than the mean, producing some positive and some negative products. When X is smaller than the mean, Y may be larger or smaller than the mean, producing some positive and some negative products. The sum of these products will tend to be close to zero because of the cancellation effect of positive and negative products.

**PROBLEMS
Section 11.8**

11.43 Determine the value of the coefficient of correlation for the following data:

X	4	6	7	11	14	17	21
Y	18	12	13	8	7	7	4

11.44 Determine the value of r for the following data:

X	2	6	8	15	19	20	23
Y	5	6	13	16	22	20	21

11.45 Determine the value of r for the following data:

X	158	296	87	110	436
Y	349	510	301	322	550

11.46 In an effort to determine whether there is any correlation between the price of stocks of airlines, an analyst sampled ten days' activity of the stock market. Using the following prices of TWA stock and Southwest Air stock, compute the coefficient of correlation:

TWA	Southwest
10⅞	23½
11½	25¾
11¼	16⅝
6½	19⅝
8¼	18¾
10	17
9⅞	19⅛
9⅞	17½

11.47 How much correlation is there between the Dow Jones Average of 30 Industrials and Lehman Brothers T-Bond Index? In an effort to find out, an analyst sampled 9 days' activity and obtained the following data:

Dow Jones	T-Bond
2,602	3,628
2,535	3,583
2,580	3,631
2,560	3,600
2,533	3,587
2,527	3,579
2,593	3,337
2,810	3,445
2,560	3,305

Compute an r value for these data. Is the correlation strong? If the analyst had wanted to develop a regression model to predict the T-Bond Index from the Dow Jones, how strong would be the model's prediction? Compute r^2 for this model.

11.48 The following data are the 1990 claims (in $ millions) for Blue Cross & Blue Shield benefits for nine states, along with the surplus (in $ millions) that the company has in assets in those states:

State	Claims	Surplus
Alabama	$1,425	$277
Colorado	273	100
Florida	915	120
Illinois	1,687	259
Maine	234	40
Montana	142	25
North Dakota	259	57
Oklahoma	258	31
Texas	894	141

Use the data to compute a correlation coefficient, r, to determine the correlation between claims and surplus.

11.49 The National Safety Council released the following data on the incidence rates for fatal or lost work-time injuries per 100 employees for several industries for the years 1985, 1987, and 1989:

Industry	1985	1987	1989
Textile	0.46	0.48	0.69
Chemical	0.52	0.62	0.63
Communication	0.90	0.72	0.81
Machinery	1.50	1.74	2.10
Services	2.89	2.03	2.46
Nonferrous metals	1.80	1.92	2.00
Food	3.29	3.18	3.17
Government	5.73	4.43	4.00

Compute r for each pair of years and determine which years are most highly correlated.

MULTIPLE REGRESSION ANALYSIS

Simple regression analysis is bivariate regression in which one dependent variable, Y, is predicted by one independent variable, X. Examples of simple regression applications include trying to predict retail sales by population density of an area, Dow Jones average by prime interest rate, and crude oil production by energy consumption. However, other independent variables, taken in con-

FIGURE 11.12

Geometric Depiction of a Multiple Regression Model with Two Predictors

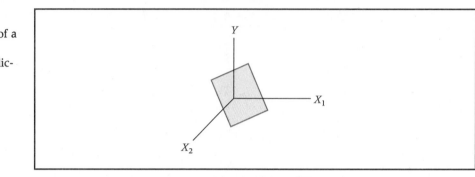

junction with the original independent variable, may make the regression model a better predictor of the dependent variable. For example, sales could be predicted by size of store and number of competitors in addition to population density. A model to predict the Dow Jones Average could include such additional predictors as yesterday's volume, bond interest rates, and Wholesale Price Index. In both cases, there is still only one dependent variable, Y, but there are multiple independent variables, X, or predictors. **Multiple regression** is *regression analysis with one dependent variable and two or more independent variables (predictors).*

multiple regression

Multiple regression analysis is similar in principle to simple regression analysis. However, it is more complex conceptually and computationally. The simple regression model is a straight line that passes through a plane of points. The most elementary multiple regression model has two independent variables and one dependent variable. Geometrically, this multiple regression model represents a plane passing through a three-dimensional space, as depicted in Figure 11.12. For multiple regression models containing three or more predictors, the geometric representation of the model requires four or more dimensions, which, of course, is impossible to depict.

Multiple regression model computations are rarely made by hand because of their complexity. This section focuses on the output from computer analysis of multiple regression. Although many of the concepts used in simple regression analysis apply in principle to multiple regression models, multiple regression provides some additional information that cannot be gleaned from simple regression.

The Regression Equation

For a population, the multiple regression equation is

$$Y = \beta_0 + \beta_1 X_1 + \beta_2 X_2 + \beta_3 X_3 + \cdots + \beta_j X_j + \epsilon,$$

where: j = number of independent variables

β_j = regression coefficient for an independent variable

β_0 = regression constant

ϵ = error of prediction

As with simple regression, the population values are rarely accessible, necessitating use of a regression equation for sample data:

$$Y = b_0 + b_1X_1 + b_2X_2 + b_3X_3 + \cdots + b_jX_j + e.$$

where: j = number of independent variables

b_j = regression coefficient for an independent variable

b_0 = regression constant

e = error of prediction

The crude oil production example presented in Section 11.1 can be expanded to a multiple regression example. The simple regression problem was to develop a regression model to predict world crude oil production by the amount of U.S. energy consumption for the previous year. Presumably, there are other predictors of crude oil production that can be added to the model to improve it. Two additional independent variables are U.S. imports of petroleum and U.S. coal production. Table 11.8 displays the world crude oil production levels for the even years 1972 through 1978 and U.S. energy consumption, U.S. imports of petroleum, and U.S. coal production for the odd years 1971 through 1987. The theory is that the values of the independent variables are more meaningful here as predictors if they are measured for the year immediately preceding the year for which the prediction is being made.

World Crude Oil Production (million bbl per day) Y	U.S. Energy Consumption (quadrillion Btu per year) X_1	U.S. Net Imports of Petroleum (quadrillion Btu per year) X_2	U.S. Coal Production (million short tons per year) X_3	
				TABLE 11.8
51	68	8	561	Data for Multiple Regression Model to Predict Oil Production
56	74	13	599	
57	71	13	655	
60	76	18	697	
59	79	17	781	
53	74	11	824	
54	71	9	782	
56	74	9	884	
58	77	13	919	

The computer software package Minitab was used to perform a multiple regression analysis for these data. The output is given in Table 11.9.

The output reveals that the equation of the multiple regression model is

$$\hat{Y} = 49.6 - 0.139X_1 + 0.828X_2 + 0.00868X_3,$$

or

$$\hat{Y} = 49.6 - 0.139(\text{U.S. energy consumption})$$
$$+ 0.828(\text{U.S. net imports of petroleum})$$
$$+ 0.00868(\text{U.S. coal production}).$$

The values -0.139, 0.828, and 0.00868 are the regression coefficients of the independent variables, and 49.6 is the constant. Each regression coefficient is analogous to the slope of the simple regression line but cannot be interpreted in the same way, and the constant is analogous to the Y intercept of the simple regression model. Note that the regression coefficients for this model vary. The magnitude and sign of a regression coefficient can be the result of that variable's units of measurement or that variable's weight (importance) in the multiple regression analysis.

For example, variable X_2 (U.S. net imports of petroleum) has a coefficient of 0.828. Thus in this multiple regression model a 1-unit increase in U.S. net imports of petroleum (quadrillion Btu per year) causes an increase of 0.828 unit in Y (million barrels of world crude oil production per day) if the other variables remain unchanged.

TABLE 11.9

Multiple Regression Output for Crude Oil Production Example

The regression equation is
$$\hat{Y} = 49.6 + -0.139X_1 + 0.828X_2 + 0.00868X_3$$

Predictor	Coef	Stdev	t ratio	p
Constant	49.60	23.59	2.10	0.089
X_1	-0.1393	0.4362	-0.32	0.762
X_2	0.8285	0.3509	2.36	0.065
X_3	0.008675	0.007890	1.10	0.322

$s = 1.485$ R-sq = 83.8%

Analysis of Variance

SOURCE	DF	SS	MS	F	p
Regression	3	56.978	18.993	8.62	0.020
Error	5	11.022	2.204		
Total	8	68.000			

The coefficient for variable X_1 (U.S. energy consumption in quadrillion Btu per day) is -0.139. For this multiple regression model, a 1-unit increase in this variable generates a reduction of 0.139 unit of Y (million barrels of world crude oil production per day). Does this result mean that, if the United States consumed more energy, world production could be reduced? The answer is no. The simple regression analysis using this variable as a predictor resulted in a coefficient of $+0.677$, indicating that as U.S. energy consumption increases, so does world production of oil.

In multiple regression, each coefficient must be interpreted in light of the other variables in the model. The -0.139 coefficient for U.S. energy consumption in the multiple regression model must be viewed also in terms of X_2 and X_3 being in the model. That is, in relation to the predictability accounted for by X_2 and X_3 in the model, X_1 has a -0.139 coefficient. The researcher needs to interpret regression coefficients carefully.

Testing the Multiple Regression Model

After developing the multiple regression model, the researcher may choose among several ways to determine the fit of the model to the data. The data from which the model was developed can be viewed as historical data in that for each of the independent variables' values, the value of Y is known. With the multiple regression model, predicted values of Y can be computed for the historical values of X. These predicted values of Y can then be compared to the historical values of Y to obtain the error of each prediction or *residual* in a manner similar to that used with simple regression. Examination of the residuals yields information about the fit of the model. The residuals for the crude oil production multiple regression model are

$$-0.621 \quad 0.742 \quad 0.839 \quad 0.028 \quad -0.454 \quad -2.553 \quad 0.051 \quad 1.584 \quad 0.384$$

Notice that the residuals for the fourth and seventh values are quite small and that the residuals for the sixth and eighth values are relatively large. Other uses, similar to those presented in Section 11.3, can be made of residual analysis.

Summing the squares of the residuals produces the sum of squares of error for the model (SSE). In the **Analysis of Variance** section of the computer printout in Table 11.9, the value of the sum of squares of error (SSE) for the crude oil production example is 11.022 (intersection of the Error row and the SS column). This SSE can then be used to compute a standard error of the estimate for multiple regression models:

$$S_e = \sqrt{\frac{\text{SSE}}{n - k}},$$

where: k = the total number of variables, including Y

For the crude oil production example, $k = 4$, because there are four variables (world crude oil production, U.S. energy consumption, U.S. imports of petroleum, and U.S. coal production). The standard error of the estimate for this multiple regression model is

$$S_e = \sqrt{\frac{SSE}{n - k}} = \sqrt{\frac{11.022}{9 - 4}} = 1.485.$$

Note that in Table 11.9, S_e is listed as s in the computer output. In Section 11.4, the standard error of the estimate was determined for the simple regression model developed to predict world crude oil production per day by annual U.S. energy consumption. The standard error of the estimate for the simple regression model was 1.928. Thus the multiple regression model, which included additional two predictors—U.S. net imports of petroleum per year and U.S. coal production per year—produced a standard error of the estimate of 1.485, which is a reduction from the 1.928 obtained previously. This multiple regression model seems to yield a somewhat better prediction than the simple regression model. In actual business situations, along with getting better predictions, keeping the model as simple as possible and still having a good fit also is important. Here, the two additional predictors reduced the standard error of the estimate by 23%. The researcher can explore other regression models to determine which model produces an acceptable standard error of the estimate using the fewest predictors. The answer is a function of the researcher's skill and preference.

Multiple regression models also generate a coefficient of determination. For multiple regression models, the coefficient of determination is denoted R^2. It is the percentage of variation of Y explained or accounted for by the X variables in the regression model. The formula for computing R^2 is

$$R^2 = 1 - \frac{SSE}{SSY} = \frac{SSE}{\Sigma Y^2 - \frac{(\Sigma Y)^2}{n}}.$$

Table 11.9 contains an R^2 of 83.8% for the crude oil production example, which was obtained for three predictors (U.S. energy consumption, U.S. net imports of petroleum, and U.S. coal production). This could have been computed by using the values of SS(Error) = SSE = 11.022 and SS(Total) = SSY = 68.000 in Table 11.9; that is, $R^2 = 1 - 11.022/68.000 = .838$. The r^2 produced by the simple regression model discussed in Section 11.5 for this example, with only U.S. energy consumption as the predictor, was 61.7%. Thus the two additional predictors increased R^2 from 61.7% to 83.8%, or by 22.1% of the total variability.

With bivariate simple regression, a t test of the slope of the regression line is used to determine whether the independent variable contributes significantly in linearly predicting the dependent variable. For multiple regression an analogous test makes use of the F statistic. The F statistic for the overall regression model is used to test the hypotheses

$$H_0: \beta_1 = \beta_2 = \beta_3 = \cdots = \beta_j = 0$$
$$H_a: \text{At least one of the } \beta\text{'s} \neq 0$$

In words, the F statistic is testing whether at least one of the regression coefficients is significantly different from zero. If the null hypothesis is not rejected, the multiple regression is adding nothing to the prediction of Y that the average Y value could not provide, and the regression model provides no linear predictability. The multiple regression model for the crude oil production example with the three predictors produced the following ANOVA (by Minitab from Table 11.9):

Analysis of Variance

SOURCE	DF	SS	MS	F	p
Regression	3	56.978	18.993	8.62	0.020
Error	5	11.022	2.204		
Total	8	68.000			

Note that the F value is 8.62. The probability of obtaining an F value this large or larger by chance is given as p, which for this example is .020. Because p is less than .05 (assuming $\alpha = .05$), for the crude oil production example at least one regression coefficient is significantly different from zero. This F test is an overall test for the multiple regression model. Is there a test for each particular regression coefficient?

Many statistical computer packages yield t tests for the slopes of each independent variable as part of the standard output. These t tests help the researcher determine whether a particular independent variable is making a significant contribution as a part of the multiple regression model. These t tests can be used in the same way that the t test of the slope is used in simple regression. The following t tests are for the slopes of the three independent variables in the crude oil production example (from Table 11.9):

Predictor	t ratio	p
X_1	−0.32	0.762
X_2	2.36	0.065
X_3	1.10	0.322

where: X_1 = U.S. energy consumption per year
X_2 = U.S. net imports of petroleum per year
X_3 = U.S. coal production per year

This table of t tests of the slopes shows that the variable U.S. net imports of petroleum per year yields a slope that is significant at $\alpha = .10$ (the actual probability is .065). This variable is the only significant predictor in this model. The slopes of the other two variables produce t tests with probabilities much larger than $\alpha = .10$ and are therefore not significant. The researcher might seriously consider dropping the two nonsignificant predictors from the model and recomputing the model using the one significant predictor. Using only X_2 as the predictor produces a regression model with an r^2 of 75.6%.

In general with multiple regression models, the F test is used as an overall test of a model to determine whether a significant linear prediction is occurring. The t tests of the slopes help to determine which variables, if any, are making significant contributions to the model.

Dummy Variables

qualitative variables
quantitative variables
dummy variables

Certain independent variables are **qualitative variables** as opposed to **quantitative variables.** Qualitative variables also are referred to as **dummy variables,** or indicator variables. Questionnaire or interview demographic questions often are coded as dummy variables because they are qualitative. Some examples are gender, religion, region of the country, occupation, marital status, and buying or renting a house. Multiple regression studies occasionally contain dummy variables. For example, in one mall location study, a variable reported whether the mall was located on the shore of Lake Erie. A site location model for pizza houses included qualitative variables of (1) does it serve beer? and (2) does the restaurant have a salad bar? These variables are all qualitative variables in that no scaled, interval measurement value can be assigned to each response. For example, if a mall is located on the shore of Lake Erie awarding it a score of 20 or 30 or 75 because of its location makes no sense. In terms of gender, what value would you assign to a man or a woman in a regression study? Qualitative or dummy variables such as these can be used in regression analysis if they are coded into a 0 or 1 format. For example, malls located on the shore of Lake Erie could be assigned a 1, and all other malls would be assigned a 0.

Many dummy variables are dichotomous, such as male/female, salad bar/ no salad bar, employed/not employed, and rent/not rent. For these variables, a value of 1 is arbitrarily assigned to one category and a value of 0 is assigned to the other category. Some qualitative variables contain several categories, such as social class: lower, middle, and upper. In this case, using coding of 1, 2, and 3 is tempting. However, this type of coding creates problems for multiple regression analysis. The social class variable should be broken into a variable for lower class where a value of 1 is assigned if a person is from the lower class and a value of 0 is assigned if they are not from the lower class. A second variable is designated for middle class where a value of 1 is assigned if a person is a member of this class and a 0 if not. A variable would not have to be assigned to the upper class, because it would be a redundant variable. Every person who did not receive a 1 for either lower or middle class is automatically a member of the upper class. This reasoning holds for all dummy variables

Northeast X_1	Midwest X_2	South X_3	TABLE 11.10
1	0	0	Coding the Qualitative Variable of Geographic Location for Regression Analysis
0	0	0	
1	0	0	
0	0	1	
0	1	0	
0	1	0	
0	0	0	
0	0	1	
1	0	0	
1	0	0	
0	1	0	

with more than two categories. If a qualitative variable has k categories, $k - 1$ dummy variables must be created and inserted into the regression analysis in order to include the qualitative variable in the multiple regression.

An example of a qualitative variable with more than two categories is the question taken from a questionnaire:

Your office is located in which region of the country?

_____ Northeast _____ Midwest _____ South _____ West

Suppose that a researcher is using a multiple regression analysis to predict the cost of doing business and believes that geographic location of the office is a potential predictor. How does the researcher insert this qualitative variable into the analysis? As $k = 4$, three dummy variables are inserted into the analysis. Table 11.10 shows one possible way to do so. Note that rows 2 and 7 contain all zeros, which indicates that these respondents have offices in the West. Thus a fourth dummy variable for the West region is not necessary. Dummy variables can be very useful and are a way in which nominal information can be recoded and incorporated into a multiple regression model.

Curvilinear Models

To this point, the discussion has centered on linear regression models. In many situations the relationship between the independent variable(s) and the dependent variable is not linear. Other such relationships include parabolic, quadratic, logarithmic, and exponential models. For example, early agricultural research indicated that the relationship between amount of fertilizer and yield might be more parabolic than linear, as shown in Figure 11.13.

FIGURE 11.13

Curvilinear Relationship
Between Yield and
Amount of Fertilizer

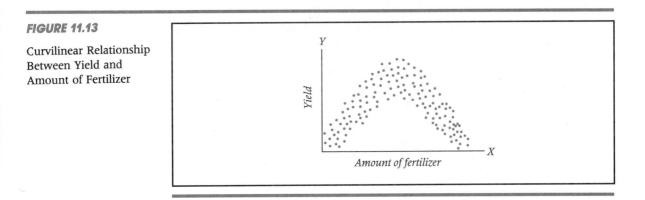

Sometimes regression analysis can produce curvilinear fits with recoded data. In the preceding example, a multiple regression model can be explored by using Y as yield, X_1 as amount of fertilizer, and X_2 as (amount of fertilizer)^2. That is, a second predictor variable, X_2, can be created from the first variable, X_1, merely by squaring the values of X_1. Most statistical computer models allow the researcher to create new and different columns (variables) from others by squaring, cubing, etc., a column of values. The second variable can then be treated as another linear variable and included in the analysis. Of course, curvilinearity has been built into the data before the variable is entered.

The researcher can explore a variety of nonlinear relationships between the dependent variable and the independent variable by coding into the data the desired relationship before entering the variable into regression. To explore the possibility of a parabolic relationship between U.S. net imports of petroleum

TABLE 11.11

Crude Oil Production
Problem with a
Curvilinear Predictor

World Crude Oil Production Y	U.S. Imports of Petroleum X_1	(Imports)^2 X_2
51	8	64
56	13	169
57	13	169
60	18	324
59	17	289
53	11	121
54	9	81
56	9	81
58	13	169

and world crude oil production in the crude oil production example, a new predictor, X_2, which is $(X_1)^2$ could be created, as shown in Table 11.11.

After the analysis, X_2 can be evaluated like any other predictor. In fact, X_2 and X_1 can be compared to determine whether the linear fit is stronger than the nonlinear fit. The multiple regression model is still linear in that the regression coefficients are still assigned on a linear basis. However, the data will already have been recoded to include nonlinear relationships and can be interpreted that way.

**Demonstration
Problem 11.7**

Demonstration Problem 11.1 to predict the FTEs of a hospital is expanded to include two new variables with the data shown. Determine the multiple regression model to predict FTEs by the three variables: number of beds, number of competing hospitals within a five-mile radius, and population density within a three-mile radius. Comment on the fit of the model by examining the residuals, S_e, R^2, and the slopes of the regression coefficients.

FTEs Y	Number of Beds X_1	Competitors X_2	Population X_3
69	23	1	800
95	29	0	750
102	29	0	900
118	35	0	1,100
126	42	1	1,300
125	46	0	1,800
138	50	2	2,000
178	54	1	2,500
156	64	1	1,500
184	66	2	2,000
176	76	3	3,000
225	78	2	5,000

Solution:

The computer package Minitab computed a multiple regression model for the following data:

The regression equation is:
$\hat{Y} = 32.9 + 1.89X_1 - 7.93X_2 + 0.0125X_3.$

The values 1.89, -7.93, and 0.0125 are the regression coefficients of the independent variables and 32.9 is the constant.

Predictor	t ratio	p
Number of Beds	4.06	0.004
Number of Competitors	-1.25	0.246
Population Density	2.07	0.073

$s = 13.37$ R-sq = 93.4%

Analysis of Variance

SOURCE	DF	SS	MS	F	p
Regression	3	20134.9	6711.6	37.57	0.000
Error	8	1429.1	178.6		
Total	11	21564.0			

The residuals are -9.37, -2.00, 3.12, 5.30, 5.53, -17.21, 1.61, 19.87, -8.49, 17.42, -14.03, and -1.75 in the order of the Y values.

The domain of the number of FTEs used in the data to develop the model is from 69 to 225. The largest residuals are 19.87 and 17.42. Two of the residuals are less than 2 FTEs. The standard error of the estimate is 13.37 FTEs. Approximately 68% of the estimates should fall within this value. Examination of the residuals reveals that 8 of the 12 residuals are within one standard error of the estimate. This value is down from the $S_e = 15.65$, which was obtained from the simple regression model using only number of beds as the predictor. The R^2 value is 93.4%; that is, over 93% of the variance of the FTEs values can be accounted for using this model, which is relatively high. The value of r^2 for the single predictor model was 88.6%. The addition of two more predictors only increased the value of R^2 by 4.8%. The F test for overall significance of the multiple regression model has a probability of less than .001. At least one of the regression slopes is significant. Examination of the t ratios, which test the slopes of each predictor, reveals that the variable, number of beds, has a significant slope at $\alpha = .01$. Another variable, population, has a slope that is significantly different from zero at $\alpha = .10$.

11.50 Examine the following data and the output generated from a multiple regression analysis by the statistical software package Minitab:

Y	X_1	X_2
27	3	9
14	11	121
11	15	225
17	8	64
18	9	81
25	2	4
10	12	144
14	16	256
16	9	81
22	5	25
24	6	36

The regression equation is:
$\hat{Y} = 32.0 - 2.30X_1 + 0.0643 X_2$

Predictor	Coef	Stdev	t ratio	p
Constant	31.963	2.826	11.31	0.000
X_1	-2.3003	0.6986	-3.29	0.011
X_2	0.06428	0.03774	1.70	0.127

$s = 2.344$ R-sq = 86.8%

Analysis of Variance

SOURCE	DF	SS	MS	F	p
Regression	2	288.03	144.02	26.20	0.000
Error	8	43.97	5.50		
Total	10	332.00			

Describe the output. Which variable seems to be a stronger predictor? Is there a relationship between X_1 and X_2? Note the sign of the coefficient of X_1. Does that coefficient have any special meaning? Is the regression model a good predictor of Y?

11.51 Examine the following data and the output generated from a multiple regression analysis with four predictor variables:

Y	X_1	X_2	X_3	X_4
9	0	20	5	12
7	1	14	6	20
6	0	15	9	26
4	0	13	11	23
2	0	9	9	22
5	0	10	8	20
11	1	17	6	9
17	1	25	4	5
10	1	8	5	8
8	0	11	8	14
8	0	9	3	15
7	1	6	7	18
6	1	8	2	20
3	0	5	1	27
2	0	6	1	29

The regression equation is:
$$\hat{Y} = 10.0 + 1.28X_1 + 0.267X_2 - 0.174X_3 - 0.318X_4$$

Predictor	Coef	Stdev	t ratio	p
Constant	10.024	2.081	4.82	0.000
X_1	1.2828	0.8110	1.58	0.145
X_2	0.26716	0.07633	3.50	0.006
X_3	-0.1742	0.1162	-1.50	0.165
X_4	-0.31818	0.06736	-4.72	0.00

s = 1.264   R-sq = 92.5%

Analysis of Variance

SOURCE	DF	SS	MS	F	p
Regression	4	196.029	49.007	30.68	0.000
Error	10	15.971	1.597		
Total	14	212.000			

Which of the variables is a dummy variable? Does the dummy variable seem to add much to the model? How do you know? Are any of the variables inversely related to *Y*? Describe the output. Which variables are the strongest predictors? Use S_e and R^2 to explain how well this model predicts *Y*.

11.52 A researcher gathered data to develop a multiple regression model to predict food store sales of a metropolitan area by three variables: city population, RMA (Ranally Metro Area population), and SMSA (standard metropolitan statistical area population). City and SMSA populations were obtained from U.S. census publications. Populations for RMAs were generated by Rand McNally Corporation. The following output was generated from computer regression analysis:

The regression equation is:
$\hat{Y} = 43{,}884.02 + 1.0875$ SMSA $- 0.2104$ City Pop. $+ 0.0374$ RMA

Predictor	Coef	Stdev	t ratio	p
Constant	43,884.02			
SMSA	1.0875	.0633	17.19	.0000
City Pop.	−0.2104	.0936	2.25	.0135
RMA	0.0374	.0615	0.61	.2717

$s = 236{,}087.7$ R-sq $= 97.7\%$

Analysis of Variance	F	p
	1295.13	0.0000

a. What is the equation of the multiple regression model?

b. What is the value of the coefficient of determination?

c. What is the standard error of the estimate?

d. Which variable is the most significant single predictor in this model?

e. Overall, is this model statistically significant?

USING REGRESSION IN FORECASTING   *11.10*

Forecasting is a useful tool in business planning and analysis. Forecasting techniques can be used to predict phenomena as near as tomorrow or as far away as thirty years. Often the financial well-being of a firm hinges on an accurate forecast of future events. Many different forecasting techniques are available for decision making, but all are imperfect and subject to error. These techniques are both qualitative (subjective) and quantitative. This section focuses on quantitative techniques and, more specifically, on regression-based quantitative techniques.

forecasting

Regression in Time-Series Data

Data gathered over a period of time are referred to as **time-series data.** Traditional business analysis of time-series data has consisted of decomposing the data into four main components: trend, cyclical, seasonal, and irregular fluctuations. The **trend** is the long-term general direction of the data. The

time-series data

trend

552

Chapter 11   Regression and Correlation Analysis

business cycle
seasonality

irregular fluctuations

cyclical trend, or **business cycle,** represents the rise and fall of business over periods of time. **Seasonality** reflects the highs and lows of business volume within a particular business cycle. Some fluctuations are not a factor of the general trend, business cycle, or seasonality. They are called **irregular fluctuations** and are the part of the model not explained by the other three components. Here, only the trend aspect of time-series data is examined.

Table 11.12 presents sales figures for a firm over a nine-year period. How can regression analysis be used to fit a trend line to these data? In this example, the time-series variable is sales. If sales are to be predicted by time, sales is the dependent variable, Y, and year is the independent variable, X. Analyzing the data from Table 11.12 by a computer regression software package produces the output displayed in Table 11.13.

TABLE 11.12

Sales Figures Over a
Nine-Year Period

Year	Sales (millions)
1983	$ 3.9
1984	4.1
1985	5.0
1986	5.5
1987	6.3
1988	7.4
1989	7.7
1990	8.4
1991	10.1

TABLE 11.13

Computer Output for
Sales Forecast

The regression equation is:
$\hat{Y} = -1484 + 0.750\ X$

Predictor	Coef	Stdev	t ratio	p
Constant	−1483.76	90.90	−16.32	0.000
X	0.75000	0.04574	16.40	0.000

$s = 0.3543$ R-sq = 97.5%

Analysis of Variance

SOURCE	DF	SS	MS	F	p
Regression	1	33.750	33.750	268.81	0.000
Error	7	0.879	0.126		
Total	8	34.629			

The regression equation given in Table 11.13 is

$$\text{Sales} = -1484 + 0.750(\text{year}).$$

This regression equation can be used to forecast by inserting the year of interest into the formula and solving for sales. For example, the forecast for 1993 sales is

$$\text{Sales} = -1484 + 0.750(1993) = 10.75.$$

Of course, caution should be exercised in interpreting this figure, because the regression model was developed for the years 1983 through 1991. There is no guarantee that the trend established for those years will continue through 1993.

Figure 11.14 depicts the sales data over time and the regression trend line. Note the extrapolation of the line to 1993, with the resulting predicted sales figure of $10.75 million.

Many nonlinear trends can be explored for time-series data, including S curves, logarithmic curves, exponential curves, quadratics, and others. Multiple regression can produce models that fit data with nonlinear shapes. Regression also can be used in forecasting by developing autoregressive models. Autoregressive models recognize a relationship between a data value for a given time period and the values for previous time periods. An example of an autoregressive model is prediction of sales data, Y, over a period of time by the same sales data but lagged one-period behind, X. These types of models have various applications but are not presented in this text. Econometric forecasters also often use multiple regression as a tool in developing models. These techniques are beyond the scope of this text.

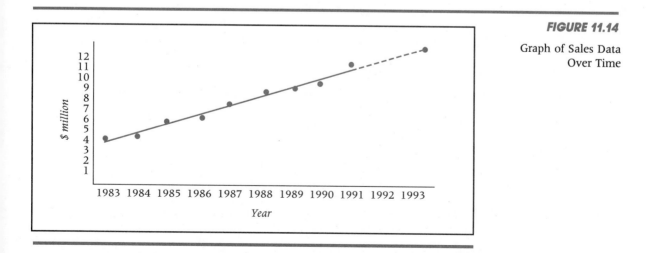

FIGURE 11.14

Graph of Sales Data Over Time

Demonstration Problem 11.8

The Federal Reserve System reports that the year-end assets of U.S. Savings Bonds have been increasing during the past several decades. Given are the total assets of the U.S. Savings Bond program for six different years. Use these data to develop a simple time-series regression model to predict the amount of U.S. Savings Bond assets for 1995.

Year	U.S. Savings Bonds (billions)
1960	$45.6
1965	49.7
1970	52.1
1975	67.4
1980	72.5
1985	79.8

Solution:

The assets of U.S. Savings Bonds are the dependent variable, Y. The years are the predictor, or independent variable, X. Following is the computer output for this problem.

The regression equation is:
$\hat{Y} = -2810 + 1.46 X$

Predictor	Coef	Stdev	t ratio	p
Constant	−2809.6	311.9	−9.01	0.001
X	1.4554	0.1581	9.20	0.001

$s = 3.308$ R-sq = 95.5%

Analysis of Variance

SOURCE	DF	SS	MS	F	p
Regression	1	926.74	926.74	84.70	0.001
Error	4	43.76	10.94		
Total	5	970.51			

The regression equation for this time-series regression line is

$$\text{Savings bonds} = -2810 + 1.46(\text{year}).$$

Substituting 1995 for the year variable produces a forecast Savings Bonds total of $102.7 billion.

11.53 Determine the equation of the trend line to fit the following time-series data, and forecast the Y value for 1992:

Year	Cost
1978	$ 2
1979	3
1980	5
1981	6
1982	9
1983	9
1984	11
1985	14
1986	16
1987	20
1988	21
1989	22
1990	24

11.54 Determine the equation for the trend line for the following time periods, and use the equation to predict the value for April 1993:

1991		1992	
Month	Sales	Month	Sales
Jan.	$ 34	Jan.	$105
Feb.	50	Feb.	109
Mar.	56	Mar.	114
Apr.	71	Apr.	121
May	80	May	134
June	85	June	138
July	87	July	146
Aug.	91	Aug.	165
Sept.	101	Sept.	182
Oct.	102	Oct.	189
Nov.	100	Nov.	199
Dec.	104	Dec.	207

11.55 Federal Reserve System asset figures for non-Savings Bond U.S. Treasury securities and mutual fund shares are presented for the years 1960 through 1985:

Year	Treasury Securities (billions)	Mutual Funds (billions)
1960	$ 24.1	$ 17.0
1965	24.9	34.4
1970	31.1	44.5
1975	51.6	38.7
1980	133.0	52.1
1985	396.4	203.0

a. Compute a time-series regression line for the Treasury securities from the data and forecast the Treasury security amount for 1990.

b. Compute a time-series regression line for the mutual fund shares data and use the line to forecast the mutual fund shares amount for the year 2000.

11.56 Shown are producer price indexes for farm products and for chemicals and allied products for 1988 through 1991.

Year	Farm Products	Chemicals and Allied Products
1988	104.8	116.4
1989	106.4	118.7
1990	112.0	123.7
1991	111.4	124.2

a. Use the indexes for farm products to predict the figure for 1992.

b. Use the indexes for chemicals and allied products to predict the index for 1993.

CHAPTER SUMMARY

Regression is a procedure that produces a mathematical model (function) that can be used to predict one variable by other variables. Correlation is a measure of the relatedness of variables. Simple regression and correlation are bivariate

Carl Gauss (1777–1855) often is referred to as the "Prince of Mathematics." He is ranked with Archimedes and Newton as one of the three greatest mathematicians of all time. Gauss was born into humble circumstances and, had his father prevailed, Gauss probably would have lived a life of manual labor. However, his mother and his uncles recognized early in Gauss's life his special talents. Reportedly, before he was three years old, he detected an error in his father's payroll calculations. In school he astonished his teachers with his skills and abilities. The Duke of Brunswick heard of Gauss's potential and became his patron.

Gauss was educated at Caroline College and the University of Gottingen. He received a PhD from the University of Helmstadt in 1799 for the proof of a geometric construction that had puzzled researchers for more than 2,000 years. Gauss contributed to every branch of pure and applied mathematics in his day. He also contributed to astronomy, geodesy, physics, and metrology. One of his greatest and most widely used contributions is that of the method of least squares regression analysis. In 1801, using least squares techniques and limited data, Gauss made accurate predictions of the orbits of some newly discovered planets. In his later years, Gauss took great pride in his contributions to the development of least squares methodology.

Source: Adapted from Dudycha, Arthur L., and Linda W. Dudycha, "Behavioral Statistics: An Historical Perspective," in *Statistical Issues: A Reader for the Behavioral Sciences*, edited by Roger Kirk (Monterey, Calif.: Brooks/Cole, 1972).

in that the analysis is of two variables. Multiple regression analysis involves three or more variables.

Simple regression analysis produces a model in which a Y variable, referred to as the dependent variable, is predicted by an X variable, referred to as the independent variable. The resulting regression model is linear. The general form of the equation of the simple regression line is the slope–intercept equation of a line. The equation of the simple regression model consists of a slope of the line as a coefficient of X and a Y intercept value as a constant.

After the equation of the line has been developed, several statistics are available that can be used to determine how well the line fits the data. Using the historical data values of X, predicted values of Y (denoted $\hat{Y}$) can be calculated by inserting values of X into the regression equation. The predicted values can then be compared to the actual values of Y to determine how well the regression equation fits the known data. The difference between a specific Y value and its associated predicted Y value is called the residual or error of prediction. Examination of the residuals can offer insight into the magnitude of the errors produced by a model. In addition, residual analysis can be used to help determine whether the assumptions underlying the regression analysis have been met. Specifically, graphs of the residuals can reveal (1) lack of linearity, (2) lack of homogeneity of error variance, and (3) independence of error terms. The residuals are geometrically the vertical distances from the Y values to the regression line. Because the equation that yields the regression line is derived in such a way that the line is in the geometric middle of the points, the sum of the residuals is zero.

A single value of error measurement called the standard error of the estimate, S_e, can be computed. It is the standard deviation of error of a model. Because the error terms are normally distributed, 68% of all errors should fall within $\pm 1 S_e$, and 95% should fall within $\pm 2 S_e$. The value of S_e can be used as a single guide to the magnitude of the error produced by the regression model.

Another widely used statistic for testing the strength of a regression model is r^2, or the coefficient of determination. The coefficient of determination is the proportion of total variance of the Y variable accounted for or predicted by X. It varies from 0 to 1. The higher the r^2 is, the stronger the prediction by the model becomes.

Testing to determine whether the slope of the regression line is different from zero is another way to judge the fit of the regression model to the data. If the slope of the regression line is not different from zero, the regression model is not adding significant predictability.

One of the most prevalent uses of a regression model is to predict the values of Y for given values of X. Recognizing that the predicted value is often not the same as the actual value, a confidence interval has been developed to yield a range within which the mean Y value for a given X should fall. A confidence interval for a single Y value for a given X value also is given. This second confidence interval is wider, because it allows for the wide diversity of individual values, whereas the confidence interval for the mean Y value reflects only the range of average Y values for a given X.

Bivariate correlation can be accomplished with several different measures. In this chapter, only one coefficient of correlation is presented: the Pearson product–moment coefficient of correlation, r. This value varies from -1 to 0 to $+1$. An r value of $+1$ is perfect positive correlation, and an r value of -1 is perfect negative correlation. Negative correlation means that, as one variable increases in value, the other variable tends to decrease. For r values near 0, there is little or no correlation.

Regression models that contain a single dependent variable and multiple independent variables are called multiple regression models. Many of the concepts of simple regression apply in principle to multiple regression. The multiple regression model has a slope or regression coefficient for each independent variable and a constant term, which is analogous to the Y intercept of simple regression. With multiple regression, the coefficient of determination is denoted R^2.

Virtually all multiple regression is done on the computer. Many of the statistical computer programs that produce multiple regression yield an F test as an overall test of the regression model and individual t values to determine the significance of the slope of each independent variable.

Simple regression models are linear, but curvilinear models can be developed by recoding data of a variable before entering it into the regression model. Qualitative or dummy variables can be analyzed in regression models by using 0 and 1 coding. If a qualitative variable has more than two categories, $k - 1$ variables must be entered into the regression analysis, where k is the number of categories.

Regression can be used in several ways as a forecasting tool. Some forecasting models represent attempts to determine a trend in time-series data. Simple and multiple regression techniques can be used effectively in exploring trends. Regression analysis can also be an important tool in the development of econometric models. Autoregression is a forecasting tool whereby regression analysis is used to predict one set of time-series data by the same set of data lagged by one or more time periods.

Key Words

Correlation	Coefficient of determination (r^2)
Regression	Pearson product–moment
Simple regression	correlation coefficient (r)
Dependent variable	Covariance
Independent variable	Multiple regression
Scatter plot	Qualitative variable
Least squares analysis	Quantitative variable
Slope of the regression line	Dummy variable
Residual	Forecasting
Outliers	Time-series data
Homoscedasticity	Trend
Heteroscedasticity	Business cycle
Sum of squares of error (SSE)	Seasonality
Standard error of the estimate (S_e)	Irregular fluctuations

USING THE COMPUTER

You can use Minitab to analyze data by both correlation and regression. The main commands for doing so are CORRELATION and REGRESSION.

Correlation

You can compute the Pearson product–moment correlation coefficient, r, for two variables or more by using the command:

MTB > CORRELATION

To do so, load the data into columns as specified in previous chapters by using either the **SET** command or the **READ** command. Correlation is computed on pairs of data, so **READ** might be the preferable command. After you have entered the data into columns, correlation calculation is possible. Suppose that you want to correlate the variable FTEs from Demonstration Problem 11.1 with number of beds. Suppose further that you have read FTE values into column 1 and number of beds into column 2. The command to correlate these two variables is

    MTB > CORRELATE C1 C2

The output is

    Correlation of C1 and C2 = 0.942

If you want to compute several correlations simultaneously, Minitab allows you to do so with the **CORRELATION** command. Merely list all variables to be correlated after the **CORRELATION** command, and Minitab produces a *correlation matrix* of the r values for all possible pairs of variables. In Section 11.9 (multiple regression), Demonstration Problem 11.1 was extended to include two other variables: population and competitors. Assuming population data are in C3 and competitors are in C4 and using the **CORRELATION** command, you can produce a correlation matrix for all intercorrelations for the problem. The command is

    MTB > CORRELATION C1 C2 C3 C4

The output is

	C1	C2	C3
C2	0.942		
C3	0.655	0.770	
C4	0.887	0.833	0.650

Regression

You can accomplish both simple regression and multiple regression by using the Minitab command **REGRESSION**. You should consider using the **PLOT** command to produce a scatter plot of the data before analyzing the data by regression. With the **PLOT** command, Minitab requires a listing of the columns of the variables to be plotted after the word **PLOT**. However, the first variable listed should be the variable that you want to appear on the ordinate or Y axis. Suppose that you want to generate a plot of Demonstration Problem 11.1 data with FTEs on the Y axis and the number of beds on the X axis. If FTEs are stored in column 1 and number of beds in column 2, the plot command is

MTB > PLOT C1 C2

The output consists of the plot.

  Simple regression is done similarly. The **REGRESSION** command requires first the location of the column containing the dependent variable, Y. Following the column location of Y is a number that represents the number of independent variables, X's, to be used in the regression. If you are using simple regression, the number will be 1. After the number of independent variables, list the column locations of the independent variables separated by spaces, commas, etc. Suppose that number of FTEs is located in column 1, and number of beds is located in column 2. The command to perform a simple regression to predict FTEs (Y) by number of beds (X) is

MTB > REGRESSION C1 1 C2

The output is

The regression equation is:
C1 = 30.9 + 2.23 C2

Predictor	Coef	Stdev	t ratio	p
Constant	30.91	13.25	2.33	0.042
C2	2.2315	0.2526	8.83	0.000

s = 15.65   R-sq = 88.6%   R-sq(adj) = 87.5%

Analysis of Variance

SOURCE	DF	SS	MS	F	p
Regression	1	19155	19155	78.05	0.000
Error	10	2449	245		
Total	11	21564			

  Note that the output contains the standard error of the estimate, s, along with R-sq, an overall test of the model, F, and tests of the slope. The residuals are not included here as output, but a Minitab command is available to compute the residuals. The **RESIDUAL** command is a subcommand of the **REGRES-SION** command. To use this subcommand, end the **REGRESSION** command with a semicolon, and the subcommand prompt **SUBC** will appear. After the prompt, use the **RESIDUAL** subcommand and enter a column location to store the residuals and a period to notify Minitab that you are finished with the subcommand. You will need to use a **PRINT** command to print the residuals from the column in which they are stored. To produce the residuals for the Demonstration Problem 11.1, use the following commands:

```
MTB > REGRESSION C1 1 C2;
SUBC > RESIDUAL C3.
MTB > PRINT C3
```

You will get the usual regression output followed by the residual output of

```
C3
   -13.2371   -0.6261   6.3739     8.9849    1.3644   -8.5617   -4.4877
    26.5863  -17.7287   5.8083   -24.5068   20.0302
```

Suppose that you want to use Minitab to perform a multiple regression analysis on Demonstration Problem 11.1 with the following dependent variable and independent variables located in the given columns:

Number of FTEs (Y) in C1
Number of beds (X_1) in C2
Number of competitors (X_2) in C3
Population (X_3) in C4

The Minitab command to accomplish this analysis is

```
MTB > REGRESSION C1 3 C2 C3 C4
```

Note the number 3, which represents the number of independent variables in the model. Note also that C1, which contains the Y variable, is listed first. The output from this command is

The regression equation is:
C1 = 32.9 + 1.89 C2 − 7.93 C3 + 0.0125 C4

Predictor	Coef	Stdev	t ratio	p
Constant	32.90	13.55	2.43	0.041
C2	1.8868	0.4645	4.06	0.004
C3	−7.933	6.344	−1.25	0.246
C4	0.012510	0.006057	2.07	0.073

s = 13.37   R-sq = 93.4%   R-sq(adj) = 90.9%

Analysis of Variance

SOURCE	DF	SS	MS	F	p
Regression	3	20134.9	6711.6	37.57	0.000
Error	8	1429.1	178.6		
Total	11	21564.0			

SOURCE	DF	SEQ SS
C2	1	19115.1
C3	1	257.8
C4	1	762.1

SUPPLEMENTARY PROBLEMS

11.57 Use the following data to perform operations (a)–(f):

X	5	7	3	16	12	9
Y	8	9	11	27	15	13

a. Determine the equation of the least squares regression line to predict Y by X.

b. Using the X values, solve for the predicted values of Y and the residuals.

c. Solve for S_e.

d. Solve for r^2.

e. Test the slope of the regression line. Use $\alpha = .01$.

f. Comment on the results determined in (b)–(e) and make a statement about the fit of the line.

11.58 Use the following data to do what is called for in (a)–(h):

X	53	47	41	50	58	62	45	60
Y	5	5	7	4	10	12	3	11

a. Determine the equation of the simple regression line to predict Y from X.

b. Using the X values, solve for the predicted values of Y and the residuals.

c. Solve for SSE.

d. Calculate the standard error of the estimate.

e. Determine the coefficient of determination.

f. Calculate the coefficient of correlation.

g. Test the slope of the regression line. Assume $\alpha = .05$. What do you conclude about the slope?

h. Comment on (d)–(f).

11.59 Solve for the value of r for the following data:

X	213	196	184	202	221	247
Y	76	65	62	68	71	75

If you were to develop a regression line to predict Y by X, what value would the coefficient of determination have?

11.60 Determine the equation of the least squares regression line to predict Y from the following data:

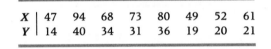

X	47	94	68	73	80	49	52	61
Y	14	40	34	31	36	19	20	21

a. Construct a 95% confidence interval to estimate the mean Y value for $X = 60$.

b. Construct a 95% confidence interval to estimate an individual Y value for $X = 70$.

c. Interpret the results obtained in (a) and (b).

11.61 Can the consumption of water in a city be predicted by temperature? The following data represent a sample of a day's water consumption and the high temperature for that day:

Water Use (million gal)	Temperature
219	103°
56	39
107	77
129	78
68	50
184	96
150	90
112	75

Develop a least squares regression line to predict the amount of water used in a day in a city by the high temperature for that day. What would the predicted water usage be for a temperature of 100°? Evaluate the regression model by calculating S_e, by calculating r^2, and by testing the slope. Let $\alpha = .01$.

11.62 Those in the aerospace industry believe that the cost of a space project is a function of the weight of the major object being sent into space.

Use the following data to develop a regression model to predict the cost of a space project by the weight of the space object. Determine r^2 and S_e.

Weight (tons)	Cost (millions)
1.897	$ 53.6
3.019	184.9
0.453	6.4
0.988	23.5
1.058	33.4
2.100	110.4
2.387	104.6

11.63 Is the amount of money spent by companies on advertising a function of the total sales of the company? Shown are sales income and advertising cost data for seven companies published by *Advertising Age:*

Company	Advertising (millions)	Sales (billions)
Philip Morris	$1,557.8	$ 25.9
Procter & Gamble	1,386.7	19.3
General Motors	1,024.9	121.1
RJR Nabisco	839.6	17.0
Pepsico	704.0	13.0
Eastman Kodak	658.2	17.0
Ford Motor	639.5	92.4

Use the data to develop a regression line to predict the amount of advertising by sales. Compute S_e and r^2. Assuming $\alpha = .05$, test the slope of the regression line. Comment on the strength of the regression model.

11.64 A computer was used to conduct a simple regression analysis to predict Y from X. The computer output is as follows:

The regression equation is:
$\hat{Y} = 122 - 0.800\ X$

Predictor	Coef	Stdev	t ratio	p
Constant	122.26	15.10	8.10	0.000
X	−0.7995	0.1279	−6.25	0.002

$s = 5.375$ R-sq = 88.7%

Analysis of Variance

SOURCE	DF	SS	MS	F	p
Regression	1	1129.0	1129.0	39.07	0.002
Error	5	144.5	28.9		
Total	6	1273.4			

a. What is the equation of the regression model?

b. What is the meaning of the coefficient of X?

c. What is the result of the test of the slope of the regression model? Let $\alpha = .10$. Why is the t ratio negative?

d. Comment on r^2 and the standard error of the estimate.

e. Comment on the relationship of the F value to the t ratio for X.

f. The correlation coefficient for these two variables is $-.942$. Is this surprising to you? Why or why not?

11.65 Determine the Pearson product–moment correlation coefficient for the following data:

X	1	10	9	6	5	3	2
Y	8	4	4	5	7	7	9

11.66 A car dealer believes that there is a relationship between the number of sales people on duty and the number of cars sold. Use the sample data collected for five different weeks at a dealership to calculate r. Is there much of a relationship? Solve for r^2. Explain what r^2 means in this problem.

Week	Number of Cars Sold	Number of Salespeople
1	79	6
2	64	6
3	49	4
4	23	2
5	52	3

11.67 How strong is the correlation between the inflation rate and thirty-year treasury yields? The following data published by Fuji Securities, Inc., are given as pairs of inflation rates and treasury yields for selected years over a thirty-five year period:

Inflation Rate	Thirty-Year Treasury Yield
1.57%	3.05%
2.23	3.93
2.17	4.68
4.53	6.57
7.25	8.27
9.25	12.01
5.00	10.27
4.62	8.45

Compute the Pearson product–moment correlation coefficient to determine the strength of the correlation between these two variables. Comment on the strength and direction of the correlation.

11.68 The following are amounts spent by nine large corporations on network television advertising and network radio advertising, as published by *Advertising Age:*

Company	Network Television (millions)	Network Radio (millions)
Philip Morris	$330,778	$ 8,937
Procter & Gamble	377,552	23,665
General Motors	272,953	18,906
Sears, Roebuck	89,973	52,701
RJR Nabisco	209,777	2,226
Pepsico	140,342	5,203
Eastman Kodak	145,961	3,941
McDonald's	216,067	0
Ford Motors	161,177	19,766

Use the data to determine the correlation between these two variables. Comment on the strength of the correlation.

11.69 Use the following data to develop a correlation matrix of intercorrelations of earnings per share for the six stocks:

Year	Abbott	Bausch & Lomb	Exxon	Motorola	Sara Lee	Tootsie Roll
1986	$2.32	$2.47	$3.71	$1.53	$2.02	$1.37
1987	2.78	2.81	3.43	2.39	2.35	1.55
1988	3.33	3.27	3.95	3.43	2.83	1.77

Which stock earnings per share were most correlated? Correlated least? Why?

11.70 Is the water consumption of a city per day a function of the time of the year? Water consumption totals for the fifteenth of each month for eight months of the year are as follows:

Month	Gallons (Millions)
January	39
February	42
March	63
April	89
May	108
June	154
July	178
August	185

Determine the equation of the trend line through these data. Note that the months January–August are used. (*Hint:* Convert the months to numbers.) What would happen to the model if you include September–December?

11.71 According to Fuji Securities, Inc., inflation increased at a relatively steady rate from the mid-1950s until the early 1980s. The following data are the average inflation rates for six of the years during this period:

Year	Inflation Rate
1955	1.57%
1960	2.23
1965	2.17
1970	4.53
1975	7.25
1980	9.25

Use these data to determine the equation of the regression line to forecast the rate of inflation during this time period. Use this model to predict the inflation rate for 1985. The average inflation rate for the 1980s was actually 5.00%. Why does the predicted inflation rate for 1985 from the forecasting model contain so much error for the 1985 prediction?

11.72 According to the Federal Deposit Insurance Corporation, the number of bank failures from 1978 through 1988 were as follows:

Year	Bank Failures
1978	7
1979	10
1980	10
1981	10
1982	42
1983	48
1984	79
1985	120
1986	138
1987	184
1988	200

Use these data to develop a time-series regression model to predict the number of bank failures for 1993.

11.73 The following data represent a breakdown of banks in the United States according to the Federal Reserve System:

Year	Total	State Banks	Mutual Savings
1940	14,955	1,234	551
1945	14,542	1,825	539
1950	14,674	1,914	527
1955	14,309	1,867	525
1960	14,006	1,675	513
1965	14,295	1,432	504
1970	14,167	1,167	496
1975	15,108	1,046	475
1980	15,145	997	460
1985	14,713	1,080	344

a. Develop a regression model to predict the total number of banks by the number of state banks.

b. Determine the correlation between the number of state banks and the number of mutual savings.

c. Develop the equation of the trend line to predict the number of mutual savings institutions for 1995 based on this model.

11.74 The National Center for Employee Ownership reports that one of the fastest growing forms of employee compensation is the employee stock ownership plan (ESOP). Listed are the number of plans in the United States and the number of employees belonging to ESOPs:

Year	Number of Plans	Number of Employees in ESOPs
1980	5,009	4,048
1981	5,680	4,537
1982	6,082	4,745
1983	6,456	5,397
1984	6,904	6,576
1985	7,402	7,353
1986	8,046	7,860
1987	8,777	8,860
1988	9,000	9,000
1989	10,000	10,000

a. Compute a correlation coefficient to determine the correlation between number of plans and number of employees in ESOPs.

b. Develop a simple regression line to predict the number of plans by the number of employees in ESOPs.

c. Develop a time-series simple regression model to predict the number of plans. Based on this model, what is the forecast number of plans for 1992?

11.75 Executives of a video rental chain want to predict the success of a potential new store. The company's researcher begins by gathering the following information from several of the chain's present outlets:

Rentals	Corner Store?	Number of Competitors (within 1-mile radius)	Average Family Income ($1,000)
710	0	3	65
529	1	1	43
314	0	0	29
504	0	2	47
619	1	0	52
428	0	4	50
317	0	1	46
205	0	1	29
468	1	1	31
545	0	4	43
607	0	3	49
694	0	2	64

Use a computer to develop a multiple regression model to predict the number of rentals per day by the other variables. Comment on the output.

11.76 The following data from four variables was used to formulate a multiple regression model to predict Y. The output from the computer analysis of these data follows:

Y	X_1	X_2	X_3
27	84	45	29
36	79	53	51
51	78	27	110
81	71	91	90
90	64	89	87
92	68	67	68
98	67	71	70
110	54	49	81
129	47	81	84
138	49	94	91

The regression equation is:
$\hat{Y} = 215 - 2.42\ X_1 + 0.268\ X_2 + 0.160\ X_3$

Predictor	Coef	Stdev	t ratio	p
Constant	214.84	37.94	5.66	0.001
X_1	-2.4155	0.3540	-6.82	0.000
X_2	0.2680	0.1818	1.47	0.191
X_3	0.1597	0.1656	0.96	0.372

$s = 10.10$ R-sq $= 95.1\%$

Analysis of Variance

SOURCE	DF	SS	MS	F	p
Regression	3	11938.1	3979.4	39.05	0.000
Error	6	611.5	101.9		
Total	9	12549.6			

Determine:
a. the regression equation;
b. R^2;
c. the standard error of the estimate;
d. the value of t for each coefficient (and comment on each); and
e. the overall test of the model for significance. Use $\alpha = .05$.

CHI-SQUARE AND OTHER NONPARAMETRIC STATISTICS

CHAPTER LEARNING OBJECTIVES

The main objective of this chapter is to present several nonparametric statistics that can be used when the level of data is insufficient to warrant the use of parametric statistics, specifically enabling you to

1. Recognize the advantages and disadvantages of nonparametric statistics.
2. Understand the chi-square goodness-of-fit test and how to use it.
3. Analyze data using contingency analysis.
4. Know when and how to use the Mann–Whitney U test, the Wilcoxon matched-pairs signed rank test, and the Kruskal–Wallis test.
5. Correlate data using Spearman's rank correlation coefficient.

JEFFERSON AND MOORE WIN A CONSULTING CONTRACT TO MEASURE ATTITUDES

Jefferson and Moore, a small Midwest management consulting firm, has been awarded a contract by Villalobos Industries, Inc., to ascertain employee attitudes toward the company. Kimberly Eshelman, a researcher with Jefferson and Moore, has been given the task of developing a measurement instrument that can be used to determine employee attitudes. She realizes that, because of the difficulty of what she is trying to measure and because of the nature of the questions, she is likely to develop a measurement instrument that will produce scores that are only ordinal level data. Furthermore, as this is a new instrument, she has no idea of the shape of the distribution of employee attitude scores. Hence when she attempts to statistically analyze small sample data, she believes that she cannot ethically use the *t* test or the *F* test because she does not know if the scores being analyzed come from a normal distribution. She wants to compare scores between men and women and to analyze the results by age bracket. If she decides to correlate attitude scores over a period of time, she cannot use the Pearson product–moment correlation coefficient, because she does not have interval level data.

Managerial Questions

- What statistical techniques are appropriate for analyzing ordinal level data?
- Are statistical techniques available that can be used to test the difference in two groups when the sample sizes are small and the distributions of the populations are not normal?
- Is a correlational analysis available for ordinal level data?

parametric statistics

V irtually all statistical techniques presented in the text thus far are parametric techniques. **Parametric statistics** are *statistical techniques based on assumptions about the population from which the sample data are selected.* For example, if a *t* statistic is being used to conduct a hypothesis test about a population mean, the assumption is that the data being analyzed are randomly selected from a *normally* distributed population. The name *parametric statistics* refers to the fact that an assumption (here, normally distributed data) is being made about the data used to test or estimate the parameter (in this case, the population mean). In addition, the use of parametric statistics requires quantitative measurements that yield interval or ratio level data.

As Kimberly Eshelman discovered in the development of the attitude scale, the data generated in an experiment sometimes do not meet the assumptions made about the population, or the level of data being measured is qualitative. For such occasions, statistical techniques have been developed that are called nonparametric or distribution-free techniques. **Nonparametric statistics** *are based on fewer assumptions about the population and the parameters than are parametric statistics.* Sometimes they are referred to as distribution-free statistics because many of them can be used regardless of the shape of the population distribution. A variety of nonparametric statistics are available for use with nominal or ordinal data. Some require at least ordinal level data, but others can be specifically targeted for use with nominal level data.

nonparametric statistics

Nonparametric techniques have the following advantages.

1. Sometimes there is no parametric alternative to the use of nonparametric statistics.
2. Certain nonparametric tests can be used to analyze nominal data.
3. Certain nonparametric tests can be used to analyze ordinal data.
4. The computations on nonparametric statistics are usually less complicated than those for parametric statistics, particularly for small samples.
5. Probability statements obtained from most nonparametric tests are exact probabilities.

Using nonparametric statistics also has some disadvantages.

1. Nonparametric tests can be wasteful of data if parametric tests are available for use with the data.
2. Nonparametric tests are usually not as widely available and known as parametric tests.
3. For large samples, the calculations for many nonparametric statistics can be tedious.

Entire courses and texts are dedicated to the study of nonparametric statistics. This text presents only some of the more important techniques: chi-square test of goodness of fit, chi-square test of independence, Mann–Whitney U test, Wilcoxon matched-pairs signed ranks test, Kruskal–Wallis test, and Spearman's rank correlation coefficient.

CHI-SQUARE GOODNESS-OF-FIT TEST | *12.1*

The chi-square statistic is widely used for a variety of analyses. One of the more prominent uses of chi-square is the goodness-of-fit test. Essentially, the **chi-square goodness-of-fit test** compares the *expected,* or theoretical, *frequencies* of categories from a population distribution to the *observed,* or actual *frequencies* from a distribution to determine whether there is a difference between what was expected and what was observed. For example, airline industry officials might theorize that the ages for airline ticket purchasers are distributed in a particular way. To validate or reject this expected distribution, an actual sample

chi-square goodness-of-fit test

of ticket purchaser ages can be randomly gathered, and the observed results can be compared to the expected results with the chi-square goodness-of-fit test. The chi-square goodness-of-fit test also can be used to determine whether the observed arrivals at teller windows at a bank are Poisson distributed, as might be expected. In the paper industry, manufacturers can use the chi-square goodness-of-fit test to determine whether the demand for paper follows a uniform distribution throughout the year.

Chi-Square Goodness-of-Fit Test

$$\chi^2 = \sum \frac{(f_o - f_e)^2}{f_e};$$

(12.1)

$$df = k - 1 - c;$$

where: f_o = frequency of observed values
f_e = frequency of expected values
k = number of categories
c = number of parameters being estimated from the sample data

---

Formula 12.1 compares the frequency of observed values to the frequency of the expected values across the distribution. The test loses one degree of freedom because the total number of expected frequencies must equal the number of observed frequencies. That is, the observed total taken from the sample is used as the total for the expected frequencies. In addition, in some instances a population parameter, such as λ, μ, or σ, is estimated from the sample data in order to determine the frequency distribution of expected values. Each time this estimation occurs, an additional degree of freedom is lost. As a rule, if a uniform distribution is being used as the expected distribution or if an expected distribution of values is *given*, $k - 1$ degrees of freedom are used in the test. In testing to determine whether an observed distribution is Poisson, the degrees of freedom are $k - 2$, because an additional degree of freedom is lost in estimating λ. In testing to determine whether an observed distribution is normally distributed, the degrees of freedom are $k - 3$, because two additional degrees of freedom are lost in estimating μ and σ from the observed sample data.

Chi-Square Distribution

chi-square distribution

Karl Pearson introduced the chi-square test in 1900. The **chi-square distribution** is the sum of the *squares* of k independent random variables and therefore can never be less than zero; it extends indefinitely in the positive direction. Actually the chi-square distributions constitute a family, with each distribution defined by the degrees of freedom (df) associated with it. For small df values the chi-square distribution is skewed considerably to the right (positive

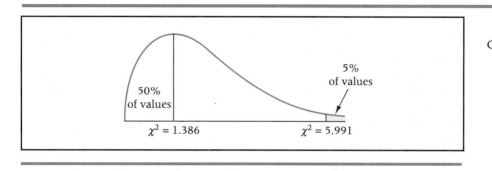

FIGURE 12.1

Chi-Square Distribution
for df = 2

values). As the df increase, the chi-square distribution begins to approach the normal curve. Table values for the chi-square distribution are given in Appendix A.8. Because of space limitations, chi-square values are listed only for certain probabilities. Figure 12.1 shows the chi-square distribution for two degrees of freedom.

How can the chi-square goodness-of-fit test be applied to business situations? One survey of U.S. consumers conducted by the *Wall Street Journal* and *NBC News* asked the question: "In general, how would you rate the level of service that American businesses provide?" The distribution of responses to this question was as follows:

Excellent   8%
Pretty good   47%
Only fair   34%
Poor   11%

Suppose that you want to find out whether the results of this consumer survey apply to customers of supermarkets in your city. To do so you interview 207 randomly selected consumers as they leave supermarkets in various parts of the city. You ask the customers how they would rate the level of service at that supermarket. The response categories are excellent, pretty good, only fair, and poor. The observed responses from this study are given in Table 12.1. You can use a chi-square goodness-of-fit test to determine whether the observed frequencies of responses from this survey are the same as the frequencies that would be expected based on the national survey.

Response	Frequency (f_o)
Excellent	21
Pretty good	109
Only fair	62
Poor	15

TABLE 12.1

Results of a Local Survey
of Consumer Satisfaction

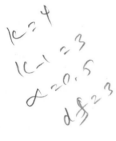

The hypotheses for this example are

H_0: The observed distribution is the same as the expected distribution
H_a: The observed distribution is not the same as the expected distribution

Chi-square goodness-of-fit tests are one-tailed, because a chi-square of zero indicates perfect agreement between distributions. Any deviation from zero difference occurs in the positive direction only, because chi-square is determined by a sum of squared values and can never be negative. With four categories in this example (excellent, pretty good, only fair, and poor), $k = 4$. The degrees of freedom are $k - 1$, because the expected distribution is given: $k - 1 = 4 - 1 = 3$. For $\alpha = .05$ and df $= 3$, the critical chi-square value is

$$\chi^2_{.05,3} = 7.815.$$

After the data have been analyzed, a calculated chi-square greater than 7.815 must be computed in order to reject the null hypothesis.

The observed values gathered in the sample data from Table 12.1 sum to 207. Thus $n = 207$. The expected *proportions* are given, but the expected *frequencies* must be calculated by multiplying the expected proportions by the sample total of the observed frequencies, as shown in Table 12.2. The chi-square goodness-of-fit can then be calculated, as shown in Table 12.3.

TABLE 12.2

Construction of Expected Values for Supermarket Service Satisfaction Study

Response	Expected Proportion	Expected Frequency (f_e) (Proportion × Sample Total)
Excellent	0.08	(0.08)(207) = 16.56
Pretty good	0.47	(0.47)(207) = 97.29
Only fair	0.34	(0.34)(207) = 70.38
Poor	0.11	(0.11)(207) = 22.77
		207.00

TABLE 12.3

Calculation of Chi-Square for Supermarket Service Satisfaction Problem

Response	f_o	f_e	$\dfrac{(f_o - f_e)^2}{f_e}$
Excellent	21	16.56	1.19
Pretty good	109	97.29	1.41
Only fair	62	70.38	1.00
Poor	15	22.77	2.65
	207	207.00	6.25

$$\chi^2 = \sum \frac{(f_o - f_e)^2}{f_e} = 6.25.$$

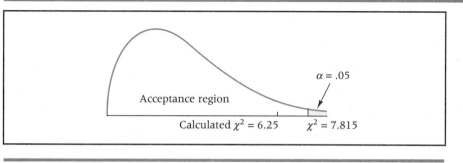

FIGURE 12.2

Graph of Chi-Square for
Supermarket Example

The calculated value of chi-square is 6.25 versus critical table value of 7.815. Because the calculated chi-square is not greater than the critical chi-square, you do not reject the null hypothesis. Thus the data gathered in the sample of 207 supermarket shoppers indicates that the distribution of responses of supermarket shoppers in your city is not significantly different from the distribution of responses to the national survey. Figure 12.2 depicts the chi-square distribution for this example, along with the calculated and critical values.

**Demonstration
Problem 12.1**

Dairies would like to know whether the sales of milk are distributed uniformly over a year, so they can plan for milk production and storage. A uniform distribution means that the frequencies are the same in all categories. In this situation, the producers are attempting to determine whether the amounts of milk sold are the same for each month of the year. They ascertain the number of gallons of milk sold by sampling one large supermarket each month during a year, obtaining the following data. Use $\alpha = .01$ to test whether the data fit a uniform distribution.

Month	Gallons	Month	Gallons
January	1,610	August	1,350
February	1,585	September	1,495
March	1,649	October	1,564
April	1,590	November	1,602
May	1,540	December	1,655
June	1,397	Total	18,447
July	1,410		

Solution:

The hypotheses are

H_0: The monthly figures for milk sales are uniformly distributed.
H_a: The monthly figures for milk sales are not uniformly distributed.

There are twelve categories and a uniform distribution is the expected distribution, so the degrees of freedom are $k - 1 = 12 - 1 = 11$. For $\alpha = .01$, the critical value is $\chi^2_{.01,11} = 24.725$. A calculated chi-square value of more than 24.725 must be obtained to reject the null hypothesis.

The first step is to determine the expected frequencies. The total for the expected frequencies must equal the total for the observed frequencies (18,447). If the frequencies are uniformly distributed, the same number of gallons of milk are expected to be sold each month. The expected monthly figure is

$$\frac{18,447}{12} = 1,537.25 \text{ gal.}$$

The following table shows the observed frequencies, the expected frequencies, and the chi-square calculations for this problem.

Month	f_o	f_e	$\dfrac{(f_o - f_e)^2}{f_e}$
January	1,610	1,537.25	3.44
February	1,585	1,537.25	1.48
March	1,649	1,537.25	8.12
April	1,590	1,537.25	1.81
May	1,540	1,537.25	0.00
June	1,397	1,537.25	12.80
July	1,410	1,537.25	10.53
August	1,350	1,537.25	22.81
September	1,495	1,537.25	1.16
October	1,564	1,537.25	0.47
November	1,602	1,537.25	2.73
December	1,655	1,537.25	9.02
Total	18,447	18,447.00	$\chi^2 = 74.37$

The calculated χ^2 value of 74.37 is greater than the critical table value of $\chi^2_{.01,11} = 24.725$, so the decision is to reject the null hypothesis. There is enough evidence in this problem to indicate that the distribution of milk sales is not uniform. The following graph depicts the chi-square distribution, critical chi-square value, and calculated chi-square value.

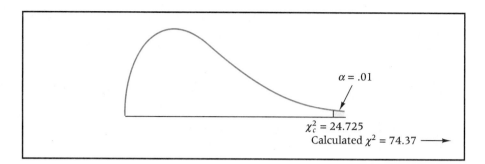

$\alpha = .01$

$\chi_c^2 = 24.725$

Calculated $\chi^2 = 74.37 \longrightarrow$

Demonstration Problem 12.2

Chapter 5 indicated that, quite often in the business world, random arrivals are Poisson distributed. This distribution is characterized by an average arrival rate, λ, per some interval. Suppose that a teller supervisor believes that the distribution of random arrivals at a local bank is Poisson and sets out to test this hypothesis by gathering information. The following data represent a distribution of frequency of arrivals during one-minute intervals at the bank. Use $\alpha = .05$ to test these data in an effort to determine whether they are Poisson distributed.

Number of Arrivals	Observed Frequencies
0	7
1	18
2	25
3	17
4	12
≥ 5	5

Solution:

The hypotheses are

H_0: The frequency distribution is Poisson.
H_a: The frequency distribution is not Poisson.

The degrees of freedom are $k - 2 = 6 - 1 - 1 = 4$, because the expected distribution is Poisson. An extra degree of freedom is lost, because the value of lambda must be calculated by using the observed sample data. For $\alpha = .05$, the critical table value is $\chi^2_{.05,4} = 9.488$. To determine the expected frequencies, the supervisor must obtain the probabilities of each category of arrivals and then multiply them by the total of the observed frequencies. These probabilities are obtained by determining lambda and then using the Poisson table. As it is the mean of a Poisson distribution, lambda can be determined from the observed data by computing the mean of the data. In this case, the supervisor computes a weighted average by summing the product of number of arrivals and frequency of those arrivals and dividing that sum by the total number of observed frequencies.

Number of Arrivals	Observed Frequencies	Arrival × Observed
0	7	0
1	18	18
2	25	50
3	17	51
4	12	48
≥5	5	25
	84	192

$$\lambda = \frac{192}{84} = 2.3.$$

With this value of lambda and the Poisson distribution table in Appendix A, the supervisor can determine the probabilities of the number of arrivals in each category. Using these probabilities and the total of 84 from the observed data, she computes the expected frequencies by multiplying each expected probability by the total (84).

Arrivals	Expected Probabilities	Expected Frequencies
0	.1003	8.42
1	.2306	19.37
2	.2652	22.28
3	.2033	17.08
4	.1169	9.82
≥5	.0837	7.03
		84.00

Using these expected frequencies and the observed frequencies, she computes the calculated value of chi-square.

Arrivals	Observed Frequencies	Expected Frequencies	$\dfrac{(f_o - f_e)^2}{f_e}$
0	7	8.42	0.24
1	18	19.37	0.10
2	25	22.28	0.33
3	17	17.08	0.00
4	12	9.82	0.48
≥ 5	5	7.03	0.59
	84	84.00	$\chi^2 = 1.74$

The calculated value is not greater than the critical chi-square value of 9.488, so the supervisor's decision is to not reject the null hypothesis. That is, she fails to reject the hypothesis that the distribution of bank arrivals is Poisson. The following graph depicts the chi-square distribution, critical value, and computed value.

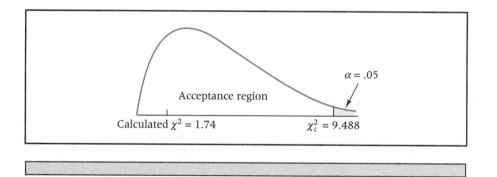

$\alpha = .05$

Acceptance region

Calculated $\chi^2 = 1.74$ $\chi_c^2 = 9.488$

Caution

When the expected value of a category is small, a large chi-square value can be obtained erroneously, leading to a Type I error. To control for this potential error, the chi-square goodness-of-fit test should not be used when any of the expected frequencies is less than 5. If the observed data produce expected values of less than 5, combining adjacent categories (when meaningful) to create larger frequencies may be possible.

Demonstration Problem 12.3

Suppose that Kimberly Eshelman developed an overall attitude scale to determine how Villalobos Industries employees feel toward their company. In theory, the scores can vary from 0 to 50. Eshelman pretests her measurement instrument on a randomly selected group of 100 employees. She tallies the scores and summarizes them into the six categories shown. Are these pretest scores approximately normally distributed? She uses $\alpha = .05$ and the chi-square goodness-of-fit test to answer that question.

Score Category	f
10–15	11
15–20	14
20–25	24
25–30	28
30–35	13
35–40	10
	100

Solution:

The hypotheses are

H_0: The attitude scores are normally distributed.

H_a: The attitude scores are not normally distributed.

Alpha is .05. With six categories, $k = 6$. To conduct a goodness-of-fit test for hypotheses about the normal distribution, the degrees of freedom for a chi-square goodness-of-fit test are $k - 3$, or df $= k - 3 = 3$. The critical table value is $\chi^2_{.05,3} = 7.815$. In order to reject the null hypothesis, the calculated chi-square value must be greater than 7.815.

To compute the calculated chi-square value, Eshelman must determine the expected frequencies. For a normal distribution, she computes the expected frequencies by using the Z table, the mean, and the standard deviation. Following the techniques presented in Chapter 3 for group statistics, the mean and standard deviation for the observed values are computed in the following manner.

Score Category	f	M	fM	fM²
10–15	11	12.5	137.5	1,718.75
15–20	14	17.5	245.0	4,287.50
20–25	24	22.5	540.0	12,150.00
25–30	28	27.5	770.0	21,175.00
30–35	13	32.5	422.5	13,731.25
35–40	10	37.5	375.0	14,062.50
	$\Sigma f = 100$		$\Sigma fM = 2{,}490.0$	$\Sigma fM^2 = 67{,}125.00$

$$\overline{X} = \frac{\Sigma fM}{n} = \frac{2{,}490}{100} = 24.90;$$

$$S = \sqrt{\frac{\Sigma fM^2 - \frac{(\Sigma fM)^2}{n}}{n-1}} = \sqrt{\frac{67{,}125 - \frac{(2{,}490)^2}{100}}{99}} = 7.194.$$

With $Z = \dfrac{X - \mu}{\sigma}$ and the techniques presented in Chapter 6, the expected probability of each category can be obtained.

For Category 10–15	P
$Z = \dfrac{10 - 24.9}{7.194} = -2.07$	.4808
$Z = \dfrac{15 - 24.9}{7.194} = -1.38$	.4162

Expected probability = .4808 − .4162 = .0646

For Category 15–20	P
$Z = \dfrac{15 - 24.9}{7.194} = -1.38$	.4162
$Z = \dfrac{20 - 24.9}{7.194} = -0.68$	.2517

Expected probability = .4162 − .2517 = .1645

For Category 20–25	P

$$Z = \frac{20 - 24.9}{7.194} = -0.68 \qquad\qquad .2517$$

$$Z = \frac{25 - 24.9}{7.194} = +0.01 \qquad\qquad .0040$$

Expected probability = .2517 + .0040 = .2557

For Category 25–30	P

$$Z = \frac{25 - 24.9}{7.194} = +0.01 \qquad\qquad .0040$$

$$Z = \frac{30 - 24.9}{7.194} = +0.71 \qquad\qquad .2611$$

Expected probability = .2611 − .0040 = .2571

For Category 30–35	P

$$Z = \frac{30 - 24.9}{7.194} = +0.71 \qquad\qquad .2611$$

$$Z = \frac{35 - 24.9}{7.194} = +1.40 \qquad\qquad .4192$$

Expected probability = .4192 − .2611 = .1581

For Category 35–40	P

$$Z = \frac{35 - 24.9}{7.194} = +1.40 \qquad\qquad .4192$$

$$Z = \frac{40 - 24.9}{7.194} = +2.10 \qquad\qquad .4821$$

Expected probability = .4821 − .4192 = .0629

These six probabilities do not sum to 1.000. Even though observed frequencies were obtained only for these six categories, getting a score <10 or >40 was also possible. Because .5000 of the probabilities lie in each half of a normal distribution and utilizing the sum of the expected probabilities on each side of the mean, 24.9, Eshelman can obtain the probability of the <10 category: .5000 − (.0646 + .1645 + .2517) = .0192. Similarly, she can obtain the probability of the >40 category: .5000 − (.0040 + .2571 + .1581 + .0629) = .0179.

She obtains the expected frequencies by multiplying each expected probability by the total frequency (100), as shown.

Score Category	P	Expected Frequency
<10	.0192	1.92
10–15	.0646	6.46
15–20	.1645	16.45
20–25	.2557	25.57
25–30	.2571	25.71
30–35	.1581	15.81
35–40	.0629	6.29
>40	.0179	1.79
	1.0000	100.00

As the <10 and >40 categories have expected values of less than 5, each must be collapsed (combined) with the adjacent category. As a result, the <10 category becomes part of the 10–15 category and the >40 category becomes part of the 35–40 category.

Score Category	P	Expected Frequency
10–15	.0838	8.38
15–20	.1645	16.45
20–25	.2557	25.57
25–30	.2571	25.71
30–35	.1581	15.81
35–40	.0808	8.08
	1.0000	100.00

The value of chi-square can then be computed.

Category	f_o	f_e	$\dfrac{(f_o - f_e)^2}{f_e}$
10–15	11	8.38	0.82
15–20	14	16.45	0.36
20–25	24	25.57	0.10
25–30	28	25.71	0.20
30–35	13	15.81	0.50
35–40	10	8.08	0.46
		$\chi^2 =$	2.44

This calculated chi-square value of 2.44 is less than the critical value of 7.815, so Eshelman does not reject the null hypothesis that these categories are normally distributed.

12.1 Use a chi-square goodness-of-fit test to determine whether the observed frequencies are distributed the same as the expected frequencies $(\alpha = .05)$:

Category	f_o	f_e
1	53	68
2	37	42
3	32	33
4	28	22
5	18	10
6	15	8

12.2 Use the following data and $\alpha = .01$ to determine whether the observed frequencies represent a uniform distribution:

Category	f_o
1	19
2	17
3	14
4	18
5	19
6	21
7	18
8	18

12.3 Are the data shown Poisson distributed? Use $\alpha = .05$ and the chi-square goodness-of-fit test to answer this question. What is your estimated lambda?

Number of Arrivals	f_o
0	28
1	17
2	11
3	5

12.4 Are the data given normally distributed? Use the chi-square goodness-of-fit to test for the distribution. Let $\alpha = .05$. What are your estimated mean and standard deviation?

Category	Observed
10–20	6
20–30	14
30–40	29
40–50	38
50–60	25
60–70	10
70–80	7

12.5 In one survey, successful women entrepreneurs were asked to state their personal definition of success in terms of several categories from which they could select. Thirty-nine percent responded that happiness was their definition, 12% said that sales/profit was their definition, 18% responded that helping others was their definition, and 31% responded that achievement/challenge was their definition of success. Suppose that you wanted to determine whether men entrepreneurs felt the same way and took a random sample of men, resulting in the data shown. Use the chi-square goodness-of-fit test to determine whether the observed frequency distribution of data for men is the same as the distribution for women. Let $\alpha = .05$.

Definition	f
Happiness	42
Sales/profit	95
Helping others	27
Achievement/challenge	63

12.6 The following percentages are from a national survey of the ages of prerecorded music shoppers:

Age	Percent from Survey	f_o
10–14	9%	22
15–19	23	50
20–24	22	43
25–29	14	29
30–34	10	19
≥35	22	49

A local survey produces the observed values. Is there evidence in the observed data to reject the national survey distribution for local music shoppers? Use $\alpha = .01$.

12.7 The general manager of a major league baseball team believes that the ages of purchasers of game tickets are normally distributed. If the following data represent the distribution of ages for a sample of observed purchasers of major league baseball game tickets, use the chi-square goodness-of-fit test to determine whether this distribution is significantly different from the normal distribution. Assume that $\alpha = .05$.

Age of Purchaser	Frequency
10–20	16
20–30	44
30–40	61
40–50	56
50–60	35
60–70	19

12.8 The Clear Lake Emergency Medical Service keeps records of emergency telephone calls. A study of 150 five-minute time intervals resulted in the distribution of number of calls shown. For example, there were 18 five-minute intervals in which there were no calls. Use the chi-square goodness-of-fit test and $\alpha = .01$ to determine whether this distribution is Poisson.

Number of Calls (per five-minute interval)	Frequency
0	18
1	28
2	47
3	21
4	16
5	11
6 or more	9

CHI-SQUARE TEST OF INDEPENDENCE | *12.2*

The chi-square goodness-of-fit test is used to analyze the distribution of frequencies for categories of *one* variable, such as age or number of bank arrivals, to determine whether the distribution of these frequencies is the same as some hypothesized or expected distribution. However, the goodness-of-fit test cannot be used to analyze *two* variables simultaneously. A different chi-square test, the **chi-square test of independence,** can be used to analyze the frequencies of *two* variables with multiple categories to determine whether the two variables are independent. Many times this type of analysis is desirable. For example, a market researcher might want to determine whether the type of soft drink preferred by a consumer is independent of the consumer's age. An organizational behaviorist might want to know whether absenteeism is independent of job classification. Financial investors might want to determine whether type of preferred stock investment is independent of the region where the investor resides.

chi-square test of independence

The chi-square test of independence can be used to analyze any level of data measurement, but it is particularly useful in analyzing nominal data. Suppose that a researcher is interested in determining whether geographic region is independent of type of financial investment. On a questionnaire, two questions that might measure geographic region and type of financial investment might be:

In which region of the country do you reside?

    A. Northeast   B. Midwest   C. South   D. West

Which type of financial investment are you most likely to make today?

      E. Stocks   F. Bonds   G. Treasury Bills

The analyst tallies the frequencies of responses to these two questions into a two-way table called a **contingency table.** Because the chi-square test of

contingency table

contingency analysis

independence uses a contingency table, this test is sometimes referred to as **contingency analysis.**

Depicted in Table 12.4 is a contingency table for these two variables. Variable 1, geographic location, has four categories: A, B, C, and D. Variable 2, type of financial investment, has three categories: E, F, and G. The observed frequency for each cell is denoted as o_{ij}, where i is the row and j is the column. Thus, o_{13} is the observed frequency for the cell in the first row and third column. The expected frequencies are denoted in a similar manner.

If the two variables are independent, they are not related. In a sense, the chi-square test of independence is a test of whether the variables are related. The null hypothesis for a chi-square test of independence is that the two variables are independent. If the null hypothesis is rejected, the conclusion is that the two variables are not independent and are related.

Let's assume at the beginning that variable 1 and variable 2 are independent. The probability of the intersection of two of their respective categories, A and F, can be found by using the multiplicative law for independent events presented in Chapter 4:

$$P(A \cap F) = P(A) \cdot P(F)$$

if A and F are independent. Then

$$P(A) = \frac{n_A}{N}, \qquad P(F) = \frac{n_F}{N}, \qquad \text{and} \qquad P(A \cap F) = \frac{n_A}{N} \cdot \frac{n_F}{N}.$$

If $P(A \cap F)$ is multiplied by the total number of frequencies, N, the expected frequency for the cell of A and F can be determined:

$$e_{AF} = \frac{n_A}{N} \cdot \frac{n_F}{N}(N) = \frac{n_A \cdot n_F}{N}.$$

TABLE 12.4

Contingency Table for
the Investment Example

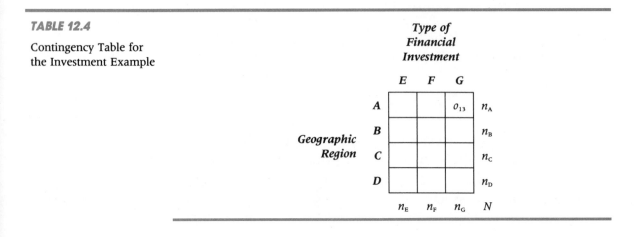

		Type of Financial Investment			
		E	*F*	*G*	
Geographic Region	*A*			o_{13}	n_A
	B				n_B
	C				n_C
	D				n_D
		n_E	n_F	n_G	N

In general, if the two variables are independent, the expected frequency values of each cell can be determined by

$$e_{ij} = \frac{(n_i)(n_j)}{N},$$

where: i is the row

j is the column

n_i is the total of row i

n_j is the total of column j

N is the total of all frequencies

(12.2)
$$\chi^2 = \sum\sum \frac{(f_o - f_e)^2}{f_e},$$

where: $df = (r - 1)(c - 1)$

r = number of rows

c = number of columns

Chi-Square Test of Independence

The null hypothesis for a chi-square test of independence is that the two variables are independent. The alternative hypothesis is that the variables are not independent. This test is one-tailed. The degrees of freedom are $(r - 1)(c - 1)$. Note that the Formula 12.2 is similar to Formula 12.1, except that the values are summed across both rows and columns and the degrees of freedom are different.

Suppose that a researcher wants to determine whether type of gasoline preferred is independent of a person's income. He could take a random survey of gasoline purchasers and ask consumers one question about gasoline preference and a second question about income. The respondent is to check whether he or she prefers (1) regular gasoline, (2) premium gasoline, or (3) extra premium gasoline. The respondent also is to check which of the following income brackets he or she belongs in: (1) less than $30,000, (2) $30,000 to $49,999, (3) $50,000 to $99,999, or (4) more than $100,000. The researcher tallies the responses, and the results are presented in Table 12.5. Using $\alpha = .01$, he can use the chi-square test of independence to determine whether type of gasoline preferred is independent of income level.

The hypotheses are

H_0: Type of gasoline is independent of income.

H_a: Type of gasoline is not independent of income.

Here, there are four rows ($r = 4$) and three columns ($c = 3$). The degrees of freedom are $(4 - 1)(3 - 1) = 6$. The critical value of chi-square for $\alpha = .01$ is $\chi^2_{.01,6} = 16.812$. In order to determine the calculated value of chi-square, the

TABLE 12.5

Contingency Table for
the Gasoline Consumer
Example

Income	Type of Gasoline		
	Regular	Premium	Extra Premium	
Less than $30,000	85	16	6	107
$30,000 to $49,999	102	27	13	142
$50,000 to $99,999	36	22	15	73
More than $100,000	15	23	25	63
	238	88	59	385

researcher must compute the expected frequencies. The expected values for
this example are calculated as follows, with the first term in the subscript (and
numerator) representing the row and the second term in the subscript (and
numerator) representing the column.

$$e_{11} = \frac{(n_1)(n_1)}{N} = \frac{(107)(238)}{385} = 66.15;$$

$$e_{12} = \frac{(n_1)(n_2)}{N} = \frac{(107)(88)}{385} = 24.46;$$

$$e_{13} = \frac{(n_1)(n_3)}{N} = \frac{(107)(59)}{385} = 16.40;$$

$$e_{21} = \frac{(n_2)(n_1)}{N} = \frac{(142)(238)}{385} = 87.78;$$

$$e_{22} = \frac{(n_2)(n_2)}{N} = \frac{(142)(88)}{385} = 32.46;$$

$$e_{23} = \frac{(n_2)(n_3)}{N} = \frac{(142)(59)}{385} = 21.76;$$

$$e_{31} = \frac{(n_3)(n_1)}{N} = \frac{(73)(238)}{385} = 45.13;$$

$$e_{32} = \frac{(n_3)(n_2)}{N} = \frac{(73)(88)}{385} = 16.69;$$

$$e_{33} = \frac{(n_3)(n_3)}{N} = \frac{(73)(59)}{385} = 11.19;$$

$$e_{41} = \frac{(n_4)(n_1)}{N} = \frac{(63)(238)}{385} = 38.95;$$

$$e_{42} = \frac{(n_4)(n_2)}{N} = \frac{(63)(88)}{385} = 14.40;$$

$$e_{43} = \frac{(n_4)(n_3)}{N} = \frac{(63)(59)}{385} = 9.65.$$

The researcher then lists the expected frequencies in the cells of the contingency tables along with observed frequencies. In this text, expected frequencies are enclosed in parentheses. Table 12.6 is the contingency table for this example. Next, the researcher computes the chi-square value by summing $(f_o - f_e)^2/f_e$ for all cells:

$$\chi^2 = \frac{(85 - 66.15)^2}{66.15} + \frac{(16 - 24.46)^2}{24.46} + \frac{(6 - 16.40)^2}{16.40} + \frac{(102 - 87.78)^2}{87.78}$$
$$+ \frac{(27 - 32.46)^2}{32.46} + \frac{(13 - 21.76)^2}{21.76} + \frac{(36 - 45.13)^2}{45.13}$$
$$+ \frac{(22 - 16.69)^2}{16.69} + \frac{(15 - 11.19)^2}{11.19} + \frac{(15 - 38.95)^2}{38.95}$$
$$+ \frac{(23 - 14.40)^2}{14.40} + \frac{(25 - 9.65)^2}{9.65}$$
$$= 5.37 + 2.93 + 6.60 + 2.30 + 0.92 + 3.53 + 1.85 + 1.69$$
$$+ 1.30 + 14.73 + 5.14 + 24.42$$
$$= 70.78.$$

The calculated value of chi-square, 70.78, is greater than the critical value of chi-square, 16.812, obtained from Table A.8. The researcher's decision is to reject the null hypothesis. That is, type of gasoline preferred is not independent of income. Having established that conclusion, the researcher can then examine the outcome to determine which people, by income brackets, tend to purchase which type of gasoline.

	Type of Gasoline				**TABLE 12.6**
Income	*Regular*	*Premium*	*Extra Premium*		Contingency Table of Observed and Expected Frequencies for Gasoline Consumer Example
Less than $30,000	(66.15) 85	(24.46) 16	(16.40) 6	107	
$30,000 to $49,999	(87.78) 102	(32.46) 27	(21.76) 13	142	
$50,000 to $99,999	(45.13) 36	(16.69) 22	(11.19) 15	73	
More than $100,000	(38.95) 15	(14.40) 23	(9.65) 25	63	
	238	88	59	385	

Demonstration Problem 12.4

Is the type of beverage ordered with lunch at a restaurant independent of the age of the consumer? A random poll of 309 lunch customers is taken, resulting in the following contingency table of observed values. Use $\alpha = .01$ to determine whether the two variables are independent.

Preferred Beverage

Age	Coffee/Tea	Soft Drink	Other (Milk, etc.)	
21–34	26	95	18	139
35–55	41	40	20	101
>55	24	13	32	69
	91	148	70	309

Solution:

The hypotheses are

   H_0: Type of beverage preferred is independent of age.
   H_a: Type of beverage preferred is not independent of age.

   The degrees of freedom are $(3 - 1)(3 - 1) = 4$, and the critical value is $\chi^2_{.01,4} = 13.277$. The expected frequencies are the product of the row and column totals divided by the grand total. The contingency table, with expected frequencies, is:

Preferred Beverage

Age	Coffee/Tea	Soft Drink	Other (Milk, etc.)	
21–34	(40.94) 26	(66.58) 95	(31.49) 18	139
35–55	(29.74) 41	(48.38) 40	(22.88) 20	101
>55	(20.32) 24	(33.05) 13	(15.63) 32	69
	91	148	70	309

For these values, the calculated χ^2 is

$$\chi^2 = \frac{(26 - 40.94)^2}{40.94} + \frac{(95 - 66.58)^2}{66.58} + \frac{(18 - 31.49)^2}{31.49}$$
$$+ \frac{(41 - 29.74)^2}{29.74} + \frac{(40 - 48.38)^2}{48.38} + \frac{(20 - 22.88)^2}{22.88}$$
$$+ \frac{(24 - 20.32)^2}{20.32} + \frac{(13 - 33.05)^2}{33.05} + \frac{(32 - 15.63)^2}{15.63}$$
$$= 5.45 + 12.13 + 5.78 + 4.26 + 1.45$$
$$+ 0.36 + 0.67 + 12.16 + 17.15$$
$$= 59.41.$$

The calculated value of chi-square, 59.41, is greater than the critical value, 13.277, so the null hypothesis is rejected. The two variables— preferred beverage and age—are not independent. The type of beverage that a customer orders with lunch is related to or dependent on age. Examination of the categories reveals that younger people tend to prefer soft drinks, and older people prefer other types of beverages.

Caution

As with the chi-square goodness-of-fit test, small expected frequencies can lead to inordinately large chi-square values with the chi-square test of independence. Hence contingency tables should not be used with expected cell values of less than 5. One way to avoid small expected values is to collapse (combine) columns or rows whenever possible and whenever doing so makes sense.

**PROBLEMS
Section 12.2**

12.9 Use the following contingency table and compute the expected frequency values for each cell. Determine the degrees of freedom.

*Variable
Two*

	24	59
Variable One	13	43
	20	35

12.10 Use the following data to determine whether variable one is independent of variable two. Let $\alpha = .05$.

	Variable Two	
Variable One	203	326
	68	110

12.11 Use the following data to test whether variable one is independent of variable two. Let $\alpha = .01$.

	Variable Two			
Variable One	24	13	47	58
	93	59	187	244

12.12 Use the data given and the chi-square test of independence to determine whether social class is independent of number of children in a family. Let $\alpha = .05$.

		Social Class		
		Lower	Middle	Upper
Number of Children	0	7	18	6
	1	9	38	23
	2 or 3	34	97	58
	More than 3	47	31	30

12.13 A group of 30-year-olds is interviewed to determine whether the type of music most listened to by people in their age category is independent of the geographic location of their residence. Use the chi-square test of independence, $\alpha = .01$, and the following data to determine whether music preference is independent of geographic location.

		Type of Music Preferred			
		Rock	Soul	Country	Classical
Geographic Region	Northeast	140	32	5	18
	South	134	41	52	8
	West	154	27	8	13

12.14 Is the transportation mode used to ship goods independent of type of industry? Suppose that the data shown represent frequency counts of types of transportation used by the publishing and the computer hardware industries. Analyze the data by using the chi-square test of independence to determine whether type of industry is independent of transportation mode. Let $\alpha = .05$.

Transportation Mode

		Air	*Train*	*Truck*
Industry	*Publishing*	32	12	41
	Computer Hardware	5	6	24

12.15 Is there a relationship between having a cellular car telephone and a person's profession? A survey of 187 members of three professions— physicians, lawyers, and accountants—results in the data shown. Use these data to test whether having a car telephone is independent of profession. Let $\alpha = .10$.

Car Telephone

		Yes	*No*
	Physician	42	39
Profession	*Lawyer*	21	34
	Accountant	13	38

12.16 In the early 1980s a study was conducted to determine the impact of a major Mexican Peso devaluation on U.S. border retailers. As a part of the study, data were gathered on the magnitude of business that American border retailers were doing with Mexican citizens. Forty-one shoppers of border city department stores were interviewed; twenty-four were Mexican citizens, and the rest were U.S. citizens. Thirty-five discount store shoppers were interviewed, as were thirty hardware store shoppers and sixty shoe store customers. In these three groups, twenty, eleven, and thirty-two, respectively, were Mexican citizens, and the remaining shoppers were U.S. citizens. Use a chi-square contingency analysis to determine whether the shoppers' citizenship (Mexican versus U.S.) is independent of type of border city retailer (department, discount, hardware, shoe) for these data. Let $\alpha = .05$.

12.3 MANN–WHITNEY *U* TEST

Mann–Whitney *U* test   The **Mann–Whitney *U* test** is a nonparametric counterpart of the *t* test used to compare the means of two independent populations. This test was developed by Henry B. Mann and D. R. Whitney in 1947. Recall that the *t* test for independent samples presented in Chapter 10 can be used when data are at least interval in measurement and the populations are normally distributed. However, if the assumption of a normally distributed population is invalid or if the data are only ordinal in measurement, the *t* test should not be used. In such cases the Mann–Whitney *U* test is an acceptable option for analyzing the data. The following assumptions underlie the use of the Mann–Whitney *U* test.

1. The samples are independent.
2. The level of data is at least ordinal.
3. If hypotheses are being tested about the means, the populations are approximately symmetric.

The Mann–Whitney techniques presented here are for large samples, that is, when n_1 and $n_2 > 10$. Mann–Whitney techniques for small samples, that is, when n_1 or $n_2 \leq 10$ are not presented.

Computation of the *U* test begins by arbitrarily designating two samples as group 1 and group 2. The data from the two groups are combined into one group, with each data value retaining some group identifier of its original group. The pooled values are then ranked from 1 to *n*, with the smallest value being assigned a rank of 1. The sum of the ranks of values from group 1 is computed and designated as W_1.

Computing a *U* Statistic

$$U = n_1 n_2 + \frac{n_1(n_1 + 1)}{2} - W_1,$$

where: n_1 = number in group 1

n_2 = number in group 2

W_1 = sum of the ranks of values in group 1

For large sample sizes (n_1, $n_2 > 10$), the value of *U* is approximately normally distributed. Using an average expected *U* value for groups of this size and a standard deviation of *U*'s allows computation of a *Z* score for the *U* value. The probability of yielding a *Z* score of this magnitude, given no differ-

ence between the groups, is computed. A decision is then made whether to reject or not reject the null hypothesis. A Z score can be calculated from U by

$$\mu_U = \frac{n_1 \cdot n_2}{2}, \quad \sigma_U = \sqrt{\frac{n_1 \cdot n_2(n_1 + n_2 + 1)}{12}}, \quad \text{and} \quad Z = \frac{U - \mu_U}{\sigma_U}.$$

For example, the Mann–Whitney U test can be used to determine whether there is a difference in the average income of viewers of PBS television and viewers of commercial television. Suppose that a sample of fourteen families that have identified themselves as PBS television viewers and a sample of thirteen families that have identified themselves as non-PBS television viewers are randomly selected. The average annual reported income for each family in the two samples is listed in Table 12.7.

The hypotheses for this example are

$$H_0: \mu_1 - \mu_2 = 0$$
$$H_a: \mu_1 - \mu_2 \neq 0$$

This example involves use of a two-tailed test of the difference of two means. Let $\alpha = .05$.

The first step toward computing a Mann–Whitney U test is to combine these two columns of data into one group and rank the data from lowest to

PBS	Non-PBS	
$24,500	$41,000	
39,400	32,500	
36,800	33,000	
43,000	21,000	
57,960	40,500	
32,000	32,400	
61,000	16,000	
34,000	21,500	
43,500	39,500	
55,000	27,600	
39,000	43,500	
62,500	51,900	
61,400	27,800	
53,000		
$n_1 = 14$	$n_2 = 13$	

TABLE 12.7

Incomes of PBS and Non-PBS Viewers

	Income	Rank	Group	Income	Rank	Group
TABLE 12.8						
Ranks of Incomes from	$16,000	1	Non-PBS	39,500	15	Non-PBS
Combined Groups of	21,000	2	Non-PBS	40,500	16	Non-PBS
PBS and Non-PBS	21,500	3	Non-PBS	41,000	17	Non-PBS
Viewers	24,500	4	PBS	43,000	18	PBS
	27,600	5	Non-PBS	43,500	19.5	PBS
	27,800	6	Non-PBS	43,500	19.5	Non-PBS
	32,000	7	PBS	51,900	21	Non-PBS
	32,400	8	Non-PBS	53,000	22	PBS
	32,500	9	Non-PBS	55,000	23	PBS
	33,000	10	Non-PBS	57,960	24	PBS
	34,000	11	PBS	61,000	25	PBS
	36,800	12	PBS	61,400	26	PBS
	39,000	13	PBS	62,500	27	PBS
	39,400	14	PBS			

highest, while maintaining the identification of each original group. Table 12.8 shows the results of this step.

Note that in the case of a tie, the ranks associated with the tie are averaged across the values that tie. For example, there are two incomes of $43,500. These incomes represent ranks 19 and 20. Each value therefore is awarded a ranking of 19.5, or the average of 19 and 20.

If PBS is designated as group 1, W_1 can be computed by summing the ranks of all the incomes of PBS viewers in the sample:

$$W_1 = 4 + 7 + 11 + 12 + 13 + 14 + 18$$
$$+ 19.5 + 22 + 23 + 24 + 25 + 26 + 27$$
$$= 245.5.$$

Then W_1 is used to compute the U value. As $n_1 = 14$ and $n_2 = 13$,

$$U = (n_1)(n_2) + \frac{n_1(n_1 + 1)}{2} - W_1$$
$$= (14)(13) + \frac{(14)(15)}{2} - 245.5 = 41.5.$$

As $n_1, n_2 > 10$, U is approximately normally distributed, with a mean of

$$\mu_U = \frac{n_1 \cdot n_2}{2} = \frac{(14)(13)}{2} = 91$$

and a standard deviation of

$$\sigma_U = \sqrt{\frac{n_1 \cdot n_2(n_1 + n_2 + 1)}{12}} = \sqrt{\frac{(14)(13)(28)}{12}} = 20.6.$$

A Z value now can be computed to determine the probability of the sample U value coming from the distribution with $\mu_U = 91$ and $\sigma_U = 20.6$ if there is no difference in the population means:

$$Z = \frac{U - \mu_U}{\sigma_U} = \frac{41.5 - 91}{20.6} = \frac{-49.5}{20.6} = -2.40.$$

For $\alpha/2 = .025$, the critical value of Z is ± 1.96. The calculated value of $Z = -2.40$, so the results fall into the rejection region. That is, there is a difference between the average income of a PBS viewer and that of a non-PBS viewer. Examination of the sample data confirms that the average income of a PBS viewer is higher than that of a non-PBS viewer.

Assignment of PBS viewers to group 1 was arbitrary. If non-PBS viewers had been designated as group 1, the results would have been the same, except that the calculated Z value would have been positive:

$$W_1 = 1 + 2 + 3 + 5 + 6 + 8 + 9$$
$$+ 10 + 15 + 16 + 17 + 19.5$$
$$+ 21 = 132.5;$$
$$U = 13(14) + \frac{(13)(14)}{2} - 132.5 = 140.5;$$
$$\mu_U = \frac{n_1 \cdot n_2}{2} = \frac{(14)(13)}{2} = 91;$$
$$\sigma_U = \sqrt{\frac{(14)(13)(28)}{12}} = 20.6;$$
$$Z = \frac{140.5 - 91}{20.6} = \frac{49.5}{20.6} = 2.40.$$

Demonstration Problem 12.5

Do construction workers who purchase lunch from street vendors spend less per meal, on average, than construction workers who go to restaurants for lunch? To test this question, a researcher selected two random samples of construction workers, one group that purchases lunch from street vendors and one group that purchases lunch from restaurants. Use the following data and a Mann–Whitney U test to analyze the data to determine whether street vendor lunches are significantly cheaper than restaurant lunches. Let $\alpha = .01$.

Vendor	Restaurant
$2.75	$4.10
3.29	4.75
4.53	3.95
3.61	3.50
3.10	4.25
4.29	4.98
2.25	5.75
2.97	4.10
4.01	2.70
3.68	3.65
3.15	5.11
2.97	4.80
4.05	6.25
3.60	3.89
	4.80
	5.50
$n_1 = 14$	$n_2 = 16$

Solution:

The researcher arbitrarily designates the vendor group as group 1 and states the hypotheses:

$$H_0: \mu_1 - \mu_2 \geq 0$$
$$H_a: \mu_1 - \mu_2 < 0$$

The alternative hypothesis that she is trying to "prove" is that the average ticket for lunches purchased from vendors is less than the average ticket for restaurant lunches. The null hypothesis is that there is no difference or that vendor lunches are more costly.

The researcher determines the value of W_1 by combining the groups, while retaining group identification, and ranking all the values from 1 to 30 (14 + 16), with 1 representing the smallest value:

Value	Rank	Group	Value	Rank	Group
$2.25	1	V	$4.01	16	V
2.70	2	R	4.05	17	V
2.75	3	V	4.10	18.5	R
2.97	4.5	V	4.10	18.5	R
2.97	4.5	V	4.25	20	R
3.10	6	V	4.29	21	V
3.15	7	V	4.53	22	V
3.29	8	V	4.75	23	R
3.50	9	R	4.80	24.5	R
3.60	10	V	4.80	24.5	R
3.61	11	V	4.98	26	R
3.65	12	R	5.11	27	R
3.68	13	V	5.50	28	R
3.89	14	R	5.75	29	R
3.95	15	R	6.25	30	R

Summing the ranks for the vendor sample gives

$$W_1 = 1 + 3 + 4.5 + 4.5 + 6 + 7 + 8$$
$$+ 10 + 11 + 13 + 16 + 17 + 21 + 22$$
$$= 144.$$

Solving for U, μ_U, and σ_U yields

$$U = (14)(16) + \frac{(14)(15)}{2} - 144 = 185;$$

$$\mu_U = \frac{(14)(16)}{2} = 112;$$

$$\sigma_U = \sqrt{\frac{(14)(16)(31)}{12}} = 24.1.$$

Solving for the calculated Z value gives

$$Z = \frac{185 - 112}{24.1} = 3.03.$$

The critical Z value for $\alpha = .01$ is 2.33. As the calculated Z value is greater than the critical value, the researcher rejects the null hypothesis. The probability method gives the probability of getting a Z score ≥ 3.03 as .0012. This value is significant at $\alpha = .01$. Thus the average cost of vendor lunches is less than the average cost of restaurant lunches.

Note:

Usually with a one-tailed Z test, the null hypothesis is rejected if a significant Z value is obtained and the sign of the Z value is opposite the direction of the null hypothesis. For example, if the null hypothesis ≥ 0, in order to reject the null hypothesis, a significant *negative Z* value must be determined. With the Mann–Whitney U test, the opposite is true. To reject a positive direction null hypothesis with a one-tailed Mann–Whitney U test requires a significant positive Z value. Similarly, a negative direction null hypothesis is rejected with a significant negative Z value. The reason is that small W_1 values produce large U values, which in turn produce positive Z values. If a null hypothesis has a positive direction and it is to be rejected, the alternative hypothesis must have a negative direction, and the average of the first group must be smaller than the average of the second group. However, the sum of the ranks for the first group, W_1, then are smaller, which results in a positive Z value.

**PROBLEMS
Section 12.3**

12.17 Use the Mann–Whitney U test and the following data to determine whether there is a significant difference between the average values of group 1 and group 2. Let $\alpha = .05$.

Group 1	Group 2
15	23
17	14
26	24
11	13
18	22
21	23
13	18
29	21
22	27
21	26

12.18 The data shown represent two random samples gathered from two populations. Is there sufficient evidence in the data to determine whether the mean of population 1 is significantly larger than the mean of population 2? Use the Mann–Whitney U test and $\alpha = .01$.

Sample 1	Sample 2
224	203
256	218
231	229
222	230
248	211
283	230
241	209
217	223
240	219
255	236
216	227
	208
	214

12.19 Results of a survey by the National Center for Health Statistics indicated that people between sixty-five and seventy-four years of age contact a physician an average of 8.2 times per year. People seventy-five and older contact doctors an average of 9.9 times per year. Suppose that you want to validate these results by taking your own samples. The following data represent the number of annual contacts people make with a physician. The samples are independent. Use a Mann–Whitney U test to determine whether the average number of contacts with physicians by people seventy-five and older is greater than the average number by people sixty-five to seventy-four years old. Let $\alpha = .01$.

65 to 74	75 and older
7	12
8	11
3	6
6	13
4	9
1	8
6	10
9	5
11	9
9	7
	13
	11

12.20 A national survey of families conducted by the National Center for Health Statistics suggested that urban households spend an average of $2,400 a year on food at home, and rural households spend $2,500 a year on food at home. Suppose that twelve urban households and twelve rural households are randomly selected and each family is asked to report the amount spent on food at home annually, with the results shown. Use a Mann–Whitney U test to determine whether there is a significant difference between the average amounts spent at home for food between urban and rural households. Use $\alpha = .05$.

Urban	Rural	Urban	Rural
$2110	$2050	$1950	$2770
2655	2800	2480	3100
2710	2975	2630	2685
2540	2075	2750	2790
2200	2490	2850	2995
2175	2585	2850	2995

12.21 Does the average male stock market investor earn significantly more than the average female stock market investor? One study by the New York Stock Exchange showed that the average male investor has an income of $46,400 and that the average female investor has an income of $39,400. Suppose that an analyst wanted to "prove" that the average male investor earns more than the average female investor. The following data represent random samples of male and female investors from across the United States. The analyst uses the Mann–Whitney U test to determine whether the average male investor earns significantly more than the average female investor for $\alpha = .01$. What does the analyst find?

Male	Female
$50,100	$41,200
47,800	36,600
45,000	44,500
51,500	47,800
55,000	42,500
53,850	47,500
51,500	40,500
63,900	28,900
57,800	48,000
61,100	42,300
51,000	40,000
	31,400

12.22 In the last quarter of 1990 according to a survey released by the Coldwell Banker Residential Group, a 2,200 square-foot house in Corpus Christi, Texas, cost $82,338. This price was the lowest for comparable houses in 219 cities surveyed. Suppose that a survey of thirteen randomly selected houses with 2,200 square feet of space is taken in Des Moines, Iowa, and fifteen randomly selected houses with 2,200 square feet of space is taken in Tucson, Arizona, with the resulting prices shown. Use a Mann–Whitney U test to determine whether there is a significant difference in the average price of a 2,200 square-foot house in these two cities. Let $\alpha = .05$.

Des Moines	Tucson
$ 90,150	$101,800
103,400	97,850
89,900	95,000
91,300	100,500
101,450	108,900
93,500	99,000
88,400	91,550
90,000	102,550
102,200	106,600
94,500	98,500
97,500	105,000
100,450	102,540
88,700	99,700
	112,500
	102,500

WILCOXON MATCHED-PAIRS SIGNED RANK TEST | 12.4

The Mann–Whitney U test presented in Section 12.3 is a nonparametric alternative to the t test for two *independent* samples. If the two samples are *related*, the U test is not applicable. Rather, the **Wilcoxon matched-pairs signed rank test** serves as a nonparametric alternative to the t test for two related samples. Developed by Frank Wilcoxon in 1945, the Wilcoxon test, like the t test for two related samples, is used to analyze several different types of studies when the data of one group are related to the data in the other group, including before and after studies, studies in which measures are taken on the same person or object under two different conditions, and studies of twins or other relatives.

Wilcoxon matched-pairs signed rank test

The Wilcoxon test utilizes the differences of the scores of the two matched groups in a manner similar to that of the t test for two related samples. After the difference scores have been computed, the Wilcoxon test ranks all differences regardless of whether the difference is positive or negative. The values are ranked from smallest to largest, with a rank of 1 assigned to the smallest difference. If a difference is negative, the rank is given a negative sign. The sum of the positive ranks is tallied along with the sum of the negative ranks. Zero differences representing ties between scores from the two groups are ignored, and the value of n is reduced accordingly. When ties occur between ranks, the ranks are averaged over the values. The smallest sum of ranks (either $+$ or $-$) is used in the analysis and is represented by T. The Wilcoxon matched-pairs signed rank test techniques presented here apply to large samples ($n > 15$) only. The value of T for large samples is approximately normally distributed.

Analysis of T for Large Samples

$$\mu_T = \frac{(n)(n + 1)}{4};$$

$$\sigma_T = \sqrt{\frac{n(n + 1)(2n + 1)}{24}};$$

$$Z = \frac{T - \mu_T}{\sigma_T};$$

where: n = number of pairs

 T = total ranks for either $+$ or $-$ differences, whichever is less in magnitude

---

This technique can be applied to the airline industry, where analysts might want to determine whether there is a difference in the cost per mile of airfares in the United States between 1979 and 1988 for various cities. The data in Table 12.9 represent the costs per mile of airline tickets for a sample of seventeen cities for both 1979 and 1988. An analyst applies a Wilcoxon matched-pairs signed rank test to the data to test the difference in cents per mile for the two periods of time and uses $\alpha = .05$.

The analyst states the hypotheses as

H_0: The population differences = 0.
H_a: The population differences ≠ 0.

She begins the process by computing a difference score, d. Which year's data are subtracted from the other does not matter, so long as there is consistency in direction. For the data in Table 12.9, the analyst subtracted the 1988 figures from the 1979 figures. The sign of the difference is left on the difference score. Next, she ranks the differences without regard to sign, but the sign is left on the rank as an identifier. Note the tie for ranks 6 and 7; thus each is

City	1979	1988	d	Rank	
					TABLE 12.9
1	20.3	22.8	−2.5	−8	Airline Ticket Costs for
2	19.5	12.7	+6.8	+17	Various Cities
3	18.6	14.1	+4.5	+13	
4	20.9	16.1	+4.8	+15	
5	19.9	25.2	−5.3	−16	
6	18.6	20.2	−1.6	−4	
7	19.6	14.9	+4.7	+14	
8	23.2	21.3	+1.9	+6.5	
9	21.8	18.7	+3.1	+10	
10	20.3	20.9	−0.6	−1	
11	19.2	22.6	−3.4	−11.5	
12	19.5	16.9	+2.6	+9	
13	18.7	20.6	−1.9	−6.5	
14	17.7	18.5	−0.8	−2	
15	21.6	23.4	−1.8	−5	
16	22.4	21.3	+1.1	+3	
17	20.8	17.4	+3.4	+11.5	

given a rank of 6.5, the average of the two ranks. The same applies to ranks 11 and 12.

After the analyst has ranked all difference values regardless of sign, she sums the positive ranks (T_+) and the negative ranks (T_-). She then determines the T value from these two sums as the smallest of T_+ or T_-:

$$T = \text{minimum } (T_+, T_-)$$

From the data,

$$T_+ = 17 + 13 + 15 + 14 + 6.5 + 10 + 9 + 3 + 11.5 = 99;$$
$$T_- = 8 + 16 + 4 + 1 + 11.5 + 6.5 + 2 + 5 = 54;$$
$$T = \text{minimum } (99, 54) = 54.$$

The T value is normally distributed for large sample sizes, with a mean and standard deviation of

$$\mu_T = \frac{(n)(n+1)}{4} = \frac{(17)(18)}{4} = 76.5;$$

$$\sigma_T = \sqrt{\frac{n(n+1)(2n+1)}{24}} = \sqrt{\frac{(17)(18)(35)}{24}} = 21.1.$$

The calculated Z value is

$$Z = \frac{T - \mu_T}{\sigma_T} = \frac{54 - 76.5}{21.1} = -1.07.$$

The critical Z value for this two-tailed test is $Z_{.025} = \pm 1.96$. The calculated $Z = -1.07$, so the analyst fails to reject the null hypothesis. There is no significant difference in the cost of airline tickets between 1979 and 1988.

Demonstration Problem 12.6

During the 1980s and 1990s, U.S. businesses have increasingly emphasized quality control. One of the arguments in favor of quality control programs is that quality control can increase productivity. Suppose that a company has implemented a quality control program and has been operating under it for two years. The company's president wants to determine whether worker productivity has significantly increased since installation of the program. Company records contain the figures for items produced per worker during a sample of production runs two years ago. Productivity figures on the same workers are gathered now and compared to the previous figures. The following data represent items produced per hour. The company's statistical analyst uses the Wilcoxon matched-pairs signed rank test to determine whether there is a significant increase in per worker production for $\alpha = .01$.

Worker	Before	After	Worker	Before	After
1	5	11	11	2	6
2	4	9	12	5	10
3	9	9	13	4	9
4	6	8	14	5	7
5	3	5	15	8	9
6	8	7	16	7	6
7	7	9	17	9	10
8	10	9	18	5	8
9	3	7	19	4	5
10	7	9	20	3	6

Solution:

The hypotheses are

H_0: The difference is ≥ 0 (workers are no more productive than before and may be less productive).

H_a: The difference is < 0 (workers are more productive after the quality control program).

The analyst computes the difference values, and, as zero differences are to be eliminated, deletes worker 3 from the study. This reduces n from 20 to 19. He then ranks the differences regardless of sign. The differences that are the same (ties) receive the average rank for those values. For example, the differences for workers 4, 5, 7, 10, and 14 are the same. The ranks for these five are 7, 8, 9, 10, and 11, so each worker receives the rank of 9, the average of these five ranks.

Worker	Before	After	d	Rank
1	5	11	−6	−19
2	4	9	−5	−17
3	9	9	0	delete
4	6	8	−2	−9
5	3	5	−2	−9
6	8	7	+1	+3.5
7	7	9	−2	−9
8	10	9	+1	+3.5
9	3	7	−4	−14.5
10	7	9	−2	−9
11	2	6	−4	−14.5
12	5	10	−5	−17
13	4	9	−5	−17
14	5	7	−2	−9
15	8	9	−1	−3.5
16	7	6	+1	+3.5
17	9	10	−1	−3.5
18	5	8	−3	−12.5
19	4	5	−1	−3.5
20	3	6	−3	−12.5

The analyst determines the values of T_+, T_-, and T to be

$T_+ = 3.5 + 3.5 + 3.5 = 10.5;$

$T_- = 19 + 17 + 9 + 9 + 9 + 14.5 + 9 + 14.5 + 17 + 17$
$\quad + 9 + 3.5 + 3.5 + 12.5 + 3.5 + 12.5 = 179.5;$

$T = \text{minimum of } (10.5, 179.5) = 10.5.$

The mean and standard deviation of T are

$$\mu_T = \frac{n(n+1)}{4} = \frac{(19)(20)}{4} = 95;$$

$$\sigma_T = \sqrt{\frac{n(n+1)(2n+1)}{24}} = \sqrt{\frac{(19)(20)(39)}{24}} = 24.8.$$

The calculated Z value is

$$Z = \frac{T - \mu_T}{\sigma_T} = \frac{10.5 - 95}{24.8} = -3.41.$$

The critical Z value for a one-tailed test and $\alpha = .01$ is -2.33. The calculated Z value (-3.41) falls into the rejection region, so the analyst rejects the null hypothesis. The productivity is significantly greater after quality control has been implemented at this company.

**PROBLEMS
Section 12.4**

12.23 Use the Wilcoxon matched-pairs signed rank test to determine whether there is a significant difference between the two groups of related data given. Use $\alpha = .10$.

1	2
212	179
234	184
219	213
199	167
194	189
206	200
234	212
225	221
220	223
218	217
234	208
212	215
219	187
196	198
178	189
213	201

12.24 Use the Wilcoxon matched-pairs signed rank test and $\alpha = .05$ to analyze the before and after measurements given.

Before	After	Before	After
49	43	54	50
41	29	46	47
47	30	50	47
39	38	44	39
53	40	49	49
51	43	45	47
51	46	52	47
49	40	42	31
38	42	36	25

12.25 A corporation owns a chain of several hundred gasoline stations on the eastern seaboard. The marketing director wants to test a proposed marketing campaign by running ads on some local television stations and determining whether gasoline sales at a sample of the company's stations increase after the advertising. The following data represent gasoline sales for a day both before and after the advertising campaign. Use the Wilcoxon matched-pairs signed rank test to determine whether sales increased significantly after the advertising campaign. Let $\alpha = .05$.

Station	Before	After
1	$10,500	$12,600
2	8,870	10,660
3	12,300	11,890
4	10,510	14,630
5	5,570	8,580
6	9,150	10,115
7	11,980	14,350
8	6,740	6,900
9	7,340	8,890
10	13,400	16,540
11	12,200	11,300
12	10,570	13,330
13	9,880	9,990
14	12,100	14,050
15	9,000	9,500
16	11,800	12,450
17	10,500	13,450

12.26 Many supermarkets across the United States have invested heavily in optical scanner systems to expedite customer checkout, increase checkout productivity, and improve product accountability. These systems are not 100% effective, and items often have to be scanned several times. Sometimes, items are manually entered into the "cash register" because the scanner cannot read the item number. In general, do optical scanners register significantly more items than manual entry systems do? The following data are from an experiment in which a supermarket selected eighteen of its best checkers and measured their productivity both when using a scanner and when working manually. The data show the number of items checked per hour by each method. Use a Wilcoxon matched-pairs signed rank test and $\alpha = .05$ to test the difference.

Checker	Manual	Scanner
1	426	473
2	387	446
3	410	421
4	506	510
5	411	465
6	398	409
7	427	414
8	449	459
9	407	502
10	438	439
11	418	456
12	482	499
13	512	517
14	402	437
15	374	408
16	451	473
17	429	455
18	492	549

12.27 American attitudes toward big business change over time and probably are cyclical. Suppose that the following data represent a survey of twenty American adults taken in 1990 and again in 1992 in which each adult was asked to rate American big business overall on a scale from 1 to 100 in terms of positive opinion. A response of 1 indicates that the person has a low opinion of big business, and a response of 100 indicates that the person has a high opinion of big business. Use a Wilcoxon matched-pairs signed rank test to determine whether the scores in 1992 are significantly higher than the scores from 1990. Use $\alpha = .10$.

Person	1990	1992
1	49	54
2	27	38
3	39	38
4	75	80
5	59	53
6	67	68
7	22	43
8	61	67
9	58	73
10	60	55
11	72	58
12	62	57
13	49	63
14	48	49
15	19	39
16	32	34
17	60	66
18	80	90
19	55	57
20	68	58

12.28 According to a survey taken by the Greater Houston Partnership, Houston business people were less optimistic about short-term local business conditions in April 1991 than they were in April 1990. The "optimism" ratings given by people in eight industries in April 1990 and April 1991 are shown. Use a Wilcoxon matched-pairs signed rank test to determine whether the Greater Houston Partnership's conclusion was correct. That is, do the data indicate significantly less optimism in April 1991 than in April 1990? Use $\alpha = .05$. The higher the score, the more positive is the business outlook.

Industry	April 1990	April 1991
Mining	63.1	57.4
Construction	67.1	66.4
Manufacturing	65.5	61.8
Utilities	68.0	65.3
Wholesale	66.6	63.5
Retail	65.7	66.4
Finance, real estate	69.2	64.9
Service	67.0	65.2

12.5 | KRUSKAL–WALLIS TEST

Kruskal–Wallis test

The nonparametric alternative to the one-way analysis of variance is the Kruskal–Wallis test. Like the one-way analysis of variance, the **Kruskal–Wallis test** is used to determine whether $C \geq 3$ samples come from the same or different populations. Whereas the one-way ANOVA is based on the assumptions of normally distributed populations, independent groups, and at least interval level data, the Kruskal–Wallis test can be used to analyze ordinal data and is not based on any assumption about population shape. The Kruskal–Wallis test is based on the assumption that the C groups are independent and that individual items are selected randomly. This test was developed in 1952 by William H. Kruskal and W. Allen Wallis. The hypotheses tested by the Kruskal–Wallis test are

H_0: The C populations are identical.
H_a: At least one of the C populations is different.

That is, this test determines whether all of the groups come from the same or equal populations or whether at least one group comes from a different population.

The process of computing a Kruskal–Wallis K statistic begins with ranking the data in all the groups together, as though they were from one group. The smallest value is awarded a 1. As usual, for ties, each value is given the average rank for those tied values. Unlike one-way ANOVA, in which the raw data are analyzed, the Kruskal–Wallis test analyzes the ranks of the data.

Kruskal–Wallis K Test

$$K = \frac{12}{n(n+1)}\left(\sum_{j=1}^{C}\frac{T_j^2}{n_j}\right) - 3(n+1),$$

where: C = number of groups
n = total number of items
T_j = total of ranks in a group
n_j = number of items in a group
$K \approx \chi^2$, with df = $C - 1$

The K value is approximately chi-square distributed, with $C - 1$ degrees of freedom so long as n_j is not less than 5 for any group.

Suppose that a researcher is interested in determining whether the number of physicians in an office produces significant differences in the number of

| | Three or More | |
Two Partners	Partners	HMO
13	24	26
15	16	22
20	19	31
18	22	27
23	25	28
	14	33
	17	

TABLE 12.10

Number of Office Patients Per Doctor

office patients seen by each physician per day. She takes a random sample of physicians from practices in which (1) there are only two partners, (2) there are three or more partners, or (3) the office is a health maintenance organization (HMO). Table 12.10 shows the data obtained.

As there are three groups in this study, $C = 3$. There are $n = 18$ physicians in the study, and the numbers of patients are ranked for these physicians. The researcher sums the ranks within each column to obtain T_j, as shown in Table 12.11.

The Kruskal–Wallis K is

$$K = \frac{12}{18(18 + 1)} (1{,}897) - 3(18 + 1) = 9.56.$$

| | Three or More | | |
Two Partners	Partners	HMO	
1	12	14	
3	4	9.5	
8	7	17	
6	9.5	15	
11	13	16	
	2	18	
	5		
$T_1 = 29$	$T_2 = 52.5$	$T_3 = 89.5$	
$n_1 = 5$	$n_2 = 7$	$n_3 = 6$	$n = 18$

TABLE 12.11

Kruskal–Wallis Analysis of Physicians' Patients

$$\sum_{j=1}^{3} \frac{T_j^2}{n_j} = \frac{(29)^2}{5} + \frac{(52.5)^2}{7} + \frac{(89.5)^2}{6} = 1{,}897.$$

The critical chi-square value is $\chi^2_{\alpha,df}$. If $\alpha = .05$ and df for $C - 1 = 3 - 1 = 2$, $\chi^2_{.05,2} = 5.991$. This test is always one-tailed, and the rejection region is always in the right-hand tail of the distribution. Because $K = 9.56$ is larger than the critical χ^2 value, the researcher rejects the null hypothesis. The number of patients seen in the office by a physician is not the same in these three sizes of offices. Examination of the values in each group reveals that physicians in two-partner offices see fewer patients per physician in the office, and HMO physicians see more patients in the office.

**Demonstration
Problem 12.7**

Agribusiness researchers are interested in determining under what conditions Christmas trees are grown fastest. A random sample of equivalent size seedlings is divided into four groups. The trees are all grown in the same field. One group is left to grow native, one group is given extra water, one group is given extra fertilizer spikes, and one group is given extra fertilizer spikes and extra water. At the end of one year, the seedlings are measured for increased growth (in height). These increases are shown for each group. Use the Kruskal–Wallis test to determine whether there is a significant difference in the growth of trees in these groups. Use $\alpha = .01$.

Group 1 (Native)	Group 2 (+ Water)	Group 3 (+ Fertilizer)	Group 4 (+ Water and Fertilizer)
8 in.	10 in.	11 in.	18 in.
5	12	14	20
7	11	10	16
11	9	16	15
9	13	17	14
6	12	12	22

Solution:

Here, $n = 24$, and $n_j = 6$ in each group. The hypotheses are

H_0: Group 1 = Group 2 = Group 3 = Group 4.
H_a: At least one group is different.

Ranking all group values yields the following:

1	2	3	4	
4	7.5	10	22	
1	13	16.5	23	
3	10	7.5	19.5	
10	5.5	19.5	18	
5.5	15	21	16.5	
2	13	13	24	
$T_1 = 25.5$	$T_2 = 64.0$	$T_3 = 87.5$	$T_4 = 123.0$	
$n_1 = 6$	$n_2 = 6$	$n_3 = 6$	$n_4 = 6$	$n = 24$

$$\sum_{j=1}^{c} \frac{T_j^2}{n_j} = \frac{(25.5)^2}{6} + \frac{(64)^2}{6} + \frac{(87.5)^2}{6} + \frac{(123)^2}{6} = 4{,}588.6;$$

$$K = \frac{12}{24(24 + 1)}(4{,}588.6) - 3(24 + 1) = 16.77.$$

The calculated K value is 16.77, df $= 4 - 1 = 3$, and the critical $\chi^2_{.01,3} = 11.345$. Because the calculated value is greater than the table value, the null hypothesis is rejected. There is a significant difference in the way the trees are grown. The following diagram shows the relationship of the calculated K value and the critical chi-square value.

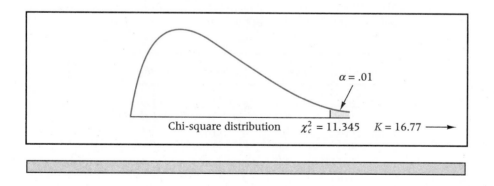

Chi-square distribution $\chi_c^2 = 11.345$ $K = 16.77 \longrightarrow$

$\alpha = .01$

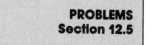

**PROBLEMS
Section 12.5**

12.29 Use the Kruskal–Wallis test to determine whether groups 1–5 come from different populations. Let $\alpha = .01$.

1	2	3	4	5
157	165	219	286	197
188	197	257	243	215
175	204	243	259	235
174	214	231	250	217
201	183	217	279	240
203		203		233
				213

12.30 Use the Kruskal–Wallis test to determine whether there is a significant difference in the following groups. Use $\alpha = .05$.

Group 1	19	21	29	22	37	43	
Group 2	30	38	35	24	29		
Group 3	39	32	41	44	30	27	33

12.31 Is there a difference in the amount of customers' initial deposits when they open savings accounts according to geographic region of the United States? To test this question, an analyst selects equivalent sized savings and loan offices from four regions of the United States. The offices selected are located in areas having similar economic and population characteristics. The analyst randomly selects adult customers who are opening their first savings accounts and obtains the following dollar amounts. Use the Kruskal–Wallis test to determine whether there is a significant difference in geographic region. Use $\alpha = .05$.

Region 1	Region 2	Region 3	Region 4
$1,200	$225	$ 675	$1,075
450	950	500	1,050
110	100	1,100	750
800	350	310	180
375	275	660	330
200			680
			425

12.32 Does the asking price of a new car vary according to whether the dealership is in a small town, a city, or a suburban area? To test this question a researcher randomly selects dealerships selling a particular make of car in the state of Illinois. The researcher goes to these dealerships posing as a prospective buyer and makes a serious inquiry as to the asking price of a new Pontiac Grand-am (each having the same equipment). The following data represent the results of this sample. Is there a significant difference between prices according to the area in which the dealership is located? Use the Kruskal–Wallis test and $\alpha = .05$.

Small Town	City	Suburb
$10,800	$11,300	$11,000
11,500	10,900	11,600
10,750	10,900	11,800
11,200	11,650	11,050
10,600	10,800	10,250
		11,550

12.33 A survey by the U.S. Travel Data Center in 1991 showed that a higher percentage of Americans travel to the ocean/beach for vacation than to any other destination. Much further behind in the survey, and virtually tied for second place, were the mountains and small/rural towns. How long do people stay at vacation destinations? Does the length of stay differ according to location? Suppose that the following data were taken from a survey of people on vacation. They were asked how many nights they stay at a destination when on vacation. Use a Kruskal–Wallis test to determine whether there is a significant difference in the duration of stay by type of vacation destination. Let $\alpha = .05$.

Amusement Park	Lake Area	City	National Park
0	3	2	2
1	2	2	4
1	3	3	3
0	5	2	4
2	4	3	3
1	4	2	5
0	3	3	4
	5	3	4
	2	1	
		3	

12.34 Do workers on different shifts get different amounts of sleep per week? Some people believe that shift workers who regularly work the grave-yard shift (12:00 A.M. to 8:00 A.M.) or swing shift (4:00 P.M. to 12:00 A.M.) are unable to get the same amount of sleep as day workers because of family schedules, noise, amount of daylight, and other factors. To test this theory, a researcher samples workers from day, swing, and graveyard shifts and asks each worker to keep a sleep journal for one week. The following data represent the number of hours of sleep per week per worker for the different shifts. Use the Kruskal–Wallis test to determine whether there is a significant difference in the number of hours of sleep per week for workers on these shifts. Use $\alpha = .05$.

Day Shift	Swing Shift	Graveyard Shift
52	45	41
57	48	46
53	44	39
56	51	49
55	48	42
50	54	35
51	49	52
	43	

12.6   SPEARMAN'S RANK CORRELATION

In Chapter 11, the Pearson product–moment correlation coefficient, r, was presented and discussed as a technique to measure the amount or degree of association between two variables. The Pearson r requires at least interval level of measurement for the data. When only ordinal level data or ranked data are available, **Spearman's rank correlation,** r_s, can be used to analyze the degree of association of two variables. Charles E. Spearman (1863–1945) developed this correlation coefficient.

Spearman's rank correlation

Suppose that someone wants to determine the correlation between the rankings of the top ten football teams as published by the Associated Press (AP) and the United Press International (UPI). The Spearman's rank correlation can be used to analyze such data.

Spearman Rank Correlation Coefficient

$$r_s = 1 - \frac{6\Sigma d^2}{n(n^2 - 1)},$$

where: n = number of pairs being correlated
  d = the difference in the ranks of each pair

The Spearman rank correlation formula is derived from the Pearson product–moment formula and utilizes the ranks of the n pairs instead of the raw data. The value of d is the difference in the ranks of each pair.

The process begins by ranking the items *within each* group, which already has been done by the AP and UPI football polls, as Table 12.12 shows. Table 12.13 contains the calculation of a Spearman's rank correlation for these data.

The interpretation of r_s values is similar to the interpretation of r values. Positive correlations indicate that high values of one variable tend to be associated with high values of the other variable, and low values of one variable tend to be associated with low values of the other variable. Correlations near $+1$ indicate high positive correlations, and correlations near -1 indicate high negative correlations. Negative correlations indicate that high values of one variable tend to be associated with low values of the other variable and vice versa. Correlations near zero indicate that there is little or no association between variables. The correlation, $r_s = +0.85$, on the previous example means that there is a relatively high positive correlation between the Associated Press poll of football teams and the United Press International poll.

University	AP	UPI		TABLE 12.12
				Top Ten Football Teams as Ranked by AP and UPI
Colorado	1	2		
Georgia Tech	2	1		
Miami	3	3		
Washington	4	6		
Notre Dame	5	7		
Penn State	6	4		
Mississippi	7	8		
Clemson	8	5		
Arizona State	9	9		
Houston	10	10		

University	AP	UPI	d	d²	TABLE 12.13
					Calculation of Spearman's Rank Correlation for Football Poll Data
Colorado	1	2	-1	1	
Georgia Tech	2	1	$+1$	1	
Miami	3	3	0	0	
Washington	4	6	-2	4	
Notre Dame	5	7	-2	4	
Penn State	6	4	$+2$	4	
Mississippi	7	8	-1	1	
Clemson	8	5	$+3$	9	
Arizona State	9	9	0	0	
Houston	10	10	0	0	
$n = 10$				$\Sigma d^2 = 24$	

$$r_s = 1 - \frac{6\Sigma d^2}{n(n^2 - 1)} = 1 - \frac{6(24)}{10(10^2 - 1)} = +.85.$$

Demonstration Problem 12.8

How strong is the correlation between crude oil prices and prices of gasoline at the pump? In an effort to estimate this association, an oil company analyst gathered the data shown over a period of several months. She lets crude oil prices be represented by the market value of a barrel of West Texas Intermediate crude and gasoline prices be the estimated average price of regular unleaded gasoline in a certain city. She computes a Spearman's rank correlation for these data.

Crude Oil	Gasoline
$14.60	$1.05
10.50	1.06
12.30	1.08
15.10	1.06
18.35	1.12
22.60	1.24
28.90	1.36
31.40	1.40
26.75	1.34

Solution:

Here, $n = 9$. When the analyst ranks the values *within* each group and computes the values of d and d^2, she obtains:

Crude Oil	Gasoline	d	d²
3	1	+2	4
1	2.5	−1.5	2.25
2	4	−2	4
4	2.5	+1.5	2.25
5	5	0	0
6	6	0	0
8	8	0	0
9	9	0	0
7	7	0	0
		$\Sigma d^2 =$	12.5

$$r_s = 1 - \frac{6\Sigma d^2}{n(n^2 - 1)} = 1 - \frac{6(12.5)}{9(9^2 - 1)} = +0.90.$$

There is a high positive correlation between the price of a barrel of West Texas Intermediate crude and a gallon of regular unleaded gasoline.

12.35 Compute a Spearman's rank correlation coefficient for the following variables to determine the degree of association between the two variables.

X	Y
23	201
41	259
37	234
29	240
25	231
17	209
33	229
41	246
40	248
28	227
19	200

12.36 The following data are the ranks for values of the two variables, X and Y. Use a Spearman's rank correlation coefficient to determine the degree of relation between the two variables.

X	Y
4	6
5	8
8	7
11	10
10	9
7	5
3	2
1	3
2	1
9	11
6	4

12.37 Compute a Spearman's rank correlation for the following data.

X	Y	X	Y
99	108	80	124
67	139	57	162
82	117	49	145
46	168	91	102

12.38 Over a period of a few months, is there a strong correlation between the value of the U.S. dollar and the prime interest rate? The following data represent a sample of these quantities over a period of time. Use a Spearman's rank correlation to determine the strength of the relationship between interest rates and the value of the dollar.

Dollar Value	Prime Rate
92	9.3
96	9.0
91	8.5
89	8.0
91	8.3
88	8.4
84	8.1
81	7.9
83	7.2

12.39 How strong is the correlation between the budget of a major motion picture and box office income? Baseline industry estimates for a sample of eight movies from 1990 are given. Use the data to compute a Spearman's rank correlation to estimate the association between a movie's budget and its income.

Movie	Budget (millions)	Income (millions)
Ghost	$24	$210
Godfather III	53	53
Days of Thunder	45	83
Another 48 Hours	45	79
Hunt for Red October	30	121
We're No Angels	20	14
Almost an Angel	28	7
The Two Jakes	25	11

12.40 During business cycles, is there a correlation between thirty-year treasury yields and real yields on bonds? Fuji Securities, Inc., released the following data for business cycles since 1954. Use these data to compute a Spearman's rank correlation. Comment on the correlation value.

Business Cycle	Thirty-Year Treasury Yields	Real Yields
1/54–10/57	3.05%	1.49%
11/57–4/60	3.93	1.70
5/60–11/69	4.68	2.51
12/69–10/73	6.57	2.04
11/73–12/79	8.27	1.02
1/80–6/81	12.01	2.77
7/81–6/90	10.27	5.27
7/90–5/91	8.45	3.83

12.41 The ranking of the top ten U.S. cities in terms of number of Hispanic-owned firms, along with the 1988 population estimates for those cities, are shown. Compute a Spearman's rank correlation between the number of Hispanic-owned firms and the 1988 population figures. If the correlation is not high, what does that mean in terms of the relationship between these two variables. What other factors might be related to the number of Hispanic-owned firms in a city?

City	Number of Hispanic-Owned Firms (thousands)	1988 Population (millions)
Los Angeles	56.7	3.353
Miami	47.0	0.371
New York	23.0	7.353
Houston	16.0	1.698
San Antonio	15.2	0.941
San Diego	10.4	1.070
Riverside, Calif.	10.2	0.211
Anaheim, Calif.	9.7	0.245
El Paso	8.2	0.511
Chicago	7.8	2.978

HISTORICAL NOTE
Karl Pearson

Karl Pearson was born in London in 1857. He was the son of a Queen's Counselor and of Quaker ancestry. When he was eighteen years old, he received a scholarship to King's College, Cambridge, from which he graduated with honors in mathematics in 1879. He had many interests, including mathematics, religion, philosophy, and poetry. During his early and mid-twenties, Pearson traveled extensively in Germany and studied German humanities. In 1884, at the age of twenty-seven, Pearson received an appointment to University College. In 1890, Pearson met Maria Sharpe, to whom he was married for 38 years. In the early 1890s, while lecturing in geometry part time at Gresham College, Pearson was drawn into areas of applied mathematics. During this period he developed much of his expertise in statistics. Between 1893 and 1901, Pearson accomplished several statistical feats worthy of mention. In 1894, he defined the population standard deviation and the normal curve. In 1895, he proved that r is the best estimate of the population correlation. He developed a paper in the late 1800s that culminated in the introduction of the χ^2 goodness-of-fit test in 1900. Pearson developed simple linear correlation, curvilinear regression and correlation, the contingency coefficient, chi-square goodness-of-fit, kurtosis, standard deviation, mode, and many variations of these methods. Pearson died in 1936 at the age of eighty-three.

Source: Adapted from Dudycha, Arthur L. and Linda W. Dudycha, "Behavioral Statistics: An Historical Perspective," in *Statistical Issues: A Reader for the Behavioral Sciences*, edited by Roger Kirk (Monterey, Calif.: Brooks/Cole, 1972).

CHAPTER SUMMARY

Nonparametric statistics are a group of techniques that were developed for statistical analysis when the data are less than interval in measurement and/or when assumptions regarding population parameters, such as shape of the distribution, cannot be met. Nonparametric tests have several advantages. Sometimes the nonparametric test is the only technique available, with no parametric alternative. Nonparametric tests can be used to analyze nominal or ordinal level data. Computations from nonparametric tests are usually simpler than those used with parametric tests. Probability statements obtained from most nonparametric tests are exact probabilities. Nonparametric techniques also have some disadvantages. Nonparametric techniques are wasteful of data whenever a parametric technique can be used. Nonparametric tests are not as widely available as parametric tests. For large samples the calculations can be tedious.

Many of the parametric techniques presented in this text have corresponding nonparametric techniques that can be used. Six nonparametric statistical techniques were presented and discussed: chi-square goodness-of-fit, chi-square test of independence, Mann–Whitney U test, Wilcoxon matched-pairs signed rank test, Kruskal–Wallis test, and Spearman's rank correlation coefficient.

The chi-square goodness-of-fit test is used to compare a theoretical or expected distribution of measurements for several categories of a variable with the actual or observed distribution of measurements. It can be used to determine whether a distribution of values fits a given distribution, such as the Poisson or normal distribution.

The chi-square test of independence is used to analyze frequencies for categories of two variables to determine whether the two variables are independent. The data used in analysis by a chi-square test of independence are arranged in a two-dimensional table called a contingency table. For this reason, the test is sometimes referred to as contingency analysis. A chi-square test of independence is computed in a manner similar to that used with the chi-square goodness-of-fit test. Expected values are computed for each cell of the contingency table and then compared to observed values with the chi-square statistic. Both the chi-square test of independence and the chi-square goodness-of-fit test require that expected values be greater than or equal to 5.

The Mann–Whitney U test is a nonparametric version of the t test of the means from two independent samples. When the assumption of normally distributed data cannot be met or if the data are only ordinal in level of measurement, the Mann–Whitney U test can be used in place of the t test. The Mann–Whitney U test—like many nonparametric tests—works with the ranks of data rather than the raw data.

The Wilcoxon matched-pairs signed rank test is used as an alternative to the t test for related measures when assumptions cannot be met or if the data are ordinal in measurement. In contrast to the Mann–Whitney U test, the Wilcoxon test is used when the data are related in some way. The Wilcoxon test is used to analyze the data by ranks of the differences of the raw data.

The Kruskal–Willis test is a nonparametric one-way analysis of variance technique. It is particularly useful when the assumptions underlying the F test of the parametric one-way ANOVA cannot be met. The Kruskal–Wallis test is usually used when the researcher wants to determine whether three or more groups or samples are from the same or equivalent populations. This test is based on the assumption that the sample items are randomly selected and that the groups are independent. The raw data are converted to ranks and the Kruskal–Wallis test is used to analyze the ranks with the equivalent of a chi-square statistic.

If two variables contain data that are ordinal in level of measurement, a Spearman's rank correlation coefficient can be used to determine the amount of relationship or association between the variables. Spearman's rank correlation coefficient is a nonparametric alternative to Pearson's product–moment correlation coefficient. Spearman's rank correlation coefficient is interpreted in a manner similar to Pearson's r.

Key Words

Parametric statistics	Contingency analysis
Nonparametric statistics	Mann–Whitney U test
Chi-square goodness-of-fit test	Wilcoxon matched-pairs signed
Chi-square distribution	rank test
Chi-square test of independence	Kruskal–Wallis test
Contingency table	Spearman's rank correlation

USING THE COMPUTER

You can compute either by Minitab directly or through relatively simple manipulation of Minitab commands most of the techniques presented in this chapter.

Chi-square Goodness-of-Fit

Minitab does not have a command that can perform a chi-square goodness-of-fit test. However, you can easily program the algorithm for calculating this test with two statements. The chi-square goodness-of-fit test compares a distribution of expected values with observed values. The first step in computing a goodness-of-fit test is to enter the data into two columns, one for the expected values and one for the observed values. You may use either the READ command or the SET command to do so because of the two columns of data in each case and the equal number of categories in each column.

The chi-square goodness-of-fit test finds the difference between the observed value and expected value, squares this difference, and divides the difference by the expected value. Use a LET command and provide the algebraic expression necessary to compute this value. Suppose that column 1 contains the observed values and column 2 contains the expected values. The Minitab computation command is

MTB > LET C3 = (C1-C2)**2/C2

Execution stores the results in column 3. As with many computer packages, the **2 is the command that squares the expression. If you sum the values in C3, the calculated chi-square results. Do so by using a SUM command:

MTB > SUM C3

The resulting chi-square answer is printed. To analyze Demonstration Problem 12.1 by Minitab in this manner, use the commands:

```
MTB  > READ C1 C2
DATA > 1610 1537.25
DATA > 1585 1537.25
      .      .      .
      .      .      .
DATA > 1655 1537.25
DATA > end
MTB  > LET C3 = (C1-C2)**2/C2
MTB  > SUM C3
```

The resulting output is

```
SUM = 74.376
```

This output is the computed chi-square value for Demonstration Problem 12.1. You can use Minitab to determine the probability of getting a chi-square value less than or equal to this value by chance by using a CDF command. In this case, the CDF command, followed by the chi-square value and a semi-colon, yields a subcommand prompt. Enter **CHISQUARE** followed by the degrees of freedom and a period. The commands for Demonstration Problem 12.1 are

```
MTB  > CDF 74.376;
SUBC > CHISQUARE 11.
```

The output is

```
74.3760   1.0000
```

The first number is the chi-square value. The second number represents the proportion of the chi-square curve to the left of the chi-square value (less than or equal to the value). In this case, the chi-square value is so large for these degrees of freedom that virtually all of the area of the curve lies to the left of that value. Thus the probability of getting a chi-square this large or larger by chance is practically zero (to the right).

Chi-Square Test of Independence

Minitab has the capability of computing more directly the chi-square test of independence than it does the goodness-of-fit test. To compute a test of independence, load the contingency table data either by columns or by rows into

Minitab. Then use a **CHISQUARE** command to produce the answer. Note that this command does not have a hyphen in it. Suppose that you want to use Minitab to analyze Demonstration Problem 12.4. The commands and output to accomplish that are

```
MTB  > READ C1 C2 C3
DATA > 26 95 18
DATA > 41 40 20
DATA > 24 13 32
DATA > end
MTB  > CHISQUARE C1-C3
```

The output is

```
Expected counts are printed below observed counts
            C1        C2        C3      Total
    1       26        95        18       139
          40.94     66.58     31.49

    2       41        40        20       101
          29.74     48.38     22.88

    3       24        13        32        69
          20.32     33.05     15.63

  Total     91       148        70       309

ChiSq = 5.449 + 12.135 +  5.778 +
        4.259 +  1.450 +  0.363 +
        0.666 + 12.162 + 17.142 = 59.405

df = 4
```

In order to determine the probability of obtaining a chi-square value of 59.405 or greater by chance, you must use the **CDF** command:

```
MTB  > CDF 59.405;
SUBC > CHISQUARE 4.
```

The output is

```
59.405   1.0000
```

The probability of obtaining a chi-square value less than or equal to 59.405 is 1.000. The probability of obtaining a chi-square value greater than 59.405 by chance is .0000.

Mann–Whitney U Test

You can make a Mann–Whitney U test directly with Minitab by using the **MANN-WHITNEY** command followed by the location of the two columns in which the data are located. This command defaults to a two-tailed test with $\alpha = .05$.

```
MTB > MANN-WHITNEY C1 C2
```

If you want to conduct a one-tailed test, place a -1 between **MANN-WHITNEY** and the first column location, if the alternative hypothesis is at the lower end of the distribution, and a $+1$ to test for the upper region. For example, to conduct a one-tailed test with a rejection region at the lower end, the command is

```
MTB > MANN-WHITNEY -1 C1 C2
```

The output includes the median values of each group, point and interval estimations of the difference in medians, a W value, and the significance of the hypothesis test.

Use the following Minitab commands to work Demonstration Problem 12.5.

```
MTB  > SET C1
DATA > 2.75 3.29 4.53 3.61 3.1 4.29 2.25 2.97 4.01 3.68 3.15 2.97
DATA > 4.05 3.6
DATA > end
MTB  > SET C2
DATA > 4.1 4.75 3.95 3.5 4.25 4.98 5.75 4.1 2.7 3.65 5.11 4.8
DATA > 6.25 3.89 4.8 5.5
DATA > end
MTB  > MANN-WHITNEY 1 C1 C2
```

The output is

```
Mann-Whitney Confidence Interval and Test

C1          N = 14        MEDIAN =       3.445
C2          N = 16        MEDIAN =       4.500
POINT ESTIMATE FOR ETA1-ETA2 IS       -1.065
95.2      PCT C.I. FOR ETA1-ETA2 IS (     -1.700,     -0.460)
W =      144.0
TEST OF ETA1 = ETA2 VS. ETA1 N.E. ETA2 IS SIGNIFICANT AT 0.0013.
```

The value of W agrees with that obtained in Demonstration Problem 12.5. However, Minitab does not convert the W value to a Z score as was done there.

Minitab determines the significance of the W value directly, as shown in the output.

Wilcoxon Matched-Pairs Signed Rank Test

Using Minitab to calculate a Wilcoxon matched-pairs signed rank test is similar to using Minitab to compute a t test for related measures. First, enter the data by using either the SET or READ command. Then use a LET command to compute the differences in the two columns. For example, for data in columns 1 and 2, the LET command to compute the column differences and store the differences in column 3 is

```
MTB > LET C3 = C1-C2
```

Next, perform a Wilcoxon test on the difference scores by using the WTEST command. The WTEST command requires only entry of the column location of the data after it. With the differences in column 3, the command is

```
MTB > WTEST C3
```

If you use Minitab to analyze Demonstration Problem 12.6 with the Wilcoxon matched-pairs signed rank test, the commands are

```
MTB  > SET C1
DATA > 5 4 9 6 3 8 7 10 3 7 2 5 4 5 5 8 7 9 5 4 3
DATA > end
MTB  > SET C2
DATA > 11 9 9 8 5 7 9 9 7 9 6 10 9 7 9 6 10 8 5 6
DATA > end
MTB  > LET C3 = C1-C2
MTB  > WTEST C3
```

The output for these commands is

```
TEST OF MEDIAN = 0.000000000 VERSUS MEDIAN N.E. 0.000000000
```

	N	N FOR TEST	WILCOXON STATISTIC	P-VALUE	ESTIMATED MEDIAN
C3	20	19	10.5	0.001	-2.000

Kruskal–Wallis Test

You can use the nonparametric equivalent of one-way analysis of variance, the Kruskal–Wallis test, to analyze data with Minitab. First, enter the multiple samples or groups to be compared into multiple columns and use the STACK command to place the data into one column. An alternative approach is to enter the data into one column stacked end to end. For example, suppose there are five columns of data. The commands to enter and stack the data would be

```
MTB  > READ C1 C2 C3 C4 C5
DATA > . . . . .
DATA > . . . . .
. .
DATA > end
MTB  > STACK C1-C5 C6
```

You need to create a column containing group identifiers. For example, if there are 7, 5, 8, 6, and 6 values in each of the five groups, respectively, you would SET the group identifier column as

```
MTB  > SET C6
DATA > 1 1 1 1 1 1 1 2 2 2 2 2 3 3 3 3 3 3 3 3 4 4 4 4 4
       4 5 5 5 5 5 5
DATA > end
```

You can run the Kruskal–Wallis test in Minitab by using the **KRUSKAL-WALLIS** command followed by the column location of the stacked data and the column location of the group identifiers. You can analyze Demonstration Problem 12.7 with Minitab by using the following commands:

```
MTB  > READ C1-C4
DATA > 8 10 11 18
DATA > 5 12 14 20
DATA > 7 11 10 16
DATA > 11 9 16 15
DATA > 9 13 17 14
DATA > 6 12 12 22
DATA > end
MTB  > STACK C1-C4 C5
MTB  > SET C6
DATA > 1 1 1 1 1 1 2 2 2 2 2 2 3 3 3 3 3 3 4 4 4 4 4 4
DATA > end
MTB  > KRUSKAL-WALLIS C5 C6
```

The output from these commands is

LEVEL	NOBS	MEDIAN	AVE. RANK	Z VALUE
1	6	7.500	4.2	−3.30
2	6	11.500	10.7	−0.73
3	6	13.000	14.6	0.83
4	6	17.000	20.5	3.20
OVERALL	24		12.5	

H = 16.77

Note that the H value yielded by Minitab is synonymous with the Kruskal–Wallis K value in the text.

Spearman's Rank Correlation Coefficient

Minitab does not directly compute a Spearman's rank correlation coefficient. You must first use the RANK command to convert raw scores to ranks. For example, if you stored the data in C1 and C2, the RANK command is

```
MTB > RANK C1 C3
MTB > RANK C2 C4
```

The RANK command requires the column in which the raw data are located and a column in which the ranks are to be stored. In this example, the raw data in columns 1 and 2 are each ranked and stored in columns 3 and 4, respectively. After ranking the data, use the CORRELATE command on the ranked data to compute a Spearman's correlation:

```
MTB > CORRELATE C3 C4
```

You may use the CORRELATE command either to generate a Pearson product–moment correlation by using the raw data (in this case, C1 and C2) or to generate a Spearman's rank correlation coefficient by using the ranked data. For more than two columns, the CORRELATE command generates a matrix of intercorrelations consisting of the correlations for all pairs.

You can use these commands to solve Demonstration Problem 12.8. The Minitab commands to accomplish this are

```
MTB  > READ C1 C2
DATA > 14.6 1.05
DATA > 10.5 1.06
DATA > 12.3 1.08
DATA > 15.1 1.06
DATA > 18.35 1.12
DATA > 22.6 1.24
DATA > 28.9 1.36
DATA > 31.4 1.4
DATA > 26.75 1.34
DATA > End
MTB  > RANK C1 C3
MTB  > RANK C2 C4
MTB  > CORRELATE C3 C4
```

The output from these commands is

Correlation of C3 and C4 = 0.895

12.42 Use the chi-square goodness-of-fit test to determine whether the following distribution is a uniform distribution. Let $\alpha = .05$.

Category	Observed Value
1	34
2	28
3	30
4	33
5	31
6	26
7	29
8	33

12.43 Use the chi-square goodness-of-fit test to determine whether the observed frequencies fit the expected frequencies. Use $\alpha = .01$.

Category	Observed	Expected
1	205	208
2	195	200
3	166	156
4	108	110
5	157	148
6	174	182
7	180	180

12.44 Suppose that the expected percentages in eight categories are 20%, 12%, 8%, 6%, 15%, 18%, 15%, and 6%, respectively. Use the chi-square goodness-of-fit test to determine whether the observed frequencies for these same categories fit the expected values. Let $\alpha = .05$.

Observed Frequencies: 242 140 75 60 155 190 162 80

12.45 Use a chi-square goodness-of-fit test to determine whether the following data are Poisson distributed. Let $\alpha = .10$.

Number of Defects	Observed Frequency
0	6
1	11
2	29
3	17
4	10
5	7
6	5

12.46 A national youth organization sells six different kinds of cookies during its annual cookie campaign. A local leader is curious about whether national sales of the six kinds of cookies are uniformly distributed. He randomly selects the amounts of each kind of cookies sold from five youths and combines them into the observed data shown. Use $\alpha = .05$ to determine whether the data indicate that sales for these six kinds of cookies are uniformly distributed.

Kind of Cookie	Observed Frequency
Chocolate chip	189
Peanut butter	168
Cheese cracker	155
Lemon flavored	161
Chocolate mint	216
Vanilla filled	165

12.47 According to *Beverage Digest*, the distribution of market share for the top six soft drinks in the United States was Coca-Cola Classic, 20.0%; Pepsi, 18.8%; Diet Coke, 9.3%; Diet Pepsi, 8.8%; Dr Pepper, 4.9%; Sprite, 3.7%; and others, 34.5%. Suppose that a marketing analyst wants to determine whether this distribution fits that of her geographic region. She randomly surveys 1,726 local people and asks them to name their favorite soft drink. The responses are: Classic Coke, 361; Pepsi, 340; Diet Coke, 192; Diet Pepsi, 153; Dr Pepper, 82; Sprite, 40; and others, 558. She then tests to determine whether the local distribution of soft drink preferences is the same or different from the national figures, using $\alpha = .05$. What does she find?

12.48 Are random arrivals at a shoe store at the local mall Poisson distributed? Suppose that a mall employee researches this question by gathering data for arrivals during one-minute intervals on a weekday night between 6:30 P.M. and 8:00 P.M. The data obtained are shown. Use $\alpha = .05$ to determine whether the observed data seem to be from a Poisson distribution.

Arrivals per Minute	Observed Frequency
0	26
1	40
2	57
3	32
4	17
5	12
6	8

12.49 Use the chi-square test of independence to determine whether variable One is independent of variable Two. Let $\alpha = .01$.

Variable Two

6	18	22
19	38	45

Variable One

12.50 Use the chi-square test of independence to determine whether the variables are independent for $\alpha = .10$.

Variable Two

32	28	14	8	17
58	43	29	15	23
40	33	19	10	22

Variable One

12.51 Is the number of children that a college student has independent of the type of college or university being attended? Suppose that students were randomly selected from three types of colleges and universities and the data shown represent the results of a survey of these students. Use a chi-square test of independence to test this question. Let $\alpha = .05$.

Type of College or University

		Community College	Large University	Small College
	0	25	178	31
Number of	**1**	49	141	12
Children	**2**	31	54	8
	3 or more	22	14	6

12.52 A researcher interviewed 2,067 people and asked whether they were the primary decision maker in the household when buying a new car last year. Two hundred seven replied that they were men and that they had bought a new car last year. Sixty-five were women and had bought a new car last year. Eight hundred eleven of the responses were from men who did not buy a car last year. Nine hundred eighty-four were women who did not buy a car last year. Use these data to determine whether gender is independent of being a major decision maker in purchasing a car last year. Let $\alpha = .05$.

12.53 Is a manufacturer's geographic location independent of type of customer? Use the following data for companies with primarily industrial customers and companies with primarily retail customers to test this question. Let $\alpha = .10$.

Geographic Location

	Northeast	West	South
Industrial Customer	230	115	68
Retail Customer	185	143	89

12.54 Are the types of professional jobs held in the computing industry independent of the number of years that a person has worked in the industry? Suppose that 246 workers are interviewed. Use the results obtained to determine whether type of professional job held in the computer industry is independent of years worked in the industry. Let $\alpha = .01$.

Professional Position

		Manager	Programmer	Operator	Systems Analyst
Years	0–3	6	37	11	13
	4–8	28	16	23	24
More than 8		47	10	12	19

12.55 Use the Mann–Whitney U test to determine whether there is a significant difference in the following two groups. Let $\alpha = .05$.

Group One	Group Two
56	48
44	49
43	51
49	55
57	47
50	53
41	42
48	54
59	58
43	46
51	52

12.56 Use the Mann–Whitney U test to determine whether the mean of population X is greater than the mean of population Y. Assume $\alpha = .01$.

X	Y
179	143
182	139
140	156
163	160
181	175
149	162
156	131
177	129
199	152
210	149

12.57 Is there a significant difference in the population means of two populations based on the following data? Use the Mann–Whitney U test and $\alpha = .01$ to draw a conclusion.

Sample 1	Sample 2
3.45	2.98
2.30	2.78
3.02	2.75
4.12	3.61
2.65	1.98
3.13	2.74
4.11	4.09
2.39	2.87
3.34	2.72
3.07	3.04
4.23	4.11
	4.01
	3.38
	3.16

12.58 Suppose that you want to take a random sample of GMAT test scores to determine whether there is any significant difference between the GMAT scores for the test given in March and the scores for the test given in June. You gather the following data from a sample of those who took each test. Use the Mann–Whitney U test to determine whether there is a significant difference in the two test results. Let $\alpha = .10$.

March	June
410	520
450	420
480	480
540	430
460	470
380	440
460	390
510	410
490	500
510	530

12.59 Should male managers wear a tie during the workday to command respect and demonstrate professionalism? Suppose that a measurement scale has been developed that generates a management professionalism score. A random sample of managers in a high-tech industry is selected for the study, some of whom wear ties at work and others who do not wear a tie at work. One subordinate is randomly selected from each manager's department and asked to complete the scale on their boss's professionalism. Analyze the data taken from these independent groups to determine whether the manager's *with* the ties received significantly higher professionalism scores. Let $\alpha = .05$.

With Tie	Without Tie
27	22
23	16
25	25
22	19
25	21
26	24
21	20
25	19
26	23
28	26
22	17

12.60 In some firefighting organizations, you must serve as a firefighter for some period of time before you can become part of the emergency medical service arm of the organization. Does that mean that EMS workers are older, on average, than traditional firefighters? Use the data shown and $\alpha = .05$ to test whether EMS workers are significantly older than firefighters. Assume that the two groups are independent and that you do not want to use a *t* test to analyze the data.

Firefighters	EMS Workers
23	27
37	29
28	30
25	33
41	28
36	36
32	39
24	33
21	30
27	28
	27
	30

12.61 Many fast-food restaurants have soft-drink dispensers with preset amounts, so that when the operator merely pushes a button for the desired drink the cup is automatically filled. This method apparently saves time and seems to increase worker productivity. To test this conclusion a researcher randomly selects twenty-two workers from the fast-food industry, eleven from a restaurant with automatic soft-drink dispensers and eleven from a comparable restaurant with manual soft-drink dispensers. The samples are independent. During a comparable hour, the amount of sales rung up by a worker is recorded. Assume that $\alpha = .01$ and that a t test is not appropriate. Test whether workers with automatic dispensers are significantly more productive (higher average sales per hour).

Automatic Dispenser	Manual Dispenser
$153	$105
128	118
143	129
110	114
152	125
168	117
144	106
137	92
118	126
146	109
151	122

12.62 Use the Wilcoxon matched-pairs signed rank test and $\alpha = .05$ to determine whether there is a significant difference in the before and after scores shown.

Before	After	Before	After
29	51	32	30
31	47	24	27
30	45	18	33
17	32	29	29
23	29	31	27
41	40	31	38
26	36	40	44
18	29	27	29
19	21	26	41

12.63 The following data are related measures. Use the Wilcoxon matched-pairs signed rank test to determine whether there is a significant difference in the two groups. Let $\alpha = .01$.

Group 1	Group 2
111	116
87	90
96	95
103	100
102	115
97	107
113	111
95	80
97	96
90	79
101	105
100	91
93	97
88	82
104	109
94	79
107	109

12.64 The scores given are husband–wife scores on a marketing measure. Use the Wilcoxon matched-pairs signed rank test to determine whether the wives' scores are significantly higher on the marketing measure than the husbands'. Assume that $\alpha = .01$.

Husbands	Wives	Husbands	Wives
27	35	18	28
22	29	20	21
28	30	24	22
19	20	23	33
28	27	25	38
29	31	22	34
18	22	16	31
21	19	23	36
25	29	30	31

12.65 Does a statistics course improve a student's mathematics skills, as measured by a national test? Suppose that a random sample of eighteen students takes the same national mathematics examination just prior to enrolling in a statistics course and just after completing the course. Listed are the students' quantitative scores from both examinations. Use $\alpha = .01$ to determine whether the scores after the statistics course are significantly higher than before.

Student	Before	After	Student	Before	After
1	430	465	10	430	430
2	485	475	11	450	460
3	520	535	12	495	500
4	360	410	13	540	530
5	440	425	14	460	475
6	500	505	15	400	420
7	425	450	16	420	445
8	470	480	17	385	380
9	515	520	18	455	475

12.66 Does deodorant sell better in a box or without additional packaging? An experiment in a large store is designed in which, for one month, all deodorants are sold packaged in a box and, during a second month, all deodorants are removed from the box and sold without packaging. Is there a significant difference in the number of units of deodorant sold with and without the additional packaging? Let $\alpha = .05$.

Deodorant	Box	No Box
1	185	170
2	109	112
3	92	90
4	105	87
5	60	51
6	45	49
7	25	11
8	58	40
9	161	165
10	108	82
11	89	94
12	123	139
13	34	21
14	68	55
15	59	60
16	78	52

12.67 Automobile dealers usually advertise in the yellow pages of the telephone book. Sometimes they have to pay to be listed in the white pages,
and some dealerships opt to save money by omitting that listing, figuring
that most people will use the yellow pages to find the telephone number.
A two-year study is conducted with twenty car dealerships where in
one year the dealer is listed in the white pages and the other year is
not. Ten of the dealerships are listed in the white pages the first year
and the other ten the second year in an attempt to control for economic
cycles. The following data represent the number of units sold per year.
Is there a significant difference between the number of units sold when
the dealership is listed in the white pages and when it is not listed?
Assume that all twenty companies are continuously listed in the yellow
pages, that the t test is not appropriate, and that $\alpha = .01$.

Dealer	With Listing	Without Listing
1	1180	1209
2	874	902
3	1071	862
4	668	503
5	889	974
6	724	675
7	880	821
8	482	567
9	796	602
10	1207	1097
11	968	962
12	1027	1045
13	1158	896
14	670	708
15	849	642
16	559	327
17	449	483
18	992	978
19	1046	973
20	852	841

12.68 Random samples of data are gathered from four independent groups.
Use a Kruskal–Wallis test to analyze the resulting data to determine whether there is a significant difference between groups. Let
$\alpha = .05$.

Group 1	Group 2	Group 3	Group 4
27	23	24	28
19	21	26	29
20	17	27	27
22	18	30	25
25	18	31	32

12.69 Use a Kruskal–Wallis test to determine whether the three samples shown come from different populations. Assume that the samples are independent and randomly selected. Let $\alpha = .05$.

Sample 1	Sample 2	Sample 3
1057	1109	1078
1049	1120	1090
1066	1092	1099
1023	1083	1101
1071	1089	1103
1026	1117	1100
	1095	1113
		1108

12.70 Analyze the following data, which have been randomly sampled as independent groups, to determine whether there is a significant difference in the groups. Use $\alpha = .10$.

Group 1	Group 2	Group 3	Group 4
3.24	1.98	2.76	2.70
3.03	1.78	2.13	2.69
2.95	2.15	2.46	2.85
3.29	1.87	2.31	2.55
3.09	2.18	2.52	2.73
3.41		2.47	
2.97		2.60	
		2.71	

12.71 The five groups shown were randomly selected as independent groups. Use the Kruskal–Wallis test and $\alpha = .05$ to determine whether the data come from different populations.

1	2	3	4	5
23.14	14.58	20.17	18.56	23.21
21.48	19.87	20.50	20.14	22.97
22.39	20.13	20.90	19.74	21.19
22.57	18.51	19.99	19.34	22.39
23.00	17.75	19.36	20.17	22.95
21.78		20.48	18.86	22.01
22.69		19.73		22.87
21.38				22.92
				22.41

12.72 A particular metal part can be produced at different temperatures. All other variables being equal, a company would like to determine whether the strength of the metal part is significantly different for different temperatures. Given are the strengths of random samples of parts produced under different temperatures. Use $\alpha = .01$ and determine whether there is a significant difference in the strength of the part for different temperatures.

45°	55°	70°	85°
216	228	219	218
215	224	220	216
218	225	221	217
216	222	223	221
219	226	224	218
214	225		217

12.73 Workers in three different but comparable companies were asked to rate the use of quality control techniques in their firms. They were given a 50-point scale to respond to, with a score of 50 representing nearly perfect implementation of quality control techniques and zero representing no implementation. Workers were divided into three independent groups. One group worked in a company that had required all its workers to attend a three-day seminar on quality control one year ago. A second group worked in a company in which each worker was part of a quality circle group that had been meeting at least once a month for a year. The third group of workers was employed by a company in which management had been actively involved in the quality control process for more than a year. Use $\alpha = .10$ to determine whether there is a significant difference between the three groups, as measured by the ratings.

Attended Three-Day Seminar	Quality Circles	Management Involved
9	27	16
11	38	21
17	25	18
10	40	28
22	31	29
15	19	20
6	35	31

12.74 Commercial fish raising is a growing industry in the United States. What makes fish raised commercially grow faster and larger? Suppose that a fish industry study is conducted over the three summer months in an effort to determine whether the amount of water allotted per fish makes any difference in the speed with which the fish grow. The following data represent the inches of growth of marked catfish in fish farms for different volumes of water per fish. Use $\alpha = .01$ to test whether there is a significant difference in fish growth by volume of allotted water.

One Gallon per Fish	Five Gallons per Fish	Ten Gallons per Fish
1.1 in.	2.9 in.	3.1 in.
1.4	2.5	2.4
1.7	2.6	3.0
1.3	2.2	2.3
1.9	2.1	2.9
1.4	2.0	1.9
2.1	2.7	

12.75 Compute a Spearman's rank correlation coefficient on the following variables.

Variable 1	Variable 2
35	91
42	88
50	86
55	90
39	87
48	80
65	73

12.76 Determine the strength of association between the two variables shown, using a Spearman's rank correlation coefficient.

Variable 1	Variable 2
1.18	1.26
1.34	1.45
1.35	1.41
1.39	1.58
1.23	1.34
1.44	1.61
1.45	1.54
1.41	1.58

12.77 The following data represent the ranks of pairs under two different rating systems. Use Spearman's rank correlation coefficient to determine how much correlation there is between the two systems.

System 1	System 2	System 1	System 2
1	4	5	2
2	1	6	7
3	3	7	8
4	5	8	6

12.78 Is there a strong correlation between the number of miles driven by a salesperson and sales volume achieved? Data were gathered from nine sales people who worked territories of similar size and potential. Determine the correlation coefficient for these data. Assume that the data are ordinal only in level of measurement.

Sales	Miles per Month
$150,000	1,500
210,000	2,100
285,000	3,200
301,000	2,400
335,000	2,200
390,000	2,500
400,000	3,300
425,000	3,100
440,000	3,600

12.79 Some people drink coffee to relieve stress on the job. Is there a correlation between the number of cups of coffee consumed on the job and perceived job stress? Suppose that the data shown represent the number of cups of coffee consumed per week and a stress rating for their jobs from a scale of 0 to 100 for nine managers in the same industry. Determine the correlation between these two variables, assuming that you do not want to use the Pearson product–moment correlation coefficient.

Cups of Coffee per Week	Job Stress
25	80
41	85
16	35
0	45
11	30
28	50
34	65
18	40
5	20

12.80 Because of their success, some television commercials have lives of several years. When a commercial is successful for several years, how much correlation is there between the ranking of the commercial one year and its ranking the next? Shown are six companies with successful television commercials, along with rankings of their commercials in 1990 and 1991. Determine the correlation of the rankings for these two years.

Brand	1990 Ranking	1991 Ranking
Pepsi/Diet Pepsi	1	2
Nike	2	1
Energizer	3	4
Coca-Cola	4	6
McDonald's	5	3
Little Caesar	6	5

TABLES

TABLE A.1   Random Numbers

12651	61646	11769	75109	86996	97669	25757	32535	07122	76763
81769	74436	02630	72310	45049	18029	07469	42341	98173	79260
36737	98863	77240	76251	00654	64688	09343	70278	67331	98729
82861	54371	76610	94934	72748	44124	05610	53750	95938	01485
21325	15732	24127	37431	09723	63529	73977	95218	96074	42138
74146	47887	62463	23045	41490	07954	22597	60012	98866	90959
90759	64410	54179	66075	61051	75385	51378	08360	95946	95547
55683	98078	02238	91540	21219	17720	87817	41705	95785	12563
79686	17969	76061	83748	55920	83612	41540	86492	06447	60568
70333	00201	86201	69716	78185	62154	77930	67663	29529	75116
14042	53536	07779	04157	41172	36473	42123	43929	50533	33437
59911	08256	06596	48416	69770	68797	56080	14223	59199	30162
62368	62623	62742	14891	39247	52242	98832	69533	91174	57979
57529	97751	54976	48957	74599	08759	78494	52785	68526	64618
15469	90574	78033	66885	13936	42117	71831	22961	94225	31816
18625	23674	53850	32827	81647	80820	00420	63555	74489	80141
74626	68394	88562	70745	23701	45630	65891	58220	35442	60414
11119	16519	27384	90199	79210	76965	99546	30323	31664	22845
41101	17336	48951	53674	17880	45260	08575	49321	36191	17095
32123	91576	84221	78902	82010	30847	62329	63898	23268	74283
26091	68409	69704	82267	14751	13151	93115	01437	56945	89661
67680	79790	48462	59278	44185	29616	76531	19589	83139	28454
15184	19260	14073	07026	25264	08388	27182	22557	61501	67481
58010	45039	57181	10238	36874	28546	37444	80824	63981	39942
56425	53996	86245	32623	78858	08143	60377	42925	42815	11159

82630	84066	13592	60642	17904	99718	63432	88642	37858	25431
14927	40909	23900	48761	44860	92467	31742	87142	03607	32059
23740	22505	07489	85986	74420	21744	97711	36648	35620	97949
32990	97446	03711	63824	07953	85965	87089	11687	92414	67257
05310	24058	91946	78437	34365	82469	12430	84754	19354	72745
21839	39937	27534	88913	49055	19218	47712	67677	51889	70926
08833	42549	93981	94051	28382	83725	72643	64233	97252	17133
58336	11139	47479	00931	91560	95372	97642	33856	54825	55680
62032	91144	75478	47431	52726	30289	42411	91886	51818	78292
45171	30557	53116	04118	58301	24375	65609	85810	18620	49198
91611	62656	60128	35609	63698	78356	50682	22505	01692	36291
55472	63819	86314	49174	93582	73604	78614	78849	23096	72825
18573	09729	74091	53994	10970	86557	65661	41854	26037	53296
60866	02955	90288	82136	83644	94455	06560	78029	98768	71296
45043	55608	82767	60890	74646	79485	13619	98868	40857	19415
17831	09737	79473	75945	28394	79334	70577	38048	03607	06932
40137	03981	07585	18128	11178	32601	27994	05641	22600	86064
77776	31343	14576	97706	16039	47517	43300	59080	80392	63189
69605	44104	40103	95635	05635	81673	68657	09559	23510	95875
19916	52934	26499	09821	97331	80993	61299	36979	73599	35055
02606	58552	07678	56619	65325	30705	99582	53390	46357	13244
65183	73160	87131	35530	47946	09854	18080	02321	05809	04893
10740	98914	44916	11322	89717	88189	30143	52687	19420	60061
98642	89822	71691	51573	83666	61642	46683	33761	47542	23551
60139	25601	93663	25547	02654	94829	48672	28736	84994	13071

TABLE A.2   Binomial Probability Distribution

n = 1

x	Probability								
	.1	.2	.3	.4	.5	.6	.7	.8	.9
0	.900	.800	.700	.600	.500	.400	.300	.200	.100
1	.100	.200	.300	.400	.500	.600	.700	.800	.900

n = 2

x	Probability								
	.1	.2	.3	.4	.5	.6	.7	.8	.9
0	.810	.640	.490	.360	.250	.160	.090	.040	.010
1	.180	.320	.420	.480	.500	.480	.420	.320	.180
2	.010	.040	.090	.160	.250	.360	.490	.640	.810

n = 3

x	Probability								
	.1	.2	.3	.4	.5	.6	.7	.8	.9
0	.729	.512	.343	.216	.125	.064	.027	.008	.001
1	.243	.384	.441	.432	.375	.288	.189	.096	.027
2	.027	.096	.189	.288	.375	.432	.441	.384	.243
3	.001	.008	.027	.064	.125	.216	.343	.512	.729

n = 4

x	Probability								
	.1	.2	.3	.4	.5	.6	.7	.8	.9
0	.656	.410	.240	.130	.063	.026	.008	.002	.000
1	.292	.410	.412	.346	.250	.154	.076	.026	.004
2	.049	.154	.265	.346	.375	.346	.265	.154	.049
3	.004	.026	.076	.154	.250	.346	.412	.410	.292
4	.000	.002	.008	.026	.063	.130	.240	.410	.656

n = 5

x	Probability								
	.1	.2	.3	.4	.5	.6	.7	.8	.9
0	.590	.328	.168	.078	.031	.010	.002	.000	.000
1	.328	.410	.360	.259	.156	.077	.028	.006	.000
2	.073	.205	.309	.346	.313	.230	.132	.051	.008
3	.008	.051	.132	.230	.313	.346	.309	.205	.073
4	.000	.006	.028	.077	.156	.259	.360	.410	.328
5	.000	.000	.002	.010	.031	.078	.168	.328	.590

n = 6

x	Probability								
	.1	.2	.3	.4	.5	.6	.7	.8	.9
0	.531	.262	.118	.047	.016	.004	.001	.000	.000
1	.354	.393	.303	.187	.094	.037	.010	.002	.000
2	.098	.246	.324	.311	.234	.138	.060	.015	.001
3	.015	.082	.185	.276	.313	.276	.185	.082	.015
4	.001	.015	.060	.138	.234	.311	.324	.246	.098
5	.000	.002	.010	.037	.094	.187	.303	.393	.354
6	.000	.000	.001	.004	.016	.047	.118	.262	.531

n = 7

x	Probability								
	.1	.2	.3	.4	.5	.6	.7	.8	.9
0	.478	.210	.082	.028	.008	.002	.000	.000	.000
1	.372	.367	.247	.131	.055	.017	.004	.000	.000
2	.124	.275	.318	.261	.164	.077	.025	.004	.000
3	.023	.115	.227	.290	.273	.194	.097	.029	.003
4	.003	.029	.097	.194	.273	.290	.227	.115	.023
5	.000	.004	.025	.077	.164	.261	.318	.275	.124
6	.000	.000	.004	.017	.055	.131	.247	.367	.372
7	.000	.000	.000	.002	.008	.028	.082	.210	.478

(continues)

TABLE A.2 (Continued)

n = 8

x	Probability								
	.1	.2	.3	.4	.5	.6	.7	.8	.9
0	.430	.168	.058	.017	.004	.001	.000	.000	.000
1	.383	.336	.198	.090	.031	.008	.001	.000	.000
2	.149	.294	.296	.209	.109	.041	.010	.001	.000
3	.033	.147	.254	.279	.219	.124	.047	.009	.000
4	.005	.046	.136	.232	.273	.232	.136	.046	.005
5	.000	.009	.047	.124	.219	.279	.254	.147	.033
6	.000	.001	.010	.041	.109	.209	.296	.294	.149
7	.000	.000	.001	.008	.031	.090	.198	.336	.383
8	.000	.000	.000	.001	.004	.017	.058	.168	.430

n = 9

x	Probability								
	.1	.2	.3	.4	.5	.6	.7	.8	.9
0	.387	.134	.040	.010	.002	.000	.000	.000	.000
1	.387	.302	.156	.060	.018	.004	.000	.000	.000
2	.172	.302	.267	.161	.070	.021	.004	.000	.000
3	.045	.176	.267	.251	.164	.074	.021	.003	.000
4	.007	.066	.172	.251	.246	.167	.074	.017	.001
5	.001	.017	.074	.167	.246	.251	.172	.066	.007
6	.000	.003	.021	.074	.164	.251	.267	.176	.045
7	.000	.000	.004	.021	.070	.161	.267	.302	.172
8	.000	.000	.000	.004	.018	.060	.156	.302	.387
9	.000	.000	.000	.000	.002	.010	.040	.134	.387

n = 10

x	Probability								
	.1	.2	.3	.4	.5	.6	.7	.8	.9
0	.349	.107	.028	.006	.001	.000	.000	.000	.000
1	.387	.268	.121	.040	.010	.002	.000	.000	.000
2	.194	.302	.233	.121	.044	.011	.001	.000	.000
3	.057	.201	.267	.215	.117	.042	.009	.001	.000
4	.011	.088	.200	.251	.205	.111	.037	.006	.000
5	.001	.026	.103	.201	.246	.201	.103	.026	.001
6	.000	.006	.037	.111	.205	.251	.200	.088	.011
7	.000	.001	.009	.042	.117	.215	.267	.201	.057
8	.000	.000	.001	.011	.044	.121	.233	.302	.194
9	.000	.000	.000	.002	.010	.040	.121	.268	.387
10	.000	.000	.000	.000	.001	.006	.028	.107	.349

n = 11

x	.1	.2	.3	.4	.5	.6	.7	.8	.9
0	.314	.086	.020	.004	.000	.000	.000	.000	.000
1	.384	.236	.093	.027	.005	.001	.000	.000	.000
2	.213	.295	.200	.089	.027	.005	.001	.000	.000
3	.071	.221	.257	.177	.081	.023	.004	.000	.000
4	.016	.111	.220	.236	.161	.070	.017	.002	.000
5	.002	.039	.132	.221	.226	.147	.057	.010	.000
6	.000	.010	.057	.147	.226	.221	.132	.039	.002
7	.000	.002	.017	.070	.161	.236	.220	.111	.016
8	.000	.000	.004	.023	.081	.177	.257	.221	.071
9	.000	.000	.001	.005	.027	.089	.200	.295	.213
10	.000	.000	.000	.001	.005	.027	.093	.236	.384
11	.000	.000	.000	.000	.000	.004	.020	.086	.314

n = 12

x	.1	.2	.3	.4	.5	.6	.7	.8	.9
0	.282	.069	.014	.002	.000	.000	.000	.000	.000
1	.377	.206	.071	.017	.003	.000	.000	.000	.000
2	.230	.283	.168	.064	.016	.002	.000	.000	.000
3	.085	.236	.240	.142	.054	.012	.001	.000	.000
4	.021	.133	.231	.213	.121	.042	.008	.001	.000
5	.004	.053	.158	.227	.193	.101	.029	.003	.000
6	.000	.016	.079	.177	.226	.177	.079	.016	.000
7	.000	.003	.029	.101	.193	.227	.158	.053	.004
8	.000	.001	.008	.042	.121	.213	.231	.133	.021
9	.000	.000	.001	.012	.054	.142	.240	.236	.085
10	.000	.000	.000	.002	.016	.064	.168	.283	.230
11	.000	.000	.000	.000	.003	.017	.071	.206	.377
12	.000	.000	.000	.000	.000	.002	.014	.069	.282

(continues)

TABLE A.2 (Continued)

n = 13

x	.1	.2	.3	.4	Probability .5	.6	.7	.8	.9
0	.254	.055	.010	.001	.000	.000	.000	.000	.000
1	.367	.179	.054	.011	.002	.000	.000	.000	.000
2	.245	.268	.139	.045	.010	.001	.000	.000	.000
3	.100	.246	.218	.111	.035	.006	.001	.000	.000
4	.028	.154	.234	.184	.087	.024	.003	.000	.000
5	.006	.069	.180	.221	.157	.066	.014	.001	.000
6	.001	.023	.103	.197	.209	.131	.044	.006	.000
7	.000	.006	.044	.131	.209	.197	.103	.023	.001
8	.000	.001	.014	.066	.157	.221	.180	.069	.006
9	.000	.000	.003	.024	.087	.184	.234	.154	.028
10	.000	.000	.001	.006	.035	.111	.218	.246	.100
11	.000	.000	.000	.001	.010	.045	.139	.268	.245
12	.000	.000	.000	.000	.002	.011	.054	.179	.367
13	.000	.000	.000	.000	.000	.001	.010	.055	.254

n = 14

x	.1	.2	.3	.4	Probability .5	.6	.7	.8	.9
0	.229	.044	.007	.001	.000	.000	.000	.000	.000
1	.356	.154	.041	.007	.001	.000	.000	.000	.000
2	.257	.250	.113	.032	.006	.001	.000	.000	.000
3	.114	.250	.194	.085	.022	.003	.000	.000	.000
4	.035	.172	.229	.155	.061	.014	.001	.000	.000
5	.008	.086	.196	.207	.122	.041	.007	.000	.000
6	.001	.032	.126	.207	.183	.092	.023	.002	.000
7	.000	.009	.062	.157	.209	.157	.062	.009	.000
8	.000	.002	.023	.092	.183	.207	.126	.032	.001
9	.000	.000	.007	.041	.122	.207	.196	.086	.008
10	.000	.000	.001	.014	.061	.155	.229	.172	.035
11	.000	.000	.000	.003	.022	.085	.194	.250	.114
12	.000	.000	.000	.001	.006	.032	.113	.250	.257
13	.000	.000	.000	.000	.001	.007	.041	.154	.356
14	.000	.000	.000	.000	.000	.001	.007	.044	.229

n = 15

x	.1	.2	.3	.4	.5	.6	.7	.8	.9
0	.206	.035	.005	.000	.000	.000	.000	.000	.000
1	.343	.132	.031	.005	.000	.000	.000	.000	.000
2	.267	.231	.092	.022	.003	.000	.000	.000	.000
3	.129	.250	.170	.063	.014	.002	.000	.000	.000
4	.043	.188	.219	.127	.042	.007	.001	.000	.000
5	.010	.103	.206	.186	.092	.024	.003	.000	.000
6	.002	.043	.147	.207	.153	.061	.012	.001	.000
7	.000	.014	.081	.177	.196	.118	.035	.003	.000
8	.000	.003	.035	.118	.196	.177	.081	.014	.000
9	.000	.001	.012	.061	.153	.207	.147	.043	.002
10	.000	.000	.003	.024	.092	.186	.206	.103	.010
11	.000	.000	.001	.007	.042	.127	.219	.188	.043
12	.000	.000	.000	.002	.014	.063	.170	.250	.129
13	.000	.000	.000	.000	.003	.022	.092	.231	.267
14	.000	.000	.000	.000	.000	.005	.031	.132	.343
15	.000	.000	.000	.000	.000	.000	.005	.035	.206

n = 16

x	.1	.2	.3	.4	.5	.6	.7	.8	.9
0	.185	.028	.003	.000	.000	.000	.000	.000	.000
1	.329	.113	.023	.003	.000	.000	.000	.000	.000
2	.275	.211	.073	.015	.002	.000	.000	.000	.000
3	.142	.246	.146	.047	.009	.001	.000	.000	.000
4	.051	.200	.204	.101	.028	.004	.000	.000	.000
5	.014	.120	.210	.162	.067	.014	.001	.000	.000
6	.003	.055	.165	.198	.122	.039	.006	.000	.000
7	.000	.020	.101	.189	.175	.084	.019	.001	.000
8	.000	.006	.049	.142	.196	.142	.049	.006	.000
9	.000	.001	.019	.084	.175	.189	.101	.020	.000
10	.000	.000	.006	.039	.122	.198	.165	.055	.003
11	.000	.000	.001	.014	.067	.162	.210	.120	.014
12	.000	.000	.000	.004	.028	.101	.204	.200	.051
13	.000	.000	.000	.001	.009	.047	.146	.246	.142
14	.000	.000	.000	.000	.002	.015	.073	.211	.275
15	.000	.000	.000	.000	.000	.003	.023	.113	.329
16	.000	.000	.000	.000	.000	.000	.003	.028	.185

(continues)

TABLE A.2 (Continued)

n = 17

x	.1	.2	.3	.4	Probability .5	.6	.7	.8	.9
0	.167	.023	.002	.000	.000	.000	.000	.000	.000
1	.315	.096	.017	.002	.000	.000	.000	.000	.000
2	.280	.191	.058	.010	.001	.000	.000	.000	.000
3	.156	.239	.125	.034	.005	.000	.000	.000	.000
4	.060	.209	.187	.080	.018	.002	.000	.000	.000
5	.017	.136	.208	.138	.047	.008	.001	.000	.000
6	.004	.068	.178	.184	.094	.024	.003	.000	.000
7	.001	.027	.120	.193	.148	.057	.009	.000	.000
8	.000	.008	.064	.161	.185	.107	.028	.002	.000
9	.000	.002	.028	.107	.185	.161	.064	.008	.000
10	.000	.000	.009	.057	.148	.193	.120	.027	.001
11	.000	.000	.003	.024	.094	.184	.178	.068	.004
12	.000	.000	.001	.008	.047	.138	.208	.136	.017
13	.000	.000	.000	.002	.018	.080	.187	.209	.060
14	.000	.000	.000	.000	.005	.034	.125	.239	.156
15	.000	.000	.000	.000	.001	.010	.058	.191	.280
16	.000	.000	.000	.000	.000	.002	.017	.096	.315
17	.000	.000	.000	.000	.000	.000	.002	.023	.167

n = 18

x	.1	.2	.3	.4	Probability .5	.6	.7	.8	.9
0	.150	.018	.002	.000	.000	.000	.000	.000	.000
1	.300	.081	.013	.001	.000	.000	.000	.000	.000
2	.284	.172	.046	.007	.001	.000	.000	.000	.000
3	.168	.230	.105	.025	.003	.000	.000	.000	.000
4	.070	.215	.168	.061	.012	.001	.000	.000	.000
5	.022	.151	.202	.115	.033	.004	.000	.000	.000
6	.005	.082	.187	.166	.071	.015	.001	.000	.000
7	.001	.035	.138	.189	.121	.037	.005	.000	.000
8	.000	.012	.081	.173	.167	.077	.015	.001	.000
9	.000	.003	.039	.128	.185	.128	.039	.003	.000
10	.000	.001	.015	.077	.167	.173	.081	.012	.000
11	.000	.000	.005	.037	.121	.189	.138	.035	.001
12	.000	.000	.001	.015	.071	.166	.187	.082	.005
13	.000	.000	.000	.004	.033	.115	.202	.151	.022
14	.000	.000	.000	.001	.012	.061	.168	.215	.070
15	.000	.000	.000	.000	.003	.025	.105	.230	.168
16	.000	.000	.000	.000	.001	.007	.046	.172	.284
17	.000	.000	.000	.000	.000	.001	.013	.081	.300
18	.000	.000	.000	.000	.000	.000	.002	.018	.150

n = 19

x	Probability								
	.1	.2	.3	.4	.5	.6	.7	.8	.9
0	.135	.014	.001	.000	.000	.000	.000	.000	.000
1	.285	.068	.009	.001	.000	.000	.000	.000	.000
2	.285	.154	.036	.005	.000	.000	.000	.000	.000
3	.180	.218	.087	.017	.002	.000	.000	.000	.000
4	.080	.218	.149	.047	.007	.001	.000	.000	.000
5	.027	.164	.192	.093	.022	.002	.000	.000	.000
6	.007	.095	.192	.145	.052	.008	.001	.000	.000
7	.001	.044	.153	.180	.096	.024	.002	.000	.000
8	.000	.017	.098	.180	.144	.053	.008	.000	.000
9	.000	.005	.051	.146	.176	.098	.022	.001	.000
10	.000	.001	.022	.098	.176	.146	.051	.005	.000
11	.000	.000	.008	.053	.144	.180	.098	.017	.000
12	.000	.000	.002	.024	.096	.180	.153	.044	.001
13	.000	.000	.001	.008	.052	.145	.192	.095	.007
14	.000	.000	.000	.002	.022	.093	.192	.164	.027
15	.000	.000	.000	.001	.007	.047	.149	.218	.080
16	.000	.000	.000	.000	.002	.017	.087	.218	.180
17	.000	.000	.000	.000	.000	,005	.036	.154	.285
18	.000	.000	.000	.000	.000	.001	.009	.068	.285
19	.000	.000	.000	.000	.000	.000	.001	.014	.135

n = 20

x	Probability								
	.1	.2	.3	.4	.5	.6	.7	.8	.9
0	.122	.012	.001	.000	.000	.000	.000	.000	.000
1	.270	.058	.007	.000	.000	.000	.000	.000	.000
2	.285	.137	.028	.003	.000	.000	.000	.000	.000
3	.190	.205	.072	.012	.001	.000	.000	.000	.000
4	.090	.218	.130	.035	.005	.000	.000	.000	.000
5	.032	.175	.179	.075	.015	.001	.000	.000	.000
6	.009	.109	.192	.124	.037	.005	.000	.000	.000
7	.002	.055	.164	.166	.074	.015	.001	.000	.000
8	.000	.022	.114	.180	.120	.035	.004	.000	.000
9	.000	.007	.065	.160	.160	.071	.012	.000	.000
10	.000	.002	.031	.117	.176	.117	.031	.002	.000
11	.000	.000	.012	.071	.160	.160	.065	.007	.000
12	.000	.000	.004	.035	.120	.180	.114	.022	.000
13	.000	.000	.001	.015	.074	.166	.164	.055	.002
14	.000	.000	.000	.005	.037	.124	.192	.109	.009
15	.000	.000	.000	.001	.015	.075	.179	.175	.032
16	.000	.000	.000	.000	.005	.035	.130	.218	.090
17	.000	.000	.000	.000	.001	.012	.072	.205	.190
18	.000	.000	.000	.000	.000	.003	.028	.137	.285
19	.000	.000	.000	.000	.000	.000	.007	.058	.270
20	.000	.000	.000	.000	.000	.000	.001	.012	.122

(continues)

TABLE A.2 (Continued)

$n = 25$

x	.1	.2	.3	.4	Probability .5	.6	.7	.8	.9
0	.072	.004	.000	.000	.000	.000	.000	.000	.000
1	.199	.024	.001	.000	.000	.000	.000	.000	.000
2	.266	.071	.007	.000	.000	.000	.000	.000	.000
3	.226	.136	.024	.002	.000	.000	.000	.000	.000
4	.138	.187	.057	.007	.000	.000	.000	.000	.000
5	.065	.196	.103	.020	.002	.000	.000	.000	.000
6	.024	.163	.147	.044	.005	.000	.000	.000	.000
7	.007	.111	.171	.080	.014	.001	.000	.000	.000
8	.002	.062	.165	.120	.032	.003	.000	.000	.000
9	.000	.029	.134	.151	.061	.009	.000	.000	.000
10	.000	.012	.092	.161	.097	.021	.001	.000	.000
11	.000	.004	.054	.147	.133	.043	.004	.000	.000
12	.000	.001	.027	.114	.155	.076	.011	.000	.000
13	.000	.000	.011	.076	.155	.114	.027	.001	.000
14	.000	.000	.004	.043	.133	.147	.054	.004	.000
15	.000	.000	.001	.021	.097	.161	.092	.012	.000
16	.000	.000	.000	.009	.061	.151	.134	.029	.000
17	.000	.000	.000	.003	.032	.120	.165	.062	.002
18	.000	.000	.000	.001	.014	.080	.171	.111	.007
19	.000	.000	.000	.000	.005	.044	.147	.163	.024
20	.000	.000	.000	.000	.002	.020	.103	.196	.065
21	.000	.000	.000	.000	.000	.007	.057	.187	.138
22	.000	.000	.000	.000	.000	.002	.024	.136	.226
23	.000	.000	.000	.000	.000	.000	.007	.071	.266
24	.000	.000	.000	.000	.000	.000	.001	.024	.199
25	.000	.000	.000	.000	.000	.000	.000	.004	.072

Source: Adapted from Robert D. Mason and Douglas A. Lind, *Statistical Techniques in Business and Economics,* 7th ed. (Homewood, Ill.: Richard D. Irwin, 1990), pp. 833–42.

TABLE A.3

Poisson Probabilities $\left[\dfrac{e^{-\lambda}\lambda^x}{X!}\right]$

	λ									
x	*0.005*	*0.01*	*0.02*	*0.03*	*0.04*	*0.05*	*0.06*	*0.07*	*0.08*	*0.09*
0	0.9950	0.9900	0.9802	0.9704	0.9608	0.9512	0.9418	0.9324	0.9231	0.9139
1	0.0050	0.0099	0.0192	0.0291	0.0384	0.0476	0.0565	0.0653	0.0738	0.0823
2	0.0000	0.0000	0.0002	0.0004	0.0008	0.0012	0.0017	0.0023	0.0030	0.0037
3	0.0000	0.0000	0.0000	0.0000	0.0000	0.0000	0.0000	0.0001	0.0001	0.0001

x	*0.1*	*0.2*	*0.3*	*0.4*	*0.5*	*0.6*	*0.7*	*0.8*	*0.9*	*1.0*
0	0.9048	0.8187	0.7408	0.6703	0.6065	0.5488	0.4966	0.4493	0.4066	0.3679
1	0.0905	0.1637	0.2222	0.2681	0.3033	0.3293	0.3476	0.3595	0.3659	0.3679
2	0.0045	0.0164	0.0333	0.0536	0.0758	0.0988	0.1217	0.1438	0.1647	0.1839
3	0.0002	0.0011	0.0033	0.0072	0.0126	0.0198	0.0284	0.0383	0.0494	0.0613
4	0.0000	0.0001	0.0002	0.0007	0.0016	0.0030	0.0050	0.0077	0.0111	0.0153
5	0.0000	0.0000	0.0000	0.0001	0.0002	0.0004	0.0007	0.0012	0.0020	0.0031
6	0.0000	0.0000	0.0000	0.0000	0.0000	0.0000	0.0001	0.0002	0.0003	0.0005
7	0.0000	0.0000	0.0000	0.0000	0.0000	0.0000	0.0000	0.0000	0.0000	0.0001

x	*1.1*	*1.2*	*1.3*	*1.4*	*1.5*	*1.6*	*1.7*	*1.8*	*1.9*	*2.0*
0	0.3329	0.3012	0.2725	0.2466	0.2231	0.2019	0.1827	0.1653	0.1496	0.1353
1	0.3662	0.3614	0.3543	0.3452	0.3347	0.3230	0.3106	0.2975	0.2842	0.2707
2	0.2014	0.2169	0.2303	0.2417	0.2510	0.2584	0.2640	0.2678	0.2700	0.2707
3	0.0738	0.0867	0.0998	0.1128	0.1255	0.1378	0.1496	0.1607	0.1710	0.1804
4	0.0203	0.0260	0.0324	0.0395	0.0471	0.0551	0.0636	0.0723	0.0812	0.0902
5	0.0045	0.0062	0.0084	0.0111	0.0141	0.0176	0.0216	0.0260	0.0309	0.0361
6	0.0008	0.0012	0.0018	0.0026	0.0035	0.0047	0.0061	0.0078	0.0098	0.0120
7	0.0001	0.0002	0.0003	0.0005	0.0008	0.0011	0.0015	0.0020	0.0027	0.0034
8	0.0000	0.0000	0.0001	0.0001	0.0001	0.0002	0.0003	0.0005	0.0006	0.0009
9	0.0000	0.0000	0.0000	0.0000	0.0000	0.0000	0.0001	0.0001	0.0001	0.0002

(continues)

TABLE A.3 (Continued)

					λ					
x	2.1	2.2	2.3	2.4	2.5	2.6	2.7	2.8	2.9	3.0
0	0.1225	0.1108	0.1003	0.0907	0.0821	0.0743	0.0672	0.0608	0.0050	0.0498
1	0.2572	0.2438	0.2306	0.2177	0.2052	0.1931	0.1815	0.1703	0.1596	0.1494
2	0.2700	0.2681	0.2652	0.2613	0.2565	0.2510	0.2450	0.2384	0.2314	0.2240
3	0.1890	0.1966	0.2033	0.2090	0.2138	0.2176	0.2205	0.2225	0.2237	0.2240
4	0.0992	0.1082	0.1169	0.1254	0.1336	0.1414	0.1488	0.1557	0.1622	0.1680
5	0.0417	0.0476	0.0538	0.0602	0.0668	0.0735	0.0804	0.0872	0.0940	0.1008
6	0.0146	0.0174	0.0206	0.0241	0.0278	0.0319	0.0362	0.0407	0.0455	0.0504
7	0.0044	0.0055	0.0068	0.0083	0.0099	0.0118	0.0139	0.0163	0.0188	0.0216
8	0.0011	0.0015	0.0019	0.0025	0.0031	0.0038	0.0047	0.0057	0.0068	0.0081
9	0.0003	0.0004	0.0005	0.0007	0.0009	0.0011	0.0014	0.0018	0.0022	0.0027
10	0.0001	0.0001	0.0001	0.0002	0.0002	0.0003	0.0004	0.0005	0.0006	0.0008
11	0.0000	0.0000	0.0000	0.0000	0.0000	0.0001	0.0001	0.0001	0.0002	0.0002
12	0.0000	0.0000	0.0000	0.0000	0.0000	0.0000	0.0000	0.0000	0.0000	0.0001

x	3.1	3.2	3.3	3.4	3.5	3.6	3.7	3.8	3.9	4.0
0	0.0450	0.0408	0.0369	0.0334	0.0302	0.0273	0.0247	0.0224	0.0202	0.0183
1	0.1397	0.1304	0.1217	0.1135	0.1057	0.0984	0.0915	0.0850	0.0789	0.0733
2	0.2165	0.2087	0.2008	0.1929	0.1850	0.1771	0.1692	0.1615	0.1539	0.1465
3	0.2237	0.2226	0.2209	0.2186	0.2158	0.2125	0.2087	0.2046	0.2001	0.1954
4	0.1734	0.1781	0.1823	0.1858	0.1888	0.1912	0.1931	0.1944	0.1951	0.1954
5	0.1075	0.1140	0.1203	0.1264	0.1322	0.1377	0.1429	0.1477	0.1522	0.1563
6	0.0555	0.0608	0.0662	0.0716	0.0771	0.0826	0.0881	0.0936	0.0989	0.1042
7	0.0246	0.0278	0.0312	0.0348	0.0385	0.0425	0.0466	0.0508	0.0551	0.0595
8	0.0095	0.0111	0.0129	0.0148	0.0169	0.0191	0.0215	0.0241	0.0269	0.0298
9	0.0033	0.0040	0.0047	0.0056	0.0066	0.0076	0.0089	0.0102	0.0116	0.0132
10	0.0010	0.0013	0.0016	0.0019	0.0023	0.0028	0.0033	0.0039	0.0045	0.0053
11	0.0003	0.0004	0.0005	0.0006	0.0007	0.0009	0.0011	0.0013	0.0016	0.0019
12	0.0001	0.0001	0.0001	0.0002	0.0002	0.0003	0.0003	0.0004	0.0005	0.0006
13	0.0000	0.0000	0.0000	0.0000	0.0001	0.0001	0.0001	0.0001	0.0002	0.0002
14	0.0000	0.0000	0.0000	0.0000	0.0000	0.0000	0.0000	0.0000	0.0000	0.0001

λ

x	4.1	4.2	4.3	4.4	4.5	4.6	4.7	4.8	4.9	5.0
0	0.0166	0.0150	0.0136	0.0123	0.0111	0.0101	0.0091	0.0082	0.0074	0.0067
1	0.0679	0.0630	0.0583	0.0540	0.0500	0.0462	0.0427	0.0395	0.0365	0.0337
2	0.1393	0.1323	0.1254	0.1188	0.1125	0.1063	0.1005	0.0948	0.0894	0.0842
3	0.1904	0.1852	0.1798	0.1743	0.1687	0.1631	0.1574	0.1517	0.1460	0.1404
4	0.1951	0.1944	0.1933	0.1917	0.1898	0.1875	0.1849	0.1820	0.1789	0.1755
5	0.1600	0.1633	0.1662	0.1687	0.1708	0.1725	0.1738	0.1747	0.1753	0.1755
6	0.1093	0.1143	0.1191	0.1237	0.1281	0.1323	0.1362	0.1398	0.1432	0.1462
7	0.0640	0.0686	0.0732	0.0778	0.0824	0.0869	0.0914	0.0959	0.1002	0.1044
8	0.0328	0.0360	0.0393	0.0428	0.0463	0.0500	0.0537	0.0575	0.0614	0.0653
9	0.0150	0.0168	0.0188	0.0209	0.0232	0.0255	0.0280	0.0307	0.0334	0.0363
10	0.0061	0.0071	0.0081	0.0092	0.0104	0.0118	0.0132	0.0147	0.0164	0.0181
11	0.0023	0.0027	0.0032	0.0037	0.0043	0.0049	0.0056	0.0064	0.0073	0.0082
12	0.0008	0.0009	0.0011	0.0014	0.0016	0.0019	0.0022	0.0026	0.0030	0.0034
13	0.0002	0.0003	0.0004	0.0005	0.0006	0.0007	0.0008	0.0009	0.0011	0.0013
14	0.0001	0.0001	0.0001	0.0001	0.0002	0.0002	0.0003	0.0003	0.0004	0.0005
15	0.0000	0.0000	0.0000	0.0000	0.0001	0.0001	0.0001	0.0001	0.0001	0.0002

x	5.1	5.2	5.3	5.4	5.5	5.6	5.7	5.8	5.9	6.0
0	0.0061	0.0055	0.0050	0.0045	0.0041	0.0037	0.0033	0.0030	0.0027	0.0025
1	0.0311	0.0287	0.0265	0.0244	0.0225	0.0207	0.0191	0.0176	0.0162	0.0149
2	0.0793	0.0746	0.0701	0.0659	0.0618	0.0580	0.0544	0.0509	0.0477	0.0446
3	0.1348	0.1293	0.1239	0.1185	0.1133	0.1082	0.1033	0.0985	0.0938	0.0892
4	0.1719	0.1681	0.1641	0.1600	0.1558	0.1515	0.1472	0.1428	0.1383	0.1339
5	0.1753	0.1748	0.1740	0.1728	0.1714	0.1697	0.1678	0.1656	0.1632	0.1606
6	0.1490	0.1515	0.1537	0.1555	0.1571	0.1584	0.1594	0.1601	0.1605	0.1606
7	0.1086	0.1125	0.1163	0.1200	0.1234	0.1267	0.1298	0.1326	0.1353	0.1377
8	0.0692	0.0731	0.0771	0.0810	0.0849	0.0887	0.0925	0.0962	0.0998	0.1033
9	0.0392	0.0423	0.0454	0.0486	0.0519	0.0552	0.0586	0.0620	0.0654	0.0688
10	0.0200	0.0220	0.0241	0.0262	0.0285	0.0309	0.0334	0.0359	0.0386	0.0413
11	0.0093	0.0104	0.0116	0.0129	0.0143	0.0157	0.0173	0.0190	0.0207	0.0225
12	0.0039	0.0045	0.0051	0.0058	0.0065	0.0073	0.0082	0.0092	0.0102	0.0113
13	0.0015	0.0018	0.0021	0.0024	0.0028	0.0032	0.0036	0.0041	0.0046	0.0052
14	0.0006	0.0007	0.0008	0.0009	0.0011	0.0013	0.0015	0.0017	0.0019	0.0022
15	0.0002	0.0002	0.0003	0.0003	0.0004	0.0005	0.0006	0.0007	0.0008	0.0009
16	0.0001	0.0001	0.0001	0.0001	0.0001	0.0002	0.0002	0.0002	0.0003	0.0003
17	0.0000	0.0000	0.0000	0.0000	0.0000	0.0001	0.0001	0.0001	0.0001	0.0001

(continues)

TABLE A.3 (Continued)

x	6.1	6.2	6.3	6.4	6.5	6.6	6.7	6.8	6.9	7.0
0	0.0022	0.0020	0.0018	0.0017	0.0015	0.0014	0.0012	0.0011	0.0010	0.0009
1	0.0137	0.0126	0.0116	0.0106	0.0098	0.0090	0.0082	0.0076	0.0070	0.0064
2	0.0417	0.0390	0.0364	0.0340	0.0318	0.0296	0.0276	0.0258	0.0240	0.0223
3	0.0848	0.0806	0.0765	0.0726	0.0688	0.0652	0.0617	0.0584	0.0552	0.0521
4	0.1294	0.1269	0.1205	0.1162	0.1118	0.1076	0.1034	0.0992	0.0952	0.0912
5	0.1579	0.1549	0.1519	0.1487	0.1454	0.1420	0.1385	0.1349	0.1314	0.1277
6	0.1605	0.1601	0.1595	0.1586	0.1575	0.1562	0.1546	0.1529	0.1511	0.1490
7	0.1399	0.1418	0.1435	0.1450	0.1462	0.1472	0.1480	0.1486	0.1489	0.1490
8	0.1066	0.1099	0.1130	0.1160	0.1188	0.1215	0.1240	0.1263	0.1284	0.1304
9	0.0723	0.0757	0.0791	0.0825	0.0858	0.0891	0.0923	0.0954	0.0985	0.1014
10	0.0441	0.0469	0.0498	0.0528	0.0558	0.0588	0.0618	0.0649	0.0679	0.0710
11	0.0245	0.0265	0.0285	0.0307	0.0330	0.0353	0.0377	0.0401	0.0426	0.0452
12	0.0124	0.0137	0.0150	0.0164	0.0179	0.0194	0.0210	0.0227	0.0245	0.0264
13	0.0058	0.0065	0.0073	0.0081	0.0089	0.0098	0.0108	0.0119	0.0130	0.0142
14	0.0025	0.0029	0.0033	0.0037	0.0041	0.0046	0.0052	0.0058	0.0064	0.0071
15	0.0010	0.0012	0.0014	0.0016	0.0018	0.0020	0.0023	0.0026	0.0029	0.0033
16	0.0004	0.0005	0.0005	0.0006	0.0007	0.0008	0.0010	0.0011	0.0013	0.0014
17	0.0001	0.0002	0.0002	0.0002	0.0003	0.0003	0.0004	0.0004	0.0005	0.0006
18	0.0000	0.0001	0.0001	0.0001	0.0001	0.0001	0.0001	0.0002	0.0002	0.0002
19	0.0000	0.0000	0.0000	0.0000	0.0000	0.0000	0.0000	0.0001	0.0001	0.0001

x	7.1	7.2	7.3	7.4	7.5	7.6	7.7	7.8	7.9	8.0
0	0.0008	0.0007	0.0007	0.0006	0.0006	0.0005	0.0005	0.0004	0.0004	0.0003
1	0.0059	0.0054	0.0049	0.0045	0.0041	0.0038	0.0035	0.0032	0.0029	0.0027
2	0.0208	0.0194	0.0180	0.0167	0.0156	0.0145	0.0134	0.0125	0.0116	0.0107
3	0.0492	0.0464	0.0438	0.0413	0.0389	0.0366	0.0345	0.0324	0.0305	0.0286
4	0.0874	0.0836	0.0799	0.0764	0.0729	0.0696	0.0663	0.0632	0.0602	0.0573
5	0.1241	0.1204	0.1167	0.1130	0.1094	0.1057	0.1021	0.0986	0.0951	0.0916
6	0.1468	0.1445	0.1420	0.1394	0.1367	0.1339	0.1311	0.1282	0.1252	0.1221
7	0.1489	0.1486	0.1481	0.1474	0.1465	0.1454	0.1442	0.1428	0.1413	0.1396
8	0.1321	0.1337	0.1351	0.1363	0.1373	0.1382	0.1388	0.1392	0.1395	0.1396
9	0.1042	0.1070	0.1096	0.1121	0.1144	0.1167	0.1187	0.1207	0.1224	0.1241
10	0.0740	0.0770	0.0800	0.0829	0.0858	0.0887	0.0914	0.0941	0.0967	0.0993
11	0.0478	0.0504	0.0531	0.0558	0.0585	0.0613	0.0640	0.0667	0.0695	0.0722

λ

x	7.1	7.2	7.3	7.4	7.5	7.6	7.7	7.8	7.9	8.0
12	0.0283	0.0303	0.0323	0.0344	0.0366	0.0388	0.0411	0.0434	0.0457	0.0481
13	0.0154	0.0168	0.0181	0.0196	0.0211	0.0227	0.0243	0.0260	0.0278	0.0296
14	0.0078	0.0086	0.0095	0.0104	0.0113	0.0123	0.0134	0.0145	0.0157	0.0169
15	0.0037	0.0041	0.0046	0.0051	0.0057	0.0062	0.0069	0.0075	0.0083	0.0090
16	0.0016	0.0019	0.0021	0.0024	0.0026	0.0030	0.0033	0.0037	0.0041	0.0045
17	0.0007	0.0008	0.0009	0.0010	0.0012	0.0013	0.0015	0.0017	0.0019	0.0021
18	0.0003	0.0003	0.0004	0.0004	0.0005	0.0006	0.0006	0.0007	0.0008	0.0009
19	0.0001	0.0001	0.0001	0.0002	0.0002	0.0002	0.0003	0.0003	0.0003	0.0004
20	0.0000	0.0000	0.0001	0.0001	0.0001	0.0001	0.0001	0.0001	0.0001	0.0002
21	0.0000	0.0000	0.0000	0.0000	0.0000	0.0000	0.0000	0.0000	0.0001	0.0001

x	8.1	8.2	8.3	8.4	8.5	8.6	8.7	8.8	8.9	9.0
0	0.0003	0.0003	0.0002	0.0002	0.0002	0.0002	0.0002	0.0002	0.0001	0.0001
1	0.0025	0.0023	0.0021	0.0019	0.0017	0.0016	0.0014	0.0013	0.0012	0.0011
2	0.0100	0.0092	0.0086	0.0079	0.0074	0.0068	0.0063	0.0058	0.0054	0.0050
3	0.0269	0.0252	0.0237	0.0222	0.0208	0.0195	0.0183	0.0171	0.0160	0.0150
4	0.0544	0.0517	0.0491	0.0466	0.0443	0.0420	0.0398	0.0377	0.0357	0.0337
5	0.0882	0.0849	0.0816	0.0784	0.0752	0.0722	0.0692	0.0663	0.0635	0.0607
6	0.1191	0.1160	0.1128	0.1097	0.1066	0.1034	0.1003	0.0972	0.0941	0.0911
7	0.1378	0.1358	0.1338	0.1317	0.1294	0.1271	0.1247	0.1222	0.1197	0.1171
8	0.1395	0.1392	0.1388	0.1382	0.1375	0.1366	0.1356	0.1344	0.1332	0.1318
9	0.1256	0.1269	0.1280	0.1290	0.1299	0.1306	0.1311	0.1315	0.1317	0.1318
10	0.1017	0.1040	0.1063	0.1084	0.1104	0.1123	0.1140	0.1157	0.1172	0.1186
11	0.0749	0.0776	0.0802	0.0828	0.0853	0.0878	0.0902	0.0925	0.0948	0.0970
12	0.0505	0.0530	0.0555	0.0579	0.0604	0.0629	0.0654	0.0679	0.0703	0.0728
13	0.0315	0.0334	0.0354	0.0374	0.0395	0.0416	0.0438	0.0459	0.0481	0.0504
14	0.0182	0.0196	0.0210	0.0225	0.0240	0.0256	0.0272	0.0289	0.0306	0.0324
15	0.0098	0.0107	0.0116	0.0126	0.0136	0.0147	0.0158	0.0169	0.0182	0.0194
16	0.0050	0.0055	0.0060	0.0066	0.0072	0.0079	0.0086	0.0093	0.0101	0.0109
17	0.0024	0.0026	0.0029	0.0033	0.0036	0.0040	0.0044	0.0048	0.0053	0.0058
18	0.0011	0.0012	0.0014	0.0015	0.0017	0.0019	0.0021	0.0024	0.0026	0.0029
19	0.0005	0.0005	0.0006	0.0007	0.0008	0.0009	0.0010	0.0011	0.0012	0.0014
20	0.0002	0.0002	0.0002	0.0003	0.0003	0.0004	0.0004	0.0005	0.0005	0.0006
21	0.0001	0.0001	0.0001	0.0001	0.0001	0.0002	0.0002	0.0002	0.0002	0.0003
22	0.0000	0.0000	0.0000	0.0000	0.0001	0.0001	0.0001	0.0001	0.0001	0.0001

(continues)

TABLE A.3 (Continued)

$$\lambda$$

x	9.1	9.2	9.3	9.4	9.5	9.6	9.7	9.8	9.9	10.0
0	0.0001	0.0001	0.0001	0.0001	0.0001	0.0001	0.0001	0.0001	0.0001	0.0000
1	0.0010	0.0009	0.0009	0.0008	0.0007	0.0007	0.0006	0.0005	0.0005	0.0005
2	0.0046	0.0043	0.0040	0.0037	0.0034	0.0031	0.0029	0.0027	0.0025	0.0023
3	0.0140	0.0131	0.0123	0.0115	0.0107	0.0100	0.0093	0.0087	0.0081	0.0076
4	0.0319	0.0302	0.0285	0.0269	0.0254	0.0240	0.0226	0.0213	0.0201	0.0189
5	0.0581	0.0555	0.0530	0.0506	0.0483	0.0460	0.0439	0.0418	0.0398	0.0378
6	0.0881	0.0851	0.0822	0.0793	0.0764	0.0736	0.0709	0.0682	0.0656	0.0631
7	0.1145	0.1118	0.1091	0.1064	0.1037	0.1010	0.0982	0.0955	0.0928	0.0901
8	0.1302	0.1286	0.1269	0.1251	0.1232	0.1212	0.1191	0.1170	0.1148	0.1126
9	0.1317	0.1315	0.1311	0.1306	0.1300	0.1293	0.1284	0.1274	0.1263	0.1251
10	0.1198	0.1210	0.1219	0.1228	0.1235	0.1241	0.1245	0.1249	0.1250	0.1251
11	0.0991	0.1012	0.1031	0.1049	0.1067	0.1083	0.1098	0.1112	0.1125	0.1137
12	0.0752	0.0776	0.0799	0.0822	0.0844	0.0866	0.0888	0.0908	0.0928	0.0948
13	0.0526	0.0549	0.0572	0.0594	0.0617	0.0640	0.0662	0.0685	0.0707	0.0729
14	0.0342	0.0361	0.0380	0.0399	0.0419	0.0439	0.0459	0.0479	0.0500	0.0521
15	0.0208	0.0221	0.0235	0.0250	0.0265	0.0281	0.0297	0.0313	0.0330	0.0347
16	0.0118	0.0127	0.0137	0.0147	0.0157	0.0168	0.0180	0.0192	0.0204	0.0217
17	0.0063	0.0069	0.0075	0.0081	0.0088	0.0095	0.0103	0.0111	0.0119	0.0128
18	0.0032	0.0035	0.0039	0.0042	0.0046	0.0051	0.0055	0.0060	0.0065	0.0071
19	0.0015	0.0017	0.0019	0.0021	0.0023	0.0026	0.0028	0.0031	0.0034	0.0037
20	0.0007	0.0008	0.0009	0.0010	0.0011	0.0012	0.0014	0.0015	0.0017	0.0019
21	0.0003	0.0003	0.0004	0.0004	0.0005	0.0006	0.0006	0.0007	0.0008	0.0009
22	0.0001	0.0001	0.0002	0.0002	0.0002	0.0002	0.0003	0.0003	0.0004	0.0004
23	0.0000	0.0001	0.0001	0.0001	0.0001	0.0001	0.0001	0.0001	0.0002	0.0002
24	0.0000	0.0000	0.0000	0.0000	0.0000	0.0000	0.0000	0.0001	0.0001	0.0001

From Robert Parsons, *Statistical Analysis: A Decision Making Approach,* 2d ed. (New York: Harper & Row, 1978). Reprinted with permission of Harper & Row.

TABLE A.4

The e^{-x} Table

Values of e^{-x} for Computing Poisson Probabilities

x	e^{-x}	x	e^{-x}	x	e^{-x}	x	e^{-x}
0.0	1.0000	3.0	0.0498	6.0	0.00248	9.0	0.00012
0.1	0.9048	3.1	0.0450	6.1	0.00224	9.1	0.00011
0.2	0.8187	3.2	0.0408	6.2	0.00203	9.2	0.00010
0.3	0.7408	3.3	0.0369	6.3	0.00184	9.3	0.00009
0.4	0.6703	3.4	0.0334	6.4	0.00166	9.4	0.00008
0.5	0.6065	3.5	0.0302	6.5	0.00150	9.5	0.00007
0.6	0.5488	3.6	0.0273	6.6	0.00136	9.6	0.00007
0.7	0.4966	3.7	0.0247	6.7	0.00123	9.7	0.00006
0.8	0.4493	3.8	0.0224	6.8	0.00111	9.8	0.00006
0.9	0.4066	3.9	0.0202	6.9	0.00101	9.9	0.00005
1.0	0.3679	4.0	0.0183	7.0	0.00091	10.0	0.00005
1.1	0.3329	4.1	0.0166	7.1	0.00083		
1.2	0.3012	4.2	0.0150	7.2	0.00075		
1.3	0.2725	4.3	0.0136	7.3	0.00068		
1.4	0.2466	4.4	0.0123	7.4	0.00061		
1.5	0.2231	4.5	0.0111	7.5	0.00055		
1.6	0.2019	4.6	0.0101	7.6	0.00050		
1.7	0.1827	4.7	0.0091	7.7	0.00045		
1.8	0.1653	4.8	0.0082	7.8	0.00041		
1.9	0.1496	4.9	0.0074	7.9	0.00037		
2.0	0.1353	5.0	0.0067	8.0	0.00034		
2.1	0.1225	5.1	0.0061	8.1	0.00030		
2.2	0.1108	5.2	0.0055	8.2	0.00027		
2.3	0.1003	5.3	0.0050	8.3	0.00025		
2.4	0.0907	5.4	0.0045	8.4	0.00022		
2.5	0.0821	5.5	0.0041	8.5	0.00020		
2.6	0.0743	5.6	0.0037	8.6	0.00018		
2.7	0.0672	5.7	0.0033	8.7	0.00017		
2.8	0.0608	5.8	0.0030	8.8	0.00015		
2.9	0.0550	5.9	0.0027	8.9	0.00014		

From Rex S. Toh and Michael Y. Hu, *Basic Business Statistics: An Intuitive Approach* (St. Paul: West Publishing Co., 1991). Reprinted with permission.

TABLE A.5
Areas of the Standard Normal Distribution

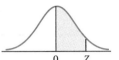

The entries in this table are the probabilities that a standard normal random variable is between 0 and Z (the shaded area).

Second Decimal Place in Z

Z	0.00	0.01	0.02	0.03	0.04	0.05	0.06	0.07	0.08	0.09
0.0	0.0000	0.0040	0.0080	0.0120	0.0160	0.0199	0.0239	0.0279	0.0319	0.0359
0.1	0.0398	0.0438	0.0478	0.0517	0.0557	0.0596	0.0636	0.0675	0.0714	0.0753
0.2	0.0793	0.0832	0.0871	0.0910	0.0948	0.0987	0.1026	0.1064	0.1103	0.1141
0.3	0.1179	0.1217	0.1255	0.1293	0.1331	0.1368	0.1406	0.1443	0.1480	0.1517
0.4	0.1554	0.1591	0.1628	0.1664	0.1700	0.1736	0.1772	0.1808	0.1844	0.1879
0.5	0.1915	0.1950	0.1985	0.2019	0.2054	0.2088	0.2123	0.2157	0.2190	0.2224
0.6	0.2257	0.2291	0.2324	0.2357	0.2389	0.2422	0.2454	0.2486	0.2517	0.2549
0.7	0.2580	0.2611	0.2642	0.2673	0.2704	0.2734	0.2764	0.2794	0.2823	0.2852
0.8	0.2881	0.2910	0.2939	0.2967	0.2995	0.3023	0.3051	0.3078	0.3106	0.3133
0.9	0.3159	0.3186	0.3212	0.3238	0.3264	0.3289	0.3315	0.3340	0.3365	0.3389
1.0	0.3413	0.3438	0.3461	0.3485	0.3508	0.3531	0.3554	0.3577	0.3599	0.3621
1.1	0.3643	0.3665	0.3686	0.3708	0.3729	0.3749	0.3770	0.3790	0.3810	0.3830
1.2	0.3849	0.3869	0.3888	0.3907	0.3925	0.3944	0.3962	0.3980	0.3997	0.4015
1.3	0.4032	0.4049	0.4066	0.4082	0.4099	0.4115	0.4131	0.4147	0.4162	0.4177
1.4	0.4192	0.4207	0.4222	0.4236	0.4251	0.4265	0.4279	0.4292	0.4306	0.4319
1.5	0.4332	0.4345	0.4357	0.4370	0.4382	0.4394	0.4406	0.4418	0.4429	0.4441
1.6	0.4452	0.4463	0.4474	0.4484	0.4495	0.4505	0.4515	0.4525	0.4535	0.4545
1.7	0.4554	0.4564	0.4573	0.4582	0.4591	0.4599	0.4608	0.4616	0.4625	0.4633
1.8	0.4641	0.4649	0.4656	0.4664	0.4671	0.4678	0.4686	0.4693	0.4699	0.4706
1.9	0.4713	0.4719	0.4726	0.4732	0.4738	0.4744	0.4750	0.4756	0.4761	0.4767
2.0	0.4772	0.4778	0.4783	0.4788	0.4793	0.4796	0.4803	0.4808	0.4812	0.4817
2.1	0.4821	0.4826	0.4830	0.4834	0.4838	0.4842	0.4846	0.4850	0.4854	0.4857
2.2	0.4861	0.4864	0.4868	0.4871	0.4875	0.4878	0.4881	0.4884	0.4887	0.4890
2.3	0.4893	0.4896	0.4898	0.4901	0.4904	0.4906	0.4909	0.4911	0.4913	0.4916
2.4	0.4918	0.4920	0.4922	0.4925	0.4927	0.4929	0.4931	0.4932	0.4934	0.4936
2.5	0.4938	0.4940	0.4941	0.4943	0.4945	0.4946	0.4948	0.4949	0.4951	0.4952
2.6	0.4953	0.4955	0.4956	0.4957	0.4959	0.4960	0.4961	0.4962	0.4963	0.4964
2.7	0.4965	0.4966	0.4967	0.4968	0.4969	0.4970	0.4971	0.4972	0.4973	0.4974
2.8	0.4974	0.4975	0.4976	0.4977	0.4977	0.4978	0.4979	0.4979	0.4980	0.4981
2.9	0.4981	0.4982	0.4982	0.4983	0.4984	0.4984	0.4985	0.4985	0.4986	0.4986
3.0	0.4987	0.4987	0.4987	0.4988	0.4988	0.4989	0.4989	0.4989	0.4990	0.4990
3.1	0.4990	0.4991	0.4991	0.4991	0.4992	0.4992	0.4992	0.4992	0.4993	0.4993
3.2	0.4993	0.4993	0.4994	0.4994	0.4994	0.4994	0.4994	0.4995	0.4995	0.4995
3.3	0.4995	0.4995	0.4995	0.4996	0.4996	0.4996	0.4996	0.4996	0.4996	0.4997
3.4	0.4997	0.4997	0.4997	0.4997	0.4997	0.4997	0.4997	0.4997	0.4997	0.4998
3.5	0.4998									
4.0	0.49997									
4.5	0.499997									
5.0	0.4999997									

TABLE A.6   Critical Values of *t*

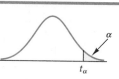

Degrees of Freedom	$t_{.100}$	$t_{.050}$	$t_{.025}$	$t_{.010}$	$t_{.005}$
1	3.078	6.314	12.706	31.821	63.657
2	1.886	2.920	4.303	6.965	9.925
3	1.638	2.353	3.182	4.541	5.841
4	1.533	2.132	2.776	3.747	4.604
5	1.476	2.015	2.571	3.365	4.032
6	1.440	1.943	2.447	3.143	3.707
7	1.415	1.895	2.365	2.998	3.499
8	1.397	1.860	2.306	2.896	3.355
9	1.383	1.833	2.262	2.821	3.250
10	1.372	1.812	2.228	2.764	3.169
11	1.363	1.796	2.201	2.718	3.106
12	1.356	1.782	2.179	2.681	3.055
13	1.350	1.771	2.160	2.650	3.012
14	1.345	1.761	2.145	2.624	2.977
15	1.341	1.753	2.131	2.602	2.947
16	1.337	1.746	2.120	2.583	2.921
17	1.333	1.740	2.110	2.567	2.898
18	1.330	1.734	2.101	2.552	2.878
19	1.328	1.729	2.093	2.539	2.861
20	1.325	1.725	2.086	2.528	2.845
21	1.323	1.721	2.080	2.518	2.831
22	1.321	1.717	2.074	2.508	2.819
23	1.319	1.714	2.069	2.500	2.808
24	1.318	1.711	2.064	2.492	2.797
25	1.316	1.708	2.060	2.485	2.787
26	1.315	1.706	2.056	2.479	2.779
27	1.314	1.703	2.052	2.473	2.771
28	1.313	1.701	2.048	2.467	2.763
29	1.311	1.699	2.045	2.462	2.756
30	1.310	1.697	2.042	2.457	2.750
40	1.303	1.684	2.021	2.423	2.704
60	1.296	1.671	2.000	2.390	2.660
120	1.289	1.658	1.980	2.358	2.617
∞	1.282	1.645	1.960	2.326	2.576

Appendix A

TABLE A.7   Percentage Points of the F Distribution

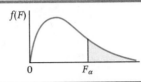

					$\alpha = .05$				
v_1				Numerator Degrees of Freedom					
v_2	1	2	3	4	5	6	7	8	9
1	161.4	199.5	215.7	224.6	230.2	234.0	236.8	238.9	240.5
2	18.51	19.00	19.16	19.25	19.30	19.33	19.35	19.37	19.38
3	10.13	9.55	9.28	9.12	9.01	8.94	8.89	8.85	8.81
4	7.71	6.94	6.59	6.39	6.26	6.16	6.09	6.04	6.00
5	6.61	5.79	5.41	5.19	5.05	4.95	4.88	4.82	4.77
6	5.99	5.14	4.76	4.53	4.39	4.28	4.21	4.15	4.10
7	5.59	4.74	4.35	4.12	3.97	3.87	3.79	3.73	3.68
8	5.32	4.46	4.07	3.84	3.69	3.58	3.50	3.44	3.39
9	5.12	4.26	3.86	3.63	3.48	3.37	3.29	3.23	3.18
10	4.96	4.10	3.71	3.48	3.33	3.22	3.14	3.07	3.02
11	4.84	3.98	3.59	3.36	3.20	3.09	3.01	2.95	2.90
12	4.75	3.89	3.49	3.26	3.11	3.00	2.91	2.85	2.80
13	4.67	3.81	3.41	3.18	3.03	2.92	2.83	2.77	2.71
14	4.60	3.74	3.34	3.11	2.96	2.85	2.76	2.70	2.65
15	4.54	3.68	3.29	3.06	2.90	2.79	2.71	2.64	2.59
16	4.49	3.63	3.24	3.01	2.85	2.74	2.66	2.59	2.54
17	4.45	3.59	3.20	2.96	2.81	2.70	2.61	2.55	2.49
18	4.41	3.55	3.16	2.93	2.77	2.66	2.58	2.51	2.46
19	4.38	3.52	3.13	2.90	2.74	2.63	2.54	2.48	2.42
20	4.35	3.49	3.10	2.87	2.71	2.60	2.51	2.45	2.39
21	4.32	3.47	3.07	2.84	2.68	2.57	2.49	2.42	2.37
22	4.30	3.44	3.05	2.82	2.66	2.55	2.46	2.40	2.34
23	4.28	3.42	3.03	2.80	2.64	2.53	2.44	2.37	2.32
24	4.26	3.40	3.01	2.78	2.62	2.51	2.42	2.36	2.30
25	4.24	3.39	2.99	2.76	2.60	2.49	2.40	2.34	2.28
26	4.23	3.37	2.98	2.74	2.59	2.47	2.39	2.32	2.27
27	4.21	3.35	2.96	2.73	2.57	2.46	2.37	2.31	2.25
28	4.20	3.34	2.95	2.71	2.56	2.45	2.36	2.29	2.24
29	4.18	3.33	2.93	2.70	2.55	2.43	2.35	2.28	2.22
30	4.17	3.32	2.92	2.69	2.53	2.42	2.33	2.27	2.21
40	4.08	3.23	2.84	2.61	2.45	2.34	2.25	2.18	2.12
60	4.00	3.15	2.76	2.53	2.37	2.25	2.17	2.10	2.04
120	3.92	3.07	2.68	2.45	2.29	2.17	2.09	2.02	1.96
∞	3.84	3.00	2.60	2.37	2.21	2.10	2.01	1.94	1.88

Denominator Degrees of Freedom

α = .05										
Numerator Degrees of Freedom										v_1
10	**12**	**15**	**20**	**24**	**30**	**40**	**60**	**120**	**∞**	v_2
241.9	243.9	245.9	248.0	249.1	250.1	251.1	252.2	253.3	254.3	1
19.40	19.41	19.43	19.45	19.45	19.46	19.47	19.48	19.49	19.50	2
8.79	8.74	8.70	8.66	8.64	8.62	8.59	8.57	8.55	8.53	3
5.96	5.91	5.86	5.80	5.77	5.75	5.72	5.69	5.66	5.63	4
4.74	4.68	4.62	4.56	4.53	4.50	4.46	4.43	4.40	4.36	5
4.06	4.00	3.94	3.87	3.84	3.81	3.77	3.74	3.70	3.67	6
3.64	3.57	3.51	3.44	3.41	3.38	3.34	3.30	3.27	3.23	7
3.35	3.28	3.22	3.15	3.12	3.08	3.04	3.01	2.97	2.93	8
3.14	3.07	3.01	2.94	2.90	2.86	2.83	2.79	2.75	2.71	9
2.98	2.91	2.85	2.77	2.74	2.70	2.66	2.62	2.58	2.54	10
2.85	2.79	2.72	2.65	2.61	2.57	2.53	2.49	2.45	2.40	11
2.75	2.69	2.62	2.54	2.51	2.47	2.43	2.38	2.34	2.30	12
2.67	2.60	2.53	2.46	2.42	2.38	2.34	2.30	2.25	2.21	13
2.60	2.53	2.46	2.39	2.35	2.31	2.27	2.22	2.18	2.13	14
2.54	2.48	2.40	2.33	2.29	2.25	2.20	2.16	2.11	2.07	15
2.49	2.42	2.35	2.28	2.24	2.19	2.15	2.11	2.06	2.01	16
2.45	2.38	2.31	2.23	2.19	2.15	2.10	2.06	2.01	1.96	17
2.41	2.34	2.27	2.19	2.15	2.11	2.06	2.02	1.97	1.92	18
2.38	2.31	2.23	2.16	2.11	2.07	2.03	1.98	1.93	1.88	19
2.35	2.28	2.20	2.12	2.08	2.04	1.99	1.95	1.90	1.84	20
2.32	2.25	2.18	2.10	2.05	2.01	1.96	1.92	1.87	1.81	21
2.30	2.23	2.15	2.07	2.03	1.98	1.94	1.89	1.84	1.78	22
2.27	2.20	2.13	2.05	2.01	1.96	1.91	1.86	1.81	1.76	23
2.25	2.18	2.11	2.03	1.98	1.94	1.89	1.84	1.79	1.73	24
2.24	2.16	2.09	2.01	1.96	1.92	1.87	1.82	1.77	1.71	25
2.22	2.15	2.07	1.99	1.95	1.90	1.85	1.80	1.75	1.69	26
2.20	2.13	2.06	1.97	1.93	1.88	1.84	1.79	1.73	1.67	27
2.19	2.12	2.04	1.96	1.91	1.87	1.82	1.77	1.71	1.65	28
2.18	2.10	2.03	1.94	1.90	1.85	1.81	1.75	1.70	1.64	29
2.16	2.09	2.01	1.93	1.89	1.84	1.79	1.74	1.68	1.62	30
2.08	2.00	1.92	1.84	1.79	1.74	1.69	1.64	1.58	1.51	40
1.99	1.92	1.84	1.75	1.70	1.65	1.59	1.53	1.47	1.39	60
1.91	1.83	1.75	1.66	1.61	1.55	1.50	1.43	1.35	1.25	120
1.83	1.75	1.67	1.57	1.52	1.46	1.39	1.32	1.22	1.00	∞

Denominator Degrees of Freedom

(continues)

TABLE A.7 (Continued)

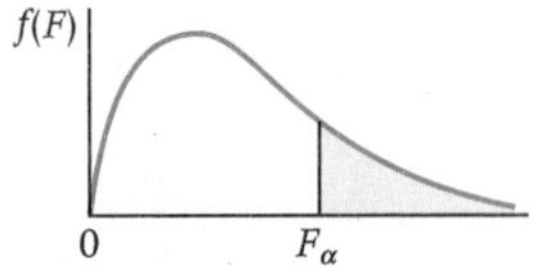

$\alpha = .01$

Numerator Degrees of Freedom

v_2 \ v_1 (Denominator Degrees of Freedom)	1	2	3	4	5	6	7	8	9
1	4,052	4,999.5	5,403	5,625	5,764	5,859	5,928	5,982	6,022
2	98.50	99.00	99.17	99.25	99.30	99.33	99.36	99.37	99.39
3	34.12	30.82	29.46	28.71	28.24	27.91	27.67	27.49	27.35
4	21.20	18.00	16.69	15.98	15.52	15.21	14.98	14.80	14.66
5	16.26	13.27	12.06	11.39	10.97	10.67	10.46	10.29	10.16
6	13.75	10.92	9.78	9.15	8.75	8.47	8.26	8.10	7.98
7	12.25	9.55	8.45	7.85	7.46	7.19	6.99	6.84	6.72
8	11.26	8.65	7.59	7.01	6.63	6.37	6.18	6.03	5.91
9	10.56	8.02	6.99	6.42	6.06	5.80	5.61	5.47	5.35
10	10.04	7.56	6.55	5.99	5.64	5.39	5.20	5.06	4.94
11	9.65	7.21	6.22	5.67	5.32	5.07	4.89	4.74	4.63
12	9.33	6.93	5.95	5.41	5.06	4.82	4.64	4.50	4.39
13	9.07	6.70	5.74	5.21	4.86	4.62	4.44	4.30	4.19
14	8.86	6.51	5.56	5.04	4.69	4.46	4.28	4.14	4.03
15	8.68	6.36	5.42	4.89	4.56	4.32	4.14	4.00	3.89
16	8.53	6.23	5.29	4.77	4.44	4.20	4.03	3.89	3.78
17	8.40	6.11	5.18	4.67	4.34	4.10	3.93	3.79	3.68
18	8.29	6.01	5.09	4.58	4.25	4.01	3.84	3.71	3.60
19	8.18	5.93	5.01	4.50	4.17	3.94	3.77	3.63	3.52
20	8.10	5.85	4.94	4.43	4.10	3.87	3.70	3.56	3.46
21	8.02	5.78	4.87	4.37	4.04	3.81	3.64	3.51	3.40
22	7.95	5.72	4.82	4.31	3.99	3.76	3.59	3.45	3.35
23	7.88	5.66	4.76	4.26	3.94	3.71	3.54	3.41	3.30
24	7.82	5.61	4.72	4.22	3.90	3.67	3.50	3.36	3.26
25	7.77	5.57	4.68	4.18	3.85	3.63	3.46	3.32	3.22
26	7.72	5.53	4.64	4.14	3.82	3.59	3.42	3.29	3.18
27	7.68	5.49	4.60	4.11	3.78	3.56	3.39	3.26	3.15
28	7.64	5.45	4.57	4.07	3.75	3.53	3.36	3.23	3.12
29	7.60	5.42	4.54	4.04	3.73	3.50	3.33	3.20	3.09
30	7.56	5.39	4.51	4.02	3.70	3.47	3.30	3.17	3.07
40	7.31	5.18	4.31	3.83	3.51	3.29	3.12	2.99	2.89
60	7.08	4.98	4.13	3.65	3.34	3.12	2.95	2.82	2.72
120	6.85	4.79	3.95	3.48	3.17	2.96	2.79	2.66	2.56
∞	6.63	4.61	3.78	3.32	3.02	2.80	2.64	2.51	2.41

$\alpha = .01$											
Numerator Degrees of Freedom										ν_1	
10	**12**	**15**	**20**	**24**	**30**	**40**	**60**	**120**	**∞**		ν_2
6,056	6,106	6,157	6,209	6,235	6,261	6,287	6,313	6,339	6,366	1	
99.40	99.42	99.43	99.45	99.46	99.47	99.47	99.48	99.49	99.50	2	
27.23	27.05	26.87	26.69	26.60	26.50	26.41	26.32	26.22	26.13	3	
14.55	14.37	14.20	14.02	13.93	13.84	13.75	13.65	13.56	13.46	4	
10.05	9.89	9.72	9.55	9.47	9.38	9.29	9.20	9.11	9.02	5	
7.87	7.72	7.56	7.40	7.31	7.23	7.14	7.06	6.97	6.88	6	
6.62	6.47	6.31	6.16	6.07	5.99	5.91	5.82	5.74	5.65	7	
5.81	5.67	5.52	5.36	5.28	5.20	5.12	5.03	4.95	4.86	8	
5.26	5.11	4.96	4.81	4.73	4.65	4.57	4.48	4.40	4.31	9	
4.85	4.71	4.56	4.41	4.33	4.25	4.17	4.08	4.00	3.91	10	
4.54	4.40	4.25	4.10	4.02	3.94	3.86	3.78	3.69	3.60	11	
4.30	4.16	4.01	3.86	3.78	3.70	3.62	3.54	3.45	3.36	12	
4.10	3.96	3.82	3.66	3.59	3.51	3.43	3.34	3.25	3.17	13	
3.94	3.80	3.66	3.51	3.43	3.35	3.27	3.18	3.09	3.00	14	
3.80	3.67	3.52	3.37	3.29	3.21	3.13	3.05	2.96	2.87	15	
3.69	3.55	3.41	3.26	3.18	3.10	3.02	2.93	2.84	2.75	16	
3.59	3.46	3.31	3.16	3.08	3.00	2.92	2.83	2.75	2.65	17	
3.51	3.37	3.23	3.08	3.00	2.92	2.84	2.75	2.66	2.57	18	
3.43	3.30	3.15	3.00	2.92	2.84	2.76	2.67	2.58	2.49	19	
3.37	3.23	3.09	2.94	2.86	2.78	2.69	2.61	2.52	2.42	20	
3.31	3.17	3.03	2.88	2.80	2.72	2.64	2.55	2.46	2.36	21	
3.26	3.12	2.98	2.83	2.75	2.67	2.58	2.50	2.40	2.31	22	
3.21	3.07	2.93	2.78	2.70	2.62	2.54	2.45	2.35	2.26	23	
3.17	3.03	2.89	2.74	2.66	2.58	2.49	2.40	2.31	2.21	24	
3.13	2.99	2.85	2.70	2.62	2.54	2.45	2.36	2.27	2.17	25	
3.09	2.96	2.81	2.66	2.58	2.50	2.42	2.33	2.23	2.13	26	
3.06	2.93	2.78	2.63	2.55	2.47	2.38	2.29	2.20	2.10	27	
3.03	2.90	2.75	2.60	2.52	2.44	2.35	2.26	2.17	2.06	28	
3.00	2.87	2.73	2.57	2.49	2.41	2.33	2.23	2.14	2.03	29	
2.98	2.84	2.70	2.55	2.47	2.39	2.30	2.21	2.11	2.01	30	
2.80	2.66	2.52	2.37	2.29	2.20	2.11	2.02	1.92	1.80	40	
2.63	2.50	2.35	2.20	2.12	2.03	1.94	1.84	1.73	1.60	60	
2.47	2.34	2.19	2.03	1.95	1.86	1.76	1.66	1.53	1.38	120	
2.32	2.18	2.04	1.88	1.79	1.70	1.59	1.47	1.32	1.00	∞	

Denominator Degrees of Freedom

TABLE A.8

The Chi-Square Table

Values of χ² for Selected Probabilities

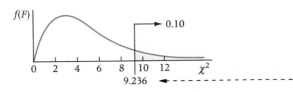

ρ = 0.5

Example: df (Number of degrees of freedom) = 5, the tail above χ² = 9.236 represents 0.10 or 10% of the area under the curve.

$\frac{\chi^2}{df}$	.90	.70	.50	.30	.20	.10	.05	.02	.01
1	.016	.148	.455	1.074	1.642	2.706	3.841	5.412	6.635
2	.211	.713	1.386	2.408	3.219	4.605	5.991	7.824	9.210
3	.584	1.424	2.366	3.665	4.642	6.251	7.815	9.837	11.345
4	1.064	2.195	3.357	4.878	5.989	7.779	9.488	11.668	13.277
5	1.610	3.000	4.351	6.064	7.289	9.236	11.070	13.388	15.086
6	2.204	3.828	5.348	7.231	8.558	10.645	12.592	15.033	16.812
7	2.833	4.671	6.346	8.383	9.803	12.017	14.067	16.622	18.475
8	3.490	5.527	7.344	9.524	11.030	13.362	15.507	18.168	20.090
9	4.168	6.393	8.343	10.656	12.242	14.684	16.919	19.679	21.666
10	4.865	7.267	9.342	11.781	13.442	15.987	18.307	21.161	23.209
11	5.578	8.148	10.341	12.899	14.631	17.275	19.675	22.618	24.725
12	6.304	9.034	11.340	14.011	15.812	18.549	21.026	24.054	26.217
13	7.042	9.926	12.340	15.119	16.985	19.812	22.362	25.472	27.688
14	7.790	10.821	13.339	16.222	18.151	21.064	23.685	26.873	29.141
15	8.547	11.721	14.339	17.322	19.311	22.307	24.996	28.259	30.578
16	9.312	12.624	15.338	18.418	20.465	23.542	26.296	29.633	32.000
17	10.085	13.531	16.338	19.511	21.615	24.769	27.587	30.995	33.409
18	10.865	14.440	17.338	20.601	22.760	25.989	28.869	33.346	34.805
19	11.651	15.352	18.338	21.689	23.900	27.204	30.144	33.687	36.191
20	12.443	16.266	19.337	22.775	25.038	28.412	31.410	35.020	37.566
21	13.240	17.182	20.337	23.858	26.171	29.615	32.671	36.343	38.932
22	14.041	18.101	21.337	24.939	27.301	30.813	33.924	37.659	40.289
23	14.848	19.021	22.337	26.018	28.429	32.007	35.172	38.968	41.638
24	15.659	19.943	23.337	27.096	29.553	33.196	36.415	40.270	42.980
25	16.473	20.867	24.337	28.172	30.675	34.382	37.652	41.566	44.314
26	17.292	21.792	25.336	29.246	31.795	35.563	38.885	42.856	45.642
27	18.114	22.719	26.336	30.319	32.912	36.741	40.113	44.140	46.963
28	18.939	23.647	27.336	31.391	34.027	37.916	41.337	45.419	48.278
29	19.768	24.577	28.336	32.461	35.139	39.087	42.557	46.693	49.588
30	20.599	25.508	29.336	33.530	36.250	40.256	43.773	47.962	50.892

Probabilities (Areas Under χ² Distribution Curve Above Given χ² Values)

From Table IV of Fisher & Yates' *Statistical Tables for Biological, Agricultural, and Medical Research,* 6th edition, 1974, published by Longman Group UK Ltd., London (previously published by Oliver & Boyd Ltd., Edinburgh), permission granted by the authors and publishers.

TABLE A.9   Factors for Control Charts

Number of Items in Sample, n	Averages Factors for Control Limits, A_2	Ranges Factors for Central Line, d_2	Ranges Factors for Control Limits D_3	Ranges Factors for Control Limits D_4
2	1.880	1.128	0	3.267
3	1.023	1.693	0	2.575
4	.729	2.059	0	2.282
5	.577	2.326	0	2.115
6	.483	2.534	0	2.004
7	.419	2.704	.076	1.924
8	.373	2.847	.136	1.864
9	.337	2.970	.184	1.816
10	.308	3.078	.223	1.777
11	.285	3.173	.256	1.744
12	.266	3.258	.284	1.716
13	.249	3.336	.308	1.692
14	.235	3.407	.329	1.671
15	.223	3.472	.348	1.652

Adapted from American Society for Testing and Materials, *Manual on Quality Control of Materials*, 1951, Table B2, p. 115. For a more detailed table and explanation, see Acheson J. Duncan, *Quality Control and Industrial Statistics*, 3d ed. (Homewood, Ill.: Richard D. Irwin, 1974), Table M, p. 927.

DATABASES

This appendix contains two databases, which are available to instructors on diskette. Both are constructed from data provided by the U.S. Bureau of the Census in its series, *Current Population Reports*.

DATABASE 1: Financial and Business Information

This database contains financial and business information from each of the fifty states. It has five variables and fifty measurements (one for each state) on each variable. The variables are as follows:

X_1 = total disposable personal income per capita for 1988

X_2 = insured commercial bank deposits per capita for 1988

X_3 = percent of mortgage loans foreclosed in FSLIC-insured savings institutions in 1988

X_4 = return on assets for FSLIC-insured savings institutions in 1988

X_5 = number of business failures per 10,000 concerns in 1988

DATABASE 1

Division and State	Disposable Personal Income per Capita[1] Total		Insured Commercial Bank Deposits per Capita[2]		FSLIC-Insured Savings Institutions[3] Percent of Mortgage Loans Foreclosed[4]		Return on Assets[5]		Business Failures per 10,000 Concerns[6]	
	Dollars	Rank	Dollars	Rank	Percent	Rank	Percent	Rank	Rate	Rank
United States	14,107	(X)	8,560	(X)	2.23	(X)	−1.08	(X)	98	(X)
New England	17,002	(X)	10,065	(X)	(NA)	(X)	(NA)	(X)	32	(X)
Maine	12,955	26	5,333	48	.48	39	.52	3	30	48
New Hampshire	17,049	4	7,840	24	.28	45	.41	11	62	35
Vermont	12,941	27	8,657	17	.02	49	.51	5	32	47
Massachusetts	17,456	3	12,244	4	.50	38	.34	17	39	46
Rhode Island	14,636	13	9,577	7	1.28	27	.51	5	17	49
Connecticut	19,096	1	9,005	13	.23	48	.02	29	17	49

2 (Continued)

Industry Group	Total Establish-ments	All Employees[2] Number (1000)	All Employees[2] Payroll Amount ($ million)	Production Workers Number (1000)	Production Workers Wages ($ million)	Value Added by Manu-facturer ($ million)
er and wood products	33,982	698.8	12,706.6	581.1	9,516.5	28,590.9
ng	11,952	87.4	1,549.8	73.6	1,227.7	4,164.3
ills and planing mills	6,696	178.9	3,265.7	156.0	2,649.4	7,634.6
ork, plywood, and struc-						
al members	7,930	240.6	4,669.2	196.8	3,429.9	9,806.3
containers	2,216	37.1	481.3	31.2	342.6	873.5
buildings and mobile						
mes	1,077	64.8	1,200.5	50.2	778.1	2,452.6
iture and fixtures	11,613	508.5	9,047.6	408.0	6,230.1	20,239.1
hold furniture	5,606	283.7	4,449.7	240.3	3,282.8	9,480.7
building and related fur-						
ure	484	20.8	377.3	15.7	244.7	844.4
ons and fixtures	2,455	73.6	1,541.4	54.5	991.3	3,094.2
llaneous furniture and fix-						
es	2,084	49.7	890.7	37.3	556.5	2,061.5
r and allied products	6,342	610.9	16,821.0	465.7	11,758.7	49,725.8
mills	39	14.2	536.5	11.1	397.5	2,246.5
mills	281	129.3	4,589.3	99.3	3,396.0	13,694.4
board mills	199	53.6	1,895.9	41.1	1,406.0	7,001.7
board containers and						
es	2,796	193.5	4,615.9	147.3	3,053.1	9,814.7
llaneous converted paper						
ducts	3,027	220.3	5,183.4	166.9	3,506.1	16,968.5
ing and publishing	61,774	1,491.9	33,515.0	796.9	15,669.9	89,207.9
papers	9,079	434.6	9,037.1	148.4	2,985.6	24,300.0
dicals	4,017	111.1	3,158.1	18.4	372.2	11,802.1
s	2,856	111.5	2,752.5	50.4	982.2	10,315.5
llaneous publishing	2,376	68.9	1,482.6	24.1	364.6	5,514.2
mercial printing	36,103	553.6	12,294.1	401.5	7,890.5	25,025.1
fold business forms	853	53.2	1,276.4	37.2	822.1	3,882.8
ing cards	162	20.7	459.8	11.2	197.3	2,196.9
books and bookbinding	1,545	68.5	1,260.9	53.9	853.5	2,918.4
ng trade services	4,783	69.7	1,793.5	51.9	1,201.8	3,252.9
micals and allied prod-						
s	12,109	816.4	25,065.3	464.3	12,327.1	121,241.8
trial inorganic chemicals	1,405	94.3	3,121.8	50.6	1,526.3	11,154.0
s materials and synthetics	680	123.4	4,034.8	84.4	2,460.7	17,882.0
s	1,356	172.2	5,312.3	79.7	1,895.5	28,176.4
cleaners, and toilet goods	2,399	119.8	3,096.1	72.6	1,576.2	21,620.4

Division and State	Disposable Personal Income per Capita[1] Dollars	Disposable Personal Income per Capita[1] Rank	Insured Commercial Bank Deposits per Capita[2] Dollars	Insured Commercial Bank Deposits per Capita[2] Rank	FSLIC-Insured Savings Institutions[3] Percent of Mortgage Loans Foreclosed[4] Percent	FSLIC-Insured Savings Institutions[3] Percent of Mortgage Loans Foreclosed[4] Rank	FSLIC-Insured Savings Institutions[3] Return on Assets[5] Percent	FSLIC-Insured Savings Institutions[3] Return on Assets[5] Rank	Business Failures per 10,000 Concerns[6] Rate	Business Failures per 10,000 Concerns[6] Rank
Middle Atlantic	15,939	(X)	11,852	(X)	(NA)	(X)	(NA)	(X)	50	(X)
New York	16,036	7	14,736	2	.44	42	.25	20	52	39
New Jersey	18,615	2	8,948	15	2.22	16	.15	25	43	43
Pennsylvania	14,072	19	9,415	8	1.21	28	.05	28	51	40
East North Central	13,929	(X)	8,280	(X)	(NA)	(X)	(NA)	(X)	96	(X)
Ohio	13,326	22	7,293	32	.72	36	.35	15	82	26
Indiana	12,834	29	7,890	23	.42	43	.40	12	77	31
Illinois	15,150	9	10,454	5	.68	37	.09	26	126	12
Michigan	14,094	18	7,435	28	.25	47	.35	15	86	23
Wisconsin	13,296	23	7,334	30	1.10	30	.51	5	91	21
West North Central	13,162	(X)	9,254	(X)	(NA)	(X)	(NA)	(X)	83	(X)
Minnesota	14,037	20	9,195	11	1.06	32	-2.30	42	48	42
Iowa	12,475	33	9,300	10	2.45	13	-1.19	40	81	28
Missouri	13,340	21	8,993	14	1.46	22	-.46	35	108	15
North Dakota	11,388	38	9,161	12	1.55	20	.09	26	86	23
South Dakota	11,611	37	12,471	3	.33	44	.39	13	69	32
Nebraska	12,773	32	9,403	9	1.53	21	-.78	37	59	37
Kansas	13,235	24	8,853	16	2.21	17	-.24	33	111	14
South Atlantic	13,735	(X)	8,031	(X)	(NA)	(X)	(NA)	(X)	73	(X)
Delaware	14,654	12	35,942	1	—	50	-.09	31	42	44
Maryland	16,397	5	7,919	22	1.31	25	.31	19	41	45
District of Columbia	17,464	(X)	20,426	(X)	—	(X)	-.23	(X)	30	(X)
Virginia	15,050	10	7,997	20	1.08	31	.01	30	78	30
West Virginia	10,306	49	7,389	29	1.31	25	.45	8	62	35
North Carolina	12,259	34	7,171	33	2.27	15	.43	9	50	41
South Carolina	11,102	41	4,421	50	.79	34	.38	14	59	37
Georgia	12,886	28	7,057	36	1.18	29	.20	22	100	18
Florida	14,338	16	8,045	19	1.70	19	-.57	36	103	17
East South Central	11,180	(X)	7,091	(X)	(NA)	(X)	(NA)	(X)	97	(X)
Kentucky	11,081	42	7,955	21	.46	41	.52	3	87	22
Tennessee	12,212	35	7,317	31	2.33	14	.16	24	117	13
Alabama	11,040	43	6,539	40	2.54	12	-.31	34	82	26
Mississippi	9,612	50	6,302	42	3.43	10	-1.71	41	95	20
West South Central	12,051	(X)	7,848	(X)	(NA)	(X)	(NA)	(X)	161	(X)
Arkansas	10,670	47	6,845	38	5.70	7	-7.26	47	65	34
Louisiana	10,890	44	6,913	37	5.63	8	-1.00	38	156	6
Oklahoma	10,875	45	7,122	35	6.53	6	-2.42	43	99	19
Texas	12,777	30	8,376	18	11.57	2	-11.32	49	188	4

(continues)

DATABASE 1 (Continued)

Division and State	Disposable Personal Income per Capita[1] — Total		Insured Commercial Bank Deposits per Capita[2]		FSLIC-Insured Savings Institutions[3] — Percent of Mortgage Loans Foreclosed[4]		Return on Assets[5]		Business Failures per 10,000 Concerns[6]	
	Dollars	Rank	Dollars	Rank	Percent	Rank	Percent	Rank	Rate	Rank
Mountain	12,570	(X)	6,328	(X)	(NA)	(X)	(NA)	(X)	177	(X)
Montana	11,264	39	7,576	26	1.80	18	.43	9	83	25
Idaho	11,190	40	6,096	44	.73	35	.32	18	133	9
Wyoming	11,667	36	7,820	25	8.34	4	−3.27	44	129	11
Colorado	14,110	17	6,408	41	7.72	5	−4.88	46	248	1
New Mexico	10,752	46	5,724	46	5.41	9	−9.62	48	107	16
Arizona	13,017	25	6,718	39	12.85	1	−3.61	45	207	2
Utah	10,564	48	5,124	49	2.74	11	−1.01	39	165	5
Nevada	14,799	11	6,177	43	.28	45	.57	2	132	10
Pacific	15,559	(X)	7,221	(X)	(NA)	(X)	(NA)	(X)	132	(X)
Washington	14,508	14	5,893	45	.96	33	.25	20	141	7
Oregon	12,776	31	5,528	47	1.40	23	−.17	32	67	33
California	16,035	8	7,500	27	1.36	24	.18	23	138	6
Alaska	16,357	6	7,138	34	8.36	3	−17.02	50	200	3
Hawaii	14,374	15	9,984	6	.47	40	.87	1	79	29

Key: NA Not available. X Not applicable. [1]See Table 704, *1990 Statistical Abstract* (U.S. Bureau of Economic Analysis). [2]See Table 806, *1990 Statistical Abstract* (Board of Governors of the Federal Reserve System). [3]See Table 820, *1990 Statistical Abstract* (U.S. Office of Thrift Supervision). [4]Foreclosures are reported as of judgement date, even if subject to a redemption period. [5]Net income after taxes as a percent of average assets. [6]See Table 877, *1990 Statistical Abstract* (Dun & Bradstreet Corporation, New York, NY).

Note: When states share the same rank, the next lower rank is omitted. Because of rounded data, states may have identical values shown, but different ranks.

DATABASE 2: U.S. Manufacturers Summary Data

This database contains 1987 information about manufacturers in the United States by industry group. It includes six variables for more than seventy-five industries. The six variables measured are as follows:

X_1 = total number of establishments in this industry in 1987
X_2 = total number of employees in this industry (000s)
X_3 = amount of payroll ($ millions) in this industry
X_4 = total number of production workers in this industry (000s)
X_5 = total wages of production workers in this industry ($ millions)
X_6 = value added by manufacture in this industry ($ millions)

DATABASE 2

SIC[1] Code	Industry Group	Total Establish-ments	All Employees[2] — Number (1000)	Payroll Amount ($ million)	Produ Numbe (1000)
(X)	All manufacturing establishments, including central administrative offices	368,817	18,933.6	474,082.9	12,259.
20	**Food and kindred products**	**20,624**	**1,448.3**	**30,232.6**	**1,029.**
201	Meat products	3,267	339.5	5,674.1	283.
202	Dairy products	2,366	141.3	3,215.7	87.
203	Preserved fruits and vegetables	1,912	208.3	3,773.4	172.
204	Grain mill products	2,610	102.7	2,708.0	70.
205	Bakery products	2,850	217.0	4,760.9	127.
206	Sugar, confectionery products	1,094	90.4	1,994.5	72.
207	Fats and oils	595	30.4	713.8	20.
208	Beverages	2,214	160.2	4,498.5	77.
209	Miscellaneous foods and kindred products	3,716	158.4	2,893.9	116.
21	**Tobacco products**	**138**	**44.7**	**1,485.9**	**32.**
211	Cigarettes	11	32.0	1,232.9	23.
212	Cigars	20	2.5	35.7	2.
213	Chewing and smoking tobacco	29	3.3	77.2	2.
214	Tobacco stemming and redrying	78	7.0	140.2	4.
22	**Textile mill products**	**6,412**	**678.0**	**11,460.1**	**580.**
221	Broadwoven fabric mills, cotton	301	72.5	1,263.2	65.
222	Broadwoven fabric mills, man-made	441	88.9	1,608.5	77.
223	Broadwoven fabric mills, wool	119	14.2	231.3	12.
224	Narrow fabric mills	277	19.1	305.8	16.
225	Knitting mills	2,130	203.5	2,990.4	176.
226	Textile finishing, except wool	971	57.5	1,057.6	46.
227	Carpets and rugs	477	53.4	1,002.4	40.
228	Yarn and thread mills	610	114.2	1,854.2	103.
229	Miscellaneous textile goods	1,086	54.6	1,146.7	42.
23	**Apparel and other textile products**	**22,872**	**1,084.9**	**13,988.6**	**913.**
231	Men's and boys' suits and coats	347	56.6	801.5	49.
232	Men's and boys' furnishings	2,195	281.8	3,278.6	247.
233	Women's and misses' outerwear	10,290	352.6	4,363.3	293.
234	Women's and children's undergarments	557	66.9	835.0	55.
235	Hats, caps, and millinery	461	16.9	198.5	14.
236	Girls' and children's outerwear	834	71.7	825.2	60.
237	Fur goods	380	2.1	48.2	1.
238	Misc. apparel and accessories	986	41.0	523.4	33.
239	Misc. fabricated textile products	6,822	195.2	3,115.0	158.

DATABAS

SIC[1] Code	
24	**Lu**
241	Log
242	Sav
243	Mil
	t
244	**Wo**
245	**Wo**
	h
25	**Fu**
251	Ho
253	Pub
	n
254	Par
259	Mis
	t
26	**Pap**
261	Pul
262	Pap
263	Pap
265	Pap
	b
267	Mis
	P
27	**Pri**
271	New
272	Per
273	Bo
274	Mis
275	Co
276	Ma
277	Gre
278	Bla
279	Pri
28	**Ch**
	w
281	Ind
282	Pla
283	Dru
284	Soa

SIC[1] Code	Industry Group	Total Establish- ments	All Employees[2]		Production Workers		Value Added by Manu- facturer ($ million)
			Number (1000)	Payroll Amount ($ million)	Number (1000)	Wages ($ million)	
	Chemicals and allied prod-ucts (Continued)						
285	Paints and allied products	1,431	55.4	1,493.5	28.3	625.4	6,238.3
286	Industrial organic chemicals	961	125.4	4,532.5	73.2	2,433.6	21,542.3
287	Agricultural chemicals	973	40.1	1,169.8	24.4	623.4	6,379.2
289	Miscellaneous chemical prod-ucts	2,904	85.7	2,304.5	51.1	1,186.1	8,249.0
29	**Petroleum and coal prod-ucts**	**2,254**	**115.9**	**3,999.9**	**76.5**	**2,462.8**	**18,398.9**
291	Petroleum refining	331	74.8	2,853.0	50.2	1,801.8	14,128.2
295	Asphalt paving and roofing ma-terials	1,367	28.1	785.0	19.7	504.0	2,882.9
299	Miscellaneous petroleum and coal products	556	13.0	361.8	6.7	157.0	1,387.7
30	**Rubber and misc. plastics products**	**14,515**	**827.9**	**17,503.4**	**640.9**	**11,644.7**	**44,293.1**
301	Tires and inner tubes	164	65.5	2,071.2	52.7	1,597.1	5,561.3
302	Rubber and plastics footwear	66	11.0	154.4	9.2	104.5	324.7
305	Hose and belting and gaskets and packing	693	53.5	1,193.2	37.7	739.1	2,756.1
306	Fabricated rubber products, n.e.c.	1,573	101.0	2,184.8	76.3	1,412.1	4,680.2
308	Miscellaneous plastics products, n.e.c.	12,019	596.9	11,899.8	464.9	7,791.8	30,970.8
31	**Leather and leather prod-ucts**	**2,193**	**127.0**	**1,798.3**	**107.4**	**1,281.7**	**4,274.9**
311	Leather tanning and finishing	344	14.6	291.3	12.1	211.6	745.2
313	Footwear cut stock	128	5.1	70.2	4.3	50.1	142.4
314	Footwear, except rubber	479	70.6	905.1	61.7	685.3	2,106.1
315	Leather gloves and mittens	77	3.1	33.6	2.7	26.1	74.5
316	Luggage	241	10.5	179.6	7.6	95.5	467.0
317	Handbags and personal leather goods	529	16.3	225.3	13.3	151.0	518.6
319	Leather goods, n.e.c.	395	7.0	93.2	5.7	62.2	221.3
32	**Stone, clay, and glass prod-ucts**	**16,166**	**521.1**	**12,274.9**	**402.7**	**8,742.5**	**33,076.4**
321	Flat glass	81	14.5	504.6	11.7	396.1	1,617.7
322	Glass and glassware, pressed or blown	522	76.5	1,938.6	65.0	1,558.8	4,943.7
323	Products of purchased glass	1,432	51.5	1,067.0	39.8	725.8	2,846.6

(continues)

DATABASE 2 (Continued)

SIC[1] Code	Industry Group	Total Establish- ments	All Employees[2]		Production Workers		Value Added by Manu- facturer ($ million)
			Number (1000)	Payroll Amount ($ million)	Number (1000)	Wages ($ million)	
324	Cement, hydraulic	215	19.2	601.7	14.5	425.3	2,284.0
325	Structural clay products	598	34.6	687.8	27.4	489.4	1,732.8
326	Pottery and related products	1,006	36.7	731.6	29.5	531.6	1,637.5
327	Concrete, gypsum, and plaster products	9,814	203.0	4,619.8	151.6	3,185.0	11,761.7
328	Cut stone and stone products	745	12.5	242.6	10.0	173.4	449.3
329	Miscellaneous nonmetallic min- eral products	1,753	72.6	1,881.3	53.3	1,257.3	5,803.0
33	**Primary metal industries**	**6,771**	**700.7**	**19,781.5**	**541.0**	**14,162.7**	**46,471.2**
331	Blast furnace and basic steel products	1,241	255.5	8,259.0	197.5	6,124.2	21,081.2
332	Iron and steel foundries	1,231	128.6	3,382.7	103.4	2,518.0	6,186.9
333	Primary nonferrous metals	169	31.3	987.4	23.8	691.8	2,975.2
334	Secondary nonferrous metals	397	12.5	310.9	9.1	185.8	947.2
335	Nonferrous rolling and drawing	1,066	161.5	4,267.5	120.8	2,898.4	10,140.2
336	Nonferrous foundries (castings)	1,687	79.2	1,796.3	64.1	1,296.6	3,382.3
34	**Fabricated metal products**	**36,105**	**1,466.6**	**35,219.8**	**1,083.7**	**22,914.8**	**75,502.9**
341	Metal cans and shipping con- tainers	538	48.2	1,529.5	39.2	1,195.5	4,224.1
342	Cutlery, handtools, and hard- ware	2,327	145.7	3,397.9	111.0	2,282.7	8,054.8
343	Plumbing and heating, except electric	828	44.0	974.9	31.4	587.3	2,779.7
344	Fabricated structural metal products	12,579	409.6	9,092.9	292.6	5,558.0	18,797.6
345	Screw machine products, bolts, etc.	2,569	94.6	2,268.0	72.7	1,551.6	4,762.4
346	Metal forgings and stampings	4,062	255.4	7,243.3	202.6	5,318.6	13,223.0
347	Metal services, n.e.c.	5,251	114.9	2,211.3	89.9	1,472.2	4,730.3
348	Ordnance and accessories, n.e.c.	374	87.5	2,457.3	54.2	1,258.3	5,342.5
349	Miscellaneous fabricated metal products	7,577	266.7	6,044.8	190.0	3,690.6	13,588.5
35	**Industrial machinery and equipment**	**52,135**	**1,853.1**	**50,749.9**	**1,145.9**	**26,077.7**	**119,214.4**
351	Engines and turbines	356	86.4	2,886.8	56.5	1,707.8	7,018.4
352	Farm and garden machinery	1,804	82.3	1,923.5	58.4	1,188.9	5,638.3
353	Construction and related ma- chinery	3,467	187.7	5,260.1	116.4	2,875.7	11,330.6
354	Metalworking machinery	11,470	269.7	7,295.3	189.4	4,636.1	13,766.2

SIC[1] Code	Industry Group	Total Establish- ments	All Employees[2]		Production Workers		Value Added by Manu- facturer ($ million)
			Number (1000)	Payroll Amount ($ million)	Number (1000)	Wages ($ million)	
	Industrial machinery and equipment (Continued)						
355	Special industry machinery	4,550	169.9	4,596.0	96.6	2,181.5	9,698.6
356	General industrial machinery	3,929	238.0	6,130.2	149.8	3,343.6	13,756.6
357	Computer and office equipment	2,134	333.8	10,865.1	123.2	2,599.9	33,166.9
358	Refrigeration and service ma- chinery	2,129	192.3	4,796.3	134.0	2,901.1	11,621.5
359	Industrial machinery, n.e.c.	22,296	292.9	6,996.7	221.5	4,643.1	13,217.5
36	**Electronic and other electric equipment**	**15,962**	**1,569.7**	**38,736.7**	**1,003.8**	**19,757.8**	**95,958.1**
361	Electric distribution equipment	766	76.6	1,777.7	53.7	1,064.8	4,577.0
362	Electrical industrial apparatus	2,213	166.7	3,920.9	110.5	2,135.4	9,020.4
363	Household appliances	480	116.7	2,633.9	92.2	1,923.3	7,444.0
364	Electric lighting and wiring equipment	1,986	169.7	3,775.4	125.6	2,438.5	10,313.6
365	Household audio and video equipment	854	44.2	844.1	33.8	522.8	3,003.5
366	Communications equipment	1,437	256.3	7,398.4	126.6	2,797.2	19,804.4
367	Electronic components and ac- cessories	5,911	550.9	13,686.7	332.3	6,158.5	30,635.2
369	Misc. electrical equipment and supplies	2,315	188.4	4,699.6	129.0	2,717.3	11,160.0
37	**Transportation equipment**	**10,500**	**1,819.7**	**58,966.3**	**1,206.3**	**34,755.1**	**135,782.7**
371	Motor vehicles and equipment	4,422	748.2	23,864.1	602.4	18,268.8	65,778.2
372	Aircraft and parts	1,618	603.0	20,834.0	329.3	9,801.2	40,188.8
373	Ship and boat building and re- pairing	2,766	177.4	4,265.6	137.6	2,933.1	7,656.7
374	Railroad equipment	173	21.0	617.5	13.7	344.2	1,285.2
375	Motorcycles, bicycles, and parts	246	7.4	158.3	5.8	110.9	367.8
376	Guided missiles, space vehicles, parts	156	213.3	8,100.9	81.8	2,606.5	18,152.0
379	Miscellaneous transportation equipment	1,119	49.3	1,125.9	35.8	690.6	2,354.0
38	**Instruments and related products**	**10,326**	**996.0**	**29,089.0**	**509.3**	**11,655.0**	**71,487.2**
381	Search and navigation equip- ment	1,137	372.3	12,446.3	159.9	4,493.6	24,647.7
382	Measuring and controlling de- vices	4,240	292.2	8,016.2	153.6	3,267.0	17,325.6
384	Medical instruments and sup- plies	3,443	206.3	5,046.7	125.1	2,287.4	14,864.9

(continues)

DATABASE 2 (Continued)

SIC[1] Code	Industry Group	Total Establish- ments	All Employees[2]		Production Workers		Value Added by Manu- facturer ($ million)
			Number (1000)	Payroll Amount ($ million)	Number (1000)	Wages ($ million)	
38	**Instruments and related products** (Continued)						
385	Ophthalmic goods	494	23.9	450.5	15.9	231.3	1,094.0
386	Photographic equipment and supplies	791	88.6	2,900.4	45.0	1,232.8	13,059.2
387	Watches, clocks, watchcases and parts	221	12.7	228.8	9.8	142.9	495.8
39	**Miscellaneous manufactur- ing industries**	**16,544**	**371.7**	**6,847.3**	**270.1**	**4,011.9**	**17,431.6**
391	Jewelry, silverware, and plated ware	2,978	50.2	957.1	35.9	545.0	2,486.9
393	Musical instruments	425	12.5	223.2	9.9	149.5	518.1
394	Toys and sporting goods	2,711	88.2	1,505.2	66.4	913.9	4,868.2
395	Pens, pencils, office, and art supplies	1,013	28.7	539.2	20.7	318.8	1,431.4
396	Costume jewelry and notions	1,020	31.2	487.2	22.0	276.6	1,155.0
399	Miscellaneous manufacturers	8,397	160.9	3,135.5	115.2	1,808.1	6,972.0
(X)	**Administrative and auxiliary**	**9,480**	**1,181.9**	**44,793.2**	—	—	—

Key: NA Not available.　X Not applicable　[1]Standard Industrial Classification Code.　[2]Average of "production workers" plus all other employees for the payroll period ended nearest the fifteenth of March.

Source: U.S. Bureau of the Census, *Census of Manufactures, 1987 Preliminary Summary*, MC87-SUM-1(P).

SUMMATION NOTATION

In Chapter 3, the symbol Σ (the Greek letter, Sigma) was introduced. In mathematics, this symbol means to sum a set of values as described by the notation following it. The value given below Σ is the beginning value and the value given above Σ is the final value of the sum. Generally,

$$\sum_{i=1}^{n} X_i = X_1 + X_2 + X_3 + \ldots + X_n. \qquad \textbf{(Rule 1)}$$

For example, if $X_1 = 3$, $X_2 = 5$, $X_3 = 7$, and $X_4 = 12$,

$$\sum_{i=1}^{4} X_i = X_1 + X_2 + X_3 + X_4 = 3 + 5 + 7 + 12 = 27.$$

The second summation rule is

$$\sum_{i=1}^{n} CX_i = C\sum_{i=1}^{n} X_i. \qquad \textbf{(Rule 2)}$$

For example, if $C = 8$, $X_1 = 3$, $X_2 = 5$, $X_3 = 7$, and $X_4 = 12$,

$$\sum_{i=1}^{4} 8X_i = 8X_1 + 8X_2 + 8X_3 + 8X_4$$
$$= 8(3) + 8(5) + 8(7) + 8(12)$$
$$= 24 + 40 + 56 + 96 = 216,$$

and

$$\sum_{i=1}^{4} 8X_i = 8\sum_{i=1}^{4} X_i = 8(X_1 + X_2 + X_3 + X_4)$$
$$= 8(3 + 5 + 7 + 12) = 8(27) = 216.$$

The third summation rule is

$$\sum_{i=1}^{n} (X_i + Y_i) = \sum_{i=1}^{n} X_i + \sum_{i=1}^{n} Y_i. \qquad \textbf{(Rule 3)}$$

For example, if $X_1 = 2$, $X_2 = 4$, $X_3 = 5$, $Y_1 = 1$, $Y_2 = 3$, and $Y_3 = 6$,

$$\sum_{i=1}^{3}(X_i + Y_i) = (X_1 + Y_1) + (X_2 + Y_2) + (X_3 + Y_3)$$

$$= (2 + 1) + (4 + 3) + (5 + 6) = 3 + 7 + 11 = 21,$$

and

$$\sum_{i=1}^{3}(X_i + Y_i) = \sum_{i=1}^{3}X_i + \sum_{i=1}^{3}Y_i = (X_1 + X_2 + X_3) + (Y_1 + Y_2 + Y_3)$$

$$= (2 + 4 + 5) + (1 + 3 + 6) = 11 + 10 = 21.$$

The fourth summation rule is

$$\sum_{i=1}^{n}C = n \cdot C. \qquad \textbf{(Rule 4)}$$

For example, if $C = 12$ and $n = 5$,

$$\sum_{i=1}^{5}12 = 12 + 12 + 12 + 12 + 12 = 60,$$

but $60 = 5(12)$, so

$$\sum_{i=1}^{5}12 = 5(12) = 60.$$

Division and State	Disposable Personal Income per Capita[1] Total		Insured Commercial Bank Deposits per Capita[2]		FSLIC-Insured Savings Institutions[3] Percent of Mortgage Loans Foreclosed[4]		Return on Assets[5]		Business Failures per 10,000 Concerns[6]	
	Dollars	Rank	Dollars	Rank	Percent	Rank	Percent	Rank	Rate	Rank
Middle Atlantic	15,939	(X)	11,852	(X)	(NA)	(X)	(NA)	(X)	50	(X)
New York	16,036	7	14,736	2	.44	42	.25	20	52	39
New Jersey	18,615	2	8,948	15	2.22	16	.15	25	43	43
Pennsylvania	14,072	19	9,415	8	1.21	28	.05	28	51	40
East North Central	13,929	(X)	8,280	(X)	(NA)	(X)	(NA)	(X)	96	(X)
Ohio	13,326	22	7,293	32	.72	36	.35	15	82	26
Indiana	12,834	29	7,890	23	.42	43	.40	12	77	31
Illinois	15,150	9	10,454	5	.68	37	.09	26	126	12
Michigan	14,094	18	7,435	28	.25	47	.35	15	86	23
Wisconsin	13,296	23	7,334	30	1.10	30	.51	5	91	21
West North Central	13,162	(X)	9,254	(X)	(NA)	(X)	(NA)	(X)	83	(X)
Minnesota	14,037	20	9,195	11	1.06	32	−2.30	42	48	42
Iowa	12,475	33	9,300	10	2.45	13	−1.19	40	81	28
Missouri	13,340	21	8,993	14	1.46	22	−.46	35	108	15
North Dakota	11,388	38	9,161	12	1.55	20	.09	26	86	23
South Dakota	11,611	37	12,471	3	.33	44	.39	13	69	32
Nebraska	12,773	32	9,403	9	1.53	21	−.78	37	59	37
Kansas	13,235	24	8,853	16	2.21	17	−.24	33	111	14
South Atlantic	13,735	(X)	8,031	(X)	(NA)	(X)	(NA)	(X)	73	(X)
Delaware	14,654	12	35,942	1	—	50	−.09	31	42	44
Maryland	16,397	5	7,919	22	1.31	25	.31	19	41	45
District of Columbia	17,464	(X)	20,426	(X)	—	(X)	−.23	(X)	30	(X)
Virginia	15,050	10	7,997	20	1.08	31	.01	30	78	30
West Virginia	10,306	49	7,389	29	1.31	25	.45	8	62	35
North Carolina	12,259	34	7,171	33	2.27	15	.43	9	50	41
South Carolina	11,102	41	4,421	50	.79	34	.38	14	59	37
Georgia	12,886	28	7,057	36	1.18	29	.20	22	100	18
Florida	14,338	16	8,045	19	1.70	19	−.57	36	103	17
East South Central	11,180	(X)	7,091	(X)	(NA)	(X)	(NA)	(X)	97	(X)
Kentucky	11,081	42	7,955	21	.46	41	.52	3	87	22
Tennessee	12,212	35	7,317	31	2.33	14	.16	24	117	13
Alabama	11,040	43	6,539	40	2.54	12	−.31	34	82	26
Mississippi	9,612	50	6,302	42	3.43	10	−1.71	41	95	20
West South Central	12,051	(X)	7,848	(X)	(NA)	(X)	(NA)	(X)	161	(X)
Arkansas	10,670	47	6,845	38	5.70	7	−7.26	47	65	34
Louisiana	10,890	44	6,913	37	5.63	8	−1.00	38	156	6
Oklahoma	10,875	45	7,122	35	6.53	6	−2.42	43	99	19
Texas	12,777	30	8,376	18	11.57	2	−11.32	49	188	4

(continues)

DATABASE 1 (Continued)

Division and State	Disposable Personal Income per Capita[1] Total		Insured Commercial Bank Deposits per Capita[2]		FSLIC-Insured Savings Institutions[3] Percent of Mortgage Loans Foreclosed[4]		Return on Assets[5]		Business Failures per 10,000 Concerns[6]	
	Dollars	Rank	Dollars	Rank	Percent	Rank	Percent	Rank	Rate	Rank
Mountain	12,570	(X)	6,328	(X)	(NA)	(X)	(NA)	(X)	177	(X)
Montana	11,264	39	7,576	26	1.80	18	.43	9	83	25
Idaho	11,190	40	6,096	44	.73	35	.32	18	133	9
Wyoming	11,667	36	7,820	25	8.34	4	−3.27	44	129	11
Colorado	14,110	17	6,408	41	7.72	5	−4.88	46	248	1
New Mexico	10,752	46	5,724	46	5.41	9	−9.62	48	107	16
Arizona	13,017	25	6,718	39	12.85	1	−3.61	45	207	2
Utah	10,564	48	5,124	49	2.74	11	−1.01	39	165	5
Nevada	14,799	11	6,177	43	.28	45	.57	2	132	10
Pacific	15,559	(X)	7,221	(X)	(NA)	(X)	(NA)	(X)	132	(X)
Washington	14,508	14	5,893	45	.96	33	.25	20	141	7
Oregon	12,776	31	5,528	47	1.40	23	−.17	32	67	33
California	16,035	8	7,500	27	1.36	24	.18	23	138	6
Alaska	16,357	6	7,138	34	8.36	3	−17.02	50	200	3
Hawaii	14,374	15	9,984	6	.47	40	.87	1	79	29

Key: NA Not available. X Not applicable. [1]See Table 704, *1990 Statistical Abstract* (U.S. Bureau of Economic Analysis). [2]See Table 806, *1990 Statistical Abstract* (Board of Governors of the Federal Reserve System). [3]See Table 820, *1990 Statistical Abstract* (U.S. Office of Thrift Supervision). [4]Foreclosures are reported as of judgement date, even if subject to a redemption period. [5]Net income after taxes as a percent of average assets. [6]See Table 877, *1990 Statistical Abstract* (Dun & Bradstreet Corporation, New York, NY).

Note: When states share the same rank, the next lower rank is omitted. Because of rounded data, states may have identical values shown, but different ranks.

DATABASE 2: U.S. Manufacturers Summary Data

This database contains 1987 information about manufacturers in the United States by industry group. It includes six variables for more than seventy-five industries. The six variables measured are as follows:

X_1 = total number of establishments in this industry in 1987

X_2 = total number of employees in this industry (000s)

X_3 = amount of payroll ($ millions) in this industry

X_4 = total number of production workers in this industry (000s)

X_5 = total wages of production workers in this industry ($ millions)

X_6 = value added by manufacture in this industry ($ millions)

DATABASE 2

SIC[1] Code	Industry Group	Total Establish- ments	All Employees[2]		Production Workers		Value Added by Manu- facturer ($ million)
			Number (1000)	Payroll Amount ($ million)	Number (1000)	Wages ($ million)	
(X)	**All manufacturing establish- ments, including central administrative offices**	**368,817**	**18,933.6**	**474,082.9**	**12,259.5**	**251,533.0**	**1,166,554.9**
20	**Food and kindred products**	**20,624**	**1,448.3**	**30,232.6**	**1,029.5**	**18,894.8**	**122,072.6**
201	Meat products	3,267	339.5	5,674.1	283.9	4,253.0	13,740.4
202	Dairy products	2,366	141.3	3,215.7	87.8	1,818.7	11,908.9
203	Preserved fruits and vegetables	1,912	208.3	3,773.4	172.9	2,767.5	17,272.1
204	Grain mill products	2,610	102.7	2,708.0	70.1	1,731.2	15,271.3
205	Bakery products	2,850	217.0	4,760.9	127.9	2,549.2	15,251.7
206	Sugar, confectionery products	1,094	90.4	1,994.5	72.4	1,423.1	8,927.1
207	Fats and oils	595	30.4	713.8	20.4	437.5	3,245.5
208	Beverages	2,214	160.2	4,498.5	77.3	2,125.4	22,693.7
209	Miscellaneous foods and kindred products	3,716	158.4	2,893.9	116.8	1,789.2	13,762.0
21	**Tobacco products**	**138**	**44.7**	**1,485.9**	**32.7**	**992.5**	**14,260.5**
211	Cigarettes	11	32.0	1,232.9	23.6	841.7	12,967.3
212	Cigars	20	2.5	35.7	2.0	26.2	106.3
213	Chewing and smoking tobacco	29	3.3	77.2	2.2	46.2	791.9
214	Tobacco stemming and redrying	78	7.0	140.2	4.8	78.4	395.1
22	**Textile mill products**	**6,412**	**678.0**	**11,460.1**	**580.2**	**8,766.8**	**26,013.9**
221	Broadwoven fabric mills, cotton	301	72.5	1,263.2	65.1	1,074.8	2,608.6
222	Broadwoven fabric mills, man- made	441	88.9	1,608.5	77.6	1,282.5	3,647.7
223	Broadwoven fabric mills, wool	119	14.2	231.3	12.4	180.7	494.1
224	Narrow fabric mills	277	19.1	305.8	16.2	217.5	612.3
225	Knitting mills	2,130	203.5	2,990.4	176.0	2,295.5	6,408.8
226	Textile finishing, except wool	971	57.5	1,057.6	46.7	754.3	2,363.7
227	Carpets and rugs	477	53.4	1,002.4	40.7	659.6	3,190.2
228	Yarn and thread mills	610	114.2	1,854.2	103.2	1,537.7	3,821.1
229	Miscellaneous textile goods	1,086	54.6	1,146.7	42.4	764.2	2,867.4
23	**Apparel and other textile products**	**22,872**	**1,084.9**	**13,988.6**	**913.3**	**9,910.2**	**33,310.8**
231	Men's and boys' suits and coats	347	56.6	801.5	49.4	614.5	1,963.5
232	Men's and boys' furnishings	2,195	281.8	3,278.6	247.4	2,534.6	8,674.6
233	Women's and misses' outerwear	10,290	352.6	4,363.3	293.0	2,876.3	10,000.2
234	Women's and children's under- garments	557	66.9	835.0	55.5	580.0	2,070.7
235	Hats, caps, and millinery	461	16.9	198.5	14.3	144.5	360.6
236	Girls' and children's outerwear	834	71.7	825.2	60.9	608.3	1,966.5
237	Fur goods	380	2.1	48.2	1.5	28.1	136.8
238	Misc. apparel and accessories	986	41.0	523.4	33.0	343.1	1,168.5
239	Misc. fabricated textile products	6,822	195.2	3,115.0	158.4	2,180.7	6,969.3

(continues)

DATABASE 2 (Continued)

SIC[1] Code	Industry Group	Total Establish- ments	All Employees[2]		Production Workers		Value Added by Manu- facturer ($ million)
			Number (1000)	Payroll Amount ($ million)	Number (1000)	Wages ($ million)	
24	**Lumber and wood products**	**33,982**	**698.8**	**12,706.6**	**581.1**	**9,516.5**	**28,590.9**
241	Logging	11,952	87.4	1,549.8	73.6	1,227.7	4,164.3
242	Sawmills and planing mills	6,696	178.9	3,265.7	156.0	2,649.4	7,634.6
243	Millwork, plywood, and struc- tural members	7,930	240.6	4,669.2	196.8	3,429.9	9,806.3
244	Wood containers	2,216	37.1	481.3	31.2	342.6	873.5
245	Wood buildings and mobile homes	1,077	64.8	1,200.5	50.2	778.1	2,452.6
25	**Furniture and fixtures**	**11,613**	**508.5**	**9,047.6**	**408.0**	**6,230.1**	**20,239.1**
251	Household furniture	5,606	283.7	4,449.7	240.3	3,282.8	9,480.7
253	Public building and related fur- niture	484	20.8	377.3	15.7	244.7	844.4
254	Partitions and fixtures	2,455	73.6	1,541.4	54.5	991.3	3,094.2
259	Miscellaneous furniture and fix- tures	2,084	49.7	890.7	37.3	556.5	2,061.5
26	**Paper and allied products**	**6,342**	**610.9**	**16,821.0**	**465.7**	**11,758.7**	**49,725.8**
261	Pulp mills	39	14.2	536.5	11.1	397.5	2,246.5
262	Paper mills	281	129.3	4,589.3	99.3	3,396.0	13,694.4
263	Paperboard mills	199	53.6	1,895.9	41.1	1,406.0	7,001.7
265	Paperboard containers and boxes	2,796	193.5	4,615.9	147.3	3,053.1	9,814.7
267	Miscellaneous converted paper products	3,027	220.3	5,183.4	166.9	3,506.1	16,968.5
27	**Printing and publishing**	**61,774**	**1,491.9**	**33,515.0**	**796.9**	**15,669.9**	**89,207.9**
271	Newspapers	9,079	434.6	9,037.1	148.4	2,985.6	24,300.0
272	Periodicals	4,017	111.1	3,158.1	18.4	372.2	11,802.1
273	Books	2,856	111.5	2,752.5	50.4	982.2	10,315.5
274	Miscellaneous publishing	2,376	68.9	1,482.6	24.1	364.6	5,514.2
275	Commercial printing	36,103	553.6	12,294.1	401.5	7,890.5	25,025.1
276	Manifold business forms	853	53.2	1,276.4	37.2	822.1	3,882.8
277	Greeting cards	162	20.7	459.8	11.2	197.3	2,196.9
278	Blankbooks and bookbinding	1,545	68.5	1,260.9	53.9	853.5	2,918.4
279	Printing trade services	4,783	69.7	1,793.5	51.9	1,201.8	3,252.9
28	**Chemicals and allied prod- ucts**	**12,109**	**816.4**	**25,065.3**	**464.3**	**12,327.1**	**121,241.8**
281	Industrial inorganic chemicals	1,405	94.3	3,121.8	50.6	1,526.3	11,154.0
282	Plastics materials and synthetics	680	123.4	4,034.8	84.4	2,460.7	17,882.0
283	Drugs	1,356	172.2	5,312.3	79.7	1,895.5	28,176.4
284	Soap, cleaners, and toilet goods	2,399	119.8	3,096.1	72.6	1,576.2	21,620.4

SIC[1] Code	Industry Group	Total Establish-ments	All Employees[2]		Production Workers		Value Added by Manu-facturer ($ million)
			Number (1000)	Payroll Amount ($ million)	Number (1000)	Wages ($ million)	
	Chemicals and allied products (Continued)						
285	Paints and allied products	1,431	55.4	1,493.5	28.3	625.4	6,238.3
286	Industrial organic chemicals	961	125.4	4,532.5	73.2	2,433.6	21,542.3
287	Agricultural chemicals	973	40.1	1,169.8	24.4	623.4	6,379.2
289	Miscellaneous chemical products	2,904	85.7	2,304.5	51.1	1,186.1	8,249.0
29	**Petroleum and coal products**	**2,254**	**115.9**	**3,999.9**	**76.5**	**2,462.8**	**18,398.9**
291	Petroleum refining	331	74.8	2,853.0	50.2	1,801.8	14,128.2
295	Asphalt paving and roofing materials	1,367	28.1	785.0	19.7	504.0	2,882.9
299	Miscellaneous petroleum and coal products	556	13.0	361.8	6.7	157.0	1,387.7
30	**Rubber and misc. plastics products**	**14,515**	**827.9**	**17,503.4**	**640.9**	**11,644.7**	**44,293.1**
301	Tires and inner tubes	164	65.5	2,071.2	52.7	1,597.1	5,561.3
302	Rubber and plastics footwear	66	11.0	154.4	9.2	104.5	324.7
305	Hose and belting and gaskets and packing	693	53.5	1,193.2	37.7	739.1	2,756.1
306	Fabricated rubber products, n.e.c.	1,573	101.0	2,184.8	76.3	1,412.1	4,680.2
308	Miscellaneous plastics products, n.e.c.	12,019	596.9	11,899.8	464.9	7,791.8	30,970.8
31	**Leather and leather products**	**2,193**	**127.0**	**1,798.3**	**107.4**	**1,281.7**	**4,274.9**
311	Leather tanning and finishing	344	14.6	291.3	12.1	211.6	745.2
313	Footwear cut stock	128	5.1	70.2	4.3	50.1	142.4
314	Footwear, except rubber	479	70.6	905.1	61.7	685.3	2,106.1
315	Leather gloves and mittens	77	3.1	33.6	2.7	26.1	74.5
316	Luggage	241	10.5	179.6	7.6	95.5	467.0
317	Handbags and personal leather goods	529	16.3	225.3	13.3	151.0	518.6
319	Leather goods, n.e.c.	395	7.0	93.2	5.7	62.2	221.3
32	**Stone, clay, and glass products**	**16,166**	**521.1**	**12,274.9**	**402.7**	**8,742.5**	**33,076.4**
321	Flat glass	81	14.5	504.6	11.7	396.1	1,617.7
322	Glass and glassware, pressed or blown	522	76.5	1,938.6	65.0	1,558.8	4,943.7
323	Products of purchased glass	1,432	51.5	1,067.0	39.8	725.8	2,846.6

(continues)

DATABASE 2 (Continued)

SIC[1] Code	Industry Group	Total Establish- ments	All Employees[2]		Production Workers		Value Added by Manu- facturer ($ million)
			Number (1000)	Payroll Amount ($ million)	Number (1000)	Wages ($ million)	
324	Cement, hydraulic	215	19.2	601.7	14.5	425.3	2,284.0
325	Structural clay products	598	34.6	687.8	27.4	489.4	1,732.8
326	Pottery and related products	1,006	36.7	731.6	29.5	531.6	1,637.5
327	Concrete, gypsum, and plaster products	9,814	203.0	4,619.8	151.6	3,185.0	11,761.7
328	Cut stone and stone products	745	12.5	242.6	10.0	173.4	449.3
329	Miscellaneous nonmetallic min- eral products	1,753	72.6	1,881.3	53.3	1,257.3	5,803.0
33	**Primary metal industries**	**6,771**	**700.7**	**19,781.5**	**541.0**	**14,162.7**	**46,471.2**
331	Blast furnace and basic steel products	1,241	255.5	8,259.0	197.5	6,124.2	21,081.2
332	Iron and steel foundries	1,231	128.6	3,382.7	103.4	2,518.0	6,186.9
333	Primary nonferrous metals	169	31.3	987.4	23.8	691.8	2,975.2
334	Secondary nonferrous metals	397	12.5	310.9	9.1	185.8	947.2
335	Nonferrous rolling and drawing	1,066	161.5	4,267.5	120.8	2,898.4	10,140.2
336	Nonferrous foundries (castings)	1,687	79.2	1,796.3	64.1	1,296.6	3,382.3
34	**Fabricated metal products**	**36,105**	**1,466.6**	**35,219.8**	**1,083.7**	**22,914.8**	**75,502.9**
341	Metal cans and shipping con- tainers	538	48.2	1,529.5	39.2	1,195.5	4,224.1
342	Cutlery, handtools, and hard- ware	2,327	145.7	3,397.9	111.0	2,282.7	8,054.8
343	Plumbing and heating, except electric	828	44.0	974.9	31.4	587.3	2,779.7
344	Fabricated structural metal products	12,579	409.6	9,092.9	292.6	5,558.0	18,797.6
345	Screw machine products, bolts, etc.	2,569	94.6	2,268.0	72.7	1,551.6	4,762.4
346	Metal forgings and stampings	4,062	255.4	7,243.3	202.6	5,318.6	13,223.0
347	Metal services, n.e.c.	5,251	114.9	2,211.3	89.9	1,472.2	4,730.3
348	Ordnance and accessories, n.e.c.	374	87.5	2,457.3	54.2	1,258.3	5,342.5
349	Miscellaneous fabricated metal products	7,577	266.7	6,044.8	190.0	3,690.6	13,588.5
35	**Industrial machinery and equipment**	**52,135**	**1,853.1**	**50,749.9**	**1,145.9**	**26,077.7**	**119,214.4**
351	Engines and turbines	356	86.4	2,886.8	56.5	1,707.8	7,018.4
352	Farm and garden machinery	1,804	82.3	1,923.5	58.4	1,188.9	5,638.3
353	Construction and related ma- chinery	3,467	187.7	5,260.1	116.4	2,875.7	11,330.6
354	Metalworking machinery	11,470	269.7	7,295.3	189.4	4,636.1	13,766.2

SIC[1] Code	Industry Group	Total Establish-ments	All Employees[2]		Production Workers		Value Added by Manu-facturer ($ million)
			Number (1000)	Payroll Amount ($ million)	Number (1000)	Wages ($ million)	
	Industrial machinery and equipment (Continued)						
355	Special industry machinery	4,550	169.9	4,596.0	96.6	2,181.5	9,698.6
356	General industrial machinery	3,929	238.0	6,130.2	149.8	3,343.6	13,756.6
357	Computer and office equipment	2,134	333.8	10,865.1	123.2	2,599.9	33,166.9
358	Refrigeration and service ma-chinery	2,129	192.3	4,796.3	134.0	2,901.1	11,621.5
359	Industrial machinery, n.e.c.	22,296	292.9	6,996.7	221.5	4,643.1	13,217.5
36	**Electronic and other electric equipment**	**15,962**	**1,569.7**	**38,736.7**	**1,003.8**	**19,757.8**	**95,958.1**
361	Electric distribution equipment	766	76.6	1,777.7	53.7	1,064.8	4,577.0
362	Electrical industrial apparatus	2,213	166.7	3,920.9	110.5	2,135.4	9,020.4
363	Household appliances	480	116.7	2,633.9	92.2	1,923.3	7,444.0
364	Electric lighting and wiring equipment	1,986	169.7	3,775.4	125.6	2,438.5	10,313.6
365	Household audio and video equipment	854	44.2	844.1	33.8	522.8	3,003.5
366	Communications equipment	1,437	256.3	7,398.4	126.6	2,797.2	19,804.4
367	Electronic components and ac-cessories	5,911	550.9	13,686.7	332.3	6,158.5	30,635.2
369	Misc. electrical equipment and supplies	2,315	188.4	4,699.6	129.0	2,717.3	11,160.0
37	**Transportation equipment**	**10,500**	**1,819.7**	**58,966.3**	**1,206.3**	**34,755.1**	**135,782.7**
371	Motor vehicles and equipment	4,422	748.2	23,864.1	602.4	18,268.8	65,778.2
372	Aircraft and parts	1,618	603.0	20,834.0	329.3	9,801.2	40,188.8
373	Ship and boat building and re-pairing	2,766	177.4	4,265.6	137.6	2,933.1	7,656.7
374	Railroad equipment	173	21.0	617.5	13.7	344.2	1,285.2
375	Motorcycles, bicycles, and parts	246	7.4	158.3	5.8	110.9	367.8
376	Guided missiles, space vehicles, parts	156	213.3	8,100.9	81.8	2,606.5	18,152.0
379	Miscellaneous transportation equipment	1,119	49.3	1,125.9	35.8	690.6	2,354.0
38	**Instruments and related products**	**10,326**	**996.0**	**29,089.0**	**509.3**	**11,655.0**	**71,487.2**
381	Search and navigation equip-ment	1,137	372.3	12,446.3	159.9	4,493.6	24,647.7
382	Measuring and controlling de-vices	4,240	292.2	8,016.2	153.6	3,267.0	17,325.6
384	Medical instruments and sup-plies	3,443	206.3	5,046.7	125.1	2,287.4	14,864.9

(continues)

DATABASE 2 (Continued)

SIC[1] Code	Industry Group	Total Establish- ments	All Employees[2]		Production Workers		Value Added by Manu- facturer ($ million)
			Number (1000)	Payroll Amount ($ million)	Number (1000)	Wages ($ million)	
38	**Instruments and related products** (Continued)						
385	Ophthalmic goods	494	23.9	450.5	15.9	231.3	1,094.0
386	Photographic equipment and supplies	791	88.6	2,900.4	45.0	1,232.8	13,059.2
387	Watches, clocks, watchcases and parts	221	12.7	228.8	9.8	142.9	495.8
39	**Miscellaneous manufactur- ing industries**	**16,544**	**371.7**	**6,847.3**	**270.1**	**4,011.9**	**17,431.6**
391	Jewelry, silverware, and plated ware	2,978	50.2	957.1	35.9	545.0	2,486.9
393	Musical instruments	425	12.5	223.2	9.9	149.5	518.1
394	Toys and sporting goods	2,711	88.2	1,505.2	66.4	913.9	4,868.2
395	Pens, pencils, office, and art supplies	1,013	28.7	539.2	20.7	318.8	1,431.4
396	Costume jewelry and notions	1,020	31.2	487.2	22.0	276.6	1,155.0
399	Miscellaneous manufacturers	8,397	160.9	3,135.5	115.2	1,808.1	6,972.0
(X)	**Administrative and auxiliary**	**9,480**	**1,181.9**	**44,793.2**	—	—	—

Key: NA Not available.   X Not applicable   [1]Standard Industrial Classification Code.   [2]Average of "production workers" plus all other employees for the payroll period ended nearest the fifteenth of March.

Source: U.S. Bureau of the Census, *Census of Manufactures, 1987 Preliminary Summary*, MC87-SUM-1(P).

SUMMATION NOTATION

In Chapter 3, the symbol Σ (the Greek letter, Sigma) was introduced. In mathematics, this symbol means to sum a set of values as described by the notation following it. The value given below Σ is the beginning value and the value given above Σ is the final value of the sum. Generally,

$$\sum_{i=1}^{n}X_i = X_1 + X_2 + X_3 + \ldots + X_n. \qquad \textbf{(Rule 1)}$$

For example, if $X_1 = 3$, $X_2 = 5$, $X_3 = 7$, and $X_4 = 12$,

$$\sum_{i=1}^{4}X_i = X_1 + X_2 + X_3 + X_4 = 3 + 5 + 7 + 12 = 27.$$

The second summation rule is

$$\sum_{i=1}^{n}CX_i = C\sum_{i=1}^{n}X_i. \qquad \textbf{(Rule 2)}$$

For example, if $C = 8$, $X_1 = 3$, $X_2 = 5$, $X_3 = 7$, and $X_4 = 12$,

$$\sum_{i=1}^{4}8X_i = 8X_1 + 8X_2 + 8X_3 + 8X_4$$
$$= 8(3) + 8(5) + 8(7) + 8(12)$$
$$= 24 + 40 + 56 + 96 = 216,$$

and

$$\sum_{i=1}^{4}8X_i = 8\sum_{i=1}^{4}X_i = 8(X_1 + X_2 + X_3 + X_4)$$
$$= 8(3 + 5 + 7 + 12) = 8(27) = 216.$$

The third summation rule is

$$\sum_{i=1}^{n}(X_i + Y_i) = \sum_{i=1}^{n}X_i + \sum_{i=1}^{n}Y_i. \qquad \textbf{(Rule 3)}$$

For example, if $X_1 = 2$, $X_2 = 4$, $X_3 = 5$, $Y_1 = 1$, $Y_2 = 3$, and $Y_3 = 6$,

$$\sum_{i=1}^{3}(X_i + Y_i) = (X_1 + Y_1) + (X_2 + Y_2) + (X_3 + Y_3)$$
$$= (2 + 1) + (4 + 3) + (5 + 6) = 3 + 7 + 11 = 21,$$

and

$$\sum_{i=1}^{3}(X_i + Y_i) = \sum_{i=1}^{3}X_i + \sum_{i=1}^{3}Y_i = (X_1 + X_2 + X_3) + (Y_1 + Y_2 + Y_3)$$
$$= (2 + 4 + 5) + (1 + 3 + 6) = 11 + 10 = 21.$$

The fourth summation rule is

$$\sum_{i=1}^{n}C = n \cdot C. \qquad \textbf{(Rule 4)}$$

For example, if $C = 12$ and $n = 5$,

$$\sum_{i=1}^{5}12 = 12 + 12 + 12 + 12 + 12 = 60,$$

but $60 = 5(12)$, so

$$\sum_{i=1}^{5}12 = 5(12) = 60.$$

A SUPPLEMENTARY *t* TEST FORMULA

In Section 10.3, a *t* test formula, Equation (10.3), is presented to test the difference in two population means for independent samples when the sample sizes are small and the population variances are unknown. An assumption underlying this test is that the population variances are approximately equal. However, meeting this assumption may not be possible. In such cases, the following alternative formula may be used. This formula is relatively straightforward and simple to use for computing the *t* value. However, the formula for determining the degrees of freedom is more complicated.

t Formula to Test the Difference in Means

$$t = \frac{\overline{X}_1 - \overline{X}_2}{\sqrt{\dfrac{S_1^2}{n_1} + \dfrac{S_2^2}{n_2}}}.$$

$$df = \frac{\left[\dfrac{S_1^2}{n_1} + \dfrac{S_2^2}{n_2}\right]^2}{\dfrac{\left(\dfrac{S_1^2}{n_1}\right)^2}{n_1 - 1} + \dfrac{\left(\dfrac{S_2^2}{n_2}\right)^2}{n_2 - 1}}.$$

ANSWERS TO ODD-NUMBERED QUANTITATIVE PROBLEMS

Chapter 1

1.5 a. Ratio **b.** Ratio **c.** Ratio
d. Ordinal **e.** Nominal **f.** Ratio
g. Ratio **h.** Ratio **i.** Ordinal
j. Ratio **k.** Nominal **l.** Nominal
m. Ratio

Chapter 2

2.3 See table.

2.11

Stem	Leaf
21	2, 8, 8, 9
22	0, 1, 2, 4, 6, 6, 7, 9, 9
23	0, 0, 4, 5, 8, 8, 9, 9, 9, 9
24	0, 0, 3, 6, 9, 9, 9
25	0, 3, 4, 5, 5, 7, 7, 8, 9
26	0, 1, 1, 2, 3, 3, 5, 6
27	0, 1, 3

2.25

Stem	Leaf
22	00, 68
23	01, 37, 44, 75
24	05, 37, 48, 60, 68
25	24, 55
26	02, 56, 70, 77
27	42, 60, 64
28	14, 30
29	22, 61, 75, 76, 90, 96
30	02, 10

Chapter 3

3.1 4

3.3 294

3.5 −1

3.7 Mean = 8,625,000; Median = 4,500,000

Solution to Problem 2.3

Class Interval	Frequency	Class Midpoint	Relative Frequency	Cumulative Frequency
0–5	6	2.5	.0698	6
5–10	8	7.5	.0930	14
10–15	17	12.5	.1977	31
15–20	23	17.5	.2674	54
20–25	18	22.5	.2093	72
25–30	10	27.5	.1163	82
30–35	4	32.5	.0465	86

3.9 Mean = 83.94; Median = 63.45

3.11 4.64

3.13 1.89

3.15 45,200

3.17 a. 14 **b.** 4 **c.** 24 **d.** 4.9

3.19 Variance = 500.67; Standard deviation = 22.38

3.21 a. 1.5 **b.** 4.01 **c.** 2.00

3.23 .75, .94, between 19.9 and 56.1

3.25 95%, 2½%, .15%, 16%

3.27 0.48, 1.52, −0.90, −2.62

3.29 CV(Mobile) = 19.67%, CV(NYC) = 24.32%

3.31 20.9, 4.57

3.33 27.5, 12.2

3.37 Mean = 2.5; mode = 2; median = 2

3.39 198.12, 14.08

3.41 Mean = 15.46; Variance = 1.38; Standard deviation = 1.18

3.43 a. 403.5 **b.** 403 **c.** 4 **d.** Variance = 24.92; Standard deviation = 4.99 **e.** −0.70

3.45 a. 1.063 **b.** 1.065 **c.** .94 and 1.15 **d.** .00813 **e.** .09 **f.** −1.37

3.47 Mean = 261,158.3; Median = 260,000; Range = 156,000; Standard deviation = 42,552.1

3.49 a. 36.56 **b.** Variance = 66.56; Standard deviation = 8.16

3.51 CV_1 = 28.3%; CV_2 = 21.2%; CV_3 = 29.7%

3.53 CV_x = 10.78%; CV_y = 6.43%

Chapter 4

4.1 $\{H_1H_2H_3, T_1H_2H_3, H_1T_2H_3, H_1H_2T_3, T_1T_2H_3, T_1H_2T_3, H_1T_2T_3, T_1T_2T_3\}$

4.3 216

4.5 a. {1, 2, 3, 4, 5, 7, 8, 9} **b.** {7, 9} **c.** {1, 3, 7} **d.** {1, 2, 3, 4, 5, 7, 8, 9} **e.** {7} **f.** {1, 2, 3, 4, 7} **g.** {2, 4, 7, 9}

4.9 {4, 8, 10, 14, 16, 18, 20, 22, 26, 28, 30}

4.11 a. .7167 **b.** .5000 **c.** .6500 **d.** 1.000 **e.** .7833

4.13 Cannot be solved without being able to determine the intersection.

4.15 a. .92 **b.** .31 **c.** .99 **d.** .01 **e.** .65

4.17 a. .44 **b.** .35 **c.** .63 **d.** .28 **e.** .37

4.19 .0278, .0556

4.21 .00018, .00048, increases

4.23 a. .09 **b.** .06 **c.** .00

4.25 a. .52 **b.** .5488 **c.** .4512 **d.** .0288 **e.** .9712

4.27 a. .2286 **b.** .2297 **c.** .3231 **d.** .0000

4.29 .0588, .0769

4.31 .2993, .0898

4.33 a. .0148 **b.** .625 **c.** .9899

4.35 a. .2143 **b.** .1341 **c.** .2632

4.37 a. .45 **b.** .05 **c.** .4743, .4269, .0988 **d.** .2748, .4533, .2719

4.39 .25, .25; Gomez = .3333; Jackson = .2500; Smith = .1944; Alvarez = .2222

4.41 .1653

4.43 a. .4431 **b.** .1691

4.45 a. .0000 **b.** .2493 **c.** .2523 **d.** .6323 **e.** around 1

4.47 a. .4211 **b.** .6316 **c.** .2105 **d.** .1250 **e.** .5263 **f.** .0000 **g.** .6667 **h.** .0000 **i.** Not independent

4.49 b. .2358 **c.** .0139 **d.** .4251 **e.** .3200 **f.** .0000 mutually exclusive **g.** Not independent

4.51 a. .30 **b.** .02 **c.** .90 **d.** .39 **e.** .1053

4.53 .0000394, .000035012, without replacement

4.55 a. .43 **b.** .189 **c.** .614 **d.** .699

4.57 a. .39 **b.** .40 **c.** .48 **d.** No **e.** No

4.59 a. .3483 **b.** .5317 **c.** .4683 **d.** .0817

4.61 Soup = .846; Breakfast meat = .115; Hot dog = .040

4.63 a. .2500   **b.** .2587   **c.** .6906

4.65 a. .0386   **b.** .9607   **c.** .0000

Chapter 5

5.1 a. .0036   **b.** .1147   **c.** .3823
   d. .5838

5.3 a. Mean = 14; standard deviation = 2.049
   b. Mean = 24.5; standard deviation = 3.991
   c. Mean = 50; standard deviation = 5

5.5 a. .0972   **b.** .1099   **c.** .0000
   d. 2.20

5.7 a. .9010   **b.** .0890   **c.** 1.00

5.9 $n = 10$ $P = .20$

5.11 a. .2608   **b.** .0254   **c.** .8027
   d. Mean = 8.25; standard
   deviation = 1.93   **e.** $4.39 \leq X \leq 12.11$

5.13 a. .0538   **b.** .1539   **c.** .4142
   d. .0672   **e.** .0244   **f.** .3702

5.15 a. Mean = 6.3; standard deviation = 2.51
   b. Mean = 1.3; standard deviation = 1.14
   c. Mean = 8.9; standard deviation = 2.98
   d. Mean = 0.6; standard deviation = 0.77

5.17 Lambda = 3.20   **a.** .0408   **b.** .1241

5.19 a. .5488   **b.** .3293   **c.** .1219
   d. .8913   **e.** .1912

5.21 a. .3012   **b.** .0000   **c.** .0336

5.23 .0567

5.25 a. .5091   **b.** .2937   **c.** .4167
   d. .0014

5.27 a. .5105   **b.** .0699   **c.** .3846

5.29 a. .3571   **b.** .4048   **c.** .1190

5.31 .0474

5.33 a. .1240   **b.** .8490   **c.** .0900
   d. .0000

5.35 a. .1607   **b.** .7626   **c.** .3504
   d. .5429

5.37 .1740

5.39 .4990, .002, 12.5

5.41 14, 14, 2.05, .031

5.43 a. .0620   **b.** .0050

5.45 a. .0723   **b.** .0972   **c.** .0273, .1653
   d. 1.8, $X = 1$

5.47 a. .0907   **b.** .0358   **c.** .1517
   d. .8781

5.49 .9463

5.51 .1353, .3233

5.53 a. .0319   **b.** .6389   **c.** .0922

5.55 a. .2098   **b.** .0010   **c.** .2697

5.57 a. .0163   **b.** .0047   **c.** .3263

Chapter 6

6.1 a. .4904   **b.** .4495   **c.** .2910
   d. .4983   **e.** .1628

6.3 a. 1.67   **b.** 0.46   **c.** −0.26
   d. −3.47

6.5 a. 188.25   **b.** 244.65   **c.** 163.81
   d. 206.11

6.7 a. .7823   **b.** .0054   **c.** .4261

6.9 756.5

6.11 6.25

6.13 a. .9332   **b.** .5865   **c.** .0030
   d. .7745

6.15 a. Mean = 21; standard deviation = 2.51;
   $X \leq 16.5$
   b. Mean = 12.5; standard deviation = 2.5;
   $10.5 \leq X \leq 20.5$
   c. Mean = 24; standard deviation = 3.10;
   $21.5 \leq X \leq 22.5$
   d. Mean = 7.2; standard deviation = 1.99;
   $X \geq 14.5$

6.17 a. .117, .120   **b.** .409, .415
   c. .1985, .196
   d. Normal approximation not close enough

6.19 .1788

6.21 .0004

6.23 a. .0000   **b.** .9993

6.25 a. 0.31, 0.31   **b.** 1.43, 1.43
   c. 0.91, 0.91   **d.** 0.17, 0.17

6.27 a. .2592   **b.** .3012   **c.** .0000

6.29 2 years

6.31 a. .89 hour, or 53.4 minutes
   b. .1065   **c.** .1703

6.33 a. .1587   **b.** .0013   **c.** .6915
   d. .9270   **e.** .0000

6.35 a. .0202 **b.** .9817 **c.** .1850
d. .4449
6.37 0.66
6.39 133.59
6.41 114.8
6.45 a. .0025 **b.** .8944 **c.** .3482
6.47 a. .0643 **b.** .2772 **c.** .0099
d. 1.28
6.49 .0000
6.51 .0016 by normal curve; .0000 by binomial; expected number = 10
6.53 33, 25.2, .5478
6.55 6.67/hour, .4264
6.57 .0498, .3834, .2212
6.59 a. 8.33 seconds **b.** .0498 **c.** .4512
d. .0007

Chapter 7

7.7 825
7.13 a. .0548 **b.** .7881 **c.** .0082
d. .8575 **e.** .1664
7.15 11.11
7.17 a. .9772 **b.** .2385 **c.** .1469
d. .1230
7.19 $67.49
7.21 a. .0107 **b.** .0301 **c.** .2651
d. .2460 **e.** 35,349.5
7.23 a. .3859 **b.** .4168 **c.** .9909
d. .0005 **e.** .0023
7.25 .26
7.27 .1251, .0000
7.29 a. .1379 **b.** .0146 **c.** .9708
d. .0005
7.31 a. .0000 **b.** .0021 **c.** .5000
d. .9979
7.33 .1635
7.35 a. .1660 **b.** .0537 **c.** .0000
7.37 .1894
7.47 55, 45, 90, 25, 35
7.49 Select every 40th outlet.
7.53 1.000, .0068, .7814

7.55 a. .0314 **b.** .2420 **c.** .2250
d. .1469 **e.** .0000
7.57 .0793
7.59 a. .1003 **b.** .0274 **c.** .0000
d. .8221
7.61 .1131
7.63 .0012
7.65 .0655
7.67 .1131
7.69 .2296

Chapter 8

8.1 $203.5 \leq \mu \leq 218.5$
8.3 $7.85 \leq \mu \leq 9.49$
8.5 $62.74 \leq \mu \leq 69.26$
8.7 5.3, $5.13 \leq \mu \leq 5.47$
8.9 $2.86 \leq \mu \leq 3.76$
8.11 $2.14, $2.11 \leq \mu \leq 2.17
8.13 a. $.37 \leq P \leq .61$ **b.** $.56 \leq P \leq .64$
c. $.39 \leq P \leq .49$ **d.** $.25 \leq P \leq .45$
8.15 .39, $.245 \leq P \leq .535$, $.344 \leq P \leq .436$
8.17 $.77 \leq P \leq .83$
8.19 $.46 \leq P \leq .62$
8.21 $-0.76 \leq \mu_1 - \mu_2 \leq 4.16$
8.23 0.20, $-0.42 \leq \mu_1 - \mu_2 \leq 0.82$
8.25 $23,000; $20,501 \leq \mu_1 - \mu_2 \leq $25,499$
8.27 a. $.19 \leq P_1 - P_2 \leq .29$
b. $-.10 \leq P_1 - P_2 \leq .00$
c. $-.23 \leq P_1 - P_2 \leq .15$
d. $-.05 \leq P_1 - P_2 \leq -.01$
8.29 $.00 \leq P_1 - P_2 \leq .10$
8.31 $.27 \leq P_1 - P_2 \leq .33$
8.33 a. 94 **b.** 38 **c.** 59
8.35 a. 85 **b.** 43 **c.** 96
8.37 106
8.39 1083
8.41 97
8.43 746
8.45 a. $24.11 \leq \mu \leq 25.89$
b. $113.2 \leq \mu \leq 126.0$

c. $3.136 \le \mu \le 3.702$
d. $54.55 \le \mu \le 58.85$

8.47 a. $-8.76 \le \mu_1 - \mu_2 \le -1.24$
b. $-98.4 \le \mu_1 - \mu_2 \le 6.4$

8.49 a. 200   **b.** 114   **c.** 299   **d.** 57

8.51 a. 174   **b.** 398   **c.** 112   **d.** 433

8.53 $3.90 \le \mu \le 5.54$

8.55 $196.3 \le \mu \le 229.7$

8.57 $.23 \le P \le .43$

8.59 $.726 \le P \le .814$

8.61 $.54 \le P \le .60$; .57

8.63 $1.35 \le \mu_1 - \mu_2 \le 1.43$

8.65 $6.3 \le \mu_1 - \mu_2 \le 9.3$

8.67 $.18 \le P_1 - P_2 \le .28$

8.69 $.06 \le P_1 - P_2 \le .26$

8.71 $.263 \le P_1 - P_2 \le .377$

8.73 196

8.75 722

8.77 110

Chapter 9

9.1 a. $Z = 2.77$; reject the null hypothesis
b. 22.11, 27.89

9.3 a. $Z = 1.59$; reject the null hypothesis
b. $P = .056$; reject the null hypothesis
c. 1212.04

9.5 $Z = 1.03$; fail to reject the null hypothesis;
Critical value = $4.51

9.7 $Z = -1.69$; reject the null hypothesis

9.9 $Z = -5.46$; reject the null hypothesis

9.11 $Z = -1.66$; fail to reject the null hypothesis

9.13 $Z = 1.41$; reject the null hypothesis

9.15 $Z = -1.17$; fail to reject the null hypothesis

9.17 $Z = -2.09$; reject the null hypothesis

9.19 $Z = 4.07$; reject the null hypothesis

9.21 $Z = 5.48$; reject the null hypothesis

9.23 $Z = -4.50$; reject the null hypothesis

9.25 $Z = 0.92$; fail to reject the null hypothesis

9.27 $Z = 2.27$; reject the null hypothesis

9.29 $Z = 0.73$; fail to reject the null hypothesis

9.31 $Z = -3.36$; reject the null hypothesis

9.33 $Z = 0.45$; fail to reject the null hypothesis

9.35 $Z = -2.56$; reject the null hypothesis

9.37 $Z = -0.40$; fail to reject the null hypothesis

9.39 a. .8133   **b.** .7389   **c.** .5596
d. .3632

9.41 a. .3483   **b.** .0102   **c.** .0000

9.43 $Z = 0.96$; fail to reject the null hypothesis;
.5832, .2514

9.45 a. $Z = -2.27$; reject the null hypothesis
b. $Z = 1.15$; fail to reject the null hypothesis
c. $Z = 3.44$; reject the null hypothesis
d. $Z = -2.73$; reject the null hypothesis
e. $Z = 3.58$; reject the null hypothesis

9.47 a. $Z = -1.18$; fail to reject the null
hypothesis
b. $Z = -0.59$; fail to reject the null
hypothesis
c. $Z = 8.43$; reject the null hypothesis
d. $Z = -0.79$; fail to reject the null
hypothesis

9.49 $Z = 5.68$; reject the null hypothesis

9.51 a. $Z = -1.75$; fail to reject the null
hypothesis   **b.** .9505

9.53 $Z = 1.05$; fail to reject the null hypothesis

9.55 a. $Z = 1.86$; fail to reject the null
hypothesis   **b.** .4880

9.57 $Z = -0.39$; fail to reject the null hypothesis

9.59 $Z = 5.85$; reject the null hypothesis

9.61 $Z = 13.07$; reject the null hypothesis

9.63 $Z = 7.37$; reject the null hypothesis

9.65 $Z = -0.26$; fail to reject the null hypothesis

9.67 $Z = -5.29$; reject the null hypothesis

9.69 $Z = +0.83$; fail to reject the null hypothesis;
.4880, .0793

Chapter 10

10.1 $t = 0.56$; fail to reject the null hypothesis

10.3 $t = 2.44$; reject the null hypothesis

10.5 $42.17 \le \mu \le 49.06$

10.7 $1.96 \le \mu \le 2.77$

10.9 $t = -2.16$; fail to reject the null hypothesis

10.11 $12.58 \le \mu \le 27.82$
10.13 $\$4.69 \le \mu \le \$5.99$
10.15 $t = -0.67$; fail to reject the null hypothesis
10.17 $\$95.78 \le \mu \le \$120.80$
10.19 $t = 0.69$; fail to reject the null hypothesis
10.21 $t = -4.66$; reject the null hypothesis
10.23 $.019 \le \mu_1 - \mu_2 \le .996$
10.25 $-118.5 \le \mu_1 - \mu_2 \le -103.5$
10.27 $t = 4.91$; reject the null hypothesis
10.29 $-4.09 \le \mu_1 - \mu_2 \le 3.29$
10.31 $\$2,258.05 \le \mu_1 - \mu_2 \le \$5,541.95$
10.33 $3.44 \le \mu_1 - \mu_2 \le 8.06$
10.35 $t = -0.74$; fail to reject the null hypothesis
10.37 $t = 2.63$; fail to reject the null hypothesis
10.39 $-19.79 \le D \le -1.07$
10.41 $-22.6 \le D \le 4.6$
10.43 $t = 6.66$; reject the null hypothesis
10.45 $t = -3.11$; reject the null hypothesis
10.47 $63.71 \le D \le 86.29$
10.49 $t = -5.81$; reject the null hypothesis
10.51 $F = 15.8$; reject the null hypothesis
10.53 $F = 17.76$, $t = 4.214$; reject the null hypothesis
10.55

Source of Variance	SS	df	MS	F
Treatment	29.64	2	14.82	3.03
Error	68.42	14	4.887	
Total	98.06	16		

Fail to reject the null hypothesis
10.57 $F = 76.8$; reject the null hypothesis
10.59 $F = 13.5$; reject the null hypothesis
10.61 $314.45 \le \mu \le 323.89$
10.63 $t = 1.02$; fail to reject the null hypothesis
10.65 $t = -0.59$; fail to reject the null hypothesis
10.67 $1.69 \le \mu \le 2.51$
10.69 $9.2 \le \mu \le 12.3$
10.71 $-0.19 \le \mu_1 - \mu_2 \le 3.69$
10.73 $-30.5 \le \mu_1 - \mu_2 \le 8.9$
10.75 $-0.01 \le \mu_1 - \mu_2 \le 9.42$

10.77 $t = 4.52$; reject the null hypothesis
10.79 $\$19,779 \le \mu_1 - \mu_2 \le \$40,221$
10.81 $9.1 \le D \le 21.5$
10.83 $t = 2.21$; reject the null hypothesis
10.85 $t = 6.71$; reject the null hypothesis
10.87 $t = 4.78$; reject the null hypothesis
10.89 $F = 8.82$; reject the null hypothesis
10.91 $F = 2.28$; fail to reject the null hypothesis
10.93 $F = 7.38$; reject the null hypothesis

Chapter 11

11.3 $\hat{Y} = -1.83 + 0.63X$
11.5 $\hat{Y} = 16.5 + 0.162X$
11.7 $\hat{Y} = -46.3 + 15.2X$
11.9 $\hat{Y} = 3.83 + 0.976X$
11.11 b. $\hat{Y} = 103,133 + 0.151X$
11.13

$\hat{Y}$	$Y - \hat{Y}$
18.46	-1.46
19.92	-4.92
21.06	0.94
17.81	1.19
19.76	4.24

11.15

$\hat{Y}$	$Y - \hat{Y}$
144.21	3.79
10.10	44.90
282.89	55.11
868.10	125.90
526.72	14.28
46.67	42.33
209.74	-83.74
581.59	-202.59

11.17 Residuals: 4.72, -0.98, -0.40, -6.75, 2.77, 0.64
11.23 $SSE = 272.1$; $S_e = 7.38$; 7 out of 8 fall within $\pm 1S_e$; all fall within $\pm 2S_e$
11.25 $SSE = 19.894$, $S_e = 2.58$
11.27 $SSE = 0.06196$, $S_e = 0.1016$
11.29 $r^2 = .123$
11.31 $r^2 = .898$
11.33 $r^2 = .909$

11.35 $t = 0.65$; fail to reject the null hypothesis—slope is not significantly different from zero

11.37 $t = 7.27$; reject the null hypothesis—slope is significantly different from zero

11.39 $12.53 \le E(Y_{25}) \le 28.57$

11.41 $133.3 \le E(Y_{20}) \le 383.7$; $-106.5 \le Y \le 621.9$

11.43 $r = -.927$

11.45 $r = .975$

11.47 $r = -.27, r^2 = .07$

11.49

	1985	1987
1987	.975	
1989	.957	.985

11.53 $\hat{Y} = -3,824.73 + 1.934X$
$\hat{Y}(1992) = 27.93$

11.55 a. $\hat{Y} = -24,757.97 + 12.607X$
$\hat{Y}(1,990) = 330.81$
b. $\hat{Y} = -10,950.62 + 5.585X$
$\hat{Y}(2,000) = 218.53$

11.57 a. $\hat{Y} = 2.69 + 1.29X$

b.

$\hat{Y}$	$Y - \hat{Y}$
9.12	-1.12
11.69	-2.69
6.55	4.45
23.26	3.74
18.12	-3.11
14.26	-1.26

c. $S_e = 3.661$ **d.** $r^2 = .777$
e. $t = 3.74$

11.59 $r = .834, r^2 = .695$

11.61 $\hat{Y} = -54.4 + 2.40X$; $\hat{Y}(100) = 185.6$; $S_e = 17.89$; $r^2 = .91$; $t = 7.80$; reject the null hypothesis—the slope is significantly different from zero

11.63 $\hat{Y} = 1020 - 1.07X$; $S_e = 400.7$; $r^2 = .016$; $t = 0.28$; fail to reject the null hypothesis—the slope is not significantly different from zero

11.65 $r = -.94$

11.67 $r = .90$

11.69 See table

11.71 $\hat{Y} = -623.08 + 0.319X$; $\hat{Y}(1985) = 10.08$

11.73 a. $\hat{Y} = 15,403 - 0.57X$
b. $r = .586$
c. $\hat{Y} = 7,087 - 3.36X$
$\hat{Y}(1995) = 383.8$

11.75 $\hat{Y} = -62.1 + 148.85X_1 + 25.72X_2 + 10.353X_3$; $S_e = 84.46$, $R^2 = .79$, $F = 10.01$

Chapter 12

12.1 $\chi^2 = 18.11$; reject the null hypothesis

12.3 $\chi^2 = 2.13$; fail to reject the null hypothesis

12.5 $\chi^2 = 198.48$; reject the null hypothesis

12.7 $\chi^2 = 2.45$; fail to reject the null hypothesis

12.9 $e_{11} = 24.4$, $e_{12} = 58.6$, $e_{21} = 16.5$, $e_{22} = 39.5$, $e_{31} = 16.2$, $e_{32} = 38.8$, df = 2

12.11 $\chi^2 = 0.24$; fail to reject the null hypothesis

12.13 $\chi^2 = 64.92$; reject the null hypothesis

12.15 $\chi^2 = 9.21$; reject the null hypothesis

12.17 $Z = 0.98$; fail to reject the null hypothesis

12.19 $Z = 2.18$; fail to reject the null hypothesis

12.21 $Z = 7.85$; reject the null hypothesis

Solution to Problem 11.69

	Abbott	Bausch & Lomb	Exxon	Motorola	Sara Lee
Bausch & Lomb	.999				
Exxon	.506	.536			
Motorola	1.000	.999	.509		
Sara Lee	.998	1.000	.553	.999	
Tootsie Roll	1.000	1.000	.511	1.000	.999

12.23 $Z = -2.59$; reject the null hypothesis
12.25 $Z = -3.20$; reject the null hypothesis
12.27 $Z = -1.75$; reject the null hypothesis
12.29 $K = 21.2$; reject the null hypothesis
12.31 $K = 2.75$; fail to reject the null hypothesis
12.33 $K = 18.99$; reject the null hypothesis
12.35 $r_s = .893$
12.37 $r_s = -.952$
12.39 $r_s = .132$
12.41 $r_s = .358$
12.43 $\chi^2 = 1.75$; fail to reject the null hypothesis
12.45 $\chi^2 = 5.27$; fail to reject the null hypothesis
12.47 $\chi^2 = 19.03$; reject the null hypothesis
12.49 $\chi^2 = 0.711$; fail to reject the null hypothesis
12.51 $\chi^2 = 54.62$; reject the null hypothesis
12.53 $\chi^2 = 10.71$; reject the null hypothesis

12.55 $Z = 0.53$; fail to reject the null hypothesis
12.57 $Z = -0.52$; fail to reject the null hypothesis
12.59 $Z = -2.43$; reject the null hypothesis
12.61 $Z = -3.15$; reject the null hypothesis
12.63 $Z = 0.26$; fail to reject the null hypothesis
12.65 $Z = 2.41$; reject the null hypothesis
12.67 $Z = -1.87$; fail to reject the null hypothesis
12.69 $K = 12.28$; reject the null hypothesis
12.71 $K = 27.22$; reject the null hypothesis
12.73 $K = 11.96$; reject the null hypothesis
12.75 $r_s = -.571$
12.77 $r_s = .690$
12.79 $r_s = .783$

GLOSSARY

a Priori Determined before or prior to the experiment.

Acceptance Region Portion of the distribution within which the researcher fails to reject the null hypothesis.

After-Process Quality Control Measurement of product attributes by inspection after the manufacturing process has been completed to determine whether the product is acceptable.

Alpha Greek letter (α) denoting the probability of committing a Type I error.

Alternative Hypothesis The hypothesis that complements the null hypothesis; usually the hypothesis that the researcher is interested in "proving."

Analysis of Variance (ANOVA) A technique for statistically analyzing the data from a completely randomized design; uses the F test to determine whether there is a significant difference in two or more independent groups.

Arithmetic Mean The average of a group of numbers.

Bayes' Rule An extension of the conditional law of probabilities that can be used to revise probabilities (discovered by and named for Thomas Bayes).

Beta Greek letter (β) denoting the probability of committing a Type II error.

Binomial Distribution Widely known discrete distribution constructed by determining the probabilities of x successes in n trials.

Business Cycle The rise and fall of business activities over periods of time.

Census A process of gathering data from the whole population for a measurement of interest.

Central Limit Theorem A theorem that states that, regardless of the shape of a population, the distributions of sample means and proportions are normal if sample sizes are large.

Chebyshev's Theorem A theorem that states that at least $1 - 1/k^2$ values will fall within $\pm k$ standard deviations of the mean regardless of the shape of the distribution.

Chi-Square Distribution A continuous distribution determined by the sum of the squares of k independent random variables.

Chi-Square Goodness-of-Fit Test A statistical test that compares expected or theoretical frequencies of categories from a population distribution to the actual or observed frequencies from a distribution.

Chi-Square Test of Independence A statistical test used to analyze the frequencies of two variables with multiple categories to determine whether the two variables are independent.

Class Midpoint For any given class interval of a frequency distribution, the value halfway across the class interval; the average of the class endpoints.

Classical Probability Probability assignment based on rules and laws.

Cluster (Area) Sampling A type of random sampling in which the population is divided into non-overlapping areas or clusters and elements are randomly sampled from the areas or clusters.

Coefficient of Determination (r^2) The proportion of variability of the dependent variable accounted for or explained by the independent variable in a regression model.

Coefficient of Variation The ratio of the standard deviation to the mean expressed in percentage.

Collectively Exhaustive Events All possible elementary events for an experiment; usually listed.

Combinations Used to determine the number of possible ways r things can happen from n total possibilities.

Complementary Events One event encompassing all the elementary events of an experiment not in the other event.

Completely Randomized Design An experiment design having one treatment or independent variable with two or more treatment levels and one dependent variable; analyzed by ANOVA.

Conditional Probability The probability of occurrence of one event if another event has occurred.

Confidence Interval An interval containing a range of values within which the analyst can declare with some confidence that the population parameter will fall.

Contingency Analysis A chi-square test of independence.

Contingency Tables Two-way tables that contain the frequencies of responses to two questions.

Continuous Distributions Distributions constructed from continuous random variables.

Continuous Random Variables Variables that take on values at every point over a specific interval.

Control Chart A graph containing an upper control limit, a lower control limit, and a centerline and depicting a particular statistic computed on several samples; used in quality control.

Convenience Sampling A nonrandom sampling technique. Items for the sample are selected for the convenience of the researcher.

Correction for Continuity A correction made when a binomial distribution problem is approximated by the normal distribution because a discrete distribution problem is being approximated by a continuous distribution.

Correlation A measure of the degree of relatedness of two or more variables.

Covariance The variance of X and Y together.

Critical Value The value that divides the acceptance region from the rejection region.

Critical Value Method A method of testing hypotheses in which the sample statistic is compared to a critical value to reach a conclusion about rejecting or failing to reject the null hypothesis.

Cumulative Frequency A running total of frequencies through the classes of a frequency distribution.

Degrees of Freedom A mathematical adjustment made to the size of sample that is used along with an α value to locate values in statistical tables.

Dependent Variable In analysis of variance, the measurement being analyzed; in regression analysis, the variable being predicted.

Descriptive Statistics Statistics gathered on a group to describe or reach conclusions about that same group.

Detail Errors When a respondent remembers an event incorrectly.

Deviation from the Mean The difference between a number and the average of the set of numbers of which the number is a part.

Discrete Distributions Distributions constructed from discrete random variables.

Discrete Random Variables Variables that take on values only at certain points within an interval.

Disproportionate Stratified Random Sampling A type of stratified random sampling in which the proportions of items selected from the strata to the final sample do not reflect the proportions of the strata in the population.

Dummy Variable A qualitative or indicator variable; usually coded as 0 or 1, representing whether or not a given item or person possesses a specified characteristic.

Elementary Events Events that cannot be decomposed or broken into other events.

Empirical Rule A guideline that states the approximate percentage of values that fall within a stated number of standard deviations of a mean of a set of data that are normally distributed.

Error of Estimation The difference between the statistic computed to estimate a parameter and the parameter.

Error Variance   The total of the variance within each of the treatments in an ANOVA; that part of the total variance unaccounted for by the treatment variance.

Event   An outcome of an experiment.

Experiment   A process that produces outcomes.

Exponential Distribution   A continuous distribution closely related to the Poisson distribution that describes the times between random occurrences.

F Distribution   A distribution based on the ratio of two random variances; used in ANOVA.

Finite Correction Factor   An adjustment made to a statistical technique to reflect that a population is finite and the size is known.

Fishbone Diagram   Sometimes referred to as an Ishikawa diagram, displays possible causes of a quality problem and several of the possible reasons for each cause; causes diagrammed along the "backbone" and possible reasons diagrammed as "ribs," giving the appearance of a fish skeleton.

Forecasting   The art or science of predicting the future.

Frame   A list, map, or directory used to represent the population in the process of sampling.

Frequency Distribution   For grouped data, a summary of data presented in the form of class intervals and frequencies.

Frequency Polygon   A graph constructed by plotting dots for frequencies at class midpoints and connecting the dots.

Grouped Data   Data organized into a frequency distribution.

Heteroscedasticity   Nonconstant error variances produced by a regression model.

Histogram   A type of vertical bar chart constructed by graphing line segments for the frequencies of classes across the class intervals and connecting each to the X axis to form a series of rectangles.

Homoscedasticity   Constant error variances produced by a regression model.

Hypergeometric Distribution   A distribution of probabilities of the occurrence of x items in a sample of n when X of that same item are in a population of N.

Hypothesis Testing   A process of testing hypotheses about parameters by setting up null and alternative hypotheses, gathering sample data, computing statistics from the samples, and using statistical techniques to reach conclusions about the hypotheses.

Independent Events   Events such that the occurrence or nonoccurrence of one has no effect on the occurrence of the others.

Independent Samples   Different samples in which items selected are related only by chance.

Independent Variable   The treatment or factor being analyzed in an analysis of variance; a predictor variable in regression analysis.

Indirect Proof   A proof having the only possible outcomes set up to be two mutually exclusive alternatives, with rejection of one outcome defaulting in acceptance or proof of the other outcome.

Inferential Statistics   Statistics gathered from a sample and used to reach conclusions about the population from which the sample was taken.

In-Process Quality Control   Product attributes measured at various intervals during the manufacturing process.

Intersection   The portion of the population that contains elements lying in two or more groups of interest.

Interval Estimate   A range of values within which the population parameter is expected to fall.

Interval Level Data   Next to highest level of data; contain all properties of ordinal level data, but, in addition, contain equal intervals between consecutive numbers.

Irregular Fluctuations   Unexplained or error variation with time-series data.

Joint Probability   The probability of intersection occurring; the probability of two or more things happening at once.

Judgment Sampling   A nonrandom sampling technique in which the researcher chooses items for the sample by judgment.

Just-in-Time Inventory System   An inventory system that stores little or no extra raw materials or parts for production.

Kruskal–Wallis Test The nonparametric alternative to one-way ANOVA; used to test whether three or more samples come from the same or different populations.

Lambda A Greek letter (λ) used to denote the long-run average of a Poisson distribution.

Least Squares Analysis The method of analysis usually used to develop a regression model; based on calculus techniques that attempt to minimize sum of the squares of error.

Level of Significance The probability of committing a Type I error; also known as α.

Mann–Whitney U Test A nonparametric counterpart of the t test used to compare the means of two independent populations.

Marginal Probability A probability computed by dividing a subtotal of the population by the total of the population.

Matched-Pairs Test A t test used to test the differences in two related or matched samples.

Mean Absolute Deviation The average of the absolute values of the deviations around the mean for a set of numbers.

Measures of Central Tendency Statistics that yield information about the center of middle of a set of numbers.

Measures of Variability Statistics that describe the spread of dispersion of a set of data.

Median The middle value of an ordered array of numbers.

Metric Data Interval and ratio level data; quantitative data.

Mode The most frequently occurring value in a set of numbers.

Multiple Comparisons Statistical techniques used to compare pairs of treatment means when ANOVA yields an overall significant difference in the treatment means.

Multiple Regression Regression analysis with one dependent variable and two or more independent variables.

Mutually Exclusive Events Events such that the occurrence of one precludes the occurrence of the other.

Nominal Level Data The lowest level of data measurement; used only to classify or categorize.

Nonmetric Data Nominal and ordinal level data; qualitative data.

Nonparametric Statistics Statistical techniques that are based on few assumptions about the population and are particularly applicable to nominal and ordinal level data.

Nonrandom Sampling Unequal probability of every unit of the population being selected for the sample.

Nonsampling Errors All errors other than sampling errors.

Normal Distribution Probably the most widely known and used of all distributions; continuous distribution; fits the measurements of many human characteristics and many machine produced items.

Null Hypothesis The hypothesis that assumes the status quo, that the old theory, method, standard is still true; the complement of the alternative hypothesis, which the researcher is usually interested in "proving."

Ogive A cumulative or decumulative frequency polygon; plotted by placing a dot at each class endpoint for the cumulative or decumulative frequency value and connecting the dots.

Omission Error An error that occurs when a respondent fails to mention past events.

One-tailed Test A statistical test in which the researcher is interested only in testing one side of the distribution.

Ordinal Level Data Next higher level of data from nominal level data; can be used to order or rank items, objects, or people.

Outliers Data points that lie apart from the rest of the points.

P Chart Graphic depiction of product proportions in noncompliance with specifications; used in quality control.

Parameter A descriptive measure of the population.

Parametric Statistics Statistical techniques that contain assumptions about the population and that are generally used only with interval and ratio level data.

Pareto Analysis   A quantitative tallying of the number and types of defects that occur with a product or service; can be graphed as a Pareto Chart, a vertical bar graph of these defects in order of magnitude.

Pearson Product-Moment Correlation Coefficient (r)   A correlation measure used to determine the degree of relatedness of two variables that are at least interval in level of measurement.

Pie Chart   A circular depiction of data, with the area of the whole pie representing 100% of the data being studied and slices representing a percentage breakdown of the parts.

Point Estimate   An estimate of a population parameter constructed from a statistic taken from a sample.

Poisson Distribution   A discrete distribution constructed from the probability of occurrence of rare events over an interval.

Population   A collection of persons, objects, or items of interest.

Power   The probability of rejecting a false null hypothesis.

Probability Method   A method of conducting statistical tests whereby the researcher determines the probability of the outcome of the test and compares that probability to the α value selected to reach a conclusion about the null hypothesis.

Proportionate Stratified Random Sampling   The proportions of the items selected for the sample from the strata reflecting the proportions of the strata in the population.

Qualitative Variables   Dummy variables or indicator variables that measure whether an item or person possesses a given characteristic; usually coded as 0 or 1.

Quantitative Variables   Variables that produce quantifiable values for each item or person; usually produce data that are interval or ratio in level of measurement.

Quality   When a product meets its specifications.

Quality Circle   A small group of workers consist-

ing of supervisors and six to ten employees who meet regularly to consider quality issues in their department or area of the business.

Quality Control   The collection of strategies, techniques, and actions taken by an organization to ensure production of a quality product.

Quota Sampling   A nonrandom sampling technique similar to stratified random sampling whereby the population is stratified on some characteristic; elements selected for the sample by nonrandom processes.

R Chart   Plot of sample ranges; used in quality control.

Random Sampling   Equal probability of every unit of the population being selected for the sample.

Random Variable   A variable that contains the outcomes of a chance experiment.

Range   The difference between the largest and smallest numbers in a set of numbers.

Ratio Level Data   Highest level of data measurement; have the same properties as interval level data, but, in addition, contain an absolute zero as smallest value.

Regression   The process of constructing a mathematical model or function that can be used to predict or determine one variable by another variable or variables.

Rejection Region   The portion of the distribution in which the null hypothesis will be rejected if the computed statistic falls within it.

Related Samples   Each item in one sample corresponding to a matched or related item in another sample.

Relative Frequency   The proportion of the total frequencies that fall within any particular class interval in a frequency distribution.

Relative Frequency of Occurrence   Assigning probability based on accumulated historical data.

Residual   The difference between the y value predicted by the regression model and the actual y value; the error of the regression model in predicting each value of the dependent variable.

Sample   A portion of the whole

Sample Proportion   The quotient of the frequency that a given characteristic occurs in a sample and the number of items in the sample.

Sample Size Estimation   An estimate of the size of sample necessary to fulfill the requirements of a particular level of confidence and to be within a specified amount of error.

Sample Space   A complete roster or listing of elementary events for an experiment.

Sampling Error   By chance the sample is not representative of the population.

Scatter Plot   A plot or graph of the pairs of data from a simple regression analysis.

Seasonality   The highs and lows of business within a particular business cycle.

Set Notation   Lists of numbers representing various groups and their relation to each other.

Simple Random Sampling   The most elementary random sampling technique; involves numbering each item in the population and using a list or roster of random numbers to select items for the sample.

Simple Regression   Bivariate, linear regression.

Skewness   Lack of the symmetry that a normal distribution of values has.

Slope of the Regression Line   The coefficient of the predictor variable in simple regression; represents the ratio of the rise of the regression line to the run of the regression line.

Spearman's Rank Correlation Coefficient   A measure of the correlation of two variables measured by data that are at least of ordinal level.

Standard Deviation   The square root of the variance.

Standard Error of the Estimate   A standard deviation of the error of a regression model.

Standardized Normal Distribution (Z distribution)   A distribution of Z scores produced for values from a normal distribution with a mean of 0 and a standard deviation of 1.

Statistic   A descriptive measure of a sample.

Statistics   A science dealing with the collection, analysis, interpretation, and presentation of numerical data.

Stem and Leaf Plot   A plot of numbers constructed by dividing the numbers into two groups—with the leftmost digits being the stem and the rightmost digits being the leaf.

Stratified Random Sampling   A type of random sampling whereby the population is divided into various strata and then items are selected for the sample randomly from each stratum.

Subjective Probability   Probability assignment based on the feelings or insights of the person determining the probability.

Sum of Squares of Error   The sum of the residuals squared for a regression model.

Systematic Sampling   A random sampling technique in which the researcher selects every kth item or person from the population.

***t* Distribution**   A distribution developed particularly to analyze the means of small samples when the population variance is unknown.

Telescoping Error   When a respondent attributes an event to a wrong time period.

Time-Series Data   Data gathered over a period of time.

Total Quality Management   A program in which all members of an organization are involved in improving quality and the goals and objectives of the organization come under the purview of quality control.

Total Variance   The total variance of the dependent variable in ANOVA.

Treatment Levels   The various subgroupings of the treatment being studied, usually by ANOVA.

Treatment Variance   The variance of the treatment means in ANOVA; the variance resulting from treatment.

Trend   Long-term general direction of the data.

Two-Stage Sampling   Sampling done in two stages; involves a first round of samples and then selecting a second sample from the first samples.

Two-tailed Test   A statistical test wherein the researcher is interested in testing both sides of the distribution.

Type I Error   An error committed by rejecting a true null hypothesis.

Type II Error   An error committed by failing to reject a false null hypothesis.

Ungrouped Data (raw data)   Data that have not been organized into a frequency distribution.

Union   A new set of elements formed by combining the elements of two or more other sets.

Union Probability   The probability of one event occurring or another event occurring or both occurring.

Variance   The average of the squared deviations about the arithmetic mean for a set of numbers.

Wilcoxon Matched-Pairs Signed Rank Test   A nonparametric alternative to the t test for two related or dependent samples.

$\bar{X}$ Chart   A graph of sample means computed for a series of small random samples over a period of time and used in quality control.

Z Distribution (a distribution of Z scores)   A normal distribution with a mean of 0 and a standard deviation of 1.

Z Score   The number of standard deviations a value is above or below the mean of a set of numbers.

Index

Boldface page number indicates a key word. *Italic f* indicates a figure; *italic t* indicates a table.

AREAS OF THE STANDARD NORMAL DISTRIBUTION

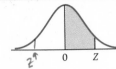

The entries in this table are the probabilities that a standard normal random variable is between 0 and Z (the shaded area).

Second Decimal Place in Z

Z	0.00	0.01	0.02	0.03	0.04	0.05	0.06	0.07	0.08	0.09
0.0	0.0000	0.0040	0.0080	0.0120	0.0160	0.0199	0.0239	0.0279	0.0319	0.0359
0.1	0.0398	0.0438	0.0478	0.0517	0.0557	0.0596	0.0636	0.0675	0.0714	0.0753
0.2	0.0793	0.0832	0.0871	0.0910	0.0948	0.0987	0.1026	0.1064	0.1103	0.1141
0.3	0.1179	0.1217	0.1255	0.1293	0.1331	0.1368	0.1406	0.1443	0.1480	0.1517
0.4	0.1554	0.1591	0.1628	0.1664	0.1700	0.1736	0.1772	0.1808	0.1844	0.1879
0.5	0.1915	0.1950	0.1985	0.2019	0.2054	0.2088	0.2123	0.2157	0.2190	0.2224
0.6	0.2257	0.2291	0.2324	0.2357	0.2389	0.2422	0.2454	0.2486	0.2517	0.2549
0.7	0.2580	0.2611	0.2642	0.2673	0.2704	0.2734	0.2764	0.2794	0.2823	0.2852
0.8	0.2881	0.2910	0.2939	0.2967	0.2995	0.3023	0.3051	0.3078	0.3106	0.3133
0.9	0.3159	0.3186	0.3212	0.3238	0.3264	0.3289	0.3315	0.3340	0.3365	0.3389
1.0	0.3413	0.3438	0.3461	0.3485	0.3508	0.3531	0.3554	0.3577	0.3599	0.3621
1.1	0.3643	0.3665	0.3686	0.3708	0.3729	0.3749	0.3770	0.3790	0.3810	0.3830
1.2	0.3849	0.3869	0.3888	0.3907	0.3925	0.3944	0.3962	0.3980	0.3997	0.4015
1.3	0.4032	0.4049	0.4066	0.4082	0.4099	0.4115	0.4131	0.4147	0.4162	0.4177
1.4	0.4192	0.4207	0.4222	0.4236	0.4251	0.4265	0.4279	0.4292	0.4306	0.4319
1.5	0.4332	0.4345	0.4357	0.4370	0.4382	0.4394	0.4406	0.4418	0.4429	0.4441
1.6	0.4452	0.4463	0.4474	0.4484	0.4495	0.4505	0.4515	0.4525	0.4535	0.4545
1.7	0.4554	0.4564	0.4573	0.4582	0.4591	0.4599	0.4608	0.4616	0.4625	0.4633
1.8	0.4641	0.4649	0.4656	0.4664	0.4671	0.4678	0.4686	0.4693	0.4699	0.4706
1.9	0.4713	0.4719	0.4726	0.4732	0.4738	0.4744	0.4750	0.4756	0.4761	0.4767
2.0	0.4772	0.4778	0.4783	0.4788	0.4793	0.4796	0.4803	0.4808	0.4812	0.4817
2.1	0.4821	0.4826	0.4830	0.4834	0.4838	0.4842	0.4846	0.4850	0.4854	0.4857
2.2	0.4861	0.4864	0.4868	0.4871	0.4875	0.4878	0.4881	0.4884	0.4887	0.4890
2.3	0.4893	0.4896	0.4898	0.4901	0.4904	0.4906	0.4909	0.4911	0.4913	0.4916
2.4	0.4918	0.4920	0.4922	0.4925	0.4927	0.4929	0.4931	0.4932	0.4934	0.4936
2.5	0.4938	0.4940	0.4941	0.4943	0.4945	0.4946	0.4948	0.4949	0.4951	0.4952
2.6	0.4953	0.4955	0.4956	0.4957	0.4959	0.4960	0.4961	0.4962	0.4963	0.4964
2.7	0.4965	0.4966	0.4967	0.4968	0.4969	0.4970	0.4971	0.4972	0.4973	0.4974
2.8	0.4974	0.4975	0.4976	0.4977	0.4977	0.4978	0.4979	0.4979	0.4980	0.4981
2.9	0.4981	0.4982	0.4982	0.4983	0.4984	0.4984	0.4985	0.4985	0.4986	0.4986
3.0	0.4987	0.4987	0.4987	0.4988	0.4988	0.4989	0.4989	0.4989	0.4990	0.4990
3.1	0.4990	0.4991	0.4991	0.4991	0.4992	0.4992	0.4992	0.4992	0.4993	0.4993
3.2	0.4993	0.4993	0.4994	0.4994	0.4994	0.4994	0.4994	0.4995	0.4995	0.4995
3.3	0.4995	0.4995	0.4995	0.4996	0.4996	0.4996	0.4996	0.4996	0.4996	0.4997
3.4	0.4997	0.4997	0.4997	0.4997	0.4997	0.4997	0.4997	0.4997	0.4997	0.4998
3.5	0.4998									
4.0	0.49997									
4.5	0.499997									
5.0	0.4999997									

Reprinted with permission from *CRC Standard Mathematical Tables*, 27th ed., © CRC Press, Inc., Boca Raton, FL.